EDUCATIONAL PSYCHOLOGY
Second Edition

SECOND EDITION

LEE J. CRONBACH *University of Illinois*

EDUCATIONAL PSYCHOLOGY

In consultation with **ERNEST R. HILGARD**
Stanford University
and
WILLARD B. SPALDING
Portland State College

Harcourt, Brace & World, Inc.   *New York and Burlingame*

DRAWINGS BY **Don Sibley**

CHARTS BY **Harry Lazarus**

To all those who have taught me educational psychology,
but most especially to
  Rick and *Bob*
  Barbara and *Joyce*
  —and *Janet Ellen,*
who caused me to revise some ideas

CONTENTS

Preface to the First Edition   xxi

Preface to the Second Edition   xxv

PART ONE
Psychology and School Problems

1. HOW PSYCHOLOGY CONTRIBUTES TO EDUCATION   2

Value of Psychological Viewpoints in Education
Are Psychological Principles Obvious?
Scientific Approaches to Educational Issues
Bases for Evaluating Assumptions, Methods Used by Psychologists
The Teaching Plan of This Book
Summary

2. WHAT TEACHERS ARE TRYING TO ACCOMPLISH   30

Education as a Part of Socialization
The Socialization Process, Special Responsibilities of the School
Aims of Socialization
Competence in Problem Solving, Confidence and Self-respect, Effective Relations with Others, Goals and Interests, Acceptance of Social Values
Reducing Educational Aims to Observable Behavior
Transferable Responses as an Educational Goal
The Kinds of Knowledge
Summary

3. AN INTRODUCTION TO THE LEARNING PROCESS   68

Seven Elements in Behavior
A Description of Active Learning
What We Mean by Learning, The Seven Elements as Aspects of Learning

A Classroom Portrait (Typing)
The Seven Elements As Seen in This Example, Problems of Teaching Seen in This Example
Summary

PART TWO
Readiness and Its Development

4. THE STREAM OF DEVELOPMENT   88

The Interaction of Biological Nature and Experience
Physical Maturing as the Base of Readiness
Physical Development Affects the Self-concept, Normal Trends in Physical Development, Neural Maturation
Cultural Pressures and Opportunities
The Environment Widens, The Child's Social Group Expands, Roles Become More Varied
The Development and Satisfaction of Needs
Need for Affection, Need for Approval by Authority, Need for Approval by Peers, Need for Independence, Need for Competence and Self-respect
A Case of Wholesome Development: Jeanne
Summary

5. DIFFERENCES IN PUPIL CHARACTERISTICS: ILLUSTRATIVE CASES   136

Pupils with Differences in Equipment
Clark, Who Has a Physical Handicap; Olive, with Low Academic Ability; Bill, a Bright Boy
Differences in Home Background
Warmth, Handling of Dependence and Independence, Training to Strive for Achievement
Portrait of Margaret, Who Felt Unloved
Summary

6. ASSESSING READINESS: PERSONALITY AND MOTIVATION   168

Classroom Observation
Seeking Fundamental Causes, Obtaining Dependable Information
Obtaining Judgments by Peers
Examining the Pupil's View of Himself
Investigation of Interests
Summary

7. ASSESSING READINESS: ABILITIES

194

Measuring Tool Skills
Reading Tests, Diagnosis in Other Areas, Study Skills and Work Methods
Measuring General Scholastic Aptitude
Individual Tests, Group Tests
General Principles of Test Usage
The Test as a Work Sample, Distinguishing Typical Performance from Ability, Use of Norms
Aptitudes and Guidance
Significance of General Scholastic Aptitude, The Ability Profile
Ability in Adulthood
Summary

8. THE INTERPRETATION AND APPLICATION OF ABILITY TESTS

233

Do Mental Tests Identify the Truly Talented?
Stability of Mental Test Scores
Changes in Score During Development, Changes Related to the Environment
The Effect of Special Stimulation on Readiness for Instruction
Adapting Schooling to Pupil Readiness
Grade Placement of Subject Matter, Ability Grouping, Diversification of Activities, Nongraded Schools
Summary

PART THREE
Acquiring Skills, Ideas, and Attitudes

9. SKILLS

270

Characteristics of Skilled Action
Change from Mediated to Immediate Response, Differentiation of Cues, Feedback and Correction, Coordination of Movements, Stability of Response Under Difficulty
Making Practice Effective
The Function of Active Practice, Selecting Appropriate Practice Tasks, Advice and Demonstration, Monitoring, Recapitulation
The Rate of Improvement with Practice
Specimen Training Records, A Theoretical Learning Curve, Individual Improvement Records
Retention, Facilitation, and Interference
Summary

10. INTELLECTUAL DEVELOPMENT AS TRANSFER OF LEARNING 314

Outmoded Views on the Transfer of Intellectual Attainments
The Decline of Formal Discipline, Emphasis on Specific Learnings
Conditions Favorable to Transfer
The Development of Intellectual Power
Learning to Learn, Stages Toward Mature Intellectual Control, Interpretation of the Theory
The Cumulative Nature of Learning
Summary

11. IMPROVING UNDERSTANDING AND THINKING 349

Meaningful Learning
Meaning as an Aid to Retention, Meaning as an Aid in Acquisition, Evidences of Meaning, Meaning of Verbal Concepts, Experience as the Base for Meaning
Learning Through Adventurous Participation
Drawing a Verbal Conclusion
Presentation vs. Discovery of Generalizations
Verbal Instruction as a Base for Performance
Improving Reasoning
Teaching of Generalizations About Reasoning, Responses That Interfere with Reasoning
Flexibility and Divergent Thinking
Summary

12. COMMUNICATING KNOWLEDGE 397

Making Presentations Effective
Use of Language, Organization, Audio-visual Devices
Automatic, Programed Instruction
Automatic Procedures, Programing, Experimental Results
Summary

13. IDENTIFICATION AND THE LEARNING OF ATTITUDES 423

Identifying Figures as a Source of Suggestions
Whom Does the Learner Imitate?, Figures with Whom the Child Identifies
Models Offered by the School
The Teacher, Teaching Materials as a Source of Models

Development of Attitudes Through Experience
*Attitudes as Meanings, Trial and Confirmation, Attitude Toward
Minorities as an Example, Conflicting Influences*
Methods for Modifying Attitudes
*Teaching Facts About the Attitude-Object, Persuasion, Activity
Programs, What Method Shall the School Use?*
Summary

PART FOUR
Planning, Motivation, and Evaluation

14. PURPOSES AND ASPIRATIONS   466

The Nature of Goals
Multiple Goals, Remote Goals
How Pupils Set Aspirations
*The Influence of Success and Failure, Personality and Goal Setting,
Group Standards*
Rewards and Punishments
Summary

15. THE TEACHER AS CLASSROOM LEADER   498

Methods of Planning and Control
*Undirected Activities, Teacher-controlled Activities, Group-con-
trolled Activities, Case Study of an Undirected Classroom (Art),
Case Study of Group Planning (English)*
Effects of Various Styles of Control
*Emotional Security, Effort and Efficiency, Learning of Course
Material, Learning to Be an Effective Group Member*
Factors Limiting the Teacher's Choice of Control Pattern
Warmth and Acceptance of the Pupil
*Descriptions of Impersonal and Supporting Teachers, Effects on
Pupil Behavior, The Interaction of Teacher Style and Pupil Needs*
Classroom Motivation
Setting Definite Goals, Competition, Marking
Disciplinary Problems as a Failure of Leadership
Summary

16. JUDGING PERFORMANCE   539

Functions of Evaluation
Evaluation Clarifies Objectives
Requirements of an Evaluation Procedure
Validity, Accuracy, Usefulness for Diagnosis

Formal Tests as Evidence of Performance
Effective Forms for Teacher-made Tests, The Use of Standardized Tests
How to Judge Educational Progress
Evaluation in Elementary Grades, Evaluation in High School
Summary

PART FIVE
Emotional Learning

17. HEALTHY ADJUSTMENT TO DIFFICULTIES   574

Immediate Reactions to Thwarting
Repetitive Response, Altered Response, Withdrawal, Pursuit of a Substitute Goal, An Example of Reactions to Thwarting, Implications for Teaching
Tension
Problem-centered Exertion, Direct and Displaced Discharge, Suppression and Related Reactions
Evaluating Mental Health
Realism, Commitment, Self-acceptance
Summary

18. CHARACTER DEVELOPMENT   616

A Definition of Character
Five Levels of Character
The Amoral Level; The Expedient Level; The Conventional Level; The Irrational-Conscientious Level; The Rational, Altruistic Level
How Character Is Unified
Mack, a Case Study of Character Structure; Evidence from Character Tests
Character and Authority
Defiance and Delinquency, Conformity, Rational Self-discipline
Procedures for Teaching Character
Providing Repetitive Practice to Form Habits, Teaching General Verbal Principles of Conduct, Efforts to Improve Emotional Adjustment, The Role of the School
Summary

Bibliography   659

Author Index   693

Subject Index   701

CASE DESCRIPTIONS

Mr. Wells and his typing class ... 76
Jeanne, a case of wholesome development ... 128
Clark, who has a physical handicap ... 137
Olive, with low academic ability ... 141
Bill, a bright boy ... 145
Margaret, who felt unloved ... 162
Charles White, whose aptitudes vary ... 225
Mr. Palmer, whose pupils create mathematical generalizations ... 374
Jim, who identifies with a male teacher ... 429
Frank, who learns liberal attitudes ... 443
Ben Blake, who learns a pattern of prejudice ... 443
Mr. Osborne, who gave his art class freedom ... 503
Miss Simmons, who plans a unit in English ... 506
Mack, a case study of character structure ... 626

ILLUSTRATIONS

1. Psychology offers new viewpoints   4
2. Eye movements of an unskilled reader in Grade III   9
3. Eye movements of a skilled reader in Grade III   10
4. Artificial reading materials simplify the learner's task   11
5. Not all educational innovations are beneficial   12
6. A chart comparing groups given different treatments   17
7. Two plans for studying how neatness affects social acceptance   19
8. How well do aptitudes forecast grades?   21
9. Higher correlation implies greater predictability   22
10. College education is increasingly reaching into lower socio-economic levels   37
11. Qualities of the socialized person   40
12. Each socializer teaches the way of life he values   47
13. Three components of action   54
14. Chemistry includes four kinds of verbal knowledge   59
15. Generalizations in isolation can oversimplify   62
16. Learning is shown in change of behavior   70
17. Aspects of the learning process   75
18. Olive lacked readiness   78
19. Strength promotes personality development in boys   91
20. The "normal" distribution   94
21. Girls mature ahead of boys   95
22. Late maturing boys overtake early maturers   96
23. Children may learn faster when training is delayed   100
24. New roles are learned   107
25. Americans expect young people to play community roles   108
26. The person must get along with authority   115
27. Sociogram for the twelfth-grade boys at Wabash High   118
28. Conflict is increased by misperception   120
29. Independence is learned gradually   122
30. Competence is satisfying   125
31. Clark has adapted to his handicap   140
32. Olive finds little satisfaction   144
33. Bill must do things his own way   146
34. Home atmospheres combine in many patterns   148

35. Homes of aggressive boys are relatively cold   149
36. Inconsistent experience generates approach-avoidance conflict   154
37. Feelings about parents generalize to teachers and peers   155
38. Achievement motivation is satisfied by a chance to exercise
    competence   158
39. Parental pressure can make the child an anxious striver   160
40. Margaret feared to assert herself   164
41. Anecdotal records showed Martie's consistency   172
42. Sociogram for a class of fourth-grade girls   178
43. The frequency of isolates and stars changes little   179
44. Preference profile of Mary Thomas   188
45. Questions to assess skill in map-reading   199
46. A representative group test of general mental ability   207
47. A general ability measure forecasts expected freshman grades   208
48. Norms indicate expected achievement   215
49. Relations among three score scales   217
50. Each college has its own ability range   220
51. Items from six subtests of the Differential Aptitude Tests   224
52. Ability profile of Charles White   225
53. Men in an occupation tend to have similar abilities   226
54. Achievement depends on the interaction between method of
    instruction and aptitude   235
55. Individual mental growth is irregular   240
56. Readiness depends on teaching method as much as on mental age   250
57. Pupils within a grade range widely in proficiency   253
58. Sectioning pupils does not do away with individual differences   254
59. The homogeneous group is a collection of unique individuals   255
60. Each child can develop according to his readiness   259
61. Fourth-graders gain more from adaptive instruction   260
62. With nongraded classes, adjustment to individual differences is a
    continuous process   263
63. Cues may be seen, heard, or felt   274
64. Feedback of consequences guides correction   275
65. Trial and correction in mirror drawing   276
66. Performance record of a trainee with increasing amounts of
    practice   278
67. Delaying feedback disrupts coordination   281
68. Task simplification aids the beginner   286
69. Three learning curves for a disk-cutting trainee   298
70. A schematic learning curve   299
71. Learning curves during three years of typing practice   303
72. Many sorts of response will transfer   319
73. With experience, information is used efficiently   324
74. A mediated response is a chain of events   327

75. The preoperational child cannot maintain a fixed point of view   330
76. The concept of order grows in power   332
77. The operation of ordering is achieved gradually   334
78. Two ways of subtracting   343
79. Results of four methods of teaching subtraction   343
80. Pupils reorganize what they recall   354
81. Meaningful associations are nearly unforgettable   355
82. People remember what fits their concepts   359
83. Understanding is shown in application   361
84. Levels of abstractness of knowledge   362
85. A person extends his concepts   365
86. To use a concept, one must discriminate   367
87. Abstract training has advantages for transfer   370
88. Mr. Palmer's pupils worked intuitively   375
89. Hints aid discovery   381
90. How to teach for transfer   387
91. A teaching machine designed by Skinner   407
92. Each step in the program is a tiny one   412
93. Programed instruction in college introductory psychology   415
94. Programed teaching of scientific theory for first-graders   418
95. Mr. Harris was an identifying figure   430
96. Pupils prefer books that satisfy their emotional hungers   432
97. An attitude is built on previous attitudes   437
98. Avoidance tendencies are much stronger when the feared object is close   438
99. Strong positive feelings outweigh mild avoidance tendencies   439
100. Meanings acceptable to one's audience are most easily learned   441
101. Students in a liberal college move away from their parents' ideas   447
102. Whose attitudes will be changed?   448
103. One-sided presentation of facts affects interpretation   450
104. The goals of any learning extend far into the future   470
105. Expectations are established by experience   475
106. Aspiration follows success   476
107. Some pupils set unrealistic goals   478
108. Aspirations depend on specific experience   479
109. Secure children set realistic goals   482
110. Mr. Osborne's pupils were free   504
111. Miss Simmons' pupils discussed things they cared about   508
112. Directed groups put forth more effort   513
113. Pupils respond to the well-organized, considerate teacher   514
114. Democratic teaching fosters initiative   515
115. Vital motives lie dormant   527
116. A sample of content in the social studies   546
117. A test of application   556

118. A test of theoretical understanding 557
119. A test of judgment about writing 558
120. Observation collects information on both divergent and convergent processes 560
121. Possible reactions to thwarting 576
122. Compensation through a substitute activity 581
123. The sources of tension vary with age and marital status 582
124. A path toward success 589
125. Stress makes problem solving inefficient 592
126. The anxious pupil shines when the task is clearly structured 594
127. Hypothetical relations of anxiety and external pressure to performance 595
128. Displaced discharge of tension 596
129. Some reactions related to suppression of emotion 599
130. The vicious circle of daydreaming 601
131. Reactions undesirable in one pupil are desirable in another 603
132. Mental health appears in many forms 611
133. Conforming behavior 620
134. Irrational-conscientious behavior 621
135. Rational, altruistic behavior 624
136. Mack is a model citizen on the surface 627
137. Forces forming Mack's attitudes 628
138. Delinquent boys have more forceful personalities 638
139. No age is too early for reasoning about values 650
140. Need fulfillment means adjustment 652
141. The architecture of character 653

TABLES

1. Scores of ten college freshmen   20
2. Conscientiousness is related to method of discipline   23
3. Two outlooks on the world   48
4. The person with achievement motivation tries when tasks seem important   49
5. Acts of the teacher associated with each aspect of learning   83
6. Some developmental tasks of American children   110
7. Effect of home treatment on dependent responses   153
8. Some "Guess Who" items used with intermediate-grade children   176
9. Correspondence of judged family adjustment to score on Minnesota Counseling Inventory   184
10. Records of high-school sophomores on two mental tests   211
11. Environment influences the similarity of people having the same heredity   241
12. Achievement scores for representative second-graders in the same class   252
13. Self-recitation during study is helpful   284
14. Active observers profit most from a demonstration   292
15. Transfer depends on the similarity of new and old tasks   307
16. Suitable teaching improves ability to memorize   325
17. Stages in the mastery of operations   336
18. Broadly significant ideas are remembered best   352
19. Pupils' concepts grow more precise   366
20. A difficult explanation   398
21. Explanation simplified   399
22. The cloze technique applied to a passage with low redundancy   400
23. The cloze technique applied to a passage with high redundancy   401
24. Schoolbooks convey the values of the writer   434
25. Pupils' attitudes shift toward the teacher's attitude   445
26. Discussion can make a change of attitude more lasting   454
27. Characteristic environmental pressures make the experience of liberal arts different from that of business administration students   487
28. Academic effort depends on peer attitudes   488
29. The pupil who is socially rewarded has greater self-satisfaction   489
30. Behavior of teachers using group control   501
31. Effects of three control patterns: a summary   517

32. Achievement depends on both teacher and pupil personalities   524
33. A report card consistent with sound motivation   533
34. The pupil learns from inspecting his corrected test paper   541
35. Sixth-graders can set definite goals   544
36. Teachers' reports are not impartial   551
37. Portion of a check list on use of the microscope   563
38. Reactions to thwarting: a summary   585
39. Which traits mark the maladjusted child?   604
40. How experts judge symptoms of adjustment   606
41. Performance of boys and girls on character tests   634
42. The child's moral interpretation varies with the situation   635
43. Delinquency expresses tensions arising in the home   639
44. Summary of common constellations of adolescent character   642
45. Disorder and truancy reflect deeper frustrations   647

PREFACE TO THE FIRST EDITION

This book seeks to bring the principles of educational psychology to teachers and prospective teachers in such a way that they can perform their vital tasks more intelligently. So vast a body of research, theory, and educational technique falls within the interest of educational psychology that attention must be focused on essential principles.

Educational psychology has grown, over several decades, by a process of accretion. Two rather separate interests of E. L. Thorndike, learning and individual differences, became the original core of the subject. As clinical studies made clear the importance of personality development, educational psychology became responsible for giving teachers a knowledge of mental hygiene. On another front, the interest in child study aroused by G. Stanley Hall and others led to a cumulation of findings about child and adolescent development. Teachers needed much of this information. Child study has recently become more important because we have discovered that it greatly benefits teachers' understanding of school processes.

The introductory course in educational psychology has hitherto presented child development, learning, measurement, and mental hygiene for the most part independently, and the instructor has been forced to deal with some of these scantily because of the limited time available. As significant new materials come along, the most recent example being the findings on group relationships and group process which the social psychologist offers to education, the instructor must try to cram them into his already bulging pack.

The evident need is for a unifying pattern to which specific concepts and bodies of evidence relate. If such a central theme is found for educational psychology, materials will be chosen which contribute to that theme. Topics which are only indirectly related will be postponed for later courses. The student may forget detail and elaboration without serious harm, provided a central understanding is so thoroughly interlocked and buttressed that it stays with him as the permanent core of his professional work.

There will, I believe, be no quarrel with the decision that the central task of educational psychology is to give the teacher an understanding of the way pupils learn. A thorough study of the learning process, its determining conditions and its results, is a sufficient aspiration for any one course. With that prime target, materials from child study, social psychology, testing, and mental hygiene are introduced as they fit into the main theme. This integration is profitable because these separate topics take on more meaning when they are treated as adjuncts to the learning process. In examining tests and measurements, for example, the basic question becomes, "What part does evaluation play in the pupil's learning?" Once this is clear, the psychological requirements of an evaluation device are easy to see, and these guide us in choosing the best practical techniques.

In order to fill the needs of the present day, any presentation of educational psychology has to possess four qualities. Many books have concentrated on some one of these as an aim, and this requires sacrificing the other qualities to some extent. In this book, all four objectives have guided the selection and organization of content, and it has been my intent to keep the four in balance.

1. *An educational psychology must be relevant to school problems.* So long as educational psychology is purely academic, it does not render the service it should. If a teacher or a teacher-in-training does not see how a principle is relevant to the schoolroom, studying the principle is unlikely to change his behavior. I have tried to present each principle in such a way that its practical importance is clear, even though people are too complex for us to reduce principles to specific "do's" and "don't's." I have omitted some topics normally covered if they seemed to have no relevance to school problems. If teachers could study the topic and still ask "So what?" the topic is not suitable content in introductory educational psychology.

I have been guided by the wisdom of many others who have clarified for me what educational psychology can do. The importance of translating psychological materials into terms significant to the teacher was particularly brought home to me by Ralph W. Tyler. At the time I became responsible for some of the educational psychology courses at the University of Chicago, Dr. Tyler as chairman of the department was the guiding spirit in a whole series of curriculum reforms, aimed to make all the courses more serviceable to educators. This aim forced a serious re-examination of traditional content which has, I think, much improved my conceptions. This thinking was reinforced by the keen interest of the teaching staff at the University of Illinois in the critical analysis of educational psychology.

2. *An educational psychology must be soundly based in research.* Too often, in an attempt to be "practical," we are tempted to dilute educational psychology with plausible suggestions which cannot be defended with evidence. Sometimes these suggestions attain wide currency, especially if they fit into whatever concepts are currently stylish in education. If there is any unique contribution of educational psychology in teacher training, however, it is that here students learn the difference between "good ideas" and ideas substantiated by experiment. The teacher will always be assailed by those who know just how he should change his procedures and aims. All these innovators (or reactionaries) speak plausibly for their ideas; but the teacher who waits for the evidence will find that only a very few of the schemes are worth taking seriously. Educational psychology should have no part in pro-

moting one educational method that happens to be popular in professional circles, when other methods are equally in accord with present evidence. An exception is made in this book to include a few ideas which are at present supported only by very fragile evidence. These ideas, notably in the area of classroom leadership, seem worth pointing out to the student as matters for thought, but always with awareness that the evidence is shaky. Most influential in teaching me to keep educational thinking close to the evidence was G. T. Buswell, whose tutelage over many years it is a pleasure to acknowledge. It will be evident to many readers that my view of learning is essentially based on that Chicago functionalism which grew with Dewey, Angell, and Judd. Dr. Buswell was my chief teacher of this psychology based on meaning.

3. *An educational psychology must be complex enough to do justice to human behavior.* To say that a science must be complex will perhaps disturb its students. The more we learn about psychology, however, the less satisfied we can be with simple generalizations about people and recipes for handling them. Students find it easy to learn, for example, that "reward teaches better than punishment." They like to believe this. Unfortunately, this facile statement misses most of the complexities of motivation and personality. Such oversimplified content is essentially false content. This is nowhere more true than in the area of personality and social relations, where so much knowledge has appeared in the postwar years. I have tried to discuss both individual differences and problems of learning in a way that will help students see how many factors must enter any judgment. In arriving at this orientation, I have depended upon so many persons working in the area of human development and child study that it is impossible to name one or two as having contributed most to my thinking.

4. *An educational psychology must be clear.* We surely cannot help students become better teachers if educational psychology cannot be understood. This requires that we avoid nonfunctional technicalities. It requires lucid writing, with realistic examples. I would not claim to have achieved this aim on my own power, but I hope I have come close to it, for it is indispensable in a textbook.

Whatever clarity this book has can be credited to the help I received from class tryouts of a draft of the book. My own classes at the University of Illinois and at Teachers College, Columbia University, made countless suggestions for improving the thinking and writing. Even more help was given by the other instructors who tried the book for me, and combined encouragement with the most helpful possible criticism. The tryout instructors were Nathan Stillman, New Paltz (N. Y.) State Teachers College; Nelson Harris, Shaw University; George D. Spindler, Stanford University; Louis V. Webb, Northwestern University; Father Trafford Maher, S.J., Saint Louis University; Frances Dillon and Jasper Valenti, Moorhead (Minn.) State Teachers College; and Raymond B. Schultz, D. J. Inabnit III, Sicily Smedsvik, R. S. Jones, Irving Lazar, and Ray H. Simpson at the University of Illinois. It is a pleasure to acknowledge the help of all these, and especially the extensive comments contributed by Dr. Dillon, Dr. Spindler, and Father Maher. I hope I have executed their suggestions well enough to do justice to their generosity in making them.

My editors, E. R. Hilgard and Willard B. Spalding, have strengthened the book in countless ways by their suggestions. I acknowledge an equal debt to Lee Deighton for exceptional editorial assistance, and to our artist, Don Sibley, whose talented sketches instruct rather than merely decorate. Bunji Tagawa has developed the excellent charts.

The case studies presented at several places in the book are based on material gathered through observation. Educational psychology students organized teams each of which studied one particular pupil as he went through his school program. The pupils' teachers assisted by contributing their insights, and I myself made enough study of the pupils to provide support and suggestions to the student investigators. Some other observations and case studies were made in connection with research projects. In presenting the cases, I have taken such liberties as suited the purposes of a textbook. Some changes were made to disguise identity of cases. To make a point clear, observations from several cases have sometimes been integrated in a single composite portrait. Other alterations have been made for the sake of brevity or emphasis. The case studies are therefore to be regarded as literary creations rather than scientific reports, although they originated in reality and are as realistic as they can be made. I owe a considerable debt to the students who worked out these studies over a period of years. It would be hard to decide whether they or I learned the most from our joint efforts.

A book can go but a short way toward making educational psychology a part of a student's thinking. He will have to think actively, comparing his preconceptions with the findings developed in the text. He will be much aided by the explanations, applications, and criticisms his instructor can provide. In the end, it is only when he tries out the concepts on real youngsters and real teaching tasks that he brings educational psychology to life for himself.

LEE J. CRONBACH

Champaign, Illinois
November, 1953

PREFACE TO THE SECOND EDITION

In planning this revision the first step was to solicit opinions of instructors familiar with the first edition. An author, like a parent, is myopic with regard to the shortcomings of his child. My correspondents, through their frank, extensive, and sympathetic comments, showed me possibilities for improving this text which I alone would never have identified. It is a pleasure to thank these advisers, and the others who responded anonymously to my inquiry:

Elton Amburn	Floyd Gilbert	Frederick J. McDonald
Paul B. Baum	Shirley C. Geldmann	Willard H. Nelson
Marjorie Carroll	M. Ray Loree	Eva Bond Wagner

There were differences in view among these critics, and some suggestions could not be accepted without changing the basic aims of the text. The most frequently recurring advice, which I was happy to follow, was to present more fully the research and the psychological theory underlying the conclusions regarding educational practice.

The last decade has seen important changes of emphasis within general psychology that make its theories more pertinent to education. Ten years ago the dominant psychology was that of Hull and his followers. Their emphasis on stimulus-response connections, reduction of primary drives, and reinforcement, while useful for explaining the learning of single tasks in the laboratory, seemed not to be very enlightening to the educator. Today the general psychologist is as concerned as the educator with meanings. Harlow demonstrates how long-continued experience facilitates learning in monkeys. Piaget and Inhelder demonstrate the emergence of disciplined thought from the child's long years of trial and error. Skinner proposes to design learning sequences such that each success on one question makes the next question more meaningful. Underwood shows that forgetting is primarily the result of interference from prior associations. Osgood, Kendler, and others advance from Hull to a theory of mediated learning. At the same time, motivational theory has broadened to recognize that mastery and understanding of the environment seems to be a basic source of satisfaction. White's paper (1959) on the need for "competence" climaxes a substantial series of advances on this front which have included Harlow's observations on manipulation and the work of McClelland and others on achievement motivation.

The same decade has seen vigorous re-examination of the purposes and quality of American education. The first great result was a marked extension of testing and counseling, of special programs for the talented and the handicapped, and, in the elementary school, of more flexible administrative arrangements for teaching. These efforts put well-established psychological knowledge to use. The second great result has been radical curriculum revision. In science and mathematics where this work has been carried furthest, the new curricula emphasize not the mastery of facts and calculations but the understanding of scientific and mathematical reasoning. The teacher is called upon to promote understanding and curiosity, and to capitalize upon the pupil's intuitions and discoveries. Cognitive development thus has become the central aim in educational reform just at the time when substantial psychological knowledge about these processes has become available.

To emphasize cognitive development in this edition required no radical change of viewpoint, since the first edition made meaning the first principle of learning. The chapters dealing with intellectual development and the attainment of concepts have been augmented to deal with the theory of Piaget and such topics as "learning by discovery" and "programed instruction." In contemporary experimentation and theory the psychology of learning and the psychology of development are inseparable. Even developments once considered to be "purely physiological" are now known to depend on experience. The teacher cannot gain a full understanding of the pupil unless every bit of learning is seen in its developmental context. I believe that it is a mistake to divide educational psychology for teachers into separate courses in "development" and "learning." In the first edition learning and development were interwoven; I hope that in this revision the treatment has become truly integrated.

Though only the chapters on intellectual learning are largely new, there have been changes and additions throughout the book. Illustrative of the concepts added or treated differently are achievement motivation and affiliation motivation, maturation, divergent or creative thinking, error of measurement, retention, persuasion and attitude change, and the school atmosphere.

I have again had the valuable assistance of Professors Ernest R. Hilgard and Willard B. Spalding, who reviewed the work at every stage from initial plan to final draft. They have drawn attention to issues requiring discussion, have helped me to select sound research and to interpret it judiciously, and have improved the clarity of presentation. I am indeed grateful for their support and interested participation.

Appreciation is expressed to the following publishers for permission to reproduce material: American Association for the Advancement of Science; American Psychological Association; Appleton-Century-Crofts, Inc.; California Test Bureau; Columbia University Press; David McKay Company, Inc.; Dembar Publications; Department of Audio-Visual Instruction of the National Education Association; Duke University Press; Educational Services Incorporated; Elementary School Journal; Harcourt, Brace & World, Inc.; Harper & Row; Harvard Educational Review; Harvard University Press; Holt, Rinehart & Winston, Inc.; Houghton Mifflin Company; Human Factors

Operations Research Laboratory; The Journal Press; McGraw-Hill Book Company; The Macmillan Company; The Ohio State University; Personnel Press, Inc.; The Psychological Corporation; Science Research Associates; Society for Research in Child Development, Inc.; State University of Iowa; Bureau of Publications, Teachers College, Columbia University; The University of Chicago Press; University of Minnesota Press. For unpublished materials I am indebted to Ralph Berdie, John Downing, John M. Stephens, Harold Seashore, and the University of Illinois High School.

In chapter reading lists, some selections are to be found in books of readings. Such sources are referred to by the name of the first editor only according to the following key:

Charters   W. W. Charters, Jr., and N. L. Gage, eds., *Readings in the Social Psychology of Education.* Boston: Allyn and Bacon, to be published in 1963.

Coladarci   A. P. Coladarci, *Educational Psychology.* New York: Dryden, 1955.

Fullager   W. A. Fullager *et al., Readings for Educational Psychology.* New York: Crowell, 1956.

Haimowitz   M. L. Haimowitz and Natalie Reader Haimowitz, *Human Development.* New York: Crowell, 1960.

Harris   T. L. Harris and W. E. Schwahn, *Selected Readings on the Learning Process.* New York: Oxford Univ. Press, 1961.

Lumsdaine   A. A. Lumsdaine and Robert Glaser, *Teaching Machines and Programed Learning.* Washington: National Education Assoc., 1960.

Maccoby   Eleanor Maccoby *et al., Readings in Social Psychology.* New York: Holt, 1958.

Loree   M. Ray Loree, *Educational Psychology.* New York: Ronald, 1959.

Noll   V. H. Noll, *Readings in Educational Psychology.* Boston: Houghton Mifflin, 1962.

Phillips   B. N. Phillips *et al., Psychology at Work in the Elementary School Classroom.* New York: Harper, 1960.

Remmers   H. H. Remmers *et al., Growth, Teaching, and Learning.* New York: Harper, 1957.

Rosenblith   Judy F. Rosenblith and Wesley Allinsmith, eds., *The Causes of Behavior: Readings in Child Development and Educational Psychology.* Boston: Allyn and Bacon, 1962.

Seidman A   J. M. Seidman, *The Adolescent.* New York: Holt, Rinehart & Winston, 1960.

Seidman C   J. M. Seidman, *The Child.* New York: Rinehart, 1958.

Seidman E   J. M. Seidman, *Readings in Educational Psychology.* New York: Houghton Mifflin, 1955.

LEE J. CRONBACH

Champaign, Illinois
August, 1962

EDUCATIONAL PSYCHOLOGY
Second Edition

PART ONE

PSYCHOLOGY AND SCHOOL PROBLEMS

CHAPTER 1 HOW PSYCHOLOGY CONTRIBUTES TO EDUCATION

This book is about people and how they learn. Since you have been learning and watching others learn nearly all your life, not much in this book will be foreign to you. Perhaps you have even done teaching—in a school, in a young people's group, or with your own children. If you already qualify as an old hand in human relations, you will want to know whether or not a book on psychology can offer you anything new. The answer is that psychology promises a new outlook on the familiar problems of education.

In every field, the informed person shows his superiority by the number of things he takes into account and the variety of concepts he uses to organize what he observes. The boy just beginning to be a baseball fan looks at the score; as he becomes more sophisticated, he looks at the batter's stance, the manager's tactics in placing the outfield, and the break on the pitcher's curve ball. But the expert on physical education, considering all these factors, superimposes yet other ways of thinking about the athlete. He thinks of the body as a mechanical system, and is able to analyze motions in terms of the principles of levers and momentum. He looks on the body as a chemical system, and so is better able to understand fatigue. Perhaps he gains further insight from psychology or anatomy. A practitioner can get along without knowing all the principles behind his craft; he follows rules and tested techniques. The person who in addition knows basic concepts can deal with problems for which there are no rules, and can improve on accepted ideas.

Some books, for example, give rules on how to be a good parent. Feed the child this way. Give him these toys. When he has a tantrum, do thus and so. Such books perform a needed service, but rules of thumb have severe limitations. A parent faces too many situations for rules to cover; no book can give enough of them. Worse than that, the rules don't work. What is right for one child is wrong for the next, what is right one day is wrong another; whoever follows blindly the advice that is best-on-the-average will make many mistakes. If, on the other hand, the parent learns general truths about child development, he can use this knowledge to interpret each particular situation. Then he can develop plans for action that take all the pertinent facts into account. Most errors come, not because parents think inaccurately, but because they consider too few angles.

Junior, age 3, says he won't eat his cereal! Mrs. Jones, seeing the situation as a problem in nutrition, is most concerned with getting the cereal into Junior's digestive system. A broader outlook would say that breakfast is not only a fueling operation, but also a learning situation. Junior is learning to like cereal, or to hate it. Some parents would see Junior's behavior as a chance to learn, or not learn, "obedience." Since everyone in our world must learn respect for authority, the parent is likely to feel that Junior's refusal calls for prompt discipline. But if the parent realizes that people also have to learn independence, he will be less eager to have Johnny take orders perfectly.

Harry, at 12, is introduced to tennis by his father. Since Harry, Sr., knows that skill depends on practicing the right thing, he makes sure that the boy uses the correct form. Are there any other goals to consider? Suppose we ask, "What attitudes is Harry developing?" instead of, "What motions is he developing?" If Harry is learning that "tennis is hard" or that "it's no fun to play a game where you have to think of all these details," he may give up as soon as Dad's pressure is off. If he is learning self-depreciation—"I can't come up to Dad's expectations"—he is losing the impetus to improve. If Harry, Sr., looks at Harry's tennis game from all sides—in terms of the champion's idea of form, in terms of Harry's idea of fun, and in terms of the psychologist's principles of learning—he has a better chance of helping Harry.

VALUE OF PSYCHOLOGICAL VIEWPOINTS IN EDUCATION

Multiple viewpoints are essential in thinking about teaching, though sometimes we fall into set ways of looking at school problems. Marie refuses to study, Marie shines up to the boys, Marie whispers in class—until the teacher is justifiably annoyed. Some teachers interpret Marie very simply: "You can't expect her to have good character, with a mother like hers," or "Marie is just plain ornery." Characterizations such as those are not valid. Psychological case studies show that (with a few pathological exceptions) people want to be good and want to be approved of by their associates. When a person does not follow accepted patterns of conduct, there must be a reason. Perhaps the cause can be discovered and treated directly. If Marie's teacher can shelve the label "discipline problem" and see Marie as a girl who wants something she is not getting out of life, the two are on the road to a good relationship. The teacher's task becomes not one of administering justice, but one of studying Marie and finding a way to help her.

Most teachers enter the profession with the hope of becoming like their own best teachers. Imitation is a fine way to learn, up to a point, but it is of little value when conditions change. Teaching methods have been handed down from generation to generation with rather little modification.

Traditions give security, stability, and a fund of tested wisdom, but they become strait jackets unless we know how to re-examine them, to apply them judiciously, and to modify them to fit the requirements of each generation.

To obtain new designs in education, it is not enough to proceed by trial and error. Trying one method after another and observing how much

"Marie is ornery!"

"Marie is bored? lacking readiness? needing approval? early maturing?"

1   *Psychology offers new viewpoints*

pupils learn under each method can lead in time to superior teaching procedures. Present education is in a remote way the result of trying out the successive inspirations of master teachers: Socrates, Comenius, Froebel, and the others. But theory and principle hasten invention. Trial and error has less error in it when new proposals spring from understanding.

If educators (and that includes parents, ministers, managers, and army officers) have lessons to learn from psychology, what are they? It is impossible to put in a nutshell the content of the remaining chapters, but samples can be given of the questions for which psychology seeks answers.

Why do different children in the same family, brought up similarly, have different personalities?

What makes a verbal presentation difficult to understand?

Why do some groups work more effectively than others?

Why do people do unwise things, like planting corn over and over in a field until the soil is worn out, even when they know that this will have undesirable consequences?

Why do some pupils find mathematics difficult even though they do well in other subjects?

Each of those questions implies the further question, "What do we do about it?" The psychological explanation will not always suggest a specific procedure for altering behavior, but it does help teachers and curriculum makers to find sounder practices. Many techniques have been suggested by psychological findings; you will learn about sociograms for studying groups, interest inventories, tests of understanding that replace examinations based on rote memory, and "teaching machines," for example. In addition, psychology calls attention to many things *not* to do. Harry's father learns that he should not criticize all the faults in Harry's tennis form. Junior's mother sees why it is unwise to punish him for saying, "I won't." The teacher learns to identify some pupils who are likely to fail algebra as he teaches it, and so spares himself and the pupils a struggle that can have no good outcome. Perhaps most important, psychology aids the teacher in continually observing the effects of his practices, so that he can modify them moment by moment and year by year to achieve better results.

The questions of educators are usually stated very concretely, and deserve straightforward answers. "At what age should children begin to study multiplication?" "What program should the high school offer a child of low-average intelligence?" "What is the best way to use motion pictures in science classes?" When questioned like this the educational psychologist answers, "It depends. . . ." The justification for such seeming evasiveness is that it really *does* depend. There are good ways and bad ways to use motion pictures, but a teacher who is merely told "the best" way will soon be in a rut, using the same method when a change of pace would serve better. The psychologist's aim is to explain as much as he can about the educational process, not to provide a magical formula for the teacher to follow.

Since the very start of modern American psychology, teachers have been coming to the study with the expectation that they will learn simple, definite, scientifically proved remedies for their troubles. William James's reply to this demand, written in 1899, applies with equal justice today:

> . . . you make a great, a very great mistake, if you think that psychology, being the science of the mind's laws, is something from which you can deduce definite programmes and schemes and methods of instruction for immediate schoolroom use. Psychology is a science, and teaching is an art; and sciences never generate arts directly out of themselves. An intermediary inventive mind must make the application, by using its originality.
>
> The science of logic never made a man reason rightly, and the science of ethics . . . never made a man behave rightly. The most such sciences can do

is to help us catch ourselves up and check ourselves, if we start to reason or to behave wrongly; and to criticize ourselves more articulately after we have made mistakes. . . .

Everywhere teaching must *agree* with the psychology, but need not necessarily be the only kind of teaching that would so agree; for many diverse methods of teaching may equally well agree with psychological laws. . . .

But, if the use of psychological principles thus be negative rather than positive, it does not follow that it may not be a great use, all the same. It certainly narrows the path for experiments and trials. We know in advance, if we are psychologists, that certain methods will be wrong, so our psychology saves us from mistakes. It makes us, moreover, more clear as to what we are about (James, 1920, pp. 7–20).

Psychologists, like other scientists, carry out one investigation at a time. Each study determines what happens under just one set of conditions, often artificial conditions established in the laboratory. The separate studies are given more significance when combined into a theoretical explanation; this, in turn, suggests practical educational procedures. But we cannot directly translate an experimental finding or a theory into decisions about teaching. A great deal of judgment and professional experience is required to judge whether or not the practical situation is enough like the experimental situation for the same principles to hold. The teacher must call to mind additional principles that modify the application. Since these judgments are not entirely dependable, the teacher must continually gather evidence in the classroom, formally or informally, to check on the soundness of his decisions.

Misunderstanding of the claims and purposes of scientific psychology has led to strong objections, particularly from those who regard the humanities as the source of wisdom about human affairs. Thus the thoughtful literary critic Gilbert Highet (1950, pp. vii–viii) has said:

It seems to me very dangerous to apply the aims and methods of science to human beings as individuals. . . . Teaching involves emotions, which cannot be systematically appraised and employed, and human values, which are quite outside the grasp of science. . . . Teaching is not like inducing a chemical reaction: it is much more like painting a picture . . . , or on a lower level like planting a garden. . . . You must throw your heart into it, you must realize that it cannot all be done by formulas, or you will spoil your work, and your pupils, and yourself.

To all this the psychologist agrees heartily, save for the very first sentence. Values, emotions, and instantaneous judgments are required in teaching, and these succeed in proportion to the depth of the teacher's understanding and compassion. But science and the humanities should join in creating that understanding. The gardener who has set his heart on planting roses must respect unsentimental facts about soil chemistry. Every dependable fact about human behavior must be respected by the teacher, even though the facts and measurements of the behavioral scientist by no means dictate exactly what to do. Teaching is indeed an art, but the best methods will be developed by those who seek to take advantage of every possible source of knowledge, particularly that knowledge which is best verified.

While we must rely on judgment in moment-to-moment work with pupils, there is danger in the sentimental view that the judgment of a teacher "with the right spirit" is always to be trusted. Mistakes in judgment are always with us, because the information available to the judge is limited, and because he is likely to give undue weight to some facts while over-looking facts that run counter to his sympathies.

Teachers and other experienced leaders frequently are misinformed about the opinions of the groups they lead. Junior-high-school teachers in one study (Amos and Washington, 1960) were asked to identify problem pupils in their homerooms. Each pupil filled out a Problem Check List (see page 181) indicating what difficulties caused him concern. The teacher also filled out the scale to show what he thought the pupil's problems were. Pupils reported, on the average, about three times as many worries as the teachers thought they had, in the areas of health, physical development, money, and work. Furthermore, the girls reported far more problems regarding home, family, and boy-girl relations than teachers recognized. Teachers tended to think of pupils as lacking interest in school and as disliking studies; they greatly underestimated the number of pupils afraid of failure and afraid of making mistakes. Another line of research (Meehl, 1954) tested the value of impressionistic judgment. Counselors were asked to predict student success by judging their total records. These impressionistic judgments were found to be much less accurate than predictions made mathematically from aptitude test scores and grades. Though the counselors knew these scores and grades, and had additional information not used in the mathematical formula, they failed to weigh the various facts properly and so made frequent overestimates and underestimates of expected performance.

These findings do not imply that all judgment about pupils should be turned over to tests and machines; teachers often can bring to bear an array of facts far richer than the machine could digest. But it is clear that we should maintain a critical rather than a trusting attitude toward our judgments. Everything that scientific investigation can do to identify truly pertinent bases for judgment will be beneficial.

1. If teaching is an art, should administrators try to regulate how the teacher conducts a class, or should the teacher be left to adopt whatever procedures feel right to him?

2. What aspects of medical treatment can be turned over to scientific laboratories and to handbooks stating how to treat a certain condition? What aspects should be left to the doctor personally? What does this suggest about the place of science in teaching?

3. How can you explain the fact that counselors made smaller errors in using a prediction formula than they did in using a full case history with the test scores?

ARE PSYCHOLOGICAL PRINCIPLES OBVIOUS?

To some beginners in educational psychology, all its principles seem obvious. When the professor enunciates a principle and reports the evidence to back it up, the student may think, "That's just common sense." And sometimes he mutters, "Why do I need to study what anyone can see?" If psychological principles were not in accord with everyday experience, however, they would be suspect, since psychology claims to account for the behavior of normal people. A formal science of psychology with experiments, special vocabulary, professors, and textbooks is necessary because on some matters the long-accepted common-sense view is wrong. Only after careful investigation do we know whether a common-sense statement is true or merely persuasive.

READING AS DESCRIBED BY COMMON SENSE AND BY SCIENCE.   Teachers have always had common-sense principles to go by, rules and sayings which they were sure contained the truth. It once seemed completely obvious that you have to read words before you read sentences, and letters before you read words. Everyone agreed on a teaching method that reflected this view. Primary children were taught the alphabet first, and then, as in the *New England Primer*, were taught the combinations: *a-b, ab,* . . . After the child learned enough syllables, he could be taught words. He accumulated many words before he read continuous stories. This logic dominated the teaching of reading until reading was studied in the psychological laboratory.

Psychologists set out about eighty years ago to determine how people actually read. They found that rapid, accurate readers do not notice the letters or syllables that make up a word. The good reader takes in a whole word or phrase at a single glance, recognizing it by its outline (Huey, 1912; M. Vernon, 1954). Good readers can even read at a glance a mutilated word like this:

$$\mathit{practical}$$

Because ordinary observation of reading could not provide detailed information, the investigators photographed the position of the eye to show where the reader was looking, moment by moment. The diagrams made from the films show that good readers lope along, taking in a large amount of material at a glance (Figures 2 and 3). Poor readers limp from one word to the next, seeing only a few letters at a time, perhaps trying to

2 *Eye movements of an unskilled reader in Grade III (G. T. Buswell, 1922; copyright 1922 by The University of Chicago)*

The upper numeral shows the order of fixations; the lower numeral shows the length of pause in twenty-fifths of a second.

patch one syllable onto another. Their technique is as awkward as recognizing a friend by identifying his features one by one: "Brown eyes, large ears, full face, heavy eyebrows—Oh! That's Perry Adams!" People recognize forms—faces, words, melodies, objects—by reacting to the pattern, not the details.

This resulted in a new common-sense principle. It suggested that beginners should from the outset recognize words as wholes. As soon as they can, they move to sentences and simple stories, where the context makes word recognition easier. This procedure, sensible as it seems, can be harmful if it neglects the techniques of word analysis. If the pupil can only guess at hard and unfamiliar words and does not learn to break words into syllables and sound them out, he cannot build up a sight vocabulary by his own efforts. Perhaps the best tactic is to introduce phonic analysis

One night Peter went to bed early. It was

not dark. The bright moon shone in at the

window. Peter could see everything in the

room. All at once he heard a noise. Peter

opened his eyes. He saw that the room had

grown dark. Something was outside the

window.

3 *Eye movements of a skilled reader in Grade III (G. T. Buswell, 1922; copyright 1922 by The University of Chicago)*

along with other reading techniques, teaching the pupil to use it as a "low gear" when he is uncertain of a word. Phonic analysis is just as integral a part of skilled reading as rhythmic eye movement; it is not a skill to be mastered *separately* before starting to read meaningful text. This recommendation may be modified when more is known about reading. Some of the selections in the reading list at the end of the chapter show that psychologists are not agreed as to the place of phonics. Even after hundreds of investigations of reading, there are unanswered questions; and ample room for invention remains, as the next section shows.

Despite its unfinished business, research on reading has turned up sensible facts that contradict what everybody once knew to be "obviously" true. The major task of educational psychology is to help teachers discard "sensible" views that are too limited or based on inaccurate observation. The principles of educational psychology should be acceptable both by rigorous scientific standards and by those of common sense.

A NEW PROPOSAL. The ceaseless search for improved methods of teaching, guided by psychological knowledge, is well illustrated by a radical proposal now undergoing experimental trial. Common sense suggests that a pupil should be trained in just the task that he is intended ultimately to perform; in technical language, that the stimuli encountered during training should be the same as those in the transfer situation. If so, the words he reads should look like the words in adult reading materials. The similarity principle does find support in psychological research, but there is another significant principle to consider: simplification of the task for the beginner benefits his learning. Such a simplification is seen in the teaching of handwriting, where it is now common to teach "manuscript writing" (printing) at the start, shifting to the adult form of cursive, connected script only after manuscript writing is well mastered (see also pages 287, 326).

In reading, the learner encounters considerable difficulty because there is no simple relation between letter form, and word sound. The letter *c*, for example, symbolizes different sounds in the words *cat, chair,* and *recess.* Hence the child is bound to be confused when he attempts to analyze an unfamiliar word. Suppose, it is suggested, that we teach him to read words printed in a special alphabet where every sound has its own symbol. If the word form remains similar to that of ordinary English text, he should be able to transfer his skill from the artificial alphabet to the ordinary one. Pitman (1961) and his associates have developed a 43-unit Augmented Roman alphabet for primers, and are now engaged in an experimental test of the new materials on a thousand pupils in England. The new text, as can be seen in Figure 4, resembles ordinary text in appearance; you would have little difficulty in transferring your reading skill to the new alphabet. It is hoped that the new training will produce faster learning, but only the full experimental trial can verify this hypothesis. It will be necessary, of course, to study the effect of the new approach on spelling and writing skills, as well as on reading, before accepting it.

Phonetic alphabets are by no means new. It may be of interest to com-

"wuns upon a tiem littl red hen livd in a barn wiŧh her fiev ɔhicks. a pig, a cat and a duck mæd ŧhær hœm in ŧhe sæm barn. ɛɔh dæ littl red hen led her ɔhicks out tω lωk for fωd. but ŧhe pig, ŧhe cat and ŧhe duck wωd not lωk for fωd."

4   *Artificial reading materials simplify the learner's task* (*From* Janet and John, Book 3, *by Mabel O'Donnell and Rona Munro, copyright 1950 by Row, Peterson & Company; the transcribed version is published by James Nisbet and Company, Ltd. Reproduced by permission.*)

A children's story printed in Pitman's "Augmented Roman Alphabet." Each character represents a different sound.

ⵔⴽⴽⴒ ⵔⵟⵉⴴ ⴱ ⵟⴶⵐ ⵐⵜⵟⵏ ⵟⵊⴱ ⵔⵊⴽ
ⵏⵜⴴⴱ ⵜⴽ ⴱ ⴴⴵⵟⴽ ⵍⵜⵏ ⵔⵟ ⵔⴶⴴ ⵛⵜⵐⴽ. ⴱ
ⵟⵜⵖ ⴱ ⵐⵊⵏ ⵊⴽⴱ ⴱ ⴴⵔⵐ ⵐⴵⴴ ⵅⵊⵟ ⵔⵐ ⵜⴽ
ⵝ ⴴⴴⵟⴽ. ⴺⵛ ⴴⴵ ⵏⵜⵏ ⵟⵊⴱ ⵔⵊⴽ ⵏⵊⴱ ⵔⵟ
ⵛⵜⵐⴽ ⴴⵏ ⵟⴽ ⵏⵟⵐ ⵔⵐⵜ ⵔⵐⴴ. ⴴⵔⵏ ⵝ ⵟⵜⵖ
ⵝ ⵐⵊⵏ ⵊⴽⴱ ⵝ ⴴⵊⵐ ⵍⵏⴴ ⴽⵊⵏ ⵏⵟⵐ ⵔⵐⵜ ⵔⵐⴴ.

5 *Not all educational innovations are beneficial*

The children's story of Figure 4 printed in an experimental alphabet tried in 1868. Each character represents a different sound.

pare the British text with an alphabet developed by the Mormon Church during the early days of the Utah settlement. Figure 5 presents the same paragraph as Figure 4, printed in the form used by a Mormon schoolbook printed in 1868.[1] This early experiment was quite unsuccessful.

4. Would it be best to teach the child to read by introducing small letters only, adding capitals after he has mastered the 26 small letters? Would it be best to introduce only a limited number of letters (say, 13) during the first six months of reading? Do you see any reasonable possibility of common-sense arguments on both sides of these questions? If everyone is agreed on one answer, does this remove the need for research?

5. Are there any possibilities of simplifying early arithmetic by new notation? What about $=$ for three, $\Box$ for five, $\Box=$ for seven? Has as much inventiveness been applied to education as to other affairs?

6. Why may the British experiment succeed where the Mormon experiment failed?

7. Can the success of Augmented Roman be judged entirely by reading tests at the end of Grade I?

SCIENTIFIC APPROACHES TO EDUCATIONAL ISSUES

Bases for Evaluating Assumptions

Some of the most firmly established ideas about education were introduced to fit conditions that no longer exist. The lecture method of instruction, for example, was introduced in medieval universities when this was the only way to bring knowledge from rare manuscripts to the student. All the other features of the schools—the organization of the elementary school by grades, the 50-minute period in high school, the presentation of

---

[1] This primer was drawn to the writer's attention by Gabriel Della Piana.

algebra before geometry and after arithmetic, and so on—were introduced because they appeared to fit conditions at some moment in the past. There is a steady stream of proposals for altering school organization and teaching method, each of which seems reasonable at least to its author. Sometimes the justification is superficial. Sometimes the proposal is well reasoned, adequately tested, and thoroughly worthwhile.

VALUE ASSUMPTIONS.   Every educational proposal rests on a *value* assumption and an *empirical* assumption. Value assumptions state what results the school should attempt to produce, and what outcomes should be given priority. Determining the goals of schooling is in the end a political decision. Only the public has the power to decide, for example, whether the local high school should give much or little attention to vocational preparation. The public view of educational goals is illuminated by a continuing debate to which many types of scholars contribute; the economist calls attention to the economic decisions that will face future citizens, the classicist speaks of the depth and current pertinence of great writings of the past, and the philosopher reduces the issues of the educational debate to a clearer form.

The psychologist makes a special contribution to value decisions by emphasizing goals that might otherwise be overlooked. For example, he draws attention to motivational outcomes: changes in the pupil's interests, in his expectation of success, and in his life aims. The educational psychologist emphasizes social behavior, personal effectiveness, and emotional adjustment just because these are inadequately considered by some specialists concerned only with "subject matter." These are not, however, the only goals he considers significant.

A second function of the psychologist is to help others to define their educational aims more clearly. He has found, for example, that ability to repeat a fact from the textbook may not imply ability to use the fact, and that ability to solve a problem presented in class does not guarantee success in solving other problems involving the same principle. The psychologist therefore fears that educators will adopt methods that produce only transient and superficial benefits. The psychologist insists that, to eliminate self-delusion, all planners should state their value assumptions in terms of the *changes in behavior* they wish to produce. This technique for bringing lofty abstractions within the range of observation will be illustrated in Chapter 2.

EMPIRICAL ASSUMPTIONS.   While the psychologist is but one of many voices in the discussion of value assumptions, he has an almost unique role to play in examining empirical assumptions. An empirical assumption is an assumption about facts. Every proponent of educational change argues that if his suggestion is followed, certain outcomes will result. This is a statement about observable events; it is empirical in the sense that it can be verified or contradicted by suitable observations. Casual observation gives insufficient proof that an educational procedure is superior. Controlled observations in laboratory, classroom, or community are needed to confirm such claims and hopes. It is the responsibility of educational research to test new ideas thoroughly and impartially.

Most educational research, though not all, is psychological. Psychologists specialize in observing behavior and measuring changes in it, and are therefore well equipped to examine empirical questions about education. In the preparation of most teachers, educational psychology is the one course whose central concern is the evidence justifying educational practices.

8. The following statements are taken from articles addressed to the general public, discussing various school reforms. Classify each statement as a value assumption or an empirical assumption, or as a combination of the two.

a. The average 5-year-old is not ready physically, mentally, or emotionally to read.

b. The 5-year-old has to learn how to get along without Mother for a while, how to get along with other children, and how to build his strength and muscular coordination.

c. Motivation and interest are more important than aptitude for success in a vocation.

d. At least two years of a foreign language should be taken by every student going to college because this develops skill in English.

e. Teaching machines can show young people how to punctuate but not how to express themselves with grace and force.

f. The purpose of studying history is to establish a perspective for the individual so that he will assume rational attitudes toward social problems.

9. Why is systematic research on a new educational proposal needed, in view of the fact that the teachers who try the new method can report how well it works in the classroom?

Methods Used by Psychologists

Dependable information about behavior is obtained in many ways. Understanding of the reading process may come from tests given throughout entire school systems, from observation of individual children as they read, or from the electronic recording of responses of the visual system. While any classification of scientific methods is somewhat arbitrary, we can draw attention to the major procedures under three headings: experimental, correlational, and case studies.

EXPERIMENTAL STUDIES.   In an experiment, the investigator administers some carefully planned treatment (e.g., some teaching procedure) under controlled conditions and observes the result. Nearly all the experiments we shall examine employ a second group, so that the investigator learns what effect one treatment has by comparing the treated group with an untreated group, or with a group given some other treatment.

Sometimes experiments are conducted in classrooms, to compare two complex systems of teaching. Sometimes comparisons are made under more controlled (laboratory) conditions. When a very high degree of control is desired, the psychologist may experiment on animals. He can make animal groups alike in every respect: degree of hunger, nature of previous experience—even heredity of the groups can be equalized.

One large-scale classroom experiment compared so-called activity and recitation methods in nine New York City elementary schools (Sells *et al.*, 1941). In the activity method, classwork grew out of interesting projects. For example, some pupils organized a window garden, giving plants controlled amounts of light and water and measuring growth. Reading, spelling, and arithmetic were practiced in the course of the activity. The recitation classes studied subject matter, formally organized with assignments and definite practice periods. Insofar as possible, equally able pupils and equally able teachers were assigned to each method.

Effects were gauged by two sets of tests. One test series measured basic skill in computation, reading, etc. A second test series measured these skills, and in addition measured other outcomes such as citizenship knowledge and the ability to find information. The result of the comparison was this:

In formal skills and knowledge the activity groups gained, on the average, about 4 per cent less than did the recitation groups.

On broader educational outcomes the activity groups gained, on the average, about 25 per cent more than did the recitation groups.

Classroom observation showed that the activity groups became markedly superior in initiative, leadership, and participation in discussion.

The differences between programs were rather small compared with the differences within either program. Many pupils in recitation classes earned high scores, and many earned low scores; likewise in the activity classes.

This study permits us to note several characteristics of experimental studies, the first being *control of treatment*. All the recitation classes had the same carefully planned program. The activity method necessarily varied from class to class, but the procedures were controlled to fit a general plan. When well-defined treatments are compared, the reader knows what was done to produce the observed results.

Second, *groups are equated* on variables other than the treatment method itself. To compare groups that happen to be using different methods would be unsatisfactory. The activity method might be found primarily in small schools, or in schools located in well-to-do neighborhoods, or in classes with bright children. If any of these characteristics might affect the results, no sound conclusion could be drawn about the treatments. To eliminate such irrelevant differences, the experimenter forms groups that are as similar as possible, before introducing differences in treatment.

The substantial overlap between final scores of the two groups in the New York study is characteristic of psychological experiments. *Variation within groups* is inevitable. Each pupil has his own pattern of ability and motivation, and hence each one responds differently to the treatment given. If two procedures are applied to each pupil at different times, some pupils are likely to respond better to one treatment and some to the other. The difference in averages tells only part of the story.

The New York experiment was superior to many other investigations because the investigators used several *measures of outcome.* Using two kinds of tests, and classroom observations in addition, they arrived at far more adequate conclusions than one measure would give. The formal tests alone suggested that the activity method was a bit inferior. On other measures the recitation method was consistently inferior. The results as they stand indicate that either method may be superior for certain purposes and in certain situations. This is most often the correct answer when we are asked, "Is classroom method A better than B?" As we said earlier, "It depends . . ." One of the most difficult problems for the investigator is to identify the conditions and value assumptions under which one approach is preferable to another.

An experimental finding never gives an exact rule for classroom procedure. The comparison of activity and recitation methods shows that activity methods can be made effective, but it by no means guarantees success for every teacher. A departure of the teacher's procedures from those used in the experiment, a difference in pupil backgrounds, or even the teacher's personality can affect the results. A conclusion must not be overgeneralized; the evidence favorable to *one* activity procedure does not provide an endorsement of all activity procedures. A research study is only indicative: it suggests *what the teacher can profitably try.* The effectiveness of the procedure, as tried by the teacher, must be judged moment by moment as the teacher proceeds.

Classroom comparison of educational methods is of considerable value, but it is at best a clumsy way to develop an understanding of learning. By comparing the health of adults, one can judge whether the Japanese diet is better than the diet in India, but it takes small-scale experiments in which one part of the diet is changed at a time in order to discover the principles that permit a nutritionist to plan the best possible diet. Laboratory experiments allow fine control that is unattainable in natural settings. Such experiments, being less costly, can be used to check one specific question at a time.

Thousands of these small studies are carried out each year on human or animal subjects. For example, Weir and Stevenson (1959) studied whether or not making an oral interpretation helps the young child to learn a simple association. The child was set the task of learning which of two push buttons would turn off a light. Above each push button a picture of an animal (monkey, cat, etc.) was placed. Certain animals were always "correct"; the child had to learn this through successive trials. The task requires observation of relations and retention of information. Such an artificial task is used because children have had no previous training on it. Their school experience should have little direct effect.

The main treatment variable was verbalization, or oral interpretation. Half the children ("verbal group") had to name the pictured animal before they pushed the corresponding button. This was expected to help them concentrate and discriminate. The other half, selected from the total group at random, did not name the pictures aloud. 32 children at each of four ages (3, 5, 7, and 9) were tested; the investigators expected verbalizing to be particularly helpful to younger children. Each child was offered a balloon or toy as a prize if he could learn to choose the correct picture in five different pairs. Children made 500 responses, learning by trial and error. The experimenter recorded the number of trials on which the pupil was correct. The averages for the various groups are presented in Figure 6.

As anticipated, naming the animals was helpful. Older children, however, did no better than those in preschool; the very best performers were the 5-year-olds. Almost every piece of research turns up some such surprise that requires further examination. In this study, the older children seemed to be looking for an obscure, complicated answer. They said, "I thought that it was going to be a pattern" and "I thought you were going to change them all around." They treated the task as a puzzle instead of a memory

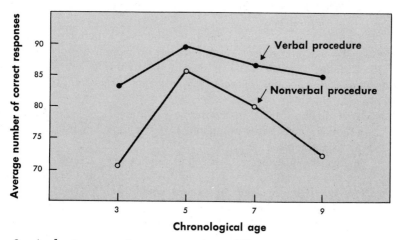

6   *A chart comparing groups given different treatments* (*Weir and Stevenson, 1959*)

task. Some of them thought the key was the position rather than the content of the pictures. One brings to a lesson some preconception as to what his task will be, and pays attention to cues pertinent to that interpretation. The 9-year-old nonverbal group had a very difficult time because they were studying the wrong things; the verbalizers had less trouble because naming the pictures drew their attention to the facts that mattered.

One experiment such as this proves very little by itself. It indicates that naming the stimulus is helpful when an arbitrary response is to be remembered. It does not indicate whether verbalizing about keyboard locations would help a typist, or whether describing works of art verbally would help a college student remember their history. The importance of each small study is that, as studies accumulate, consistent evidence will ultimately indicate when and why oral interpretation during learning is helpful (see also page 328).

    10. Do you think it would be wise to sacrifice even a small amount of progress in fundamental skills in order to obtain the advantageous outcomes that the New York activity schools showed?

    11. How do you account for the wide range of scores within either program in the New York study?

    12. Is it easier to control differences among students and among teachers in a laboratory experiment on teaching, or in a classroom experiment?

    13. Would classroom or laboratory experimentation be advantageous for investigating the following questions:

        a. To what extent does adding illustrations to reading material influence the length of time a student spends in voluntary reading?

        b. To what extent does adding illustrations to reading material improve the pupil's learning from the printed text?

        c. What kinds of illustrations most improve student comprehension of printed text?

    14. Could Weir and Stevenson have obtained a better answer to their question by teaching school lessons instead of arbitrary associations?

    15. Examine a recent issue of one of the following journals: *Journal of Educational Psychology, Journal of Experimental Education, Child Development.*

        a. Find the articles that describe experiments, as distinguished from other types of investigation. List the topics investigated by these experiments.

        b. Select one experimental report, and list the treatments compared, the outcomes measured, and the variables that the experimenter controlled to make the groups equal.

    16. To determine whether or not preschool experience affects the child's performance in grade school, what outcomes should be measured? Can conclusions be reached by investigating only the children given preschool experience, or would a "control group" also be needed? If so, what sort of group?

CORRELATIONAL STUDIES.   A correlational study is an investigation that begins with groups already differing in one respect and goes on to determine how much these groups differ in other respects. In an experiment the

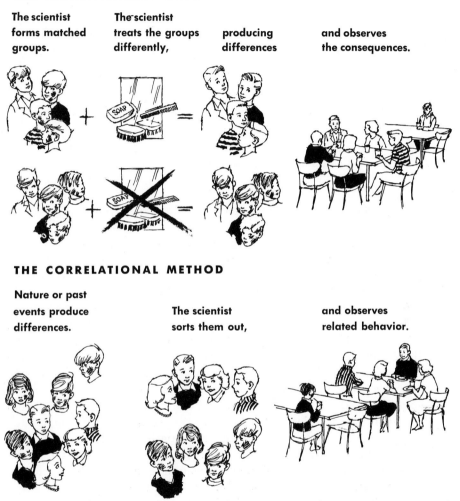

THE EXPERIMENTAL METHOD

The scientist forms matched groups. **The scientist treats the groups differently,** **producing differences** **and observes the consequences.**

THE CORRELATIONAL METHOD

Nature or past events produce differences. **The scientist sorts them out,** **and observes related behavior.**

7 *Two plans for studying how neatness affects social acceptance*

psychologist creates a difference between groups of subjects by treating them differently and then measures the resulting difference in outcome. In a correlational study the differences he measures have already been created by biological or social influences (Figure 7). The effect of home background upon emotional adjustment, for example, must be studied by comparing children who already differ in home background. The psychologist cannot

TABLE 1

Scores of ten college freshmen

College aptitude test		Reading test	High-school graduating class		Freshman grade average	
287	**1**	**2**	201	**4**	4.7	**1**
258	**3**	**1**	112	**6**	4.0	**2**
250	**4**	**3**	31	**9**	3.8	**3**
152	**9**	**8**	87	**7**	3.4	**4**
279	**2**	**6**	374	**1**	3.1	**5**
168	**8**	**7**	84	**8**	3.0	**6**
212	**5**	**5**	266	**2**	2.9	**7**
121	**10**	**10**	16	**10**	2.8	**8**
188	**7**	**9**	172	**5**	2.5	**9**
201	**6**	**4**	258	**3**	2.3	**10**

Grades are recorded on a scale where $A = 5$, $C = 3$.
Figures in **boldface** are ranks.

arbitrarily dictate what home experiences children shall have, as an experiment requires.

The correlational study compares the averages of various groups. Just as in an experimental study, it is necessary to control irrelevant differences between groups. The investigator equalizes his groups, if he can, on variables irrelevant to his inquiry. Studying effects of home background, he selects cases so that each group has a similar composition with regard to sex, age, etc. Practical difficulties prevent the control of all variables. Homes that treat children differently are likely also to differ with respect to the income and the educational level of the parents; it is hard to study the effect of parental technique in handling the child, independent of these other factors.

When there are several levels of each variable, correlational analysis is commonly used to summarize results. The *correlation coefficient* summarizes the degree of relationship between two variables (e.g., home background and adjustment). If two variables are perfectly related, so that one can be determined exactly from the other, the coefficient is +1.00. A zero coefficient (.00) indicates absolutely no relation, and a negative coefficient shows that high values on one variable are associated with low values on the other. (For example, age and health are negatively correlated among adults.)

Table 1 presents scores we can use to illustrate correlation coefficients. For each student we are given scores on two tests he took when he entered college, the size of his high-school class, and his grade average for his freshman year in college. It can be seen that the aptitude test and the reading test rank the students in about the same way. One student who ranks second in aptitude ranks sixth in reading, but he is an exception. The aptitude test also tends to agree with the grade average—but how

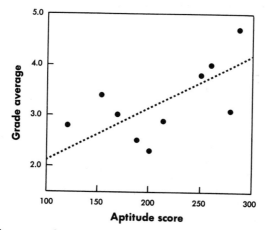

8 *How well do aptitudes forecast grades?*

Each dot in this scatter diagram shows the standing of one student, as listed in Table 1. The broken line is an indication of the trend; it can be used to estimate the expected grade average for a student whose aptitude score is known.

closely? One way to examine the relationship is to prepare a diagram such as Figure 8. Here, two scores for each student are used to locate one point. If one variable predicted the other perfectly (a correlation of 1.00), all points would fall in a straight line. In our diagram, the points show a general trend but do not fall exactly along a straight line. The coefficient is calculated by a formula, given in any elementary statistics book, which tells how close the points come to a line.

Between aptitude and grade average, the coefficient is .59. If you make a diagram comparing the reading test to the aptitude test, you will see that points fall more nearly in a line; the correlation coefficient is .74. The correlation of graduating-class size with grade average is −.10; that is, there is a very slight tendency for students from large schools to earn low grades in this sample.

Figure 9 is a chart helpful in interpreting the correlations that you will encounter in research reports. There are two measures: X and Y. Each scale interval contains one quarter of the group. The chart shows how the people who fall into the highest quarter, say, on X perform on Y, for each degree of correlation.

Correlations between −.30 and +.30 indicate weak relations—too weak, ordinarily, to be a basis for prediction about individuals. Low correlations often have theoretical significance. The value of low correlations in developing theory is illustrated by a study in which the parents of several hundred young children were interviewed. One set of questions asked how much "conscience" the child showed. Other questions dealt with the parents'

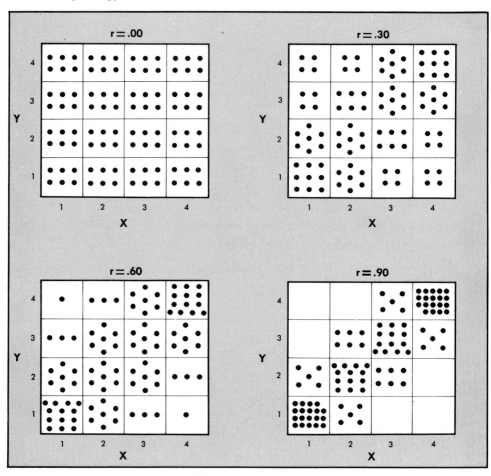

9   *Higher correlation implies greater predictability*

Each dot represents one person in a group of 96. The score range is divided so that each level includes one-fourth of the group.

methods of disciplining the child. The results (Table 2) are shown in two forms: percentage and correlation. The percentages show, for example, that differences in conscience were associated with type of discipline. Parents who gave frequent praise reported that the child was concerned to do the right thing almost twice as often as did parents who gave praise rarely. The percentages and the correlations tell the same story in somewhat different ways. The percentages tell how often conscientiousness is to be expected. A single correlation summarizes two or more percentages, indicating the direction and strength of the relation. Here it tells what kinds of rewards are positively related to conscience and indicates that the relation is far from perfect.

TABLE 2

Conscientiousness is related to method of discipline (*R. R. Sears et al., 1957, p. 386*)

Method used to train child		Number of families	Percentage having conscientious children	Correlation *
Praise	Much used	181	32	.18
	Little used	192	17	
Reasoning with child	Much used	192	30	.18
	Little used	91	16	
Tangible rewards	Much used	188	20	−.04
	Little used	181	28	
Physical punishment	Much used	175	15	−.20
	Little used	197	32	

* Based on high, low, and middle groups.

The correlations in the table are small, indicating that no one technique of control can by itself guarantee that the child will develop a high degree of conscience. The correlations (together with three others not reproduced here) imply that loving attention to the child through praise and reason strengthens conscientiousness, while punishment tends to retard its development. The authors conclude (R. R. Sears *et al.*, 1957, p. 388):

> Six of the seven [correlations] are in the theoretically expected direction. . . . The consistency of these findings, rather than the amount of influence of each separate dimension, gives us some confidence in the significance of the final results. The findings all support the theory that love-oriented techniques aid in the development of conscience.

In interpreting a study, it is unsafe to conclude that "since *A* and *B* are correlated, *A* causes *B*." There are two other possibilities to be considered: *B* may cause *A*, or some third cause may affect both *A* and *B*. The last sentence in the foregoing quotation is justified only on the basis of a substantial compilation of other research. From this one correlation, it might be argued that having a conscientious child leads parents to give more loving treatment ("*B* causes *A*"). It might be that higher intelligence in parents (a third factor) produces more conscientious children and also is associated with more loving discipline. There are similar hazards in interpreting an experimental study. Sometimes a new teaching method gives better results in a tryout than a conventional method, not because it is truly superior, but because the teachers and pupils are more interested when trying something new.

17. In the investigations sketched in Figure 7:
   a. Can the outcome be expressed as a numerical score, suitable for averaging or correlating?
   b. What variables need to be controlled in matching experimental groups? Do these variables influence the correlational study?
   c. What advantage does the correlational method have over the experimental method in this study?

18. If it is found that neatness increases social acceptance, is this information important to a teacher? If social acceptance has no relation to neatness, is this information important?

19. Using Table 1, prepare the scatter diagram relating aptitude test to reading test. Prepare one for class size and grades.

20. Can one conclude from the negative correlation between high-school-class size and college grades that small high schools are more beneficial than large ones? What variables have not been controlled?

21. How could a diagram comparing aptitude score and freshman grade in college for several hundred students be used by a high-school counselor?

22. It is reported that college students who smoke have lower grade averages than those who do not; those who smoke most tend to have the lowest grades. What explanations can you offer for this correlation?

23. Suppose it is found that the score on a test of anxiety correlates .30 with subsequent success in a certain educational program. What use does this finding have for the administrator of the program? How would your answer change if the correlation were .60? If it were −.30?

24. Among college entrants, rank in high school correlates .60 with grade in a certain course. What prediction would be made regarding a student whose high-school record is a bit below the average of the group? (Use Figure 9.)

25. A predictive test is given to sophomores applying to enter teacher training. What correlation with success in teaching should this test have, if it is to be used to eliminate the least promising quarter of the group? (Refer to Figure 9.)

CASE STUDIES.   Experimental and correlational studies are statistical. They investigate relationships found on the average, usually in a sizable group of persons. A case study is an intimate, detailed investigation of one person at a time. While tests and laboratory measurements may be used, emphasis is ordinarily placed on observation in everyday situations, interviews with the subject, and interviews with parents and teachers. A case study is made whenever detailed knowledge of the individual is required in order to solve his particular problems. Case studies also have general scientific value. After accumulating many cases of one type we can analyze the records correlationally. Thus a basis exists for tracing the effects of formative influences. An example is the study (page 446) where Newcomb identified girls who changed their social and political attitudes while in college, and by case studies showed what factors in their backgrounds predisposed them to profit from college, and what past experiences limited the readiness of others to learn.

26. In investigating what causes a person to become a scientist, what advantage would a collection of case studies have over a correlational study of a larger number of persons using a single questionnaire?

27. What advantages and what disadvantages would the case-study method have as compared with the experimental method of studying the effect of preschool on subsequent school performance?

THE TEACHING PLAN OF THIS BOOK

A few suggestions for using this book, and a few comments on its design, may be helpful at this point. If you are using the book in a course in educational psychology, the organization and activities of that course will determine your approach to the book. One class may skim the entire volume quickly to identify problems for intensive study. Another class may begin with problems arising out of teaching experience and refer to the book for answers. Most readers, however, will probably want to study one topic thoroughly and then proceed to the next. The book is organized to assist study of this kind.

Psychological topics cannot be separated from one another. Each of the important areas—emotional reactions, social learning, reasoning, etc.—affects all the others, so that we must study the *relation* of emotion to social experience and to intellectual performance. This means that the text can be fully comprehended only when taken as a whole. A topic introduced in an early chapter is still being discussed in the last chapter, with new ideas and specific findings being introduced all the way through.

The organization of topics is deliberately repetitive. A topic is introduced in a general overview that shows its importance and clarifies it somewhat. Then we consider it in connection with other topics. In some later chapter, we take up the same concept a second time, making a more thorough examination of detailed questions and findings. Chapter topics have been chosen to present important principles each time in a new context. For example, you should become aware of the importance of the child's feeling that his parents accept him and approve of him. In Chapter 4 this is introduced in connection with the over-all story of social and emotional development. We go further in Chapter 13, showing that this feeling of acceptance impels the child to learn his parents' attitudes and that the child-parent relation determines how easily the school can teach him new attitudes, values, and goals. The same concept enters again in Chapter 18, where we analyze character formation. Each chapter goes deeper than the previous treatment.

This planned review is one of several means by which the book tries to apply the principles of educational psychology. The questions imbedded in the text are another attempt to assist learning. The questions are intended to make you stop and think. They are placed in the midst of the text because you should understand one section before going on to the next. The questions are not usually so simple that you can "look back" for a key sentence that gives the answer. The principles of the text should help you think about real educational problems; any real problem requires you to combine many concepts rather than simply to recall one phrase. Our questions call for this kind of integration. Occasionally a question is intended to arouse interest in a topic that the text will discuss later.

Many educational issues lack simple answers, and you should not be surprised that you are uncertain as to the "correct" answer to some questions. Equally intelligent students will be able to defend different answers. People with different values will prefer different solutions. Often, a book problem must omit the detailed information that would affect an actual decision. Therefore, a good answer is one that takes more things into account. A good answer will not be "Yes" or "No." It will begin, "I'd want to know these things before deciding . . ." or "I'd say 'Yes,' provided that . . ."

Many examples are given in the text. They are not themselves the content to be studied most seriously. The examples are given to illustrate principles and to show their meaning in terms of real learners and real schools. The principle, not the example, is what will be most helpful in new situations.

At several points in the book we give lengthy case reports. Such reports tell a great deal about a single person or classroom situation. While the report emphasizes certain principles relevant at that point, it also illustrates many other parts of the book. The list of case descriptions (page xiii) will help you to keep the cases in mind. The case reports are based on observations, but they are not accurate scientific reports. Limitations of space have made it necessary to simplify, omitting detailed information and minor features of each case. Moreover, to disguise the identity of teachers and pupils, observed facts have been altered where this could be done without falsifying the general picture.

Research described in the text is similarly illustrative. From the many studies that support each important principle, only one or two are reported. The studies selected are those easiest to comprehend or those most important to teachers, preferably both. In reading, therefore, you should recognize that most conclusions are based on considerable research in addition to the studies described. Since the research reported is chiefly illustrative, there is little reason to try to remember the details of each study. The principles and the general method of attack, as illustrative of psychological investigation, are the important concern.

SUMMARY

The chapter has indicated the kind of contribution psychology makes to the improvement of education, and it has described the ways in which the psychologist reaches his conclusions. Psychology broadens the educator's outlook by suggesting factors to be taken into account in directing educational activities. It thus equips the teacher to design procedures to meet changing conditions, where traditional methods are unsatisfactory. Psychological principles do not always lead to direct recommendations for educational practice. As James said, psychology is a science, and teaching is an art. The science provides principles to which the teaching method should conform, it draws attention to erroneous practices and suggests new possibilities, and it aids the teacher in evaluating the soundness of his trial procedures.

A scientific approach to education is inconsistent with blind faith in tradition, with enthusiasm for untested innovations, or with reliance on impressionistic judgments. Comparisons of impressionistic judgments with judgments reached by controlled techniques show that the more systematic judgment is generally more accurate. Scientific conclusions do not eliminate the necessity for continual judgment by the teacher who applies them, but it is important to maintain a critical attitude about such judgments.

Psychological principles and proposals based on them should be consistent with everyday experience. But commonly held, plausible beliefs are frequently incorrect. As one example, the psychology of reading was discussed. The skilled reader identifies words as wholes, in terms of their general outline, rather than—as was once believed—by seeing the separate letters and combining them. Breaking a word into syllables or letters is a reserve technique, learned for use when a word is not familiar enough to be instantly recognized. The common-sense principle that the learner should practice by reading regular text is being challenged by current British studies using an artificial alphabet for beginning instruction.

Every educational practice and proposal rests on value assumptions and empirical assumptions. Value assumptions state what results are wanted. The psychologist is one of many who contribute to decisions about values. He draws attention to certain outcomes—for example, social effectiveness, and the pupil's expectations about himself—that may be neglected by specialists in other branches of knowledge. Secondly, he increases the clarity of educational aims by insisting that they be stated in terms of desired changes in behavior. An empirical assumption is an assumption about facts, capable of being verified or contradicted by observation. Psychologists, trained to observe changes in behavior, have a unique responsibility for identifying and testing empirical assumptions about education.

Psychological research methods are discussed under three headings: experimental, correlational, and case studies. In an experiment, comparable groups are formed and each one is given a different treatment. Experiments can be conducted in classrooms or, where more perfect control is required, in the laboratory. Two illustrative experiments are described. One, comparing activity and recitation methods of instruction, showed the recitation groups to be very slightly superior in formal skills and knowledge, and considerably inferior with regard to other outcomes, including citizenship knowledge, leadership, and ability to locate information. The second study showed that verbalizing the correct response can be valuable in learning a nonverbal response. Older pupils had unanticipated difficulties because their complex hypotheses interfered with learning. Features of experimental method to which attention was drawn are the control of treatment, the equating of groups on variables other than treatment, the existence of variation within groups, and the importance of measuring multiple outcomes.

Correlational studies are those in which the investigator observes connections among already existing differences. An example is the Sears study of conscientiousness in children, which concluded that parental giving and withholding of love has more effect on development of conscience than material rewards and forceful punishments. The interpretation of the correlation coefficient was discussed, Figure 7 being provided to show the degree of relationship indicated by a correlation of a certain magnitude.

The case study is an intimate, detailed investigation of a single person. It is useful for understanding the specific individual and also as a basis for generalizations.

Reading List 1

Roger Brown, "Methods of Learning to Read," in *Words and Things* (Glencoe, Illinois: Free Press, 1958), pp. 65–80.

John B. Carroll, "The Case of Dr. Flesch," *American Psychologist*, 11 (1956), 158–63.

Rudolf Flesch, "Phonics vs. No Phonics," Chapter 5 in *Why Johnny Can't Read, and What You Can Do About It* (New York: Harper, 1955), pp. 60–68.

This set of papers gives a unique opportunity to examine a debate about the educational use of psychological findings. All three writers are trained psychologists. Flesch's best seller was an all-out attack on the schools for not teaching beginning reading by phonic analysis. Carroll disagrees with Flesch, arriving at a quite different interpretation of the studies. Brown looks at the research and comes up with a still different conclusion. It will be highly instructive to study these papers, both to learn about phonics and to form an opinion as to how much educators should trust the psychologist as an authority on school policy.

> John B. Carroll, "Wanted: A Research Basis for Educational Policy on Foreign Language Teaching," *Harvard Educational Review*, 30 (1960), 128–40.

In an address prepared for teachers of modern languages, Carroll notes questions now being asked about curriculum and method, or questions that ought to be asked, and shows how the answers depend upon facts that must be determined by investigation. Parallel questions could be asked regarding other fields of instruction.

> Stephen M. Corey, "The Conant Report on the American High School," *Educational Forum*, 24 (1959), 7–9.

Corey, an educational psychologist, criticizes the famous report on what high schools should teach. What questions does he raise that might be overlooked by a nonpsychologist? Are his objections matters of opinion or matters that can be settled by investigation?

> Francis J. DiVesta, "Balance in Teaching Methods and Learning Processes," in *Balance in the Curriculum*, Yearbook, Association for Supervision and Curriculum Development (Washington, D. C.: National Education Association, 1961), pp. 66–94.

This remarkable. chapter is very nearly a complete overview of what educational psychology has to say about the current issues and difficulties in education. As such, it gives a preview of this book.

CHAPTER 2 WHAT TEACHERS ARE TRYING TO ACCOMPLISH

Before studying *how* people learn and what can be done to help them learn more, we need to discuss *what* we want them to learn. How we teach and how we judge our effectiveness depend upon what we are trying to teach. It is easy to list quickly some things the schools should be teaching. When the man in the street makes such a list, however, he is likely to omit many things important for pupils to learn in school. Teachers themselves sometimes overlook important objectives. If we fail to keep all the purposes of schooling in mind, we miss opportunities for giving the best possible education.

What should education try to develop in the student? Some people answer by listing subjects they wish taught. Such a list is unsatisfactory, however, because some important performances and attitudes are not identified with any one field of study, and any one subject can be taught with many different aims. In the New York investigation described in the last chapter, the conclusions would have been incomplete if the only accomplishments examined had been arithmetic, spelling, and reading. Health knowledge, citizenship knowledge, the ability to read tables and draw conclusions, and the ability to apply principles to new problems had to be considered. In order to arrive at a comprehensive list of the possible school objectives, this chapter examines the fundamental question, "What must people learn in order to function well in our society?"

MULTIPLE OUTCOMES OF A LESSON. An example will illustrate some of the concepts one must take into account in judging a particular learning experience. One student from an educational psychology class visited a high-school English class to observe teaching procedures and returned with a critical report. "They weren't working on English. Instead of having lessons on sentence structure and things like that, they were sitting with their chairs in a circle listening to reports and talking about them. There didn't seem to be anything they were trying to learn, and I don't see how the teacher thought she was teaching English! That's why students get into the University without knowing how to write." This student reacted with so harsh an opinion because he did not recognize that the school was aiming to produce many changes in pupils besides increased knowledge of sentence structure.

When the educational psychology class examined carefully what was going on in this high-school session, it found many purposes behind the activities. Each activity had a definite aim, as outlined below:

Activity	*Changes resulting*
The pupils prepared the reports.	They learned to use the library, and to select material from reference books.
The pupils gave the reports and answered questions. When the speaker mumbled or spoke too fast, students who could not follow him requested a repetition. The teacher commented on the organization of the reports.	They learned to speak to an audience, to use good diction and delivery. They learned to "think on their feet" and to express themselves.
The reports dealt with feudal England. There was much discussion of knightly tradition and courtly love.	The pupils learned enough so that they would understand Chaucer's stories, which they were to take up next. They developed an interest in the period. They learned the source of traditions about manners and romantic love that affect their own lives. Moreover, they used this discussion to clarify their feelings about the different standards set for men and women in our own day.
The pupils raised questions, discussed the meaning of unclear points, and contributed additional information.	They learned to examine disagreements and reach conclusions, to think for themselves, and to voice their opinions with confidence.

At the end of this analysis, the student who originally complained had changed his view. "Use of the library is certainly something students need to learn, and English classes ought to teach them how to speak and to prepare reports. Studying about the feudal era before reading the stories sounds good too. But I still think that some time—perhaps on other days or later in the year—should be spent on grammar." Perhaps the student is wrong in this final opinion, since formal grammar lessons have often been unprofitable (see page 316). But that question is aside from our concern in this chapter.

The function of this chapter is to broaden your conception of the tasks of the school. The theme of the chapter is voiced in a famous statement by John Dewey (1938):

Perhaps the greatest of all pedagogical fallacies is the notion that a person learns only what he is studying at the time. Collateral learning in the way of formation of enduring attitudes, of likes and dislikes, may be and often is much more important than the spelling lesson or lesson in geography or history that is learned. For these attitudes are fundamentally what count in the future. The most important thing that can be formed is the desire to go on learning.

EDUCATION AS A PART OF SOCIALIZATION

The Socialization Process

The process of preparing a person for a role in a society is called socialization. Every group of people, whether on the tiniest island of the Pacific or in a modern city, has some plan for changing human raw material into whatever type of adult is needed to make its society run. Human behavior varies from one society to another, being determined by the society's religion, its ideas about proper treatment of other people, its economic system, and its accumulated knowledge. Sometimes children are socialized largely by the parents, as they were on the American frontier, where boys acquired knowledge by helping their fathers around the homestead and in the hunting field, and at the same time learned character traits appropriate for that self-reliant life. As society becomes more complex, we rely more on formal social institutions to accomplish socialization.

Socialization refers to "the whole process by which an individual, born with behavioral potentialities of enormously wide range, is led to develop actual behavior which is confined within a much narrower range—the range of what is customary and acceptable for him according to the standards of his group" (Child, 1954, p. 655). Some people misunderstand the term, thinking that to socialize is to create the good fellow for whom nothing in life is important save fitting into the group. Learning to work with others and enjoy their company is indeed a part of socialization for an interdependent community. But socialization includes all the training a society provides. A person must make a productive contribution. He must think for himself. He must be content when it is appropriate for him to be alone. He must oppose majority opinion at times. He must accept responsibility for making others unhappy when an unpopular decision is called for. Proper socialization produces all of these. *Socialization* is far from being a synonym for "having fun in a group." Some societies teach cooperation and equality while others insist on independence and even fierce competitiveness, but either training process is called *socialization.*

Socialization is lifelong. It is easy to think of socialization as a preparatory activity, needed before one steps out into the world on his own. This view is too limited. While it is true that more lessons must be learned in youth than later, socialization continues throughout adulthood. It must continue,

for society changes. As new knowledge is acquired and new inventions appear, society must adapt to them. Furthermore, the individual's life changes as he grows older and takes on the new roles of parent, supervisor, retired worker, etc. To fulfill these roles requires new learning.

> **1.** Is "socialization" the same as "Americanization"?
>
> **2.** Should the aims of socialization be the same for every American child?
>
> **3.** Professor Travis is a scholar whose translations of Greek poetry are famous. He is shy, uneasy when he must attend a social gathering or make a public appearance, and so formal and undramatic that undergraduate students avoid his classes. He has never married, and spends most of his time happily at work on manuscripts in the library or in discussions with his graduate students. Is it correct to speak of Professor Travis as having been *socialized*?

Special Responsibilities of the School

The responsibility for socialization is shared by many institutions. Some things are still taught chiefly in the home: how to speak our language, how to dress, how to eat, how to be kind to others. Sunday school and church teach how to gain satisfaction and guidance from religious rituals, and they teach some of the basic attitudes and principles of conduct. Employers teach skills of business and trade. Newspapers, motion pictures, and other mass media educate too: about care of children, about political issues, and about fashions. All these agencies provide ideas, skills, and attitudes that help a person meet the demands of his culture and contribute to it.

The school has two concerns in the socialization process. First, it is assigned primary responsibility for intellectual learning and for certain skills. For instance, all people have to know the system of numerical symbols that plays such a large part in business and science. The school therefore is asked to teach arithmetic and, more broadly, quantitative thinking. The school is likewise the place where people get an organized conception of the world through geography, science, and history.

Second, the school is expected to supplement the work of other socializing agencies. The home and neighborhood teach the child a great deal about working with others, for example. School continues these lessons. Well-planned school activities can do much to compensate for an inadequate home. The school can, for example, teach the quarrelsome child how to attain satisfaction without annoying others. On the other hand, school events may interfere with desirable socialization; some school practices, for example, encourage hostile competitiveness rather than respect for others.

Possible objectives for the school are identified by answering two questions. What must people know to be an effective part of our society (or of the better society that education could promote)? Which of these types of learning are not being attained through agencies other than the school? As we said earlier, the behavioral sciences give a valuable perspective from which to review value assumptions. Anthropologists compare the goals of socialization in different cultures; these comparisons sometimes suggest that our own traditions are unwise (Mead and Wolfenstein, 1955; Benedict, 1934). Only by a keen and detached study of its traditions and social organization can a nation wisely decide what should be perpetuated as it is, and what should give way to new patterns of behavior.

One way to find out what people ought to learn is to study how members of our society act. If we compare those who are effective with those who break down or who make no contribution, we find where our socializing machinery has been faulty. Consider family life as an example. Homes are less stable and divorces more frequent than they were formerly. A high divorce rate appears undesirable, for studies of divorced couples and their children show that many of them remain unsettled and unhappy. Even though divorce may be the best way to resolve a particular family conflict, a high divorce rate is a sign that there are many unwise marriages. Having identified a social weakness such as this, the next step is to look for causes and possible remedies, e.g., lack of sex education. Whenever the home and other unorganized socializing agencies fail to teach ways of thinking and acting that are good for the community as a whole, the community protects itself by asking some agency under its control to teach them. This explains the trend in recent years toward introducing the study of family problems into the school.

The school, in its long history, has added on many obligations, each worthy in itself. In one century the school has been charged with preparing scholars for a life of the mind, in another with integrating children of immigrants into the American tradition, and in yet another with preparation for industrial and technical work. There are, however, too many fields of useful knowledge and too many important attitudes for all of them to be seriously considered as school objectives. The school cannot find time to make up for all the deficiencies of other socializers.

Even when there is complete agreement as to what is of highest importance, it is difficult to decide how much to concentrate effort in order to accomplish these most vital objectives thoroughly, and how much to spread effort to give some attention to other high-ranking objectives. This issue arises, for example, when a legislature proposes that every high-school pupil be instructed on the consequences of drinking. It can also arise in allocating the time within a particular course—the English teacher above, for instance, chose to emphasize oral discussion at the expense of added work on composition. Psychology can contribute toward such decisions (for example, by investigating whether or not information about physiological effects of alcohol affects an adult's drinking habits). The final decisions, however, depend primarily on the values held by those directing the schools and by the public.

    4. List contributions to socialization made by each of the following:
        a. a study of the solar system in Grade VII.
        b. Little League baseball
        c. individual music lessons
    5. In our society, what means are used for the socialization of adults after they end their continuous schooling?
    6. Each portion of the school program is intended to fulfill a socializing function. What aspects of American life (out of school) would you examine to determine whether or not a good job is being done by each of the following?
        a. the mathematics curriculum
        b. the music curriculum
        c. the curriculum in vocational agriculture
        d. vocational guidance
    7. The curriculum should not duplicate socialization adequately provided for outside the school. Which of the following do you think are being taught adequately by the home and other out-of-school agencies?
        a. homemaking and child rearing
        b. automobile driving
        c. recreational skills and interests

THE SCHOOL AND SOCIAL OPPORTUNITY.   Some social functions of the school are not recognized as conscious objectives. One of the chief attractions of college for young women, for example, is the fact that it affords an opportunity to meet more desirable prospective husbands than they might find at home. Likewise, some boys are sent to college to form acquaintances who will be useful when they enter the family business, rather than because they or their parents value education. Assisting young people to rise in the social-class system is one school function of particular significance.

The social-class system of the United States is far different from that of a feudal society where a person's station in life, his way of living, and even the person he is allowed to marry are determined by the status of his ancestors. Our system allows great mobility; "poor boy to President" is a tradition rather than a myth. Until recently, sociologists saw American society as marked off into three major classes corresponding roughly to blue-collar workers, white-collar workers, and persons with inherited wealth and social position. Within these "lower," "middle," and "upper" classes, further distinctions were made. The "upper lowers" were established and productive, whereas the "lower lowers" were outcasts, ne'er-do-wells, often unemployable. As late as 1950, one could identify marked differences in manner of living and basic attitudes toward life, which could be summarized a bit superficially by saying that the lower classes typically lived for the present moment while the middle classes were always concerned with the future consequences of their acts. Hence the middle classes were more concerned with education, with manners, with saving and building up capital, with taking civic responsibility.

In the last decade many of these class differences have faded almost to the vanishing point. The change has been so rapid that we have no good sociological description of the current situation. Much of the research prior to 1958, and current research outside the United States, found important differences in child-rearing practices and in attitudes toward education between the middle and lower social classes. Today, although different homes teach different values, sociologists report that the attitudes are not closely related to socioeconomic levels. Instead, the differences are related to size and type of community; a big city fosters one set of attitudes, a remote town another, but within the setting the attitudes are much more homogeneous than they were a decade ago (Kimball, 1961; Gold and Slater, 1958; Havighurst, 1961).

The wife of the plumber and the wife of the physician shop at the same supermarket. Professional men send their children to comprehensive community high schools although they themselves attended exclusive private, academic schools. The same cultural stimulation (or absence of stimulation) pours into the living rooms on every street in town, thanks to the all-absorbing power of television. The forces that made the socioeconomic levels of society more homogeneous in outlook are many: the veteran's benefits and scholarship programs that made education widely available, the cheap and persuasive books on child rearing, which taught lower-class mothers the same theories that middle-class mothers were following, the virtual elimination of personal servants, the shorter work week and the reduction of fatigue in factory and home, the spread of installment buying, and so on.

The important stratification in American society today is associated primarily with levels of education. Positions of power and respectability go to the person who "has a college education." Among men, a college degree opens the way to employment even in positions where the college work may be irrelevant. It is hard to show that college makes a man a better sales manager, but the firm is likely to try to recruit a graduate just because the manager will associate with college-trained persons in other departments and other firms, and he must "belong." Among girls, there is less demand that the college course be completed; the girl who joins a good sorority and eventually marries a college-class husband will circulate at as privileged a level as the girl who completes professional training. The privileged position of the college group is not without its obligations and pressures—to provide leadership in community and business affairs, to carry work and worries home from the office, to encourage their children to the same level of achievement and responsibility.

The educated members of society, especially those who have more education than their parents had, know very well that rewards come to the man who is educated to the B.A. level. Indeed, this recognition, spreading through the entire society, accounts for our movement toward post-high-school training for everyone. The average parent supports radically increased outlays for education not because he wants to develop the nation's talent, but because he sees schooling as the gateway to a good life for Junior. It is still true that the children of professional men are more likely to go to college than the children of factory workers, but rapid change is occurring. Havighurst's estimates, in Figure 10, show that college is increasingly drawing boys from the lower social classes. The trend for girls is similar, though a smaller percentage of each female group goes to college.

Positive response to the school program, adequate success in college preparatory subjects, and, finally, survival in college are hurdles the child must surmount if he is to rise easily to a superior job and a position of

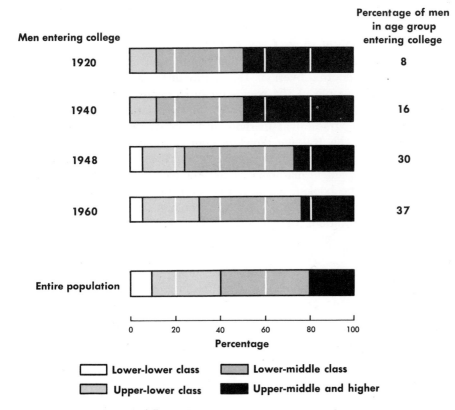

10 *College education is increasingly reaching into lower socioeconomic levels (Havighurst, 1961)*

All data are estimates.

respect and influence. The school thus is a sorting agency. It has the power to decide which persons in the next generation will rise to the top and to reject others, pushing them out into routine jobs and "common-man" status. As Gardner (1961, p. 71) puts it, "Who should go to college?" translates itself into "Who is going to manage the society?" The school record becomes a stamp of approval not just on intellectual performance but on the person as a whole.

School tasks are a proper basis for selecting people for power and prestige only if the talents needed in the adult are identical to those rewarded by the school. McClelland (1958, p. 251; 1961) urges that the sorting function be recognized in planning school programs. Perhaps, he says, the school rewards some children for talents that are of little ultimate importance, and discourages others who have talents that the school is not set to recognize. There is considerable reason to think that the best school records now belong to pupils whose eventual contributions to society will be good rather than outstanding. According to J. L. Holland (1961), those with the best achievement records in school are persevering and responsible, but they are not usually creative. Creative performers are most often independent, asocial, and consciously original (see pages 234, 390). These pupils may give little of themselves to assigned tasks that have no intrinsic interest or challenge, and teachers often overlook their individualistic talent.

As a specific example of the way educators' decisions favor one talent rather than another, consider the program in arithmetic. Able pupils often find distasteful the traditional method of teaching, with its emphasis on perfect accuracy. This training develops computational skills, but it repels pupils who dislike routine, unimaginative work. These are the pupils most likely to become excellent mathematicians. The true mathematician (as distinguished from the bookkeeper and the surveyor) works intuitively, not systematically; he grapples with a vague problem and imaginatively constructs plausible solutions (Polya, 1954). Detailed proof or checking for accuracy comes only after the mathematician is satisfied with his general comprehension. Indeed, unless he can ignore troublesome details for a time, he will rarely solve a new problem. More generally, it is found that the highly creative adult in any field is not much interested in small detail and in practical and concrete knowledge; what captures his attention is the meanings and symbolic transformations of things and ideas (MacKinnon, 1960). The teacher who insists on step-by-step precision with every detail in its place discourages the intuitive leap. He turns mathematics into drudgery for creative youngsters, a subject to be escaped as soon as possible. Such teaching, moreover, may impair the ability to reason intuitively. Several current experiments in arithmetic teaching (see Chapter 11) seek to encourage intuitive talent. Such a program would be expected to discover talent in some of the pupils who appear mediocre when taught conventionally.

8. The Rockefeller Report on Education (*The Pursuit of Excellence*, 1958, p. 47) makes the following statement:

"With rare exceptions, it is probably true that a society only produces great men in those fields in which it understands greatness. Spain in the sixteenth century produced Cortez and Pizarro and a dozen more who rank with the most extraordinary explorer-conquerors who ever strode the pages of history. It is unthinkable that the same society at the same time would have produced a Jefferson. The society that produced Jefferson produced Franklin, Monroe, Benjamin Rush, John Adams, and other philosopher-statesmen of breadth and brilliance. It is less easy to believe that it could have produced a Mozart."

What sorts of excellence are most likely to be developed in the present American culture? Can the school do anything to bring a greater diversity of talent to full development?

9. Should the fact that many girls come to college to seek a mate be acknowledged by an institution in planning its program, or ignored?

10. Do you agree with the following statement? "The purpose of *public* education *today* is *what it has always been:* to *raise the intellectual level* of the American people *as a whole* (Bestor, 1955, p. 17; italics ours). Consider separately each italicized word or phrase.

11. "We need to know to what extent the role requirements of being a student are the same as or different from those of various other status systems in later life" (McClelland, 1958, p. 251). What are the personality and behavior characteristics that bring reward in school? Do you think these are also the qualities that should be rewarded in adult society?

AIMS OF SOCIALIZATION

We need an image of the mature individual toward which our socializing aims. The following pages describe the person who may be considered properly socialized for our culture. In broad outline, his most important qualities are these:

He solves problems as well as the available facts permit.

He has self-respect and self-confidence.

He is effective in dealing with other people, he respects their rights, and he helps his associates to live satisfying lives.

He has some absorbing goals, interests, and sources of satisfaction.

He wants his actions to be praiseworthy, but he examines values critically before conforming to them.

A person must develop along all these lines. An adult who does not satisfy this description is an incomplete and handicapped person. The five qualities do not operate independently. Skill in solving problems, for example, leads to nothing, unless the choice of problems for attention is guided by worthy interests and values. Moreover, one quality contributes to another: interest to self-respect, self-confidence to problem-solving ability, and so on.

. . . . accepts social values

"Let's leave a clean campsite."

. . . . solves problems

"How much insurance can I afford?"

11   *Qualities of the socialized person*

In describing the goals of education, we must recognize the diversity of individuals and the fact that they may properly have different ways of contributing to society. As the Rockefeller Report (*The Pursuit of Excellence,* 1958, p. 32) says:

> What constitutes opportunity for one man is a stone wall for the next. If we are to do justice to the individual we must seek for him the kind of education which will open *his* eyes, stimulate *his* mind and unlock *his* potentialities. We should seek to develop many educational patterns—each geared to the particular capacities of the student for whom it is designed.
>
> But though the educational patterns may differ, the goals remain much the same for all: enabling each young person to go as far as his aptitude will permit in fundamental knowledge and skills, and motivating him to continue his own self-development to the full along similar lines.

12. Would these same five behaviors have been equally important in the culture of the Plains Indians, 200 years ago? Would they demand any characteristics that we do not?

. . . . has self-respect and self-confidence

"I think we ought to . . ."

. . . . has personal goals, interests

. . . . is effective with others

"Bill, can we work it this way?"

13. Does the foregoing list imply that intellectual development is an unimportant aspect of socialization? To how many of these qualities could the study of philosophy (for example) contribute?

14. To which of the five qualities of the well-socialized person can each of the following contribute?

    a. learning to compute percentages

    b. studying Latin

    c. writing to a pen pal in Norway

    d. attending meetings of a Future Farmers group

    e. learning to draw

Competence in Problem Solving

In a primitive culture where everyone plants corn, mends fish nets, and raises children as preceding generations did, education prepares the growing person for routines and crises that can largely be anticipated. Our student, on the other hand, must be equipped to deal with situations that we cannot now foresee. He is to be educated for a place in society even though his future role is uncertain. Inventions, the growth of cities, shifting social values, and new leisure confront each adult with decisions and problems unknown to the preceding generation. Standardized skills and recipes for living have only a very limited function in socialization. In all his roles— as citizen, father, professional man, and consumer—modern man must solve one problem after another, finding the right solution for his immediate circumstances.

The problems that the adult must solve range from small, everyday choices to major decisions and creations. Problem solving includes the behavior of the man trying to start a balky car on a cold morning, the bride choosing curtains for her new home, the governor seeking a tax policy, and the dramatist creating a plot for a play. The school cannot anticipate all these problems and teach how to solve each one. Somehow, while giving direct instruction on a limited number of problems, it must prepare the pupil to solve the many, many others not discussed in school.

Every subject taught in school, save for the narrowest of vocational and recreational courses, is to be applied primarily in unfamiliar situations. Knowledge is a storehouse of possible solutions to problems and of materials out of which solutions may be constructed. The educated man is not just one who *knows*, but one who gains from his knowledge the power to *do*. Later in the chapter we shall make a more thorough analysis of different kinds of knowledge and of the contribution each kind can make to effective behavior.

Problem solving calls for emotional as well as intellectual resources. The socialized person's interests and values turn his attention to problems worth solving. His security and self-confidence determine whether or not he will be thoughtful, adequately persevering, and able to break away from the patterns of the past. The school cannot teach the pupil what he should do as a citizen in 1990. But it can make him alert to civic problems and proud of his responsibility for forming and voicing opinions. It can give him confidence that he is able to influence civic decisions and knowledge about how to do it. The school may, on the other hand, present government as something remote, which he should understand "from outside." It may encourage him to accept opinions from power figures and to suppress his own doubts. Schools encourage pupils in *not* thinking, when they reward them for "looking up" the answer to every question (J. Henry, 1955).

Confidence and Self-respect

The person who aims too low or who gives up at the first difficulty is lacking in some ingredient required for effectiveness. He finds quitting and accepting failure less unpleasant than continuing to try. If he felt that he would satisfy his wants by persisting, he would consider the effort worth making. If he thinks that further effort will expose him to further criticism, he may give up to escape unpleasantness.

The school and home can make a person confident that his tries will bring him to his goals, and confident also that he will lose nothing save his effort if he tries and fails. Confidence and respect for one's own capabilities develop continuously. Through successful performance the pupil learns that he can master reading or the balancing of chemical equations; in addition, he develops a more general faith that he can master intellectual tasks.

Adults often make trying unpleasant when they criticize, or when they scold a child who takes initiative and thereby gets into difficulty. Soon the child learns that his impulses get him into trouble. He learns to follow where led, but not to direct himself.

Effective Relations with Others

Whenever we observe people in groups, we find that some of them are ineffective in personal relations. Sanders manages an industrial laboratory. He likes his workers, thinks the jobs they do are important, and sincerely tries to be a good leader. Nonetheless, he is plagued by high turnover, resistance to his suggestions, and slipshod work. A trained observer who studied Sanders' laboratory reports that Sanders' mistakes are simple. Sanders explains his policies, but always in terms of what *he* is trying to obtain instead of the benefits the policies would mean to the workers. Sometimes the failure is just in not keeping the workers informed, as when some of the men were transferred to other duties on two days' notice. Though some of the men had applied for such transfers long before, and although the new work was seemingly desirable, the abrupt transfer was received with resentment. Two of the men quit a short time later. Sanders has the common fault of not making sure that the people involved are prepared for his solution.

One who is effective in interpersonal relations trusts and respects other people. He thinks that they have a will to do good and that their reasoning will be as good as his if they have all the facts. The poor leader is likely to argue stubbornly for his views instead of trying to reconcile the opposing positions. One source of inappropriate social response is fear. Perhaps Sanders thinks the men dislike him and would be antagonistic if he discussed plans openly with them. Skill in working with others rests on a foundation of emotional security, on ability to interpret the cues one's associates present, and on concern for the welfare of the group.

The attempt of schools to promote effective social interaction has been much criticized. For example: "The children are supposed to learn democracy by underplaying the skills of intellect and overplaying the skills of gregariousness and amiability. . . . Respect for ability to do something tends to survive only in athletics" (Riesman, 1950, p. 64). Such criticisms have a valid point. A person who is overly concerned with "fitting in" does not develop his full potential or make his full contribution. It is one thing to teach a child to phrase his ideas so that they will get a hearing; it is quite another to teach him to remain quiet when in disagreement with his fellows. The person effective in social relations is not a passive floater. He helps to shape the aims of his group and opposes others when necessary to achieve the aims.

Goals and Interests

Living should be more than vegetating, waiting for crises that demand adjustment. Rich living involves striving for and making progress toward goals. Some find their satisfaction in helping others (as in teaching or homemaking); some find it in designing houses or building up a business. Boredom and depression are frequent companions of one who lacks goals and interests. His momentary problems solved, he has no way to occupy himself. Faced with major personal decisions, he has no answer to the question, "Why am I doing all this anyway?" Enthusiastic acceptance of some larger ends stabilizes life, gives excitement to daily activities, and keeps one going amid difficulties.

The school promotes interests by the contagious example of an admired teacher, by exposure to stimulating models in literature, and by opportunities to gain a sense of competence. The school develops vocational and recreational interests, pleasure in artistic self-expression, and pride in craftsmanship.

Acceptance of Social Values

The core of "good behavior" is acceptance of values consistent with one's culture. One familiar set of values emphasizes ambition, civic responsibility, thrift, cleanliness, striving for education, and respect for truth. In fact, most people going into teaching so thoroughly accept these values that it is hard for them to see how anyone could approve any other code. But other cultures, and some segments of American culture, live with very different values. Some of the competing systems are based on pleasure: "Have fun while you can." Some are based on spiritual values; kindness is placed above cleverness, and inner peace above achievement.

Values affect all thinking and all satisfaction and discontent. They determine what problems one thinks about and what solutions one accepts. When we share values with other persons, we receive and give respect, and arguments can be resolved rationally; a group without shared values disintegrates because the members pull in different directions. A person whose values are not accepted by his associates is certain to be in conflict. The psychopaths, some criminals, and some delinquents become rebels and live by a code of "every-man-for-himself." Others who outwardly conform may secretly wish to violate some standard of behavior. If a person does not believe in the values he publicly conforms to, he must deceive others and perhaps must deceive himself. Neurotic disorders often arise out of just such internal conflicts.

The socialized person embraces the value system of his group, but this does not mean that he never challenges the opinions of others. The successful reformer is ordinarily one who shares most of the values of the people of his time. One who respects others and shares many beliefs with them can communicate and defend opinions that are unconventional, even revolutionary.

The goal of socialization is not to impose one uniform set of attitudes. The American ideal of society is one in which people who consider religion the key to life and others who have no religious convictions can both be respected. Cultural values are shifting, and new values are challenging the old ones. The pioneer's insistence on independence and self-reliance is gradually giving way to some form of central planning and control, as evidenced in federal social security, the regulation of the stock exchange, price-support laws and labor unions. Thrift and the postponement of gratification are giving way before installment payments which make it easy to enjoy today what you hope to pay for tomorrow.

If values are so important, and at the same time we have no uniform code to teach, what is the school to do? The school's function is to teach certain core values, such as consideration for others and loyalty to the nation, and to encourage pupils to challenge traditions that are harmful. Fundamentally, *each person must want to do right and be willing to defend even his heresies to his group*. This central attitude is essential to social stability. Without it, people are morally irresponsible.

CONFLICTING VALUES AMONG EDUCATORS.   Each teacher has his own value system and it is natural that he should pass these beliefs on to his students, but teachers' values differ. The anthropologist Margaret Mead (1951) comments provocatively about the values of American teachers. She identifies three types (though she admits that few teachers fit any one pattern exclusively):

The "child-nurse" who helps the learner to be himself and enjoy his present activities.

The "parent" who is making a success and wants to prepare the child to succeed in the uncharted future.

The "grandparent" whose memories run far back and who enjoys bringing children to appreciate their traditions.

This somewhat humorous, somewhat irritating, classification is based on Mead's observations in other cultures. She points to the Indian tribes whose children are reared chiefly by grandparents, to the Samoans whose children are left in the charge of older sisters, and to the "efficient, profit-seeking" fishermen of the South Pacific Admiralty Islands where the parents are the socializers.

Pleasure

Practicality

Tradition

12   *Each socializer teaches the way of life he values*

According to Mead, the teacher of the "child-nurse" type finds her satisfaction in sharing the child's joy in today's pleasure. Anything that makes school life less pleasant to the child, she too finds unacceptable. She fulfills her needs by permissively encouraging young children in brief, entertaining, unsystematic activities. The teacher of the "parent" type has found satisfaction and prestige in moving ahead and meeting new challenges. This teacher preaches the gospel of progress and ambition:

> She teaches her pupils to acquire habits of hygiene and of industry, to apply themselves diligently to prepare to succeed, and to make the sacrifices necessary to success, to turn a deaf ear to the immediate impulse, to shatter any tradition which seems to block the path to the goal, but to shatter it . . . [as an] entrepreneur.

Finally, Mead characterizes the teacher who serves as does the grandparent in the Indian tribes. This teacher, who has found stability and pleasure in the arts and traditions, stresses the immutable past. This teacher cares little about whether or not the material is "useful" in solving practical problems.

> The gifted teacher of the classics conveys to the child a sense of the roundedness and relatedness of life, of the way in which each period repeats in its own way an old story that has already been written in a more gracious and finished way in the past. Any budding desire to explore the new, to make new conquests, can be gently, benignly reduced to the expected, by a reference to Diogenes or to Alexander.

15. Which school subjects would teachers of each of Mead's types most enjoy teaching?

16. If a teacher has a keen appreciation of history and tradition, should he attempt to teach pupils his own values at a time when this outlook is becoming less common among educators and in the culture generally?

17. It is said that European schools and homes train the young person to believe that adults are right and superior, and that their values should be accepted. American homes and schools more often encourage children to form independent judgments, and values are established anew in each generation. What are the hazards in each system?

THE ACHIEVEMENT ETHIC AND THE AFFILIATION ETHIC. Mead's description draws attention to a fundamental conflict within our culture. Few Americans regard tradition as the best guide for conduct; their world is changing too rapidly for that. But there are many who, like Mead's fisherman, regard sustained achievement as the main thing in life, and there are others who live mostly for pleasure. This conflict between *the achievement ethic* and *the affiliation ethic* has been described in many recent criticisms of American society. (See *The Organization Man* (Whyte, 1956), and *The Lonely Crowd* (Riesman, 1950); the achievement ethic is the philosophy of Riesman's "inner-directed" man, and affiliation that of the "other-directed" man.)

The achievement ethic dominated American thought in the century following the industrial revolution (D. Miller and Swanson, 1958; Strodtbeck,

1958). Opening a frontier demanded self-reliance and responsibility; the rewards went to the man who carried out his own ideas and outdid his competitors. Since parents owed their success to self-control and fore-thought, these were primary virtues to be taught to the children.

In the affiliation ethic the highest good is the passive enjoyment of pleasant social activity. This value system emerged only recently in America. It is fostered by a wealthy, economically stable society where mere reasonable conformity to the demands of an employer brings secure living, and the products of work are identified with a team rather than with the individual. An office manager snug in his suburban niche and a factory worker with comfortable seniority and a union contract are likely to encourage their children to "fit in." In school these affiliation-oriented children reject the hard workers: "they don't know how to have any fun." And the achievement-oriented pupils say in turn that the others are "irresponsible, and don't know what is good for them" (Kahl, 1953).

The philosophical roots of each ethic run deep. The achievement ethic expresses attitudes fostered by the Protestant Reformation and, for somewhat different reasons, by traditional Jewish culture. The differences are not specifically religious; while the Catholic family in southern Italy is likely to live by the undemanding affiliation ethic, the French Catholic family sternly demands achievement in its children (Strodtbeck, 1958; Wolfenstein, 1955a; Dolto, 1955). Contrasting beliefs within the two systems are summarized in Table 3.

The American school was created to serve the achievement ethic, cultivating talent so that the young person can contribute in proportion to his

TABLE 3

Two outlooks on the world (after Strodtbeck, 1958)

Achievement Ethic	Affiliation Ethic
We live in an orderly universe, where difficulties can be overcome by intelligently directed effort.	One's fortunes are subject to the whims of destiny; luck counts more than effort.
Impulses to seek gratification are temptations; one must keep them under control to avoid future unpleasantness.	One should accept impulses, taking present pleasure without concern for the future.
Each person is responsible for establishing his individual worth through his contributions.	One progresses as part of a closely interdependent group rather than as an individual.
Personal conscience should determine one's choices.	Group standards should determine one's choices.

merit regardless of his family status. The public college in particular was designed for the youth struggling up a steep trail to a position of responsibility. Today, however, the college plays host to no small number of affiliation-oriented young men who regard the college as a gentle escalator to comfortable corporation jobs (and to the young women whose ambition is to share such a life). These students "want social security, not great achievements. They want approval, not fame. They are not eager to develop talents that might bring them into conflict, whereas the inner-directed young person tended to push himself to the limit of his talents and beyond." So speaks Riesman (1950, p. 270; see also Jacob, 1960). It is hard to say what fraction of today's young people deserve this acid description.

Elizabeth French (1955) used an indirect personality measure to identify which Air Force officer candidates were high or low in achievement motivation. Then she asked them to do a simple code-substitution task under one of three levels of incentive. In one condition ("relaxed"), the men were told that the experimenter just wanted to see what kind of scores people would make on such a test. In a second group ("task oriented") it was emphasized that every man should do his best because the ability tested would be important in his career. In a third group ("external incentive"), it was promised that the men who did best would be allowed to leave early, but nothing was said about the importance of the test. The three groups were equal in ability; their average performance, however, varied as shown in Table 4. Those who had accepted achievement as a motive for life did markedly better when the task "mattered" in some significant way. The group with less inner drive perked up when offered some immediate reward, but would not strive merely to show how well they could do.

A subsequent experiment with a similar procedure (E. French, 1958) emphasizes the difference between achievement and affiliation motivation. Airmen were identified who had strong achievement motivation and weak

TABLE 4

The person with achievement motivation tries when tasks seem important (*E. French, 1955*)

| | Average performance scores among men with | |
Condition under which task was performed	strong achievement motivation	weak achievement motivation
Relaxed: "See what you can do."	17.7	15.5
Task-oriented: "Do your best; this ability affects your career."	29.8	16.6
Immediate goal: "Do well and you may leave."	18.2	22.5

affiliation motivation; others were chosen who were stronger in affiliation. (This omits the minority high in both, or low in both.) Four men with the same motivation pattern were asked to fit together a story, using phrases or sentences provided by the experimenter. Each phrase was written on a card, and each man had 5 of the 20 cards. The men could reconstruct the story only by communicating and cooperating intelligently. Halfway through the task the experimenter interrupted the group and told the men that they were working efficiently, and drew attention to things they had been doing (e.g., using grammatical cues) that reflected well-organized behavior. Half the groups were praised in this way for effectiveness. The other half of the groups (chosen randomly) were praised for their friendliness. The experimenter drew attention to such social, affiliative behaviors as giving everyone a chance to contribute and keeping arguments friendly. The groups then worked further on their stories. Each group's final story was judged for completeness and correctness. The average scores, for eight groups of each type, were:

Achievement-motivated men praised for efficiency	40.5
Achievement-motivated men praised for friendliness	29.2
Affiliation-motivated men praised for efficiency	29.1
Affiliation-motivated men praised for friendliness	38.4

The men with achievement motivation were obviously impatient when told how fine their social conduct was, but they listened keenly when the investigator talked about their efficient procedures. And the men who valued affiliation worked better after being told that they were in a friendly group! The effect of praise is to improve performance, but only if the praise means something to the individual.

In some communities the public wants a program that will teach vocational and social skills without emancipating pupils intellectually and emotionally. These communities are content with affiliative values. But the school exists to serve the larger society, and can do its job only by teaching some things that the local community values little. The American school strengthened the nation when it taught national patriotism at a time when parents placed local and sectional loyalties first, and later when it taught the interdependence of nations in isolationist communities. The college looks beyond the trade-school motivation of the average student to introduce him to the liberal arts, even though neither he nor his parents seek them out.

Today's school can do its best for society by pointing the pupil in the direction of the achievement ethic, while avoiding the neurotic overtone of such slogans as "*Never* do less than your best." This recommendation is consistent with our emphasis on problem solving as a goal of socialization. A society loses vitality when its members suppress ideas for the sake of harmony, waste resources for the sake of present satisfactions, demand no more of science than additions to their daily comforts, and require of the arts only that they soothe. Professional educators should therefore pull against the current of other-directedness, aiming to fire the enthusiasm of individual children and to instill those values which serve community progress. Social skills, security in relations with others, and enjoyment of affiliation are all worthwhile goals, contributing both to effectiveness and to satisfaction; but these values by themselves do not constitute an adequate philosophy of life.

One may win pupils from a passive, uncommitted conformity without endorsing the extremes of the individualistic-competitive way of life. While the achievement ethic contributes to progress, in its traditional form it imposes great strains. As D. Miller and Swanson say (1958, pp. 206–07):

> The man who constantly denies himself for the sake of future gain finds less pleasure in his life. He is likely to know spasmodic waves of depression. His control and his striving become excessive. . . . Sunday, without the ordered and familiar channels of work, can become a bore or a nightmare. . . . [When he grows tired,] the result is guilt and uneasiness, not relaxation. . . . Easy relations with other people are also hindered by the kind of control and manipulative activity fostered by an entrepreneurial society.

The achievement ethic is damaging insofar as it prevents enjoyment or generates dissatisfaction with self and others. We shall have many occasions in subsequent chapters to consider the attitudes that make it possible for a person to attain *satisfaction through achievement*. This, not achievement alone, is the proper goal.

18. What changes in American life have contributed to the rise of the affiliation ethic?

19. An "ethic" is a point of view about what is right and wrong, rather than merely a preference for a particular type of satisfaction. Why can this term be applied to "the affiliation ethic?"

20. What behavior by the adolescent would be most distressing to the achievement-oriented parent? What behavior would be most a violation of the wishes of the affiliation-oriented parent?

21. The founder of behavioristic psychology, John Watson (1928, pp. 186–87), summarized his aims in socialization as follows:

> "We have tried to sketch . . . a child as free as possible of sensitivities to people and one who, almost from birth, is relatively independent of the family situation. Above all, we have tried to create a problem-solving child. We believe that a problem-solving technique . . . plus boundless absorption in activity . . . have worked in many civilizations of the past and . . . will work equally well in . . . the future."

    a. Is this consistent with the achievement ethic, the affiliation ethic, or neither?

    b. What sort of school program would be consistent with Watson's goals? What sort would he criticize?

    c. Some would argue that Watson was seeking to prepare the child for a world that no longer exists. What do you think?

22. Discuss this comment by Riesman (1954):

"A generation or so ago it made sense for teachers to be preoccupied with social skills, and there are still many underprivileged childen who lack access to those skills. But today, for the most part, many situations and devices outside the school are cultivating those abilities. Children in the home are listened to—they are no longer seen and not heard; they become good little communicators very early. . . . Nevertheless, . . . both parents and teachers, conscious of their own childhood inadequacies and gaucheries, are giving many children what amounts to postgraduate education in sociability, when what they need, for the most part, is something very different, namely, protection for those long-term intellectual and humanistic interests that are momentarily at a discount [i.e., unfashionable in the adult society]."

REDUCING EDUCATIONAL AIMS TO OBSERVABLE BEHAVIOR

For the experimental study of teaching problems, we phrase educational purposes *in terms of behavior*. There are other ways to state purposes: "to develop the mind," "to instill good character," "to promote patriotism," for example. But these phrases are not meaningful until they are defined so as to indicate precisely what we want the person to do after we have taught him. Soviet schools seek "to develop the mind," but their goal appears to be a mind that never questions a statement from a high Communist source. Their schools develop "character"—but it is a particular breed of character, which can only be described by telling just what a Soviet citizen is supposed to do in particular situations.

Any educational objective that is to be studied experimentally must be defined by stating the situations that the person is expected to encounter and the way the educator wishes him to respond. If our objective is to teach a boy to bat a ball, we must describe the sorts of pitches he is likely to meet. He is to respond by hitting the ball. But more than that, at different stages of his training he should learn to hit the ball a long distance, to hit it on a low arc, to place his hit at a selected spot in the outfield, and so on. And he should learn attitudes; e.g., that he should try to advance runners rather than just try to get on base, and should sometimes wait for a base on balls even though a hit would be more dramatic. Such definite objectives help in teaching and in assessing the teacher's success; a general aim "to develop ball-playing ability" does not.

Psychologists place greater emphasis on behavioral definitions than do others concerned with education, because the psychologist bases his conclusions on observation. Only in behavior can he observe the effects of treatment. The psychologist cannot obtain evidence about vaguely described goals. The broad aims of education—appreciation of the arts, mental hygiene, democratic citizenship, and so on—must be reduced to behavioral descriptions before they can be investigated and before psychological research can be used as a basis for educational planning.

Thus a broad intention "to develop the mind" must be reduced to specific subgoals such as "to teach the pupil to define significant terms precisely." Even more specifically: "whenever (situation) the student is using a word crucial to his argument that may be misunderstood, then (response) he will relate the word to concepts or examples within the experience of his audience." Once the objective is defined in this way, we can tell how well students are performing, can identify things the teacher does that encourage the response of *not* defining terms, and can suggest beneficial teaching methods.

Note, first, that our statement of the desired response is not, "He will give a definition." There must be different definitions for different audiences; formal definition may or may not be preferable to definition by example; and the explanation must be suited to the audience. Hence our objective is an adaptive response rather than a fixed pattern of behavior. Second, note that the statement of the objective tells when the response is desired: "Whenever a word is crucial and may be misunderstood." A speaker who pedantically defined every word he used, or even every word fundamental to his argument, would drive off his audience. There is little merit in teaching a response unless the person also learns when and where it should be used. Third, note that this objective is defined as a habit (how he will act) rather than merely as a skill (how he can act). This point is elaborated in the next paragraph.

TYPICAL RESPONSE DISTINGUISHED FROM ABILITY.　When teachers list objectives, they usually list facts or principles to be learned and skills to be developed. Facts and skills are important, because without them one is certain to act incorrectly or inefficiently. But a list of purposes that stops with ability to perform on demand is incomplete. Making a skill or fact available is only a first step toward teaching the pupil to use it consistently in appropriate situations. If the student's actions are to change, he must see what his newly acquired response is good for and must feel comfortable in using it. There is no merit in teaching a boy legible handwriting if his work outside the penmanship lesson is a scrawl. School programs are intended to alter the person's usual or typical behavior. Teachers are concerned about pupil actions that involve attitudes, habits, and emotional responses:

> When I criticize Mary, she keeps quiet and does not participate in the discussion for the remainder of the hour.

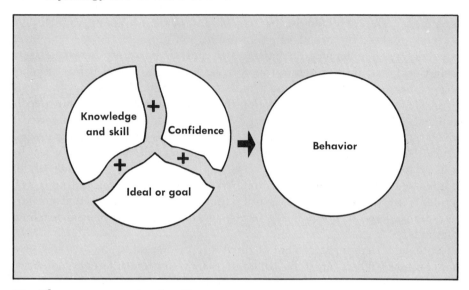

13   *Three components of action*

Our second-string quarterback, Hansen, almost always calls for a pass on the third down, but the first-string man, Harris, thinks the situation over and decides whether to punt, pass, or run.

Tom usually chooses a cowboy book when he has time for free reading.

The school alters many forms of typical behavior: goals selected, ways of doing tasks, emotional reactions, etc.

"Education of the whole person" can easily become a hollow slogan, but the phrase can also be a reminder that behavior depends on much more than the acquisition of ideas. Even the college, which has frequently thought of education as purely intellectual, will fail of its purposes unless it concerns itself with the student's typical behavior and underlying personality. As Nevitt Sanford (1962, pp. 36–37) emphasizes:

One could say that education is the transmission of symbols. . . . [and] has as its sole object the inculcation of skills and knowledge respecting civilization, society, and culture. Education in this sense does not necessarily change the developmental status of the individual personality. The skills and knowledge acquired may remain peripheral in the sense that they never become integrated with the major or central processes of the person. Students may learn a great deal without changing their personalities in any important way. . . . A person might put great resources of academic learning into the service of his need to exhibit himself and to score points at the expense of the less well tutored. . . . The difference between the uneducated anti-Semite and the educated one would be that the former might engage in overt actions against the Jews while the latter could invent clever remarks in parlor discussions, or perhaps write learned essays on why the Jews "get themselves into so much trouble." In short, the person who is educated in the narrow sense of this word has been given a set of terms in which to carry out his functions as a personality; if he is immature or psychopathic he may now display these characteristics in an educated way.

Stember (1961), to make the same point, quotes a Japanese proverb: "Learning without wisdom is a load of books on an ass's back."

23. Differentiate "outcomes of education" from "objectives of education."

24. A college plans a course in art for people who will not use it professionally. What actions and feelings might such a course seek to develop? Consider attitudes toward oneself, attitudes toward others and their ideas, and habits of working and thinking.

25. Restate each of the following objectives in terms of desired responses to situations:

    a. to develop neatness in handwriting
    b. to develop leadership potential
    c. to promote understanding of labor-management problems
    d. to develop appreciation of the importance of science in the modern world
    e. to teach scientific methods of farming

26. What do we ordinarily mean when we say that one adult behaves more intelligently than another? Can such "intelligence" be learned?

27. Is it the responsibility of the college to consider how the student will use his education and what goals he will pursue with it? Is "changing the personality" an objective, and if so, what teacher is responsible for attaining it?

28. Mayer (1961, pp. 29–32) takes a position opposite to that of this chapter: "In the context of the classroom, nobody except an incompetent, doctrinaire teacher is ever going to worry much about 'the aims of education.' " He goes on to quote a mathematician who has invented several dramatic improvements in teaching method for arithmetic classes:

"After I finish my demonstration, there's a question period, and somebody always asks the same question. Usually it's the first one. She gets up and says, 'What are your objectives? What are your aims in teaching arithmetic the way you do?'

"Which is, to anyone who's been around at all, like saying, 'Explain the universe.' Finally, I found the right answer. Now, whenever I'm asked that question, I say, 'What are *your* objectives? They're mine, too. Whatever you want to accomplish, I want *that*, too.' "

    a. Do arithmetic teachers make any decisions that promote one objective at the expense of others? Is it conceivable that the methods being demonstrated are equally suited for all objectives?
    b. Would the following statements be reasonable? Compare them with Mayer's statement on education.

"In working with a patient, no competent psychiatrist would concern himself about what it means to say that a patient is 'cured.' "

"When he is planning a college dormitory building, it is stupid for the architect to ask the college administrators, 'What do you want this building to accomplish?' "

TRANSFERABLE RESPONSES AS AN EDUCATIONAL GOAL

When we teach a pupil how to respond to a certain situation, we are interested both in improving his response to that situation and in facilitating his adaptation to other situations. We refer to such improved ability to deal with a situation not encountered during training as *transfer of learning*. Since schooling can at best reproduce only a few of the situations to which adults must respond, most school learning is aimed at transfer. The transfer required may be small, as in the transition from typing classroom to office, or it may be enormous, as when college lectures are somehow to equip a man to explore and understand an island, or to find the source of a kind of radiation never before observed. The role of transfer is particularly evident when we try to define the intellectual aims of education in terms of situation-and-desired-response.

One function of the science course is to develop what are sometimes called "scientific patterns of thought." How should science instruction change one's response when, for example, he sees an advertisement offering "Hi-Grade Tablets," which claim to release mental energy and improve performance in school? The active ingredient, glutamic acid, "has been tested by scientists who find that it can raise the intelligence quotient as much as ten points." Does he buy the family-size bottle, accepting the drug as a new miracle of science, or does he ask critically, "If this works so well, why has it not been described in newspapers and dependable magazines? Why don't schools and doctors recommend it?" He might take further steps such as asking his physician or looking in reference books. He should also bring to bear scientific information—for example, that most drugs and dietary supplements are remedies for specific deficiencies, and not capable of boosting the health and performance of normal, well-fed individuals. If he reads a description of an investigation, he should raise questions about the number of cases, the adequacy of controls, and the methods of measurement. All of these attitudes and reasoning processes are desirable outcomes of science education. (For your information: Although several studies have reported glutamic acid beneficial to the mentally defective, these studies were poorly controlled; in well-conducted studies, treated children did not improve more than a control group given no drug—Astin and Ross, 1960.)

It is hopeless to try to duplicate in school every significant situation where an idea or skill will later be used. This is most nearly accomplished in vocational training, where a student may work with equipment just like that he will later employ as, say, a printer. Even when the training situation is very much like the situation in which a response is later to be used, some adaptation of the response is required. A skilled action is performed differently as the conditions and goals of performance vary. A performer practices a piano selection until it seems as if every movement is automatic, yet he plays differently on a new piano or in a room with different acoustics. If he could not make these adaptations, he would not be a good performer.

There are many views on transfer of learning. At one extreme, some have claimed that "transfer occurs only to the extent that the application situation duplicates the training situation"; at the other, that "if the school teaches worthwhile responses, transfer will take care of itself." The teacher who regards transfer to an unfamiliar situation as unlikely makes school experiences as "close to life" as possible; his chemistry course, for example, would be expected to deal principally with specific, directly applicable knowledge about baking powder and fire extinguishers. The one who expects transfer to come readily will build his curriculum around general ideas such as molecular structure and systems in equilibrium, in the expectation that the pupil will transfer these abstract conceptions to concrete situations.

This chapter is not the place to examine the evidence on transfer. We can anticipate the later discussion of this important topic (Chapter 9, pages 308 ff.; Chapter 10) by denying both of the extreme views on transfer. Transfer often occurs from one situation to others that are superficially quite different, but knowledge certainly does not always transfer. Transfer of ideas and skills occurs if a person understands them and recognizes their relevance to the situation he faces. A widely applicable principle makes good educational content, but the goal is not to teach the principle in the abstract. The success of teaching should be judged by whether or not the learner makes effective use of the principle whenever it is pertinent at any time during his life. Although the teacher must have clearly in mind the immediate changes of behavior that constitute short-run classroom objectives, these are of minor importance compared to long-run transfer effects.

29. Are the following intended to prepare the student to deal with future situations? Explain.
  a. the study of English grammar
  b. a study of the United Nations
  c. a high-school biology unit on insects
  d. a third-grade unit on insects

30. How would each of the following courses be planned by a teacher who believes that transfer is readily achieved, and by a teacher who regards transfer as unlikely?
  a. agricultural education
  b. the education of girls for care of infants

    c. the teaching of junior-high-school English where one objective is ability to write business letters

    d. a first course in German for college freshmen

The Kinds of Knowledge

Most people identify education with the acquisition of knowledge, though we have seen that this is only one aspect of socialization. There are several kinds of knowledge, each with its own significance for future behavior (McMurray and Cronbach, 1955; Broudy, 1961). There is, first, the pre-verbal knowledge that comes from first-hand experience. Verbal knowledge—experience put into words by the learner or statements presented to him in verbal form—may be classified under four headings: descriptions, prescriptions, principles, and systematized knowledge. The last two have the greatest potential for wide transfer.

What a rose looks like, how a headache feels, what the properties of glass are—knowledge of this type grows out of direct experience with objects. Indeed, we cannot put such *preverbal*, perceptual knowledge into words. No instructor can communicate in words just how hard to press the brake to bring the car to a smooth stop; this knowledge must arise directly from muscular sensation. Verbal knowledge is a code that helps us to communicate, once concepts are connected to reality through preverbal learning. When the person has become acquainted with glass, and has attached the word *glass* to the experience, we can connect those ideas to something else; for example, we can tell him that certain lava resembles black glass. Verbal knowledge does not affect behavior unless the symbols relate to preverbal knowledge.

The school is chiefly concerned with the four types of verbal knowledge. Until experience is translated into words it has limited transfer value. In the cafeteria line, a man can, by recollections that need no words, pick out the foods he has enjoyed before. But if a vegetable is prepared in a different way, so that its appearance is changed, he must inquire what it is. Only when it is named can he draw on his file of past experience: "I like squash; I don't like carrots." This statement is a very simple verbal generalization.

Descriptions provide a substitute for direct, personal experience. A description tells what a single event or object is like, attempting to communicate impressions the individual might form for himself if he were to observe it. We convey descriptive knowledge when we recount the events of the Civil War, when we describe lava, and when we have a pupil read *Huckleberry Finn*. There is pleasure to be had in visiting faraway scenes and sharing others' experiences through the aid of descriptions. Moreover, descriptive information can affect responses to the situation described, as when a person traveling in a foreign country uses knowledge about that country gained in school. But specific information can ordinarily be acquired more efficiently as the need arises.

The more important function of descriptive information is transfer; one bit of knowledge gives insight into other situations. Describing the steps in constructing the Grand Coulee Dam illustrates difficulties engineers face on other jobs. Reacting with admiration or distress to a report on the

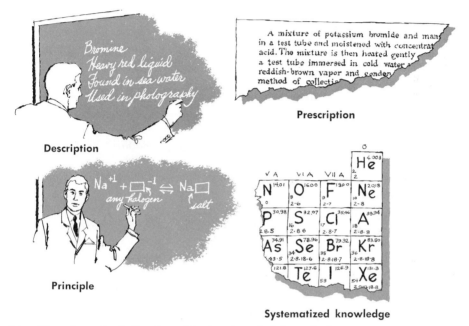

Description

Prescription

Principle

Systematized knowledge

14 *Chemistry includes four kinds of verbal knowledge*

Athenian Greeks or the Germans of 1935 influences our view of our own government. Our case studies of pupils (Chapter 5) are descriptive information, intended to transfer. Descriptions, though valuable in forming impressions and attitudes, are less useful for systematic thought (e.g., designing a bridge or a government) than exact principles.

A *prescription* tells exactly what to do to achieve a specific goal; e.g., how to give artificial respiration, how to spell *friend*. A prescription is profitable when there is one particular correct response to a situation. We can teach prescriptions for removing stains from cloth, for capitalizing words, or for bringing a boat about in a light breeze. Prescriptive teaching has limited value. One can give a prescription for calculating interest on a bank loan, but not for deciding whether to take on the debt. A prescription can tell how to copy a bridge, not how to design one for a new situation. Prescriptions are useful only for repetitive, stereotyped situations.

A *principle or broad generalization* is a higher type of knowledge than a description or a prescription; it gives information about many different situations and, unlike the prescription, can be applied differently as one's purpose changes. A principle is a statement connecting two or more concepts. The simplest principles are little more than descriptions ("Glass is harder than wood.") or prescriptions ("A moving vehicle takes longer to stop when the pavement is wet."). With the use of increasingly broad and abstract concepts we arrive at principles that are powerful aids to thought. Rather than teach descriptively all the separate facts about each chemical compound—copper combines with one or two chlorine molecules, one sulphur combines with one or two coppers, and so on for all combinations—we teach the concept of *valence*. Copper has valence $+1$ or $+2$, chlorine has -1, sulphur -2. There is no economy so far, but as soon as the pupil learns the valence of a new element such as boron ($+3$), he can immediately figure out its compounds (one boron with three chlorines, for instance). The man in the cafeteria line used a simple generalization: "I like squash." With more abstract concepts such as *protein* and *vitamin*, he can make a more intelligent choice of his meal.

Systematized knowledge is the outcome of extended scholarly investigation. A science is not just a shelfful of principles. It is a system in which each concept relates to many others; principles form a network, supporting each other. The physicist has a view of the universe in which the central concepts are *mass, energy, time,* and *position*. Derived from these are less fundamental concepts, such as *velocity, power,* and *magnetic attraction*. The system of principles relating these concepts permits predictions about the physical behavior of all sorts of objects: droplets in a cloud, molecules in the blood stream, or a metal casting under stress.

A discipline is a logically ordered body of knowledge, so stated as to exhibit to one who understands it the sources (axioms, observations, definitions, rules of analysis) from which it follows and the conclusion (generalization, prescription, or decision) to which it points (Dewey, 1916, p. 256). It is one thing to "know" the descriptive statement that "the American economy is expanding at the rate of 3 per cent per year," and quite another to know why the statement is true and, in the fullest sense, what it means.

The connectedness and precision of thought which characterize a discipline are well illustrated in this paragraph (Pei, 1949, p. 86) on phonetics:

> The technical terminology used in defining the various kinds of speech-sounds is involved and precise. . . . Two of the more widely-known terms are "vowel," a sound produced without friction or stoppage, and "consonant," a sound characterized by friction, squeezing or stoppage of the breath in some part of the vocal passage. Vowel-sounds are always accompanied by vibration of the vocal cords; consonant sounds may or may not have this vibration, the presence or absence of which we can easily perceive by putting our fingers to our Adam's apple and uttering in turn the sound of *d* and that of *t*, or *b* and

p, or *v* and *f*. Vowel-sounds are often described as front, middle and back, according to the part of the mouth where they are articulated. Consonant-sounds, in addition to being voiced or unvoiced (that is, accompanied or not by vibration of the vocal cords), are also said to be plosive (where the breath-stream is gathered up behind a complete obstruction, then suddenly released, as when we pronounce *p* or *b*), and fricative (when the obstruction is only partial, and the breath-stream escapes gradually, as in the case of *f* or *v*). . . . A sound like that of *p*, for example, is plosive (full obstruction, suddenly removed), labial (the obstruction is produced by the lips), and unvoiced. . . .

Systematic understanding is valuable because it gives central place to the most general, most powerful principles, it adds meaning to each subordinate principle, and it provides a way of coming to grips with unprecedented situations. When, for example, a new disease appears, germ theory and the systematic knowledge of microbiology help immediately to bring the disease under control. Health investigators set out to look for a bacillus or a virus, rather than casting about randomly for an explanation of the illness. The systematic viewpoint of the discipline focuses thought on the most pertinent inquiries.

In learning a discipline, one masters an integrated network of principles and a method of inquiry, rather than generalizations one at a time. Indeed, generalizations learned in isolation can be misleading (Bruner, 1960, pp. 22–23; see Figure 15 below).

A good case in point is to be found in the usual attempt to explain the nature of tides. Ask the majority of high school students to explain tides and they will speak of the gravitational pull of the moon on the surface of the earth and how it pulls the water on the moon's side into a bulge. Ask them now why there is also a bulge of less magnitude on the side of the earth opposite to the moon, and they will almost always be without a satisfactory answer. Or ask them where the maximum bulge of the incoming tide is with respect to the relative position of the earth and moon, and the answer will usually be that it is at the point on the earth's surface nearest the moon. If the student knows there is a lag in the tidal crest, he will usually not know why. The failure in both cases comes from an inadequate picture of how gravity acts upon a free-moving elastic body, and a failure to connect the idea of inertia with the idea of gravitational action.

The explanation is really understood only when all the pertinent concepts and laws are used at once.

Understanding a discipline requires one to understand principles about the nature of knowledge itself. It is important to teach that science is growing and changing, that it is not a collection of final answers. It is good for the fourth-grader to learn that he himself can discover similarities among the seed pods of various plants. It is even better if he learns that his schoolmates see other ways to classify them, so that he must decide which

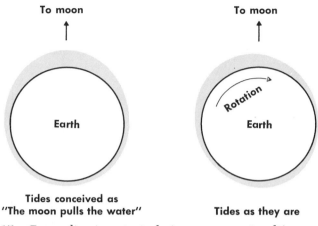

15   *Generalizations in isolation can oversimplify*

classification serves best. Now he is learning more than the facts of science; he is learning what it means to speak of knowledge as scientific. In high school the pupil should grasp such generalizations about the nature of science as these (Physical Science Study Committee, 1957):

Observation of regularities must precede formulation of laws.

To establish a law solidly, many independent arguments using different sources of evidence are required.

A physical law is established over a certain range of phenomena and within a certain range of accuracy.

Knowledge at this level is valuable because it helps one to understand additions to knowledge during one's lifetime (and contradictions of accepted knowledge), and reduces the tendency to accept viewpoints solely on the word of the scientist. The quotations earlier in this chapter, from Dewey and from the Rockefeller Report, placed a proper emphasis on the ability to go on learning after schooling ends. Systematic understanding is far better suited to promote this continued growth than is knowledge of the other sorts. Prescriptions and single generalizations are fixed answers; disciplined knowledge is a living structure, of inquiry and interpretation, continually open to influence from new observation and insight.

In pointing out the value of disciplined knowledge, we run the risk of seeming to endorse various false educational ideas to which the word "discipline" has been connected at times. The above description does not support the ancient notion that merely using the mind on difficult lessons is beneficial. It does not identify the mastery of a discipline with the accumulation of thousands of unconnected facts. And it does not argue that every academic subject is worthy of attention from every learner, or even from every above-average student. It is very dramatic to proclaim that "the wisdom of mankind has been set down in a multitude of languages, and he [man] has cultivated the linguistic disciplines so that he may unlock this storehouse, and then add it to his own ideas, expressed with precision and vigor" (Bestor, 1955, p. 35). But this passage confuses skill with discipline. The student who is not to become an anthropologist or a specialist in the evolution of languages can ignore most of phonetics, syntactics, and the other theoretical aspects of language. The disciplines worthy of study are the ones that bear on the problems one actually expects to face.

31. How does the discipline of phonetics, partially described in the quotation from Pei, help an investigator studying the strange language of an Eskimo tribe? a teacher working with a foreign student whose English pronunciation is unclear?

32. Classify each of the following as description, prescription, principle, or systematic knowledge.

   a. The observation of a paramecium by a pupil shows the structures it uses for food intake and for locomotion.

   b. The equinox that marks the official beginning of autumn occurs when the sun crosses the equator.

   c. Yellow fruits or vegetables should be included in one's menu every day.

   d. In typing, the fingers should be placed over the middle row of the keyboard.

33. To what extent does the education of the physician require each type of knowledge, from preverbal to systematized principles?

34. What nonscientific studies lead to systematized knowledge?

35. Broudy (1961) distinguishes between (a) knowing *that* something or other is true (existential), (b) knowing *what* a thing is (classificatory), and (c) knowing *why* some statement is true or reasonable (theoretical or explanatory). How do these relate to our types of knowledge?

SUMMARY

Judgments about educational procedures require an understanding of the function education is to perform. This chapter has discussed the purposes of schooling, drawing on sociology and anthropology, and on philosophy of education. It has necessarily been devoted more to opinions about American education and about the good life than to facts from psychological research.

The fundamental position of the chapter is represented in the quotation from John Dewey given earlier, to the effect that collateral learning, such as the formation of attitudes, may have more enduring and more significant effects than the specific content of lessons. The good or harm done by an educational experience can only be judged by considering all the changes in behavior, feeling, and understanding that it produces.

The school is one of many agencies responsible for socializing the child. Socialization is the process of preparing a person for a role in a society. It is not concerned solely with helping him to get along with other persons; rather, it includes all the training that brings out certain of his potentialities and suppresses others. Socialization continues throughout life, as a person's behavior is reshaped by changing roles. Since much of socialization is accomplished by other agencies—the home, the church, the employer, etc.—the school needs to concentrate its efforts. The primary responsibility of the school is to promote certain skills and to convey knowledge. It is the only agency specifically planned for intellectual learning. But it cannot confine attention solely to the intellectual. Intellectual knowledge may be harmful unless turned to a good social purpose. As Sanford says, a highly prejudiced person, given a complete intellectual education, may only become able to express his prejudices in a more elegant way. The school cannot take primary responsibility for character development, but it should supplement the efforts of other agencies and take advantage of its opportunities to strengthen character. The school that thinks solely about intellectual outcomes may impede socialization.

One unique responsibility of the school is that it selects the individuals who will as adults "manage" the society. The person with a college education has a far greater opportunity of rising to a position of leadership and influence than the person who leaves school earlier. The school, by the aptitudes it demands and by the behaviors it rewards, selects certain types of persons. Hopefully, the persons who do well in school are those who have the talents needed in responsible positions; in that sense, the school is a screening agency that sifts the talented from the untalented. Critics have argued that the school favors some pupils and discourages others who might make equally important contributions. In particular, it is said that assignments that emphasize following prescriptions discourage the creative youngster, while showing the persistent child at his best. It is said that true mathematical talent is intuitive rather than systematic, yet the usual teaching methods demand systematic, step-by-step reasoning.

Consideration of the values of our society, and of the successes and failures of individuals within it, suggest five qualities to be sought as aims of socialization:

A person should solve problems as well as the available facts permit.

He should have self-respect and self-confidence.

He should be effective in dealing with other people, respect their rights, and help his associates to live satisfying lives.

He should have some absorbing goals, interests, and sources of satisfaction.

He should aim to act in a praiseworthy manner, but should examine values critically before conforming to them.

These aims include knowledge, but they go far beyond it. The distinction between ability and typical response is helpful: the aim of the school is generally to change what the student does, rather than merely to give him the ability to act correctly. How the person behaves depends upon his goal (which ultimately rests on his value system), his knowledge and skill, and his confidence. Unless all of these develop properly, he will not be an effective person.

Most of the actions for which the school seeks to prepare persons call for problem solving, i.e., for transfer of responses into new situations for which no specific correct response has been learned. This is inevitable in a changing society. Knowledge is to be looked upon as a storehouse of possible solutions and of materials from which solutions can be created. But effectiveness depends on the choice of worthwhile problems, on persistence, and on willingness to take an independent position. Problem solving is by no means purely intellectual.

Several kinds of knowledge contribute to problem solving. Preverbal knowledge permits the recognition of objects, the recall of colors, flavors, and other experiences, and the control of muscles. It is developed from direct experience with reality; until one has had experiences that give meaning to his words, he cannot employ verbal knowledge. But preverbal knowledge is not easily transferred to new situations.

Within verbal knowledge, there are four levels of complexity: descriptions, prescriptions, generalizations, and systematized knowledge. The description is a partial substitute for firsthand experience; it conveys in words what a specific object or event is like. One can base decisions on descriptive knowledge about some similar event in the past, but general principles are usually more potent. The prescription is likewise specific; it tells what to do to accomplish a particular result in a certain type of situation. The calculating routines of arithmetic and the rules for spelling are typical prescriptions. In contrast to descriptions and prescriptions, a broad generalization can be used in many situations and for many purposes. The generalization describes relations between abstract concepts, such as *valence*.

Concepts and principles are organized into systems of thought, or disciplines. Knowledge of a discipline requires understanding of the way the separate principles lock together (thus, the principles of gravitation and of inertia are both required to account for the tides). Secondly, to understand a discipline one must understand how its knowledge is achieved, i.e., what sources of evidence and methods of reasoning it uses. The disciplined knowledge is more powerful than the isolated prescription because it permits effective analysis of completely strange situations. The young child can make some progress toward understanding how knowledge is organized and where it comes from. Even in the early grades, for example, he can begin to discover regularities in nature for himself, and to organize his discoveries into a miniature scientific system.

Decisions about what values to emphasize in school are necessarily controversial. There is no uniform set of values to present. Some educators want children to learn respect for tradition, while others are trying to shatter tradition and to encourage admiration for new ways of doing things; some want to encourage productive efficiency, while others want to encourage relaxed enjoyment. But all educators want to teach values and appreciations, and the pupil who does not develop values will be an aimless drifter. We have emphasized the importance of developing some system of values, not necessarily those held by the rest of society, and of being willing to defend those values to others.

We have examined the distinction between the achievement ethic and the affiliation ethic. The achievement ethic stresses productivity and self-reliance. As Table 3 indicates, the achievement-oriented person is a striver, working toward future goals even if he must sacrifice present pleasures. French's experiment shows achievement-motivated men working much harder on tasks labeled "important" than on tasks where a small immediate reward is offered. And she finds them more interested in how to be efficient than in how well they are getting on with others. The contrasting affiliation ethic has apparently been growing in prominence as society becomes more stable and more affluent, and work becomes more a team effort than an individual effort. The affiliation-oriented student is most interested in getting along with others and having fun with them. He seems not to believe in his own power to overcome obstacles, seeing success as largely a matter of luck. It appears that the school should strive to promote motivation for achievement and the associated attitudes. But enjoyment of one's competence is not the same as neurotic perfectionism. Satisfaction through achievement, not achievement alone, is the proper goal.

In discussing educational aims, the importance of defining aims in terms of behavior has been stressed. Only then can one collect evidence to decide whether or not the school is reaching its goals. A clear statement as to the types of situation the student should cope with, and the responses that are considered desirable, guides the planning of school activities.

Reading List 2

H. S. Broudy, "Mastery," Chapter 5 in B. O. Smith and Robert O. Ennis, eds., *Language and Concepts in Education* (Chicago: Rand McNally, 1961), pp. 72–84.

A philosopher distinguishes types of knowledge and skill, and discusses how teachers should judge whether or not a pupil has a high degree of mastery of them.

Jerome S. Bruner, "The Importance of Structure," Chapter 2 in *The Process of Education* (Cambridge: Harvard Univ. Press, 1960), pp. 17–32.

Bruner argues that a curriculum which presents the fundamental structure of a discipline does more to make future performance efficient than a curriculum which concentrates on specific facts and skills.

Nolan C. Kearney, *Elementary School Objectives* (New York: Russell Sage Foundation, 1953).

Will French and others, *Behavioral Goals of General Education in High School* (New York: Russell Sage Foundation, 1957).

These are companion reports listing objectives important for every pupil. The first of the two is especially influenced by psychological studies.

Daniel R. Miller and Guy E. Swanson, "Changes in Society and Child Training in the United States," Chapter 2 in *The Changing American Parent* (New York: Wiley, 1958), pp. 30–60.

The authors describe the social conditions that fostered the achievement ethic and, more recently, the affiliation ethic. The section on bureaucracy and child training is particularly important. Are the goals pictured appropriate under present conditions?

David Riesman, "Secondary Education and 'Counter-cyclical' Policy," Chapter 3 in *Constraint and Variety in American Education* (Lincoln: Univ. of Nebraska Press, 1956), pp. 107–54.

Here the writer of the famous *Lonely Crowd* argues for a high-school program that will "buck the trend" of the community, so as to contribute to the pupil's development whatever inspiration he will *not* get from his other experiences. He contrasts the contributions made, in different times and places, by the British school for the elite, by progressive education, and by a demanding academic curriculum.

George D. Spindler, *The Transmission of American Culture* (Cambridge: Harvard Univ. Press), 1959, 51 pp.

Spindler amplifies the themes of Mead and Riesman, that each teacher expresses achievement values or affiliative values in his educational theory and practice. Especially startling are Spindler's quotations from a well-motivated teacher whose identification with superior ability and achievement is so great that he is unable to be encouraging and sympathetic to children from poor Mexican-American families. His biases color even his remarks to pupils on the value of studying typewriting.

CHAPTER 3 AN INTRODUCTION
TO THE LEARNING PROCESS

The next few pages present a highly concentrated description of learning. If you do not let the flood of new concepts bewilder you, you will not find the material difficult. This section introduces concepts that all the rest of the book will be explaining much more thoroughly. Our approach is rather like what happens when you go to a party where there are many strangers. The host takes you around and presents you to everyone, helps you with a sentence or two of identification, and at the end releases you to make a more leisurely acquaintance with each guest. That is our plan here: first a quick survey of the most important ideas, then a chance to study each one carefully.

To study learning systematically, we need to select appropriate concepts and state their relations to each other. Our theoretical explanation will use seven chief concepts that can be used to describe any sequence of behavior: situation, personal characteristics, goal, interpretation, action, consequence, and reaction to thwarting. This chapter defines each concept and also defines learning itself. A case study of a typing class shows how these elements are found in classroom learning. This chapter is compact, and you will need to reread some sections, and later to review the chapter from time to time.

SEVEN ELEMENTS IN BEHAVIOR

Behavior is a series of choices among possible actions. Think of a man walking across country. He is at each step confronted with alternatives, since there is no single path to follow. As he comes onto the crest of a hill he sees before him many choices: he may go straight ahead, plunging directly toward his destination; he may circle to the left, staying on top of a ridge that promises better views and less climbing; or he may drop down and follow a gully that leads off to the right, on the theory that this will in the long run require the least exertion. The hiker selects and tries the alternative that he thinks will give him the greatest satisfaction. If his expectation is confirmed, he goes on toward his goal and makes further choices as they are called for. If plunging straight ahead brings him to an impassable thicket, he must make a new interpretation and try a new path.

Whether we are examining the performance of a thoroughly familiar task, or a learner's early attempts to solve a strange problem, we find that any act involves these seven elements:

1. *Situation. The situation presents alternatives requiring choice.* Situations offer opportunities to satisfy wants. The hiker finds interesting views which will add to his pleasure, or a berry patch he can raid. The situation also presents challenges or threats; if the hiker does not take appropriate action, he faces relatively unpleasant consequences.

2. *Personal characteristics. A person's abilities and attitudes limit the ways in which he can respond.* The person has a repertory of possible responses; within those possibilities, there are some he is more likely to try than others. He will fail to cope with the situation if he is too weak, too ignorant, or too inhibited by fears. Then we would say that he lacks readiness to deal with the situation.

3. *Goal. The person sees some possibility of acting on the situation so as to gain satisfaction.* Action is directed toward goals. Sometimes the aim is an immediate gratification: the relief of having an assignment done, or the joy of receiving a smile from the girl across the aisle. There are also long-range goals: a better job, a pleasant home, etc. Almost always several wants are active at the same time. The hiker wants to see a pleasant view, to increase the esteem in which his companions hold him, to stay dry, to get back to base by dinnertime, etc.

4. *Interpretation. The person interprets the situation.* Before one acts, he must decide what actions are possible, and what actions promise the best consequences. Choices are based on interpretations. An interpretation is a prediction that this situation resembles some earlier one and that actions will have the effects they had before. One alternative for the hiker is a roundabout and seemingly interesting path. But he notes that the clouds are becoming heavier and considers a short path toward shelter. He predicts that, with clouds like these, the longer path may lead to a drenching.

5. *Action. The person takes whatever action he expects will lead to the greatest net satisfaction.* Having considered what he can expect from several possible actions, he tries the one that seems to offer the best combination of pleasures and annoyances. Going by the ridge will delay him, but he will have pleasure from the view. He must decide whether that advantage is worth the risk of a soaking. The action he chooses is the one he expects to best satisfy his whole pattern of desires.

6. *Consequence: confirmation or contradiction. The action is followed by consequences which confirm or contradict the interpretation.* If the hiker follows the short path and barely beats the storm, his interpretation is

confirmed. Such confirmation tends to reinforce the interpretation, making it more likely to be used another time.

If he optimistically takes the long path and is caught by the storm, his expectation is contradicted. This "negative reinforcement" discourages optimistic interpretation in the future; next time he will be more concerned when clouds appear.

Contradiction may occur immediately, while the person is still in very nearly the same situation. Thus, he may head down the short path only to find it blocked by thorn bushes. The situation now demands a new choice.

16   *Learning is shown in change of behavior*

7. Reaction to thwarting. When the person's actions fail to produce an adequately satisfying set of consequences, we say that he is thwarted. He may reinterpret and try a new response. He may decide that his goal cannot be reached. He may become emotionally upset. The essential difference between a well-adjusted person and a maladjusted one is that the maladjusted one becomes emotionally disorganized when prevented from reaching a goal, whereas the adjusted person responds with appropriate reinterpretations and new tries.

Reaction to thwarting is not really the end of the sequence, although we have had to place it there. Always, the thwarting is followed by other behavior. The person makes a new interpretation and finds some new way toward his goal. Or, if he cannot, he abandons that goal and tests some other expectation, until an interpretation is confirmed.

These seven concepts describe a person's reaction to any problem: an assignment from the physics teacher, a broken toy brought to him by a child, or a challenge from a business competitor. Even in an action as routine as tying a shoelace, the same concepts apply. Here, however, interpretation proceeds very rapidly, and the performer gives little attention to alternatives unless he encounters difficulty.

A DESCRIPTION OF ACTIVE LEARNING

What We Mean by Learning

Behavior involves response to a situation. If the person consistently makes different responses this month from the responses he made a month ago, we say that he has learned something. More precisely, *learning is shown by a change in behavior as a result of experience*.

The sound of an ice-cream wagon coming down the street is to the child a signal. Various responses are possible. Different children may be observed to call to the man to stop, or to run into the house for a dime, or to scamper along beside the wagon, or to go on with whatever game they are playing. Observing a single child on dozens of days, we find that his response is not always the same. He makes one response 50 per cent of the time, a second response on 30 per cent of the occasions, a third response 10 per cent of the time, and other responses rarely. The day-to-day changes reflect small differences in the situation or in his desires (he isn't hungry, or he is especially hot, or he knows that his mother is in a bad mood and he had better not ask for money).

Learning is shown when some actions became more frequent than before. A child moving into the neighborhood, who has not previously seen an ice-cream wagon of this kind, may during his first week merely glance at the wagon and go back to his game. Then, from the other children, he finds out that the wagon is a source of ice cream and that their mothers sometimes give them money. So his interpretation changes, and during the next week we find him streaking home to request a dime whenever the wagon is heard. If his mother refuses the money, this trial action will be dropped, but he probably will not go back to his original indifference. Instead, we may find him stopping his play and watching the others with envy, biting his nails, or becoming irritable for a spell. Some responses have become more frequent and others less frequent. Learning has taken place.

Many changes occur through learning. We acquire new goals that make a response more attractive than it used to be (example: a boy detouring past the house of a girl to whom he paid no attention a month before). We become sensitive to new signals or we discover new interpretations. We learn emotional reactions. In each case a change in response can be observed.

It is somewhat unusual to say that a person learns the misinterpretation that causes him to act wrongly, but this also is learning and can be explained by the same laws as successful learning. If a pupil consistently says that the capital of Kentucky is Lexington, he obviously has learned this response, even though his teacher prefers the response "Frankfort."

The frequency of an action can increase or decrease. There are occasions when the hardest job of the teacher is to break up a response pattern that is already fixed, reducing its probability of occurrence. When Johnny learns not to hit a child who annoys him, the way is paved for teaching him more intelligent ways of handling conflicts. He has learned something when he abandons the old response, even though he has not learned what he should do.

1. "Learning has been too often considered . . . as synonymous with memorizing or, at best, as the acquisition of knowledge or skill. While these are legitimately considered forms of learning, they are not the whole of it; they are not even the most important aspects of it." What other aspects do you think the writers of this statement might have in mind?

2. How does the definition given in the text differ from this one: "Learning occurs when, as a result of experience, a person acquires a new response"?

3. In the definition given for learning, there occurs the phrase "as a result of experience." What sorts of changes in behavior, not considered to be learned, are ruled out by this phrase?

4. How does our definition differ from this one, given for skill learning: "Learning is the improvement of score with practice."

5. Some writers say that learning is characterized by reduction of the variability of responses in a recurring situation (Lawson, 1960, p. 14). Is this consistent with our definition? Can learning take place when a person's response to some set of situations becomes *more* variable?

The Seven Elements as Aspects of Learning

The seven elements of our description express in miniature a theory of behavior, and we shall also use them as the base for a theory of learning. Learning is shown by change in behavior, that is, by new interpretations and altered responses. Every experience teaches something, because it either confirms or contradicts an interpretation. To examine learning, then, we need to examine the seven elements of behavior, beginning with a formal definition of each and a brief description of the part it plays in learning.[1]

1. *Situation. The situation consists of all the objects, persons, and symbols in the learner's environment.* Experience in one situation prepares a person to respond to similar situations in the future. Curriculum planning is, in essence, the selection of situations (tasks, lessons, questions, objects) to which the pupil should learn to respond, and the arrangement of them in the best sequence.

2. *Personal characteristics.* Under this heading we include *all the abilities and all the typical responses that the person brings to the situation.* "Abilities" include such physical qualities and skills as strength, reach, and ability to swim, and intellectual attainments such as ability to hold a long sentence in mind after one hearing and knowledge about how a treaty is ratified. The phrase "typical responses" (see page 53) refers to what the person usually does. Does he tend to use short sentences? To spell carelessly? To quarrel when another person points out an error he has made? These abilities and typical responses indicate how the pupil is likely to interpret and respond to a situation arranged by the teacher. Certain characteristics are needed if the pupil is to profit from the experience; we refer to this as the *readiness* required for the activity. If the pupil does not have the abilities and typical responses suited to the activity proposed, some other task must be found for which he does have readiness.

3. *Goal. The goal of the learner is some consequence (i.e., state of affairs) that he wishes to attain.* His desire may be for an object, a certain response from another person, or some internal feeling. The goal is defined by an opportunity or a threat he perceives in the situation. The person has many goals at the same time, and usually sees any immediate goal (such as completing an assigned task) as related to a whole series of future goals (earning a respectable grade in the course, finishing school, and succeeding in a career). Since goals direct effort, the teacher's problem of motivation is essentially one of arranging situations in which the learner will see goals he wants to attain.

4. *Interpretation. Interpretation is a process of directing attention to parts of the situation, relating observations to past experiences, and predict-*

---

[1] The statement we present is less formal than the technical "theories of learning" of the psychologist. The laboratory psychologist seeks a highly refined theory, which describes very precisely the particular (usually simple) form of learning he is investigating. We, however, need a description that will apply to all forms of learning, and especially to those complex responses for which no technical learning theory has been completely worked out. Among formal theories, our "elements" are most closely related to E. C. Tolman's conception of purposive behavior (1959); the statement is also much influenced by E. R. Hilgard's summary of points of agreement among formal theories (Hilgard, 1956, pp. 457 ff.). A recent theory of behavior, which resembles ours particularly in its emphasis on the regulation of behavior by consequences, is that of G. A. Miller *et al.*, 1960.

ing what can be expected to happen if various actions are taken. Interpretation may be conscious and deliberate, but a person makes many interpretations without putting them into words or giving them his full attention. The interpretation suggests what action to try. (Logically, the goal is part of the learner's interpretation, but for the sake of emphasis we have listed it separately.)

5. *Action. The person's actions include movements and statements; they are observable responses.* A person chooses whatever action he expects to give him the greatest satisfaction. (There are involuntary actions, such as the opening and closing of the iris of the eye, but these are rarely of concern in school.)

If the learner is in doubt about his interpretation in a strange situation, he acts tentatively. We speak of his act as a *provisional try.* Then he is especially likely to look at the consequences of his act and to learn from them. This questioning, experimental attitude is one of the traits that sets apart the creative person, and the one who continues his learning long after he leaves school.

6. *Consequence: confirmation or contradiction. Some events that follow the action are regarded by the learner as consequences of it.* Consequences include the direct effect of the action, such as getting the basketball through the hoop, and less direct accompaniments, such as the popularity attained by a good player. If the consequences are those he predicted, the learner's interpretation is confirmed. Then he is likely to make a similar interpretation on another occasion. For the teacher, one of the important problems is to help the learner observe consequences accurately, and sometimes to arrange pleasant consequences so that correct interpretations and actions will be reinforced.

If the consequences are not what the person expected, his interpretation is contradicted and he does not reach his goal. He learns not to make this interpretation in the future.

7. *Reaction to thwarting: adaptive or nonadaptive. Thwarting occurs when the person fails to attain a goal.* If his first try is not confirmed, he may make a new interpretation and change his action. Through such *adaptive behavior,* he will usually hit on some action that brings him closer to the goal. At the same time, his goal may also be modified as he changes his idea of what he can attain.

The learner may instead respond nonadaptively, stubbornly repeating the same unsuccessful act, giving up entirely, or acting erratically and thoughtlessly. To distinguish between adaptive and nonadaptive behavior is difficult, because giving up, for example, is sometimes sensible.

On page 75 is a series of sketches to help you remember this analysis of the learning process. Most learning situations are more complex than the pictured problem of the boy at the cookie jar. A motive may be as simple as the desire for a cookie, but more often behavior is directed by

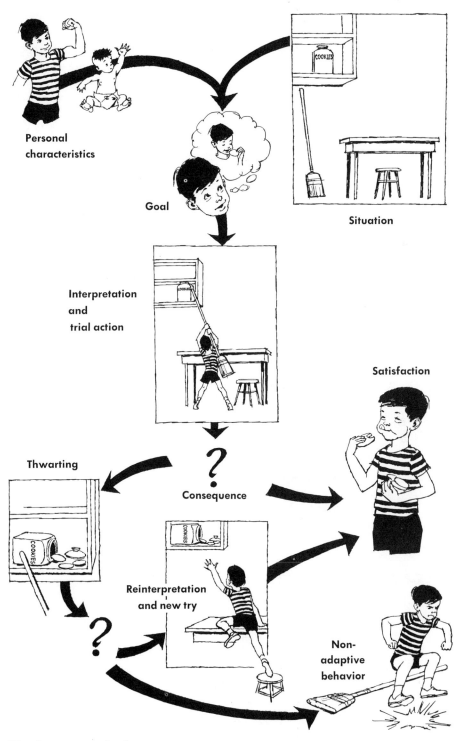

Personal characteristics

Situation

Goal

Interpretation and trial action

Satisfaction

Thwarting

?

Consequence

Reinterpretation and new try

Non-adaptive behavior

?

17 *Aspects of the learning process*

a mixture of desires. Nor is the consequence as simple as getting the cookie or not getting it. Instead of reaching total satisfaction or failing to get any reward, the person usually attains a partial measure of satisfaction.

6. Describe the learner's possible actions in this situation so as to illustrate each aspect of the learning process.

  a. A fourth-grader is trying to make a scrapbook of pictures to illustrate how people in Asia live.

  b. A high-school student takes as a project the development of a plan for handling parking in his community.

7. A 6-year-old goes to school for the first time. If this is a new situation, on what basis can he make interpretations (predictions as to what will probably happen)?

8. Sometimes it is said that "the learner keeps trying until one of his responses is successful. He then learns that response." How does this differ from our statement about consequences?

9. Each of the following pairs contrasts an element in our theory with a related term used in other psychological writing. What fact about the learning process do we emphasize when we choose the first term of the pair for our description?

  a. situation—stimulus

  b. goal—drive (as in "hunger drive")

  c. confirmation—reward

  d. contradiction—punishment

10. "When a learner has a need or want, and is placed in an unfamiliar situation, he tries one response after another at random, and finally discovers which one reaches his goal. In the future he is more likely to use that successful response."

  a. How does this statement differ from the conception of learning outlined above?

  b. According to this theory, how should you coach basketball?

  c. According to this theory, how should you teach primary pupils to draw?

A CLASSROOM PORTRAIT (TYPING)

To show how our seven concepts apply to a classroom, we examine here a typing class. Typing is a skill, hence easily observed, and every pupil is expected to learn much the same responses. Most of the practice and study takes place in the classroom. The typing class does relatively little to develop attitudes or reasoning abilities. This simplicity makes the typing class suitable for an introductory chapter.

When we discuss skill-learning more fully in Chapter 9, we will reconsider some features of the teaching method described. Mr. Wells's teaching method is probably better than that of many other teachers of typing, but his method is not ideal. He avoids some common errors, but, on the other hand, the case report shows at least one serious mistake in judgment.

Mr. Wells's class contained about thirty pupils, most of them juniors and seniors. On the opening day of the semester, Wells made an inquiry or two and found that few pupils had ever worked with the typewriter. Therefore he let them spend several days merely exploring the machine. For instance, they fed paper into the machine and, when they encountered difficulty, learned what the paper guide was for and how it could be used. Wells made no attempt to point out all the knobs and adjustments; only when pupils asked how to obtain a certain result did he introduce his knowledge. By the end of the week, the group was at home with the machine, and turning out small messages with considerable satisfaction. But the novelty was wearing off, hunt-and-peck was beginning to seem tedious, and several of the boys and girls were wasting time. An observer might have been concerned about the pupils' bad techniques of performance—poor posture, watching the keyboard, using the index finger for all keys, and the like.

At this point, Wells described good typing procedure. Had he demonstrated posture and hand placement the first day, he would have found pupils far more eager to start punching keys than to worry about refinements. As they discovered that their methods were slow and tedious, they became more ready to hear about efficient procedures.

Wells now taught formally the positions of the fingers. Beginning with the "home" positions a-s-d-f, j-k-l-;, pupils performed a limited number of exercises for practice in locating the keys. After a few trials with each letter, pupils began to type words. As new letters were introduced, Wells encouraged pupils to make lists of words they could type with those letters. One pupil would prepare a list (typing it, of course) and give it to his neighbor to practice on. Pupils also practiced by composing directly on the machine. The entire alphabet was brought in rapidly. By the end of the third week all the letters were in use even though most pupils had to look for them on the keyboard.

Wells left pupils largely to themselves while they were finding their way about the keyboard. They practiced from lists of simple sentences. Wells allowed them to look for letters whose location they did not recall. He called attention only to the most gross lapses from proper posture and fingering methods.

By the end of the fourth week, differences in performance were notable. Some pupils were at home with all three rows of the keyboard and were progressing steadily. Some were shaky in their knowledge of the less-used keys, and a few were confused about even the letters first introduced. For pupils having trouble with common letters, Wells provided lists of words that used chiefly those letters. As they became proficient, pupils moved ahead to more complicated words and sentences. Variations for the sake of interest and technique were introduced at times; for example, to encourage prompt stroking, Wells occasionally dictated a series of letters, which the class typed in unison.

As soon as pupils had mastered the keyboard well enough to type words without marked pauses to search for letters, class time was given chiefly to practice from continuous copy. They were urged to work as fast as they comfortably could, even if they made errors in so doing. At this time also, Wells introduced weekly three-minute speed tests. The pupils were slow at this, but so much better than they had been at the start of the course that all had a feeling of substantial progress.

18   *Olive lacked readiness*

As individual pupils moved from word-practice to straight copy, Wells's work became more varied. He observed each pupil, and now drew attention to incorrect posture, faulty attack on the keys, and similar errors that earlier he had let pass without comment. He now insisted that pupils try to type without looking at the keyboard.

Martha had been a laggard throughout and now was in a state of marked confusion. Observing her carefully, Wells found that Martha knew the approximate location of the letter *u*, for instance, but could not put her finger on it directly. Unless Martha looked at the keys, she could only try some letter in the general region, and so she hit *y* or *i* frequently instead of *u*. Wells observed that Martha was quite erratic in finger placement; for example, she used either her first or second finger for *h*. Since she never knew by feel where her hand was on the keyboard, she could not always light on *u* by reaching out with the first finger. Wells corrected this by watching Martha as she practiced and warning her whenever she let her hands wander from the proper home position. Once persuaded that using the correct finger was just as important as striking the correct key, she reduced her errors and began to overtake the class. The majority remained well ahead of her, and she continued to be somewhat discouraged. This difficulty might have been avoided if Wells had checked on individuals early in their practice to correct serious faults before they became fixed.

According to the tests, a few pupils seemed to be stalled on a particular level, making no improvement for several weeks. Some of them seemed merely to be having difficulty because their memory for certain letters was shaky, and Wells concluded that further practice would correct that. Others were inefficient in practice. To two students he suggested practice using any work they wished to bring in instead of preplanned drills; there was an immediate increase in their interest and progress.

James, on the other hand, did not respond to attempts to interest him, saying that he "didn't care whether he learned typing or not." James was taking the course only because he had a free hour at that time and could find no other class that better fitted his plan to finish high school and go into his father's store. Wells, unable to arouse James to real effort, decided that nagging would be unwise. James, for his part, put in his time dutifully and created no disturbance. Neither Wells nor the boy, however, was satisfied. This problem is only to be solved by a more diversified curriculum.

Olive had gone into a slump when the class began work on normal copy. She used excellent stroking and had a good knowledge of the keyboard, but her typing was hesitant because whenever she reached a complicated word, she had to read it from the copy letter by letter. Other pupils could hold the word in mind and type it straight off with only occasional hesitation. Olive, however, had always been a poor speller, so that thinking of the word as a whole did not permit her to type it. Wells was unable to bring Olive to the level of the rest of the class on standard copy. By giving her more practice on simple words, he was able to develop her typing skills. A supplementary study of spelling, worked out by Wells with Olive's English teacher, brought some improvement, but her spelling vocabulary remained so low that her typing was seriously handicapped.

The Seven Elements As Seen in This Example

In Wells's class, each of the seven aspects of learning can be observed. To learn typing, the students had to be placed in a *situation* where typing actions could be practiced. The situation involves more than being seated at a typewriter. Wells was careful to have pupils react to the whole natural task of typing. They practiced from copy, rather than by typing over and over a memorized sentence about "the quick brown fox." The copy was not nonsense; instead, it resembled what they would later type outside the course. The situation was not, however, identical to typing in an office. For example, early in the course Wells had pupils make up their own word lists so that having to look at copy would not complicate their work. Teachers generally must modify, not duplicate, out-of-school situations.

The *characteristics of the pupils* varied. Some were more mature and better coordinated than others; some were better prepared in such fundamentals as reading and spelling; some learned faster because they had better attitudes toward their work, more patience, and better concentration.

Pupils had many *goals* to which success in typing could contribute, so that good performance became a goal in itself. There were girls who looked forward to using typing as a way of earning a living; with each week's progress they gained pride in seeing themselves as nearly independent and self-supporting. Others were striving to win praise from the teacher or to feel superior to the group. Pupils' goals determine what they try to do and how they react to difficulties. The students with great need to excel, for example, are likely to be disorganized if they fail to make progress. Wells tried to make it possible for pupils to fulfill their wants.

Wells, when he suggested better finger placement, was suggesting an *interpretation* of the relation between the hands and the machine. The pupil, learning to strike *i*, uses this interpretation or some other. He will be most successful if he learns its position as "above the third finger in the home row." Thinking of letters in this way, he will come close to the right stroke as he types. Martha had only the dim interpretation "*i* is somewhere in the upper right"; as a result, her typing involved much error. Faulty interpretation leads to faulty practice. If left to themselves, pupils would regard typing as similar to other tasks requiring poking of buttons. One teacher, trying to substitute a correct stroke for the beginner's tendency to punch or poke, interprets it to them as "a tiger stroke." His vivid picture of the reach and swipe "with velvet paw" makes it less likely that in practice they will rest the finger on top of the key before striking it.

Having an interpretation of the situation, the pupil *tries the action* he considers appropriate. Trying to strike *i*, he reaches what he thinks is the correct distance, but his finger glances off the key to the left because his stroke is wrong. On another trial, he corrects his movement by striking farther to the right.

The *consequence* of the typing stroke includes the appearance of the material typed, and the confirming "feel" when the finger lands solidly on the key. The consequence is confirming or contradicting, depending on what the typist expects. Martha, you recall, was satisfied even though her strokes often missed the proper key. She hoped only that her stroke would bring her into the neighborhood of the correct key each time, and she did not set a higher goal. When she finally felt a need for more perfect technique, she had already learned her faulty method and had to unlearn it.

Thwarting occurs when one's goal is not reached. In the typing class, Martha, Olive, and others were at least temporarily thwarted. James reacted by giving up, since the rewards he could obtain were unimportant to him. Thanks to Wells's skill, both Martha and Olive made constructive adaptations. They might instead have become annoyed and discouraged.

11. Pupils differ substantially in their readiness. What steps did Wells take to adjust his teaching to individual differences?

12. What advantage would there be in having pupils begin their straight-copy practice with material selected by the teacher, instead of material they bring in?

Problems of Teaching Seen in This Example

The methods Wells used are in some ways different from those of other effective teachers of typing, and they certainly are not exactly like those useful in other subjects or grades. His work, however, is like that of the other teachers, for he has essentially the same problems to solve, namely, organizing curriculum materials, motivating pupils, evaluating their work (and his own), and providing for individual differences. All of these problems will be examined in subsequent chapters.

ORGANIZING CURRICULUM MATERIALS.   Arranging the learning situation calls for many decisions. The teacher must choose (with or without aid from pupils and professional superiors) the topics to be included and the text materials and activities to be used. Thus Wells had to decide whether pupils should work on business letters or on other sorts of copy. In making such a decision, it is especially necessary to consider the personal characteristics of the class.

How to arrange lessons is likewise a matter of concern. The teacher must decide how rapidly to introduce new ideas, in what order to introduce them, and how long to stay with them. Wells decided to introduce letters in groups, following the rows of the keyboard. He did this at a rapid rate, and some students were more confused than they would have been with fewer letters at once. Wells organized the work around continuous sensible copy, whereas some teachers emphasize jumbled-letter sequences, and others have pupils practice mostly on sentences out of their own heads. All of these decisions require knowledge of research findings, ability to estimate what is appropriate for a particular class, and alertness to modify tentative plans wherever they work badly.

Every plan is a response by the teacher based on his interpretation of his subject and his class. He should regard it as a provisional try which is likely to require modification. The teacher is running a continuous informal experiment, in which the reactions of the class reveal the need for changes in procedure or timing. Wells adjusted his plans, for example, by giving special practice lists to pupils having trouble with certain letters.

MOTIVATION.   The teacher wants pupils to direct their efforts to worthwhile goals. He decides whether to use competition, reprimands, pep talks, or other devices. Some teachers arouse motivation by group planning that makes goals clear and attractive.

Wells assumed that pupils wanted to type and would try if they felt able to make progress. Many of his procedures (such as delaying criticism) were intended to make the typing rewarding. The reward came from accomplishment and mastery, not from gold stars or special commendation. Wells relied also on social satisfactions. Letting pupils write messages to each other added interest to the early weeks before the skills themselves became a matter of pride. Interchanging lists of words to be typed made the work more fun. When Wells's assumption was incorrect, learning suffered. James did not care about typing and made only as much effort as was needed to keep out of trouble.

EVALUATION. Evaluation is a process of noting consequences of an action. Evaluation by the teacher is the basis on which he modifies his procedure; evaluation that makes consequences apparent to the pupil is necessary to his improvement. One of Wells's major tasks was the monitoring of practice to identify successes and errors.

It is important to know when to evaluate. Wells did not measure speed of typing until pupils had gained a reasonable amount of skill, on the assumption that an earlier test would have discouraged them. He criticized posture, but only after pupils had overcome their initial strangeness to their task. Some delays of evaluation seem to have been unwise. If Wells had observed Martha's hand placement before she practiced her error over and over, it could have been more easily corrected. One of the teacher's hardest decisions is between being critical enough to remove errors, and being lenient enough to give the pupil encouragement and a chance to develop his individual style of work.

Some teachers evaluate entirely by measures of performance, such as speed of typing. Progress records kept week by week do evaluate growth in skill, but Wells used several additional bases for judgment. Knowing that the score sometimes stays constant while the pupil is making significant gains in form, Wells watched *how* pupils typed more than *how much*. Wells ignored some results that other teachers would have assessed carefully. Apparently he did not direct pupils' attention to the way they organized their desks nor to how they spaced letters on the page. Nor did Wells direct attention to the amount of fatigue their typing produced. Talking over this problem might suggest postural improvement and could in the end increase both skill and enjoyment.

Having measured learning, the teacher is faced with the problem of what to do with the results. Wells did not use test results to encourage competition. Each pupil watched his own rate of improvement, but the pupils were not compared with one another. Wells chose to analyze weak performance, rather than to praise or blame the pupil.

INDIVIDUAL DIFFERENCES. Every learner is different from his fellows in interests, social effectiveness, ability, and the sort of errors he makes. As soon as the teacher tries a plan for his class, he finds that some pupils do not respond as the majority do. Some, like Martha and Olive, have trouble, and some who have adequate ability find the work unchallenging.

Wells dealt with individuals separately. He watched each one's errors and provided practice suited to his difficulties. This procedure works better in teaching typing, shopwork, or creative writing than it does in teaching social studies or science. The typical classroom teacher cannot isolate individuals from the group, and cannot find time to organize special lessons for each one. In many classes, furthermore, learning to work in a group is an important objective.

Some problems of individual differences are dealt with by guidance. With better guidance, James would not have elected typing or would have taken the course with a real purpose. As we shall see later, Olive's problems stemmed also from an inappropriate school program.

Table 5 provides a summary statement, organized according to the seven elements of learning. As we have seen, each element poses tasks for the

TABLE 5

Acts of the teacher associated with each aspect of learning

Situation	Selects and arranges material to which the pupil is to respond.
Personal characteristics	Uses aptitude tests and other data to judge what method and material the pupil is ready for.
Goal	Helps the pupil to understand what constitutes a desirable performance. Provides an encouraging atmosphere, sets attainable standards. Shows connections between the pupil's classwork and his personal aims.
Interpretation	Makes clear the characteristics of a desirable response. Arranges material meaningfully, and elaborates meanings by suitable explanation. Suggests suitable trial responses or methods of attack.
Action	Provides for the pupil to make active responses through practice, recitation, projects, etc.
Consequence	Monitors the pupil's performance to detect misunderstanding or faulty technique. Uses tests to show the pupil what progress he is making and what faults need to be overcome.
Reaction to thwarting	Reduces emotional tension. Assists the pupil to reinterpret. Studies the pupil individually to identify causes of difficulty.

teacher. Our subsequent chapters will consider how these tasks can be performed successfully. Chapters 4 through 8 will deal with personal characteristics, that is, with facts about development, readiness, and individual differences. Chapters 6 through 8 will be especially concerned with practical procedures. Chapters 9 through 13 deal with the selection and organization of curriculum materials and class activities. Particular attention will be given to the selection of situations likely to have "transfer value," i.e., likely to prepare the pupil to deal with situations not encountered in school. Chapters 9 through 13 also consider how the teacher can improve the pupil's interpretations and trial actions.

Goals and consequences are closely linked. They are discussed together in Chapters 14 through 16. The three chapters examine how goals arise, how planning and classroom control contribute to motivation, and how measurement helps the pupil evaluate his action. Reactions to thwarting lead into the study of emotional behavior in Chapter 17. The related topics of character development and mental health, in Chapter 18, provide an opportunity to review the entire learning process in a new context.

SUMMARY

Learning is shown by a change in behavior as a result of experience. The child has learned when he shows a new ability, and also when he changes his typical behavior so that some response becomes more probable, or less probable, than before.

Seven concepts central to the learning process, and indeed to nearly all behavior, are introduced:

Situation. The situation consists of all the objects, persons, and symbols in the learner's environment. The situation offers an opportunity to satisfy some want by choosing a suitable response. Curriculum planning is essentially a problem of selecting and arranging situations to which the pupil should learn to respond.

Personal characteristics. These include all the abilities and all the typical responses that the person brings to the situation. These characteristics limit the ways he can and will respond. The characteristics needed to profit from a learning experience are said to constitute "readiness" for the experience.

Goal. The goal of the learner is some consequence that he wishes to attain. He may seek some concrete object, a friendly response from someone else, an intellectually satisfying solution to a problem, etc. The goal is some possibility he perceives in the situation, which he expects to be gratifying. Effort is directed toward goals; hence the problem of motivating the learner is one of helping him to see, in the situation, goals he wants and thinks he can attain.

Interpretation. Interpretation is a process of directing attention to parts of the situation, relating observations to past experience, and predicting what result various actions will lead to. The interpretation is a part of the response to the situation.

Action. The person's actions include movements and statements; they are the observable parts of his response. Among the possible actions, the person chooses the one he expects to produce the most satisfying consequence. When uncertain whether or not he can attain his goal, the person makes what we call a provisional try, a tentative response that is quickly changed if early consequences prove unsatisfactory.

Consequence. The consequence may confirm the person's expectations, in which case he is likely to make a similar interpretation in the next such situation. The teacher, helping the learner to judge his performance, should make certain that he observes consequences accurately. The teacher who praises a good response is reinforcing the interpretation and action used. Contradiction of expectation is spoken of as "negative reinforcement"; there may be various reactions to this contradiction or thwarting.

Reaction to thwarting. Thwarting occurs when the person fails to attain a goal. His reaction may be adaptive. That is to say, he may make a new interpretation and alter his response in a reasonable way. Such adaptive behavior will usually bring a more satisfying consequence. He can also adapt by changing his goal to one he can attain. The reaction may be non-adaptive: stubborn repetition of the original response, thoughtless variation of the response, or abandonment of goal.

A typing class is described to show how these aspects of performance may be observed in the classroom. The example draws attention to decisions about curriculum, motivating procedures, evaluation, and the handling of individual differences. Table 5 summarizes particular teaching acts relevant to each aspect of the learning process.

Reading List 3

G. Lester Anderson, "Basic Learning Theory for Teachers," Chapter 14 in C. E. Skinner, ed., *Educational Psychology* (New York: Prentice-Hall, 1959), pp. 389–416.

Although Anderson's own view of learning is not unlike ours, in this chapter he contrasts four historically separate "learning theories" and discusses how education would be changed if each theory were adopted. What does each theory emphasize that our chapter does not, and vice versa?

G. Lester Anderson and Arthur I. Gates, "The General Nature of Learning," Chapter 1 in Nelson B. Henry, ed., *Learning and Instruc-*

tion, Forty-ninth Yearbook of the National Society for the Study of Education, Part I (Chicago: Univ. of Chicago Press, 1950), pp. 12–35. Reprinted in Harris.[2]

This selection describes the learning process as an attempt to get around obstacles and attain goals. A careful comparison of the key terms in this presentation with our seven concepts will be instructive.

Ernest E. Bayles, "The Idea of Learning as Development of Insight," *Educational Theory*, 2 (1952), 65–71. Reprinted in Fullagar.

"Learning means development of insight, and that alone." Bayles compares his theory with some previous interpretations of learning theory. Is his theory the same as that of the present chapter? Was Mr. Wells's class developing insight, according to Bayles's definition?

Herbert J. Klausmeier, "Human Abilities and Teaching-Learning Processes," Chapter 1, in *Learning and Human Abilities* (New York: Harper, 1961), pp. 3–33.

Klausmeier describes several types of learning (purposeful, imitative, conditioned), and shows how the process may be modified by the guidance of the teacher. His discussion of purposeful learning is much like that of this chapter, giving additional examples and summary charts. You should consider carefully whether his other "types" of learning represent processes missing from our chapter.

Neal E. Miller, "Graphic Communication and the Crisis in Learning," *Audio-Visual Communication Review*, 5 (1957), 61–103. (Also published as a separate book by National Education Association, Washington, 1957.)

A prominent learning theorist makes recommendations regarding education by means of films and similar devices, using a learning theory in which the key concepts are *drive, cue, response, reward.* How do these fit into our scheme of seven concepts? What have we added?

J. B. Stroud, "The Role of Practice in Learning," Chapter 10 in Nelson B. Henry, ed., *The Psychology of Learning*, Forty-first Yearbook of the National Society for the Study of Education, Part II (Bloomington: Illinois, Public School Pub. Co., 1942), pp. 353–76.

Stroud discusses the proper type and organization of practice in school, and contrasts this with misconceptions arising from oversimplified views of learning. Note especially his opinion on drill.

[2] References such as this indicate books of "readings" whose full titles are given in the Preface, p. xxvii.

PART TWO

READINESS AND ITS DEVELOPMENT

CHAPTER 4 THE STREAM OF DEVELOPMENT

Readiness is the central concern behind questions of educational planning such as: "What works of literature are appropriate for junior high school?" "In what grade should fractions be introduced?" "Can Stephen succeed in a precollege curriculum?" We shall devote the next five chapters to examining the sources of readiness, what pupils are ready for at different ages, how to judge readiness, and how to use information on readiness. The even more significant topic—how to promote readiness—will enter into these chapters but must obviously be a major theme also of later chapters on intellectual and emotional learning.

One's reaction to a situation depends on his repertoire of possible responses, his past experience in related situations, and general traits such as his goals and values and his level of anxiety. These characteristics also determine whether he adapts or gives up when a provisional try fails. Hence the characteristics of the pupil determine how he will respond to each learning opportunity the school offers. Readiness is affected by all the characteristics of the pupil including, specifically, his biological equipment, his ideas and skills, his habits, and his attitudes and values. We sometimes speak of readiness as being present or absent; thus, "Mary is ready for the study of French, but Susan is not." This is an oversimplified statement, however. Readiness is not readiness merely for certain subject matter. One is ready or unready for the total learning situation, taking into account the method of teaching and the satisfactions offered as well as the subject matter. One can learn French at age 2 under certain conditions of instruction, and not until high school under others. This view is expressed in the recent contention (Bruner, 1960, p. 22) that calculus can be taught, in some form and by some suitably chosen method, in any grade, even the first.

It is insufficient to say that a pupil "lacks readiness" for instruction. The pupil who lacks readiness for the instruction we propose is ready for *some* learning experience. To speak of what he lacks is to miss the point. For every pupil, we can find some worthwhile activity at which he can succeed —hopefully, one that will remedy his present deficiency. The study of readiness is much more than an attempt to forecast success and failure; it is an attempt to match instruction to pupil characteristics. The teacher in any grade must be acquainted with all aspects of development and with all periods of life. What went on before the pupil enters this teacher's classroom affects what he can and will do, and what happens to him here must be judged in terms of what it contributes to his subsequent readiness.

THE INTERACTION OF BIOLOGICAL NATURE AND EXPERIENCE

At first thought it might seem that physical development would affect only the learning of motor skills. But physical immaturity, poor coordination, or lack of endurance can interfere with any type of learning. The pupil who is readily exhausted, for example, will have a shorter span of concentration, will be more upset by difficulty, and will be less willing to persevere. He should have extra help, and tasks that he can complete in a relatively short time. On the other hand, physical difficulties sometimes *increase* readiness for academic learning. The child who has no success in games may take special pride in his reading and rely on it for much of his satisfaction. His success in reading may cause him to prefer books to games, with the result that he withdraws more and more from the play group and so drifts further behind in physical skill and social development.

The characteristics of the pupil change with his experience and continued biological development. Readiness in first grade depends in part on things that happened in infancy. The elementary grades create (or sometimes impede) readiness for high-school learning. Taking responsibility in a high-school project teaches self-reliance and skill in planning; these increase readiness for professional training. Four principles will be illustrated over and over in this and later chapters:

All aspects of development interact. A change in any facet of the child's readiness can alter his whole system of responses. When the normal sequence of development is interrupted in any way, effects are to be seen throughout the child's development.

Physiological maturing prepares one to profit from experience. Biological changes, especially in the nervous system, influence what one can learn. Pupils who differ in rate of maturing have different experiences and develop different personalities.

Experiences have a cumulative effect. Each experience affects the child's reaction to the next similar situation. A single success tends to make the next success more likely, a series of successes snowballing to build up great readiness in a particular direction. Cumulation of failures holds back development.

Certain times in life are formative periods, which have a great effect on readiness for a particular activity. The period when a person first has a chance to engage in an activity is especially important. The formative period for physical skill is, roughly, from age 1 to age 4. From the time he learns to creep through the "runabout age," the child is establishing a basic coordination pattern and developing confidence or timidity. The usual formative period for attitudes regarding one's intellectual abilities, reading, work with numbers, and school work in general is the first year or so of schooling. Success, failure, challenge, and conflict at that time precondition the reaction to all later schooling.

Inadequate development during a formative period need not blight a child's life; with a later opportunity to learn, he can overcome early setbacks. Social relationships are much influenced by attitudes and skills acquired from ages 3 to 7. But the child who has not learned to get along with playmates even by age 10 may do so later, under the guidance of a teacher or scoutmaster. It ordinarily takes special effort and skilled teaching, however, to eradicate responses acquired during the formative period and practiced repeatedly thereafter.

    1. When would you expect the formative period to come for each of the following:
        a. relations with the opposite sex; love and courtship
        b. managing money
        c. being interested in books and ideas
        d. defending one's own rights
    2. Show that physical, intellectual, and attitudinal characteristics would all be of concern in teaching:
        a. handwriting
        b. high-school English
        c. auto mechanics
    3. A fourth-grade girl of average-to-superior mental ability is chosen by her group to take the principal part in a play they are presenting. She does well and receives great praise for her acting. What effect is this likely to have on her future behavior? How will she be affected by the time she reaches high school if she has further experiences of this sort?
    4. "Readiness is more important in the elementary-school classroom than in high school or college." Do you agree or disagree?

PHYSICAL MATURING AS THE BASE OF READINESS

Physical Development Affects the Self-concept

Children grow at different rates. Some are larger than others, and some mature more rapidly. The direct effect of these differences is seen in their ability to play games and to hold their own in fights. The indirect social and psychological effects are even more important.

⟩ Physical superiority tends to have a beneficial effect on personality. The larger children acquire confidence in their physical competence; by winning approval they also gain social assurance. Larger children are more apt to be selected as leaders. The child with a slight physique, less capable of batting a ball solidly, finds himself unwanted when his playmates are choosing teams. Again and again he is in the awkward position of making the crucial out, of being greeted with "Here's an easy out!" when he comes to bat.⟩ Physical size is particularly important to the boy, whose strength affects all of his social relationships. Around age 12, his social influence is closely related to how well the other boys think he can fight (Lippitt *et al.*, 1952). Stronger boys are superior in buoyancy, appearance, and masculinity. Figure 19 charts average ratings of boys of age 11–12; even greater differences were found late in high school.

⟩ One's attitude toward his physical endowments is an element in self-confidence at all ages.⟩ During adolescence in particular we find boys comparing themselves with athletes, and girls checking their good points against those of movie actresses. The judgment of self is complicated by many false ideas, such as the girl's notion that she is unattractive because she wears glasses. Stolz and Stolz (1944; see also Frazier and Lisonbee, 1950) report that 30 to 40 per cent of adolescents are at some time "definitely disturbed concerning their physical characteristics." Tallness in girls, shortness in boys, and fatness in both sexes lead the list of causes of self-disap-

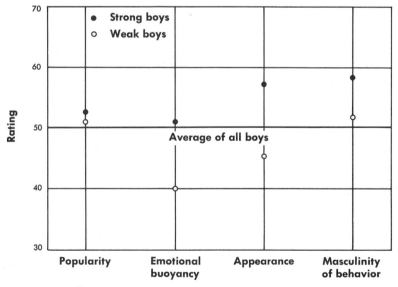

19   *Strength promotes personality development in boys* (H. E. *Jones, 1946*)

proval. As the Stolzes say, the changing body becomes for a time "the symbol of the self."

Physical superiority does not necessarily mean behavioral superiority. Sometimes the large boy finds it so easy to get his way by force that he is overbearing and unpopular. The relatively small adolescent who is attractive and mature may be popular with both sexes. For the adolescent girl, a large frame is often a handicap because boys favor average-size and small girls. Thus the effect of a physical characteristic depends upon the meaning attached to it by the person and his group.

The contrasting histories of Walter and Stanley illustrate all four of our principles regarding development. When Stanley was small, just beginning to crawl about, climb, and otherwise learn motor skills, he showed remarkable security. Whether because of inborn temperament or because he had learned to be at ease and optimistic, Stanley would try anything. As he tried various feats of jumping and climbing, he had many successes. When he fell, he picked himself up and started over. His falls seemed not to hurt, and with his relaxed carriage he probably did fall "soft." Outgoing and seeking activity, he developed superior coordination and took great delight in bodily contact. In preschool, he participated vigorously in games even when the others tended to hold back. More than that, when larger children jostled him he was ready to shove back or even to attack them. His words expressed his concept of himself: "I'm tough." At 6, Stanley was adept in learning new sports, eager to learn boxing and ready to take the punishment of such a contact sport, unafraid of children of any age—but somewhat inclined to be overbearing.

Walter, though also large for his age, showed just the opposite pattern. At 10, Walter had an opportunity to learn boxing. He began with what seemed like keen interest, but he came sidling in with face averted. The instant his opponent began punching, Walter was ready to turn his back, bury his head in his arms, and retreat. Stanley from the start threw his fists with a free and powerful movement; Walter's boxing was a matter of poking and jerking. This behavior was characteristic of Walter. From very early childhood Walter had sought sympathy to an unusual degree. Early explorations brought him many falls, each of which he fussed over. His anxiety increased his physical tenseness; this made him more awkward so that he had more falls and played games badly. Finding his world a source of discomfort (where Stanley's was a source of adventure and accomplishment), Walter's reaction was to seek adult support. He learned to think of vigorous physical activity as dangerous. Later, when his school group played active games, Walter was overcontrolled and dodged bodily contact. His companions teased him, so he became unhappy in the group and disliked school. Thus his physical handicap reached out into all other areas of adjustment.

Normal Trends in Physical Development

SIZE. Change in height and weight is most striking in early adolescence, when the rate of growth changes markedly. Adolescence is the period that bridges from childhood to adulthood. Adolescent biological changes include great increase in height, change from childish to adult body proportions, development of the sexual organs and changes in glandular functions, and change in voice. The child in effect acquires a new body, which can do new things and admit him to new social relationships. These biological changes extend over several years and have no definite beginning or end point. It is customary to consider the appearance of adult sexual characteristics as the start of adolescence. This development, known as *puberty*, is dramatically signaled for the girl by the first menstruation (menarche), and less suddenly for the boy by the appearance of pubic hair. The child does not leap abruptly into adolescence. Many physiological and social changes proceed very gradually.

Growth in height is fairly steady during childhood, but there is a pause before puberty, and then a spurt. Girls enter this cycle ahead of boys, and remain ahead in this and other indicators of maturity. The peak growth for the girl comes somewhere between ages 10 and 15, most often at about 12—eighteen months ahead of the average boy (Tanner, 1955; Stolz and Stolz, 1951). The more rapid growth of girls presents special problems during Grades V to VIII. Physically, the typical girl is at this time as mature as the boy two grades ahead. The girl who matures early has less in common with her classmates than at any other time in her school life. Social unity in the classroom suffers when physical maturity and interests are too diverse.

Both before and after puberty children of the same age and sex differ markedly. Whatever the quality measured, some children are physically like the average child two years older, and some like the average child two years younger.

INDIVIDUAL DIFFERENCES. Many of the traits that concern teachers fall into the pattern known as a normal distribution. The *normal distribution* is symmetrical, with many people close to the average and a few ranging far out on either side (Figure 20). The distributions of height in Figure 22 below are approximately normal in form. Mental test scores also have nearly normal distributions in representative groups.

By remembering that measures of individual differences are distributed more or less normally we can eliminate two fallacies in reasoning. One fallacy is to recognize only those differences that represent deviation from the average in an undesirable direction. Too often, individual attention is given only to the inferior pupil. The normal curve reminds us that superiority in any characteristic will be about as common as inferiority. The second

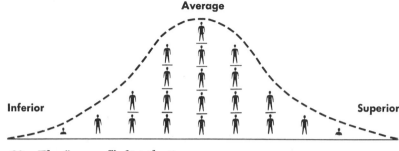

20   *The "normal" distribution*

fallacy is to think of people as falling into distinct "normal," "inferior," and "superior" groups. Nearly all the qualities of concern to teachers have continuous distributions. There are no gaps in the height distribution, separating "tall" from "normal"; nor in the intelligence distribution, between bright and normal. Whenever we separate "exceptional" children for special treatment, our dividing line is arbitrary. Great variation remains within each group.

The pupil who is advanced in some physical characteristic has a good chance of remaining above average as he grows older; for example, height at ages 6 through 10 correlates .75 with height at maturity (Shuttleworth, 1939; Tuddenham and Snyder, 1954). Despite this consistency, positions shift considerably from year to year. Some children spurt in size or strength while others seem to be marking time. Illness or an emotional upset may delay development, and such a physical setback may influence all learning and social adjustment. Size as such is no indication of mental ability or probable academic success; size, strength, and measures of skeletal maturity have negligible correlations (.00 to .20) with measures of academic ability (Abernethy, 1936; Klausmeier *et al.*, 1958).

TIMING OF ADOLESCENT CHANGES.   Individual differences in growth are of special importance during adolescence. As Figure 21 shows, there are great individual differences in the timing of adolescent development. Some girls enter adolescence at age 11 (about Grade V) and some do not make the transition until four years later. Among boys, even many high school juniors are still children physically.

The age of puberty has changed and presumably is continuing to change. Tanner (1955) summarizes evidence from many Western countries showing that puberty occurred in 1940 at an average two years earlier than the average age of puberty in 1880. There has probably been a further change of at least three months since 1940, though no good current data are available. The data charted in Figure 21 are therefore not perfectly representative of the present situation, though the average shift of a few months is of small importance in view of the range of individual differences. The fact that the age of puberty has shifted by a full year, however, since the junior high school was introduced early in this century as a special institution for the early adolescent, makes it clear that educators must be ready to modify their institutions to fit changing developmental norms.

The social consequences of delayed puberty are long-lasting (M. C. Jones and Bayley, 1950). The early maturing boys become far "smoother" socially: each success gives confidence and prestige, which helps them further. At a ninth-grade graduation party they come at a sophisticated late hour, they dance well and daringly, and act condescendingly. Boys of the same age

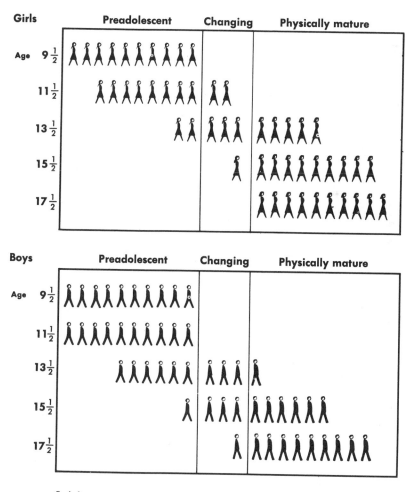

Each figure represents 10 per cent of the age group

21   *Girls mature ahead of boys (From* Life and Growth, *by Alice V. Keliher. Copyright 1938, 1941, D. Appleton-Century Co., Inc. By permission of Appleton-Century-Crofts, Inc.)*

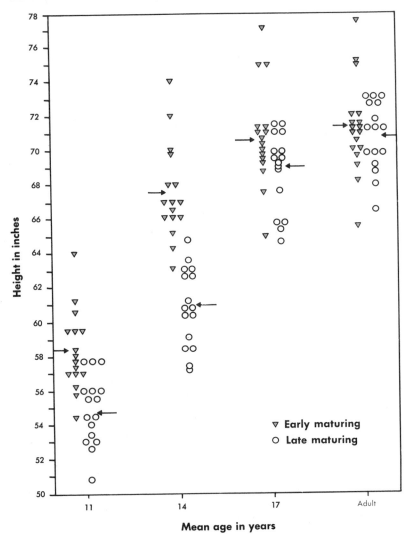

22 *Late maturing boys overtake early maturers (Mary C. Jones and Nancy Bayley, 1950)*

who are not as far into physical adolescence show childish, bouncing enthusiasm, giggling, and silliness. They do not dance well or know how to talk to girls. They are not popular, do not succeed in athletics, and are not chosen for class office. They are apt to be troublesome to teachers. They tend to be restless, energetic, and bossy. Twelve out of eighteen late maturers were rated by observers as having a strong desire to attack others by ridicule and criticism, an indicator of insecurity found only half as often among early maturers. By age 17, late maturers are described as straining to be popular and to be accepted in groups.

Further studies were made of both groups when they reached the age of 30. On a questionnaire the early maturers described themselves as relatively high in responsibility, sociability, dominance, and self-control. Others depended on them for advice and reassurance; they had become influential. There was no marked difference in the professional success of the two groups (M. C. Jones and Bayley, 1950; M. C. Jones, 1957; Mussen and Jones, 1958). Every difference observed favors the early maturing boy; the only criticism that might be made is that as a group they appear a bit stuffy in their easily won adjustment. Their superiority is not the direct result of a biological advantage. Rather, it is a psychological by-product: they were physically ready in early adolescence to take a full part in a new social environment and to learn from it.

The years around puberty are stressful for girls, the peak tension evidently coming in the year or so immediately before menarche. Frequent disturbing dreams are reported by 39 per cent of the girls two years before menarche, and by only 9 per cent two years after. There is a prepubertal peak of shyness, emotional dependence, and irritability (Macfarlane *et al.*, 1954). The early maturing girl has more of these problems than the late maturer. In Grades V and VI her interest turns to boys, but she gets no encouragement from the boys in her class. She is socially out of step until Grades VII to IX. By age 17, the early maturing girl is likely to be superior in self-acceptance and poise. In high school, it is the late maturing girl who is at a disadvantage (Faust, 1960; M. C. Jones and Mussen, 1958).

EDUCATIONAL IMPLICATIONS OF GROWTH. Because feelings about physical characteristics play an important role in personality development, the instructional program should help the pupil to appreciate his own qualities. For example, primary pupils can be taught to place proper valuation on differences in size. Rearing a family of animals can convey that one's size is usually like his parents', and that small size is not a mark of inferiority. Curriculum material urging certain foods "to make you big" suggests that the child who is not big has something to apologize for.

The program of physical activity should be sufficiently varied to give each pupil a chance to do well. Small boys or girls can perform well in sports where size is less important than agility. With suitable roles to play, even awkward children can achieve self-respect, as the following incident demonstrates (Tryon and Henry, 1950, p. 157).

> John went with his class and teacher one spring day across the neighboring fields to gather specimens for their aquarium. The children clustered along the bank of a stream seeking to catch the prized crayfish. Only the nimble fingered had occasional successes.
>
> John, clumsy of body and slow in reaction time, after five minutes of no success turned to the teacher and said, "Don't you think it would be a good idea if I gathered some moss and leaves to line the baskets we are going to carry these crayfish in?" The teacher nodded approval of this sugges-

tion and John, accompanied by a half dozen others, set happily about the task. In other sections of the teacher's record about John, we find him holding the tape for racing matches or refereeing a game.

The school that encourages chief attention to competitive sports intensifies the adjustment problems of the undersized and underskilled child. Interscholastic competition in basketball in the elementary school, for instance, stresses the difference between those who are "good enough for the team" and those who are not. The less able boys have little chance to develop fundamental skills. Some of the undersized or clumsy preadolescents will be tall and well coordinated five years later, so that the competitive program is not ideal even for developing champions. Discouraging the less adept boys cuts out some who might be star performers in high school and college if they were given an early start (Knapp and Combes, 1949). A physical education program that offers rewards only to the large, fast, and adept is as inimical to the development of all pupils as is an academic program in which the duller pupils find nothing they can do. Varied sports calling on different types of physical readiness are needed; activities that minimize comparison and competition should be part of the program.

Because of the wide range in size of pupils at any age, and the differences in maturity at adolescence, it is valuable to arrange school activities so that pupils of different ages can mingle and sort themselves into groups of corresponding development. Clubs and recreational activities based on interests rather than age classification help toward this goal.

Growth is more than enlargement. Parts of the body change in relative size, glands take on new functions, and innumerable changes take place in the body's microanatomy and biochemistry. A decline in metabolism, for example, might cause a girl to put on fat and to have consequent difficulties in adjustment (Shock, 1951). The teacher who suspects a marked change in a pupil's physical functioning will do well to recommend a physical examination. Sometimes drugs or glandular therapy can be of great benefit to health and to learning (C. H. Lawrence, 1942).

> **5.** What methods can be suggested for dealing with the girl who reaches adolescence while in the fifth grade, and loses interest in the activities of her classmates?
>
> **6.** How can you account for the fact that the early maturing girl gains in popularity and adjustment between the ages of 12 and 17?
>
> **7.** Should all pupils move into the junior high school at the same age? Would it be wiser to base this transfer on the pupil's physical maturity?

Neural Maturation

It is amply clear that the neurophysiology and biochemistry of the brain and nervous system change as the child grows older, and that these have much to do with his performance and learning (Harlow and Woolsey, 1958; Rosenzweig *et al.*, 1960). But our knowledge of these physiological topics is seriously incomplete, and in any event we would no more expect the teacher to apply them directly than we would expect the chef to become an expert in food chemistry. The teacher needs only to be aware of the significance of neural development and of the interpretations that have been made of the findings.

The brain changes in size and structure. One important change is the deposit of a fatty substance *myelin*, which appears to act as an insulator between the nerve cells, thus permitting more precise control of motor responses. There are no doubt many more subtle changes in the fine structure of the brain, not yet identified.

It is reasonable to suppose that a good deal of the change in the nervous system that occurs during early childhood is an unfolding of more or less predetermined structures according to the timetable natural to the species. This biological pacing of development is referred to as *maturation*. More formally, maturation is defined as the emergence of any characteristic whose form and timing are chiefly controlled genetically, by heredity (Eichorn and Jones, 1958). The word "chiefly" should be noted; every characteristic depends to some extent on diet, exercise, maternal care, and other aspects of the environment. If brain structures unfold in some predetermined manner, this should set limits regarding the age at which we can teach various things, and there is research to support this view.

Most of the studies on maturation have been done with lower animals, where no ethical questions arise if half the subjects are deprived of some experience. For example, one can raise salamanders in an anaesthetic solution to see if this delays the development of swimming reactions. Swimming emerges promptly when, at the normal age for swimming, the anaesthetic is allowed to wear off; this suggests that the swimming response merely "unfolds" biologically. (For this and other studies supporting the maturation hypothesis, see McGraw, 1946.) A number of less extensive studies of young children have compared development with and without training. J. R. Hilgard (1932) gave 2-year-olds twelve weeks of training and practice in such activities as cutting with scissors. Each child had from 25 to 30 practice periods. A second group of the same age was trained only during the last week of the experiment. As Figure 23 shows, Group B gained a great deal between December and April just from growth and everyday experience. Four sessions of specific training then produced almost as much gain as Group A achieved from mid-January to mid-March. The children profited more when they were more mature—but nonetheless the group with longer training was more proficient in the end. Studies like this were interpreted as showing that there is some point at which the child becomes biologically ready for a certain learning, and that practice before this time may be wasted. Worse than that, if the child is pressed to learn prematurely,

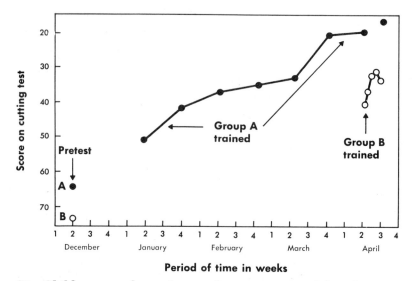

23   *Children may learn faster when training is delayed* (*Josephine R. Hilgard, 1932*)

his failures may give him a negative attitude that will impede learning at the proper time. This view has had great influence on educational thinking, and has often been translated into a policy of "waiting for maturation" whenever a child has trouble in learning.

Although the facts established in the experiments described are not in dispute, other biological evidence speaks against a "waiting" policy. (There are other sorts of evidence to be discussed in Chapters 8 and 10.) In the first place, there is no substantial evidence that neural maturation continues into the school ages. The 6-year-old has 95 per cent of the myelin he will have as an adult. The last 5 per cent may be highly important, and there may be other subtle changes yet to come; this is an unsettled question. But surely studies of early development give us no evidence on maturation during school ages.

Even in the early years when neural development is proceeding rapidly, experience is evidently necessary to promote and direct that development. Sperry (1951) tells us that using a part of the brain speeds up myelinization in that area. Riesen (1960) tells us that the physiological development of the retina proceeds normally only if the eyes are used early in life. This is dramatically evidenced in persons born blind whose sight is later made normal by an operation. The person who has had no opportunity to compare patterns in childhood finds it very difficult to make such discriminations when he finally can see (von Senden, 1960). A girl with vision blocked by cataracts was cured by an operation. Although she was intelligent, having completed high school while blind, after the operation she could not learn to recognize the faces of her associates. Hebb (1958, p. 123), having described this girl, extends such findings into the general conclusion that "perceptual development depends essentially on exposure to the patterned stimulation of the early environment. . . . It is rare that an adult learns a language so well that he can pass in every respect as a native. . . . One's 'ear' for the rhythms and nuances of speech must be acquired early." Despite the fact that some developments are highly dependent upon biological processes, a normal range of varied experience appears to be necessary if these processes are to do their work.

The eminent neurosurgeon Wilder Penfield, drawing on anatomical rather than experimental evidence, declares that as the brain ages it becomes unable to learn what it could have learned at an early age. Specifically, "for the purposes of learning languages, the human brain becomes progressively stiff and rigid after the age of nine" (Penfield and Roberts, 1959, p. 236). Particularly during the second year of life, the child is building, through practice, the neural connections required to pronounce syllables. Simultaneously, he builds neural "programs"—systems of interconnections—to produce the speech rhythm and sentence structure.

This word *program* will play an important part in our later discussions of complex performance, being used in several related ways. An electric computer is controlled by a program, that is, a sequence of orders telling the machine what steps to take next, at what instant to send an impulse through a particular circuit. A similar sequence of orders controls the movements of the diaphragm, voice box, and mouth that shape a sound. The program is like a well-designed football play: each player has his assignment, and if he comes in at the correct instant, the play succeeds.

Practice at the right age develops circuits that instantly bring forth, by a coordinated sequence of actions, the sounds and structures of the language as the child calls for them. The child develops a basic program only for the sounds of his own language. It is quite difficult for the older person to pronounce new sounds; instead, he speaks a French word by putting together the sounds from his native language that come close to the French sounds. The Hawaiian language possesses only seven consonants (h, k, l, m, n, p, w). The person who as a child learned no language save Hawaiian may find it necessary to say *Mele Kalikimaka* as his best approximation to *Merry Christmas*. If Penfield is correct, the child learning a language before age 10 does so by creating *new* circuits in the syllable-producing areas of the brain; the older person can only recombine the syllable-circuits of his first tongue. Consequently, the person who acquires a second language in high school or college is unlikely to speak without an accent.

The educator, trying to base a policy on such research as this, encounters two difficulties. First, the research is quite insufficient to establish a theory. At most, we know that providing training too early is wasted effort, and may be harmful. On the other hand, delaying an experience may let the child drift past the point of greatest readiness to profit from it. Second, the educator faces difficult value judgments as to what expenditure of effort is justified. Penfield's proposal raises such a question. Suppose that his tentative conclusions about language learning are fully correct; does this mean that every preschool child should be taught a second language? This writer is unwilling to accept such a recommendation. Even if we could forecast what language will be most useful to the child in later years, perfect diction does not seem very important to anyone save an undercover agent. Penfield does not imply that early instruction improves ability to comprehend and to formulate thoughts in a second language. Only evidence to *this* effect would warrant spending some hours each week, throughout childhood, on language instruction. An equal instructional effort to support concept development or creative activities should have greater ultimate benefits.

The studies seem to show a substantial maturational element in the acquisition of sensorimotor control: learning to interpret information coming to our sense organs. and learning to make our muscles act as we wish. While there may be maturational developments after age 6 that affect conceptual learning and reasoning, there is no present biological evidence on the point. Hence curriculum plans must rest on psychological evidence regarding the child's response to various forms of instruction. The evidence to appear in Chapter 10 seems to support a conclusion like this: Whatever you wish to teach a child, some experience can be provided at any school age that will carry him toward your objective. Early childhood stimulation has more value than it was credited with when maturational experiments were first reported.

8. Foreign languages are now being added to the curriculum for Grade IV or V in many places. Would Penfield endorse this?

9. For what functions, other than vision and speech, is "patterned stimulation" in very early childhood likely to form circuits for interpretation and control?

10. What is your opinion of this statement: "There is no harm in offering the child a very rich and stimulating environment, regardless of his level of maturation, unless the parent or teacher puts pressure on him to develop mastery"?

11. A maze task requires a person to study a printed square maze until he can trace the path along a circuitous route, from center to exit, without ever entering a blind alley. A certain maze of high complexity contains ten choice points. Suppose it is found that children given this task never solve it on the first trial before age 12. Would this imply that the performance requires some biological maturation that occurs around age 11?

12. In the Hilgard experiment, Group A, with 30 training sessions, finished at a higher level than Group B, with four sessions. If other studies confirm this finding, does it argue for helping the 2-year-old with training in cutting?

CULTURAL PRESSURES AND OPPORTUNITIES

What a child becomes depends upon the culture in which he is reared. In one setting, children grow into the New Guinea tribesmen who are gentle, contented, and possess only simple arts and skills. Another setting develops the competitive, aggressive Alaskan Indian whose highest goal is to humiliate and subjugate his rivals. The Balinese consider dancing important and develop exceptional skill in it; the Italians are famed for fun and music-making; and American mechanical ingenuity is a well-founded legend. The stimulation and constraints imposed by a culture encourage certain activities and discourage others, thus shaping mental development, interests, tastes, and character traits.

The Environment Widens

The environment of the growing child expands in many ways, three of which merit special attention. The most obvious expansion is in the child's geographical range. As he grows older, he ranges over a larger area and encounters a far wider variety of stimulation. A second change is in the number of persons who mold his thinking. At first, his parents are his only guides, but his social environment gradually takes in more people. Eventually those in his own age group become the most important influence. A third and more subtle change is in the roles open to him. In a social gathering the young child is likely to be confined to passing the cookie plate and looking pleasant. In later years, he is expected to respond intelligently in conversation, and by late adolescence it is appropriate for him to initiate topics of serious conversation. While this expansion continues into adulthood, sometime in the 50's and early 60's the process is reversed: the contraction of physical mobility, social interaction, and accessible roles is almost synonymous with social aging (Cumming *et al.*, 1960).

The infant's first environment is little more than his mother's face and voice. As his maturation permits him to focus his eyes, reach, sit up, and creep about, he widens the range he can explore. American children ordinarily make plentiful contacts with others of like age during the years from 2 to 5. Billy learns about conflict and power when Harry wants the tricycle. He learns that he is "too little" for certain activities; even at this age, a social role is defined for him. Babyhood, he finds, has its pleasures as well as its restrictions. He may cling to its indulgence and protection like Robin, age 3, who tells his mother solemnly after a misdemeanor: "You won't spank me. I'm too little to understand."

Entrance into school is a significant step toward independence. In this (one writer calls it the "first adolescence"), the child comes out of the home into society. Before the age of 5 or 6, most of his activities are linked to the home and supervised by the parent. Once in school and in free contact with other children, he enters into a life over which parents have little control. He makes his way among strangers and joins social groups on his own. The first grade is by no means the beginning of intellectual learning, but the school presents a more insistent demand for "work" than most children have experienced. He must achieve if he is to fill his role successfully and win approval.

The preschool child deals almost entirely with events and objects within his immediate experience. Stories, television, and the like make him familiar with only a few figures from the wider world. After age 6, he adds concepts by reading and his wider exploration of the community. He notices more in what he sees. The western drama, once just the excitement of horses and guns, now communicates a dozen cultural values and taboos. Stereotyped though it is, it acquaints the child with motives he might never observe in his daily life—greed, revenge, public service—and lines up his emotions on the side of justice, property rights, and the law. Such stimulation stretches the child's horizon across the earth's surface, backward into history, and forward into time and space.

With the increased physical interaction with the environment comes a firmer intellectual grasp. The same event carries a different meaning for the older child than it does for the younger one. This is illustrated by children's responses to questions about the flag (Weinstein, 1957; see also Piaget and Weil, 1951). At 5, the child sees the flag as an object with pretty colors; he knows of no connection between flags and nations. A year later, he associates flags with the idea of "good" and "bad" countries. By 8 or 9, he is aware that there are flags for many governments, and he begins to speak of ideas of honor, loyalty, and pride in connection with the flag. By age 12, his vague ideas coalesce into a logical system. He sees the flag as an agreed symbol of the people and their government.

> **13.** A. B. Guthrie, who wrote such first-rate novels on western history as *The Big Sky* and *Ten Thousand Hills*, criticizes the westerns of television for presenting a false picture of the West. The Indians shown are efficient, organized warriors, not the starving nomads of the real West. TV lawmen are brave and honest; but Guthrie says many of the marshals ignored the law and plundered as much as any masked bandit. What forces work against portraying this true West in television?

The Child's Social Group Expands

The circle of others who influence one's life is constantly widening. Three categories of persons have a socializing influence: those in power who present explicit demands and reward compliance (authority figures), those who present an image of behavior that can be copied (models), and those companions whose favorable and unfavorable reactions are rewarding or punishing.

The infant begins with but a single socializer, his mother; in the second or third year the father begins to be significant. Later the parents are joined by many other adult socializers, teachers being most prominent. Gradually authority figures outside the home come to have greater influence.

PEER INFLUENCES.   Associates of one's own age and status are referred to as "peers." The peer group is a powerful source of rewards. The power to reward is in itself the power to demand, so that the peer group acts as an authority figure. Unlike other authority figures—parents, teachers, older brothers and sisters, bosses—the peer group is not delegated its authority by the adult culture. The peer group represents its own interests and values, even working in opposition to the more official socializers. Here, for example, is the plaintive report of a university faculty who arrange a "Talent Series" of concert artists as a contribution to the cultural development of students:

> It was once considered fashionable—"the thing to do"—to attend the Talent Series. Those who did not attend were just not quite "in style." Undergraduate attitudes have changed. Of 1,900 season tickets sold this year, only 200 were sold to undergraduates. In contrast, special programs such as jazz concerts are often patronized almost exclusively by undergraduates. About 4,200 of the 5,000 who attended a jazz concert by Stan Kenton last year were undergraduates. Are students redefining what is cultural? Who is to say that the Cleveland Orchestra is "cultural" while a jazz band is not?

Peers first enter the child's life as models whose actions suggest provisional responses; if Timmy is playing in the snow, Sharon wants to go out, too. This suggestive force is gradually transformed into a positive need for doing things with others and being accepted by them. In the preschool years, children pair off in ever-changing small groups; there is no group spirit and no concentration of activities. As intellectual development makes it possible for a large group to operate effectively, group approval becomes a coercive force. If marbles become the ruling passion of the fourth-graders, the boy who wants to make a kite in a new design must turn his back on the group. It takes strong interest in the kite (or a fear of unpleasantness if he joins the group) to outweigh the attractions of the noisy, happy group.

Peers are more significant in American childhood than in some other countries. Boehm (1957) tested elementary pupils in Geneva and in Winnetka, Illinois, with stories such as this:

A group of children of your age want to give a surprise birthday party to their scout leader. One boy has accepted the responsibility of decorating the room. He wonders whom he could ask for advice.

In an interview, 70 per cent of the Swiss children insisted that teachers and parents always give the best advice. Only 7 per cent of the Americans considered the teachers' advice superior to that of an artistically talented pupil. Says Boehm: "The American child matures earlier than does the Swiss child [and] seems to transfer his parent dependence to a peer dependence at an earlier age. . . . Whereas the American child's conscience is turned primarily toward social adaptation, the Swiss child's is geared toward character improvement."

Roles Become More Varied

Each setting into which the child moves calls for new relationships and styles of response; each experience is a training ground for future roles. The 5-year-old who takes her turn as center of attention during "show and tell time" is learning a new role; when she hands out the class drawing materials she learns another. As Havighurst and Neugarten (1962, p. 78) say:

> The individual . . . incorporates the role behaviors into his personality and into "himself." In this sense, the social self consists, in large part, of the behavior the individual expresses in his various roles. In this sense, too, the well-socialized individual is one who fills his various social roles successfully. While every person has his idiosyncratic pattern of role behaviors (thus no two women fill the role of mother in exactly the same ways) still the well-socialized person is one whose role behaviors are appropriate to the expectations set by the social groups with which he interacts.

Roles are defined by the group; thus in one sense they are sockets into which a person must fit. On the other hand, a person has much latitude to write his own part. At a party, he may be the one who organizes games, the one who remembers to encourage the wallflower, or the one who makes the others laugh. As club president, he may dominate or he may be a figurehead.

Successive roles carry with them increasing power; the person acquires steadily increasing latitude for making decisions and is allowed to control increasing resources. The child is allowed few choices before age 3. The parent chooses his food, tells him when to go out and when to play indoors, is firm against his wandering about the neighborhood. Gradually, one restriction after another is removed. The child selects his games and his playmates; he decides which of his clothes he will wear and how he will spend his allowance. He may be consulted about how the family will spend Sunday afternoon or what project his class will next undertake. By adolescence, parents usually allow great freedom in leisure activities. The adolescent may be allowed to spend money on clothes or recreation in amounts that are substantial in relation to his family's income.

There are great differences among communities in the significance of the roles open to individuals, and the opportunities for learning they provide. In a small town, the 10-year-old has a good chance to do things that "mean something" to the adult community—making an announcement in a

24 *New roles are learned*

church meeting, playing Little League ball before a neighborhood audience, helping in a UNICEF campaign. In a metropolis he has little chance to engage in anything but childish activities. Barker (1960) compares two small towns: Midwest, Kansas (715 people) and Yorodale, in rural Yorkshire, England (1,300 people). He counted all the roles essential to community activities: participant roles as distinct from audience or customer roles. In a year's time, the Kansas residents fill, on the average, three times as many responsible roles as those in Yorkshire. There is more activity there and fewer people to carry it on. The distribution by ages showed that Midwest gave especially great opportunity to adolescents (Figure 25). Even in Yorodale the adolescents have more varied experiences than adults.

> According to the Midwest theory of education, children are prepared for adulthood by participating to the maximum of their abilities in the regular behavior settings of the town along with adults; it is of particular value to children to undertake important and responsible roles even before they can discharge them with complete adequacy. . . . According to the Yorodale theory of education, children are prepared for adulthood by removing them from the community settings. . . . Children do not disturb community settings until the requisite skills and responsibilities have been imparted to them [by the school] so they can take their parts smoothly.

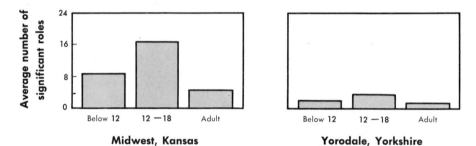

Midwest, Kansas   **Yorodale, Yorkshire**

25   *Americans expect young people to play community roles* (*Barker, 1960*)

14. Some people describe personality as a collection of habits; others describe personality as a repertoire of role behaviors. Which comes closer to your view?

15. A teacher plays many roles during the school day. Illustrate this.

16. How would the 15-year-old in Yorodale differ from the 15-year-old in Midwest?

17. Barker regards the Midwestern "use" of children in community affairs as a heritage from the underpopulated frontier, where children were needed to carry out community functions. What does this imply regarding the function of the school today in Midwest and in a crowded American city?

DEVELOPMENTAL TASKS.   Certain roles around which the culture is organized take on special importance, and failure to master one of them at the appropriate time may lead to a permanent handicap. In contrast to the developmental opportunities, which a child may or may not take advantage of (e.g., opportunities for leadership), the *developmental tasks* are very nearly obligatory. Havighurst (1953, p. 5) has stated eloquently the place of developmental tasks in the thinking of educators:

When the body is ripe, and society requires, and the self is ready to achieve a certain task, the teachable moment has come. Efforts at teaching which would have been largely wasted if they had come earlier give gratifying results when they come at *the teachable moment*.

Table 6 summarizes the major tasks of each age. Down the side of the table the life-span is divided into stages, though such a division is only a convenience. Development is continuous, and there is no overnight change at any birthday. The periods are marked off to correspond to major changes in behavior and social role (English, 1957). The demands upon children of a given age change from time to time; for example, marriage now occurs much earlier than it did a decade ago, and more children enter school at age 5 than formerly. There are differences in timing and emphasis among regions and social classes; the table most closely fits the middle-class suburban family in the United States.

LATER ADOLESCENCE AS AN EXAMPLE.   To become acquainted with the table, we shall examine one row. In the period labeled "later adolescence" the boy and girl break free from direct adult supervision. The 16-year-old, with his driving permit and a part-time job, is able to go where he chooses and to gratify his own tastes. Parents impose some restrictions, but they find standards difficult to enforce unless they are accepted as sensible by the young people themselves. In this period, many young people leave school to take jobs, enter the armed services, or marry; others go to college or enter technical training. The final years of high school are therefore years of serious and nearly irreversible decisions.

Close ties of affection and understanding replace the casual dating of earlier adolescence. The first love will give way to others, but sharing affection has been tried and found satisfying. Being important to someone (and being able to give happiness) aids the young person casting off into an otherwise impersonal world. Opportunities for finding a companion and discovering love are great at these ages, where school and youth groups facilitate social contacts. Marriage is often delayed; but the person who does not learn, by his early twenties, to make a place in his life for a loved companion is likely instead to learn self-centered attitudes that become crustier with time. A man may learn to exploit women for momentary physical satisfaction, he may become suspicious that women are trying to "trap" him, or he may decide that he is unattractive. He may find pleasure in work that tends to crowd out social-sex activities. Moreover, as his friends settle down he finds fewer and fewer opportunities to meet possible partners.

The shift from subordination to self-direction is rapid in late adolescence. Young people begin to manage an income or a living allowance. They choose jobs, college majors, friends, and living quarters. Self-direction is required to an increasing degree by the school; the teacher makes assign-

TABLE 6

Some developmental tasks of American children

Age	Physical landmarks	Characteri-zation	Need for affection
0 - 1½ Infancy	Creeps by age 1	Dependent Learns to interpret sensory impressions	Establish feeding schedule, weaning Develop confidence in adult care
2 - 4 Early childhood	Walks and talks by age 2	Energetic play Social regulation imposed with or without understanding	Accept newborn brother or sister Form secure identification with likesex parent
5 - 9 Early schooling		Adapts to organization Develops tool skills	
10 - 11 Middle childhood	Growth spurts	Stable group activities Projects extending over longer periods	
12 - 16 Early adolescence	*Puberty:* Girls 10–15 Boys 12–17	Dating begins Increased sense of unique personality, planning for future	
17 - 20 Later adolescence	Growth tapers off	Car gives freedom from supervision Serious preparation for work Courtship	Form close comradeship with member(s) of opposite sex
21 - 26 Transition		Mating Establishment of own home, start of career	Attain sex adjustment in marriage Devote self to infant (girls)

Need for approval by authority figures	Need for approval by peers	Need for independence	Need for competence and self-respect
			Master objects within reach Gain eye-hand coordination
Accept rules, schedules, denial of wishes Begin to understand principles behind regulations	Develop social skills: share, take turns, inhibit aggression Learn property rights	Accept separation from parent Express own desires via requests Successfully make demands on others	Accept and meet parental performance standards Successfully make demands on environment
Accept rules and procedures Control emotions Understand rights of others Accept teacher as model and guide	Care for own appearance Win acceptance in school group Develop play skills		Master schoolwork Master physical skills for games Accept own physical characteristics, aptitude for school
Make effort toward school achievement	Conform to sex role Accept group code Learn to compete within the code	Carry on tasks without supervision Enjoy own industriousness Accept some conflict with authority	Develop interests Find means of earning pocket money
Accept more impersonal direction in departmentalized school	Gain acceptance from opposite sex Acquire new sex roles	Find satisfaction in non-family recreations	Accept own body, role of own sex Accept own abilities and talents Find vocational direction
Hold self to schedule, complete tasks defined in general terms Apply standards set by authority to one's own work with minimal supervision		Make serious decisions without reliance on adults Take responsibility for car, job Make decisions despite parental opposition Plan with spouse	Choose specific vocational goal and develop vocational skill Find part-time job Establish self in "respectable" job

ments less specific and asks for papers and projects to be worked out over a period of several weeks. Many college students have difficulty because they have not previously learned to schedule their time and spread work evenly over the semester. Young people who have been gradually learning self-direction do not fear responsibility. For them, learning to make decisions is primarily a matter of gaining perspective on each specific problem, rather than of casting off fearfully into unfamiliar seas.

Some vocational and educational decisions are made in early adolescence, but the late adolescent is still choosing among alternatives (Super and Overstreet, 1960). Choice of occupation is usually a major concern around age 17. Uncertainty, at a time when a decision is urgently demanded, arouses confusion and tension. The pupil is well aware that a faulty or delayed choice may waste the years when training must be acquired.

> **18.** Fill in two additional columns for Table 6, listing the developmental tasks that you think would be important in middle maturity (ages 40–50) and at retirement (ages 60–70). In middle maturity, children are leaving the home, occupational skill and economic power are at their height, and physical and sexual power are declining. At retirement, loss of occupation and health are major concerns.

THE DEVELOPMENT AND SATISFACTION OF NEEDS

Accomplishing one developmental task paves the way for later developmental learnings. Each major developmental task is related to a continuously developing need. A single task, such as courtship, is part of a long process of satisfying the need for affection.

It is convenient to explain behavior and personality in terms of needs. Whenever a person acts, he is presumably trying to attain a goal, and the goals chosen on various occasions often seem to have a common element. The goals people seem to be rushing toward at noon on a given day are remarkably diverse in location and substance, but they all have to do with eating. We can summarize this consistency by speaking of a need for food. A *need* is a broad motive that makes certain types of goals attractive and important to the individual. If we identify needs that are especially strong, we can appeal to them and help the person to satisfy them. If John insists on his way whenever he serves on a committee, the remedy does not lie in scolding or removing him from all committees. He may need to prove to himself that he is grown up and intelligent. The teacher can help him by acknowledging the merit of his ideas, and seeing that he gets rewards for his independent contributions. After John feels accepted he can be taught that a good leader helps others to develop their ideas, too.

The needs most frequently important in school, as sources of positive motivation or of troublesome behavior, are those for affection, adult approval, peer approval, independence, and competence and self-respect. This list is not exhaustive, nor is it the only way to classify motives. Some writers compress the list to three or four needs, and some expand it to twenty or more. We disregard physiological needs, though a hungry child will be as maladjusted in school as a child who lacks affection.

Need for Affection

Close affectional ties with a few persons provide the chief satisfaction of living for most Americans. The home and family are our central institutions, to which work, recreational life, and creative activities are secondary. While achievement can be satisfying in itself, most people find greater pleasure in the appreciation given by family and friends.

Some people work out acceptable substitutes for a warm home life. Sometimes a child from a cold or rejecting home finds affection in a teacher. Some adults find an emotionally significant purpose in community service or in a career where they can give and get affection. Many people, however, do not find a way to fulfill this need. Among the adults and children who require help from clinical psychologists, the feeling of rejection is a common trouble.

The developments that bear most directly on affection are grouped in one column of Table 6. The need for affection is manifested early. In the baby's first months he is engulfed in a meaningless swirl of sensations. Many are unpleasant: hunger, wetness, muscular cramping. These are attended to by his mother, and her tender and smiling care accompanies the routines that give him comfort. Soon the infant begins to show pleasure in the presence of his mother and stops crying when she appears. He has learned to find affection gratifying and to want it when it is absent.

During infancy, the mother introduces the first pressures or demands. The child must adjust to a feeding schedule, must drink from a cup, must control his bowel and bladder. The infant emerges from the state where he could do no wrong to one where affection and pleasantness depend on his conduct (Parsons, 1955, pp. 63 ff.). The child who smoothly accomplishes the early learnings connected with feeding and elimination will usually retain his secure trust in parental affection (Erikson, 1950). But what if he does not? It appears that along with new feeding and toilet habits, many infants learn that "adults withdraw affection unless you do what they want" (Fries, 1946). These babies can no longer take for granted the support and love of their parents. To act upon their own wishes and impulses arouses anxiety.

The desire for a full share of parental affection is again threatened when a brother or sister is born. The baby requires disproportionate care and often the older child feels that he has been robbed of affection. Through wise parental handling, the child can learn that the baby is his to enjoy and to be loved by. It is significant that second and third children in a family exhibit less need for affection and support, even in adulthood, than do only children or first-born children (Schachter, 1959). The need of the first born is intensified by being able to monopolize his parents at an early age.

Boys and girls learn different roles. To the girl, "You got your clothes dirty" is usually a reprimand. The mother says the same words to the boy in a laughing and tolerant manner, more proud than rueful that her boy is so normal. Even at 3, boys and girls show differences forecasting later "masculine" and "feminine" styles of behavior. The father becomes increasingly important in the boy's life as a model and source of approval. The warmer the relation, the more quickly and confidently the boy develops the masculine qualities of the "real boy" (Bronson, 1959; Mussen and Distler, 1960).

No dramatic events during the remainder of childhood need be singled out as hurdles in affectional development. The child who feels accepted and wanted during the preschool years usually remains trusting as he works out later social relationships. The necessity to establish independence leads to a shifting emotional focus in late adolescence. In courtship, the person comes to depend on a partner of his own age for emotional assurance and purpose. Achieving a stable and satisfying marriage requires faith in the unwavering affection of the mate. As in childhood, security is threatened if disagreements on routine decisions lead to a feeling that one's partner will withdraw his love. Affectional security established with the parents helps one to establish emotional security in marriage.

A succeeding stage in the maturing of affectional relations is the sharing of affection with children. Even in adulthood, the person is still meeting new affectional demands and learning new roles.

In the activities related to affection, five principles applying to all social needs are illustrated:

An experience associated with other gratifications comes to be desired for itself. Thus social needs are learned. They are acquired or secondary motives, as distinct from such primary physiological drives as hunger and a desire for sweet tastes. While a secondary motive may have an instinctive base (this is difficult to investigate), its strength and the goals sought are a product of experience.

From time to time changes in a person's social surroundings and in the demands upon him make it impossible for him to satisfy his needs by the actions that formerly satisfied them.

If a person fails to master the developmental tasks at one age, satisfying the same need at later ages is more difficult.

The development of a person is interlocked with the needs and development of others around him.

Development continues throughout life. Important adjustments and learning remain to be accomplished in adulthood.

Need for Approval by Authority

The child doing what his parents demand, the worker keeping on the good side of the boss, and the citizen driving with unusual care behind a police car are all concerned with approval from authority figures. Parents and teachers command and restrict. The child must learn to conform and to fit his actions to the purposes of others. There will necessarily be conflict between his own impulses and the pressures for obedience.

"You'll have to do this problem over."

"Pick up your toys before you eat."   *"You'll have to work overtime."*

26   *The person must get along with authority*

When he first begins to explore his home, the infant encounters prohibitions and regulations. Pretty as the vase is, he must not touch. He must pick up his toys before he may eat. During the first five years the child establishes an attitude toward authority. If he balks and gets round the prohibitions, he concludes that adult mandates can be disregarded. If severely punished for violations, he is likely to conclude that he dare not risk disapproval. He may learn to regard authorities as arbitrary, unreasonable, and threatening. A more wholesome resolution to the conflict between desires and restrictions is for the child to learn that parental judgments are consistent and predictable.

The child who learns at home to be rigidly obedient, or to act on his own momentary impulses, reacts similarly to the more impersonal authority at school. If he thinks of parents as willing to hear his suggestions and willing to modify rules when he can give a good reason, he will try these approaches with new adults.

The techniques of leadership and control used by the teacher make it easy for some children to adapt, and hard for others. If the teacher reduces rules to the minimum in order to give children experience in planning and self-regulation, some children make good use of their opportunity. Other children, however, have learned that to get along they must do just what the adult wants. They become insecure when the teacher does not state rules and goals; instead of developing goals for themselves they try to find out "what is wanted."

The pupil finds demands of teachers difficult to satisfy when they run counter to his other training. Boys are especially likely to be in conflict with teachers because the teacher disapproves of pupils who are rough, noisy, and unmanageable. Yet in middle childhood these traits are encouraged by peers and, more subtly, by parents. Meyer and Thompson (1956) find that sixth-grade teachers scold or reprove boys four times as often as girls. Boys, on the average, receive equal amounts of approval and disapproval, whereas girls receive about twice as much favorable as unfavorable attention. Meyer and Thompson suggest that this constant threat of punishment for normal role behavior produces conflict in boys and contributes to a dislike for school.

Attitudes toward authority develop year by year in a continuous fashion. A person learns a consistent method of dealing with authority—by dependency, by rebellion, or by some other pattern. Macfarlane *et al.* (1954) report that overdependency is more persistent over the years from 5 to 14 than any other personality problem. Attitudes toward authority learned during school carry over into relations with superiors on an adult job (Friend and Haggard, 1948).

Need for Approval by Peers

Each child learns early that getting along with others of his own age is pleasurable and that their disapproval is unpleasant. This experience generates in him a need for peer approval: a desire to be liked and included in activities, to have his accomplishments praised and his ideas listened to. Getting along without friction is not enough. For full pleasure in group activities and comfort in dealing with others, one must feel that he "belongs," that his group positively welcomes him.

Accepted patterns of social behavior change as the character of the social group changes. The young child plays with one or two other children at a time. His games are loosely organized; everyone may be playing with blocks, but Jimmy stops work on Mary's tower to pile blocks in Joe's wagon. Then Joe wants to pull the wagon before it is loaded. In such a situation children adjust by taking dominant or submissive roles, as some one determined child learns that he can control the situation (Ames, 1952). Parents and preschool teachers suggest interpretations and ways of acting: sharing, asking the owner of a toy for permission, acknowledging that Joe had the wagon first and is for the moment in charge. During this preschool period, children are expected to become aware of others' feelings and to act so others will also be happy. By school age we expect the child to understand how other people feel and to sympathize with them.

In the school years more stable social relations form. Children have particular friends. Individuals are "typed": the boy who is good at ball games, the bully, the boy everyone teases, and so on. As reputations crystallize, they become harder and harder to change. The popular and able boy can be irritable and uncooperative for a time without losing his status; the outcast can be cheerful and helpful without being accepted.

Popularity is an aid to learning and development. The popular child can more easily be daring and creative because others are unlikely to make fun of him. He has more encouragement to communicate and so develops more varied, more connected, and more meaningful language (Rosenthal, 1957). The popular child sent to the store on an errand stops by a friend's house, takes him along, and so gains one more bit of social experience. The child who is uncertain of his reception by others simply does the errand, with no loitering to exchange gossip and hence no social learning. Likewise, the child who feels accepted converts schoolwork into a social activity while the insecure child works by himself (Elkins, 1958). Deficiencies are cumulative, not self-healing.

Popularity depends on ability to do the things that command prestige in one's group. A "real boy"—a leader, good at games, who takes chances— is likely to be popular. For girls, requirements change. To be a "little lady" makes for great popularity in Grade I, but not later. Being quiet is always mildly approved, but at later ages the demure and tidy girl is less popular than the girl who is active and relatively dominant. As pupils approach adolescence, good looks and attractiveness as dates become important for popularity (Tryon, 1939; Tuddenham, 1951). In general, popularity goes to the ones who can best contribute to the goals of group activity. In choosing a work partner, a child often picks one who can help with the specific assignment, whether or not he is generally popular. Moreover, the pupil tends to select someone above him (but not too far above) in ability; the pupil only slightly above average may be preferred over the very able pupil, by a chooser who is below average. Even the relatively unpopular pupil has some talents that can make him a sought-after partner, if the teacher arranges an activity that calls for his assets.

Positive contribution, rather than mere passive cooperation, is important. Bonney (1943a, p. 471) finds that "a child is well accepted in a group much more because of what he is and what he does than because of what he refrains from doing. . . . It follows that any type of moral or religious education which places great emphasis upon docility, nicety, and submission to authority may be a handicap to a child's social acceptance." Popularity correlates about .50 with other advantages: higher socioeconomic level, better school performance, and smoother relations at home (Northway, 1952; Elkins, 1958).

With age the proportion of *mutual* choices (liking given and received) rises slightly. About 80 per cent have at least one such exchange in Grades III to VI, and around 90 per cent in Grades VII to XII (Gronlund, 1959, p. 108).

GROUP STRUCTURE.   Popularity is not just a matter of being "in the swim." The social life of a school is a complicated flow of main currents, isolated eddies, and backwaters. Each pupil finds his friends in a particular pool, and the nature of that subgroup does much to shape his actions. One counselor traced friendship patterns in a large suburban high school. Each pupil was asked to name his three best friends (for further discussion of this procedure, see page 177). Figure 27 diagrams the choices made by boys in

27   *Sociogram for the twelfth-grade boys at Wabash High (data from C. W. Gordon, 1957)*

Each boy was asked to name his three best friends. A double line indicates a mutual choice. Where fewer than three choices are shown, the boy chose someone in another grade, someone out of school, a twelfth-grade girl, or someone who did not take the test. Numbers are assigned arbitrarily; numbers over 50 indicate boys who went to college. Larger circles indicate boys who received three or more choices. Dotted circles indicate boys in another grade who belong to the crowd.

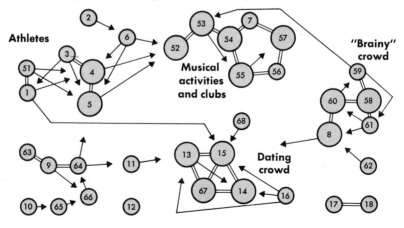

Grade XII, and the choices they received from others. The great majority of the choices of these boys are to others in their own sex and grade group.

In this school each year-group tends to be a self-contained system, with limited influence upon the next. High school teachers often observe that "this year's junior class has its own personality"—eager or apathetic, keen on dances or passing them up, centered on school affairs or interested chiefly in out-of-school clubs. This may depend on the style of the student pace setters, on the history of the first class dances in Grade IX or on the energy and talent of the class adviser. Class-to-class differences are similarly found in the grades, and also in medical schools and graduate seminars.

As is typical in large groups, Figure 27 exhibits distinct, almost unconnected clusters of social influence. One group dominates the school clubs and musical activities, the athletes associate chiefly with each other, and off in a third section of the chart we find a "studious" crowd. Each crowd values and encourages certain things; the athletes are driving to the next town to find girls and beer while the "brains" are exchanging gossip about the newly launched satellite or worrying about the extra-credit math problem. In the studious group four of the five went to college, and in the activity group six of the seven; but only one of the daters and one of the athletes went to college.

Details of Figure 27 merit attention. Some boys (e.g., 36) receive no choices from others and find no one in the sex-grade group whom they regard as a friend. Gordon reports each pupil's academic record and involvement in school activities. Each clique tends to have its own academic level: the brainy group are in the top fifth of the class, the athletes in the lowest fifth, and the hunting-fishing crowd at or slightly below the average. The outdoor sportsmen take little part in school activities, and in this class the "brains" have a large role.

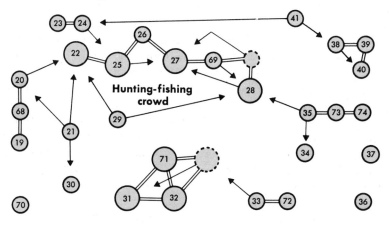

Hunting-fishing crowd

ADULT INFLUENCE AND PEER INFLUENCE.   The teacher plays a large part in the social acceptance of the pupil, particularly before adolescence. The teacher damages a child's acceptance if she treats his comments as worthless or gives all the prestige-building assignments to others. While young children tend to accept the teacher's evaluation, in later elementary school and in high school a pupil may become unpopular when he is too eager to satisfy the teacher.

28   *Conflict is increased by misperception*

Even in preschool one can observe the child caught between the adults' disapproval of fighting and his peers' expectation that he will stand up for himself (Fite, 1940; Frankel, 1946). By mid-adolescence, youths frequently disagree with adults because adult ideas about dress, language, and the importance of study differ from those the adolescent crowd reinforces. Marks (1954), in one of many studies supporting this view, found that the most popular adolescent girls are those with relatively few intellectual-cultural interests, and with a strong interest in things parents disapprove. Similar but smaller differences were found for boys. (This is not, however, an indication that the credit of adults has been wiped out. Adolescents say that they consider parents' opinions more valuable than peers' regarding politics, the spending of money, and personal problems, but not in matters of dress and recreation. Adults retain substantial influence, so long as domination does not become an issue in itself.)

Conflict between youths and adults is intensified by the fact that both groups expect conflict. When adolescents and their parents describe how teen-agers actually behave, they agree well. For example, on a scale ranging from 7 (most desirable) to 1, adolescents rate "the average teen-ager" at 4.6 on responsibility, and adults rate the teen-ager at 4.9. But parents believe that adolescents think much too highly of themselves—they *predict* that the rating by adolescents will average 6.0. And adolescents expect parents to rate them at 2.8! In general, parents expect adolescents to overrate themselves, and adolescents expect parents to be overcritical (Hess and Goldblatt, 1957).

We hear much of the conformity of American adolescents; this is easily exaggerated. Remmers and Radler (1957, p. 236) find that adolescents divide nearly evenly between conformist and independent attitudes. Turner (1960) measured competitiveness and preoccupation with group approval among 1,400 American and 300 British university students. The score distributions were identical, save that more Americans piled up at both the high and the low extremes. The most nearly typical responses are: "A little zest is always added to any accomplishment if I am also outdoing some friend or associate," and "I often find that I am unintentionally thinking about whether my actions are getting people to like me or dislike me." Some Americans are too indifferent to others and some are too conformist, but there is little to criticize in the average.

19. A third-grade teacher appoints monitors who are to keep records of children who talk, drop papers on the floor, etc. What will the monitors learn from this experience?

20. What does adolescent concern with peer approval suggest regarding ways to develop tastes in high school?

21. What does Figure 27 tell about boy 6, whose grades and participation are above average? Why is this information of interest to his teachers?

22. Which is more nearly correct: "A pupil's values determine the friends he chooses?" or "A pupil's friends determine his values?"

Need for Independence

The requirement that one become more responsible and decide more matters for oneself is in conflict with training for dependence and obedience. Independence requires that the person express his own will and act spontaneously upon impulse while retaining a balance of self-control.

The young child first experiences independence in exploration. If his choice of objects to clutch brings adult criticism, he may learn that independent acts bring trouble. The child who is not frightened into undue dependence develops interests of his own and occupies himself for long periods. With satisfaction in these activities and confidence that no harm will come to him, he can accept the absence of his mother. By the age of 6, we expect him to leave the sheltering home for a full day of school.

In his social relations we wish him to be an autonomous member of the group. He learns to fit in with group plans, but he should learn also to disagree and obtain a hearing for his reasons for dissent. If he finds that others listen, and sometimes are converted to his opinion, he is rewarded

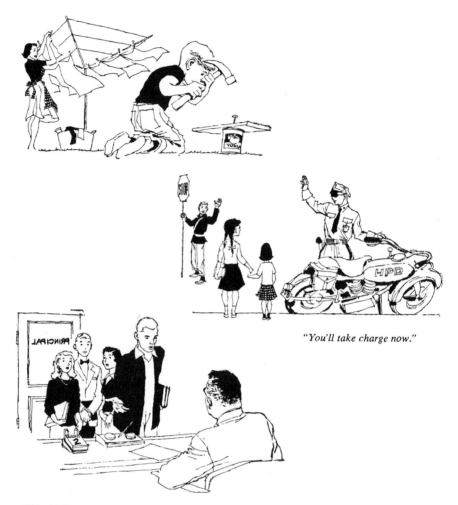

"You'll take charge now."

"We think you should change your rule about . . ."

29   *Independence is learned gradually*

for thinking for himself. The teacher or parent who seeks evidence for settling a disagreement encourages the child to accept reality as a "higher authority." Havighurst and More (1953, p. 87) list the following behaviors, among others, as indicating that a 9-year-old is making adequate progress toward autonomy, "changing from a morality of constraint to one of consent."

Works for an hour or more at tasks which interest him.

Occasionally shows displeasure at the arbitrary way in which parents, teachers, and other authority figures direct his behavior, expresses rebellion by such actions as disregarding commands, disobeying rules occasionally, arguing with adults.

Works for the approval of teachers, but is not slavishly dependent on such approval as motivation for doing his best.

Independence is fostered by the widening environment. As a child mingles with children from other homes and with community groups, his interests and activities are less tied to his own family. He carries on with limited supervision, though his parents ordinarily take care to know what he is doing and help him judge which activities are right and which are wrong. He has more frequent occasion to go among strangers, and his assurance is the outgrowth of his experience over many years that as he enters a new group he is accepted and treated pleasantly.

We have spoken of the continuity of development of various needs and patterns of adjustment. This is shown strikingly in the findings of Schoeppe and Havighurst (1952), who rated boys and girls at age 10 on their accomplishment of developmental tasks, and again at ages 13 and 16. The degree to which the pupil had attained emotional independence from others at 10 correlated .78 with independence at 16. Equally high predictive correlation was found for ability to establish relations with peers, to master intellectual requirements, and to rely on his own conscience. The much lower age-to-age correlation (.42) for mastery of an appropriate sex role reflects what we have already discussed: that behavior appropriate to the girl or boy in adolescence is achieved only through a complicated learning process in which many falter. It is worth reporting also that success in one task is only moderately correlated with success in another task at the same age; emotional independence correlates around .45 with conscientiousness, for example.

> **23.** What satisfactions are these pupils gaining in the following incident? Why are some of them nonparticipants?
>
> The sophomore girls, in the interval between classes, are engaged in their usual clamor. This time, Frances is trying to borrow Julie's sweater so that her clothes will have the most clashing color scheme. Some of the others have already traded socks and other items. The girls who have changed are chattering briskly about who has the loudest combination. Some of the others have not changed, and Barbara mutters to one beside her, "I think that is so stupid!" (This goes on until the teacher calls the group to order to discuss the Protestant Reformation.)

Need for Competence and Self-respect

The fifth area of motivational development is concerned with attitude toward the self in relation to the external world. The happy, effective person is committed to goals, active in his approach to living, accepting of his real limitations, but otherwise optimistic. The defective personality is often plagued by feelings of inadequacy, uselessness, and guilt.

Before discussing this need developmentally, a side remark about recent motivational theory may be illuminating. As you probably know from study of general psychology, in most "theories of learning" developed in the laboratory primary physiological needs or drives hold the central place. Motivation to run a maze is controlled by leaving an animal without food for a certain number of hours or by applying an electric shock. So learning theory has emphasized the desire to reduce some tension as the source of motivation. The clinical psychologist or psychiatrist has likewise seen deprivation as the prominent source of motivation, though his attention is on social needs. This reflects the fact that his observations are on persons in trouble. His observations, along with research of social psychologists, have led to considerable knowledge about social motives, some of which we have summarized above. Theory is now expanding to give far more attention to the positive motives behind behavior (E. R. Hilgard, 1956, Ch. 12; Berlyne, 1960; Young, 1961).

One important part of that motivation in man and the higher animals is what (following R. W. White, 1959, 1960) we refer to as "need for competence."

Most simply, "need for competence" is a phrase that draws attention to control of the environment as a source of pleasure. To be sure, such control is often a means to a practical end and a source of pride in self. But, more fundamentally, the higher animal enjoys producing change in the environment, especially when he can predict and control that change. Higher organisms like activity and adventure; taking steps three at a time is fun even if it involves a bit of risk.

As compelling as any single line of research in drawing attention to the desire for competence is that of Harlow *et al.* (1950; see also Harlow, 1953). Everyone knows that animals solve mechanical problems to escape confinement or to get food. But Harlow's monkeys manipulate pieces of equipment just because they like to. Nail a hasp and staple to the cage wall. Put a hook through it, and push a pin into a hole so that the hook is blocked in place. The monkeys will learn to disassemble the device, and will do so time after time, even though they get no prize and are left with nothing save the parts of the device hanging on the wall. Manipulating things to see what they will do can easily be understood to have "survival value," in the Darwinian sense, just as the desire to avoid an empty stomach does.

The human infant does a great deal of manipulation, observing its effect. Most early crawling and walking is exploratory rather than directed toward a "useful" goal object. At all ages, play is action which is in some ways familiar, in some ways unfamiliar, and thus takes one always onto new ground and enlarges his competence. As White says (p. 322), "Interest wanes when action begins to have less effect; . . . motivation subsides when a situation has been explored to the point that it no longer presents new possibilities." The game of tick-tack-toe loses its charm when one has learned all the moves and countermoves; not even the addict of crossword

30 *Competence is satisfying*

puzzles wants to fill in the same puzzle twice. The satisfaction found in manipulating objects has its counterpart in manipulating abstractions. The preschool child is observed making long strings of rhymes, or singing a song in which the same phrase is put to one tune after another. This is joy in invention, reinforced by no reward except that of performance itself. The act has a goal, in that the person strives toward a certain orderliness or equilibrium (Piaget, 1957; see Berlyne, 1960, p. 301). The child prefers rhyme to an unconstrained sequence of words. He makes his games more challenging by adopting rules.

The importance of this exploratory action for intellectual development cannot be overstated. This passage by Meredith (1956, pp. 260–61), though not fully understandable by itself, will introduce a point of view to which Chapter 10 will give extended attention.

> Rignano has suggested that thinking may be regarded as *inner experimentation*. I would describe thinking more generally as the *introjection of bodily actions*. . . . Language plays a crucial role. It enables actions to be given symbolic representation in the inner world, thus setting them free from the limitations of specific imagery. In so far as the child is helped by his parents to as-

sociate his own movements with precise verbs, adverbs and prepositions, the introjections of these movements become precise *mental operations.*

Bodily actions include not only the whole range of locomotor actions of limbs and trunk but also the extremely varied actions of the hands, in manipulation of all that the environment offers—materials hard and soft, plastic and elastic, greasy and sticky, clean and dirty, inanimate, living and human, powders and liquids, froths and jellies, winds and flames, in all manner of inter-relations and inter-actions—the fitting of lids on saucepans, of buttons into buttonholes, the turning of handles and the pressing of switches, the folding of paper . . . —one could continue the list indefinitely. The quantity of self-pedagogy in which the child indulges in the early years is prodigious. He establishes all the experiential foundations of physics, chemistry, biology, sociology and mathematics. . . . He is hungry for the knowledge of the properties of matter. And thus he develops a labyrinth of fine structure in his inner space.

As the child approaches school age and is given more tasks to perform, the motivation to explore and master things for their own sake becomes overlaid with ideas of duty and approval. The child's early joy in exploratory learning may be stamped out by the puritanical distinction between work and play he encounters in school and home. In a sense, "fooling around" with indefinite aim is the essence of creativity, and it may be that the key to producing more curious, more inventive adults lies in the cultivation of a playful attitude toward topics the school now treats with somber dedication to "the right answer."

The child's work is constantly evaluated, praised, and criticized. He learns that some performances and some people win praise and others do not. He acquires standards by which to judge himself, and an ideal of what a good person ought to do. If his performance and conduct are usually accepted and he makes steady improvement toward the ideal, he comes to believe that he is good. If he seems never to come near the ideal, he sprouts a sense of inadequacy. Self-respect does not mean smugness. A healthy self-concept is, "I am adequate to meet present demands upon me, and where I want to do better, I am capable of improving."

Favorable responses from others do much to direct energies into a certain channel. What this motivation can produce at its best is seen in the genius Blaise Pascal (1623–62). His father was a nobleman actively engaged in government and a promoter of the new scientific interests of the period. (C. M. Cox, 1926, p. 691. This statement is partly quoted by Cox from biographies.)

> Pascal early showed much interest in his surroundings and wanted to know a reason for everything. . . . Even at an early age he took great pleasure in conversations upon the subject of natural science.
>
> His genius for geometry made its appearance before he was 12 years old and in an extraordinary manner. His father wished him to learn languages before undertaking mathematics and in consequence put away all his books on the subject and refrained from mentioning it in his son's presence. This

precaution did not prevent the child's curiosity from being aroused, however, and he begged his father to teach him mathematics. He refused [though he did tell the boy that it was the way of making accurate figures and studying their relation to each other.] At the same time he forbade his son ever to think or speak of it again. Pascal, however, began to dream over the subject and . . . he used to mark with charcoal on the walls of his playroom, seeking a means of making a circle perfectly round and a triangle whose sides and angles were all equal. He discovered these things for himself and then began to seek the relationship which existed between them. He did not know any mathematical terms and so he made up his own, calling circles *rounds*, lines *bars*, etc. Using these names he made axioms and finally developed perfect demonstrations . . . until he had come to the thirty-second proposition of Euclid ("the sum of the angles of a triangle . . ."). One day the father came in unexpectedly and asked his son what he was doing. The child explained, showing him some demonstrations he had made. . . . The father left the room, without saying a word, and unbosomed himself in tears of joy to a friend who lived close by.

Being labeled a failure instills a sense of unworthiness that eliminates trying. Many Americans have never developed even the most routine skill in drawing because, during childhood, they learned that others considered them deficient as artists. Difficulties in learning social regulations produce guilt and a sense of moral inadequacy. Neurotic symptoms in an adult often have their origin in severe condemnation during early childhood. By following impulses, a child "gets into trouble." He takes things that are not his own, he is openly curious about sex—quite innocent of any intent to do wrong. If a parent views this conduct as a perverse tendency that must be stamped out, he punishes the child emphatically and the child comes to identify his own impulses with sinfulness.

No single incident and no single type of failure destroys the sense of worth. After failure in one activity, the child tries others. But when a child encounters criticism over and over, either because he does poorly or because adults hold very high standards for him, he learns to think of himself as inadequate (Schoeppe *et al.*, 1953). He tackles a new job "as if he were licked before he starts." Constructive criticism helps him to accept his impulses as reasonable without approving his conduct. It shows him a better way to deal with impulses: "Yes, I know you were very angry at Tommy, but the next time you feel that way you had better just go play elsewhere."

Our list of needs (affection, approval from authority, approval by peers, independence, and competence and self-respect) may be compared with the qualities of the socialized person of Chapter 2: competence in problem-solving, confidence and self-respect, effective relations with others, goals and interests, and acceptance of social values. It is evident that these lists have a great deal of overlap; indeed, each quality named in Chapter 2 reappears here, under one need or another. We are discussing the development of the whole person, and we can "slice" our information in many ways. As we said earlier, there is no one list of needs, and the needs we have described do not act in isolation from each other. The present chapter has listed some important collateral learnings that the teacher should consider in evaluating an experience and that constitute an important source of individual differences in readiness to respond to the teacher's efforts. This will be illustrated more fully in Chapter 5.

24. An elementary school has numerous service positions (safety squad, stage crew, library assistants, milk distributors, student council, etc.). These positions are regarded as honors to be earned by successful academic work during the preceding school year. In general, the oldest and most responsible pupils are chosen. What assumptions are reflected in this method of filling positions? How can these positions be assigned so as to make a greater contribution to pupil development?

25. What relevance to Pascal's motivation does each of these facts have?
   a. His mother died when he was 3 years old.
   b. His father personally supervised his education from age 3.
   c. His father's acquaintances showed amazement and delight at his questions and conversation from an early age.
   d. His father refused to instruct him in mathematics.

26. What does each of the following generalizations suggest to a person choosing suitable excursions for the preschool child?
   a. The child learns from interacting with his environment.
   b. Enjoyment comes from variation that shows new possibilities in a familiar situation.
   c. Creativity is the expression of one's own purposes.

27. How does the phrase "variation about a familiar pattern" account for differences in musical preferences at different ages and in different persons of the same age?

A CASE OF WHOLESOME DEVELOPMENT: JEANNE

For a realistic picture of what wholesome development can be like, consider Jeanne Allison. Jeanne's personality development and readiness for the future are nearly ideal. Fourteen years old, in Grade IX, she is popular with both teachers and fellow pupils. Her schoolwork is consistently superior, and her mental test scores place her in the topmost group. Her IQ of 154 is at a level reached by fewer than one pupil in a hundred.

Her needs seem in balance with her attainment. Her home is evidently generous with affection, and Jeanne has always felt secure. She is the oldest of three children in a moderately well-to-do family. Mrs. Allison's prime interest is in her family, and she has always had time to share the children's interests. Jeanne not only feels loved; she returns the love wholeheartedly and has a keen pride in her brother and sister. Two of the teachers recall hearing her talk about her brother's photography. When Jeanne was one of a group rehearsing a play, she had to take care of her 7-year-old sister after school. So she brought her sister to the rehearsal, and with the other girls kept her happily entertained.

Jeanne is pretty, and will no doubt be successful with the boys in a year or so. She is on the petite side, and looks younger than her age. Since dating is uncommon among the girls of Jeanne's group, she has had little attention from boys and shows no special awareness of them. Her social relations with the other girls are free, but rather casual. Her class contains two competitive social hives, each of which has its reigning queen, but Jeanne has friends in both camps. Her closest friends are Ellen and Carol, both of whom the teachers think of as pleasant but not very prominent. That phrase characterizes Jeanne as well. While Jeanne engages in many activities (tennis, dramatics, a club), contributes an average amount in class discussion, and seems to occupy her time, she never pushes toward a prominent position.

In a conversation among the teachers, one happened to comment on Jeanne's charm and seeming adjustment. The music teacher, Miss Winton, replied with considerable astonishment: "How can you call her so well adjusted? With her ability, she could be a real leader. Instead, she lets Ruth and Sandra be the social leaders. In dramatics, she seems content to take a minor role and let others be stars who are no better than she. Why—even the chums she runs around with are really secondary, compared to the outstanding kids in the class. I don't think all this quietness is healthy. Beneath that placidity she must have some problems or she'd do more." Mrs. Baldwin, who had made the first comment, said that she found it a relief to deal with a bright adolescent who could enjoy just being herself instead of having to impress everyone all the time. "Her quietness is just a sign that she's not driven. She always does whatever is necessary to attain a real goal, but she sizes up the situation realistically and doesn't exert herself without such a purpose." "Well," muttered Miss Winton as the group broke up, "you may be right. But it seems to me she needs more drive. Having all this potentiality and not using it. It just seems to be a waste."

This conversation reveals how different value systems lead to different judgments on the same child. Sometimes the quiet child is indeed maladjusted, but Jeanne is not retiring. She works into whatever activities are current, always with a sense of fun and purpose. She tosses ideas into a discussion that interests her and accepts disagreement impersonally. One teacher remembers a particularly glaring blunder Jeanne made in talking about Joan of Arc. When another pupil pointed out the error, and not too politely, Jeanne admitted the error, laughing at her own stupidity, and went easily on to another comment.

Jeanne's balanced development must be credited in part to her rich endowment of health, appearance, and intellect. Her warm and stimulating home gave her assurance at an early age, and when she first entered school, the primary teacher noted her quick adjustment to a strange setting. Throughout childhood, she seems to have escaped emotional blocking. Learning came readily, friends were easily made, and her own quick enjoyment of any activity made boredom foreign to her. Jeanne settled into a somewhat passive pattern, which became pronounced in Grades III and IV when a few other pupils began to exert themselves as class leaders. Jeanne was amenable to any suggestion and was at home in activities ranging from drawing to outdoor camping. She developed no "specialty," either in school or recreation, perhaps because so many things came easily to her.

Jeanne comes about as close as any child to ideal development for her age. Favored as she was, and lucky enough to capitalize on her assets, Jeanne demonstrates what a pleasant person a child can become. But a caution is needed, lest you assume that easy, natural development comes only to those with good family income and high intelligence. Any school has dozens of Mikes and Saras who can match Jeanne's healthy enjoyment of every moment. Neither money nor intelligence is the source of inner stability, although both of these made things easier for Jeanne. The most unusual thing about Jeanne, compared to other well-adjusted students, is her uniform reaction to all activities. More commonly, even with fine emotional adjustment, there is concentration upon some interests and abilities and relative lack of development in others. In the next chapter, we shall study pupils whose patterns are more differentiated. We shall see how some students with handicaps achieve adjustment, how some with assets like Jeanne's develop rough-edged personalities, and how some are emotionally disrupted by their experience. Perhaps the total of all these cases provides the most truthful picture of typical development.

28. In what specific ways might an above-average family income have assisted Jeanne's development, directly or indirectly?

29. How can a teacher decide whether quietness shows adjustment or underlying conflict?

30. Would one describe a personality like Jeanne's as "ideal" in a boy of her age?

31. Does the foregoing discussion of wholesome development imply that there is a single personality pattern that socializers should aim to produce?

SUMMARY

The characteristics of the pupil determine how he will respond to any educational experience. Hence, to plan school activities the teacher requires knowledge of all aspects of readiness: biological equipment, ideas and skills, habits, attitudes, and values. The present interpretation of developmental studies is summarized in four general principles:

All aspects of development interact.

Physiological maturing prepares one to profit from experience.

Experiences have a cumulative effect.

Certain times in life are formative periods, which have a great effect on readiness for a particular activity.

Changes in physique are important for the teacher primarily because of the psychological consequences of physical proficiency. Larger children are more successful, more popular, and more confident. Physique is not correlated directly with academic ability. Physical deficiencies can be a source of distress, notably in adolescence.

The adolescent cycle begins at puberty, the point where adult sexual characteristics appear. Prior to this, there is a slowing of growth; after puberty, there is a marked increase in height and a change of body proportions. For girls, the peak growth comes more often at 12 or 13 than at any other age. Puberty comes later for boys, with the peak growth most often at 14. Some pupils enter adolescence five years later than others of the same sex. There are numerous changes in relative size and strength, due to differences in timing and other factors. Adult size is fairly consistent with size in middle childhood, a correlation of .75 being reported. But in early adolescence there are temporary changes in rank, since some whose final height will be only average shoot up earlier than their fellows. Attention is drawn to the so-called normal distribution: in nearly all characteristics there is a continuous range of scores, with few scores far above and far below average.

Whether a pupil matures early or late has an important effect on his adjustment. Early maturing boys have lasting advantages: they learn to dance, to talk to girls, to take leadership. The late maturers are ineffective and often insecure. Even as late as age 30, the early maturers excel in responsibility and sociability as a result of the cumulative benefits of early success. Among girls, there appears to be marked tension just before puberty. The early maturer has some difficulties because her interests develop ahead of her group, but by age 17 she tends to be superior in self-acceptance and poise.

The changes in the nervous system that accompany maturing are little understood. One that is known to be important is the depositing of the insulating substance myelin. Biological development cannot be considered a process acting by itself. We apply the term maturation to those developments whose form and timing is determined *chiefly* by heredity, but little or none of human development is an unfolding of fully predetermined structures. Early research on maturation, such as Hilgard's study of children's use of scissors, showed that learning was more rapid when training was delayed. But the children given an earlier start, and therefore a greater amount of training, were more proficient than the late starters. Experience at the right time is required even for biological development, as is shown in the studies of the blind who have difficulty recognizing patterns when they finally can see.

There is a time when the organism is ready to profit from an experience; if the experience is delayed until later, readiness may be lost. This, says Penfield, happens in the speech-producing mechanism. *Programs*—neural interconnections—for forming sounds are developed early in life through practice in saying the words one hears. After about age 10, new words are formed entirely by assembling the established sound programs into units; the new sounds required by a foreign language cannot be mastered.

The pupil should be encouraged to appreciate and make use of his own good qualities; a uniform ideal for everyone leads to dissatisfaction for some. A competitive program in sports can be harmful in the elementary grades, depriving some pupils of an opportunity to gain in proficiency and pride. The teacher should note individual differences and recommend a physical examination where therapy might be desirable. With regard to the implications of maturation for curriculum-planning, it was concluded that decisions must be made on the basis of direct experimentation with proposed instruction, since biological knowledge is too incomplete to provide an educational timetable. Indeed, there is little present evidence regarding the structural changes, if any, that occur during school ages; myelinization, for example, is nearly complete at age 6. Very early teaching of a second language was criticized because the chief benefit claimed is learning to speak without an accent; this gain seems not to compare in value with outcomes to be expected from other educational activities that could occupy the same time.

The child's environment continually widens. He encounters a wider range of experiences that bring new concepts to his attention. The gradual emergence of concepts is seen in the child's response to the flag: at 5, a pretty object; at 6, a sign of a country; at 9, a focus for ideas of patriotism; and at 12, part of a logical concept of government established by people. As his environment widens his range of acquaintance also expands. Peer influences are particularly important; indeed, the peers become a source of reward and authority rivaling the parents and teachers.

In each setting the child is expected to play certain roles. In learning these roles he acquires competence and confidence; one role paves the way for the next. Barker's studies show the American small town as providing a greater variety of roles for young people, and hence greater opportunity for learning, than he finds in a similar town in Yorkshire. The roles upon which a culture places particular value are called *developmental tasks*. The child who fails to master these tasks at the normal time will suffer penalties. Havighurst speaks of the teachable moment as the point where "the body is ripe, society requires, and the self is ready to achieve." Table 6 presents in outline form the principal developmental tasks.

In presenting the developmental tasks, we make use of the concept of *needs,* as motivations that underlie much behavior. Many tasks contribute to instill the same need and to provide ways of satisfying it. While any list of needs is somewhat arbitrary, the following list emphasizes matters important to the educator: affection, adult approval, peer approval, independence, and competence and self-respect. Five principles are noted, which apply to all needs:

An experience associated with other gratifications comes to be desired for itself.

From time to time, changes in a person's social surroundings and in the demands on him make it impossible for him to satisfy his needs by the actions that formerly satisfied them.

If a person fails to master the developmental tasks at one age, he will find it more difficult to satisfy the same need at a later age.

Development of the person is interlocked with the needs and development of others around him.

Development continues throughout life.

The need for affection emerges from the infant's desire for physical comfort. Trust in his mother is established and hopefully is maintained even during the period when she is frustrating him by imposing demands and pressures. The father also is an important molding influence: the warmer the boy's relation with his father, the more he becomes "a real boy." Affectional development continues into courtship and marriage, and into parenthood. There is a comparable series of developments for each of the other needs.

Sometimes needs pull against each other; adult approval may be sacrificed, for example, as the youngster tries to increase his independence and self-respect. Some of this conflict is unnecessary, arising from misperceptions such as the adolescent's feeling that his parents are more critical of him than they are. The "real boy" encounters disapproval from the teacher for acts his peers reward.

Popularity depends on ability to do things: it derives from competence and it contributes to competence. The structure of peer relations, as shown in sociograms, is far too complex to be summarized by a single scale of popularity. Each group rewards somewhat different types of competence, so shapes its members in a different mold. Yet the complaints about adolescent "conformity" seem to be overdrawn. There are both conformers and nonconformers, but the modal response is balanced between concern for others' views and for one's independent judgment.

Recent changes in theory of motivation have reduced the emphasis on "tension reduction," and give prominence to the positive desire for competence, for ability to alter one's environment and control it. Even in the infant's play, one observes a continued attempt to move things about and obtain a predictable result. But once the response is mastered, the infant loses interest and goes on to something more challenging. A passage quoted from Meredith previews the argument of Chapter 10 that these exploratory actions are a form of "self-pedagogy." This same exploration is seen as an important feature of creative talent. Self-respect is damaged by failure; stern disapproval for violations of rules is particularly likely to develop a sense of guilt.

Reading List 4

Leonore Boehm, "The Development of Independence: a Comparative Study," *Child Development,* 28 (1957), 85–102.

This report gives further details regarding the comparison of Swiss and American children referred to in the text. The introduction summarizes the reasons for suspecting that American parents and teachers encourage conformity.

"Cecilia," in Kenneth Soddy, ed., *Mental Health and Infant Development* (New York: Basic Books, 1956) Vol. 2, pp. 31–42.

All the case studies in this volume are worth reading, covering as they do French, British, and Americans from many backgrounds and with many varieties of adjustment. Cecilia was followed from childhood to adulthood, with detailed psychological observations. She is much like our Jeanne, and the record covers many specific topics treated in this chapter. For example, why did early toilet-training not damage Cecilia? How did her early maturing create problems during high school?

A Healthy Personality for Every Child (Raleigh, North Carolina: Health Publications Inst., 1951). Reprinted in Coladarci, Rosenblith, Seidman *A*, Seidman *E*.

This essay prepared by a White House conference seeks to define "healthy personality." Largely influenced by the theory of Erik Erikson, it covers the topics we discuss as needs and developmental tasks, but organizes them in another manner. Can you fit Erikson's eight stages into Table 6?

Herbert R. Stolz and Lois Meek Stolz, "Adolescent Problems Related to Somatic Variations," Chapter 5 in Nelson B. Henry, ed., *Adolescence,* Forty-third Yearbook of the National Society for the Study of Education (Chicago: Univ. of Chicago, 1944), Part I, pp. 80–99.

The significance of physical changes to the adolescent is described. Social influences that increase difficulties of self-acceptance are noted. Two questions arise: Why are these facts important for the school? If a school wishes to reduce anxiety associated with bodily changes, what procedures can it use?

Joseph Stone and Joseph Church, "Adolescence: 1," Chapter 10 in *Childhood and Adolescence* (New York: Random House, 1957), pp. 268–95.

These authors speak of adolescence as a "cultural invention," a role created because the adult culture is uncertain how to make a place for the teen-ager. Conflicts regarding authority, self-understanding, and pressures from peers are described. Questions are raised regarding recent trends in the adolescent role, with the implication that the traditional parent-adolescent conflict may be replaced by an unhealthy docility.

CHAPTER 5 DIFFERENCES IN PUPIL CHARACTERISTICS: ILLUSTRATIVE CASES

In every teacher's life one of the really exciting moments comes when he sits at his desk in an empty classroom and waits for a strange group of pupils to appear. One minute the places are empty. A bell rings, and the room begins to swarm with activity. Some pupils come in laughing pairs and chattering clusters. Some enter singly, shy and silent. Two boys rush in, one chasing the other with evident intent to crown him with a book. The glances of the teacher, sizing up the pupils, are matched by their glances in his direction and their behind-the-hand exchange of impressions.

To the layman, the pupils seem much alike. True, there are differences in dress, and some children are quieter than others. But when you put together 30 fourth-graders, all much of a size, with much the same social development, eager and giving voice to their vitality, the first impression is one of homogeneity. Such an age-uniform group is indeed more alike than the random cluster of children seen on the neighborhood street or the school playground. At higher levels of education, selection causes even greater uniformity.

The thoughts of the teacher, however, quickly dismiss the seeming uniformities. The test of his skill lies in the individual challenges the pupils will present. There will be some who have difficulties in learning, and others so quick mentally that they will be bored by tasks that challenge most pupils. One of the boys in this group will choose the teacher as a close friend and rely on him for the support he does not get at home. And there is likely to be a girl who feels that she is less attractive than the others and needs her self-respect bolstered.

The teacher will need to evaluate and take into account the readiness of each individual for the classwork. The teacher will consider the pupil's success in accomplishing developmental tasks, for difficulties with these tasks will alter the learner's response to class activities. Teachers find it easy to think *separately* about intellectual development, social adjustment, and other single elements. It is harder to recognize how these relate to each other, a given problem in development having quite different effects on different children. In order to show how aspects of development influence each other, we shall consider several individual cases in this chapter.

Some of the pupils we will study have deficiencies or advantages in physical and mental equipment. Clark has a congenital physical defect that impedes him in all bodily activity, and this affects his school learning, his social relations, and his feelings about himself. Bill is a very rapid learner, Olive a very slow one. In each case, the way in which parents, peers, and teachers respond to the pupil affects what he learns and what he finds satisfying. We shall therefore place considerable emphasis on the pressures found in different environments. A report on Margaret and a much briefer one on Barbara serve as illustrations. The most important new principles in this chapter describe types of home environment that shape pupil motivation.

PUPILS WITH DIFFERENCES IN EQUIPMENT

Clark, Who Has a Physical Handicap

Clark, the first and only child of a pharmacist, was born 12 years ago with a physical defect. Because of damage in the motor control centers of his brain, he has grown up without full command of his legs. He has learned to walk, and can even run in an awkward, lurching fashion, but has limited control over his hip and leg muscles. Medical treatment has failed to improve his condition, but he is otherwise in excellent health.

Clark entered school at the usual age and has made regular progress. Mental tests show him to be one of the brighter pupils in the class, and he is highly superior in reading. His interests set him apart somewhat from other boys. He devours science and geography, and is fascinated by small construction and repair projects. He is, however, quite uninterested in fiction of any sort, even comic books. He never participates in games and sports, save when these are a scheduled activity, and he is equally out of things when sports are a topic of conversation. His schoolwork varies from passive meeting of requirements to a positive distaste for art, dramatics, and class discussions. Socially, he is accepted but not sought out. Three of the boys who have some interest in his construction hobbies are his nearest friends, but none of them thinks of Clark as a close chum. They spend some afternoons or Saturdays with him, but he has no regular companion. Clark is calm and self-controlled in contacts with others.

Clark's interests and social reactions are not random developments; neither are they the inevitable consequence of his original limitations. Rather, they are patterns of adaptation he has learned. These patterns took root in babyhood. The influences at that time were subtle, since Clark's life seemed not to differ greatly from that of any other child in his neighborhood. His parents were like other educated parents, concerned for his welfare and moderately well informed regarding ways of child-rearing. When a doctor's examination showed that Clark had a defect whose probable course and significance could not be predicted, their alarm must have altered their treatment of him, though they made every effort to provide him with normal stimulation. Because his mother did not wish him to build up a sense of inadequacy, she did provide more supervision than another child might have had. She was usually on hand to help Clark reach things, to pick him up when he fell or to praise him for a small accomplishment. Certainly Clark received plentiful affection and made normal progress through the early developments of learning to talk and acquiring toilet habits. Praise for accomplishment hastened his skill in dressing himself, feeding himself, and other small acts of independence.

His behavior during the preschool years was not like that of the other children in the neighborhood. Most of them ranged over a larger area and mixed with other children freely, but Clark held back. When the group was close to his home, he would play with them, but as soon as the tricycles and scooters headed for another location, Clark turned back to his own yard. He learned to manage a tricycle but could not handle scooter or skates. His father spent considerable time encouraging him in ball games, and Clark did learn to catch and throw his large rubber ball. The ability of the other children to run for the ball so far surpassed Clark's that he soon learned to stay in one place and let them do the running.

Clark's mother taught him about property rights, taking turns, and other codes to govern his relations with others. With his usual obedience and understanding of parental suggestions, he grasped these ideas and lived by them, so that he rarely had trouble with other children.

Clark did not seem to enjoy social contacts much. When his mother left him with the group, he followed her with his eyes and quickly found a reason to seek her help. He appeared content to play indoors near her; to encourage him in social participation she had to go outdoors with him. Clark seemed to have a reasonable degree of self-confidence. He accepted the spills that came with his awkwardness and went on with his game. He worked for long periods on bead stringing or other tasks that interested him without seeking help so long as his mother was nearby. If she was several rooms removed, he would soon take some difficulty to her for help.

We would conclude that Clark had no difficulty in satisfying his needs for affection and parent-approval. These indeed had become his main satisfactions in life. He learned skills required in peer relations, but he did not learn to enjoy group activities because full participation pulled him away from his mother's orbit. His self-respect seems to have been adequate; he apparently knew his limitations but expected to succeed wherever his handicap did not affect the results. Clark's serious failure was in the development of independence.

It was during this early period that his interest in tools and handwork developed. At some point between the ages of 2 and 3, it was noted that Clark was especially fond of hammering and that he was bringing in scraps of wood to "work on," imitating his father. Clark could do his carpentry near his mother, he could take pleasure in the results, and his parents encouraged it. As he learned to use more tools, his interest broadened. By age 5 he was successfully handling screwdriver and pliers and had learned to take things apart and reassemble them. He showed (acquired?) real talent for this work, grasping how things operated and learning rapidly from explanation.

Clark, at 6, had no reluctance to attend school; during his later preschool years he had been willing to spend more and more time away from his mother. His parents had talked enthusiastically of school and Clark accepted it at their valuation. The teacher was for him an extension of his parents, armed with the same powers of conferring pleasure through approval and pain through criticism, and to Clark that pleasure or pain was important. Clark participated in whatever way the teacher suggested. If the group set out to make a mural showing the fire department, Clark painted his section diligently. If the group was talking about the visit to the firehouse, Clark was properly attentive. Clark had what the teacher, Miss Baron, thought of as good work habits. Left to himself, he kept busy far longer than the others, who were all too prone to forget their work for play or chatter.

Miss Baron felt that Clark was more dependent on her than he should be. She noted, for instance, that he learned to read easily but would ask for help rather than try to figure out a puzzling word for himself. Similarly, he would bring his drawing to her several times for comment, whereas the others compared drawings with each other or simply settled down to work out their ideas. In order to keep him from developing a "teacher's pet" relationship, Miss Baron was careful not to give Clark more affection than she did the others. She urged self-reliance and made it seem important to the class by referring to it as "growing up." She gave Clark help when he needed it but told him to seek his own answers since she could not give too much of her time to him alone. Clark's response was quite satisfactory, Miss Baron felt. He stayed at his own work more and mastered his own problems. It did seem that he became more critical of his own drawing and was less eager to draw than he had been during the early period when, as Miss Baron put it, "he used it as an excuse to get attention."

Clark's relations with the other pupils were fairly smooth. He never got into conflict with them, he did his share of the work, and he was respected as a member of any task group. On the other hand, he was on the fringe whenever activities were informal. He had one brief phase of social difficulty in Grade II. Over a period of several weeks, he came to the nearest teacher on the playground several times to report that some pupil was not doing what he should. This seemed to be the result of an excessive desire to do right and to make sure that everyone else did right, not an attempt to hurt the others by reporting on them. The teachers recognized that tattling would hurt Clark's acceptance in the group, and they therefore listened to his reports calmly and with neither approval nor criticism. When the teachers did not respond to these reports, they ceased. He, however, continued to behave more "properly" than the others.

Between his inevitable incapacity in running games and his lack of a shared interest with the other pupils, Clark spent more and more spare time on his craft work. During the next several years, as reading opened up new avenues of interest, he was especially attracted to books that suggested things to do. Instead of confining himself to mechanical and carpentry

31   *Clark has adapted to his handicap*

projects, he went off in a variety of directions, from explorations with a lens to building a chipmunk cage complete with exercise wheel. Reading along scientific lines was strongly encouraged by his parents, who were inclined to think scientific accomplishment more meritorious than skill with tools. His father was quick to respond to Clark's desire to talk about his reading and discoveries in new areas, or to help him plan on getting new equipment he needed.

Realizing that Clark spent much time alone and that he had no group of companions, his parents introduced him to Cub Scouting at age 9. He accepted this as he did school, without conspicuous enthusiasm. Some aspects of scouting were barred from him by his handicap, and others, such as a trip through a gun factory, interested him greatly. When the group tried archery, he responded with only mild interest. A few of the younger boys, but not Clark, took it as a chance to play Indian, brandishing their bows with appropriate shouts and dances. Most of the boys responded to the competition and tried to score higher than the others. Clark seemed interested in the score and shot fairly well, but he expressed no competitive spirit. When the group moved to its next activity, Clark seemed neither regretful nor eager to change. Clark, who had been a good group member under adult direction, proved to be equally cooperative when the boys directed their own activities. He did not contend for leadership, but when he had an idea to offer he did so. His interest, consistently, was in the task, unlike others who enjoyed the meetings as get-togethers and were as satisfied with horseplay as with projects. As he became one of the senior members of the den, Clark necessarily took more responsibility. He was not the one with fun-making ideas nor the one who intervened when two smaller boys got in a squabble. But he proved a competent work-director. You could count on Clark to urge others to "stop fooling around" and to discourage impractical plans.

Looking back over the 12 years of Clark's development, we see that he has solved most of the developmental problems. His need for affection was satisfied early and continually. His needs for parent-approval and later for teacher-approval were also satisfied. His early attempts to get a larger amount of approval from his teachers were unsuccessful, and he adapted by a pattern of school behavior that can best be described as dutiful. He places no great weight on peer-approval, but shows adequate social skill. He is more independent at age 12 than he was at age 6, but he still tends toward conformity, trying very hard to do the right thing. He can be content when left to his own devices. His preference for familiar areas and areas where he receives direct encouragement rather than new ones suggests some sense of inadequacy; but he does not refuse to try new things. His insistence on doing something useful is notable. Possibly it reflects a feeling that he wins love by his accomplishment rather than just for being himself, or it may be merely a sign that he has never learned to enjoy idle social intercourse.

1. How might different treatment by Clark's parents have led him to a different personality, as good as or better than his present one? How might they have caused him to develop a less wholesome pattern?

2. How did Miss Baron change Clark? How might she have had a better effect on his adjustment?

3. In second grade, how might teachers have treated Clark's tattling differently? What needs did his tattling reflect? What treatment might therefore have been wisest?

4. In what ways has Clark's pattern of development altered his readiness for learning things that his physical handicap itself does not affect?

5. Judge Clark's development in terms of the "characteristics of socialized persons."

Olive, with Low Academic Ability

Of all the differences pupils present, teachers are usually most concerned with brightness and dullness. Olive is below average in aptitude. Her problem was somewhat aggravated by the character of the school she was attending, but many high schools are like this, so her history is a valuable example.

Olive lives on a farm outside Thornhill, a community of 40,000 with two high schools. Thornhill High, which serves the older and poorer sections of town, tries to provide courses for pupils at all levels of ability. At Thornhill, a pupil can prepare for college, or he can take, for example, four years' work in science, mathematics, and their practical applications designed for pupils who will be employed in factories or on farms. At the other end of town, in an area of more expensive homes, is Bishop High. Bishop is newer and smaller; its existence reflects some local class consciousness. When Thornhill became intolerably crowded and the need for building became evident, influential parents obtained the new building for a school with a college preparatory emphasis instead of expanding at Thornhill. Bishop High, staffed by good teachers, serves able students well. But Olive is different.

Bishop High School recognized trouble the day Olive enrolled. Routinely, she and the other entrants were given a group intelligence test. (We shall consider such tests specifically in Chapter 7 and note their limitations.) Olive's IQ was 63, much below the average of 100 we would find if we tested every person of a given age. The select Bishop pupils had an average near 115. The freshman adviser talked to Olive and examined her past record; Olive certainly acted normal and competent, and her elementary-school record was mediocre but passable. Olive strongly desired to attend Bishop, and since she lived in a rural area she was eligible to choose her school. Olive said that her main reason for choosing Bishop was that her chum Velma was going there. Olive and Velma lived on neighboring farms and had attended the same elementary school.[1] Olive enrolled in the least taxing courses the adviser could find at Bishop: English, history, typing, home economics, and art.

As soon as possible, Olive was given an individual intelligence test, the Stanford-Binet, which placed her IQ at 85. In view of her earlier school record, and because the individual test is more dependable than the group test, this score is probably a better estimate of her intellectual readiness than the score of 63. During her year's work, Olive received grades of C in English, history, typing, and art, and B in home economics. The B was based on her satisfactory completion of sewing projects. Her difficulties in typing were described in our portrait of Mr. Wells's class (see page 79); Olive remained irretrievably at the tail end of that group. In art she completed her work but showed no special ability or imagination. In English and history life was a continual struggle. Her success was far below average,

---

[1] Do not conclude that all farm children are dull. Where economic conditions are at all comparable, average differences between rural and urban children are small. Velma's IQ was 121, and she did well at Bishop.

but she had tried and the teachers saw nothing to be gained by grading her below C.

Olive was well aware of her deficiencies. Any question from the teacher was answered by silence or "I don't know," though occasionally with encouragement and patience the teacher would get an answer. Olive's reticence was out of proportion to her learning difficulties, since her written work showed that she knew something of each topic. She was obviously diligent. When it was time to study, she plunged into work more quickly than the others and rarely turned from it. Yet, for all her concentration, the results were meager. One teacher timed her covertly during a class period when she was reading a book of her own choice. The choice, *Hans Brinker,* should not have been too hard for her—yet she read only 15 pages in the hour.

Olive is a very poor reader. She moves her lips while she reads as if she were reading aloud. Probably she originally acquired a poor technique. The school has little information on Olive's early schoolwork; poor teaching in the early grades may have reduced her ability to acquire new ideas. Inadequate spelling reduced Olive's readiness for typing, and other specific defects were probably also present. When trouble with beginning reading causes the pupil to believe that he is a poor learner, he expects less of himself in the future. Some pupils stop trying. Olive did not, but her hesitant recitations do show that she stopped expecting much of herself.

Socially, life at Bishop offered Olive nothing. She always entered the room alone, always kept to herself. Yet, as in the sewing class, she welcomed any advance from another pupil. Her face would light up; she would show her work with pleasure and converse easily. Such contacts were casual and infrequent. While Olive usually went home immediately after school, one day each week she stayed for the Girls' Athletic Association. She seemed to enjoy the sports, but the others treated her almost as a stranger.

Olive's parents do not participate in Thornhill community life and the school has little information about them. They visited school toward the end of the year and in talking with one of the teachers said they thought Olive "could do better if she only tried." This comment, in the light of Olive's determined effort during school study periods, indicates that Olive's family is probably too critical. Neither they nor Olive has any plan for Olive's future after high school.

Olive has not found ways of satisfying the major needs. She has no evident way of attaining self-respect at school and has little self-confidence. She is unaccepted and knows it (though we do not know how she would act with adolescents of her own background). There is reason to suspect some friction at home. She seems to have no interests, no life goals, and no aim in school. During the school year the teachers were continually aware of Olive's struggles with her schoolwork and her lack of progress. They concluded that her feeling of hopelessness was intensified by being among pupils who could do the work much more easily. At the end of the year a class adviser discussed Olive's work with her, and she agreed, almost with relief, that she would be better satisfied at Thornhill High in a curriculum not directed toward college.

Olive is not at all unique. Most pupils who enter high school are confronted with a heavily academic curriculum, and many schools make less effort than Bishop High to adapt the work for less able pupils. The teachers

32   Olive finds little satisfaction

at Bishop are competent in planning work for superior pupils, but they have no experience in meeting the needs of the few like Olive who reach the school. If pupils like Olive are to be educated rather than frustrated, the curriculum must have a bearing on their present and future lives, the teaching methods and materials must be within their comprehension, and they must have a place in the social life of the school.

6. What developmental tasks did Olive find difficult?

7. What sort of program would be best for Olive at Thornhill High? What individual help might teachers there give Olive?

8. For an English composition Olive chose "Australia and Its Views" from a list of suggested topics. Was this an appropriate assignment for Olive?

9. Was it wise for the teachers to give Olive "C" grades, in view of her accomplishment?

10. Should Olive be encouraged to remain in high school until she graduates?

Bill, a Bright Boy

Bill Chelten, like Clark and Jeanne, is well toward the top of the group in tested intelligence. Unlike them, his record is mediocre, all his grades being B or C. His file from previous years—he is now a high-school sopho-more—shows that many teachers have complained of his indifference or his inability to concentrate. Bill shows consistent patterns of behavior repre-sented in the following incidents reported by an observer.

Bill is belligerent and out of step.

His German teacher opens class with a comment on the deadline for an assign-ment. Bill calls out, "But you said that wasn't due till Thursday!" The other pupils squelch him with polite and impolite comments that it was due Tues-day and everyone else knew it. Bill subsides, mumbling to himself. Minutes later, pupils are reading orally in turn from the prepared assignment. No one else has trouble, but when Bill's turn comes, he falters repeatedly, knowing much of the passage but requiring help on several words. When helped, he says petulantly, "I can *translate* it, but it still doesn't make sense." Two minutes later, when called on again, he has no idea what is to be read next. As soon as the oral work is done, Bill reopens the matter of the assignment with "We voted for *Thursday* last week." The class in chorus: "We voted for Tuesday." Bill: "Well, let's vote again." The teacher firmly ends the debate and intro-duces a new activity. (Fifteen minutes of class time are covered by these incidents.)

Bill volunteers occasionally, apparently with real interest.

In English, he follows up the teacher's comment on Sweden with a long story about smorgasbord. Another time he offers to run a motion-picture projector. He volunteers to report to the German class about a book he has been reading.

Bill does not work seriously on group activities.

When the class is discussing ways to improve the school, five or six of the boys offer facetious comments; Bill says the school should put in an elevator. When the boys are practicing basketball, Bill tosses the ball in a perfunctory manner, seeming not to try or care. The observer comments, "On one occasion he astonished me by offering to answer three questions in regular geometry work. The only reason I could see was that, because the rest of the class was stumped, he found it a chance to show off."

If we translate Bill's actions into the needs they represent, it appears that independence is very important to him. He continually argues with the teacher or with the group. He dawdles through assigned work, but is quick to participate when he can do so voluntarily. His favorite subject is art, where the teacher allows individual choice of projects. Apart from that, his only continuing interest is his pet cocker spaniel and all related topics; he talks seriously of studying veterinary medicine. Bill is not warmly accepted by his classmates, though they tolerate his quarreling and horse-play. He has few habits that win approval from peers or adults. His self-respect and self-confidence are hard to judge. While his moments of lively participation are a favorable sign, the reports that he dislikes criticism and puts off difficult jobs are unfavorable.

The crucial element in Bill's development, according to a case study, seems to be his relations with his parents. There has been conflict over many matters and for several years: arguments over his clothes, restriction on his excessive reading, criticism of his schoolwork, and distress over his un-

"I decided to do this experiment."

33   *Bill must do things his own way*

willingness to become a physician like his father. Bill's parents have visited the school repeatedly to learn how he is doing and what the school is doing for him. Dr. Chelten is a prominent local personage and expects others to accept his ideas. He is as blunt as Bill and has much to say about what is wrong with the school. Mostly, his criticism centers on the fact that Bill doesn't have homework every night and that Bill is studying local community problems instead of history. From the Cheltens' comments, it is clear that they expect much of Bill and keep steady pressure on him.

Conversations with Bill's elementary-school teachers confirm the hunch that Bill has had continual trouble in peer relations and in developing independence. During his early school years, Bill worked hard and well. He was quiet and alert. His social relations were less successful: he had few close friends and tended to work alone. (Bill and Clark both preferred to work alone, but this is certainly not true of all bright boys.) One factor impeding his social development was his comparative clumsiness. He did not play games well and seemed hesitant to take part in them after the fourth grade. Even now he is chubby and underdeveloped. From Grades VII to IX he was noted for squabbling, but in Grade X his behavior is comparatively peaceable. He still quarrels with any authority but he criticizes classmates less. His original conformity gave way over a period of years to his present combination of intractability and indifference. No one noticed a sharp break, but the cooperative boy his fourth-grade teacher recalls does not resemble Bill in Grade X.

As his growing interests and intelligence led him to make demands his parents would not accede to, Bill set out to test his strength against theirs. Defeated on every ground by their firmness and power, he found no way of being independent and retaining their approval. Dr. and Mrs. Chelten criticize Bill steadily but they cannot make him work. His stubborn and ill-conceived resistance, an assertion of his will, makes his life harder. Partly because his ability keeps him from falling far behind, partly because the teachers encourage his initiative, he is better adjusted to school than he was last year. If he begins to succeed in some activity and enjoy it, he may devote himself to purposeful work and accept his parents' pressure as a cross to be borne. Or he may become more and more a social outcast, lose his present spontaneous interest, and find neither success nor happiness.

11. What methods used by Bill's teachers seem to produce especially good results with him? Could these methods be used more?

12. Last year Bill's English class was scheduled to read *David Copperfield*. Bill had already read it, and wanted the class to take up another book. His teacher refused, and during the next two months there was continual conflict, with Bill complaining and neglecting the work. Who was right? Could the situation have been handled better?

13. Describe the German class incident in terms of the stages in learning. What was Bill trying to attain? Why did he use this trial response? What did he learn from the incident?

14. Each of the following statements was made by one of Bill's present teachers. How do you account for the wide differences? Which statement do you agree with?

"Bill has a chip on his shoulder and is frustrated within himself. His manner is really a defense."

"Somewhere along the line he has got the idea that he is so intelligent he does not need to put forth any effort. No one knows what Bill's IQ is better than Bill."

"Bill is very personable, an excellent scholar, and well adjusted. He had trouble last year, but now he's found his place in the group."

DIFFERENCES IN HOME BACKGROUND

The treatment of the child at home, both before and during the school years, has marked effects on his personality and response to school. One parent is nagging and critical, where another smothers the child with reassurance and suggestions. One parent follows where his child drags him, another ignores the child's wishes. Each home has its own individuality, neither totally good nor totally bad, which leaves a unique impression on the child. We shall study those effects for two reasons. They explain many individual differences, particularly in the needs discussed in Chapter 4, and they illustrate principles of learning that are relevant to the actions of teachers as authority figures.

Warmth

Homes differ in many respects: warmth, indulgence, acceleration, democracy, activity, and so on (Baldwin *et al.*, 1945). Warm parents express their own love and encourage the child to express his feelings; family

Autocratic indulgent high activity　　　　**Autocratic rejectant low activity**

"Come on! We're all going fishing!"　　　　*"Don't bother me. Can't you see I'm busy?"*

34　*Home atmospheres combine in many patterns*

members react to each other on an emotional level, their feelings being alive and open. Indulgence is contrasted with rejection. The indulgent parent protects the child from difficulty and rarely demands that he take responsibility or meet standards. Indulgent homes are generally warm rather than unemotional, but not all warm homes are indulgent. At the opposite extreme is hostile rejection, where the parent dislikes the child and is continually critical and punitive. Some homes are accelerating, encouraging rapid maturing and rapid development of interests and ideas. Other homes let the child freely follow his own interests and his own pace; at the extreme are parents who, like Clark's mother, help the child remain immature and dependent. The democratic home takes children's preferences into account. Policies are worked out between parent and child, or are explained carefully. In an autocratic home the child has little influence and little freedom.

Traits of homes combine in many patterns. Bill's home, for example, was fairly warm, not at all indulgent, not democratic, rather strongly accelerating, and rather low in family activity. One might find such other combinations as a cold democratic home, or a warm-indulgent-autocratic-accelerating-active home. Indeed, a single home may not be entirely consistent. Isolated practices taught by such widely read authors as Gesell and Spock are grafted onto patterns arising from ethnic traditions, social-class attitudes, value orientations, and the emotional needs of the parents. Thus, in families moving upward from the lower class, mothers adopted a permissive feeding schedule when that was the recommended policy, but their anxiety over their own status led them to maintain strict control over certain other behavior, such as aggressiveness (R. Sears, 1950).

The warmth of the home is evidently the most important factor in promoting adjustment. The consequences of a cold, rejecting home appear in early infancy and continue into adulthood: feeding problems, slow development of behavior appropriate to the child's sex and age, and unusual aggressiveness (R. Sears *et al.*, 1957, p. 482; Mussen and Distler, 1960; Bandura and Walters, 1959). Moreover, the child lacking a warm relation with his mother is more likely to have language difficulties. Lisping, baby talk, and other speech disorders are associated with poor parent-child relations, and some reading difficulties as late as Grade V can be traced back to rejection or overprotection in early childhood (McCarthy, 1959; Wood, 1946).

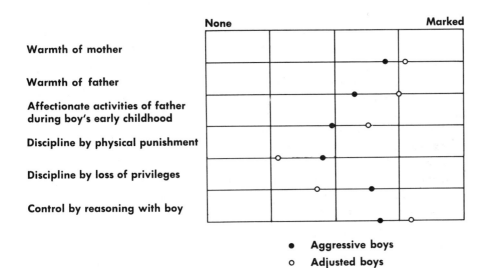

35   *Homes of aggressive boys are relatively cold (Bandura and Walters, 1959)*

The widely radiating effects of parental coldness are illustrated by Bandura and Walters (1959), who compared adolescent boys carefully matched with respect to age, ability, and social class. One group consisted of "aggressive" boys in trouble with the law, all from reasonably good neighborhoods, living with both parents, and in the normal range of mental ability. The control boys, similar in intelligence and family status, were chosen by school counselors as neither markedly aggressive nor markedly withdrawn. Information was obtained from interviews with both boys and parents, and from disguised tests of attitudes. Some ratings of the two groups are shown in Figure 35. Warmth of relations, especially with the father, is strongly associated with better-controlled behavior. (The difference for mothers was not large because most mothers in both groups expressed warmth.) The aggressive boys felt rejected and consequently avoided their parents; they did not seek help or encouragement and resisted their parents' help when it was offered. As so often occurs when developmental learning goes wrong, this situation led to further troubles; the parents sensed the boys' hostility and became even more rejecting.

A parenthetical remark needs to be made regarding all studies of parent-child relations to be discussed in this chapter. We present general conclusions, not tracing separately the development of each sex. Though boys and girls show many similarities, studies that consider the sexes separately find noteworthy differences. Thus Marshall (1961) finds popularity with peers correlated positively with parental coldness among boys and negatively among girls. Since there is still not enough systematic evidence on such sex differences for a reasonable interpretation, the conclusions offered in this chapter are incomplete.

A steady flow of affection and care during the first two years gives the child assurance and protection. This makes it possible for him to act confidently, knowing that he has sympathy and help to fall back on. In addition, it makes his mother important to him, so that he values her approval. This desire for approval extends later to his father also. In the warm home the child identifies with his parents; that is, he adopts many of their acts as trial responses and uses their standards to guide his conduct. Early development of conscience is the product of a warm home where the chief response to the child's actions is the giving or withdrawal of love, rather than more tangible reward or punishment (Sears *et al.*, 1957; see p. 23). In such a home the child learns to regulate himself instead of waiting for external pressure to modify his actions.

The child in a rejecting home, where nothing he does brings parental support, is unable to develop affectional security and a clear understanding of how to behave. Chance (1959, p. 154) reports that among children referred for psychotherapy there is a recurrent family pattern: a mother who gives little affection and support, and a father who is passive and powerless. The mothers are themselves badly adjusted—resentful of their burdens, inclined to accuse others of imposing on them, and secretly wishing for more affection than they receive. The greater the mother's unfulfilled need for love and help, the less she can free her child to express such needs. The emotionally underprivileged child may become aggressive, passive and dependent, or inhibited and withdrawn; the consequences of rejection are difficult to predict.

15. Is early development of conscience desirable? Can conscientiousness be too strongly developed?

16. Of the five traits of homes—warmth, indulgence, acceleration, democracy, and activity—which ones also could describe differences among classrooms?

Handling of Dependence and Independence

The most crucial period for the development of independence occurs when parents begin to impose regulations and demands. In infancy most children learn to depend on their mothers for consistent, unconditional affection. When it is time for weaning, for playing alone, or for sharing attention with a brother or sister, the relation is placed under strain. The child has learned in infancy that his wishes will be gratified; by crying for food, he controls his mother. Now he finds that she wishes to control him. His wants are fulfilled only occasionally, tasks are set for him, and when he seeks help or affection he may be scolded for "acting like a baby."

Initial dependence should ideally give way to an alternation between dependence and independence, according to what is reasonable in the immediate situation. The child needs to be able to discriminate where dependence is appropriate. This development is fostered by the warm home that is consistent in its requirements and makes clear when independence is allowable. Such a home imposes demands and rewards compliance, but it also encourages independent action. Dependent responses, made where they are inappropriate, lead to no care and approval, and simply fade out. In the words of the learning theorist, absence of reinforcement is enough to extinguish the dependent response in this situation.

This conclusion is supported by several studies. Dependency is lowest among kindergarten children and first-graders who at home have been often rewarded for dependency—presumably in appropriate situations—and never directly punished for it (Sears *et al.*, 1957, p. 256; Medinnus, 1961). Hoffman *et al.* (1960) found that boys who come from homes which combined firmness with opportunities for independence are superior in schoolwork in Grades III to VI, more successful as leaders, and more friendly. Neither independence training nor firm discipline alone leads to such desirable development. In another study adolescent boys were placed under a firm adult leader who set out interesting activities but gave no chance for self-expression; the ones who adjusted to the leader's demands were those from firm and warm homes (Lewin, 1946, p. 837). They had learned that cooperating with authority gets rewards.

Homes differ greatly in the degree to which they encourage independence. Some parents are eager to have the 8-year-old circulate through the town by himself, while others are reluctant. Some parents demand from the adolescent a full account of his social plans, and some give him no supervision at all. Social class has much to do with these differences. Psathas (1957) found the lower social classes more permissive in allowing adolescents to choose their own clothes, to make their own social plans, and to regulate their own lives. It is the home on a higher educational and economic level that encourages the adolescent to share in planning family activities and listens to his opinions with respect. Thus one home encourages independence *from* the family while the other encourages independence *within* the family.

Again, anxiety of the parents has a great influence. Barbara Singer's home is subtly autocratic, even though her parents "believe in democracy." The Singers think they want to make Barbara independent; she is encouraged to voice her opinions and to make her own decisions. But Mrs. Singer, who feels inadequate to her executive's-wife role, cannot risk Barbara's becoming truly independent. The Singers have climbed from modest origins, and they fear that Barbara may be "contaminated" by any attitude that does not contribute to social status. If one of Barbara's companions makes an unconventional proposal, Mrs. Singer makes the child seem inferior or ridiculous by casual hints; Barbara can usually be counted upon to drop that friendship. Barbara has been taught to be reserved in social relations, not to share her bicycle because "ordinary children don't take care of nice things such as you have." She has had swimming lessons, dancing lessons, music lessons, even roller-skating lessons—anything they thought would give her polish. Under these doting but determined parents, Barbara finds it easy to conform. Says the observer (Baldwin *et al.*, 1945, p. 420):

> She has developed into a neat, prim, adult-child, smug and self-satisfied. She . . . takes it for granted that in the intellectual area she can do whatever she sets out to do. . . . She realizes that she is unpopular with other children in general and is experiencing a social isolation that makes her miserable and confused. Admittedly the brightest child in her class, she knows so well how little her scholarship contributes toward popularity that she is contemptuous of this success, in fact, almost resents it.

Independence training can go wrong in many ways. Strenuous pressure for compliance can cause the child to over-react toward either slavishness or rebellious independence. The preschool children most dependent on the teacher are those who some years before have been weaned most abruptly—i.e., whose dependency needs have been most frustrated (R. R. Sears, 1950; Sears *et al.*, 1953). Indulgence or inconsistent discipline can delay maturity and make the eventual shift to self-direction more difficult. Inconsistent discipline also hinders learning of independence. Those of Sears' kindergartners who had received little reward for dependency at home were highly dependent, implying that they were left with unsatisfied dependency needs. Dependency was also high among those who were often rewarded *and* often punished for dependent behavior. Cases of "school phobia" (panicky resistance to going to school, often accompanied by physical upset) are traced to homes where the mother keeps the child dependent, so that he feels threatened when on his own (Waldfogel, 1957). Table 7 summarizes some of the effects of different home treatments during the early years. It should be recognized that this is a summary of statistical trends, not of inevitable effects.

Frustration of dependency wishes creates "approach-avoidance" conflict. The child desires help and encouragement (so he is tempted to approach the strong adult), but he expects criticism or punishment for clinging to adults (which threat produces an avoidance tendency). Similar conflict arises if he wishes to express his own views and follow his own plans yet

TABLE 7

Effect of home treatment on dependent responses

Home atmosphere	Handling of dependent response	Immediate consequence	Resulting pattern
Firm, warm	Gratifies dependency when appropriate. Neither gratifies nor punishes when inappropriate.	If gratified, dependent response to situation is reinforced. If not, child tries another response.	Realistic compliance or independence, as situation changes.
Indulgent, protective	Gratifies dependency.	Dependency is reinforced. Independence is less practiced.	Inadequate self-regulation. Relatively low self-reliance.
Stern, autocratic	Gratifies dependency when appropriate. Punishes when inappropriate.	Child sees parental reaction as arbitrary. Conflict over dependency results.	Irrational conformity or aggressive independence. Inability to discriminate where to be dependent.

anticipates unpleasantness whenever he violates the wishes of authority. Conflict is marked by anxiety, which has four consequences:

The anxious child is less sensitive to the subtle cues that would help him to identify where dependency is acceptable.

He acts in a way that reduces his anxiety about what will happen. He must escape uncertainty at all costs. When he goes to one extreme or the other, consequences are predictable even if not pleasant. Conflict over dependency is often resolved by rushing headlong toward violent, irrational independence or slavish dependence.

A need that is erratically gratified becomes stronger.

The need generalizes widely, determining response in situations quite unlike those in which it originated.

Monday

"Here's the way to fix it ..."

Tuesday

"Figure it out for yourself..."

Wednesday

36 *Inconsistent experience generates approach-avoidance conflict*

Conflicts regarding dependence and independence have profound effects upon reactions to all authority. When adolescents are rated as to maturity of character, the two facets of the home atmosphere that correlate .60 with maturity are consistency and mutual trust. Given these two stabilizers, either the strict or the lenient parent, either the democratic or the dominant parent, is likely to produce a responsible, self-disciplined adolescent (Peck and Havighurst, 1960, p. 107).

The Bandura-Walters delinquents, unable to find the path to approval, have resolved their conflict by exaggerated independence. They resist in-

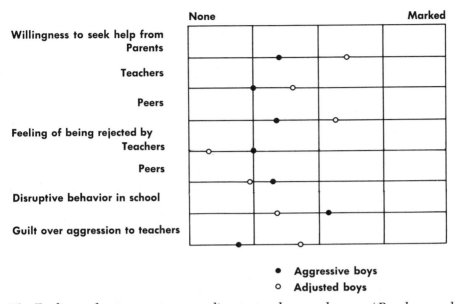

37 *Feelings about parents generalize to teachers and peers (Bandura and Walters, 1959)*

fluence from both peers and teachers: avoiding help, not seeking praise, making nuisances of themselves by tossing paper airplanes and smoking. Beneath this bravado is considerable anxiety, as we see in this reply of one boy asked how he feels about getting help from a teacher or counselor: "I just don't like it. I just, I don't know. I just don't like asking them for help. I don't want to. I don't know why. I just don't like it." The adult world is an enemy camp to be avoided (see also M. L. Hoffman, 1960).

Other children, impressed by the penalties for independence, react with irrational conformity. They dare not be independent. One test of conformity used in laboratory studies presents an intellectual problem (estimating which of three lines is longest, say); the subject is seated among several other persons who are confederates of the experimenter and have been coached to give the wrong answer. A subject who cannot risk being different changes from the correct answer to agree with the group (Asch, 1956). Mussen and Kagan (1958) find that college students who in this task are unreasonably dependent on their peers' opinions are those who recall their parents as harsh and restrictive.

Some children disciplined sternly at home positively demand strong adult direction outside the home. Frenkel-Brunswik (1955) describes one such 11-year-old who, though he felt threatened by authority, preferred strict teachers over warm and tolerant teachers. For him, demands reduced anxiety because they told what to do to avoid trouble. His fears were so great that he could not trust the teacher who tried to provide a reassuring, permissive environment.

The effect of the autocratic home is described by Frenkel-Brunswik (pp. 383–84) as follows:

> Family relations in such homes are commonly based on roles clearly defined in terms of demands and submission. Execution of obligations rather than affection is the basis of smooth functioning. Furthermore, there is a stress on stereotyped behavior and on adherence to a set of conventional and rigid rules. The intimidating, punitive, and paralyzing influence of an overdisciplined, totalitarian home atmosphere may well exert a decisive influence upon the thinking and creativity of the growing child.
>
> The rules are bound to be beyond the scope and understanding of the child. To compel the child into an obedience of the rules which he is thus unable to internalize may be considered one of the major interferences with the development of a clear-cut personal identity.
>
> It seems to be largely the resultant fear and dependency which discourage conscious criticism and which lead to an unquestioning acceptance of punishment. . . . [But] children who seem most unquestioningly to accept parental authority at the same time tend to harbor an underlying resentment. . . . The existing surface conformity . . . [is] devoid of genuine affection.

As we shall see in later chapters, these emotional reactions impede the child's thinking, his learning, and his character development. But there are some types of learning that make a positive appeal to fearfully docile pupils. Haggard (1957) describes a group of very bright preadolescents from well-to-do homes whose profiles show excellent accomplishment in spelling and the mechanics of English, and relatively lower performance in other areas. They are described just as Frenkel-Brunswik's cases are: fearful of authority, untrusting, passive, rule-bound, lacking in independent judgment. This is entirely different from the freedom and self-acceptance shown by pupils who are strong in reading and arithmetic reasoning, and relatively lower in spelling and language usage. The pupil unadjusted to authority "has readiness" for typical instruction in spelling and language usage just because the instruction is highly structured and calls for dutiful study rather than understanding.

> **17.** Lucito (1959) finds that among school-age children the mentally retarded far more often change their responses on the length-estimation task to conform to group opinion than do those of normal mentality, even though the retarded ones are capable of judging length correctly when alone. Explain this result.
>
> **18.** How can a teacher decide whether a pupil's conformity to authority is desirable or undesirable?
>
> **19.** Some homes discipline by means of physical punishment rather than by withdrawal of love and "reasoning." The child "gets his thrashings regularly and learns not to fear them. Because his punishment is chiefly physical,

he is spared the constant attacks of prolonged guilt, and the fears of losing parental love, which middle-class parents continually seek to arouse . . . in training their children" (A. Davis and Havighurst, 1947). How would this situation affect the reaction of the child to the disciplinary methods of the teacher?

Training to Strive for Achievement

The person motivated to achieve enjoys challenges, intellectual or non-intellectual. He adopts, consciously or unconsciously, the "achievement ethic" described in Chapter 2 (McClelland *et al.*, 1953; E. G. French, 1956). His self-respect is attached to growing competence and responsibility, rather than to attractiveness and popularity. He competes vigorously, puts forth effort beyond that demanded, persists when a task is difficult, and rejects unsound opinions from associates. "Disrespect [for parents] is not nearly so serious a vice for the subjects high in achievement motivation as is lack of courage. Courage is apparently symbolic for them of their independent, self-reliant achievement urges" (McClelland *et al.*, 1953, p. 286).

Adolescents and adults motivated to achieve have less than average attachment to their families. Adolescent underachievers endorse the statement that "nothing in life is worth the sacrifice of moving away from your parents." College students with strong achievement motivation recall their parents as less friendly, less helpful, and more severe than others do (McClelland *et al.*, 1953, pp. 279 ff.; Dynes *et al.*, 1956; Strodtbeck, 1958).

Development of achievement motivation is fostered by parents who set high standards and expectations, who keep emotional ties loose, and who encourage the child to master the environment and go his own way. According to McClelland *et al.* (1953, pp. 302–04; see also Winterbottom, 1958, pp. 453–78):

> The mothers of sons with high [achievement motivation] . . . represent an "individualistic" family pattern in that they stress early independent achievement. They also make more [early] restrictions. . . . The restrictions fall off more markedly after age 8, presumably after the child has mastered the necessary skills. The picture here is of a parent who urges her child to master a skill early (e.g., "to know his way around the city"), restricts him until he does (e.g., "not to play away from home"), and then lets him alone. . . . In short, she has faith in her son's ability to master something and do it on his own. . . . [She] is interested in her son's developing away from her.

The active democratic family that encourages self-expression and experimentation produces a preschool child with greater than average curiosity (Baldwin, 1949; Pentony, 1956). There are also positive changes in mental-test scores, which we shall examine in Chapter 8. These changes are accompanied by greater competitiveness, excitability, and impatience, but these are not serious faults because at later ages it will be easier to acquire control than to acquire spontaneity. In fact, these "faults" promise good adjustment. When we look back at the nursery-school ratings of men who, at age 30, have made good adjustments despite serious stress in their lives, and compare them with men who have been seriously upset by stress, we find that at age 5 the well-adjusted ones were described as more active, more turbulent, more demonstrative, and more dominant. The findings

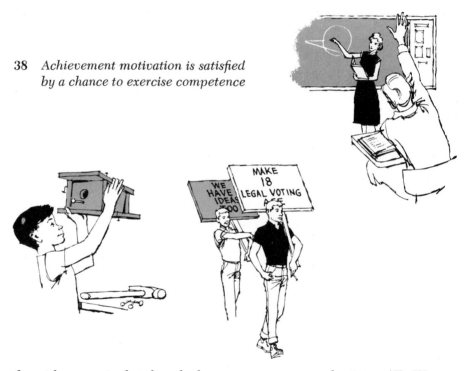

38   *Achievement motivation is satisfied by a chance to exercise competence*

for girls were similar though the pattern was more feminine (E. Werner, 1959).

The home that generates achievement motivation is the home where the parents care passionately about what the child does with his own resources. Rosen and d'Andrade (1959) observed equally able boys with high and low drive toward achievement. Visiting in the home, they asked the boy to take tests in the presence of both parents. The parents were free to talk with the boy when and how they wished. Some parents urged the child forward, others gave specific hints and directions. Compared with parents of boys with low drive, fathers and mothers of achievement-motivated boys showed more warmth, gave fewer specific directions, stated higher expectations regarding the boy's score, and when the task requirements were indefinite, demanded more from him. The parent who makes few demands and is too quick to set things right with specific help does not train the child to stand on his own feet.

Mothers and fathers have different influences. The typical rising business executive recalls his mother as strong, supporting, and strict rather than tender, i.e., as more concerned with his development than with his happiness. His father he recalls as inept, and perhaps as hostile. Not finding his father a model to admire, he broke away from him emotionally (Abegglen, 1958). Strodtbeck (1958) finds achievement motivation stronger where an achievement-oriented mother dominates the home. According to Rosen and d'Andrade, mothers of achievement-motivated boys become highly involved in their performance and highly demanding. Compared with mothers of unmotivated boys, "these mothers are likely to give their sons more option as to exactly what to do, [but] they give them less option about doing something and doing it well." The fathers put on *less* pressure than do fathers of unmotivated boys. A powerful father who demands that his son meet his standards is seemingly perceived as an invincible competitor, so that the boy is unwilling to accept the challenge. A demanding mother, on the other hand, is evidently seen as a source of attainable reward. All these results are tentative and say nothing about development of achievement motivation in girls, a subject that is as yet little understood.

The direct concern of some homes for intellectual achievement has a powerful effect. Even in the cradle, the child begins to hear of the importance of learning, as in the traditional Jewish lullaby quoted by Zborowsky (1955):

> The Law shall baby learn,
> Great books shall my Yankele write.

There are two types of strivers, those interested in competence and those interested in avoiding disapproval. Generalized, deeply felt motivation for competence is by no means the same as a conformist desire for good grades (de Charms *et al.*, 1953). The pupil who *says* that he has high educational goals may be more desirous of adult approval than of mastery. The pupil whose actions reveal a strong drive toward mastery may say that he has only average motivation. The fundamental difference is that the pupil with genuine motivation to achieve enjoys mastering the environment whether or not this brings external rewards. The compulsive, driven striver is far more concerned with satisfying those in power and with escaping from his own guilt feelings (McClelland *et al.*, 1953, p. 79).

Striving may be an expression of insecurity. A good many homes generate anxiety by their steady pressure for accomplishment (A. Davis, 1944). The parents feel that they must make the child ambitious and industrious, and sometimes the pupil feels that he will lose affection if he does not do well enough. Anxious, he may strive more than is reasonable. He may be irrationally competitive. He may be unable to accept anything short of perfection (example: a professor's brilliant daughter, who copies from a neighbor when unable to answer a question on a history test). Sometimes the symptom is prodigious effort. In any college class, there is likely to be a student whose papers are twice the length called for. This greater volume is not entirely to his credit. It is usually a sign that his insecurity forces him to go on and on after the job is really finished. Even when praised, he experiences no fulfillment. On a treadmill, he must run furiously toward the next goal and the next.

"I'm sure you can do better than this."

39   *Parental pressure can make the child an anxious striver*

The teacher finds it easy to appeal to the neurotic, overdependent striver. Clear assignments with grades to signal when he has done well provide an environment to which he can contentedly conform. His work is not creative or insightful, but he can learn a great deal. The teacher should help him relax and find value in what he does for its own sake. The more deeply motivated student who values his own performance needs fewer external guides, and indeed may rebel against routine that permits no personal expression. The teacher will find him easily challenged, more imaginative, and able to make a sustained effort.

The hardest problems arise in dealing with students whose motivation to achieve is low. These students find their prime satisfaction in social relationships. They live for the present moment; the teacher's explanation that something "will be useful when you get to college" is worse than wasted. Parents who have little education want their children to become good citizens and insist that they make an effort in school, but the value is usually placed on "being respectable" or "keeping out of trouble," not on the learning itself. The school tells Pete that learning to read is important, but Pete's father may be nearly unable to read, and certainly never reads beyond the racing and baseball news. The school says that proper citizens are concerned over civic problems, but Pete's father has no contact with government he can avoid, and never discusses community affairs in the home. Grammar will not help Pete to talk right as rightness is judged in his neighborhood. Behaving nicely on the playground and speaking respectfully to the teachers will—in some neighborhoods—make his friends scorn him.

We have no dependable tactics for reaching the pupil who lacks achievement motivation and does not fear failure. A demanding, strictly administered program will only make him certain that learning is not for him; a lenient, play-oriented program may keep him contented without teaching him. To the extent that the teacher connects activities to immediately pleasurable ends, the pupil is likely to be motivated enough to participate energetically; if the activity is well chosen, he will learn from it.

Teachers may be able to develop achievement motivation in some pupils where the home has not laid the groundwork, but this miracle is performed neither frequently nor rapidly. Indeed, the entire school structure—except the athletic program—is geared so that the pupil from the "good" home gets more than his share of the rewards and the lower-class pupil more than his share of unfavorable attention (Havighurst and Taba, 1949; Abrahamson, 1952). The middle-class pupil dominates most clubs and activities—in part because he has the verbal skills and social graces these call for, in part because he has the time and money to spare, and in part because teachers tend to favor him. These are scarcely the circumstances that would make the lower-class pupil want to increase his contact with teachers and extend his education.

20. Why does a certain type of home atmosphere (e.g., rejecting, and demanding independence) not have the same effect on all children?

21. McClelland emphasizes that verbal understanding helps one to discriminate so as to react in ways appropriate to each situation. In the child who does not understand, however, reward and punishment form intense motives which impel him to make certain responses regardless of the situation. Illustrate the relevance of this to the teacher's work.

22. Some writers speak of "need for achievement." Is this distinct from the needs described in Chapter 4?

23. Some home conditions foster achievement motivation and some foster neurotic striving. What conditions lead to the absence of both these motivations?

24. Explain in detail how living in an indulgent home would cause a child's personality to take one form rather than another.

25. How would it help an English teacher to know the home atmosphere from which a pupil comes?

26. Illustrate dependent behavior as you might encounter it in the situation where you expect to teach. What actions by the teacher would have a beneficial effect on dependency in the future? What actions would have a detrimental effect?

PORTRAIT OF MARGARET, WHO FELT UNLOVED [2]

Our final case in this chapter has several special values. First, because the most important factor in Margaret's development was the treatment in her home, she exemplifies the learning process described above. Second, the failure of her school to help her is food for thought. Third, the record carries her from infancy to adulthood and therefore presents a long perspective of development. Margaret is seriously maladjusted; her story is a needed contrast to the successful Jeannes and Clarks, and also to Bill and Olive, who are emotionally whole despite their troubles.

In the average home children are desired and cherished, and Margaret's was no exception. Her parents meant to bring her up to be a good and happy woman. Yet at age 23, when she first received psychological help, she was a tense and ineffectual girl, living out a drab routine. Margaret reacted to daily defeats by taking to bed with a sick headache. The headaches, which were genuinely distressing, brought her to a clinic where medical tests and interviews disclosed that her trouble was psychological. In the beginning Margaret failed to develop ways of meeting her basic needs. This deficiency was made worse by later experiences until as an adult she was unable to command rich affection, lacked satisfying relation with peers, could not afford even small acts of independence, and was unable to compete or to defend herself.

The first two years of Margaret's life were if anything too warm and affectionate. Her mother had time to care for her and give her companionship, but she supervised Margaret so closely that Margaret learned an unrealistic dependence. Parents properly take sharp scissors from children, but Margaret's mother worried about trivial hazards; she "protected" Margaret from so many perils that Margaret was taught never to experiment, never to explore. So Margaret stayed close to her mother and basked in approval.

Margaret's life, centered as it was on affection and approval, crumbled when a sister was born. Preoccupied with the new tasks, her mother now suddenly demanded that Margaret (whom she had kept immature) act more than normally mature. Margaret must keep out of the way; Margaret must stay out of trouble. Another child with internal sources of satisfaction might have taken this deprivation easily. Margaret, taught to hunger for adult attention, found the reduced ration a severe punishment. Determined

[2] Presented in the film *The Feeling of Rejection* produced by the National Film Board of Canada.

that she should be "grown-up" (at the age of 4!), the parents left her without emotional support. If she drew, they looked at her drawings perfunctorily. If she danced to capture attention away from the baby, they told her not to show off; that is to say, they punished her for dependency, thereby intensifying the conflict. What approval she got was given for occupying herself and keeping out of trouble.

By eight, Margaret was a "model" child. Forced to choose between serving as caretaker for her sister and playing with others of her age, she chose the adult-pleasing course. If speaking to adolescent acquaintances might seem like intruding, Margaret would walk past whereas any secure person would speak without hesitating. As an adult in an office, Margaret carried extra burdens, because insisting on her rights would have challenged authority. Margaret learned early that any independence or self-assertion was dangerous. By adulthood, she automatically took the safe, submissive course, despite the strong needs it left unsatisfied.

Spontaneous people are gay, colorful, fun to be with. Those like Margaret, gray and anxious, make few friends and miss much of the fun. Resenting those who imposed on her but unable to risk voicing her anger, Margaret was charged with emotion which she could not acknowledge even to herself. In therapy, a psychiatrist was able to help Margaret slowly to a new sense of her own merit, an acceptance of her own feelings, and a flicker of self-confidence. Then, by helping her join groups where she could be accepted, where she was encouraged to speak out, and where no punishing adult loomed over her, he arranged conditions in which she could learn a new personality.

EFFECT OF THE SCHOOL ON MARGARET.   Most Margarets do not reach a therapist because no one recognizes their depression and overcontrol as symptoms of emotional "deficiency diseases." Habits reinforced for twenty years are hard to modify even in therapy. The school can help such people, especially if it works with them while they are young and still making provisional tries. The school did nothing to help Margaret. One incident we know of was positively harmful. When Margaret was finishing elementary school, she caught the enthusiasm of the others for the school play. This was a great event, and if she had won a part she would have been prominent and happy for a time. Making a great effort, Margaret tried for the part of the princess. Unsure of herself, fearing that winning the part might cause her rival to dislike her, she made a miserable showing. The teacher was kind when deciding against her, but that defeat was the end of any striving to win attention. The school had punished Margaret for trying, just as the home had.

What might the school better have done? The competition Margaret entered was disastrous because winning meant too much. If there is only one play, and only one stellar part in the play, only one child can triumph while many feel inferior. If plays large and small had been common from the first grade, no one play would have been crucial to Margaret. If this final play had had several parts of similar importance, Margaret could have tried for one of them without conflict between the virtue of doing well and the evil of depriving a classmate. The teacher encouraged Margaret to try a hurdle for which she was unprepared and set so great a prize that stumbling was painful. If Margaret had been prepared by smaller successes and

40   *Margaret feared to assert herself*

partial failures in other small performances, she would have done better. Also, because participation would have built self-respect and the assurance that others thought well of her, the big failure would have been less crushing.

We have learned a good deal about Jeanne, Clark, Olive, and our other cases. Each one is interesting—but what have we learned from them that applies to pupils in general? First and foremost, we have learned that teachers must consider all the aspects of development in understanding any particular difficulty. Clark, Bill, and Jeanne had fairly similar intelligence, but each achieved less than his full potentiality. Why Jeanne was relaxed, Bill negative, and Clark withdrawn could only be explained in terms of home background and peer relations. Second, our cases give substance to the statement that development is a continuous, cumulative process. Events in the first few years of life clearly made Clark and Margaret what they are today. Something apparently went wrong in Bill's early adolescence when he first began to reach out for independence. What teachers do today may mar a pupil's readiness for important activities in the future, as is illustrated both by the play tryout in Margaret's life, and by Miss Baron's treatment of Clark, which made him self-reliant but emotionally isolated.

27. Characterize Margaret's home with respect to warmth, democracy, acceleration, and indulgence.

28. Margaret in high school was a bystander, having casual friendships and passively doing acceptable work. What might a teacher who recognized her lack of initiative and self-acceptance have done to help her?

29. Margaret sacrificed independence to ensure approval. Bill worked for independence but lost approval in doing it. Which pattern seems more desirable to you?

30. Suppose that a single class included all the pupils described in this chapter (at the same age): Clark, Olive, Bill, Margaret, Barbara. Would they react to the teacher's personality in the same way? Would they react to a particular lesson in the same way? What conclusions about the school program and teaching methods does this suggest?

31. Schools sponsor dances for adolescents because they believe them to have educative value, yet half the pupils never attend the dances. How do you account for their difference in responding to this opportunity? Would you expect those who miss the dances to be those who do not need this experience?

SUMMARY

Each home can be described in terms of "traits" such as warmth and democracy, which combine in a great many patterns. The cold, rejecting home is responsible for a disproportionate share of feeding problems, aggressiveness, language difficulties, and lack of self-assurance. The child who does not receive normal affection may show his disturbance by excessive inhibition, by aggressiveness, or by passive dependency. Warmth has much to do with the development of conscience; the child who identifies with parents adopts their standards of conduct and works for their approval.

Homes handle independence and dependence in various ways. When the child seeks comfort or approval, one parent may give it freely, even indulgently. Another may brush the "babyish" action aside; a third may punish it. The child needs to discriminate between situations where dependency is appropriate and situations where it should be replaced by independence. Table 7 summarizes the effects of different techniques of reward and punishment. Approach-avoidance conflict occurs when one perceives that a situation may result in either a valued reward or a severe punishment. Such perceptions come from inconsistent experience, which makes it difficult to discriminate when a given act will be rewarded and when it will be punished. Conflict is accompanied by anxiety, which has these consequences:

Failure to observe subtle cues useful in guiding response.

Such action as will reduce anxiety and end the conflict. The child is likely to rush to one extreme or the other, instead of considering his choice and planning a response intelligently.

Strengthening of the need as it is erratically gratified.

Generalization of the need so that it determines responses in a variety of situations.

Consistency and mutual trust in the childhood home is strongly correlated with maturity of character in adolescence. A group of delinquents who do not trust their parents show generalized distrust of other adults, and some distrust of their peers.

Frenkel-Brunswik describes the "paralyzing influence" of the overpunitive authoritarian home, which inhibits all efforts toward independence. Insistence on rules that the child cannot understand damages his sense of worth and lays the base for an irrational fear of authority.

The home that teaches the child to work for achievement encourages independence. The child is encouraged to master his environment and to go his own way. Parents of an achievement-motivated boy may be warm, but his emotional ties with them are so loose that he is likely later to recall his parents as distant and severe. The parents expect substantial accomplishment. Achievement motivation in the boy is produced by pressure from the mother more than from the father; a strong father may be a threatening competitor. The home that encourages self-expression tends to produce a more spontaneous child, who at the time of school entrance may also be less self-controlled. Control is expected to come later. The submissive, timid pupil is often superior in spelling and language usage, but lacks the flexibility of thought needed to understand arithmetic and reading. Here the spontaneous child has an advantage.

There is a distinction between interest in performing competently and interest in avoiding disapproval. Only the former is identified as achievement motivation. The pupil who states a high goal may be more interested in gaining approval from others and from himself, less interested in the task. Some whose performance and fantasies display achievement motivation do not think of themselves as strongly motivated. The anxious striver often is dissatisfied with his work and is unlikely to think creatively. Pupils from lower-class homes often have very little interest either in intellectual competence or in conformity to the demands of authority. The school provides few social rewards for such pupils and they often perform poorly, so that their motivation is not likely to be increased by the school experience.

Reading List 5

Alfred L. Baldwin, "Impact of the Home," Chapter 21 in *Behavior and Development in Childhood* (New York: Dryden, 1955), pp. 521–36.

A summary of the chief findings regarding the effects of parental attitudes and disciplinary techniques on children.

Howard S. Becker, "Social Class Variations in the Teacher-Pupil Relationship," *Journal of Educational Sociology,* 25 (1952), 451–65.

Interviews with sixty Chicago schoolteachers indicate how children from different backgrounds appear to the teacher, and what problems of classroom discipline and motivation he encounters. Read these reports closely to decide whether the problems are inevitable or are aggravated by school policies and the teacher's attitudes.

Else Frenkel-Brunswik, "Differential Patterns of Social Outlook and Personality in Family and Children," Chapter 22 in Margaret Mead and Martha Wolfenstein, eds., *Childhood in Contemporary Cultures* (Chicago: Univ. of Chicago Press, 1955), pp. 369–402.

Case studies of two children, a boy raised in an authoritarian home and a girl in an equalitarian home. The studies trace the effects of the home on motivation, as discussed in this chapter, and also on the child's reasoning.

Dorothy Lee, "Developing the Drive to Learn and the Questioning Mind," in Alexander Frazier, ed., *Freeing the Capacity to Learn* (Washington: Association for Supervision and Curriculum Development, 1960), pp. 10–21.

Mrs. Lee, an anthropologist, describes how cultures with strongly established intellectual values—the Oglala Sioux and the eastern European Jews—conveyed those values to the child. These methods succeeded in spite of a faulty educational system.

David C. McClelland, "Motivation: Experimental Approach," Chapter 12 in *Personality* (Princeton: Van Nostrand, 1951), pp. 431–77. Reprinted in John W. Atkinson, ed., *Motives in Fantasy, Action, and Society* (Princeton: Van Nostrand, 1958), pp. 437–52.

An extended theoretical explanation of the process by which needs are developed in early childhood. Requires a good background in general psychology.

Fred L. Strodtbeck, "Family Interaction, Values, and Achievement," Chapter 4 in David C. McClelland, ed., *Talent and Society* (Princeton: Van Nostrand, 1958), pp. 135–94.

A comparison of Jewish and Italian boys in New Haven, which shows how overachievement or underachievement in school is related to the values of the family and the power relations in the home.

CHAPTER 6 ASSESSING READINESS: PERSONALITY AND MOTIVATION

Even the most selected group of pupils is varied. It will contain rebellious pupils like Bill, retiring ones like Clark, pupils who work effectively, and those who fool away their time or are quickly discouraged. Some pupils are not ready for the reading materials and ideas the teacher thinks appropriate for their grade. A topic that excites some will be only another dull assignment for others. Even among pupils high in ability and interest, emotional needs cause some to welcome challenges and high hurdles, whereas others must be coaxed along with emotional support and reassurance.

The pupils who fail to learn at a normal rate and the pupils who create disturbance in the classroom are pupils to whose personal characteristics the subject matter or the teaching method is unsuited. Bill Chelten, for example, caused friction all semester after the teacher insisted that he reread *David Copperfield*, which had been chosen for the class to study. Not only did he lack interest, but his need for independence was too great for him to submit passively to the teacher's order. He was engrossed in establishing his independence, and the only teachers who could handle him were those who gave him a chance to perform independently.

This chapter describes techniques for obtaining information on the pupil's motivation and emotional needs. In some pupils the roots of misconduct or confusion lie too deep to be brought to light by techniques the teacher can use. Psychologists have additional procedures for obtaining insight into these buried elements of personality, and teachers frequently request the counselor or school psychologist to study a puzzling case by these methods. This discussion will concentrate on methods by which the classroom teacher studies personality and motivation, and will offer only a brief introduction to the techniques requiring more specialized training.

CLASSROOM OBSERVATION

Seeking Fundamental Causes

Three basic principles are helpful in diagnosing behavior:

Any action is an attempt to satisfy some need.

Consistent behavior patterns run through the pupil's actions in many situations (Newcomb, 1939). These patterns are stable over long periods of time (Macfarlane *et al.*, 1954; Kelly, 1955; Tuddenham, 1959).

Any pattern is the result of many causes, and any single cause may lead to many different adaptations.

Bill's belligerence is annoying, and the teacher's first impulse may be to put him in his place and end the trouble. But if Bill's unruly behavior expresses an urgent need, stamping out his trial responses may be like tying down the safety valve on a boiler. The tension is sure to explode in some other action, perhaps more harmful than his argumentativeness. If the teacher looks for the need that is the cardinal cause of Bill's unusual behavior, perhaps this need can be satisfied in some legitimate way, substituting a desirable and successful act for the disturbing one. Such a strategy of "diagnose—then work on the cause" was followed by the teachers who discovered that Bill was striving for independence and encouraged him to take initiative. They allowed him to satisfy his need in a way that contributed to class progress.

Instead of looking for basic needs, some teachers try to deal with the surface behavior directly. This rarely works. When Bill is punished for speaking out of turn or for voicing his opinions, he becomes even more convinced that adults are against him. Thus he becomes less ready to discuss his problems with them, and less likely to volunteer helpful ideas in class. If Olive is regarded only as a girl who does failing work and is punished by being required to repeat courses, she is made more unhappy but not more adequate.

The English teacher who demanded that Bill reread *David Copperfield* thwarted his campaign for independence. In fact, this teacher thought she was performing a service by "teaching Bill that he must do as he is told," though this was the same tactic that had led to difficulty between Bill and his father. Instead, she might have recognized his need for independence and tried to teach him how to be independent and cooperative at the same time. For example, Bill might have been allowed to read *Great Expectations* or *Oliver Twist*. Then, in class discussion, whenever a question about plot or character development arose in connection with *David,* Bill could be asked to tell how Dickens handled similar problems in the other novel (see also page 430). Bill would thus have had a chance to be independent and yet remain an important member of the group. Such a solution can come only when the teacher discovers the dominant aim in the student's striving, as reaching for independence was the aim at this time for Bill.

1. What are the consistent behavior patterns of Jeanne? of Olive?

2. Is Clark's pattern adequately described by classifying him as an introvert?

3. Show that a single cause leads to different personalities by suggesting another pattern Clark might have developed, given his handicap and his parents.

4. Drawing illustrative material from Jeanne, Clark, Olive, or Margaret, discuss the question: How stable are personality patterns?

Obtaining Dependable Information

Judging pupils accurately is difficult. Skill in observing and interpreting behavior is developed through training in sound procedures, and through experience. The need for training in observation is indicated by Prescott's list (1957, p. 100) of ten errors that occur frequently when teachers judge children:

1. Faulty knowledge. They employ mistaken ideas about human behavior and development.

2. Uncritical acceptance of data. They accept rumors and prejudiced descriptions as facts; they do not distinguish between fact and opinion.

3. Leaping to conclusions. They draw conclusions from a single incident, neglecting facts that would cast doubt on the conclusions.

4. Overlooking situational modifiers. Teachers observe some frequent behavior (e.g., timidity) and interpret it as characteristic of the child, failing to recognize which situations do and which do not elicit the behavior.

5. Confusing hypothesis with fact. Having interpreted a few incidents as reflecting some cause, they accept that suspected cause as a fact without collecting sufficient evidence.

6. Excessive certainty. Teachers accept interpretations as established truths when the facts establish only a probability of truth. This closes their minds and freezes their attitudes.

7. Oversimplification. When teachers identify one probable cause, they accept this as the sole and sufficient cause for all the child's behavior.

8. Emotional thinking. In drawing conclusions teachers give excessive weight to incidents that have disturbed them.

9. Projection of their own experience. They reason from their own experience, not realizing that the child's experience may have been quite different.

10. Expressing their own needs in interpretation. Teachers attribute to pupils motives that the teachers, to justify their own feelings, "want" them to have. (For example, a teacher may see a pupil as hostile to justify the teacher's own insecurity and antagonism.)

To avoid these errors, a teacher is advised to be objective. This means, particularly: Begin with a factual description of behavior rather than with impressions of traits, and evaluations. Premature interpretation often causes the observer to report falsely what the pupil does. From watching Bill in his German class, an observer might remember only: "Bill is lazy. He kept trying to get out of finishing his work on time." This is an incorrect description of Bill as a whole, for the total picture shows plenty of energy and effort. Recollections of this kind are superficial. Suppose one person reports, "Bill is lazy," while another one says, "I saw Bill and he is energetic"; contradictory impressions cannot be reconciled. If we have uncolored factual descriptions of each situation and Bill's behavior in it, the separate scraps of evidence combine to give a more valid image.

One excellent procedure is to accumulate a folder of *anecdotal records* describing incidents factually. The teacher should make full notes of each significant incident. A detailed written record is especially helpful in comparing situations to which the pupil responds differently to see what conditions account for the difference. Observation reports always carry the date, locality, and general activity in which the behavior occurred. A note that says "Tom got in trouble because he shoved Mark in class" is unrevealing. If the full facts are that all pupils were writing papers and that both boys had finished ten minutes before the pushing began, we can understand Tom's boredom and can suggest how to prevent future trouble.

In recording an incident, it is often wise to put down a preliminary interpretation and carefully note it as such; a useful device is to set interpretative comments in brackets. Here is an example from a report on Clark made by a student observer:

> After lunch, before the class had been called to order, James asked the teacher if he could show the fossil rocks he had brought from home during the lunch hour. She consented, and he talked for two or three minutes, holding up the rocks. Clark said nothing during this, but, like the others, he watched Jim closely. [Seemed much interested.] When Jim was finished, the teacher took two of the boys to get books from across the hall, and the group as a whole became noisy. Clark got up, went across the room to Jim's place, and engaged him in conversation while handling the fossils. As Miss Gordon came back, he turned and started for his seat. Mike stuck out his foot and Clark stumbled slightly over it. Clark looked apologetically at Miss Gordon, made a face at Mike, and took his seat. [I don't think he was embarrassed at being out of his seat, but he knew he should go back. Mike seemed to be teasing Clark; Clark was good-natured about the tripping. Maybe Mike was trying to get Clark in trouble.]

This one incident offers information on Clark's intellectual interests, his relations with other pupils, and his security in relations with the teacher.

Figure 41 shows a portion of a record form developed to assist the teacher in rapidly noting significant incidents. The blocks at the left of the figure are used to record and classify incidents. In addition to the sections shown here, there are spaces for incidents on social behavior, and spaces for giving greater detail on certain events. The right side of the figure is taken from the summary page. While the jottings illustrated here are less colorful than the complete anecdotal record, the convenience of the form offsets this disadvantage when the teacher is trying to keep an eye on every pupil in the class.

The observer should see the child in a wide range of situations and. also call on what other persons know (V. White, 1958). The teacher sees behavior in one classroom, but needs to know about the pupil's entire life. How does he react to other adults? How when there is no adult leader? Some of the most revealing information comes from watching the pupils in the cafeteria, in the hall before school, or in the bleachers at a basket-

41 *Anecdotal records showed Martie's consistency (Flanagan, 1956. Reproduced courtesy of Science Research Associates.)*

Part of a specimen record using the Performance Record of the Personal and Social Development Program.

	DATE	ITEM	WHAT HAPPENED
PERSONAL ADJUSTMENT			
A. Reacted in a calm manner to threatening criticism, suggestion, or punishment	¹¹/₁₀	D	upset this morning—but controlled
B. Handled teasing, attacks of others in a humorous or unruffled manner			
C. Reacted to failure in a constructive manner			
D. Adjusted well to difficult situation			
PERSONAL ADJUSTMENT			
a. Reacted to suggestion, punishment, or teasing with:	¹¹/₈	e	"sickness" on arriving at school
a-1. sulking, hostile remarks, tantrum, crying, door slamming, etc.	¹¹/₉	e	same as yesterday
a-2. running away from situation, hiding face, etc.	¹¹/₁₂	b	message for Miss Allen
b. Cried, complained, or was upset over small matter	¹¹/₁₅	e	"sickness" again
c. Had difficulty adjusting to situation	12/5	b	minor incident of broken pencil
d. Failed to participate with group, withdrew			*(see page 4)*
e. Feigned sickness or gave excuse to avoid distasteful situation			
CREATIVITY AND INITIATIVE			
A. Made up poem, song, or carried out some original or creative project	10/5	F	the missed spelling test
B. Worked out satisfactory solution when faced by unfamiliar or un-expected situation	10/25	A	musical composition
C. Took over in response to special needs	10/29	E	to clean up broken milk bottle
D. Attempted to learn special skills on own initiative	12/19	C	ad lib in Xmas play
E. Volunteered to do some task			
F. Asked to make up work			
G. Sought additional work			
CREATIVITY AND INITIATIVE			
a. Was unable to develop even very simple idea when presented to him			
b. Was unable to work out plan of action when faced by unexpected or unfamiliar situation			
c. Had to be told to undertake something that obviously needed doing			

ball game. This does not require the teacher to skulk behind pillars like a fictional detective. Pupils behave naturally in the presence of an adult so long as the adult does not stare or pointedly take notes.

Wherever community conditions permit, the teacher should find out about the pupil's home and his nonschool activities. A visit to the home, conversation with the pupil's Sunday School teacher, or merely a stroll down the block where the pupil lives adds to the teacher's knowledge of his background. Although often tinged with deceptive biases, reports from other teachers provide essential information. A medical report, or information from a social agency, may shed light on behavior in school.

When a large number of incidents have been recorded, consistent patterns come out. This process never fails to amaze beginning observers. The first time they see a child, they form an impression and think they under-

---

MEMORANDA ON PROGRESS

PERIOD I: From *October 5* **to** *November 16*

Summary of Incidents

Headings	1	2	3	4	5	6	7	8
Number of BLUE entries			3		1			
Number of RED entries	4			1	3	2	2	

SUMMARY NOTES ON . . .

Child's strong points: *Creativity and initiative — musical — volunteers*

Needs for improvement; sources of problems: *Recent "sick spells" and crying + fussing over nothing — Also tattles, insists on being first (see notes on p. 4)*

Actions taken by child, parent, and teacher: *Parent Interview 11/16 Mrs. C. will give Martie errands so she can earn money to repay Winston — At school Martie will be "chairman of missed assignments."*

Results; actions found effective and ineffective: *11/2: Talking to Martie ineffective — 11/16 She is pleased with her new assignment.*

PERIOD II: From *November 19* **to** *December 21*

Summary of Incidents

Headings	1	2	3	4	5	6	7	8
Number of BLUE entries	1	1	1	1	1	2		
Number of RED entries		1					1	

SUMMARY NOTES ON . . .

Child's strong points: *She tries very hard — becoming more sensitive to others*

Needs for improvement; sources of problems: *Still jealous of little sister — learning to control emotions but don't let her become too controlled.*

Actions taken by child, parent, and teacher: *12/2 Talked to Mrs. C. on phone — Martie helps dress sister now and tries to teach her; does errands promptly. — At school Martie is very competent helping others with missed assignments.*

Results; actions found effective and ineffective: *Giving her responsibility is effective both at home and at school — good response to praise — Note improvement shown by summary boxes.*

stand him. A few observations later, they have found so many inconsistencies that they cannot imagine an underlying unity. When behaviors are studied over many situations, consistent relationships do emerge. Bill is troublesome and quarrelsome, but there are contrasting moments when he takes initiative and helps the teacher. When we see how those situations differ, we arrive at his unifying pattern; Bill is negativistic when *required* to do something.

The observer's first impressions are of surface characteristics. These characteristics—tenseness, aggressiveness, devotion to sports, etc.—have slight explanatory value; primarily, they define the problem to be studied. As soon as there is sufficient evidence to support a preliminary characterization, it is desirable to start thinking about causes. Causal thinking counteracts any tendency to regard the pupil's traits as fixed and his personal difficulties as beyond help. If probable causes are identified, treatment suggestions follow. Early in his observation of a pupil, the teacher is advised to make a list of possible causes. This list should be wide-ranging and speculative. Bill's difficulties may stem in part from retarded physical development, insecurity in relations with girls, inefficient study skills, or a dozen other sources. Subsequent observation and tests can be directed to verify the hypotheses listed. Only a broad list offers the teacher a good chance of turning up the truly critical information. As facts accumulate, some hypotheses are found unreasonable and others are given support. At the same time, as it becomes clearer which situations bring out desired behaviors and which ones trigger undesirable responses, the description of the pupil is itself revised.

Anyone who knows the practical situation in which teachers operate is skeptical about proposals to make numerous case studies. Teachers who want to do the best possible job sometimes feel guilty when they realize that they never get around to making individual studies. Just what can a busy teacher hope to do? It is good training to make one or two full-scale case studies. By such work, a teacher learns how to extract information from minor incidents, and sees for himself how behavior is organized into consistent patterns. After this initial experience, however, teachers rarely make formal case reports. Instead, when a pupil seems to need special attention, the teacher collects information in the course of his regular activities. The teacher will record key incidents, especially if other teachers are also likely to need information about the pupil. In practice, then, the teacher observes everyone as opportunity permits, but looks deliberately for facts about one or two pupils at a time. In this way, the teacher's limited time is concentrated effectively.

It is unfortunately true that thorough studies of pupils are uncommon in the secondary school. The high-school teacher traditionally has a more impersonal relationship with pupils than the elementary-school teacher, partly because of the greater emphasis on subject matter, and partly because the teacher may face 150 different pupils in the course of the day.

The school counselors study many pupils intensively, but even they must rely on the teacher for critically important information. Because adolescents can be taught more effectively when teachers understand pupils individually, it is important for the secondary-school teacher to develop skill in observation and interpretation of pupils' personalities.

5. Of the ten errors listed by Prescott, which might be overcome by appropriate training?

6. One of the principal devices in training teachers to interpret behavior is to ask them to list as many possible explanations as they can for the behavior pattern observed, even if the explanations are conflicting. Which of the ten errors might this device overcome?

7. Prescott (1957, p. 429) recommends that in the elementary school anecdotal records be kept in a locked box in the classroom. What advantage does this have over keeping them in a central office?

8. What could be done by a high-school principal to make it possible for teachers to become more familiar with characteristics of individual pupils?

9. In post-high-school education is it desirable for teachers to concern themselves with individual differences in personality?

10. If teachers collect anecdotal records seriously, the file can become so bulky that no one uses it. What principle can you suggest for weeding out observations? How long does such information remain useful?

OBTAINING JUDGMENTS BY PEERS

Some pupils are left on the sidelines when sports or parties are starting; some are popular and in demand; some are "natural leaders." Information about social relations gives valuable suggestions for classroom goals. The teacher will see that Herbert has to develop greater social assurance before he will participate freely in class discussion, and that Jerry's brains are not making their full contribution because he placidly follows the proposals of a popular boy with less ability. The fact that Sara becomes highstrung and quarrelsome has already drawn the teacher's attention. When he finds that Sara and Julie are rivals in popularity and leadership and notes that Sara's outbreaks always occur when Julie is getting the spotlight, he knows that a new social pattern will have to emerge before Sara's tension can subside.

PEER RATINGS.   Teachers use two formal procedures—peer ratings and the sociogram—to find out what his fellows think about a pupil, i.e., what his reputation is. This information is valuable because companions usually know a pupil better than the teacher does. Even when the reputation is undeserved, it is still significant, since peer attitudes influence adjustment.

Peer ratings can cover many aspects of personality. The method has been used successfully at all levels from the primary room to the college dormitory, with directions and questions modified to fit the group. The test may consist of a series of descriptions worded in student language (see Table 8). The instructions are to think over the members of the group, and after each description to name whomever it fits. Sometimes the directions are cast in "Guess Who" form. Usually the rater is left free to put no name, one name, or several names after the item.

The teacher tabulates how many mentions each pupil gets for each characteristic. No attention is paid if a given child is mentioned two or three times as "a poor sport," since such random mentions do not show a crystallized reputation. But if a third of the class nominate Patrick as a poor sport, the information is significant. It does not necessarily show that Pat *is* a poor sport; perhaps he does not know how to play the games, or perhaps the others are prejudiced and judge him unfairly. The remedy may be to work on Pat's behavior, or it may be to develop group acceptance of Pat.

The teacher will find differences between his own view and the group view of the same boys and girls. Teachers naming class leaders may give undue attention to brighter pupils or to the ones they like, only to find that the pupils themselves name a much less conspicuous boy as the one who has good ideas about what to do and who can take charge and get things done. Teachers are often very wrong when they name their most popular pupils (Ausubel *et al.*, 1952; Gronlund, 1959, p. 11).

To be effective, the peer-rating questionnaire must be given to groups of 20 or more students who are well acquainted. Pupils are a little disturbed by questions that require them to rate each other, especially when the

TABLE 8

Some "Guess Who" items used with intermediate-grade children
(Cunningham et al., 1951, pp. 419–22)

Here is someone who likes to talk a lot, always has something to say . . . .

Here is someone who always seems rather sad, worried, or unhappy, who hardly ever laughs or smiles . . . .

Here is someone who waits for somebody else to think of something to do and always likes to follow the suggestions which others make . . . .

Here is a girl who likes to read boys' books, play boys' games, or would prefer to be a boy . . . .

Here is someone who can appreciate a joke and see the fun in it even when the joke is on himself (or herself) . . . .

Here is someone who is very friendly, who has lots of friends, who is nice to everybody . . . .

procedure is new to them. If care is taken in introducing the questions, however, students are glad to participate (Tuddenham, 1952). (Said one primary pupil, "I wish I could have two turns.") Ordinarily, responses are left unsigned. The teacher or counselor explains why the questions are being asked. With older pupils, the teacher can explain that this information is used in guidance and in providing experiences which will "improve personality." Adolescents are so much concerned with self-analysis that such an explanation makes the test seem genuinely important. Pupils must be sure that no other pupil will see the results, and the plan is likely to backfire into complaints unless the students like the teacher and welcome his personal interest. To reduce anxiety one may present items that describe only favorable traits.

THE SOCIOGRAM.   The sociogram portrays social structure. To obtain the needed information one may request each pupil to write down his own name and the names of three, four, or five best friends. The teacher then prepares a chart in which he lists every pupil, and draws arrows to show choices. The first sketch is jumbled, but if the names are then rearranged to put mutual friends together and to shorten the lines between choices as much as possible, a definite choice network appears, as in Figures 27 (page 118) and 42.

The structure often comes as a surprise to the teacher. Because 30 pupils means 435 possible pairings, the teacher rarely observes the elaborate social structure of his class. He has spotted certain chums and certain rivalries, and knows that Jane is going around with Emily's crowd this fall. The sociogram brings the relations into view like a microscope turned abruptly into sharp focus. Jane is seen to be on the outskirts of Emily's crowd, able to count on friendship only from Emily and ignored by the other four. The quiet Ann seems to follow the dashing Agnes around, but the sociogram shows her as the real "star" whom everyone thinks of as a friend. Lurline and Rena may be seen by the teacher as indistinguishable, well-mannered girls. Yet Lurline is one of a warmly knit social group, while Rena is ignored and wistfully casting about for a friend.

Again, the teacher must convince the pupils that through the inquiry about their friends he intends to help them rather than to pry into their affairs. Ordinarily, the teacher explains frankly that if he knows their friends, he can understand them better, plan activities at which they will work with their friends, and so make life pleasanter. Often the inquiry is connected with an immediate problem: for example, "We are going to work in committees for the next two weeks. Please list the five people you would most like to work with. I'll arrange for you to have as many of your choices as I can. If there is someone you don't want on your committee, you may tell me that also. (This last inquiry should be casual, if included at all,

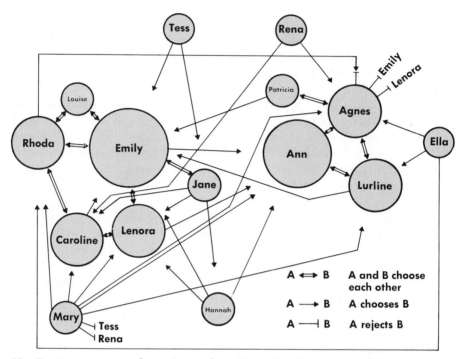

42 *Sociogram for a class of fourth-grade girls (Data from* Helping Teachers Understand Children, *1945, p. 297)*

This drawing appeared in Cronbach, 1960, p. 521.

since the thought of blackballs is threatening.) To maintain confidence the choices should really be used in making up committees. Good work is obtained from such compatible committee members; moreover, the teacher who notes that Charles wants to work with Bruce and Mike can put him on their committee and give him a chance to build a friendship.

The number of choices the pupil receives is an index of acceptance or popularity. The meaning of the data depends on the question asked; there is a substantial, but far from perfect, relation between acceptability as a co-worker and acceptability as a friend. Always, several pupils ("stars") receive more than their proportionate share of choices, and others ("isolates") receive none.

Gronlund asked pupils in Grades III to XII to list their five preferred work companions or seating companions. Figure 43 shows how many pupils fell at or below each level of acceptance. These are composite results; the frequency of isolates, stars, etc., changed very little from grade to grade. While the sociometric information helps to identify influential class members, Gronlund (1959, p. 23) warns against overinterpreting it. Being frequently chosen "presents no evidence concerning [the pupil's] emotional stability or his ability or power as a leader."

The individual's status does not change often under conventional school procedures. Bonney (1943b) found that sociometric scores are nearly as stable as aptitude and achievement tests, correlations being about .80 between one year's measure and the next. (See also R. Wertheimer, 1957; Cannon, 1958). Popularity returns to much the same level when pupils are reshuffled into new classes and given time to become acquainted (Laughlin, 1954). Individual popularity is more likely to shift when the teacher plans activities to promote the acceptance of underchosen children (E. A. Taylor, 1952). Change is not always for the better. Sometimes a popular person slips as he fails to adapt his social techniques to the shifting interests and ideals of the group.

Even though popularity is not very changeable, the friendship linkages are continually shifting (Taba, 1955b, p. 62). Especially if the teacher gives pupils a chance to work together and help each other, the sociogram may shift from one with cliques and rival stars to one where choices spread over the whole group, with no tight clusters or cleavages.

The teacher whose September sociogram for her fourth-graders is shown above obtained a second sociometric report in December. Important

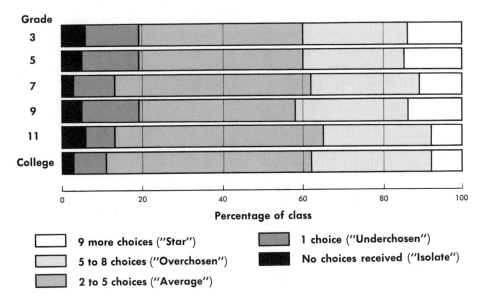

43   *The frequency of isolates and stars changes little (Gronlund, 1959, p. 97)*

Choices were made in classes of about 30 members, with five choices allowed each member.

changes were found. For one thing, seven of the girls "rejected" others, whereas in September there had been only two such expressions of antagonism. By December Rena had found a mutual friend in a new girl, Edna May, and isolates Mary, Tess, and Ella received at least one choice each. Lenora, once very popular, was chosen by no one in December. Some of her closest friends had been ill or had moved away, and Lenora had found no way to replace them with new social relationships. Loss of social position is hard to accept and is likely to result in emotional disturbance, compensatory engrossment in schoolwork, or some other behavior important to the teacher.

As a by-product of its detailed information on individuals and social clusters, the sociogram offers a survey of the school or the grade group as a whole. A count of how many pupils receive no choices, 1 choice, etc., is almost a census of the degree of social adjustment in the population. Thus in Westlake High School, in a prosperous residential neighborhood of a city, 19 per cent of the girls and 37 per cent of the boys were chosen by no one. This high frequency of social isolation reflected the influence of out-of-school clubs and sororities in which newcomers, poorer pupils, and those of a minority religion had no place. An uninspired program of school activities in which only the athletics appealed to the boys was a contributing factor. Upon inquiry, it was found that students frequently transferred away from Westlake because they were "miserably unhappy" (Taba, 1955a). The sociometric survey, by detecting an unhealthy social atmosphere, encourages a deeper inquiry and remedial action. Survey results may also be reassuring. In an elementary school studied by Taba, a cleavage between Jewish and Gentile children anticipated by the staff did not appear in friendship choices.

11. Considering either primary, junior-high-school, or college students, write several peer-rating descriptions that would give the teacher significant information.

12. What individuals represented in Figure 42 seem to be having social difficulties? Should the school be concerned about those who have only one mutual choice?

13. "Teacher judgments of social acceptance are about as accurate as their judgments of intelligence. It would seem just as important to obtain accurate information on interpersonal relations as to give an objective intelligence test." Do you agree?

14. How often should a teacher of fourth-graders obtain a sociogram?

15. If a girl who shows a loss of social acceptance turns to reading as an outlet, what is best for the teacher to do?

16. May a frequently chosen pupil be maladjusted?

17. What further inquiries are needed before modifying the Westlake program? What changes in the program might be desirable?

18. What opportunities does a high-school science teacher have to use sociometric information (Buck, 1952)?

EXAMINING THE PUPIL'S VIEW OF HIMSELF

Educators and psychologists have wanted dependable personality tests very badly. Hundreds of instruments have been invented, and many are used in schools. Properly interpreted, some of these devices are useful, but few do all that their inventors intended. Personality tests are especially useful to study the aspects of the pupil that are hard to observe. The pupil's awareness of his own limitations, for example, can be known only if he will tell us frankly what he thinks of himself.

PROBLEM INVENTORIES.   Most personality measurement employs the "self-report" principle, asking the pupil about himself. He may not judge himself accurately, but even so his statement is important, for his self-concept has great influence on his actions. The teacher must remember that the questionnaire result is no more than a pupil's statement about himself. It is not necessarily his "true personality" nor even a truthful report of his self-concept.

The pupil's cooperation is essential. If he resents a question or feels that he will be penalized for admitting some fault, he will not tell what he thinks. It is necessary to explain questionnaires so that the pupil will not be threatened. Fortunately, most pupils are interested in learning about themselves and look forward to the results of personality tests. A test whose results can be discussed frankly with the pupil is easier to employ than one which analyzes responses in terms of "neurotic tendencies" or some other threatening language.

For the teacher, the most important type of questionnaire is the so-called problem inventory, which lists two hundred or more concerns found among pupils at a given level and asks the pupil to check those that bother him. Typical items from the Mooney Problem Checklist (junior-high level) are: [1]

Don't get enough sleep	Ill at ease at social affairs
Not good looking	Giving in to temptations
Afraid of tests	Not having as much fun as other
So often feel restless in classes	kids have
Being treated like an outsider	Family worried about money

There are other forms of the checklist for Grades IV–VI, senior high, and college.

One may count the concerns marked in such areas as health, school, home, money-work, and boy-girl relations. High scores indicate that certain pupils are, so to speak, signaling for help. While prior attention will usually go to these "emergency cases," the number of problems a pupil marks is

[1] Items copyright 1950 by The Psychological Corporation and reproduced by permission.

not an accurate indication of his degree of disturbance. A pupil's adjustment may be drastically upset by one single problem. Moreover, one pupil may check every slight concern while another may check only matters that worry him greatly. Pupils with similar adjustment therefore receive different scores.

The most effective use of the checklist is to find out *what* concerns the pupil. Even a seemingly trivial problem like an outbreak of pimples can undermine self-respect. The problems may be such that the teacher can provide direct help, or they may be beyond any solution the school can suggest.

Even when the teacher can give no practical help, he may do substantial good merely by encouraging the pupil to talk further about his problem. Pupils generally welcome the chance to discuss their worries with a mature person. A common reaction to a counseling conference is, "Thanks very much. Just talking about the problem made me feel better." Children sometimes hesitate to talk with their parents about a problem, particularly when their struggle for independence is near its height or when their parents seem remote. A teacher whose attitude makes clear his readiness to listen will find much demand for that service.

Checklist responses can be analyzed item by item to locate problems common in the group. By counting how many pupils check each item, the teacher obtains a picture of the most prevalent concerns. Such a list can be used in planning classwork. If the ninth grade is concerned about conflicts with parents and their own desire for more freedom, discussion of the problem may be appropriate in a home economics class, an English class, or a homeroom. Class activities might include panel discussions with parents, reading of relevant literary works or sociological and psychological materials, or small research studies on freedoms allowed pupils at different ages. Appropriately planned work of this type develops ability to outline written material, to express oneself orally, and to use library resources, while at the same time giving insight into an area of present and future importance. If 80 per cent of an adolescent group check "Lack of places to go for recreation" as a serious problem, this finding suggests a source of social disorganization that community leaders should work on. It also suggests a genuine problem about which a social studies teacher can center citizenship education. Depending on the teacher and the community, the subsequent activities might range from surveying facilities to acquaint students with them to spearheading a campaign to organize a youth center and a program for it.

Information about adjustment is by no means obvious to the casually observing teacher. Pupils' self-reports are often far from what teachers expect (see page 7). The teacher is prone to confuse success with adjustment, and to assume that the pupil whose classwork is good has no problems. Sarason *et al.* (1960, p. 265) report:

If a child is bright, highly motivated, and clearly adequate to his classwork, it is difficult for his teacher to believe that this child may be highly anxious about his abilities and his classwork. We have had occasion many times to discuss high anxiety children with their teachers, and, particularly in the case of the bright child, we have encountered a reaction of near-disbelief that such a child answered the questionnaires as he did.

This comment is more easily understood if we recall Haggard's finding that children afraid of authority and lacking self-acceptance are definitely superior in some schoolwork.

Even if the child's fears are based on a false self-evaluation, information about them is highly significant to the teacher, because they influence the pupil's preferences among tasks, his mental flexibility, and his reaction to criticism.

DESCRIPTIVE QUESTIONNAIRES.   More elaborate personality questionnaires yield several descriptive scores. The Minnesota Counseling Inventory for high schools, for example, has scores on family adjustment, school adjustment, morale, conformity or responsibility, emotional stability, etc. These scores are obtained from responses (in true-false form) to 355 statements such as these: [2]

> I seek to meet the important person at a reception or tea.
> I am subject to eyestrain.
> I hesitate to volunteer in class recitation.
> I have been quite independent and free from family rule.

The five scores named above have intercorrelations ranging from about .10 to .65; this means that aspects of good adjustment have some degree of association, but that the individual profile usually has high and low points. The pupil who surpasses 75 per cent of the class on one scale may fall in the lowest quarter on another. Adjustment is not an all-or-none matter.

Unfortunately, questionnaire scores do not correspond closely to other evidence supposedly indicating the same personality traits. Principals, counselors, and visiting teachers named pupils in each grade and sex thought to have exceptionally poor family adjustment; these were compared with the total school population. The results in Table 9 were obtained for ninth- and tenth-grade boys; they are representative of results for other grades, for other scales, and for girls. While poorer scores indicate a relatively high frequency of poor adjustment, at no score level is it possible to say, "A pupil with this score probably has poor relations with his family." At best one can say, "Pupils at this score level have more than the usual probability of poor family adjustment." All of the better personality questionnaires show a similarly positive but weak correspondence of scores to external evidence.

[2] Items copyright 1953 by The Psychological Corporation and reproduced by permission.

TABLE 9

Correspondence of judged family adjustment to score on Minnesota Counseling Inventory (data supplied by R. F. Berdie, based on boys in Grades IX and X)

Score: "Family Adjustment Problems"	Number of boys at this level		Probability that a boy at this score is in the maladjusted group
	All boys	Boys judged maladjusted	
30–	17	3	18
25–29	43	2	5
20–24	187	9	5
15–19	329	21	6
10–14	591	16	3
5–9	902	12	1.3
0–4	744	4	.5
Total	2813	67	2.4

Several reasons can be given for the inconsistency between questionnaires and observed personality: deliberate concealment on the part of the pupil, his lack of self-understanding, insufficient information on the part of the person supplying the criterion rating, and imperfect correspondence between inner adjustment and outer behavior. Because descriptive questionnaires are hard to interpret, they should be used only by a trained counselor. The scores are useful as part of his thorough study of a pupil, but they are rarely of direct benefit to the teacher who lacks special training in personality theory.

The association between school accomplishment and personality measures is shown by Ullman (1957). As a measure of accomplishment he examined two questions: did the student complete high school, and did he attain the honor roll at graduation? The composite measure of accomplishment correlated with ninth-grade scores as follows:

	Boys	Girls
Adjustment as rated by teachers	.50	.40
Number of problems checked on a problem checklist	−.08	−.28
Number of self-favorable statements made on a questionnaire ("self-adjustment" score on the California Test of Personality)	.16	.30
Number of choices received in a sociometric test	.44	.31

There is some association between adjustment measures and academic success. The association suggests that adjustment helps one in school, but it is also likely that previous accomplishment affected the judgments of teachers and peers in Grade IX. While noting the positive correlation, we should emphasize that it is not very large; among students with excellent accomplishment there is a wide range of adjustment, and vice versa.

It is of further interest to compare maladjusted boys (as judged by ninth-grade teachers) who later graduated from high school with maladjusted boys who did not. These groups describe themselves quite differently. Here are self-descriptions accepted more often by the graduates:

> I'm easily excited (32% of graduates, 8% of nongraduates)
> I'm afraid of failure (24%, 8%)
> I wish I were a good listener (40%, 16%)

Statements more often marked by nongraduates were:

> I hate school (8% of graduates, 28% of nongraduates)
> I lack drive (4%, 20%)
> I feel like leaving home (8%, 24%)

The graduates are dissatisfied strivers, the nongraduates seem to be rejecting the role cut out for them.

PROJECTIVE TECHNIQUES. The pupil can usually recognize the "good" answers to a questionnaire, and faking is easy. If a test can be devised where the pupil cannot guess what is desirable, he will presumably give the answer that is natural for him. Foremost among subtle procedures are the so-called *projective* techniques. The pupil may be asked to interpret an inkblot, or to make up a story to fit a picture of, say, an adult looking out a window on an adolescent boy and girl. The assumption underlying projective tests is that the pupil has a certain outlook on the world which he uses to make sense of the ambiguous test materials. If in a picture test he repeatedly offers stories centering around conflicts between adults and youth, it is clear that he regards such conflict as common and important.

It is hard for the pupil to tell how his answers to a projective technique will be interpreted, and distortion is therefore difficult. Often the responses reveal attitudes of which the pupil is not consciously aware. Though such tests have been useful in the clinical analysis of individuals by psychologists, they are difficult to interpret and are not very trustworthy. They are more useful in comparison of groups for research purposes.

A simple projective method useful for school counselors is the Sentence Completion Test. If a pupil is asked to complete unfinished sentences rapidly, he often reveals attitudes without realizing that he is doing so. Typical sentences are:

> My mother and I . . .
> I believe I have the ability to . . .
> My schoolwork . . .

The responses suggest areas of emotional conflict and methods by which the pupil copes with blocking. There is no adequate, standardized sentence-completion instrument for use below the college level.

Because tests do not always give dependable information, teachers selecting and using tests should take advantage of critical reviews. A review describes a test, gives an expert evaluation of its content and the evidence supporting its interpretation, and summarizes uses for which the test can be recommended. The most important source of reviews is the *Mental Measurements Yearbook*, edited by O. K. Buros (1959), which covers tests of personality, achievement, and mental abilities. In a test review, the most important issues are those concerned with validity, i.e., with, "What does the test really measure?"

19. Questionnaire measures of adjustment usually have only low correlations with the number of sociometric choices received. Explain.

20. We have proposed that adolescents use class time to gain a better understanding of their conflicts with their parents. This is one form of "education for adjustment," which has been much criticized. Is there a legitimate argument against such an educational activity? Is the activity consistent with the school's responsibility to promote academic learning?

21. According to Table 9, would it be profitable to give the Minnesota Counseling Inventory to all pupils to screen out for individual attention those likely to have family problems?

22. Examine the review (Buros, 1959) for one of the following tests and answer the question: Would it be desirable to use this test in the grade I teach? If so, who should interpret it and for what purposes?

    a. California Test of Personality (Kindergarten–college)
    b. Family Adjustment Test (age 12 and over)
    c. Kuder Preference Record—Personal (Grade IX–college)

23. Some nonpsychologists have questioned the propriety of personality testing in the school, objecting particularly to questions such as: "Do you feel that your parents have been unduly strict with you?" and "Have there been frequent quarrels in your home?" What do you think of the following editorial comment?

It is not difficult to suggest to a young child that he has problems he has not recognized before, or drive a wedge into family relationships where none existed. Family linen becomes part of the child's "permanent record." What justifies a wholesale, dragnet inquiry into the home life of a community?

INVESTIGATION OF INTERESTS

Of all the psychological traits of the pupil, his interests are the easiest to find out about. He enjoys telling about his hobbies, about stories he has liked, and about interesting things he did in previous classes. True, there are some barriers to an accurate self-report. If urged to make a public avowal before the class, the pupil has to tell a story that will make him look good in the eyes of his fellows. If the pupil thinks it tactful or profitable to say he is fond of the subject the teacher is presenting, his report is less than frank. Frankness is encouraged when the pupil's report will be used to select his future work, and he knows it.

One technique, useful from age 11 through college, is to request an autobiography. This may be written as a composition assignment. It may be a self-appraisal connected with a study of personality development, in which case it takes on intrinsic interest. Instead of asking for a general autobiography, the teacher may inquire about background in a single area. A science teacher might open a course, for example, by asking the pupil to list things of a scientific or mechanical nature he has done. Properly primed by class discussion, this helps the pupil to see connections between science and his past experience and tells the teacher which topics will be familiar and which unfamiliar. The teacher could also ask the pupil to list topics he wants to know more about.

Published interest inventories are intended chiefly for use in vocational guidance and curriculum choice at the secondary or college level. The systematic questions lead the pupil to take stock of himself, reviewing information that he otherwise is unlikely to add up into an accurate balance sheet. Interest inventories are a good device with which to encourage the adolescent's self-appraisal, because one is usually satisfied with one's own interests, and discussing them is less threatening than discussing personality or aptitudes. This makes a good first step in the study of occupations or in individual counseling.

In one such inventory, the *Kuder Preference Record,* each item lists three activities, e.g.:

> Build birdhouses
> Write articles about birds
> Draw sketches of birds

The student marks which of the three he would prefer. These three alternatives are counted as showing mechanical, literary, and artistic interest, respectively. The profile shows how many items the pupil checked in each interest area, compared with others of his age and sex.

Mary Thomas, a college student majoring in child development, came to a counselor because her grades were low, and he administered various tests to determine what readiness she had for the work she was taking. Her Kuder scores produced the profile chart shown. Her interest in Mechanical activities is greater than average; 69 per cent of college girls have lower scores. Mary is below average in liking for Social Service and Persuasive activities, which call for work with people. Her peak interests, Clerical and Computational, were not engaged in child development courses.

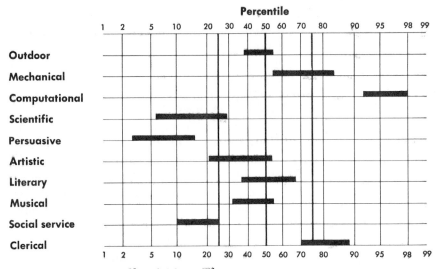

44   *Preference profile of Mary Thomas*

Each bar indicates Mary's location relative to other girls; because measurement is not perfectly accurate, her position is indicated by a band rather than as a point (see page 210).

Yet when questioned Mary explained that she had set her heart on work in an orphanage. She chose this goal in early childhood after reading a book about a woman who helped orphan children; this seemed to her a "wonderful" life. During the years when her mind was fixed on this goal, she had held various summer jobs in offices. She had, she said, "just loved" her job of the previous summer as a file clerk. Supplementary evidence showed that Mary had far more aptitude for secretarial work than for the field of child development. The counselor's function here was to lead Mary to examine deliberately a vocational choice about which she had never thought realistically. The outcome in Mary's case was a trial enrollment in secretarial training to see if she would succeed and like it. Girls as misdirected as Mary are common, though their number is reduced when school programs encourage continual self-appraisal and career planning.

Around ages 13–14, an examination of interests helps the pupil to form a realistic self-concept and to choose activities for exploration. It illuminates a preliminary study of careers. But there is no single point at which career decisions are made. The ninth-grader is often asked to make a rather definite vocational choice, but he has barely become aware of the need to make a choice and to learn about himself. He will require some time to collect pertinent information, and to make provisional tries through such activities as part-time jobs. Super and Overstreet (1960) surveyed the boys in a typical community in New York State, and came to these conclusions, among others (pp. 152 ff.):

Most ninth-grade boys in this study were aware of the immediate choices which they were being required to make . . . and many of these boys were aware of intermediate choices, but there was minimal awareness of the more remote choices to be made after leaving school. . . . At this stage of development, . . . they need experiences which help them to develop better self-understanding and self-acceptance. . . . Taking the student's vocational aspirations at face value is often a mistake, . . . seeking to help him formulate a specific occupational objective at the ninth-grade level may be a strategic error. Vocational preferences are unstable at this stage, and often unwise when judged by intellectual and other requirements. . . . However, these vocational preferences may be significant for exploratory purposes.

Interests become increasingly well defined as adolescence progresses, so that the pupil can select a broad field that is appealing, and then narrow his choice. By age 16–18, the typical boy has well-defined and fairly permanent interests. Among men tested at age 38, three-fourths had about the same profile as the one they showed as college freshmen (Strong, 1955; Kelly, 1955). One-fourth, though, had markedly changed in what they liked and disliked.

Guidance is by no means complete if the student enters college with a definite vocational aim. Many high-school graduates were inadequately counseled, and many others ignore the evidence of tests while pursuing a plan growing out of family tradition or childish fantasy. Dropout rates in law curricula are notoriously high. Only 28 per cent of Harvard seniors finish in the natural sciences, though as freshmen 50 per cent had planned to be science majors. Many students find law or science courses more difficult than they had expected, and many discover new fields of interest (especially social sciences). Those who stay with legal training must accept a new goal, modifying their adolescent visions of the dramatic clash in the courtroom with an acceptance of routine paper work. In many unfortunate cases the discovery that life as a lawyer is difficult and "not intellectually stimulating" does not occur until after the young man finishes law school and takes his first position (Lortie, 1959).

Even after leaving college and entering upon a career, a person has opportunities to shape it to fit his interests. Medical students, though they have many interests in common with each other, have diverse interest patterns. A few are interested chiefly in the intellectual and research aspects of medicine; some are organizers and managers at heart; some are chiefly motivated by the desire to serve the weak and ill; and a large number give the impression that they chose medicine primarily to achieve a high standard of living (Kelly, 1957). The available professional roles range from medical missionary to society doctor. Choosing a curriculum is only part of developing a career plan. A man is most likely to find fulfillment if he understands his own interests and values, and shapes his career accordingly. This self-understanding is the chief objective in use of interest measures.

24. Can men of different interest patterns be satisfied in engineering? in work where they use training in the maintenance of electronic apparatus?

25. If physicians differ in interest patterns, on what basis can one advise a boy that his interests make a medical career a doubtful choice?

26. To what extent is a girl's identification of her interests useful if she will not go to college and is likely to become a housewife shortly after high-school graduation?

27. If the school accepts vocational guidance as a responsibility, who should investigate the pupil's interests and discuss them with him?

SUMMARY

The teacher tries to identify individual differences because the pupil's characteristics determine whether or not he will profit from the lessons planned. This chapter describes techniques used by teachers to obtain information on motivational characteristics. Emphasis is placed on three principles:

Any action is an attempt to satisfy some need.

Consistent behavior patterns run through the pupil's actions in many situations. These patterns are stable over long periods of time.

Any pattern is the result of many causes, and any single cause may lead to many different adaptations.

The view that an action is rooted in the personality suggests that one can deal with undesirable behavior only after diagnosing the underlying forces.

Teachers often make unsound judgments about pupils; ten sources of error are listed on page 170. Many of these errors take the form of oversimplification; others arise from insufficiently careful reasoning. The teacher can reduce errors if in observing he seeks an accurate factual description of behavior, leaving interpretation until later. Accumulating anecdotal records of significant incidents is a desirable technique. Only as numerous incidents accumulate in a variety of situations can one expect consistencies to come to light.

Judgments from peers are collected in part because these are valid statements about what the pupil is like, and in part because his reputation—deserved or undeserved—is an important fact. Peer ratings are obtained by questions fitted to the maturity of the group. The "Guess Who" technique is employed in the lower grades. One may also ask pupils to indicate their friends or their preferred work partners. The resulting choices, plotted in the form of a sociogram, map the social structure of the group. Even if five choices are given by each member of the group, usually about 5 per cent of the group turn out to be isolates, receiving no choices. At the other extreme, some 10 per cent are stars, receiving at least double their "fair share" of choices. Although many factors can change sociometric status, the standings are about as stable from one year to the next as school achievement. The teacher promotes desirable changes by devising activities in which the underchosen pupil can contribute to the group.

The self-description is important even when it does not correspond to the pupil's behavior, because his self-concept influences his reactions. Self-reports are not necessarily frank. By selecting an instrument wisely and by making its purpose clear to the pupil, the teacher can increase the pupil's cooperation. The "problem inventory" is particularly recommended; it highlights troubles the pupil wants to call to the teacher's attention. A tabulation of the responses of the group to each item can suggest problems for discussion and sometimes can point to desirable alterations in school procedure. Information given by self-reports and peer ratings often disagrees with the impression the teacher has acquired by casual observation. For example, teachers are unwilling to believe that many able pupils are anxious about schoolwork.

The descriptive questionnaire, which gives trait scores for the pupil, does not correlate highly with other evidence. Many pupils having poor family adjustment earn average "family adjustment" scores. The questionnaire is primarily of value when it is part of a case study by a counselor or a psychologist.

Adjustment as rated by teachers and popularity with peers are related to school achievement, correlations reported by Ullman being in the range .30–.50. This may, however, be as much a sign that achievement produces good ratings as that adjustment produces achievement. A follow-up showed that graduates and nongraduates had had different symptoms of maladjustment in Grade IX, the former being more self-critical, the latter more antagonistic and withdrawing.

Projective techniques are primarily of value in research and in case studies by psychologists. They present an ambiguous problem in which the pupil's response indicates something about his way of interpreting the world. One of the simpler techniques is the Sentence Completion Test, which can suggest areas of emotional conflict.

Interest tests, and such alternative procedures as the autobiographical essay, give information relevant both to planning classwork and to individual counseling. Vocational interest inventories frequently reveal concentrations of interest of which the pupil had not become aware. An examination of his interests helps the early adolescent acquire self-understanding, but he cannot choose a vocation as early as Grade IX. Choices stabilize during high school; among college freshmen, about three-fourths are expected to exhibit the same interests that they will exhibit 20 years later. Even students who announce definite aims, however, may have made unsound choices. Dropout rates in certain "glamorous" college curricula, and shifts into fields students had not considered in high school, show the need for continuing guidance during college. Even after a person has entered upon his career, he has many opportunities to shape his work to his characteristics, if he understands himself. This self-understanding is the chief function of interest testing.

Reading List 6

John G. Darley and Theda Haganah, "The Strong Vocational Interest Blank in Individual Cases," Chapter 6 in *Vocational Interest Measurement: Theory and Practice* (Minneapolis: Univ. of Minnesota Press, 1955), pp. 194–263.

Browsing through the numerous cases presented here will make clear the importance of measuring the interests of older students and will indicate some of the problems of interpreting interest profiles. Some cases show a marked discrepancy between what the student believes he is interested in and the test profile. Other records compare interests with abilities.

Edgar Z. Friedenberg, "Five Exemplary Boys," Chapter 5 in *The Vanishing Adolescent* (New York: Norton, 1959), pp. 92–113.

Friedenberg shows how Sentence Completion tests may be used by a psychologist to gain an impression of a boy's internal resources and attitudes. These descriptions of individuals are used to point up biting criticism of a disciplinary system in whch a "student court" passes out sentences to those who violate rules (his pages 88–91).

Daniel A. Prescott, "Obtaining Information," Chapter 6 in *The Child in the Educative Process* (New York: McGraw-Hill, 1957), pp. 151–67.

Advice on the nature of useful anecdotes and how to record them, followed by advice on home visits. Other chapters of this book include case studies in which these techniques are applied.

Edward K. Strong, Jr., "Use of the Strong Vocational Interest Blank in Counseling," in W. L. Layton, ed., *The Strong Vocational Interest Blank* (*Minnesota Studies in Student Personnel Work*, No. 10, 1960), pp. 178–91.

The chief contributor to the development of interest measurement summarizes the ways in which interest scales should be used and presents evidence of their effectiveness.

Hilda Taba, *School Culture,* Studies in Intergroup Relations (Washington: American Council on Education, 1955).

Illustrates how surveys of friendship, interests, and participation can identify needed improvements, and describes how the process of change can be initiated through group discussion of the surveys.

Verna E. White, "How Should Data Gathered for an Individual Be Synthesized and Interpreted?" Chapter 5 in *Studying the Individual Pupil* (New York: Harper, 1958), pp. 123–65.

Cases are presented to show representative interpretations. Data from various sources supplement each other and sometimes seem to be in conflict. A search for consistent patterns produces an explanatory hypothesis that makes it possible to help the pupil.

CHAPTER 7 ASSESSING READINESS: ABILITIES

In this chapter you will become acquainted with tests of aptitudes and work skills. Tests of general scholastic aptitude (the name "intelligence test" is dropping out of use) receive a great deal of attention because of their importance in educational decisions. Other aptitude tests are especially significant as indicators of vocational potential. The chapter will begin, however, with procedures used to analyze study skills, since the discussion of these can be less technical.

A second aim of the chapter is to prepare you for the responsibilities most teachers have for testing programs. Every classroom teacher administers some tests to his entire class. Pupils' records on these tests, and on other tests given by an administrator or counselor, are used by the teacher. Still other tests are called upon when a case study of a single pupil is being made. The teacher therefore has these responsibilities:

He must administer group tests in the proper way, so that accurate information is obtained.

He must interpret test results placed in files for use by teachers.

He must use information from less-common tests, obtaining help in interpreting from the counselor or some other trained person.

He must know what kinds of tests would aid in understanding a pupil so that he can ask a qualified person to administer them.

In addition, the teacher sometimes selects tests related to the subject he teaches, serves on a committee to plan guidance services, or has other duties requiring an understanding of tests. This chapter is no more than an introduction, and does not qualify the teacher to choose and interpret tests. For further information, more specialized books such as the following should be consulted:

Lee J. Cronbach, *Essentials of Psychological Testing* (New York: Harper, 1960).

H. H. Remmers, N. L. Gage, and J. Francis Rummel, *A Practical Introduction to Measurement and Evaluation* (New York: Harper, 1960).

Robert L. Thorndike and Elizabeth Hagen, *Measurement and Evaluation in Psychology and Education* (New York: Wiley, 1961).

MEASURING TOOL SKILLS

One common cause of difficulty in learning is inadequate fundamental skills. This is true in the later elementary grades, and also true as high as graduate school. The skills required for educational success include, first and foremost, reading; second, arithmetic, written expression, and other tool subjects; third, ability to plan study, to organize work, and to concentrate; fourth, skill in finding information and in using the library. These abilities should be developed gradually throughout schooling.

Reading Tests

Educators once assumed that the ability to read was developed in the elementary grades and could be taken for granted when the student reached high school or college. Now we know, after testing thousands of students, that a large fraction of them are struggling along without the reading skills they need. Many more can read only well enough to keep up with school demands; few students in any grade read with ideal efficiency. Where the efficient reader can understand a particular reading assignment in 30 minutes, some students require two or three times as long.

A standardized reading test is a carefully developed instrument for assessing competence in reading. The teacher can, of course, identify some poor readers from their confused contribution in class discussion. He can locate more of them by requesting each student to read orally, or by timing silent reading. A published test is easier to administer and more impartial. Moreover, such tests have equivalent forms, which permit measurement of gains from year to year.

The usual nationally distributed test provides a standard by which the teacher can compare one class with other pupils of the same grade. A teacher whose class reads less well than the norm may have to use simpler reading materials than the books ordinarily employed in that grade. If a group is superior, the teacher will not hesitate to bring in difficult reading matter when it is appropriate.

Reading tests come in many styles. Pupils who do well on one test will usually perform adequately on another, but there is some variation because the tests measure different reading skills. Some tests measure speed in reading simple sentences. Others require the exact comprehension and interpretation of difficult passages. Some tests involve unusual vocabulary, while others use only common words. To interpret the reading test, the teacher should know just what type of reading ability it demands. The pupil is not fully described as "a good reader," or "a poor reader"; no single score tells about all his different reading abilities. We have many types of test so that the teacher can measure the type of ability most relevant to a particular program. The most appropriate test is usually the one whose reading tasks resemble those demanded by the materials and methods of instruction.

READING DIAGNOSIS.   A diagnostic test breaks down a complex performance into many parts and thereby indicates the pupil's areas of strength and weakness. If a teacher wishes to know only which students have the greatest difficulty in reading, a test that provides a single score will detect them. If one stops with predicting that Helen will do well but Jane will do poorly, little has been done to help Jane. The most the single-score test can do is detect the student who needs further attention. To plan remedial instruction, a diagnostic procedure is required.

A diagnostic reading test will show that some pupils have excellent comprehension but cover the page too slowly. Some have good reading technique but have trouble with uncommon words. Some are baffled by a long and unfamiliar word because they do not know how to "sound it out" so that it can be recognized. The pupil whose total score is average usually shows weakness in one or more specific reading skills. Many weaknesses can be overcome by small amounts of intensive instruction. The regular classroom work provides opportunities to build vocabularies or to train pupils to skim for a central thought. The teacher may prescribe for individual students special exercises to develop these or other skills. The diagnostic test aids in deciding which pupils can be helped sufficiently by the class teacher, and which ones should work with a remedial reading specialist.

Here is part of a diagnostic report (Gates, 1947, pp. 532–34) for a sixth-grader:

> His scores in five silent-reading tests center closely about grade 3.7, or three grades lower than his grade position in school. . . . Oral reading is even poorer, grade 3.1.
>
> He read in an artificially high-pitched voice with signs of emotional tension. When he encountered unfamiliar words his concern was obvious and he appeared to attempt to work them out by a detailed study of the word form as a whole and the technique of naming and sounding letters, usually with little success. . . .
>
> He is very poor in dividing words into syllables and phonograms and working out the recognition of unfamiliar words by syllabication. Note that when words are "flashed" and must be recognized as wholes, he gets a grade score of 3.5, but in Syllabication, Recognition of Syllables, and Recognition of Phonograms, his grade score is about 2.5, a grade lower. He is better in Blending Letter Sounds (grade 3.2) and he got perfect scores in Giving Letter Sounds and Reading Letters. Here is a boy whose techniques are limited to recognizing words as wholes, and failing in this, he resorts to letter-naming and sound-

ing. . . . The tests of Auditory Techniques show that [he] . . . has a good basis for working with word sounds and a test showed his hearing to be normal. . . .

The pupil's difficulty was diagnosed, therefore, as due to failure to acquire the more advanced types of word-analysis techniques and to sheer lack of experience in reading.

This diagnosis was followed by special training in word analysis and encouragement of reading for fun. Three months later this boy's scores had advanced a whole grade. His morale and attitude improved correspondingly.

Diagnosis in Other Areas

Each subject depends on certain fundamental ideas and skills. Information about the pupil's achievement in these respects can and should be obtained from the reports of previous teachers. Such reports, however, are usually indefinite. Jeff's low mark in arithmetic is a warning signal to the algebra teacher. But the teacher needs to know more: whether the trouble lies in Jeff's ability to think through problems, in his skill in fundamentals, or in a few special topics such as percentage.

To be most helpful for guidance, the school record should contain diagnostic statements. Sometimes the school's report to parents contains a partial description of the pupil's special interests and assets and of the areas of behavior where he particularly needs to improve. In other schools, the teacher files a descriptive statement, which future teachers of this pupil can use. Even these reports may have faults. Each teacher stresses certain aspects of the pupil's development and may overlook weaknesses in other areas. The teacher may have given relatively little attention to some pupils, so he will not know their individual weaknesses. Finally, despite all care in note-writing, the description is likely to be ambiguous. "Needs drill in fundamentals" may be written when the teacher finds that the pupil is erratic in adding (which may or may not indicate a need for drill). In another case the phrase may be only an exasperated substitute for, "I've tried my best and can't determine where his difficulty lies."

The teacher who begins work with a new class will find past records most helpful in locating pupils for early diagnostic study. A standardized survey test given to all pupils is frequently helpful; the shorthand teacher can take advantage of a test of ability in English given for general guidance purposes, or may give such a test himself. More analytic tests may be applied to individuals who show weakness. Tests identifying specific areas of strength and weakness are available in many fields, the most widely used being tests of mathematical competence, English usage, and reading.

The teacher who understands the possible causes of difficulty can often make a sound diagnosis by observing a pupil individually. If a pupil is confused about his algebra, the teacher should observe as he works various problems aloud. Faulty reading and interpretation, weakness in fundamental concepts, failure to organize work, or erratic computation may be noticed. Skill in diagnostic observation is built up through practice or special training and is one of the chief differences between a person who merely knows his subject and one who can teach it well.

Just as certain personality problems require analysis by the school psychologist or some other specialist, there are some intellectual difficulties beyond the teacher's power to diagnose. Nelson (1961) discusses subtle brain damage as a disorder that can easily remain unrecognized unless the teacher asks for a specialist's evaluation. One sign is writing disturbances. Nelson mentions a 12-year-old who was asked to write from dictation, "The weather becomes cold in winter," and wrote, "The wearthe become cold in wather." Less severe symptoms of brain damage include short attention span, inflexibility of ideas, and poor sound discrimination. Diagnosis of such problems requires the help of medical specialists, psychologists, and speech pathologists, among others.

No pupil is just "poor in arithmetic" or "unable to spell." Even a seemingly general weakness is a sign of specific faults, of particular responses to particular situations that this pupil has not mastered. If the teacher can locate where the pupil goes off the track, he can then reteach the critical response. When Ralph attempts problems in bookkeeping, he tries to find percentages by guessing which number to divide into the other. The bookkeeping teacher who discovers this fault in procedure has a manageable task of reteaching; there would be no hope for Ralph if his teacher defined the problem only as, "Ralph is weak in arithmetic."

> **1.** Are the purposes of the teacher testing achievement at the end of the term the same as the purposes of a teacher testing the same pupils at the beginning of the next term? Should the tests used on the two occasions be similar?
>
> **2.** What specific difficulties might be mentioned in a record describing a student who is poor in written expression?
>
> **3.** Does "diagnosing" spelling mean anything other than listing all the words a pupil misses?

Study Skills and Work Methods

Study skills play the same part in schoolwork that handling hammer and plane play in carpentry. Map-reading, for example, is a study skill consisting of specific responses to situations. The pupil must recognize such conventions as the placement of north at the top of the map and the use of color to indicate altitude; he must be able to determine distances using the scale;

The map below shows an imaginary continent. The principal cities appear in alphabetical order, beginning near the top.

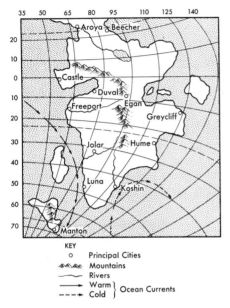

KEY
o   Principal Cities
⩕⩕⩕   Mountains
⌒⌒⌒   Rivers
⟶   Warm ⎫
╌╌►   Cold   ⎭ Ocean Currents

1. Which of these cities would probably have the highest average temperature?
   1) Duval   3) Jolar
   2) Hume   4) Koshin

2. Which of these most accurately describes the location of Aroya?
   1) 25°N, 90°W   3) 25°N, 70°E
   2) 25°N, 70°W   4) 25°S, 70°E

3. The river which goes through Koshin flows in what general direction?
   1) North   3) Southeast
   2) South   4) Southwest

45   *Questions to assess skill in map-reading (From the Iowa Test of Work-Study Skills. Copyright 1955 by the State University of Iowa and reproduced by permission.)*

and, in advanced work, he must make allowance for distortions introduced by projection. Pupils fail to profit as they should from atlases and geographies until they are taught map-reading.

Study skills are measured either in special tests for that purpose or in sections of general achievement batteries. One example is the "Work-Study Skills" section of the Iowa Every Pupil Tests. The form of this test intended for Grades III–IX contains sections on reading maps, graphs, tables, and charts and using indexes and dictionaries.

As with other achievements, the teacher can obtain evidence on study skills simply by alert observation. The teacher who finds a class confused about distances among the American colonies may suspect poor map-reading as a cause and check this suspicion by an informal exercise. Similarly, a discussion of library procedures or a small assignment in which information must be located will reveal gaps in library skills. Faults in these skills are readily identified and it is not hard to design activities that will lead to improvement.

In some ways more important, and much harder to identify and remedy, are faulty *habits* of work. The pupil can show skills on a test that he fails to use in his daily work. High-school and college students fail to schedule adequate time for study. Some who can write a well-organized theme for an English class neglect to outline their thoughts before writing a report in another subject. Pupils who are capable of checking arithmetic, and who know they must do this in their mathematics classes, turn in erroneous computations in the science laboratory rather than take the trouble of checking.

Teachers perform an important service by helping pupils to become critical of their own study practices. This is usually recognized as an objective in Grades IV through VII, though continual emphasis is needed at much higher levels. A questionnaire on which the student describes his customary methods of work, a log in which he records his study activities, and the critical inspection of actual work in progress are useful in the process of self-appraisal.

For secondary schools and colleges there are published questionnaires to identify students with inappropriate habits and attitudes. The California Study Methods Survey, for example, was formed by trying out numerous self-description items to find those which differentiate high-achieving pupils from low-achieving pupils of similar mental ability (Carter, 1958a). The questionnaire score correlates substantially with marks, but much less highly with general mental ability; in one sample, the correlations were .55 and .36, respectively (Carter, 1958b). Many of the responses that predict success are expressions of attitude: "I like school"; "teachers are fair"; "I believe in doing as well as I can." (A surprising number of pupils frankly express a negative attitude on such questions.) The study procedures associated with success are perhaps of greater significance, since they can be taught directly.

Among the techniques more commonly used by effective students are these:

Trying to foresee questions that might be asked about a reading assignment

Planning an orderly sequence for papers and essay test answers

Looking for relationships among ideas, within a subject, and from one subject to another

Drilling themselves deliberately on details in foreign language and geography

Studying alone when possible

Studying by reciting material to themselves

Studying each subject nearly every day

These statements, put together, present a picture of determined effort. The effective student tries to understand as much of his assignment as he can, then turns to memorization to master elusive details. Some techniques that

on the surface appear to represent diligent study are associated with inferior attainment, including the following:

Repeated reading of the assignment
Writing down rules of grammar or summaries of chapters of novels
Copying extensive notes from books
Talking the lesson over with another person

Ineffective students do not concentrate, because their work seems purposeless or hopelessly difficult. They ignore parts of the assigned work
because they do not expect to be tested on it. Thinking that teachers want
them to memorize details, they lose sight of the central theme of an assigned passage. They wait until the last minute to write a paper, instead
of allowing it to mature through successive outlines and drafts. In sum,
they are unable to recognize what is important.

Bad study habits are in large measure created by teaching that rewards
bad practices (Bruner, 1959).

> In a social studies class of an elementary school in a well-to-do suburb of
> one of our great eastern cities, I saw groups of twelve-year-old children doing
> a "project" on the southeastern states. Each team was gathering facts that
> might eventually end up on a . . . chart. . . . The fact-gathering was atom-
> ized and episodic. Here were the industrial products of North Carolina. There
> was the list of the five principal cities of Georgia. I asked the children of one
> team what life would be like and what people would worry about in a place
> where the principal products were peanuts, cotton, and peaches. The question
> was greeted as "unfair."

College students flock to reading clinics because they are unable to cover
their assignments. Those coming to the reading clinic at Harvard rank in
the top 15 per cent of all college freshmen in the nation in reading ability.
They work diligently. But when asked to sit down and study a chapter of
history as he would for an assignment, only one in ten makes any effort
to look ahead, to read the chapter summary first, or to make sense of the
chapter as a whole before slogging off into the marsh of disorganized facts
(W. G. Perry, 1959).

Further evidence that they cannot judge what learning is worthwhile
appeared when they were asked to grade two essay responses to this test
question:

> "From 1066–1272, the Norman and Angevin kings laid the foundations of Eng-
> lish self-government both by their strengths and by their weaknesses." Discuss.
> (Twenty minutes)

One essay was as factual as an encyclopedia and as little pointed toward
the quotation: any fact, about any king, tossed onto the collection plate.
The other was a neat essay going to the heart of the question, with no

names of kings and dates of incidents on display. About a third of the students thought the first essay deserved a higher grade, or preferred the second essay and gave the wrong reason. "A C-minus," says Perry, "for the attainment of useless knowledge is perhaps less of a kindness in the long run than congratulations for effort and a clean *E* for expending it in the wrong game."

4. What specific knowledge is called for in each map-reading item (Figure 45)?

5. On the basis of the information given about the Iowa Test of Work-Study Skills, when do you think would be the best time to administer it? To which pupils? To whom should the results be given?

6. Some students need the ability to read shop drawings. List several specific skills included in this type of readiness.

7. What explanations can be suggested for the fact that writing down rules of grammar is associated with ineffective study?

8. What explanation can be suggested for the fact that studying alone tends to be correlated with higher marks among pupils matched in ability?

MEASURING GENERAL SCHOLASTIC APTITUDE

To judge a pupil's potentialities for succeeding in a course of instruction we need information on the abilities the instruction will require. Some of these are measured in reading tests, tests of study skills, and the tests of knowledge acquired in previous courses. Ability to perform school tasks, however, depends on more than knowledge of school subject matter from previous years. The pupil must comprehend words, think in abstract terms, see relationships quickly, and so on. One who can do these things best will have an advantage in studying almost any new material.

General scholastic aptitude refers to a group of mental abilities that work together to increase success in intellectual activities. An important discovery made about 1900 is that mental performances hang together. It was once a popular belief that Nature had kindly provided for compensation in abilities. This theory held that the person who is inept in one area need only continue searching to discover another area in which he is richly endowed. The idea that abilities are uncorrelated, or even that one great ability implies severe deficiencies elsewhere, is found in the folk beliefs that beauties tend to be dumb and brilliant children to be weaklings. A related idea is that those who excel at school tasks are not likely to do well in practical affairs. Test results show that correlation rather than compensation is the rule. Good memory tends to be accompanied by superior comprehension and flexibility of thought. A child superior in vocabulary tends also to do well on a nonverbal task such as a jigsaw puzzle. A person who has the intellectual powers required by one school subject can be expected to succeed in most other subjects, though there are some specialized aptitudes.

It is often convenient to use a single, heterogeneous mental test to estimate the pupil's probable success in all intellectual activities. We refer to such tests as measures of general scholastic aptitude rather than as intelligence tests for two reasons. Too often "intelligence" is thought of as something inborn and unchangeable, whereas performance on these tests is substantially affected by experience. We want to emphasize too that these tests stress abilities more relevant to the verbal, symbolic, convergent problems of the school than to other types of intelligent action. Although abilities hang together, there is more than one important talent. Every person does better on some types of problems than on others.

Individual Tests

The best-established tests of general ability are the Stanford-Binet and Wechsler scales. These are individual tests that can only be administered by a specially trained tester. They are important in the clinical study of individual children and in research. Group tests are economical, but they afford no opportunity for observation and cover a relatively limited variety of tasks.

The first successful mental test, by the French psychologist Alfred Binet, was developed about 1905 to decide whether a pupil's educational difficulties should be attributed to intellectual limitations rather than to insufficient effort or poor teaching. There have been numerous revisions of the scale to increase its accuracy; the latest version is "Form L-M of the Stanford Revision of the Binet Scale"—Stanford-Binet L-M, for short (Terman and Merrill, 1960). This test, requiring about an hour, is a "ladder" beginning with tasks suitable for 2-year-olds ("Put the button in the box") and ascending in difficulty to problems that tax average college students. The tester presents items a bit below the subject's expected level to give him a running start, and continues up the scale until he fails several tasks in a row.

A few of the tasks in the scale are as follows:

YEAR IV

Recalls name of simple object (e.g., a toy dog) after it is covered by a box.
Completes *Brother is a boy; sister is a* _____.

YEAR IX

Examiner folds paper over twice and cuts notch from one corner; child draws sketch to show how the paper will look when unfolded.
Repeats *8-5-2-6* backward.

YEAR XIV

Tells how to get 13 pints of water, using 9-pint and 5-pint cans.
Tells how *beginning* and *end* are alike.

Most of the items require a performance that has not been practiced; they require the subject to take ideas from his past experience, apply them to a novel situation or question, and work out an answer. A few items call for straight recall of vocabulary, or arithmetic reasoning. The tester has opportunities to observe the child's carefulness and reaction to difficulty, and to note specific errors that may suggest an explanation for his difficulties.

An even better basis for observation is provided by the Wechsler scales (WISC for children, WAIS for adults). These scales are organized into subtests, each of which contains a different type of task. Half the tasks are "performance tests" in which the responses are actions or very simple verbal expressions. These are likely to be an important supplement to verbal tasks, especially for testing persons who have little familiarity with English. The subtests of the WISC are as follows:

VERBAL SCALE

Information	What makes water boil? Where is Argentina? What does the heart do?
Comprehension	Understanding of everyday affairs is tested: e.g., why a promise should be kept, why cloth is made from cotton fiber.
Similarities	How are *mountain* and *lake* alike?
Arithmetic	Eighteen is two-thirds of what number?
Vocabulary	Defines words ranging from *bicycle* to *traduce*.

PERFORMANCE SCALE

Coding	Translates a simple message using a letter-substitution code.
Mazes	Traces, without error, the path through a maze.
Picture Arrangement	Arrange in sensible order six cards carrying cartoons that make a story.
Picture Completion	Simple drawings are shown in which something is missing (e.g., the buttonholes in a coat).
Object Assembly	A cutout face is chopped into about eight segments; the child is to assemble the picture within three minutes.
Block Design	Arranges cubical blocks to match a mosaic pattern.

The WISC is recommended for ages 7 to 15, after which the similarly designed adult scale is used.

A single IQ is obtained for the test as a whole. The verbal and performance sections of the Wechsler can also be scored separately. Verbal IQ and Performance IQ correlate about .60 among pupils of the same age; these superficially distinct intellectual performances have a good deal in common.

Quite a few pupils, however, do much better on one section than on the other, and such a discrepancy may be highly significant. If the performance score is much higher than the verbal, one suspects that the pupil's verbal development has been impaired by, for example, hearing little English at home. When the verbal score is much higher than the performance score, one explanation to consider is that emotional difficulties are reducing the pupil's efficiency and causing careless mistakes.

Group Tests

A group test is limited to items that can be administered by reading simple directions and answered by a mark on paper. With a very few exceptions designed for the early grades, group tests are in a multiple-choice form that can be scored mechanically. Objective, high-speed scoring is especially important in college admissions and scholarship testing where thousands of scores must be compiled.

A representative test of particular interest is the Scholastic Aptitude Test (SAT) of the College Entrance Examination Board. This has separately scored verbal and quantitative sections. The verbal items call for judicious use of vocabulary. Items such as the following will, it is hoped, favor the intellectually competent student rather than the one who has merely crammed his head with uncommon words.

COMPLETION: [1] In college courses we expose students to the _____ of art, but in lower schools we often think that the creative activities of children would be _____ by knowledge of the past.

(a) techniques . . . inspired　　(b) masterpieces . . . contaminated
(c) prospects . . . decreased　　(d) fertility . . . restrained
(e) significance . . . suggested

FIND THE OPPOSITE: Exaggeration: (a) slight misunderstanding　(b) silence
(c) accurate representation　(d) truth　(e) understatement

ANALOGY: Bicycle is to locomotion as _____ is to _____.
(a) canoe: paddle　(b) hero: worship　(c) hay: horse　(d) spectacles: vision
(e) statement: contention

In another type of verbal item the student selects the best of several interpretations for a paragraph from college text material.

The quantitative section calls for mathematical reasoning. The specific mathematical principles to be applied are common subject matter that all pupils with two years of high-school mathematics have probably studied, but they must be applied intelligently. In problems like the following, the given information must be combined in just the right way:

[1] Items here and below, copyright 1956, 1960 by the College Entrace Examination Board and reproduced by permission.

The mortality rates for three diseases are as follows: disease X, 7 per 100,000; disease Y, 2 per 10,000; disease Z, 11 per 1,000,000. (Five statements are made regarding the relative seriousness of the diseases; the student is to pick the best interpretation.)

Which of the following fractions is greater than ⅔ and less than ¾?

(a) ⅝   (b) ⅘   (c) ⁷⁄₁₂   (d) ⁹⁄₁₆   (e) ⁷⁄₁₀

If the 9″ x 12″ piece of paper shown in this figure were folded flat by creasing along the line PQ, how many inches closer would the points R and S be?

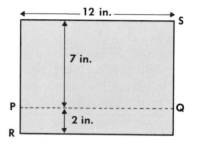

It can be seen that the SAT is very nearly a work sample of the interpretation and problem-solving required in college, leaving out knowledge of specific subject matter. A person who cannot do these tests will have great trouble in college.

General scholastic aptitude tests for lower grades are sometimes very much like SAT. They measure developed abilities (e.g., reasoning with fractions and exact word usage) that can be turned directly to use in comprehending tomorrow's lesson. Other tests include more varied tasks, ranging from highly verbal, school-like items to problems independent of past schooling. The Kuhlmann-Anderson items in Figure 46 are used from kindergarten through high school. Each pupil takes subtests appropriate for his own level; tests 8 to 17 are rated as suitable for Grade II, but a second-grader who does well on these can be given advanced tests to appraise his full range of ability. A test of this sort, requiring controlled manipulation of ideas, undoubtedly measures intellectual development.

Most pupils rank on this test as they do on an achievement test. When both tests are given at the same time to pupils in a single grade, correlations above .80 are expected. This correlation is high enough to indicate that the group aptitude test and the achievement test reflect much the same abilities. The general aptitude measure is primarily used in testing groups of students who have diverse educational backgrounds—for example, when several elementary schools feed into the same junior high school. If the elementary schools have different programs, no achievement test gives a completely fair opportunity to all the pupils.

There are always a few pupils whose aptitude and achievement scores are noticeably unequal. Some of these discrepancies are random variations

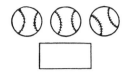

Test 2. Picture errors. "Put a dot on the part that is wrong."	Test 5. Pattern Completion. "Put in the stick that is left out of the second figure."	Test 8. Counting. "Put as many dots in the box as there are balls"

Test 10. Copying. (The square with lines is held up before the class for 10 seconds.)

top rattle doll
sled playing

Test 21. Classification. "Find the one that does not belong with the others."

old rich wide
poor green full

Test 23. Opposites. "Find the two opposites."

robin winter horse
song squirrel fence

Test 26. Similarities. "Find the three things which are alike."

N-B-U-M-E-R
N_ _ _ _ _ _ _ _

Test 28. Anagrams. "You are given the first letter. Write the rest of the word."

inaudible distinct
deafening faint loud

Test 32. Arrangement. "If these were arranged in order, which would be the middle one?"

Basket
Picture

Test 34. Directions. "If the word contains E but not R nor I write 3 after it."

5 6 8 11 15

Test 39. Number series. "Write the two numbers which should come next."

46 *A representative group test of general mental ability (Items copyright 1952, 1960, 1962, by Personnel Press, Inc. and reproduced by permission.)*

Items selected from the 7th edition of the Kuhlmann-Anderson test series. The directions used in testing are much simpler and more complete than these abbreviated quotations suggest.

due, for example, to change in effort from day to day. But the test detects a small residual group of "underachievers" with greater mental ability than their achievement suggests. When our interest is in predicting who will do best in subsequent schoolwork, we are wise to bet on the pupil whose demonstrated achievement is high, rather than the pupil whose aptitude is above his achievement. The former's abilities are already harnessed to production. But the pupil who shows to advantage on the mental test is

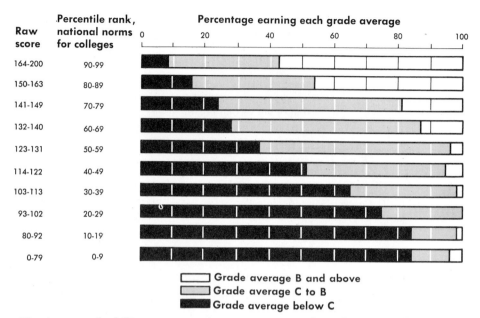

47   *A general ability measure forecasts expected freshman grades (Data courtesy of The Psychological Corporation.)*

Based on a study of the College Qualification Test, showing first-semester grade averages earned at a midwestern state university by men at each score level.

well worth careful study. If an impediment (vision? reading? tension? poor relations with teachers?) can be found and removed, he should achieve at a much higher level.

It should be obvious that all the tests depend on learned concepts and attitudes, and not solely on the biological development of the brain. To follow directions calls not only for verbal comprehension, but also for the attitude that in the test it is important to be self-critical. Even the idea that one should do one's best must be learned.

9. Wechsler says (1949, p. 5):

"It is not possible to identify or equate general intelligence with intellectual ability. . . . Intelligence is part of a larger whole, namely personality itself. The theory underlying the *WISC* is that intelligence cannot be separated from the rest of the personality, and a deliberate attempt has been made to take into account the other factors which contribute to the total effective intelligence of the individual."

What does this mean? In what way do "nonintellective factors" appear in the Wechsler scale? Is this an advantage or disadvantage in judging the readiness of a possibly retarded child for regular schooling?

10. A Puerto Rican boy, age 9, has recently come to the mainland with his family. When he enters school, his WISC Performance score is slightly below average for his age and his Verbal score is below the average for 7-year-olds. What interpretation can be made?

11. Explain the finding that a nonverbal performance test predicts adjustment in the community by mentally retarded young men better than the Stanford-Binet does (Porteus, 1939).

GENERAL PRINCIPLES OF TEST USAGE

We now turn to a general statement about what tests try to do and what errors of measurement are likely to occur.

The Test as a Work Sample

When we want to know if there is enough gold in a hill to be worth bringing ore to market, we take a sample of all the ore; when we want to know whether a certain brand of canned peaches is Grade A or Grade B, we sample from the total pack of peaches. We examine the sample carefully, and from the sample judge the quality of the whole. The teacher who wants to know about all of a pupil's behavior must be content with observing a sample. All testing procedures for psychological analysis and educational evaluation are based on the *work sample* principle. Out of all the tasks or topics in an area, we present a small sample as a test. It is essential that the sample be fairly representative of the defined area, and large enough so that the results are little affected by accidental factors.

VALIDITY.   The first critical question about a testing procedure is how well it represents the segment of behavior it is intended to measure. A social-studies teacher might use the Iowa test (Figure 45) to determine which pupils are likely to have difficulty in using maps during his course. The test is appropriate only if the map-reading skills required by the test are those his course calls for. If technical geographic vocabulary (*Tropic of Cancer, meridian*) will be needed in class discussions, vocabulary items measure something important to readiness. If, instead, the class will be studying trade routes, perhaps items on estimation of distances should appear in the work sample. A published test distributes items over a broad field. This is like drawing the sample of ore from various parts of the mountain, or drawing the peaches to be examined from different boxes. If the tasks presented by a test are a sample of the situations the pupil will encounter in the future, and credit is given for the type of response one wishes to know about, the test is said to be a *valid* measure. (For further discussion, see page 544.)

No test is valid for every purpose. A reading test that measures ability to obtain facts rapidly from a passage will be useful to some teachers. It is not very pertinent, however, in deciding how well pupils identify the central thought running through many sentences. As another example, you will recall that problem checklist responses are a useful catalogue of the pupil's concerns, but that the total numerical score signifies little.

ACCURACY.   No test is perfectly accurate. The lucky pupil encounters several questions he is familiar with and gets a higher score than classmates with equal ability. Another pupil becomes confused and earns a lower score than he deserves. Interpretation must bear in mind that any single test is only an estimate based on a sample of performance; other questions, another day, or another examiner would produce a somewhat different score.

One principal of a small school wondered how much faith he could put in IQs from group tests, and investigated by following one test with another a month later. First he used the Henmon-Nelson Test, then the California Test of Mental Maturity. The roll of the sophomore class in Table 10 shows important discrepancies. If only the first test had been given, teachers would expect Doug Axton to do normal work. If they had only the second record, they would probably regard him as a borderline case, unable to carry a regular high-school program. Francis Howard, who seemed certain to present problems according to the first measure, is reported as normal on the second. Accuracy of interpretation is increased by using especially long tests for important decisions such as college admission, retesting where there is any reason to regard the pupil's score as unrepresentative of his ability, and considering the score along with all other facts about his ability. Another important aspect of interpretation—stability over time—is left for discussion in the next chapter.

Accuracy is primarily determined by test length, because taking a larger sample of performance improves the estimate. Ambiguous questions, inexact scoring, and momentary confusion of the pupil also lower accuracy. Test manuals describe accuracy of measurement in two ways. A *reliability coefficient* is the correlation between two measurements, usually with two forms of the test. When a test provides several scores, as the Kuder Preference Record does, each score has its own reliability. For women, such reliability coefficients as the following are reported: Computational, .88; Persuasive, .87; Literary, .90. Though these values fall short of 1.00, they are high enough to indicate that the score obtained on one testing would probably be confirmed by a second testing.

TABLE 10

Records of high-school sophomores on two mental tests (*Knezevich, 1946*)

Name	Henmon-Nelson IQ	California IQ one mo. later	Difference
1. Axton, Doug	95	80	−15
2. Barnes, Glenn	119	121	2
3. Borden, May	109	110	1
4. Charles, Ernest	88	86	−2
5. Davis, Marshall	96	93	−3
6. Duncan, James	91	98	7
7. Edgerton, Dorothy	87	85	−2
8. Filson, Donald	117	92	−25
9. Gorham, Helen	98	95	−3
10. Grant, Lloyd	127	115	−12
11. Harris, Cora	103	87	−16
12. Howard, Francis	69	107	39
13. Hurt, George	124	106	−18
14. Kirk, George	108	104	−4
15. Lawrence, Kenneth	99	103	4
16. Lee, Max	102	87	−15
17. Logan, Gertrude	99	97	−2
18. Meadow, Adolph	99	104	5
19. Olsen, Ralph	110	100	−10
20. Petersen, Lola	118	118	0
21. Pollack, Mary	107	99	−8
22. Sanders, Willa	103	94	−9
23. Smith, Viola	105	88	−17
24. Stroup, Guy	95	84	−11
25. Tanner, Charles	93	83	−10
26. Thompson, Jerry	101	92	−9
27. Vance, Marie	122	116	−6
28. Wilson, William	123	114	−9

The accuracy of a single score may be described by the *standard error of measurement*. Testers can use the standard error to set limits to the "true" score that would be obtained from a very long, perfectly accurate test. The chances are two to one that the true score is within one standard error of the score actually obtained. (This statement depends upon mathematical assumptions that we cannot examine here. See Gulliksen, 1950.) If Mary's score on computational interests is 36 points, and the standard error of measurement is 3 points, her true score is likely to fall in the range 33 to 39 (36 plus or minus 3). The corresponding range in percentiles is 92 to 98, according to the norms for women. Figure 44 showed Mary's interests by plotting a band on each scale; the width of the band reminds us that we do not know the precise strength of each interest. Seeing the overlap of bands, we are not tempted, for example, to conclude that her clerical interest is truly higher than her mechanical interest.

Although the older practice in recording scores and profiles was to write down the pupil's exact score, it is better to record the uncertainty band whenever the standard error is known. One recent achievement test (Sequential Tests of Educational Progress) has designed its norm table so that, knowing the pupil's score, one reads the corresponding uncertainty band directly from the table. This practice will be increasingly common.

The person selecting a test must ask two questions. First, is the test accurate enough (reliable enough) for my purposes? For some decisions an approximate measure serves well enough. Approximate measures are suitable to determine a class or school average because in the average errors of measurement tend to balance out. They are also suitable for preliminary estimates that can be checked by later observation or interview. A short, not too reliable interest inventory, for example, can be confirmed or contradicted in the counseling interview.

Second, does the test give the information I want? That is, is it relevant to my purposes? The question about reliability asks whether or not the sample of behavior taken by the test is large enough to give a dependable estimate. The question about relevance (i.e., about validity) asks whether or not the test samples the right things. An accurate test is not of much value if it gives precise information about an irrelevant quality.

12. Is a composition on the assigned topic "A Happy Holiday" a valid and accurate work sample of ability to write well?

13. In what sense is a personality questionnaire dealing with social relationships a work sample?

14. Can a test manual provide information from which to judge validity, or must this be judged by the teacher through a study of the test items?

15. The reliability of subtests of the Test of Work-Study Skills is lower than that for the total score (e.g., in Grade IV, .84 for Map Reading compared with .93 for Work-Study total). Explain.

16. Colleges usually ask a high school to provide a rating of seniors who apply for admission. How can the accuracy of such information be studied? What factors would lower the accuracy of ratings?

17. A pupil's reading score is reported as 60 and his vocabulary score as 75, comparable scales being used for the two measures. What do we gain from the information that the standard error of each score is approximately 2 points? What if the standard error were 15 points?

18. On October 1, a reading test gave an uncertainty band for Leon of 250–282 words per minute. On November 1, after special reading exercises, the uncertainty band is 262–291. What interpretation appears to be warranted by these facts?

19. Are we certain that the true score falls within one standard error of the observed score for the individual?

Distinguishing Typical Performance from Ability

We may seek information either about a pupil's ability (how well he can do a task if he tries) or about his typical performance (how well he usually does). A person does not ordinarily put forth all-out effort; his normal reading speed, his normal concentration during study, or the grammatical quality of his everyday speech falls short of his ability. The usual test of ability indicates what a person *can* do but not what he *will* do.

MEASURING ABILITY.   In order to sample ability, we need only set up a situation in which pupils know what they are to do and are motivated to try. Pupils learn, even in the primary grades, to try hard on a school test. The ability test gives a sample of the pupil's *performance-on-this-task-with-strong-school-motivation.*

Test performance does not reflect ability when a pupil does not care about school, feels that he cannot win the teacher's approval, or for some reason does not want a good score. Sometimes a pupil holds back because the rewards for a poor performance (as seen by the pupil) seem to be greater than those for a good one. There was, for example, the boy who gave stupid answers on a test because, knowing that his closest friend would not be promoted, he wished to be kept in the same grade also. Seeing a low test score, the teacher cannot know whether it represents low ability or faulty motivation. The low score is only a signal that something is amiss.

MEASURING TYPICAL PERFORMANCE.   In order to sample typical performance, we must somehow estimate the pupil's *performance-on-this-task-with-ordinary-motivation.* Ordinary motivation is not constant, so we can at best sample performance on many different occasions and take an average. To learn how consistently a boy concentrates during study periods, we have to observe him when he is rested and when he is tired, when his friends are in the room and when they are absent, when he is preparing for a test and when he has no special goal. The more samples of performance we take, the more likely it is that the over-all impression will truly represent his average behavior. We cannot observe normal study habits if he knows we are testing him; if he did, he would quickly put on his best behavior. For this reason, the teacher observes inconspicuously. Since the teacher must observe over and over again to obtain a composite picture that represents any pupil's typical performance, precise data will rarely be gathered.

A self-report is used as a substitute; instead of placing an observer on the pupil's trail, we ask him to describe his own behavior, as in the interest inventory. As we saw in the preceding chapter, self-report cannot be taken at face value. Discrepancies between actual behavior and a report arise in several ways. The pupil may not realize how he acts. He may not be willing to reveal the truth. He will find some questions ambiguous. His report is most likely to be truthful if he does not expect criticism, whatever his answer. The self-report is probably best seen as a statement of how the pupil wants the school to view him.

> **20.** On which of the following would you expect self-report to be relatively accurate: intelligence, subjects causing greatest difficulty, interests, names of best friends, use of slang in conversation?
>
> **21.** When a teacher administers a questionnaire on study methods, what can be done to increase the number of truthful reports?

Use of Norms

Scores are generally interpreted on a comparative basis. If we know that Anna expresses liking for 18 persuasive activities out of 30, we cannot immediately say whether this is an unusually strong interest or a weak one. No one likes every activity in a category. We therefore take the average for similar pupils into account. If Anna's score of 18 is much above average for girls, we can think of her as showing exceptional readiness to enjoy persuasive activity. But the average is not the sole basis for judgment. The teacher may decide that 18 "likes" out of 30 possible is a rather low level of enthusiasm even though it is *relatively* high.

In order to find out what performance is to be expected on a published test, the teacher often has recourse to *norms* based on other pupils of the same age and grade. Such norms show how difficult a test proved to be for a large number of pupils in a given grade. They guard against the teacher's possible tendency to set unreasonably high expectations for his class. Supervisors wishing to judge the success of instruction use norms to compare the school or community average with the national average for the same grade. Unless the comparison is made with schools enrolling comparable pupils, such interpretations may be misleading. The bright children in a well-to-do suburb are likely to surpass in achievement the national average for all schools even if their school's program is inferior. The national average, moreover, is by no means as good as it could or should be.

Just as the school should be compared with schools "in its own league," the pupil's accomplishment can best be judged by comparing him with others of similar ability. A bright boy who reads slightly *better* than the average pupil still should have special assistance. To facilitate such interpretations, some tests are now provided with tables or charts such as Figure 48. The achievement normally found among pupils in a certain grade and with a certain mental age is indicated by the "anticipated score" line on the chart. The individual pupil's mental age (defined below) and achievement score are used to locate a point. If the point falls far to the right of the line (e.g., Mental age 180, Reading 65), he is performing better than typical pupils of like general aptitude; he would be called an overachiever

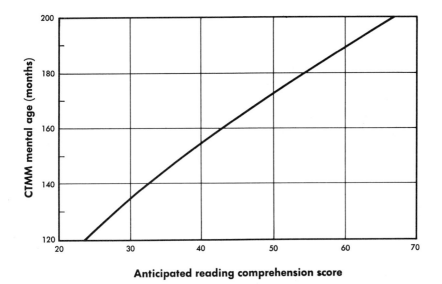

Anticipated reading comprehension score

48 *Norms indicate expected achievement*

Redesigned from the Grade VII expectancy chart for the California Achievement Tests. Mental age is based on the California Test of Mental Maturity.

If he falls far to the left, he is doing less well than others like him. Note that the pupil is compared with others of the same mental age, not the same IQ; the reason for this will appear in the next section.

SCORE INTERPRETATION.   Test scores are reported in various forms, the most prominent being raw scores, age or grade equivalents, percentiles, and standard scores. The *raw score* is the number obtained by applying the scoring key to the test. Usually it is a count of the number of right answers. On a multiple-choice test a special formula is used. If four choices are allowed, the scoring formula is usually $R - \frac{1}{3} W$; with three choices, $R - \frac{1}{2} W$. More generally, if there are n alternatives, the raw score is $R - (1/n - 1)W$. This is a correction intended to permit a fairer comparison of the cautious pupil and the pupil who takes more chances and hence gets more items right. The raw score depends on the number and difficulty of test items.

The raw score may be converted to an age or grade equivalent. If the pupil does as well as the average 9-year-old, we say that his mental age is 9. The pupil's *mental age* (MA) is the age at which the average child earns this pupil's raw score. One could similarly express any characteristic that increases with age (height, reading, etc.) in terms of age equivalents. For educational attainments *grade equivalents* are used. Whatever raw score the average pupil earns at the start of the fourth grade, for example, is converted to a grade equivalent score of 4.0.

Scores in percentile form are often most useful for teachers. Such a score compares the pupil directly with his fellows. The percentile (or centile) scale gives a ranking, expressed on a scale from 1 (low) to 99 (high). If 25 per cent of a reference group surpasses a certain raw score, that score is said to fall at the 75th percentile. That is to say, the *percentile score* tells what proportion of some reference group the pupil surpasses. One may calculate percentile standing within a single class, or from a national sample of pupils from a certain grade, or from any other group whose score distribution is known.

Another scale that compares the pupil with a reference group is the *standard score*. This is less easily explained than the percentile scale. The standard-score scale is based on the standard deviation, which is a measure of the spread of scores in the reference group. For our purposes, we can think of the standard deviation as half the distance between the 16th and 84th percentiles. (A more fundamental formula is given in statistics texts.) The mean raw score—i.e., the average—is arbitrarily set equal to 50 on the standard-score scale. Whatever raw score is one standard deviation (s.d.) above the mean is changed to a standard score of 60 (see Figure 49). A standard score of 80 is immediately interpretable as falling 3 s.d. above the mean of the reference group. This type of conversion will be clarified by an example.

> John takes a reading test, earning a raw score of 64.
> For his grade, the national average is 50.
> The s.d. of the national sample is 7.

John is 14 points—2 standard deviations—above the mean, so his standard score is 70, or $50 + (2 \times 10)$. Teachers never have to make such conversions. A conversion table is provided in the test manual, where the teacher can read directly that in this grade the raw score 64 equals the standard score 70.

The standard-score scale serves much the same purpose as the percentile scale. When scores are normally distributed there is a direct correspondence between the two, as Figure 49 shows. The table also shows that IQs (intelligence quotients) are a type of standard score. Instead of setting the mean equal to 50, we set it at 100. And instead of adding 10 points for each standard deviation, we add 16 points to get an IQ. An IQ of 132 indicates that the pupil's raw score is 2 s.d. above the mean for his age group. This unique scale has a 50-year history; the quotient was originally actually obtained in quite a different manner, now obsolete. The only reason for using the IQ scale rather than ordinary standard scores is that teachers and laymen have become familiar with IQs and are not yet familiar with the 50 ± 10 scale.

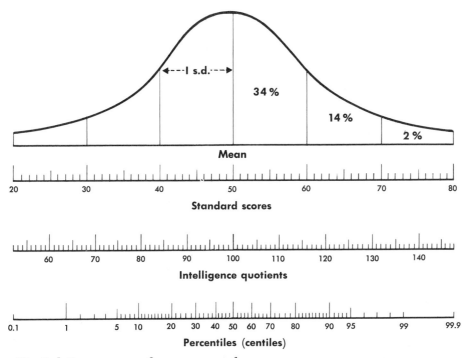

49 *Relations among three score scales*

This figure is helpful in answering such questions as these, which any teacher encounters from time to time:

Fred's IQ is 120. His mechanical comprehension is reported as at the 80th percentile. How do these scores compare?

Is Jerry's IQ of 130 very unusual?

Equal steps on the standard-score scale do not correspond to equal steps on the percentile scale. A small rise from the 98th to the 99th percentile ordinarily implies a large difference in standard score and in raw score. Because there are few pupils toward the extremes of the distribution, neighboring ranks represent large differences in ability.

The IQ, the standard score, and the percentile are all statements about the pupil's performance relative to others of the same age or grade. In comparing pupils of mixed age, the mental age predicts performance better than the IQ does. Consider three girls in Grade VI. Ethel is 10½ years old, Ruth is 12, and Joan is 13. (Such differences arise through variation in admission and promotion policies, transfer of pupils from school to school, loss of time through illness, and other causes.) If these girls solve exactly the same problems on a scholastic aptitude test, they will have the same raw score and the same mental age—say, 13. So far as we can judge from this test, we would expect them to do equally well in this year's schoolwork. Their minds seem well matched at present. But their IQs differ a great deal because each girl is compared to a different age group. Ethel's IQ is about 120, Ruth's is 107, and Joan's is 100. For grouping pupils or for predicting individual achievement in the near future, the raw score or the mental age is a better index of present readiness than the IQ or the standard score. When the group is uniform in age, of course, the IQ and the MA lead to the same conclusion.

22. Could superior high-school instruction raise the graduate's SAT score? If so, how? Does this mean that his aptitude for college has been improved?

23. A pupil in Grade VII has a mental age of 140 months and a reading score of 40. What interpretation can be made, knowing that the class average in reading is 50? How does the interpretation change when the information in Figure 48 is used?

24. Should an expectancy chart such as Figure 48 be based on national norms, on norms for the school system, or on the performance of the class to which the pupil belongs?

25. A pupil who falls to the right of the line in Figure 48 is often called an overachiever. Is overachievement good or bad? Is it possible for a pupil to achieve "beyond his capacity"?

26. Mental ages of 12-year-olds spread much more widely than those of 6-year-olds. Why?

27. Interpret each of these scores as fully as possible using Figure 49.
   a. Pete is at the 40th percentile for his grade.
   b. Steve has a standard score of 75.
   c. Mike has an IQ of 110 and is 10 years old.

APTITUDES AND GUIDANCE

Significance of General Scholastic Aptitude

Tests of general scholastic aptitude usually collect norms for all children of a given age in the nation (or of all children in school) by testing a representative sample. These norms do not describe the distribution in a community or in a class. Though an IQ of 90 is near the 45th percentile nationally, in an underprivileged community this score is likely to be above average. An IQ of 90 may be in the bottom 10 per cent of pupils in a high school serving mostly professional families. Dropouts are much more common at the lower end of the scale, especially at the legal age for leaving school. A study made during the 1940's (Dillon, 1949) found that 86 per cent of the seventh-graders with IQs above 115 continued to graduation. In the IQ range 85–94, only 54 per cent remained that long, dropouts being most numerous in Grades IX and X. The median IQ of high-school graduates is about 105.

College students are a selected group, though college attendance is determined by many factors other than ability. An able girl is less likely to go to college than an average boy from the same graduating class, and she is more likely to drop out after a year or two than a male student of equal ability. Family attitude, financial resources, and the pupil's insight into his own ability are important determiners (Kahl, 1953).

Although the rising tide of applications is forcing long-established colleges to become increasingly selective, there is at the same time a rapid growth in the number of collegiate institutions, particularly community colleges that provide both vocational and liberal arts instruction. Each college has its own ability range; a freshman who would rank in the lowest quarter at one institution might be superior in another school. Figure 50 reports score distributions in several institutions. No one mental-test level defines the college-capable student; even a pupil with IQ 95 may succeed if he selects a suitable college and a suitable curriculum, if he is strongly motivated, and if he gets help in overcoming emotional problems or deficiencies in his basic skills. Harmon (1961) indeed finds that one out of every 30 Ph.D.'s was recorded by his high school as having an IQ below 100. Cantoni (1954) tells of a boy with an IQ of 93 (according to repeated tests in Grade IX) who ultimately became a lawyer. This boy showed evident signs of maladjustment, which no doubt impaired both his test score and his schoolwork. Encouragement from a counselor helped him toward a more positive attitude in school; an intermission for military service also contributed to his maturity. Such exceptional cases warn against taking the mental test or academic record as a final verdict on a student's promise. But these cases *are* exceptions. Considering any large number of students, the risk of failure in college increases with each step down the IQ scale (see Figure 47).

A reasonable guide for interpreting mental test scores is this rule: Every pupil above standard-score 60 (IQ 116) should think seriously about going to college; no pupil below standard-score 50 (IQ 100) should plan on a four-year college course unless the counselor has evidence that his score is held down by specific handicaps that remedial help can remove. This rule is deliberately left inexact; it recognizes that neither a favorable nor an unfavorable prediction can be made in the borderline 50–60 range, that final decisions must rest on many facts other than the test score, and that education can be continued in other ways than a four-year college course.

TIMING OF DECISIONS.   Decisions about college are not to be made at any single moment in the pupil's career. Over many years he and his parents should form a realistic picture of his probable performance, and should set their eyes on a suitable educational goal. Grade IV is none too early

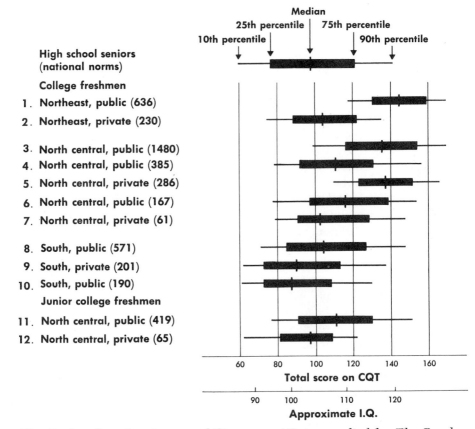

50 *Each college has its own ability range (Data supplied by The Psychological Corporation, through the courtesy of Harold Seashore.)*

Score distribution for all men in the freshman classes of selected institutions during a year in the late 1950's. The test used is the College Qualification Test.

to begin the systematic identification and encouragement of talent. An able pupil often does well in the elementary grades, coasting through without realizing his own competence. About Grade VII, the work becomes harder and he can do well only by making a serious effort. He encounters the stiffer demands and more systematic assignments of the junior high school just at the age when sports, dating, and a part-time job put in competing bids for time and interest. Some families have a tradition that makes it fairly certain that their sons will choose an academic curriculum and put forth a reasonable effort. But other boys may receive more parental encouragement in their recreations and their jobs than in determined study. Parents teach many American boys that the only reason for finishing high school is that this promises a more satisfactory job.

When parents have low aspirations, a boy is unlikely to choose an academic curriculum and make the most of his ability unless the school reaches him and his parents early. If achievement opens the way to interesting activities—for example, in a science club—this provides a stronger incentive than any amount of listing on honor rolls. The heart of the problem of talent development is to convince nonaspiring parents that their child can have a better and more valuable life if he prepares for college (see page 246). At best, it is hard to establish motivation for achievement in the child whose home has laid no foundation in early years (Kahl, 1953; T. Parsons, 1959).

The crucial importance of arousing parental interest is shown by recent British studies (Wall and Miller, 1961). Social-class divisions are still strongly marked in Great Britain, and these investigators therefore made comparisons both with regard to social status of the home and the degree to which parents were actively interested in the pupil's educational development. Three strong effects emerge from tests given at ages 8 and 11:

Pupils from the higher social classes move higher in the group in mental test performance; those whose fathers are manual workers hold the same position or decline in relative position.

Within each class, the standing of pupils with encouraging parents rises more rapidly than that of pupils whose parents care little about education.

Holding mental ability constant, achievement in arithmetic is strongly associated with degree of parental encouragement.

The American school requires formal decisions about educational plans in Grade VIII or IX. But plans regarding college must be reviewed periodically. There are pupils who improve in performance and become more interested in schooling (and others who decline in performance). It should be made easy for the pupil to transfer into a college-preparatory program as late as Grade XI. This is a critical point, because the senior year provides a final opportunity to repair gaps in preparation for a job or for further education. The choice of college is made at this time. This choice should be guided by the pupil's demonstrated ability and by the match between the nature of the college and his motivational pattern. The right choice will greatly increase his chance of survival and of his being stimulated to develop to his full potential.

> **28.** While it is agreed that the increasing demand for trained persons makes it desirable for most high-school graduates to continue their education, there is much disagreement regarding the desirability of a college education for everyone. What are the reasonable goals of post-high-school education for the pupil of IQ 100?
>
> **29.** Suppose that the average ability in College A is represented by a score of 100 on the CQT (cf. Figure 50). Should the admissions officer recruit the most able students he can attract, or should he encourage applicants with ability far above 100 to apply elsewhere?

OCCUPATION AND IQ.   General mental tests have significance for occupational guidance as well as for academic success. Where a person eventually settles—in professional, skilled, or unskilled work—is appreciably related to his general ability. One of the many pieces of evidence is a follow-up study of young candidates for flight training tested by the Air Force in 1943. About 10,000 of these men were questioned ten years after they had been discharged to determine what occupation they had settled in. The 1943 test scores for various occupational groups were compared (Thorndike and Hagen, 1959). Occupational averages for the largest groups ranked as follows:

Highest level: engineers, physicians, scientists
Second level: accountants, dentists, managers, lawyers
Third level (roughly, IQ 95–105): carpenters, clerical workers, farmers, wholesale salesmen
Fourth level: bus and truck drivers, machine operators, mechanics

These group averages do not tell the whole story. Every group had a wide range; one quarter or more of the accountants, for example, came from the top level, and another quarter fell below IQ 100. The wide range within an occupation demonstrates that IQ does not alone determine one's status. To put it in another way: men with an IQ of 120 are found in every occupational level from semiskilled laborer to professional.

> **30.** How can a teacher encourage a fifth-grader to think of himself as academically able without arousing jealousy in the class and without giving him false impressions of his ability?
>
> **31.** Mental-test performance is sometimes lowered by emotional disturbance. Does this make the tests more or less satisfactory as a basis for judging readiness?
>
> **32.** Is it legitimate for a teacher or counselor to discourage the ambition of an eighth-grader who has poor marks and poor test scores, yet plans to be an engineer?

The Ability Profile

The test of general scholastic aptitude emphasizes comprehension of words and other symbols. But mental ability has many facets, and sometimes these are important enough to be measured separately. The would-be architect, for example, must have a different ability pattern from that required for general college work: he must have a good mastery of the fundamentals of mathematics, and, for engineering drawing, an ability to reason about shapes and structures.

To discuss plural abilities seems to contradict the earlier statement that mental abilities hang together and can be represented by a general or composite score. But it is true both that (a) most pupils who do well in one subject do well in other subjects, and that (b) each pupil does better in some subjects than in others. When verbal, numerical, mechanical, and other aptitudes are measured separately, they correlate about .40, a moderate relation that supports both statement a and statement b. To judge how much education the pupil should plan on, general ability is most important, since all schooling depends on abstract and verbal reasoning. To judge what he should major in and what work he should consider, we need to know the shape of his ability profile.

There are a surprisingly large number of specialized aptitudes. The Air Force found more than 20 distinct abilities that contribute to success as a pilot. The United States Employment Service tried to develop tests to measure all the aptitudes needed in different types of jobs, but abandoned the effort when the collection reached the unwieldy size of 100 tests. There are a dozen or more distinct physical and psychomotor aptitudes. And studies of creative performance make it clear that numerous talents presently lie outside the scope of aptitude testing.

For guidance, it is usual to examine just those aptitudes that can be dependably measured and have widespread importance. The five most commonly included in test batteries are verbal, numerical, spatial, mechanical reasoning, and clerical perception. A test "battery" is a collection of tests that have been administered to the same norm group so that the pupil's standing in each ability is expressed on the same scale. There are several such batteries; the Differential Aptitude Tests (Figure 51) are primarily for Grades VIII–XII and require about four and a half hours of testing. In addition to the six subtests illustrated in the figure, scores are obtained on spelling and language usage because these are important for commercial and office work.

Verbal ability requires a well-developed vocabulary and ability to understand relations among concepts. The SAT Verbal section and many tasks of the Binet and Wechsler scales depend on verbal ability. Numerical ability involves facility in arithmetic operations. Tests usually emphasize reasoning rather than sheer computational speed. The specimen DAT item, you will note, can be answered intuitively, without calculation.

Spatial tests require ability to think about geometric forms and relationships. Spatial judgment is required in some mathematics courses, in engineering, engineering drawing, sheet metal work, and dressmaking.

Mechanical reasoning tests ask how machinery operates and how physical principles work. The tests can be passed on the basis of everyday experience, although training in shop or science tends to improve the pupil's score. A reasoning test of this sort is distinguished from a test that requires the pupil to name shop tools and give other information, and from tests of manipulative skill.

VERBAL REASONING   Pick out a numbered word for the first blank, and a lettered word for the second blank, so that the sentence will make sense.

. . . . . is to water as eat is to . . . . .

1. continue	2. drink	3. foot	4. girl
A. drive	B. enemy	C. food	D. industry

NUMERICAL ABILITY   Pick out the correct answer.

$$? = \frac{4}{9} \text{ of } 648$$

A   14.58
B   72
C   218
D   1458
E   none of these

ABSTRACT REASONING   The four pictures at the left make a series. Pick out the picture which would be the fifth one in the series.

SPACE RELATIONS   Which figures can be made from the pattern shown?

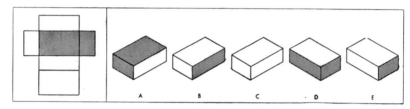

MECHANICAL REASONING

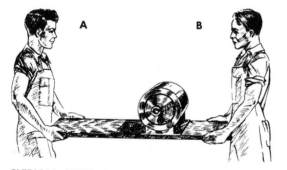

Which man has the heavier load?
(If equal, mark C.)

CLERICAL SPEED AND ACCURACY   Underline at right the symbol which is just like the underlined symbol at left.

AB	AC	AD	AE	AF		AC	AE	AF	AB	AD
A7	7A	B7	7B	AB		7B	B7	AB	7A	A7
Aa	Ba	bA	BA	bB		Aa	bA	bB	Ba	BA

51 *Items from six subtests of the Differential Aptitude Tests (Items copyright 1947 by The Psychological Corporation and reproduced by permission.)*

Clerical perception calls for rapid detection of errors. It does not require reasoning, but it does require careful, rapid work of a routine nature. This ability predicts success in simple office jobs, but it is only one of the aptitudes pertinent in more responsible work such as bookkeeping and stenography.

AN ILLUSTRATIVE COUNSELING RECORD.   The record of Charles White illustrates how these tests can be used. He earned an IQ of 104 on a group mental test. His DAT scores in Grade X are charted in Figure 52. A test of reading comprehension and speed placed him at about the 30th percentile, compared to the national norm for his grade. (You should try to interpret these scores and draw your own conclusions about Charles before you read further.)

According to the counselor's records (Bennett *et al.*, 1951):

Charles entered the college preparatory program in senior high school. During the first semester he experienced great difficulty in his studies of English, world history, and Latin. Conferences with Charles and his mother revealed that the family was determined that Charles should have a college education. Charles wished to oblige his family and was working very diligently toward this goal. By the end of this semester, however, his failure in Latin and his

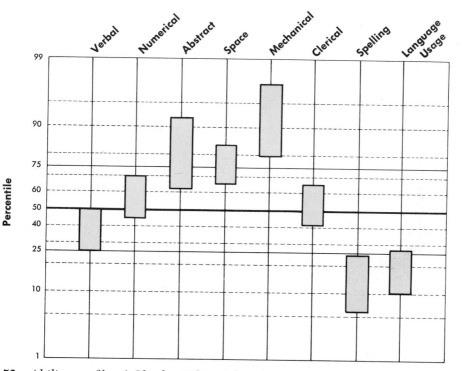

52 *Ability profile of Charles White (data from Bennett et al., 1951, p. 61)*

low grades in English and history seemed to climax the discouragement under which he had been laboring through the past few years in school.

When he entered senior high, reading tests, junior-high-school achievement tests, and intelligence tests had cast doubt on the advisability of his pursuing an academic program. At that time, the Differential Aptitude Test results also became available. They seemed to confirm the previous indications of Charles' limited verbal ability. At the same time they pointed out areas of superior ability, a positive starting point from which to plan revisions in Charles' high-school program.

In the light of this new information, it was decided that Charles might further explore his interests in mechanical and technical work. He was assigned to less demanding class sections in English and history. Latin was replaced by mechanical drawing. At the end of the year, his marks and his disposition had improved considerably. In Grade 11 he is pursuing a high-school program made up chiefly of shop, science, and mathematics courses, and his work is entirely satisfactory. His present goal, in which his family now concurs, is to enter a technical training institute in a two-year college. There is good reason to believe he can complete such a course successfully.

For evidence of the pertinence of the ability profile to vocational guidance we may again turn to the study of former Air Force men. The average

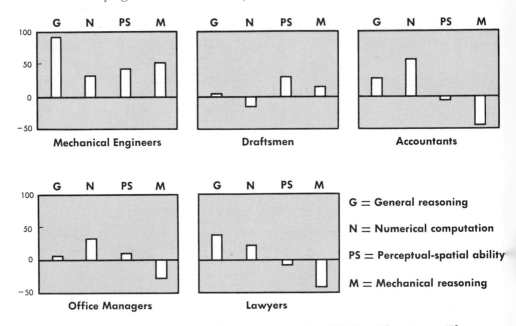

53   *Men in an occupation tend to have similar abilities (data from Thorndike and Hagen, 1959)*

Mean profile of men in an occupation, based on tests given during Air Force training fifteen years earlier. The heavy line indicates the average score among all men tested.

profiles for several occupational groups are shown in Figure 53. The general reasoning score here includes both verbal and numerical reasoning; the numerical score emphasizes computational facility. The perceptual-spatial score includes spatial reasoning and speed in interpreting visual signals. It is evident that these men who have survived training and the initial years of practice in an occupation tend to have a pattern of ability suited to that work (see also Bennett, 1955).

Interest profiles are significant in predicting success and persistence in a college curriculum or in a professional career. Comparing the students who complete one college curriculum with those who complete another, investigators find greater differences in interests than in abilities (J. W. French, 1961; R. G. King, 1958). The best indicator of probable success in advanced training is strong general ability plus strong interest in the field, based on a realistic image of it. In several fields of study, competence in mathematics is essential. While deficiencies in other specialized aptitudes will be a handicap in some work, the bright and well-motivated student usually can survive despite one or two such inadequacies.

> **33.** Which specific aptitudes are represented in the items illustrated from the Kuhlmann-Anderson test (page 207)?
> **34.** Why were the Differential tests more helpful in counseling Charles than the IQ?
> **35.** At what point in the pupil's high-school career would it be most valuable to administer and interpret a battery such as the Differential Aptitude Tests?
> **36.** Select one of the following types of test that especially interests you, and find out what the tests are like, how dependable they are, and how they may be used. Information may be obtained from *The Mental Measurements Yearbook*, and sample copies of the tests can probably be examined in a library or a departmental collection.
>   **a.** reading readiness tests for beginning readers
>   **b.** musical aptitude tests
>   **c.** artistic aptitude tests
>   **d.** mechanical aptitude tests
>   **e.** nonverbal mental tests for individual administration

ABILITY IN ADULTHOOD

A few words should be said about the trend of intellectual development in adulthood. Research on the change of ability with age requires repeated retesting of the same persons. It is quicker to compare random samples of persons of different ages, but this method is unacceptable because in this century older adults have had much less schooling than younger adults and are at a disadvantage on tests. A fixed group of subjects is difficult to follow after its members leave school and scatter about the country, and retest studies require decades to complete.

The evidence from retests is still scanty, but several conclusions are beginning to emerge (Bradway and Thompson, 1962; Bayley, 1960; Owens, 1953):

The average score on a general mental test rises from year to year; this rise continues at least into the thirties.

There is a decline in test performance for elderly subjects.

Different abilities exhibit different trends. Abstract reasoning appears to stabilize in late adolescence, but vocabulary and information continue to increase.

With time, the individual's profile becomes more irregular, his high and low abilities being more separated. The correlation among abilities declines during adolescence, and probably in adulthood.

The adult's understanding of and ability to apply concepts is as great as that of the adolescent, a fact highly encouraging to adult education. To be sure, the adult may be less motivated than the schoolboy. His experience may have taught him misinformation or faulty habits that interfere with new learning, but his greater stock of knowledge offsets these disadvantages.

37. The findings now appearing contradict the belief once held that general scholastic aptitude reaches its peak about age 20 and then declines. Should the educational system be planned the same way under the new conclusion as under the former belief?

38. So far as is known, the average general mental test score for males and females is about the same at each age (though the averages on special aptitudes are not). In view of their social and biological roles, should women delay their post-high-school education until age 35, when their children are in school?

39. What does the greater irregularity of adult aptitude profiles imply for adult education programs?

SUMMARY

The responsibilities of the teacher are to administer group tests properly, to interpret test results for more common tests, to interpret certain less common tests with the aid of a counselor or other trained interpreter, and to request that suitable tests be administered when needed to understand a pupil.

Testing procedures evaluate the pupil by means of a work sample. This sample needs to be representative of the pertinent situations, and reasonably large. If the situations encountered in the test are representative of the situations to be encountered in the future, a test is said to be valid. A test valid (relevant) for one purpose is likely not to be valid for other purposes. Accuracy is lowered by any momentary confusion, by any poor question, or by incorrect testing procedure. Using a large sample of items allows variations of this sort to average out so that a better measure can be obtained. Accuracy is reported in the form of a reliability coefficient, usually the correlation between two forms of the test. An obtained score represents a somewhat indefinite band within which the true score lies; in profile interpretation the uncertainty band is taken as twice the standard error.

The ability test tries to measure what a person can do. The tester tries to motivate him to do his best. This is in contrast to the measure of typical performance, which seeks to determine how the pupil behaves under ordinary motivating conditions. Measures of study habits, emotional tension, friendliness, etc., may best be interpreted as measures of typical behavior. Where it is impractical to observe actual behavior, self-report is a substitute, not fully dependable.

Norms are used to compare one particular pupil or class with typical pupils. This keeps the teacher from setting unrealistic expectations. In judging the quality of a program, it is important to compare the class with similar classes, not with the national norm. In judging the attainment of an individual, it is desirable to judge him against others with similar initial ability. A pupil who does better than the average pupil with the same aptitude is referred to as an overachiever.

Scores are transformed in various ways in order to simplify interpretation. The raw score is a count of items correct, or perhaps a score in the form $R - (1/n - 1)W$. To offset the advantage of the pupil who guesses, all, half, a third, or a quarter of the wrong answers are subtracted from the number of right answers—depending on whether the test items have two, three, four, or five alternatives. An age-equivalent score indicates the age at which typical pupils earn a given raw score; thus a mental age of 7 is assigned to any one, young or old, who does as well as the average 7-year-old. The percentile scale compares the pupil with a reference group. On a certain test for fourth-grade boys, a raw score of 74 ranks at the 90th percentile; this means that just 90 per cent of fourth-grade boys score below 74. A standard-score scale is calculated by a formula based on the mean (average) and the standard deviation (a measure of the spread of scores). In the usual scale, a person scoring at the mean is assigned a standard score of 50, and a person one s.d. above the mean is assigned a standard score of 60 (see Figure 49). The well-known IQ is nothing more than a peculiar standard-score scale in which 100 and 16 are used for the mean and s.d. instead of 50 and 10. This scale continues in use only because of its familiarity. In comparing pupils mixed in age, it is necessary to examine raw scores or age equivalents; percentiles and standard scores are useful for comparing different scores of the same pupil or for comparing pupils of similar age and grade.

Among ability tests, reading tests have special importance as measures of readiness. Tests are of many types; it is best to use one whose content and questions resemble those to be encountered in the classroom. Diagnostic tests are used to study pupils whose over-all performance is weak. The diagnostic test of reading breaks reading into subskills and determines which constitute the source of the pupil's difficulties. Diagnosis is equally important in other areas; no pupil is just "poor in arithmetic" or any other subject. While the teacher can diagnose many difficulties by so simple a step as observing the pupil at work, diagnosis by a specialist is required for other disorders.

Faulty study skills may be neglected unless they are directly appraised. Numerous studies have tried to identify the habits that characterize the effective learner. Items listed on page 200 give a picture of the better learner as diligent and well directed. He is selective; he looks for relationships and meanings; he drills himself on the details he needs to know. Poor students characteristically cannot identify what is important and fail to realize that the material before them can make sense. They fail to organize their written work about main ideas.

The test of general scholastic aptitude covers various important mental performances. Abilities such as memory, reasoning, and vocabulary tend to hang together; the person superior in one is likely to be average or superior in the others. The Stanford-Binet and Wechsler scales are individual measures; the Wechsler has a separate Performance section. Both tests provide good opportunities for observing how the person thinks. Group tests do not allow for observation. The SAT is very nearly a representative sample of types of thinking needed in college; the reasoning tasks of the Kuhlmann-Anderson, on the other hand, make little use of school learning. General-ability tests correlate .80 with tests of achievement given at the same time. If pupils come from different educational backgrounds, the general-aptitude test gives a fairer comparison than a measure of achievement. The correlation of an aptitude test or an achievement test with subsequent college marks is likely to be .60 or higher.

There is no IQ level that marks the college-capable student. Colleges draw on different ranges of ability; the student below average in one college would be superior in some other institutions in the same state. Changes over time must also be taken into account; a few pupils with low IQs will rise to a superior level if emotional and other difficulties are remedied. As a rule of thumb, we advise that every pupil above standard-score 60 (IQ 116) should consider college, and that the pupil below 50 (IQ 100) should not be encouraged to plan on a four-year college course unless remediable handicaps are identified and corrected. Decisions about educational plans should be continuous, starting as early as Grade IV and being revised as late as the last year of high school. The heart of the problem of talent development is to reach the parent of the able child. The school is likely to raise the parent's aspirations for his child only if it approaches him early. Parental attitudes affect the pupil's development; the child whose home encourages intellectual effort gains in performance relative to his classmates.

Even though abilities hang together, a profile shows relative strengths and weaknesses. The abilities most commonly measured in test batteries are verbal, numerical, spatial, and mechanical reasoning, and clerical perception, but many other aptitudes have been identified. Men in different occupations have different ability levels, and distinctive profiles. Lawyers, for example, tend to be superior in general and numerical reasoning, but weak in mechanical reasoning.

Retests during adulthood indicate that measured ability increases from year to year, at least into the 30's. In old age, test scores decline. The profile becomes more irregular with time, abilities becoming less closely correlated.

Reading List 7

Leo J. Brueckner and Guy L. Bond, "Diagnosis in Arithmetic," Chapter 8 in *The Diagnosis and Treatment of Learning Difficulties* (New York: Appleton-Century-Crofts, 1955), pp. 192–239.

Learning difficulties can be understood only through an examination of the specific faults and successes in the pupil's performance. This chapter illustrates how such an analysis is made. Especially valuable are pp. 219 ff., on case-study procedures and the diagnosis of performance on verbal problems.

John W. Gardner, "The Identification of Talent," Chapter 5 in *Excellence* (New York: Harper, 1961), pp. 46–53.

The idea that the school is the "sorting agent" for society was introduced in our Chapter 2. Gardner summarizes the reasons for placing greater reliance on tests than on teachers' judgment, and comments on the fact that tests used in this way are inevitably unpopular. He points out major cautions in the use of tests to select talent.

Katrina de Hirsch, "Tests Designed to Discover Potential Reading Difficulties at the Six-Year-Old Level," *American Journal of Orthopsychiatry*, 27 (1957), 566–76.

The full complexity of readiness is brought out by this description of a dozen aspects of behavior through which a clinic appraises perception, understanding, and coordination. Although the procedures cannot be used without special training, the clear discussion and the close connection between each test finding and suggested educational treatment make the article valuable for teachers.

William G. Perry, Jr., "Students' Use and Misuse of Reading Skills: A Report to a Faculty," *Harvard Educational Review*, 29 (1959), 193–200.

Perry surveys deficiencies among highly able college students. What he says about how to improve thinking and study procedures applies equally in high schools.

Calvin W. Taylor, "A Tentative Description of the Creative Individual," in Walter B. Waetjen, ed., *Human Variability and Learning* (Washington: Assoc. for Supervision and Curriculum Development, 1961), pp. 62–79.

Taylor's theme is that the conventional mental test identifies only one type of giftedness, and that if only this type of talent is encouraged the creative individual will often be lost. He reviews the research of a dozen other investigators on the nature of creative talent.

Lewis M. Terman, "The Discovery and Encouragement of Exceptional Talent," *American Psychologist*, 9 (1954), 221–30. Reprinted in Haimowitz, Noll, Remmers, and Rosenblith.

The developer of the Stanford revision of the Binet scale reviews a lifetime of research on the significance of tested mental ability for later achievement.

CHAPTER 8 THE INTERPRETATION AND APPLICATION OF ABILITY TESTS

The content of present ability tests and their customary uses were examined in Chapter 7. We now go on to some of the more controversial issues in test interpretation. There has been much disagreement about whether or not present aptitude tests measure the right things, about how they are best interpreted, and about the advisability of such practices as grouping pupils on the basis of test scores. On some of these issues research offers a clear conclusion; other questions remain open, to be settled either by policy decisions or by further investigation.

DO MENTAL TESTS IDENTIFY THE TRULY TALENTED?

Mental tests are highly successful as predictors of academic grades and progress in school, but they have been criticized on the ground that they do not properly identify talent. The argument of McClelland that schools are the "screening agency" for society will be recalled (see page 38). Pupils who do not attain the expected educational standards are marked as inferior. They are given less encouragement, are often barred from school activities, and are shunted into positions of low status after they leave school. Poor school performance is a passport to obscurity. If a pupil does well on a mental test and poorly in school, teachers will make great efforts to find out what is wrong. If both his school record and his test scores are poor, he will be allowed to fall by the wayside as one of the "untalented."

CONVERGENT AND DIVERGENT THINKING.   Some critics believe that the customary scholastic aptitude test in which one manipulates ideas to conform to external requirements does not identify the pupils who will be creative as adults. The most extensive studies have been those of J. P. Guilford, who has been trying to identify distinct intellectual processes or operations that can be measured to form a profile describing how the individual thinks. The "content" profile of present aptitude batteries shows *what* the individual is most effective in dealing with (words, numbers, machinery, or spatial forms), not *how* he deals with them. While the processes that might be distinguished have not been conclusively identified, Guilford (1959, p. 360) suggests this list: memory, cognition (recognizing events and ideas, as in reading and picture completion), evaluation (judging the soundness of conclusions), and convergent and divergent thinking. It is these last two that raise the sharpest questions about current practice.

In convergent thinking a person starts with given facts and proceeds logically to construct the one correct solution to a problem. The facts must be rearranged or transformed by means of concepts, rules of logic, arithmetic techniques, etc. This type of thinking is most emphasized in current mental tests; the SAT items and Tests 28, 34, and 39 of the Kuhlmann-Anderson Test are clear examples. In divergent thinking, one deals with a situation for which there are many reasonable solutions. This calls for fluency, imagination, and integration. The mind must cast about to find one possibility after another and choose the responses that "fit" on the basis of intuitions as much as by rigorous logic. Possible tests requiring divergent thinking are these:

Write a sentence using four given words (e.g., *policeman, snowball, cook, found*).

Suggest valuable uses of a new ink that fades away completely a month after it is applied.

Sketch a picture within a square, using as part of the drawing three lines that already appear there.

Divergent thinking is rarely measured by any mental test used in schools. Convergent thinking is emphasized in scholastic aptitude tests and also in the school program. Ordinary general ability tests and school achievement tests are unlikely to identify outstanding "divergent thinkers." Though the two types of ability are correlated, it is estimated that only one out of three pupils in the top fifth on divergent thinking will be included in the top fifth on an ordinary mental test. Teachers know which of their pupils are good at convergent thinking and regard them as desirable pupils. Teachers do not recognize pupils competent in divergent thinking, and are less likely to rate them as "the sort of pupil I like to have" (Torrance, 1959). In later chapters we shall encounter further findings regarding divergent thinking.

Caution is required in identifying tests such as Guilford's as measures of "creativity." While these tests measure an intellectual process, there is as yet no substantial evidence that they predict creative contributions. But since both convergent and divergent thinking are clearly intellectual performances, it is reasonable to ask: Is the school neglecting pupils superior in divergent thinking who could make an important social contribution if they were identified and encouraged?

A test of convergent thinking is highly appropriate to select pupils having readiness for present schooling. Most present instruction emphasizes controlled thinking and the mastery of techniques and principles that reach the one right answer. This is true of science instruction, arithmetic, foreign language, and all other subjects save the arts. Information on tests of divergent thinking /is still fragmentary, but they seem less correlated with achievement than convergent tests, under present methods of schooling.

This last phrase brings us to a fundamental question: Is there some other educational method for which the pupil who excels in divergent thinking has superior readiness? To understand that question we need to see what sort of experimental results would warrant an affirmative answer.

THE INTERACTION OF ABILITY AND INSTRUCTIONAL METHOD. Consider the hypothetical results pictured in Figure 54. Two methods of instruction are applied to comparable classes. We have a test score on convergent thinking and another representing divergent thinking. The left chart shows the end-of-course achievement of those above average in convergent thinking, and of those below average. In the right-hand chart the same pupils are classified according to their scores in divergent thinking. The left-hand chart leads us to think that Method 1 is the better teaching method at both high and low aptitude levels. It also indicates that convergent thinking identifies pupils who do well under Method 1. The right-hand chart shows that divergent thinking has a modest correlation with success under Method 1. All these results for Method 1 are similar to those we would expect to find for the curriculum and methods in general use.

Look further at the right-hand chart. The order of merit of the two methods is reversed at the two ends of the divergent thinking scale. The persons

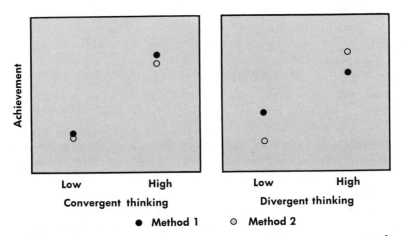

| | Low | High | | Low | High |

Convergent thinking   **Divergent thinking**

● **Method 1**   ○ **Method 2**

54 *Achievement depends on the interaction between method of instruction and aptitude*

high on divergent thinking do better on the average under Method 2, and those low on divergent thinking do better under Method 1. This is called an *interaction* between aptitude and method. The pupil's prospects of success are determined by aptitude and treatment together, not by aptitude alone. Experimental comparisons that determine only which educational method is best on the average are not an adequate basis for selecting educational methods for different types of pupils.

These data are purely hypothetical. Can treatments be found that interact with individual differences? Certainly. Think of a class containing both sighted and blind children: it is obvious that a test that predicts readiness for conventional instruction will not be suitable for predicting readiness for instruction in Braille.

The logic of the foregoing argument is unquestionable. If an ability is truly intellectual, even if it does not predict success in present schooling, it should be possible to invent a teaching method that does capitalize on this ability. Here present knowledge stops. There are special methods for the pupil with an identified deficiency, but there are no validated instructional methods for capitalizing on particular positive talents. Divergent thinking is not the only talent on which a different sort of instruction might be based. Perhaps a method could be found for teaching pupils who are superior in concrete, nonsymbolic reasoning. Perhaps one could design a method for teaching science and mathematics to pupils having superior spatial and mechanical reasoning (Edgerton, 1956, 1958). Personality also interacts with treatment; we may find it fruitful to modify teaching method according to pupil personality (McKeachie, 1962). Questions such as these were neglected so long as psychologists and educators asked only that tests predict which children would do well in schooling as it now exists. But if we regard as reasonable the hypothesis that some instructional method can be found to capitalize on any intellectual ability, we will need to classify pupils according to their best aptitudes, and to find a method for each type of pupil (Cronbach, 1957).

Another current discussion bears on this matter. The traditional place of convergent thinking as the prime educational objective is being seriously questioned. Specialists in many subjects consider that the curriculum has placed too much emphasis on answers laid down by tradition, and too little on the creation of knowledge for oneself through intuition and speculation followed by verification (see page 371). This argument seems likely to lead toward teaching methods where divergent thinking is an important part of readiness.

It would be wrong to carry away the impression that those who do well in the present tests and in the present curriculum are lacking in socially significant talent. Terman and Oden (1959), who followed into adulthood 1,500 children with high Stanford-Binet scores, found them to be exceptionally successful in school and exceptionally productive as adults. In business, community leadership, and professional work (especially science), they have made far more numerous contributions than typical college graduates. Of the men, 70 are listed in *American Men of Science* and three have achieved the rare honor of election to the National Academy of Sciences. They hold over 200 patents; they have written over 30 novels, as well as plays, motion picture scripts, and articles. But the group includes no great composer, no great artist, and "not more than three or four with a high order of literary creativity." The women have less often pursued full-time careers, but seven of them are eminent scientists, and one is an outstanding poet.

Children who do very well in school are expected to make superior contributions later. This does not, however, rule out the possibility that a significant number of potentially creative individuals are lost because they are in the average range on present school tasks.

    1. In high-school instruction in written English, what types of assignments or problems call for convergent thinking? for divergent thinking?

    2. What place is there for divergent thinking in the following:

        a. an elementary-school study of exploration and colonization

        b. instruction in food preparation

        c. the study of fractions

    3. "If a student is high in Aptitude A and below average in Aptitude B, his program should consist of subjects that depend chiefly on Aptitude A." What are the advantages and dangers of this policy?

STABILITY OF MENTAL TEST SCORES

The next issue to be considered is whether aptitudes should be regarded as fixed or as likely to change with time. This leads to the even more important question: Can anything be done to raise the level of ability? This inquiry is of desperate importance to the parent who discovers that his young child has low mental ability. It is of equal practical significance for any teacher who must help a ninth-grader of borderline ability decide whether or not he should plan on going to college, and for the curriculum-planner who would want the school to develop intellect if that is possible. This is not just a question about test scores. It is is a basic question about transfer of learning, i.e., about providing experience that will make a person better able to comprehend future situations.

Before going into specific investigations, we shall state briefly the major conclusions. First, the matter of definition. If you *define* "intelligence" as inborn capacity, it is illogical to talk about improving an individual's intelligence. More than that, it is impossible to do research on such a hypothetical capacity since there is no way to measure it. We can study improvement only in observed performance. It is obvious that success on mental-test items depends upon experience as well as upon the construction of the brain. Test performance is not to be equated with innate capacity.

Second, the facts about consistency of scores. Ranks in general scholastic aptitude change gradually with the passage of time, even when all pupils are given similar education. Despite these changes, individual tests at age 6 predict standing in high school (correlation = .80).

Third, the contribution of heredity. Children tend to be bright who have bright ancestors. Superior or inferior power to develop is passed along through heredity.

Fourth, the role of experience. Hereditary potential must be stimulated and trained. Solving problems calls for concepts, techniques, and attitudes that must be learned. Someone put it this way: "Heredity deals the cards, but environment plays them." This is an echo of the point made in Chapter 4 that biological development and experience interact.

Opportunities to observe, to try interpretations and responses, and to receive satisfying confirmation are necessary for intellectual development (Hunt, 1961). Any major deprivation in a child's experience, compared to that of the average child, is likely to depress his test scores and his readiness for school. Remedial treatment can often repair much of the damage. Theoretically, it should be possible to set up experiences that would promote greater all-round mental development than present "good environments" produce, but no technique for achieving this end is yet available. Hereditary disadvantages cannot be wiped out, nor, even with the best of in-school and out-of-school environments, can we bring the average child up to the level of the quickest learner. The child who comprehends best will ordinarily gain the most from *any* experience; when all children have the same rich opportunities, the abler child usually extends his lead.

Changes in Score During Development

The child who starts out above average in mental ability usually stays superior to others of his age; those who start inferior tend to remain inferior. But it does not follow that each individual's standing is fixed. Some individuals make important changes over time. On an immediate retest with the same instrument it is rare that mental-test standing shifts one standard deviation (16 IQ points). Over long intervals, shifts are larger (R. R. Brown, 1933; Bayley, 1949; Terman and Merrill, 1960). At least 10 per cent of children change at least one standard deviation during an interval of six to eight years. The correlation between an individual test around ages 6–9 and a second test after an interval depends on the interval between tests, as follows:

few days' interval   .91
one-year interval   .88
three-year interval   .84
six-year interval   .80
twelve-year interval   .79

The greater the passage of time, the more numerous the important changes in standing.

While individual tests give reasonably stable information down to the age of 4, tests during the first four years are quite undependable, as Figure 55 shows. Measurement is very difficult before language and work habits are stabilized (Bayley, 1960, p. 819).

> During the stormy, early part of the preschool period it is often difficult to get an intelligence-test score on a child: his understanding may outstrip his language facility and thus be inaccessible for measuring . . . ; his attention span may still be too short to hold his interest, or his tolerance of frustration may be so low as to prevent controlled effort on difficult tasks.

Group tests are especially unstable during the first two years of school, when children are still learning to settle down to pencil-and-paper tasks.

The IQ of the girl in Figure 55 hovers around 85 to 90 from ages 3 to 12. All her IQs after age 12 are above 90. The increase is small but consistent. Evidently some development in adolescence enabled this girl to gain faster than her agemates. The boy swings up and down, going as low as an IQ of 97 in the school years. Yet he rises as high as 120, and his curve ends with a strong rise in adolescence. No final judgment about any child should be made on the basis of a test at one age.

Because school experience is cumulative, the pupil who does well in the early grades will be better prepared for the higher grades; test scores therefore become quite stable in the later school years. This warrants our earlier recommendation that plans for higher education be considered in the junior high school. But a decision for or against college should not be irreversible. Ninth-graders are sometimes asked to decide, once and for all, whether they are going to college. One decision places them on the college-preparatory track, and the other shunts them into subjects that will not be accepted for college admission. The door should be kept open as long as possible for a change in plans if a pupil's performance shows an upward trend.

We have to this point confined attention to changes in general ability. A further important question is, When do the peaks and valleys of the aptitude profile stabilize? The profile in Grade I has no resemblance to that of the same pupil in Grade IV (L. Tyler, 1958). If, for example, a child's numerical ability is below his general performance in Grade I, that deficiency is as likely as not to change to a superiority. At the primary level, spe-

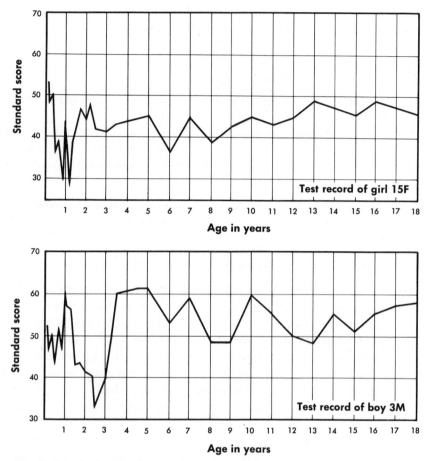

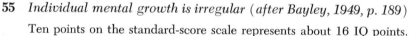

55   *Individual mental growth is irregular (after Bayley, 1949, p. 189)*

Ten points on the standard-score scale represents about 16 IQ points.

cialized aptitude measures are useful only in appraising immediate readiness. By Grade IV differences within the individual (e.g., Verbal high, Numerical low, Spatial average) are moderately stable. And by Grade VIII the *marked* peaks and valleys in the boy's profile forecast his adult aptitudes (Bennett and Doppelt, 1951; W. J. Meyer, 1960). Findings now available for girls are inconsistent (W. J. Meyer and Bendig, 1961). Changes in profiles are fairly common for both boys and girls during high school. This finding reinforces the recommendation that guidance should include a periodic review of performance, aptitudes, and interests.

   4. In view of the stability of the mental test score and the profile, and of the decisions to be made about pupils, in what grades should mental tests be given?

5. In junior high school, a pupil is one standard deviation above the average (IQ 116) and his marks are good. He plans on a college preparatory course. On a group mental test in Grade XI his score is slightly below average, and his marks are around the average. What steps should the school take? Should his plans be changed?

Changes Related to the Environment

That heredity has much to do with ability was suspected from the fact that some families produce eminent men generation after generation. This is uncertain evidence, however, since a distinguished father can provide many advantages for his children. To arrive at firm conclusions it is necessary to investigate twins. Identical twins receive precisely the same genes. When they are reared in the same home, their experiences also have much in common. But in some cases death or other misfortune makes it necessary to separate the children, and then the twins are exposed to different stimulation and emotional climates as they grow up. Some foster homes provide more favorable environments than others.

In the study reported in Table 11, the "same environment" twins are much alike as adults. The correlations for height, weight, general ability, and school achievement are nearly perfect. The mental test scores for the twins reared together agree as closely as two measures of the same person would. When we look at the pairs with differing environments, we find that height correlates about the same as in the first row. The differences in environment among these foster families were not large enough to have a noticeable effect on height. This phrasing is important. Height reflects heredity, but environment also could have significant influence, as is made obvious by the unusual average height of the current generation of young Americans.

TABLE 11

Environment influences the similarity of people having the same heredity (Newman et al., 1937)

			Correlation between twins			
	Heredity	*Environ-ment*	*Height*	*Weight*	*General Scholastic Aptitude (IQ)*	*Achievement test*
Identical twins reared together	Same	Same	.98	.97	.91	.96
Identical twins reared separately	Same	Different	.97	.89	.67	.51

Achievement is affected by environment, the correlation in the second row being much lower than that in the first. Though mental ability is less associated with difference in environment than is achievement, it is clear that heredity by no means predetermines test score. This study of course reflects only the differences among the homes in which these twins were raised. If one twin from each pair were adopted into a very fine environment, and the other grew up in a remote community where he received little schooling, the correlation would be far lower than the .67 reported. P. E. Vernon (1958) found (in a study that unfortunately could not be adequately controlled) that even in adolescence the quality of the school program has marked effects on how rapidly mental ability grows.

Consistent opportunities to use a type of reasoning or discrimination, with appropriate reward, enhance that ability. One of the many types of evidence is the discovery that Samoans earn extremely high scores on a Navy test of aptitude for learning radio code, which calls for memory of rhythmic patterns. Ford (1957) explains the result as follows:

> The basic elements of Samoan music are percussive rhythm instruments, principally sticks, hollowed logs, rolled-up bundles of matting, and empty biscuit tins. Any group of Samoans engaged in group dancing will employ several of these rhythm instruments producing a total effect of very complex rhythmic patterns, against the background of which dancing and singing are performed. Consequently, from childhood the Samoan is accustomed to highly varied and rapid systems of rhythmic beats similar to that found in radio transmission. So proficient do the Samoans become as radio operators that on the Naval circuits between Samoa and Hawaii, which are in use to this day, it was customary to employ Samoans at the Hawaiian end because of the difficulty in obtaining any other kind of personnel who could receive messages sent from Samoa, so great was the rapidity of the Samoan operators in Pago. Since nearly everything in Samoa is done rhythmically, it is not at all surprising that the Samoan radio operators are among the finest transmitters of [code] messages in the world.

Conversely, restricted experience retards development. It is repeatedly found that rural children, Negroes, and children from remote regions such as the Kentucky mountains earn, on the average, lower scores than white city children. (While these facts are important, differences within groups are much larger than those between groups. There are many high scores among the underprivileged.)

The effect of restricted environment becomes worse the longer a person remains within it. Wheeler (1932, 1942) tested children in Tennessee mountain hamlets. In 1930, he found the 6-year-olds near the national norm, their average IQ being 95. But the average dropped steadily with age, the average IQ at age 12 being 80. In a second study a decade later, after roads had opened the area to permit consolidated schools, and after industrial employment had improved the standard of living, the decline with age was much less; the mean IQ at age 12 was 90. Other studies report that Northern Negroes do better on mental tests than Southern Negroes. Negroes who have been longer in the North do better than those who moved north more recently. This too implies that test scores reflect the advantages one has had.

It oversimplifies to say that good environments or poor environments account for changes in ability. This explanation would lead us to predict a steady rise in standing for some children (good environment) and a steady decline for others. But individual retest records are of many different shapes; we observe some steep declines, some up-and-down patterns, some records that run level for many years and then start marching upward. Perhaps hereditary patterns of physiological development control this timing of mental growth to some degree. The few pairs of identical twins who have been retested repeatedly show sufficiently similar mental-growth curves to support this speculation (Sontag *et al.*, 1958, p. 122).

Some increases or declines reflect radical changes in the child's emotional relations with his world, as in the case of Danny (Lowell, 1941). Danny's mother, having to work, left him in the care of aging grandparents who were irritable and easily disturbed. Therefore Danny was restricted and discouraged when he sought to satisfy his curiosity through questions and exploratory play. A nervous disorder was an additional complication. At age 5, Danny was one s.d. below average in mental ability. His mother, suddenly realizing that his situation was chaining him down intellectually and emotionally, moved away from the grandparents. Over the next several years Danny received proper medical care, superior schooling, and much greater attention, affection, and encouragement. His scores showed a steady, gradual rise, until he was 2 s.d. above average at age 12.

Parental attitudes and techniques affect intellectual development. It will be recalled that children from "democratic" homes tend to be more curious and competitive when they enter school. While present evidence is based on small samples and inadequate techniques, increases in tested ability from age 3 to 6 or from age 6 to 10 appear to be associated with democracy in the home and with parental attempts to accelerate the child's growth toward independence. It is also found that a rise in ability from age 6 to 10 is strongly associated with the personality at age 6; the one who gains tends to be aggressive, competitive, and self-initiating (finding occupation for his time without adult or peer suggestions). Children who improve are not consistently above or below average in affiliative behavior. The independent child is emotionally free to gain more from his environment (Sontag *et al.*, 1958, pp. 116, 126–29; Baldwin *et al.*, 1945; Eva Grant, 1939). It is reasonable to think that independence continues to promote intellectual growth at later ages, but formal evidence has not been collected to demonstrate this.

6. The warmth and affection of parents appears not to be correlated with change in ability from age 3 to 10. How can this be explained?

7. "Aggressive" children in the Sontag study were also characterized as dominating and strong-willed at age 6. Those rated unaggressive were quiet, sometimes shy and withdrawn, and submissive. What explanation can be offered for the fact that the more aggressive children tended to rise in ability between ages 6 and 10?

8. "Probably there is no more fallacious belief about the role of environment than . . . that two children in the same family have the same environment" (Hunt, 1961). What does this mean? Do children in the same school-room have the same environment?

THE EFFECT OF SPECIAL STIMULATION ON READINESS FOR INSTRUCTION

In the past, impressed by the stability of the IQ and the correlation of mental age with school performance, educators have often reasoned as follows about pupils with low test scores:

These pupils lack readiness for the regular school curriculum.

Pupils cannot learn unless they are given tasks for which they have readiness.

Therefore, these pupils should be given relatively little verbal work or work requiring abstract thinking.

In accordance with this conclusion, some schools routinely assign pupils with subaverage mental-test scores to vocational training. In the social-studies class, while the others are using the library to prepare reports, the teacher encourages these slow pupils to cut out pictures for a scrap-book. When it is recognized that readiness for schooling consists of concepts, attitudes toward work, techniques of concentrating attention, and other *learned* performance, one looks for ways to increase readiness rather than resignedly accepting the low test score as an immutable fact.

EARLY TRAINING FOR THE MENTALLY HANDICAPPED. The possible effect of special school experience is shown in Kirk's (1958) experiment with institutionalized children. These children, about 4½ years old at the start of the study, had IQs between 45 and 80. One group spent six hours per day in a preschool that provided group experience, opportunity to draw, to tell stories, etc., and gave individual tutoring in those abilities that seemed especially weak. After one to three years of such instruction the pupils entered Grade I. The most important finding comes from the follow-up test given after one year in school (average age 7½):

	Gain in Stanford Binet IQ over initial test	Percentage above IQ 85 on follow-up test
Institution children in preschool	10.2	27
Comparable untrained institution children	−6.5	0

Similar results for institution children are reported by others (Dawe, 1943; Skeels and Dye, 1939). It is noteworthy that six of Kirk's 15 preschool children, and not one of the 12 untrained controls, could later be paroled from the institution.

Remedial programs to remove well-identified handicaps are helpful for children outside institutions. Herr (1946) reports a great increase in readiness among Spanish-American children given preschool work which offered experience in English that their homes did not offer. Programs to improve reading readiness are common. Pupils make up stories, read picture stories, and listen to stories read by the teacher. In addition, exercises to develop ability are provided (G. L. Anderson and Gates, 1950, p. 22).

> The child who is not ready to begin reading may achieve the necessary status more quickly if he is trained in such component abilities as detecting common sounds, noting the visible features of small word-like characters, following the thread of a story, and getting the meaning of pictorial illustrations. On the other hand, some component abilities . . . [are not much improved by known methods of teaching.] In any event, knowing the nature of the child's developmental pattern enables the teacher to adjust teaching to secure maximum progress. For example, if the child's auditory discrimination of words is poor and not easily improved at the time, the teacher may choose a procedure which capitalizes on a superior ability such as visual analysis.

Bradley (1956) found it profitable to delay reading instruction of first-graders until the various components of their reading readiness had been brought to a satisfactory level. Though their start was delayed, the pupils made up their disadvantage by more rapid progress in Grades II and III. Some form of therapeutic help is valuable in cases of emotional difficulty (Bills, 1950).

Enriched experience shows much less benefit where no specific deficiency is identified. Kirk provided preschool experience for retarded children living at home and compared their development to that of similar untrained children, with these results:

	Gain in Stanford-Binet IQ		Percentage above IQ 85 on follow-up test
	at school entrance	after one year of school	
Children living at home who attended preschool	11.2	11.8	60
Comparable untrained children	−0.6	6.9	58

The special training produced marked gains during the preschool period. The children who had been left in their normal environments made up much of the difference during the first school year. The trained group very likely did gain in readiness, but their advantage did not last. In first-grade achievement they were not superior to the control group except in art and writing, where their early creative experience was beneficial. Kirk notes that improvement was less common among children where there was evidence of brain damage and among children whose parents were restrictive and uninterested in their development. Among untrained children also, first-grade progress was least among those from "psychosocially inadequate" homes.

A PROGRAM FOR THE CULTURALLY DEPRIVED. We are almost entirely without techniques for helping the older child who has been deprived of stimulation during his early development. Fundamental change in attitude toward education, achievement, and one's own worth is rare after the elementary grades. Great interest therefore attaches to the pioneering experiment of a New York City junior high school, where the student body is largely Negro and Puerto Rican, and where prior to the experiment few graduates did well in high school or went to college. Beginning in 1954, these "culturally deprived" children were subjected to an invigorated program of counseling and remedial instruction. Parent education was carried out simultaneously. Perhaps most important, pupils took field trips to entertainments, museums, colleges, and the larger world whose excitement had never penetrated their tenement neighborhood. Nonverbal mental tests were used to guide the counseling and remedial efforts. As a formal study, the experiment was loosely controlled and incompletely evaluated (Wrightstone, 1960). Many of the results, however, were so dramatic that the only question left to answer is just what the limits of the approach may be; that it works appears to be beyond question (Morse, 1960, pp. 41 ff.; Mayer, 1961, p. 124). There are stories of children who gained 40 points in IQ (remedial reading is a large part of the story) and carried off college scholarships. On the average, the IQs rose about seven points, and the average gains in reading were one and a half times the normal rate. Since progress in arithmetic was no better than the usual rate, that part of the program is being changed (an example of the importance of careful investigation, even in a program that justifies enthusiasm). All reports on pupil motivation and parent interest in their education are favorable. It remains to be seen what these pupils will do after high school to participate in New York's cultural resources and opportunities for achievement.

No successful method for speeding up the mental development of average and superior children, beyond that attained through the regular school program, has been reported. It was hoped for a time that preschool experience would have marked effects on IQ and readiness for first-grade work. In nine studies comparing normal children who did and did not have preschool training, the preschool group was found to show more mental growth in every study (Whipple, 1940). The gains, however, were very slight, and the investigators properly concluded that the preschool had little effect on general scholastic aptitude.

Socialization equips the human organism with all the intellectual armament of our civilization; modern man overcomes problems that would have utterly baffled the man of five centuries ago. With this conception of ability as something acquired, it is natural to seek some way of speeding up or forcing the growth process. The methods attempted fall into two classes: the undirected and the directed. The undirected methods try to provide a rich and encouraging environment, but they do not set out to teach particular responses. In the more directed methods, the student is taught responses to carefully chosen situations. From studies such as Kirk's we are forced to conclude that, while accelerating mental development by a richer environment is theoretically possible, we have not found undirected stimulation very effective. The environment of the average child is sufficiently rich to allow great mental development, since he is stimulated by adults, peers, newspapers, and television. As a bonus, we can take him to a museum or a farm, or buy him an encyclopedia. Such little "enrichments" provide only a very small surplus over the benefits that almost all children have.

In remedial work, directed methods have marked success in increasing readiness. Special experience is directed to correct whatever specific weakness the pupil shows. We can similarly help anyone who makes a persistent error in reasoning or lacks a needed concept. The best method we have found for increasing the capacity to learn is to teach useful techniques, concepts, and habits in place of inefficient ones. *Instead of hoping for incidental learning as a result of general stimulation, we teach the improved responses deliberately.* Methods for improving reasoning and teaching concepts will be discussed in Chapters 10–12.

Conclusions about what can be accomplished in the early years are likely to be drastically modified when evidence from a current experiment becomes available. O. K. Moore and his colleagues state that young children permitted to experiment with electric typewriters, under carefully controlled conditions, learn to read and spell at age three. This directed training in mechanical associations of forms with sounds may conceivably do more to increase readiness for later intellectual learning than the preschool "enrichment" assessed in previous research.

9. The following playful passage comes from a story by Daniel Keyes (1960). Comment in the light of what this text has said. A patient in a mental hospital says:

"I'm not sure what an IQ is. Dr. Nemur said it was something that measured how intelligent you were—like a scale in the drugstore weighs pounds. But Dr. Strauss had a big argument with him and said an IQ didn't weigh intelligence at all. He said an IQ showed how much intelligence you could get, like the numbers on the outside of a measuring cup. You still had to fill the cup up with stuff."

10. Bradley found it profitable to delay reading instruction. Can this be described as an example of "waiting for maturation"?

11. Does the New York program for the culturally handicapped suggest any procedures that would be desirable in a midwestern community of 40,000 where the children of professional and managerial families go on to college, but other pupils typically do not?

12. How would a directed program to improve physical fitness differ from an undirected program of enriched physical experience?

ADAPTING SCHOOLING TO PUPIL READINESS

Grade Placement of Subject Matter

The school program is organized on the basis of assumptions about readiness, some of which have a solid experimental foundation. Others are traditions that have never been adequately scrutinized. The basic organization is *age-grading.* Children are classified according to age, and certain branches of learning are placed in the curriculum for each age level. Reading is assigned to age 6, psychology to the second year of college, the world of careers to Grade IX. Assignments to any grade are justified only if it can be contended that this placement fits the intellectual development and interests of these pupils. The very organization of the school, with distinct units beginning at ages 6, 12, 14 or 15, and 18, reflects assumptions about the mental abilities, interests, and social characteristics of those years.

The placement of an educational experience is sometimes an echo of intellectual and educational history. Classical languages entered the American curriculum as a vocational subject for ministers, lawyers, and scholars; they were later supposed to sharpen the intellect of the advanced student. Languages, including modern languages, were therefore made a secondary-school subject, reserved for the minority going on to college. Yet a second language can be learned by preschool children and by the feebleminded, when the method of instruction does not call for reading, writing, or grammatical analysis (Angiolillo, 1942). Schools in many other countries begin language instruction in the early grades. We have already encountered Penfield's statement (page 101) that languages need to be acquired before age 9 in order to develop perfect speech. Awakened to the fact that starting language instruction in Grade IX has no justification, American schools now find themselves with no clear policy; introductory work in modern languages may be found in any grade, depending on the school system.

Mathematics provides a second example. Introductory courses deal with the most ancient content; the newest branch to develop must fall in at the end of the line. The principles of set theory were developed a century ago, but as recently as 1940 it was highly unusual for a student to encounter them unless he went as far as graduate school. This placement was challenged by mathematicians who believe that set theory provides a particularly useful mathematical system, more significant for understanding mathematics than such time-honored content as the solution of right triangles and the "mixture" problems of arithmetic. (How many pupils will become surveyors or grocers?) Today the traditional engineering mathematics for freshmen has been replaced in many colleges by a course based largely on set theory. Experimental instruction in set theory is being carried out successfully as early as Grade I.

The traditional placement of subject matter is being challenged today more radically than it has been at any time in American history. Bruner (1960, pp. 12, 33) speaks for a conference of physicists, psychologists, historians, and other scholars with these words:

> We begin with the hypothesis that any subject can be taught effectively in some intellectually honest form to any child at any stage of development. . . . Experience over the past decade points to the fact that our schools may be wasting precious years by postponing the teaching of many important subjects on the ground that they are too difficult. . . . The basic ideas that lie at the heart of all science and mathematics and the basic themes that give form to life and literature are as simple as they are powerful. To be in command of these basic ideas, to use them effectively, requires a continual deepening of one's understanding . . . that comes from learning to use them in progressively more complex forms. It is only when such basic ideas are put in formalized terms as equations or elaborated verbal concepts that they are out of reach of the young child. . . . Fourth-grade children can play absorbing games governed by the principles of topology and set theory, even discovering new "moves" or theorems.

The influence of psychologists during the past 40 years has often been on the side of postponing instruction. Studies of the maturation of neural processes suggested that growth could not be accelerated. The correspondence between mental age and success in school implied that pupils fail if asked to do work "beyond their ability." Failure was known to produce loss of confidence, emotional interference with thinking, and a high dropout rate. Investigators concerned with reading failures found that the pupil was likely to fail if his mental age was below $6\frac{1}{2}$; consequently, prereading instruction replaced the primer as the first semester's work for most children. Investigators identified topics in arithmetic that pupils found difficult and moved the topics to a later grade. These studies were sound, and their lessons are not to be neglected. It is not good for a child to encounter frequent failure, and we have not been able to change the timetable of mental development greatly.

But a significant fact is overlooked by those who wait for readiness to develop. Readiness is not readiness for a subject or a topic; it is readiness for a certain learning experience. As Arthur Gates said (1937), even at the height of educational concern for maturation, "The age for learning to read under one program or with the method employed by one teacher may be entirely different from that required under other circumstances." Here are some of his supporting data: Figure 56 shows the percentages of children achieving below a "grade equivalent" of 1.75 in reading (2.0 is the approximate norm after one year of school). The four programs, in different communities, varied in important ways. Schools A, B, and C had good teachers; in A and B, special materials including supplementary easy books and diagnostic aids were used. School D had poorly qualified teachers and a poor selection of materials; the teachers seldom worked with individual children. If we were to say that a mental age indicates "readiness" if 75 per cent of pupils at that level succeed in reading, a mental age of 5 is sufficient in schools A and B, a mental age of 6 in C, and a mental age of 6½ in D.

The teaching of fractions, according to some, should be delayed until Grade IV or later; but H. E. Moser (1947) found that if teachers continually explain the meanings of the fractions and of the operations, even second-graders have little difficulty. The mental age required to learn French through conversation about pictures and events is certainly less than that required for learning by conjugating verbs. The force of current attempts to place intellectual content earlier in the curriculum lies in the assumption that methods can be adapted to the readiness of the younger child. This is especially well illustrated by a study in progress that is preparing texts and classroom procedures for teaching the same topic (coordinate geometry) in every grade from I to VI; the aim is to study how the approach should differ for younger and older pupils.

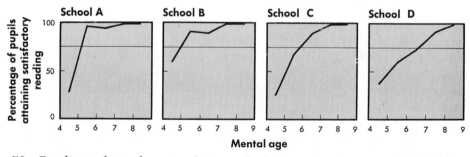

56   *Readiness depends on teaching method as much as on mental age (data from Gates, 1937)*

Experimental curricula are finding ways to bring abstract ideas within the reach of pupils. The principles underlying current experiments are not novel, but they have rarely been applied as carefully, or with such technical resources. Intuitive understanding is placed ahead of formalization. Concrete objects or visual aids are substituted for verbal or mathematical symbols until the phenomenon under study is familiar to the pupil. The "ripple tank" of the Physical Sciences Study Committee, for example, permits the pupil to become thoroughly at home with the interference and summation of waves, reflection, and other phenomena. The teaching encourages the pupil to estimate and to speculate. Pupils are far more likely to fail when they can reach an acceptable answer only by following blindly the steps of an elaborate routine. They are far more likely to succeed if the goal is to obtain a reasonable—though perhaps inexact—answer. After a strange topic has lost its strangeness, the pupil is more ready for a formal, highly efficient technique.

No basic idea or skill belongs exclusively to one year of the curriculum. A basic idea can be considered many times, taking on new significance or greater depth in each new context. Take the inheritance of traits as an example. For the fourth-grader, a study of his family tree gives personal meaning to the topic. The high-school senior deals with the idea quite differently when carrying out a study of his own with fruit flies, or discussing the population explosion.

The real problem is not when a particular *subject* is to be taught, but when certain types of *understanding* or *performance* can be developed by the best methods of teaching. It makes sense to break up a subject such as biology or economics so as to introduce some concepts years earlier than others. Students do not learn to type at an employable level until high school, but primary children can begin to type and this beginning helps them in all language learning (B. D. Wood and Freeman, 1932; O. K. Moore, unpublished).

While the trials so far made are encouraging, none of the proposals discussed has been adequately tested. The worth of the proposals will be fully known only when we have been able to see what levels of mathematical competence, for example, typical pupils attain in high school, after starting with set theory in the first grade.

13. Is the following comment sound?

"The fact that children seldom master long division and fractions by the time they leave school should be proof enough that the learning was beyond their comprehension."

14. As a child learns his native tongue, is he rewarded or punished when his sentences are partially wrong in structure? Is the ability to form sentences acquired intuitively or formally?

15. If a fixed total time were to be devoted to foreign-language study, what arguments could be given for and against starting instruction in Grade IV rather than in Grade IX? Assume that pupils will remain in school 12 years.

16. If we find that several important scientific ideas can be taught in Grade II, on what basis should the ones for study at that level be selected?

17. Many adults need to know how to choose annuities and similar investments wisely. They could learn in high school or alternatively in an adult education program. Discuss which would be psychologically the best location for the material, taking into account readiness, the opportunity for learning through practice, and forgetting.

Ability Grouping

No matter what the curriculum, the school cannot properly assign pupils to learning experiences solely on the basis of age. People do not develop at a uniform rate or according to a fixed sequence. Some boys have made their vocational decision, sound or unsound, before they reach junior high school, and some have no concern about vocation until age twenty. Comparable differences in development are found for any other interest. An interest in dating and courtship emerges rather suddenly in an individual, but the age when it emerges may be 11 or it may be 18.

The wide range of abilities is seen in this table of scores for a class of second-graders tested in the spring. The achievement test offers "grade equivalent" scores; a score of 4.0, for example, represents performance equal to that of the average pupil at the start of Grade IV. The scores listed for a few representative pupils give an impression of the individual differences usually found. Two pupils can read materials appropriate for fourth-graders; one is still below the level of the second grade. The range in other

TABLE 12

Achievement scores for representative second-graders in the same class (Goodlad and Anderson, 1958, p. 10)

Child	Mental age [*]	Paragraph meaning	Word meaning	Spelling	Arithmetic reasoning	Arithmetic computation	Achievement (total)
A	8-11	4.2	4.2	4.6	4.1	2.5	4.2
B	8-10	3.7	4.7	4.2	3.9	2.5	3.9
C	6-11	3.3	3.5	3.2	2.2	2.1	3.2
D	7-7	2.5	2.2	3.2	2.8	2.2	2.5
E	8-1	2.0	2.4	2.7	2.6	2.3	2.4
F	5-1	1.5	1.7	1.5	1.5	1.3	1.5

[*] Pupils range from 7-5 to 7-9 in age. At the time these pupils were tested, the norm group averaged around 2.8 on each test.

subjects is equally wide, save for arithmetic computation (where pupils have had no chance to learn more advanced processes). Differences between the most and least advanced pupils increase in higher grades; by Grade VI, some pupils are equal to eighth-graders and others are still no better than the average third-grader.

Figure 57, charting information from the national norms of the California Achievement Tests, reinforces these statements. In reading comprehension, the pupil has to read passages and answer multiple-choice questions about them; in spelling, he chooses the correct spellings of words. The number of points at the left side shows the number of questions answered correctly. In each test, the lower half of the sixth grade occupies the same range of scores as the upper half of the fourth grade.

An obvious suggestion to cope with this wide range is ability grouping. Second-graders might be allocated to different classes according to total ability and achievement scores, or a single class might be subdivided. This procedure has been condemned by those who regard it as a caste system within the school. The self-respect of the pupil who knows he is in the lower group is indeed threatened, but this difficulty is not caused by the grouping. Pupils who cannot do normal work feel inferior under any plan.

Ability grouping of this type does not create a class with uniform readiness. Because different aspects of readiness are no more than moderately correlated, *pupils who are homogeneous in one respect differ in other dimensions almost as much as unselected pupils.* Within a group selected so that all pupils are above average in mental ability, there are still differences in reading and arithmetic ability that require adaptation in teaching. Figure 58 s¹ ows the typical relation between abilities. The superior group (right of chart) is homogeneous in reading ability, but its members vary from superior to poor in arithmetic. The lower section, where no one is superior in reading ability, contains quite a few pupils superior in arithmetic. As more abilities—art, spelling, oral communication, com-

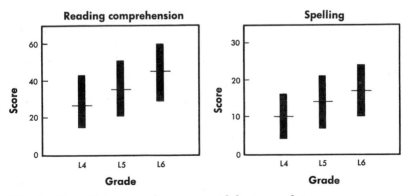

57 *Pupils within a grade range widely in proficiency*

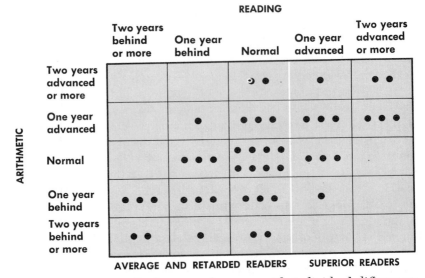

58   *Sectioning pupils does not do away with individual differences*

mittee work—are considered, it is quickly seen that the "homogeneous" group is a collection of unique individuals, nearly as varied in ability as the original pool from which they were chosen. Furthermore, the personality differences that require the teacher to restrain one pupil, inspire a second, and give emotional support to a third will be found no matter how selected the group is in ability.

Some children do not have enough ability to remain in the regular instructional program. Pupils with IQs below 50 are nearly always assigned to a special school or a special class. Pupils with IQs above 75 are ordinarily retained in the regular school program. Many pupils in the IQ range 50–75 should be in special, small classes under specially trained teachers. The advantage of keeping such children in the regular class, apart from the possible reduction in school costs, is that they might obtain a broader social experience and feel less stigma; but this advantage cannot be counted upon, since the child of low IQ is likely to be rejected and isolated (G. O. Johnson and Kirk, 1950; R. V. Miller, 1956). Whether a child should be in a regular or a special class depends upon his ability and personality, the program of the regular class, and the skill of its teacher (Dunn, 1960).

Under some circumstances, placing the exceptionally able pupils in a special program is beneficial (Lorge, 1954; for descriptions of several such programs see De Haan and Havighurst, 1961, pp. 115–45). This type of ability grouping has long been familiar in the very selective admission policies of certain colleges. Some cities have established similarly selective high schools, the Bronx High School of Science being the most famous example. In smaller communities and in lower grades, the advantages of special classes for the gifted are often better attained by establishing interest groups (e.g., creative writing clubs and advanced science classes), which form only a part of any one pupil's program.

Grouping for instruction in a single subject has substantial value. The primary teacher forms groups that use quite different reading and prereading materials. Ninth-grade algebra students are divided into sections that proceed at different rates and cover different amounts of material. Students in the same section for algebra may be in different sections for history or biology. In high schools and colleges grouping has been represented primarily by special "slow sections" or courses diluted to serve the

| Age 10 | Age 10 | Age 10 | Age 10 |
| IQ 110 | IQ 110 | IQ 110 | IQ 110 |

59   *The homogeneous group is a collection of unique individuals*

weaker pupils. Today there is a comparable interest in special sections for the talented (see below).

Whether a class is selected or is a cross section of the school, there is much to be gained by subdividing it for particular activities: five pupils who have trouble with division may be taken aside for several weeks of special instruction, while continuing as regular members of the class in all other work. Pupils grouped together for reading fall at different ability levels for dramatics or drawing.

There is no educational magic in grouping itself. Having a somewhat uniform group is no more than an opportunity to find the educational method for which that group is most ready. Little is gained by grouping if the group is taught the usual material in the usual way. In working with an unselected class, the teacher takes advantage of materials and a course of study that have, over a long period, been adjusted to fit the typical pupil. With a select group the teacher has to take the full responsibility for adapting content, method, and pace. If he pitches the work too high because he knows he has a superior group, or if he goes too far in the other direction with a supposedly slow group, pupil achievement and motivation are likely to be less than they would be in an unselected group (Cronbach and Gleser, 1957, p. 71).

ACCELERATION.   Closely related to ability grouping is the acceleration of superior pupils. The bright child tends to resemble somewhat older pupils in interests and social development as well as in achievement. Moving him through school faster has been suggested as an easy way to give him a better program. Sometimes acceleration is achieved by double promotion, i.e., skipping over a grade. Sometimes bright pupils are taught the work of two grades in one year to prepare them for promotion to more advanced groups.

Whether or not to accelerate must be decided individually, since some bright children are immature physically and socially. Skipping Bill Chelten (p. 145), for example, would probably have intensified his difficulties with his peers. Another very bright pupil accelerated a year or two may still be superior or equal to the group in most respects. Keys (1938) found that such educational acceleration tends to accelerate social development. More extreme acceleration is usually unwise. Placing a pupil permanently with others who are several years older leads to difficulty because he encounters developmental demands before he can meet them. It is hard for a 12-year-old, for example, to find a part-time job that compares with the jobs of 16-year-olds, though he is involved in their activities and needs to earn spending money.

Opinions regarding acceleration have gone through three stages since mental testing was introduced. First it was held that pupils with similar educational *achievement* should be placed together. In this period, acceleration was common and some pupils finished school far ahead of the normal age. Then, as educators became concerned with social adjustment, acceleration became taboo. Pupils of each *age* were kept together, and teachers were advised to invent special activities to keep the brighter ones interested and busy. The present view is that pupils of similar *maturity* should be placed together, maturity being judged in terms of social, physical, emotional, and intellectual characteristics.

Many bright children are bored with schoolwork paced by the readiness of the average child. Furthermore, bright pupils show excellent records of achievement and social adjustment after they have been accelerated (Pressey, 1949; Terman and Oden, 1959; Worcester, 1955). Acceleration permits the able student to finish an undergraduate course one or more years before the normal age. This makes it more likely that he will go on to graduate study or professional training.

One can accelerate the academic learning of the bright child without pushing him into a higher grade by bringing work from the higher levels down to him. The Advanced Placement program common in high schools permits the pupil to take certain college courses while participating in the regular courses and taking advantage of the social life of pupils of his own age. When he enters college he will be able to take some second- or third-year courses at the outset. Honors programs, special research projects, conversation groups in foreign languages—many devices can be used to challenge and encourage the superior student. To be beneficial, the accelerated program must be continuous. There is no virtue in carrying a selected group of sixth-graders through a good deal of algebra and then transferring them to a junior high school where they must rejoin average pupils and sit through two years of review.

NONPROMOTION.   Holding pupils back instead of promoting them to the next grade is also, on its face, a move toward a homogeneous group. This puts the weak pupil with those a year younger, whose achievement and mental age are more like his own. In theory, "repeating" the work in which he has had difficulty provides a good opportunity for mastering it. In actuality, the repeater makes less progress than the pupil with similarly low achievement who, in another school, is promoted with his class. There is a large body of research that Goodlad and R. B. Anderson (1959, p. 35) summarize as follows:

> At all grade levels, promoted low achievers generally do better than their nonpromoted counterparts. In all these studies, a number of nonpromoted children did show reasonable growth in achievement during the repeated year, but to offset this, a much larger percentage actually did worse on achievement tests after a year of repetition than they had done when tested just before the impact of failure or the subsequent deadening effect of repetition, or both, destroyed the will to learn and impaired some of the learning that already had occurred.

Many schools responded to this evidence by a policy of 100 per cent promotion, that is, by grouping pupils strictly according to seniority. This policy rightly recognizes that the child who "fails" in first-grade reading probably is more like the rest of his class than like next year's first-graders in every aspect of development except reading. However, the weak pupil has considerable difficulty if he is promoted. Goodlad (1952) studied unsuccessful first-graders in a dozen schools, half of which held pupils back and half of which had a nonfailure policy. He found that *both* groups were maladjusted during the next year. Both groups continued to have trouble with schoolwork, and members of both groups had relatively poor social acceptance and self-confidence. The adjustment problems were more extreme among the nonpromoted children, which supports the conclusion that holding the pupil back is self-defeating. But several of the promoted children worried about schoolwork to the point of cheating. It is obvious that trying to move all children through the same lessons at the same pace denies all we know about readiness and gives each successive teacher a wider range of differences to cope with.

18. In view of the sex differences in development and role in society, would acceleration have the same consequences and advantages for girls as for boys?

19. There is some evidence (Worcester, 1955, p. 37) that keeping a bright child with his own age group, in a school where lessons are the same for all pupils in a grade, damages social-emotional adjustment. Explain.

20. What are the advantages and disadvantages of giving a pupil like Olive a failing mark in a high-school course?

21. Which of the following policies would you endorse for high schools?

   a. Separate classes should be organized for slow-learning (distinctly below average) pupils.

   b. Slow-learning pupils should be encouraged to leave school at the earliest age legally allowable.

   c. Slow-learning pupils who fail to show satisfactory accomplishment in a particular subject should repeat the work in that subject.

   d. Slow-learning pupils should be given less classwork or easier classwork than the average pupil.

   e. Pupils of low ability should participate less in extracurricular activities than the average pupil.

   f. Slow learners should take vocational courses rather than courses in social studies and science.

Diversification of Activities

Regardless of school policies on promotion, the teacher must find ways of adapting instruction to individuals. Even within supposedly homogeneous groups, there are such great differences in interests, in specific intellectual skills, and in need for support, critical supervision, or independence that uniform treatment is at best a compromise which fits few students well.

Individual instruction—the teacher working differently with every pupil—is a good way to allow for differences in readiness. Individual methods are invariably used in remedial work and have an important place in teaching skills because of the importance of observing the performer. But in a large class little of the work can be individualized. Moreover, working in a group gives pupils an opportunity for learning from others that a strictly individual method cannot offer.

Often the teacher can devise a group activity within which every pupil works at his own level. He then has the self-respect and interest that comes from contributing to a group project, without the frustration of a too-difficult task or the tedium of work that is too easy. Within the main unit each pupil can work on a subdivision that arouses his interest. If he has a special weakness or a strong talent that merits encouragement, he can be directed into a task which will develop that area. Instead of reading from the same source as every other pupil, he reads what is suited to his skill.

In a sixth-grade unit on railroads, some children may be making a map of early American railroads while others are drawing people in the costumes of 1890 meeting a train. The first group will need less creative skill than the second. Both groups will have to do library work to get the necessary information, and the harder investigations can be allotted to the more capable pupils. Boys will be more concerned about the train in the mural, and girls with the costumes, but both can develop artistic skill. Pupils can take various social roles. Terry is the chairman of a committee; Babs is secretary; Frank arranges a visit to the roundhouse; Jill serves as classroom librarian. Brad, who lacks confidence and persistence, gets the rather simple task of collecting timetables for use by several of the committees; their constant "Have you got the one for us yet?" keeps him aware of his responsibility

60   *Each child can develop according to his readiness*

until he completes it. Claude is a good worker and skilled at lettering, but he tends to work by himself. In addition to his work on the map, he is asked to assist the others in improving their lettering on the charts and graphs of railroad services they are making.

Activities of this sort require ingenuity. The teacher cannot plan a lesson or a lecture and use it year after year, nor can he purchase the plans from a school supply house. Each time the unit is studied with a new class, the unique social structure and interests of that group call for somewhat different emphasis, organization, and source materials. Differentiated activities make teaching easier in some ways, since they result in greater interest and fewer problems of discipline. Moreover, the fact that each pupil is working on material he can master makes helping him far less of an uphill job.

The benefits to be obtained from adapting instruction are demonstrated by Daisy M. Jones's (1948) study in Grade IV (Figure 61). In five experimental classrooms the lessons, textbooks, and procedures were chosen for individuals on the basis of pretests. The texts ranged from second- to sixth-grade level. In the control groups, where pupils were closely similar to the experimental pupils initially, the customary fourth-grade materials were used;

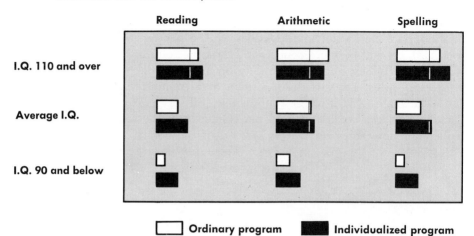

61 *Fourth-graders gain more from adaptive instruction (data from Daisy M. Jones, 1948)*

supplementary materials were also chosen to "fit the group as a whole." Gains were measured by a standardized achievement test; in one year, a gain of 1.00 on the grade-equivalent scale is normally expected. In eight out of nine comparisons the experimental group did better than the control group. In this study the low-ability pupils were helped most by individualization. It is to be emphasized that this result was accomplished with no special selection of teachers and no special budget; the experimental teachers merely used a superior plan.

The newly emerging proposals for "automatic teaching" adapt to individual differences in another way. In a later chapter (see page 406) we shall describe these techniques, the chief feature of which is a carefully arranged sequence of explanations and questions to carry the learner through a body of factual material. The material may be presented by a machine or a workbook. Progress is continuously checked; if the pupil fails to grasp an idea, he misses certain questions. Since he is not ready to move ahead to the next concept or the next application of the idea, he is turned back for review or for study of the same idea in another form. This scheme differs from the traditional use of homework questions, recitations, and workbooks because every pupil answers every question in the main sequence, learns at once of his errors, and is held on one small body of material until he masters it. The material he is to work on during any study session is selected automatically, according to his record on the preceding trials.

There are endless questions to be raised regarding the proper role of such instruction, many of which we shall examine later. For the present, it is worthwhile to see this proposal as a radically new idea in individualized instruction that does not impose an impossible burden on the teacher. Each pupil moves at his own rate. The pupil with a good background can push ahead rapidly, until he reaches material that challenges him. The pupil who finds a certain concept confusing puts extra time on it without holding up the class. Each pupil can spend extra time on whichever subject is most troublesome for him.

Automatic instruction does not remove the problem of individual differences. The pupil who is weak in arithmetic must work on different materials than the advanced pupil, and if each moves ahead efficiently the weaker pupil may never catch up. Nothing in the method as it presently exists copes with differences in motivation. But, for those aspects of school learning where intensive study of defined "fundamental content" is appropriate, presenting questions adjusted day by day to the pupil's current understanding should be of great assistance.

22. Can activities involving differentiated assignments be used in a college class?

23. How might a high-school civics class be organized to allow for differences in interests and abilities?

Nongraded Schools

As we have seen, age-grading is inconsistent with the facts about pupil differences, and allocating pupils to grades according to their over-all ability or their ability in one subject does little to improve the situation. In high school and college the problem is alleviated by assigning the pupil to an appropriate section of each course; the same high-school senior may be doing advanced projects in drafting and working in a low-ability section in first-year algebra at the same time. In the elementary school, however, the tradition of keeping each class physically together greatly limits the flexibility of grouping.

This tradition is now being challenged. As specialist teachers come into the elementary school, they find it appropriate to form ability groups that cut across grades. The music teacher can form a successful ensemble by combining the most advanced players from the fourth through sixth grades, to provide a learning opportunity that neither within-grade instruction nor individual lessons could offer. Science specialists may similarly form clubs or work groups of children who, regardless of grade, are capable of working effectively on a particular experiment. Such grouping outside the regular classroom is most commonly intended to serve superior pupils.

A more radical innovation is to erase grade designations. A class is made up of pupils who have much the same readiness, particularly in reading and general intellectual development. The class carries forward as a unit, perhaps for three years, but individuals are moved to another class whenever they are found to be far ahead or behind the group. The class may include some who would be first-graders and some who would be third-graders in the conventional school. Under a nongraded plan, learning activities are determined by readiness, not by seniority. Fred, with one year of seniority in the school, finds himself working with five other children in a reading group. Two of these entered the school a few months ago, two came in with Fred, and one entered a year before Fred came. Fred helps a group paint a mural, and in that group all the others may be a year older than Fred. The teacher sets up committees and work groups so that pupils ready for the same experience get it. Flexible grouping makes it possible for a child who needs two years to master first-grade reading to do so. The plan eliminates the decision to promote or not to promote at the end of first grade, when many children in the graded school receive a pointed, crushing setback. The pupils have little awareness of seniority. An immature child can, if necessary, spend four years in the primary section without the social dislocation nonpromotion usually inflicts. Next year he can stay with a class most of whom are old friends, whereas in a formally graded school he would be torn from all his friends and publicly labeled a failure.

Figure 62 indicates one way of organizing primary work. Here there are seven classes, ranging from the least skilled in Miss Black's room to pupils working on the usual third-year course of study in Miss Gray's. Henry, who is finding work in Miss Smith's room easier than most other pupils, is moved to Miss Jones's room if it is felt that he can make the social adjustment successfully. In that group he will be about average in attainment; he will therefore suffer less dislocation than the child who skips a grade and finds himself behind his new group in many ways. Harry, on the other hand, is moved from Miss Brown's class, where he is at a disadvantage, to a group where he will be more comfortable. Harry does not know that he was moved "down," and if his problem is a transient one he will move out of the primary unit after three years, just as he would have done under Miss Brown.

There is practically no formal evidence regarding the effectiveness of the nongraded school, though teachers give encouraging reports (Goodlad and Anderson, p. 57). One small study (Skapski, 1960) finds that nongraded primary reading instruction produces an advantage equal to an extra six months of graded instruction by the end of the third year of school. For the very superior pupil, the gain is a full year.

The two- or three-year primary unit has been widely adopted because the inability of some pupils to read after one year in school has made the first grade a particularly unsatisfactory administrative unit. An intermediate unit can replace Grades IV–VI. It appears to the writer that many problems of instructing pupils at ages 11–14 would be reduced by instituting a nongraded unit in place of the junior high school. Differences in biological maturity and interests might be recognized by moving pupils into this unit shortly after puberty, assuming appropriate educational maturity, and moving them on to the ninth grade when their social and intellectual perfor-

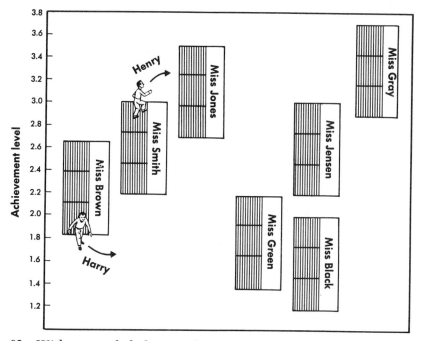

62 *With nongraded classes, adjustment to individual differences is a continuous process* (*Goodlad and Anderson, 1958, p. 74*)

mance warrants. The average girl would move out of the intermediate unit earlier than the average boy. Some intellectually able boys, physically and socially immature, would be retained beyond the point where they now move to the junior high school. The radical alteration of both elementary and secondary curricula now under way (notably in science, languages, and mathematics) will call for a redefinition of the junior-high-school curriculum. Along with this reform, it would be wise to seek an administrative plan that will provide proper early-adolescent experiences for those who *are* early adolescents, rather than for those who happen to have spent six years in school.

 24. What would happen under a graded plan and under a nongraded three-year primary plan
  a. to a girl who is very bright and learns the fundamentals of reading after two months of school?
  b. to a girl who is of average general ability but has special difficulty in reading and scores far below the norm on a reading test after one year?
 25. Describe a detailed plan for organizing a nongraded "early adolescent" unit. What advantages would such a plan have compared to the 6-3-3 organization? what disadvantages?

SUMMARY

While scholastic aptitude tests identify pupils likely to succeed in the school as it now exists, such tests can be criticized from two points of view. The first criticism is that some of the pupils who seem untalented might be superior performers if given a different type of instruction. Present tests and present schooling demand convergent thinking, presenting problems that have just one correct solution. Some writers speculate that a school program that capitalizes upon divergent thinking would fit some pupils better than the present one. A test of divergent thinking calls for fluency in finding reasonable solutions where there is no one "right" answer. If creativity in adulthood calls for divergent thinking, a school program that neglects this talent is faulty. At present, there is little evidence that tests of divergent thinking do have socially important correlates, and no educational program based on divergent thinking has been established. The speculations on this matter illustrate the unquestionably valid point that talents are of different types, and that our ultimate aim should be to find a method of instruction fitted to each pupil's talent. This means also that we should identify aptitudes that interact with instructional methods, not solely the aptitudes that predict success within one fixed method.

The second criticism of tests is that they are used at an early age to identify the talented and to place low-scorers in a nonintellectual program, as if ability were fixed. But there is no way to measure intellectual "capacity." A test shows only the performance the child has so far developed. Though fairly stable, mental test standing is not fixed. A significant minority of pupils change as much as one standard deviation (16 or more IQ points) in eight years. The aptitude profile does not begin to stabilize until about age 10; changes in profile shape continue throughout high school. This means that plans for a pupil must be reviewed periodically as he develops.

Differences in environment may have important effects on ability. Studies of identical twins, of emotionally disturbed children, of children in backward communities, and of children raised in different home atmospheres all testify to environmental influences. Heredity also contributes to differences in ability level and perhaps is responsible even for some spurts and declines in mental growth. Little is known about the environment best for mental growth. The democratic and accelerating home promotes independence and curiosity; this seems to have a positive effect on ability. For children coming from seriously deficient environments, especially stimulating preschool or primary experience is found to have great and lasting value. Kirk raised the IQs of institutionalized mental defectives, and Herr helped children of Spanish-American parentage by a special prereading program. A junior-high-school program for the culturally deprived in a New York slum appears to be stimulating talent and remedying deficiencies in readiness. But for children of more or less normal background supplementary enrichment does not seem to yield permanent gains. The research warrants hope that educational methods for increasing the rate of intellectual development can be devised. These methods are more likely to take the form of the direct teaching of skills, concepts, generalizations, and techniques of thinking than of vaguely defined "enrichments."

х The traditional method of adapting schooling to readiness is age-grading, assigning certain content to be learned at a certain age. The traditional placement of subject matter does not necessarily match what pupils can do; on the contrary, it appears that by changing the method of teaching one can successfully teach material much earlier than is customary. The idea that neural maturation dictates the timing of mental development has suggested postponing any subject that the young pupil finds difficult. This evades the problem of inventing a method of teaching that subject from which the younger pupils will profit. Current curriculum experiments are bringing advanced ideas within the reach even of school beginners. No basic idea or subject belongs exclusively to one year of the curriculum. A significant idea should reappear in the curriculum many times, in new contexts and with increasingly thorough treatment.

While improved curricula can better fit typical development, individual differences remain a problem. In Grade VI, some pupils reach the eighth-grade average in achievement, and others are no better than the average third-grader. Sectioning pupils is not the solution. Pupils selected as having similar test scores will not be homogeneous. Some in a good group have serious deficiencies in reading or arithmetic; some in a poor group are above average in particular subjects. The child with an IQ below 75 is often taught more easily in a special program. Above that level it is necessary to regroup pupils for each subject to obtain a reasonably uniform group. Even when there is ability grouping for a single subject, the benefit follows from devising an educational plan fitted to the group, not from the uniformity itself.

Double promotion and other methods of accelerating the bright child can be beneficial. The child put with an older group gains academically and often achieves better social adjustment. Placing a pupil a year or two ahead of his age-group can be recommended when his maturity level, taking into account interests and social-emotional maturity as well as intellect, is similar to that of the new group. Special programs can accelerate the pupil's learning without removing him from his age-group. These accelerated programs should be continuous. It is pointless to give advanced work in Grades V and VI if the pupil will move into a lock-step junior high school.

The evidence is unfavorable to a policy of holding back the failing pupil.

The first-grader who is promoted despite a poor record tends to do better than the one who is required to repeat the first year's work.

Two approaches are particularly successful in recognizing individual differences. Within a classroom, the teacher can diversify activities, allowing pupils to use different materials and to work on assignments matched to their educational needs. This may be facilitated by "automatic" teaching aids. The school organized on a nongraded principle achieves flexibility. It adjusts the pupil's rate of progress through school without conspicuous points of failure or "skipping." In the nongraded school, pupils of similar development are placed in the same room. The pupil may be moved to a more advanced group at any time during the year. This plan has been most used at the primary level, but it may have equal benefits during early adolescence.

Reading List 8

John I. Goodlad and Robert Anderson, "Toward Realistic Standards and Sound Mental Health," Chapter 7 in *The Nongraded Elementary School* (New York: Harcourt, Brace & World, 1959), pp. 142–69.

This chapter traces the progress of the pupil under conventional and nongraded plans, showing the presumed effect of each plan on the motivation of fast and slow learners. Note also chapters on "To Promote or Not To Promote" and "The Nongraded School in Operation."

Robert J. Havighurst and Bernice J. Neugarten, "The School as a Sorting and Selecting Agency," Chapter 9 in *Society and Education*, 2nd ed. (Boston: Allyn and Bacon, 1962), pp. 227–48.

Case studies and statistics describe how pupils from different social-class levels fare in school. Particularly important is the evidence that plans for grouping often discriminate against pupils from poorer homes.

Arthur D. Morse, "The Search for Hidden Talent," Chapter 3 in *Schools of Tomorrow—Today* (Garden City: Doubleday, 1960), pp. 41–60.

A report on the New York City experiment with special stimulation for underprivileged junior-high-school pupils. What are the circumstances that made this program necessary? How widely should other schools adopt such a method?

A. Harry Passow, "Enrichment of Education for the Gifted," in Nelson B. Henry, ed., *Education for the Gifted*, Fifty-seventh Yearbook of the National Society for the Study of Education, Part 2 (Chicago: Univ. of Chicago Press, 1958), pp. 193–221.

Arguments comparing enrichment, acceleration, and special schools for the gifted. Enrichment practices at various levels of schooling are described in other chapters.

Pauline S. Sears, "Problems in the Investigation of Achievement and Self-esteem Motivation," in M. R. Jones, ed., *Nebraska Symposium on Motivation* (Lincoln: Univ. of Nebraska Press, 1957), pp. 265–339.

One section of this lecture (pp. 280–319) describes three sixth-grade boys with very different abilities and needs. A different list of educational goals was set for each child (e.g., for Alex: less dominance, less defensiveness, greater care in written work). The teacher's technique in handling each child was adjusted to promote these developments.

D. A. Worcester, *The Education of Children of Above-Average Mentality* (Lincoln: Univ. of Nebraska Press, 1955).

A summary of research on acceleration and enrichment, with recommendations for practice.

PART THREE

ACQUIRING SKILLS, IDEAS, AND ATTITUDES

CHAPTER 9 SKILLS

Skilled performance is shown whenever we run through a complex series of well-practiced actions to accomplish a familiar task. A man rises from bed, dresses, shaves, walks downstairs, feeds himself, and drives to his office. Each of these is a highly developed skill. Even so simple an act as rising from bed consists of carefully selected movements, each appropriate in force and direction. If the man had not learned, he would be reduced to clumsy, slow trial and error, but thanks to experience he can perform rapidly and accurately without giving the act his full attention.

The word *skill* may be applied loosely to any performance. We might say, for example, "This painter was skillful in conveying the excitement of the fiesta." We, however, will confine the term to repetitive behavior in which a complex sequence of actions is carried out in a more or less fixed way. Such well-defined sequences of action can be observed in diving, typing, singing, sawing a straight cut, and assembly work in a factory. These are clearly to be classed as psychomotor skills. This chapter will be mostly concerned with psychomotor skills, important in vocational proficiency, the performing arts, and sports. Some psychomotor skills, such as speech and handwriting, concern almost all teachers.

A skilled performance involves interpreting and making a trial response directed toward a goal; the process of learning a skill is therefore much the same as any other learning. Skill learning is relatively simple since one ordinarily develops skill through experience with a limited range of tasks. A well-defined response pattern is polished, often nearly to perfection. Many of the principles of psychomotor learning apply also to performance where the motor element is unimportant. Surveying, for example, calls for a sequence of operations more intellectual than motor, but most of the principles of skill learning apply to it.

This chapter will be especially concerned with questions about practice. What conditions make practice most beneficial? What is the function of supervision by the instructor? Should skills be developed in a situation just like that where the actions will be used after training, or should the situation be simplified for teaching purposes? Should the learner begin his practice without help, so that he will discover the correct pattern of movement for himself, or does it help to demonstrate the best pattern before he starts?

CHARACTERISTICS OF SKILLED ACTION

A person in an unfamiliar situation must find out what to do. His actions are likely to be hesitant, with many pauses to examine consequences. In a familiar situation, actions are direct and usually successful. Only when a person encounters difficulty will he act indecisively and pause to think about what he is doing. Problem solving is required when a person driving in strange territory is uncertain which turn to take. He makes a trial decision and pushes hesitantly down the chosen route, watching closely for signs by which to check his decision. On a well-known road, however, he sails along. He shifts gears, gives the car extra gas on a hill, and takes curves without interrupting his conversation with his companion. Both his handling of the car and his pathfinding performance (for he is selecting his path moment by moment) illustrate mature skills.

One person is said to be more skilled than another when he reaches his goal with fewer pauses to make choices or to correct errors. We can describe skilled performance by such words as "automatic" and "smooth." Any skilled performance, even writing the letter *a*, is a complex, integrated series of hundreds of nerve-muscle coordinations.

Change from Mediated to Immediate Response

The change from conscious step-by-step direction to an automatic performance is in large part due to the dropping out of *mediating responses* (mediating = "in the middle"). When the beginner takes up a new piano selection, he must use a chain of stimulus-response associations like this:

    a. Sight of note produces thought: "That stands for B♭."

    b. Thought of note produces image of position B♭ on keyboard: "Of the three black keys, the one farthest to the right."

    c. Sight of keyboard and hand produces thought: "B♭ is next to the little finger."

    d. Player directs self to move little finger up and to the right; stroke on B♭ key with little finger follows.

Each of the mediating responses at this early stage is a thought leading the performer one step along the way. In a chain such as this a response is also a stimulus for the next step. The beginner's performance, broken into steps, is clumsy. With practice the separate mediating responses become unnecessary. For example, after the beginner practices for a while with his hand in the same base position, the thought "B♭" leads without a pause to movement of the proper finger. Later, the sight of the note becomes a sufficient stimulus for the movement. Stimulus substitution has occurred. Once the needed stimulus for the act was the thought, "Strike the black key with the little finger"; now only the note is required.

Mediation translates the concrete into the abstract; i.e., it changes sensed reality into symbols that refer to stored verbal knowledge. And, as the end product of thought, mediation provides a verbal order directing action (abstract to concrete). The engineer may know a great deal about the mathematical theory of positive feedback in oscillations. Surveying the channel where he will build a bridge, he senses the peculiar winds and "recognizes them"—i.e., translates his impression into a concept: "forces that start oscillations." This verbal label tells him what theory to call upon; if he fails to make this translation, he will never think to use the theory. Likewise, if he knows the theory but cannot derive from it a concrete rule for action, he will never achieve an adequate design. By analogy with an electronic computer, we can speak of these processes as *encoding, data processing,* and *decoding.* In every verbally mediated action we can identify four stages:

a. Intake: stimuli set off nervous impulses.

b. Encoding: stimulus information (cues) is turned into symbols meaningful to the individual. (Wind on cheek is labeled "force"; black key is labeled "B♭").

c. Data processing: associations and reasoning operations are used to derive from the information a symbolically stated prescription for action ("strike with middle finger").

d. Decoding: the symbolic order is turned into nervous impulses directing muscles to act on the physical situation (finger movement at the piano; bracing the bridge at a certain point).

The symbolic processes may be highly explicit if one is dealing with a situation for the first time. Later, they receive less attention. In a thoroughly practiced skill the step from sensory information to action is taken immediately, without symbolic interpretation. A specialized neural program (see page 101), below the level of conscious attention, is set up for performing the familiar act.

1. Which of the following performances would be called skills?
   a. John Smith signs his name to a check.
   b. On the check stub he subtracts $2.40 from $15.00 without error or difficulty.
   c. A quarterback notices that an opponent is out of position and calls a successful play through that spot.
   d. The quarterback throws passes that consistently "lead" the runner by just the right amount, though the direction, distance, and wind conditions change from occasion to occasion.

    e. A child on his third trip to a small zoo names all the animals correctly.

    2. Show that a sequence of decisions or actions is involved in each of the following skilled performances.

        a. Mrs. Brown fries an egg.

        b. Terry Tuttle goes to the library and locates information on the presidential election of 1940.

        c. A child sings the familiar "Yankee Doodle."

        d. A German student translates, "Der Hund seht den Fleisch."

    3. What mediating responses that are present in early ballroom dancing drop out with practice?

Differentiation of Cues

In learning a skill three processes can be noted: differentiating the cues, bringing the needed elementary responses under control, and interconnecting the responses. A pianist cannot make the stroking response on signal until he is able to perform it on his own command. Once he can make the response promptly on signal, he begins to associate the response with stimuli that occur early in the sequence. The beginner identifies only a few of the signals or potential cues in the situation and forms a rough conception of the desired combination of actions. With practice, he becomes familiar with additional directing cues, reacts faster (gives less time to mediating responses), and coordinates his actions.

An action is guided by cues from the situation. The cues may be seen, heard, or felt. *A relevant cue is any stimulus from outside or from within the body that can help a person to recognize a situation or direct an action.* (Irrelevant stimuli, which he should learn to ignore, may be thought of as false cues.) The person who sits at a typewriter for the first time will guide his response almost entirely by sight cues. The letter on the key says to him, "Strike here and you will print the letter you want." The trained typist guides his action by muscular cues. At each instant he can sense where his fingers are, relative to the keyboard, and how he must move them to strike the desired letter.

With experience more and more cues become useful in selecting the right response. A beginner depends upon the most obvious cues. Later he makes use of many additional cues. He finds that one particular reach on the piano keyboard (yielding a muscular cue) is equivalent to a movement from the seen position of A to the seen position of B♭ (a visual cue). The boy starting to play a horn can judge whether or not his action is right only by the tone that comes out. Soon he finds that the right action *feels* different from the wrong. His lips feel right in one position, wrong in another, and if he uses this wrong position the wrong tone comes out. Lip-muscle cues are now as significant as the sound cues. The muscle cues are more useful, because they are available before he blows and they permit him to correct without sounding a false note.

The experienced person can select the most appropriate response on the basis of fewer cues than can the inexperienced person. We need many cues to recognize a near-stranger. If he so much as leaves off the hat he wore on previous occasions, we may not recognize him. We sometimes recognize a friend, however, from no better cue than the sound of his footsteps

63   *Cues may be seen, heard, or felt*

in the hall. The skilled performer takes advantage of the multitude of cues he knows to be relevant; if only a few of them are present, he nonetheless responds successfully. The performer usually is confronted with dozens or hundreds of stimuli. Some are fundamental cues, which one must notice to respond at all successfully; others are secondary, helpful in regulating the response; and still others are irrelevant. For the shortstop, the swing of the bat and the initial motion of the ball are fundamental cues that send him into action. The spin on the ball and the conditions of the infield are of no help to the beginner, but they help the expert to anticipate the hop of the ball. The position of the umpire, the roar of the crowd, and a million other stimuli are to be ignored. In understanding spoken Spanish, the listener must first detect the sounds carrying the central nouns and verbs; endings, adverbs, and the speaker's emphasis are somewhat secondary; and the fact that the voice is soprano or contralto is irrelevant.

The expert gives more of his attention to the secondary regulating cues. A toddler put upon a stage would have to give his full attention to the rim of the platform and to his muscular sensations to avoid toppling off. A 10-year-old giving a talk needs to give no attention to standing and balancing; however, *he* will have to think very hard about what he is trying to say. Getting words in the right order and remembering a series of ideas will take concentration. A more experienced speaker, master of what he is trying to say, can arrange the words with little conscious choice, and his postural reactions need no conscious direction. He is therefore free to watch the expressions and reactions of his audience and to alter his speaking adaptively. Repeated practice on recurring elements makes the basic response second nature. After that, more attention can be given to subtle discriminations.

> **4.** In rifle marksmanship are any cues pertinent save the visual cues from the target?
>
> **5.** Which of the following statements is (are) illustrated in attaching a two-prong plug to an electric cord?
>> **a.** The expert makes use of cues that the beginner ignores.
>> **b.** The expert makes more precise judgments than the beginner.
>> **c.** Many aspects of the situation are ignored by the expert.
>
> **6.** Suppose that building a campfire is a skill important enough that we wish to develop an ideal training program. What cues are fundamental, what cues secondary? Is the best procedure simply to have the learner build campfires under natural conditions?

Feedback and Correction

A skilled act may look like a single motion, but it is not. If we could put behavior under a microscope—something like this can be done by recording electrically the actions of separate muscles—we would see that the smooth motion is a chain of impulses. Each impulse checks, redirects, or augments the preceding action. Even in so simple an act as throwing a dart, no two performances are identical.

In the middle of the act, trials and corrections take place. This is obvious in steering a car. We do not—indeed, cannot—point the car down the road and hold it straight. We aim it more or less well, and then judge whether we are drifting to the right or the left. As soon as we sense the drift, we turn the wheel to correct it. Usually we correct too far, and soon must move the wheel back. Our path is a zigzag, never a straight line.

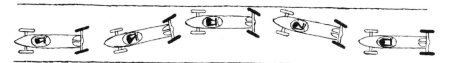

64 *Feedback of consequences guides correction*

The expert comes closer to the ideal path than does the novice, and his corrections involve less conscious attention. But his action consists of repeated sensing and correcting—what we call a *feedback* process. The driver's action has certain consequences. Knowledge of these consequences is fed back to the driver by visual and other cues. If he is dissatisfied he takes a further action; soon its consequences in turn are fed back.

Feedback is easily observed in mirror drawing because the unfamiliarity of the task reduces performance to a primitive level. The subject is asked to trace a path, looking not at his hand but at its reflection in a mirror. The reflected hand seems to move away when the real hand is pulled closer. The person produces a jagged, zigzag line quite unlike regular drawing (Figure 65). He is like the man blundering across a strange room in the dark, who starts in the direction that seems best, comes up short when he brushes an obstacle, turns on a new tack, cracks his shin and turns again, and so on. Feedback in the drawing experiment keeps the person near his proper path, but errors and too-strong corrections slow the performance. With practice much smoother lines are produced. There is still wavering as the person goes too far to the right or the left and

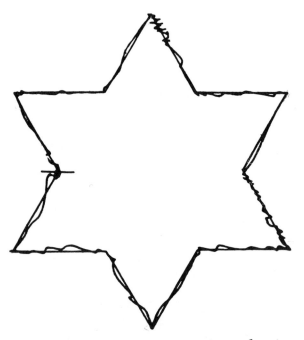

65   *Trial and correction in mirror drawing (Dearborn, 1910)*

checks himself. Eventually he becomes so adept at sensing the faintest deviation that mirror drawing becomes as smooth as adult penmanship.

Feedback occurs even in the middle of an act. The unskilled pianist reaches for an octave. As his hand comes down, he touches a black key where no key is expected. Receiving this warning, he stretches his fingers wider and continues the stroke. Cues received halfway through the action cause him to change the provisional try before he has finished it. A better pianist uses feedback from muscular stretch and contraction.

An expert does not do everything perfectly; rather, he detects and corrects errors during the action itself. He catches the mistake before it "comes out." Like the pianist, a person skilled in arithmetic checks himself while doing the problem. If at any intermediate stage he gets a number that is unreasonable (i.e., contrary to his expectation), he backtracks almost without thinking to the point of error, long before the wrong number is written down. As a person becomes sensitive to more delicate cues, he becomes able to correct a motion or an interpretation the instant it begins to go wrong. There is an anecdote about a teacher of bridge who, after watching Charles Goren and his partner win a national championship, sniffed, "He's not so wonderful. He didn't do a single thing that I wouldn't have done." Goren's comment was, "But the question is, would she have done everything we did for 36 straight hands?" The player who commits the fewest overt errors is the one who wins.

Improvement during practice is shown by Figure 66. These records show the learning of an industrial skill. The worker presses a foot treadle that drives a cutter, which in turn slices disks from the end of a rod. He is supposed to come down smoothly, follow through after the cut, and return to position for the next cut. Jerky action breaks cutting wheels and produces jagged disks, which have to be discarded. The performance records were made by fastening a recorder to the treadle. A steep line shows a rapid movement. In each stroke we see the starting pause at top, the rightward slant of the cutting stroke, the follow-through, and the upward return. Even in the final record, each stroke is a bit different. If you look closely, you can see the tiny wobbles that indicate sensing and correcting.

Feedback is the regulator of expert performance, and it is also the regulator of learning, for it tells the novice when he is improving and when he is wrong. At best it also tells him what to change. Thus it is not surprising that Bilodeau and Bilodeau (1961) say, "Studies of feedback or knowledge of results show it to be the strongest, most important variable controlling performance and learning [of motor skill]. It has been shown repeatedly that there is no improvement without knowledge of results, progressive improvement with it, and deterioration after its withdrawal." In intellectual learning, meaning is the "most important variable," but knowledge of results remains extremely important.

7. Show that feedback takes place in handwriting.

8. A chemistry class carries out an experiment, setting up flasks to generate hydrogen when acid is poured onto zinc. The instructions are clearly given in the laboratory manual, and the pupils work individually at their benches as the instructor circulates. When does feedback occur?

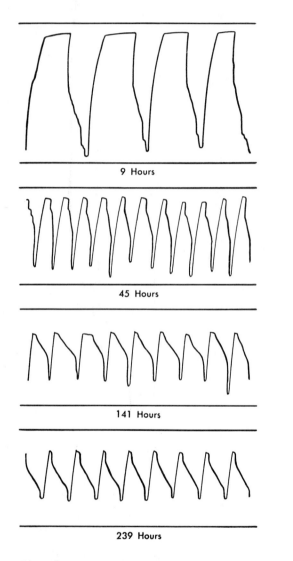

66 *Performance record of a trainee with increasing amounts of practice (Lindahl, 1945)*

Coordination of Movements

In a well-coordinated movement, each subordinate act occurs at just the right time. Its force is in correct proportion to the force of the other movements. Even putting a period after a sentence calls for many muscles pulling against each other to move the pen straight to the paper. The superior pianist keeps his eyes on the printed music well ahead of his fingers. Seeing what is coming, he can be in position for it. He sees and comprehends a whole phrase at a time, and plays it expressively as a phrase rather than note by note.

Actions organize into longer and longer sequences or programs—another use of that valuable word. The program of a ceremony is a list of things to be done in order: musical selection, invocation, flag salute, speech of welcome, and so on. The word has been applied in developing computers and automatic machines; seeing how it applies in this use will help us to understand its place in the description of human behavior.

An automatic dishwasher has a very simple program. It is "instructed" to rinse for, say, 45 seconds, close the drain, tip the soap dish, add water until a certain level is reached, spray the soapy water over the dishes for eight minutes, and so on until it turns off a signal light to end the cycle. Every action is performed at a certain time, regulated by a series of cams. A slightly more elaborate program is required for a clothes washer, which can be reset for different fabrics; each switch setting alters the timing of the various acts.

Still more complex is the program whereby a desk calculator carries out automatic division. The operator wishing to divide 22 by 3 places 22 in the dial and 3 in the keyboard, and presses the button. The machine then performs three acts repeatedly: subtracts 3 from 22, moves the counter ahead once, checks whether the remainder has "gone past" zero. The machine can do this seven times, and each time the remainder is decreased. After the eighth subtraction, the remainder is -2—"past zero." Now the machine follows a further order to correct its oversubtraction, shift to the next column, and continue working on the remainder to form a decimal fraction. This program specifies a sequence of actions with an important self-regulating or feedback step. In a large enough calculator it could continue forever, giving the answer 7.333 . . . A person doing long division follows a very similar program, save that he uses a trial divisor. The program he has learned tells him the steps to take, in order. If he has mastered the program, he never pauses to inquire, "What do I do next?" Programing is the arrangement of actions in a predetermined sequence. Later, in discussing teaching machines (page 412), we shall speak of them as providing "programed instruction," since the questions and explanations are arranged in a definite, carefully planned sequence.

In motor skill, the timing and the regulation of force become critically important parts of the program. You can observe this when you pick up a pencil from the desk. The eye locates the pencil, directs the hand into position so that the fingers come down an inch or two from the point. The thumb comes down opposite the first two fingers. You grasp the pencil between thumb and fingers, then between the two fingers, and without thought turn the pencil past the thumb into writing position. You have performed this act thousands of times without being aware of what you did. Even our description is incomplete. Did you notice that your thumb had its own part to play while the two fingers were rotating the pencil? The action is regulated by feedback. The same general program handles a slender pencil from a memo pad, or a marking pencil half an inch thick. The fingers close until the pressure seems right for lifting the pencil, each pencil requiring a different finger position.

In a rhythmic or coordinated movement, one action gives the signal for later ones. The driver who is learning to shift gears must consciously step on the clutch, shift to low, release the clutch, press it again, shift to second, and so on. The accomplished driver does all these in one fluid motion; while the clutch pedal is being released for low gear, the hand is already preparing to push the gearshift lever upward into second—just as in picking up the pencil your fingers and wrist were coming into position before the arm movement had been completed. In skilled action, the muscular cues of the first step give the signal for starting the second and third. The muscles used in the later parts of the action are poised and ready to act as soon as the right amount of time has elapsed. The expert makes use of signals far in advance of the action, his movements being tied together in long sequences. The beginner depends on cues closer to the time of the action, so that his responses are less integrated (Hartson, 1939; Bartlett, 1958, p. 15). Every expert develops an individualized program. Good tennis players making a forehand drive time their various muscle contractions differently, each having his own consistent coordination pattern (Slater-Hammel, 1949).

The importance of feedback for coordination is shown by experiments in which the feedback is disturbed. In one investigation, the subject's hand was shielded so that he could not watch it as he wrote. Instead, he was allowed to watch the hand on a TV screen. In the important experimental condition the TV image was electronically delayed one-half second. Having to watch the screen for cues produced only a slight loss of legibility and speed, but adding this delay disrupted the performance. The time necessary to write a word increased three- to tenfold, and writing became illegible (Figure 67). In speech, delayed feedback through earphones produces a stumbling, disorganized pattern similar to stuttering (Fairbanks and Guttman, 1958).

Programing is so essential a feature of skill that we might define a skilled performance as one in which a definite sequence of actions can be observed. The skilled performer need not, however, know *about* the program; often he is not aware of the movements he is making, nor of the cues he responds to. Conscious analysis of his own program sometimes helps the learner to improve, sometimes creates confusion. It is important that the teacher know what the program for successful performance should

No TV **TV - IMMEDIATE** **TV - DELAY**

67 *Delaying feedback disrupts coordination (Smith et al., 1960; reprinted from* Science *by permission.)*

Subjects wrote or traced normally, watching themselves on a television screen, or watching themselves with the image delayed one-half second.

be, however. Knowing the actions to be performed and the cues that guide them is the first step toward designing practice situations and identifying the learner's errors.

9. Show that a program of actions is used in diving from a high board. In balancing a chemical equation.

10. Examine an automatic pinsetter in a bowling alley and try to list the signals to which it responds and the sequence of actions it performs. How does this differ from what a human pinsetter would do?

11. The definition of a skill as programed behavior says nothing about the correctness of the technique, the speed of the performance, or the quality of the product. Why?

12. Show that when an expert types the words *died, hidden, did,* and *board* the act of striking *d* is different each time.

Stability of Response Under Difficulty

Men who earn equal scores are not necessarily equally expert. To decide which man is the most skilled, we would have to know who performs the most consistently. The British Air Force found that some men who seemed to be excellent pilots under normal conditions lost much of their skill when fatigued or ill. They were likely to crash or to be shot down because their skill was unstable. The best pilots maintain their performance under adverse conditions (Bartlett, 1948). Among the stresses that upset the person who is only half-expert are fatigue, illness, emotional pressure, and a confusing external situation.

Errors increase also when one performs several complicated acts simultaneously. For example, Horn (1961) finds that when elementary-school pupils try to express complex thoughts, they often misspell words that they write correctly in isolation. The expert maintains correct spelling while putting most of his attention on the ideas to be expressed.

The expert has several advantages (Castenada, 1956; Lazarus *et al.*, 1952; Fitts *et al.*, 1961; Fuchs, 1962):

He can perform even when, under abnormal conditions, discrimination becomes difficult. Some of the usual cues may be missing (e.g., driving in a snowstorm). Distractions cause signals to be missed. Discomfort or stress reduces the performer's ability to take in information. The expert can get by with fewer, fainter cues. His responses, "locked in place" as a sequence, do not depend solely on cues at the instant of action; he can continue smoothly past a temporary interference.

The expert is able to anticipate a possible hazard. He knows what to expect and takes advantage of cues when they first become available. By making an earlier adjustment (e.g., slowing before he comes to a slick place), he avoids what would create an emergency for the novice.

Under stress, errors occur or responses fail to get the expected result. This forces the performer to "shift down" to a more primitive performance, giving attention to mediating responses. The expert can recall correct mediating responses. The less expert performer is often uncertain which mediating response is correct ("Let me see, which key *is* B♭?").

Whereas stress upsets the nonexpert performer, it often brings the expert to his peak. The higher tension level of a public performance elicits more perfect responses from the experienced performer than does a rehearsal, just because he comes nearer to giving 100 per cent of his energy and attention.

13. How might one use the idea that quality of performance under stress is a sign of expertness
   a. to measure the proficiency of truck drivers at the end of an Army training course?
   b. to measure proficiency in speaking a foreign language?
14. What types of stress does the college student encounter that are likely to reduce his reading efficiency unless he is quite expert?

MAKING PRACTICE EFFECTIVE

The term *practice* refers to any repeated attempts to perform a task. Practice may take the form of a systematic drill, or it may be incidental to other school activities. It may be routine and repetitious, or every trial may be an adventure. We are primarily interested in what happens when a person has a series of systematically scheduled opportunities to attempt the same performance. In setting up lesson plans, the teacher selects tasks and arranges conditions so that the pupils will practice useful discriminations and response sequences.

The Function of Active Practice

The child who goes to market for his mother learns to make change faster than the one who only does arithmetic problems in school. The boy who tinkers with a radio set learns more about electricity than if he simply reads what the physics text says on the subject. The child who writes thoughtfully, three or four times, the word he has misspelled is much more likely to learn it than his neighbor who listens to other children spelling in chorus. The extrovert in the front row who talks continually learns more French than the shy boy in the back seat who recites only rarely (Pressey and Robinson, 1944).

By active trial the learner finds out how adequate his interpretation is. If he does less well than he expected, this suggests that he has overlooked or misinterpreted something. It is then profitable for him to watch someone demonstrate.

Though the value of plentiful practice seems obvious, the school sometimes fails to encourage active trial. The lecture method, for instance, makes no provision for trial. Students usually study by reading the text over and over. But trying to answer questions put to oneself (self-recitation) produces greater mastery than trying to absorb by reading, particularly with material difficult to understand. Most of the evidence on this point comes from studies of factual learning and memorization.

Gates asked pupils to memorize numerous statements. Some were told to read the statements over repeatedly. Other groups were told to use a certain portion of the time for testing their recall. As you can see (Table 13), 60 per cent recitation proved best for this material. Some other percentage would probably be better under other conditions. H. A. Peterson (1944) found 33 per cent self-recitation better than 50 per cent for long, connected passages where time was limited. Too short a reading period did not allow for adequate examination of the material.

TABLE 13

Self-recitation during study is helpful (Gates, 1917)

Percentage of study time used for self-recitation	Average score on memory test		
	Grade III	Grade V	Grade VIII
0	4.8	7.2	9.6
20	5.8	8.2	11.6
40	8.2	10.5	15.3
60	9.4	12.3	15.8
80	8.9	10.8	15.5
90	8.7	11.6	14.5

Practice is no guarantee of desirable learning. With extended experience in a situation one's response tends to stabilize, but the response acquired may be awkward, inefficient, even totally unsuccessful. What actions are learned, and at what level of mastery, depend on many factors, among them the situation, the method used to explain the task to the learner, the method of monitoring or evaluation, and the amount and spacing of practice.

Practice periods should be properly located in relation to explanations. If a person practices before he knows the correct general pattern of the task, he is likely to practice wrong actions. If he is given large amounts of explanation before he knows the task at first hand, he will understand little of the explanation. There must be an interplay between explanation, practice, and further explanation.

The amount of practice will need to be great if a response is hard to explain or demonstrate to the learner. A small amount may suffice if the explanation can be very clear and the cues are obvious. A skill that requires delicate discrimination or very exact timing needs large amounts of practice.

For some performances the external signals directing the task are essentially the same on all occasions. Playing a piano sonata from the written music is an example. In learning such a selection the musician is often wise to devote considerable time to studying the music before he begins physical practice. Activity, bringing in response-produced muscular cues, complicates the situation at a time when the player needs to give his full attention to getting the music in mind and thinking out the fingering for hard passages (von Wright, 1957a, 1957b). Once the interpretation is in mind, it serves to direct a suitably patterned motor performance, which is polished by physical practice. Such an explanation probably accounts for the finding that in shooting baskets from the foul line small amounts of "mental practice," in which the person merely imagines himself going through the act, are a beneficial supplement to motor trials (Vandell *et al.*, 1943; Twining,

1949; Waterland, 1956). There is no evidence that such "sitting and think-ing" improves those motor skills where the situation changes on each trial, as in dribbling through an opposing team. Nor is there evidence that it helps after the basic pattern of a coordination has been acquired.

Selecting Appropriate Practice Tasks

PRACTICE IN CONTEXT.   The teacher (along with the curriculum maker and the author of text material) arranges tasks for the pupil. He identifies re-sponses-to-situations to be developed within a broad area, such as the use of the library. He decides whether practice should take place in connection with larger projects, such as a class discussion on the United Nations, or through formal exercises in library skills. Each method has advantages; the choice depends on the complexity of the skill, the extent to which the correct response varies with the context, the value of the suggested projects, and the maturity of the learner.

Using a response in the context of a significant problem is often a supe-rior form of practice. The student will generally be interested in doing well when the act is necessary to a larger undertaking. When he performs correctly, progress on the larger problem encourages him. Furthermore, a lifelike context gives varied experience. A boy learning to catch flies during an actual ball game must take into account new wind and sun conditions every time he plays. Fifty flies in two dozen different games are far more varied than 50 flies hit to him in the same practice session.

Practice incidental to a larger activity may be too scattered and too little thought about, and the conditions too varied, for successful learning. If the pupil "practices" only once the use of the dictionary key to pronun-ciation, he probably will not remember what to do when, weeks later, pro-nunciation is pertinent to another report. When he uses the library, he may be rewarded in the end by completing his report to the class on time. But unless he or the librarian pauses to evaluate the library work, he may not realize how he wasted time or what resources he neglected. Without this attention to the performance, the practice leads to little improvement.

15. Discuss the advantage, if any, of formal exercises in teaching the fol-lowing:
   a. proper capitalization of titles
   b. outlining of a composition or talk
   c. focusing of a microscope

REALISTIC CUES.   As our analysis of skilled performance suggests, the situation must present the cues that can later be used in applying the skill. The teacher must decide how perfectly he should duplicate the future situation in which the skill will be used. He might reproduce that situation in every detail, simulate only parts of it, or use tasks that have little in common with the application situation. The decisions required are well illustrated in the design of "simulators." Psychologists and engineers develop extremely expensive pieces of apparatus to train men for military duties. This expense is justified because the only alternative is to allocate real airplanes, submarines, and rockets for training use. A simulator can, for example, present an image on a radar scope identical to that an approaching plane would make.

The cues that direct significant action should be realistically reproduced; other aspects of the situation need not be. Thus the radar screen should carry, along with the target image, the flashes and specks of interference that appear during normal operations; otherwise, the operator will not learn to locate a faint target through interference. Likewise, the brightness controls and other adjustments should resemble operational equipment in shape and location, since the operator will form the habit of reaching to a certain knob without looking. The timing of successive events should be the same as they are in combat. On the other hand, there is no need to reproduce the noise of a plane in motion, or the jar when a missile hits the ship; these cues are not the ones that regulate the actions being trained. The simulator can also neglect cues to which adaptation is easily learned on the job.

68 *Task simplification aids the beginner*

What apparatus would be required if we wished to substitute classroom training for a part of the road training of drivers? What, for example, would be the merit of showing a motion picture of a road, as seen through the windshield, and giving the pupil a steering wheel and brakes so that he could respond to the cues presented? This device might be of some use in teaching the quick application of brakes (e.g., when children suddenly appear beside the road). It would not be at all useful in teaching motor skills, however, because the learner would not have the true visual and motion cues that regulate steering and braking. One cannot give the "feel" of bringing a car to a gentle stop at the stop sign, or of taking an icy corner, without building a simulator that—like the Link trainer for pilots—responds with whatever motion his actions would give to a real car.

In discussing the importance of realism, we should not lose sight of the fact that while practice can be perfectly realistic, *instruction* is deliberately-unrealistic. The teacher alters the natural situation in order to speed up learning. At times this calls for simplifying the task, providing additional conspicuous feedback, or isolating a part skill for separate attention. In training typists, for example, flashing a phrase of copy on a screen for a fraction of a second is a valuable supplement to ordinary practice from a page of copy (Winger, 1951; Palmer, 1955). The explanation appears to be that this prevents any read-a-letter-type-the-letter-read-another-letter sequence of response. Forcing the pupil to grasp a whole phrase at once, this exercise encourages longer uninterrupted sequences of movement. Lindahl's recorder (see above) is another example of profitable artificiality.

Any simplification must conform to the principle of realism, however. If a task is changed in some fundamental way when it is made easier, practice loses much of its value. It "simplifies" the handwriting task to have a beginner trace well-formed letters through a tissue overlay, but he is no longer calling to his mind an image of the correct shape and no longer directing his muscles to produce it. He is responding to cues not present in the usual writing situation. Manuscript writing, on the other hand, *is* a reasonable preliminary to cursive writing just because the perceptual cues, the mediating image of a good response, and the motions used in writing

all resemble those present in the more complex response

Simplification is especially valuable early in learning, to help the learner to isolate and discriminate the most pertinent cues or to sense the essential pattern of the task. We make language learning easier, for example, by using simple sentences in which a limited number of main words are used (see also page 326). Usually, the best sequence for training is to begin with easy discriminations that help the learner to identify the major cues, and then to move gradually toward more subtle discriminations

(D. H. Lawrence, 1952; Baker and Osgood, 1954; von Wright, 1957a, 1957b). In a paced task, for example, it may be desirable to perform for a time at a slow speed to consolidate one's interpretation, before practicing at speeds where information comes too fast to be given full attention (D. H. Lawrence and Goodwin, 1954).

> **16.** It has been shown that in learning to type the pupil should practice striking the key with a quick movement even though a slower, more controlled movement would hit the key more squarely. What cues does he use in each kind of practice?
>
> **17.** Why is it better for the student to practice typing words and sentences rather than nonsense syllables? (L. J. West, 1956; 1957, p. 17).
>
> **18.** Pupils are to learn to fill out and to interpret bank checks. Which of the following is important to reproduce in the teaching situation?
>
> > **a.** A space is provided for the amount in both numerical and verbal form.
> >
> > **b.** The phrase "Pay to the order of" is always present.
> >
> > **c.** A number identifying the bank, as well as the bank's name, is always present.

VARIED PRACTICE MATERIALS.   Should practice materials and conditions be uniform so that the person will learn an instantaneous, fixed response? Or should the materials be varied so that he is constantly judging and adapting? This question is important because most drill procedures are designed to promote automatic response to uniform stimuli. Thus our question asks what value drill may have and how it should be planned.

Sometimes it is our intention to "train" the learner so that he will act always in the same way. This is proper if we can anticipate exactly the problem he will face in the future. Rarely in education, however, can the future be so neatly anticipated. Even in military training one wants a man to adapt to the unexpected.

We are never training a response alone; we are always developing ability to adapt to diverse situations. This may be illustrated with reference to English usage. Some teachers have tried to teach grammar as a set of unvarying "good responses." But language forms are associated with purposes. Formal, elaborate sentences suitable to compositions are awkward in informal communication. If the student learns only formal sentences, his speech will often fail to achieve his goal. Adaptive learning would be promoted by considering alternative expressions, such as:

> I sure done good on my last job.
> I sure hit the ball on my last job.
> I worked diligently and effectively on my last job.
> I worked hard and effectively on my last job.

To provoke discrimination rather than mechanical response, one might ask where each sentence would be appropriate—In a literary work? In a letter of application for an executive job? In a political campaign speech? In a personal interview with a factory foreman? (Deighton, 1949) This procedure develops skill in making a response where it is appropriate. Modification of response according to the situation, instead of stereotyped response, is sought.

The old idea of drill was that one should practice precisely the same response until it became completely mechanical. Over and over the student faced essentially the same stimulus and was to make the same response, preferably with no pause to analyze or consider the unique features of the situation. It was even suggested that all arithmetic problems requiring a given operation (say, subtracting cost price from selling price) be worded in the same way so that the student would never puzzle over what operation to use.

The modern view is that the student should practice in the greatest variety of situations he can cope with. This requires him to isolate the essential elements. Learning becomes not forming one mechanical reaction, but acquiring familiarity with a type of situation in all its guises. No one recommends helter-skelter variation that leaves the learner continually off balance. He should attain a reasonable degree of success with one situation before going on to another variation. Often it is beneficial to alter one element of the situation at a time to gradually extend skill. More adaptive training leads to much greater skill in dealing with new situations. The person who learns to fish with one lure in one stream is less versatile and less accomplished than the fisherman who has acquired his experience over a range of fishing grounds, even if the total amount of practice is the same for both.

> **19.** The teacher requires each fourth-grader to write 50 times each word he misspells from the day's assignment. Is this sound procedure?
>
> **20.** How would practice designed to produce an unvarying habit and practice designed to produce an adaptive habit differ for each of the following?
>> **a.** a girl learning to put up her hair
>> **b.** an advanced student learning to play a violin selection
>> **c.** a boy learning to smooth wooden surfaces with a plane

Advice and Demonstration

Some skill learning is accomplished through trial and error, unaided by instruction. This is particularly true of the attainment of muscular control. A person learns to move his hand to a certain point only by repeated trial. Such basic control patterns are acquired early in life by means of thousands of reaches toward a toy or a bright spot in the crib. They are made more precise by further extensive practice at each new stage in maturity (Piaget, 1952). There is little or nothing an instructor can tell a person, young or old, about how to bring under control an untrained set of muscles. Nor is the performer aware of precisely what adjustments he makes to attain a desired result. How do *you* make the sounds for *t* and *d*? Although you have spoken English for many years you probably are unaware that the chief difference between the two is that a vibration in the vocal cords is added to make the sound of *d*. A teacher can do little to help the individual discover the basic movement patterns of the hands, the tongue, and other motor organs. At best, the teacher can give some slight direction to the process of discovery by trial and confirmation.

It is quite another matter when the learner needs to combine responses into a complex sequence. To be sure, he might discover the best pattern, but it is more likely that left to his own devices he will settle upon a relatively inefficient pattern. Demonstration or verbal explanation tells him which of the many responses already under his control he should employ and what cues he should react to.

One college archery class was told how to stand, how to hold the bow, and how to release the arrow; these aspects of their performance were inspected by the teacher. This class did consistently better than another class left to trial-and-error learning. After 18 periods, the demonstration group was hitting on 65 per cent of its shots, compared to 45 per cent in the uninstructed group (Davies, 1945). The demonstration group paid more attention to correct form. According to the investigator:

> The non-tuition group members concentrated mostly on aim throughout the entire experiment. They thought about form only when they were not being as successful as they thought they should be, and their concentration upon aim had not helped them. The students did not seem to realize the necessity for perfecting the parts of the technique in order to raise their scores.

With preschool children learning ring-toss it was found valuable not only to show the correct technique, but also to prevent them from trying any other technique (Goodenough and Brian, 1929).

Motion pictures, which can enlarge and slow action, are a superior way of demonstrating. In teaching lathe operation, boys who saw a film demonstration learned faster than another group where the instructor merely explained verbally what to do (Vander Meer, 1945; T. Anderson, 1942). Using films to teach the "western roll" style of high jumping eliminates a great deal of the erratic trial and error that boys normally show in learning it (Priebe and Burton, 1939). Clarification is especially valuable early in learning.

Cox (1933) provided evidence of the value of explanation and specially designed exercises for teaching industrial assembly skills. The assembly of an electric lamp was broken into subtasks. Each group of subjects practiced one of the subskills and of course improved. But there was no transfer from one subtask to an unpracticed one (e.g., practice on wiring did not improve skill in fitting wooden wedges into place at the top of the lamp). In a new training experiment, subjects went through lessons outlined as follows:

Exercises on arrangement of parts on workbench, manner of holding parts, etc.

"Eye observation exercises" on what to observe; noticing spatial relationships

"Finger observation exercises" to notice muscular sensations accompanying action

Exercises in control of attention and effort

Practice in applying the various exercises to the task

The observation exercises were directed toward increasing the conscious analysis of cues. In the training experiment, all these exercises were applied to just one of the subskills (container assembly). No other subskill was practiced. Yet at the end of this training *all* of the subskills had improved substantially. General techniques of efficient work had been acquired.

A still more striking result was the record of a group trained on the container task, which then began to practice the wedge task. Their learning curve was compared with that for a group of equal pretest ability who began practice on wedges directly, with no training on another subskill. The scores in successive practice sessions were as follows (expressed as average time to complete a block of work):

	1	2	3	4	5	6	7	8	Gain (8-1)
Pretrained	56	48	44	42	39	38	36	35	21
Practice only	61	52	49	47	47	44	47	44	17

The training program caused the workers to profit more from practice on subsequent tasks. To use a term we shall emphasize in the next chapter, they "learned to learn."

A demonstration is most effective when the learner gives it his full attention and sees just what goes on. Fifth-graders were asked to learn to assemble a complex jigsaw puzzle. Each child individually was shown how to do the puzzle, and after the demonstration practiced until he could do the puzzle without error. Table 14 outlines the experiment. Some children merely looked on silently. Others were asked to describe aloud what the demonstrator was doing, which required close attention. Some children were asked to count aloud during the demonstration, and thus were prevented from describing the actions of the demonstrator to themselves. The demonstrator helped some pupils by telling what she was doing or by correcting the child's misstatement. The results show much faster learning by the describers, who observed the demonstration most closely and saw

TABLE 14

Active observers profit most from a demonstration (*L. Thompson* [1])

Group	What child did as he watched	Amount of verbal explanation given by demonstrator	Time required to do easy puzzle	Time required to do hard puzzle
1	Counted to 100 by 2's	None	5.7	25 [2]
2	Said what demonstrator was doing	None	3.1	22
3	Kept silent	Incomplete description	3.5	16
4	Kept silent	Full description	3.2	14
5	Said what demonstrator was doing	None except to correct child's errors	2.2	12

[1] See May and Lumsdaine, 1958.
[2] Only three pupils out of twenty-five could finish the puzzle at all under these conditions.

most clearly what was happening (L. Thompson; see May and Lumsdaine, 1958). There is evidence, indeed, that watching another person perform, with close attention, may produce better orientation to a task than trying it oneself from the outset (Galperin, 1957; see also page 284 above).

A desired response should be introduced in such a way that it will be comprehended. Recall how Mr. Wells taught his class to type (Chapter 3). It may seem strange to you that he allowed the pupils to watch the keyboard during the first weeks of the course. They did not respond to the same cues as the mature typist, who relies almost wholly on muscular cues. But Wells's procedure helped the beginners interpret their task. He allowed them to guide themselves by eye until they built up a mental map of the keyboard, which became a useful mediator in interpreting muscular sensations from the hands (L. J. West, 1957, pp. 13–15). Wells's students were taught to type by touch (muscular cues) as soon as they had reasonable comprehension of the keyboard. You may also recall that during the first week Wells's group experimented with the typewriter without guidance. This is contrary to the suggestion that guidance precede practice, but the exception is justified. In this preliminary period pupils discovered useful facts for themselves. Demonstrations on the first day would have been over the heads of the beginners because the machine was quite unfamiliar. A few days later they were ready to observe a demonstration intelligently.

The evidence is consistent that leaving the worker to discover a psychomotor response for himself is a poor teaching technique, compared to demonstrating the action he should perform. Another type of explanation emphasizes not the action but the underlying scientific principles. Does it help, for example, to instruct the billiard player regarding the laws of reflection? This topic is sufficiently complicated that we must leave it for discussion in Chapter 11, where we will also consider some of the positive values of discovery by the learner.

21. In Table 14, why did Group 5 do better than Group 2 on the easy puzzle?

22. Why did Group 2 fall behind Group 4 on the hard puzzle?

23. Would explanation or practice be more helpful in learning to bake cakes? What cues must be differentiated for skilled performance?

Monitoring

Always it is the *perceived* consequence of the trial that determines whether an interpretation is retained or altered (Ammons, 1956; Bilodeau and Bilodeau, 1961). How well the learner thinks he is doing determines what he learns. If he lacks knowledge of results he cannot improve. If accurate information on the quality of his performance is not provided by the teacher or by a scoring device, he can usually make a judgment, but that judgment may be unrealistic. Pupils who are quite able to distinguish good from bad performance in someone else may not yet be able to apply the same judgment to themselves. Berko and Brown (1961, p. 531) give this illustration:

> One of us, for instance, spoke to a child who called his inflated plastic fish a *fis*. In imitation of the child's pronunciation, the observer said, "That is your *fis*?" "No," said the child, "my *fis*." He continued to reject the adult's imitation until he was told, "That is your *fish*." "Yes," he said, "my *fis*."

Learning to discriminate cues arising within one's own performance is a distinct aspect of skill learning. It may require direct training (with the aid of a tape recorder, for example).

Practice should always be arranged so that the learner has prompt and accurate information about his success. Preferably he should be taught to use indicators of success that will be available to him outside the training situation (Annett, 1959). Prompt knowledge of results has a powerful motivating effect. Delayed reports (such as scores or critiques handed back on a later day) are ordinarily much less influential than immediate feedback. Delayed feedback is useful if the learner can recall vividly the situation to which he initially responded and can reinstate his interpretations. Loree and Koch (1960) conducted panel discussions among students in educational psychology. The panel heard a playback of its discussion a day or so later. Whenever a good technique of discussion was used (e.g., paraphrasing another panelist's remark for the sake of clarification) the teacher stopped the record and drew attention to the good example. There were 24 discussions, each reviewed with the class. A final discussion was used to test the effect of the training. Skill in discussion advanced from an initial mean of 70 on a 146-point scale to a final mean of 103. A control class who practiced panel discussion without feedback did not improve.

The teacher has an especially important part to play in monitoring aspects of the performance where the pupil's judgment of consequences is inadequate. Martha, learning to type, fixed an incorrect technique because she was not corrected at the right time. She moved her right hand about while she typed, striking a key with any convenient finger. An expert could have told Martha at the outset that this was inefficient, but Martha, pleased because her errors were decreasing, established a faulty habit. Pupils practice faulty procedures because they do not comprehend what is recommended, do not realize the importance of the suggestion, or are unable to observe themselves while performing a complex act. With many things to attend to, some error of technique is likely to be overlooked until it is firmly rooted.

The learner tends to judge his success by his product: how many words he types correctly, how far he drives the golf ball, how long it takes him to adjust his microscope. When he thinks he is gaining he rarely worries about form. The teacher should remind him to judge progress in terms of technique rather than output. If the learner knows the marks of good form, he can judge himself to some extent. He should think occasionally of his foot placement and the slope of the racket as he drives a tennis ball. He should check his own posture and finger placement as he types.

The instructor's monitoring should be moderate in amount so that the pupil does not think, "I can't ever do anything well enough to please this instructor," or so that he becomes dependent on the monitor. Attention should be called to consistent faults, not to every random departure from the ideal.

Devices to record what the learner did are an important feature of training machines and simulators. Speech teachers use tape recorders to monitor students. Coaches take motion pictures to point out faulty performance and improved performance (Priebe and Burton, 1939). The tracings of a disk-cutting performance (Figure 69) had teaching value because they showed workers their errors. The workers became interested in making a good tracing instead of trying to see how fast they could cut. As their patterns became better, they broke fewer cutting wheels, spoiled fewer disks, and attained a higher rate of output (Lindahl, 1945).

While correct technique should be encouraged, this does not mean that the beginner should perform by exactly the same technique as the expert.

It is usually necessary and desirable for him to make additional mediating responses, which have the effect of subdividing the task (Brownell, 1933). The beginner, sight-reading piano music, has to play note by note, thinking or saying the name of the note before striking it. While learning to subtract, writing 7 in place of 8 to indicate that "1 has been borrrowed" eliminates a demand upon memory and helps the beginner avoid error. It is now generally recommended that the teacher encourage the learner to use mediating responses within a sequence of acts. The teacher should make sure, however, that the sequence will be consistent with the desirable pattern when the mediators fade out. The mediators usually do vanish after considerable practice. If they do not, a special effort to extinguish them must be made. The use of a flash technique in typing is an example of such a remedial procedure.

24. Would it be desirable to have learners take turns monitoring each other?

25. In bowling, what consequences besides the score confirm (or disconfirm) the provisional try?

26. List possible uses of video tape recording in the classroom teaching of skills. (Disregard questions of cost.)

THE PRACTICE SCHEDULE.   There are many ways to schedule practice on a skill: one hour per day, ten minutes per week, etc. It ought to be possible to arrive at general principles that would guide the scheduling of training. Unfortunately, the research that has been done on this topic has little bearing on educational schedules (Underwood, 1961). The advantages of "massed" versus "distributed" practice have often been studied, but the experiments have usually dealt with very short training programs. A typical experiment is likely to investigate whether or not 20 one-minute trials, with one-minute rests between, are superior to ten two-minute trials, with one-minute intervals. This gives little guidance to the planning of a year-long training schedule.

There is an occasional study with educational relevance. College women had nine practice sessions in which to learn billiards. Three groups practiced with a uniform spacing of sessions: a daily session for nine consecutive days, sessions spaced on a M-W-F sequence, and weekly sessions. The best results were obtained by a fourth group on a schedule with increasing intertrial intervals, e.g., January 1, 2, 3, 5, 8, 13, 21, and February 3, 24 (J. Harmon and Miller, 1950).

With a longer interval, weaknesses or confusions are more likely to reveal themselves so that they can be corrected. A technique or interpretation that is shaky is more likely to be identified after a forgetting period.

Long practice sessions lead to fatigue and boredom. Consider a boy who is trying to purse his lips properly for blowing a horn. For ten minutes he obtains good tones. Then his lips tire and he more often makes the sound incorrectly. This is frustrating. It reduces his confidence and interest. If he tries to force the horn into tone by pressing his lips harder, he may get the right effect in the wrong way and learn a bad technique.

Short, widely spaced practices are generally recommended, but these cautions are to be noted:

Within a school year, to increase intervals between practices is to reduce the total amount of practice. There are few training programs where the total amount of practice reaches the point of diminishing returns.

Intervals can become so long that there is excessive forgetting. We generally judge practice sessions to be too far apart if the average pupil is unable to regain his level of previous trials fairly early in the next session.

In many tasks effective practice comes only after a warming-up period, both physiological and psychological. The time needed to loosen muscles, recapture interpretations, re-establish timing, etc., varies with the skill. A practice period is too short if it does not extend well beyond the warming-up period.

The practice period may be too short if it does not allow one to complete a whole performance. Assembling a piece of equipment may require twenty minutes. A beginner will take much longer than that. Therefore his practice period probably should be an hour or more, unless the task can be broken into psychologically independent segments. What constitutes a unit for practice depends on the stage of learning.

> 27. Should practice periods become longer or shorter as the person becomes more expert?
>
> 28. Might there be a warming-up effect in practice on addition, where muscular factors are not very important?

Recapitulation

We may bring together the chief recommendations for the teacher introduced in the preceding pages:

Confront the learner with the cues that he will respond to in using the skill. Additional cues to aid discrimination are sometimes beneficial.

Simplify the task at the start of practice. Such simplification should not violate the pattern of the task as a whole.

Provide occasion for adapting responses to different purposes and different contexts.

Analyze the task to determine the best pattern of response. Demonstrate it or give a clear verbal prescription. Direct the pupil's attention to important cues. The timing of explanations and demonstrations has to be worked out for each task; explanation usually has the greatest value early in training.

Monitor to make certain that the basic form of response is correctly practiced.

Give prompt feedback until the pupil can judge himself.

Teach the pupil to judge his own performance, especially its form.

Favor relatively short practice periods, with increasing intervals between practices.

THE RATE OF IMPROVEMENT WITH PRACTICE

Specimen Training Records

A *learning curve* is a record of an individual's improvement made by measuring his ability at different stages of practice and plotting his scores. Some teachers post such charts to encourage improvement in typing, reading, and other skills. Theoretically, it would be possible to develop learning curves for knowledge, attitudes, and other types of learning, but teachers rarely take enough measures to allow this.

To begin, let us consider the improvement in disk-cutting recorded in Figure 66 (page 278). How might this be summarized in a score? A good over-all measure would be the number of acceptable disks cut per hour, but that would not describe change in the performance itself. Looking at the movement tracings, we can study improvement in speed (strokes per minute), smoothness (number of visible jerks per stroke), or overthrow (length of stroke beyond rod). Speed should rise with practice; jerkiness and overthrow should decline. When we count the number of complete strokes per line in Figure 65 as a measure of speed, the results are:

Hours of Practice	9	45	141	239
Strokes	4	11	9	8

These numbers, plotted, form Figure 69a. Evidently this man acquired speed early in training. In fact, to improve in disk-cutting he had to reduce his speed. Now consider smoothness and overthrow:

Hours of Practice	9	45	141	239
Smoothness (jerks per stroke)	6.0	1.8	.9	.6
Length of Overthrow (arbitrary units)	4.5	4.1	.7	.1

Smoothness (curve b) shows rapid early improvement. There was little improvement after 100 hours because jerks were nearly eliminated, save for the one at the top of the return stroke. This subskill could be mastered later; perhaps at 1,000 hours all jerks would be gone. The overthrow curve dropped markedly between 50 and 150 hours. After that progress was slower.

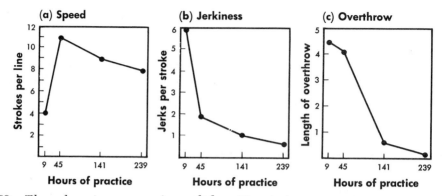

69   *Three learning curves for a disk-cutting trainee*

Based on the performance record in Figure 66, page 278, from Lindahl's 1945 study.

What principles are illustrated here? The following observations are supported by many studies:

Parts of a skill develop at different rates or at different points in training. (Speed and smoothness developed early; overthrow took longer to bring under control.)

While one part of a skill is showing little improvement, the person may be mastering another important element.

The speed of performance may increase while the form remains poor or deteriorates. (The speed was too high at 45 hours; overthrow became better controlled when the cutter slowed his movements.)

> **29.** How might the record shown at 239 hours improve with much more practice?
>
> **30.** What part skills in arithmetic computation might conceivably be measured separately?

A Theoretical Learning Curve

The theoretical learning curve in Figure 70 is a scheme to summarize many features of learning. No actual curve looks like this. Improvement is always irregular. The usual curve of improvement resembles just a part of this schematic curve. Curves for various subskills or aspects of a performance have different shapes (Culler and Girden, 1951; Krueger, 1947).

Our general curve is divided into six stages:

1. *Negligible progress.* Very little improvement in score.
2. *Increasing gains.* The rate of learning increases as the learner grasps the essentials of the task.

3. *Decreasing gains.* The rate of measured improvement is slower.
4. *Plateau.* A period of no systematic change in score.
5. *Renewed gains.* Performance again rises.
6. *Approach to limit.* Progress becomes negligible.

Looking again at disk-cutting, we see that the smoothness curve illustrates two of these stages: rapid improvement as in 3, followed by a period of little progress like 4 or 6. Overthrow gives an S-shaped curve containing sections like 2 and 3. In an actual record, we would perhaps find several periods where learning nearly stops for a time, and then moves forward. The whole curve would then be a series of gradually climbing S-shapes.

THE PREREADINESS PERIOD.   The left end of the curve shows a long period of negligible progress. If we begin a record in infancy, the performance curve always shows this prereadiness period. The child must develop attention, manipulation, perceptual skills, and an understanding of how goals are reached before he can profit from practice on a task. There may be a similar period of very slow progress for an older learner who has difficulty in making certain key discriminations.

Relevant learning takes place during the prereadiness period, even though there is no advance in the score we are plotting (Bahrick *et al.*, 1957). From birth to 18 months (or thereabouts) the child acquires readiness for walking. If we measured steps per minute, his score would stay at zero for the first year. Nevertheless, he is learning the skills of balance he needs in walking. During period 1, the learning that is taking place does

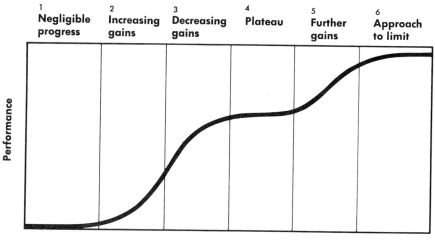

70   *A schematic learning curve*

not show in the measured performance because the person is not yet ready to perform the entire task.

THE PERIOD OF RAPID GAINS.   In period 2, the score rises rapidly. The person becomes aware of the cues to attend to, the goals that he may attain, or the ways to organize responses effectively. The child learning to count illustrates this. His first counting involves learning one word after another and memorizing the correct (but nonsensical) order. Then he discovers an underlying regularity from 13 upward. As he masters first the notion that the 30's are followed by the 40's, later the pattern by which we build numbers into the hundreds and thousands, his counting ability leaps upward. He may master the numbers from 20 to 99 in a few days, whereas it may have taken years to get the first 20 numbers in order.

Mastery of a coordination is another source of rapid progress. Until a boy is able to stand balanced, hold his wrists firm, and swing a bat horizontally, his batting average remains close to zero. As soon as he masters this basic coordination, his batting becomes controlled rather than erratic. He can now improve in aim, judgment, and timing.

Sometimes the rapid rise indicates a change in motivation. The boy who suddenly reforms, astonishing his mother by regularly washing his face, combing his hair, and expressing concern over clothes illustrates this. The "discovery" that grooming is a source of approval and pride brings a spurt of performance that the child was capable of at a much earlier age.

THE PERIOD OF DECREASING GAINS.   Period 3 is a period of refinement in which improvement per practice session becomes less and less. Such slowing is inevitable, since the easier aspects of the task are mastered first. It is not completely correct to say that learning is slower during this period. The person is now learning tinier changes in response, each of which has a small effect on his total score, but he is nonetheless making many changes in his program of responses.

Many observed learning curves start out like period 3 of our curve. There is much improvement at the start, then slower and slower progress. This is to be expected when the person starts practice with adequate readiness and understanding. The learner transfers to the new task his accomplishment in other performances, and phases 1 and 2 do not appear. The disk-cutters had already learned general bodily coordination and control of foot movements. Their smoothness improved chiefly through learning to use cues found only in this task—a typical period 3 refinement.

LEVELING OFF.   Sooner or later, the rate of progress becomes negligible, and the person's score remains at about the same level. It is always possible that learning will be resumed, as in stage 5 of our curve. For purposes of discussion we distinguish between a plateau (4) and performance that has reached its limit (6). A plateau is a period of negligible improvement in score, which is followed by further gains. Obviously, until the plateau has ended, we do not know whether further gains are possible. The "limit" of stage 6 is only a hypothetical limit. Even when a performer reaches the world's record, we are not sure that he cannot improve further.

Learners often rise from plateaus without help from a teacher. Sometimes this gain is due to renewed interest or to physical development. Often it is due to improved comprehension, altered technique, or coordination of larger segments of the performance. During the time he is on the plateau, the learner is making small changes in balance, timing, and other components of the response (M. D. Smith, 1930). He may be connecting responses with more remote cues and reducing his dependence on mediators. If so, he will later be able to run off a larger sequence of actions as a unit. The smoothness curve of the disk-cutter (Figure 69b) shows a plateau that he will probably overcome when he discovers how to make his return stroke correctly. L. J. West (1957, p. 24) comments as follows on progress in the later stages of learning typing:

> It is known that changes in rate are accomplished by changes in work methods, in finger-movement paths. . . . It is characteristic for improvements in work method to be hit upon accidentally, stumbled on in the course of practice. The typist does not consciously contrive a new stroking method. When he does fall into improved motion patterns, he is (more often than not) quite unaware of the change in his work method. He may sense that things feel different, better, smoother, easier—but usually he will not be able to identify what has produced the change.

Plateaus are not observed in all learning curves, and perhaps they would not occur under an ideal teaching method. In a sense, the very idea of a "period of no progress" is false; the person is modifying subskills even though his total score is stable. Probably there never is a period when all aspects of the response are stable. The curve representing over-all rate or quality of performance combines many part skills.

Individual Improvement Records

Individual learning curves are characteristically irregular, quite unlike the smooth theoretical curve. The fluctuations reflect momentary shifts in interest, energy, or ability to combine part skills. The teacher and learner should not place much weight on a single striking success or a brief slump. The peak of each fluctuation shows what the person can do when all conditions are favorable, but the athlete is unrealistic if he is discontented with 14-foot pole vaults after he has once made 15 feet. If he is distressed by what is really an admirable average, he may worry himself into a serious slump. He may start experimenting with his already excellent technique and thereby spoil it.

Among pupils all instructed in the same way, there are wide differences in results. These differences are significant for the teacher: first, because he will need to diagnose the pupils showing atypical performance; second, because each pupil tends to judge his progress in terms of his standing in the group.

If a pupil sees that he is poorer than the average, his attitude toward the task is altered. One common interpretation is, "If I'm below average now, I'll probably remain at about that level no matter how I work on this task." The pupil may be satisfied merely to hold his place in the group, though perhaps he could do much better. Sometimes the pupil who is lagging behind will drop out, assuming that if he is poor at the beginning he will always be poor.

Performance early in training is not a dependable predictor of ultimate proficiency in psychomotor skills. The learner who catches on quickly, either because he transfers related past experience or because he has superior intellectual ability, gets off to a head start. These initial intellectual differences are likely to count for rather little in the end, however, since those slower to understand a complex situation often overtake the early star performers. Differences late in training depend on coordination and speed more than on abstract thinking (Dunnette, 1962, p. 296).

A rapidly rising learning curve may not reflect desirable learning. The pupil who continues to look at the keyboard will improve faster than the pupil who begins to type by touch, but he reaches a plateau earlier and stays on it longer. Because they center attention on the product, measures of rate of improvement are best delayed until basic form has been acquired. When the learner focuses on quantity or rate of performance (e.g., when winning the next race is of first importance), he is more likely to practice poor techniques than when he is commended for improvement in form.

To improve form frequently requires a temporary sacrifice of product. The learner may have been using his faulty technique at a high level of "efficiency," whereas he is awkward and slow in using the new method. He resists suggestions regarding technique because the familiar method feels more natural, and mastering the new method will require extended practice. If the pupil does try the recommended change, he finds to his distress that his score becomes lower, not higher than before. The teacher can minimize these difficulties by emphasizing technique from the outset and by saying little about speed or relative standing of the group.

Individual progress during long-continued practice is illustrated in Figure 71. The records show what these girls did during three years of steady practice in typing. Virginia remained fairly close to the class average throughout. Carol was consistently below average in the first year, but when school resumed the next fall she showed fast progress. During the second

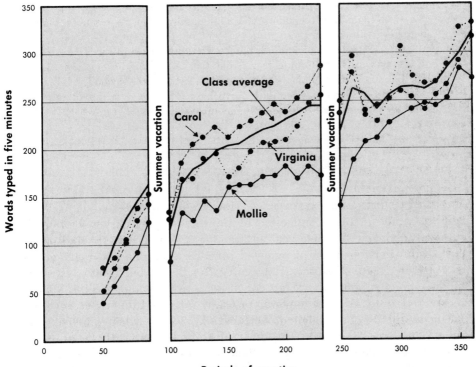

71 *Learning curves during three years of typing practice (from Sandiford, 1928, p. 208; the original study is by W. G. Edwards)*

year, she sailed ahead of the class, only to remain on a plateau in the third year, which permitted the rest of the class to overtake and pass her. We cannot be sure what caused these changes. Greater maturity in the second year may have helped Carol; loss of interest or faulty technique may have caused her third-year stagnation. Mollie learned typing slowly. Her progress was relatively poor from the start, and she made little gain in the second year. In the third year she hit a rapid stride. She ended the year only forty strokes behind the average, although she had been seventy strokes behind at the end of the second year. In view of her steady climb, there is no reason to think that Mollie has neared her limit; with further practice on the job, she has a good chance of attaining average speed.

31. In a classic study of the learning of telegraphy, a plateau was found when the operator reached a receiving rate just exceeding that required for main-line receiving (Bryan and Harter, 1897). How can such a plateau be accounted for?

32. If tests were given on successive weeks to typical adults to see how rapidly they can walk, their rates of performance would change little. They

would be on a flat portion of the learning curve. Does this most probably represent a plateau or their limit of walking ability? If it represents a plateau, can it be attributed to motivation or to technique?

33. After two years of typing practice, students' scores on speed tests were only a few words per minute faster than at the end of the first year. Is this a fair basis for concluding that they learned little in the second year?

34. Does the idea of a learning curve have any meaning in a subject such as history, where a new topic is taken up each week?

RETENTION, FACILITATION, AND INTERFERENCE

AMOUNT OF RETENTION EXPECTED.   How well skills are retained over an interval of no practice is suggested by the three typing curves. During the summer following the first year of training, every girl dropped substantially; but after ten hours of renewed practice, each one had regained her end-of-year speed. This occurred again after the second year. Systematic investigations support the same conclusion: psychomotor skill is quickly recaptured even after an interval of many years (Ammons *et al.*, 1958; Battig *et al.*, 1957). Though proficiency may be low when practice is resumed, the losses are quickly made up. The armed services can train men in tracking or gunnery, discharge them into the inactive reserve, and yet have confidence that brief refresher training will bring back their skills when they are needed. Once the child is taught to swim, his skill will remain permanently useful even if he has little or no further practice.

It is not possible to make a well-founded statement about the long-term retention of performances that are primarily intellectual, such as sketching, judging cattle, trouble-shooting on electronic apparatus, or adding fractions with unlike denominators. Recall tests have occasionally been given a year or more after instruction ends, but we do not know how rapidly such abilities are recovered with renewed practice. From an educational point of view, speed of recovery is the most important evidence on retention or loss. The studies available (page 352) suggest that an intellectual performance is likely to be well retained if it is an organized, meaningful whole, if it was thoroughly learned originally, or if there are occasional opportunities for practicing with feedback during the intervening years.

MEASUREMENT OF "SAVINGS."   We have suggested that retention can be observed not just by a measure of proficiency long after training, but by the amount of further practice required to bring the person back to his original level. This is called the "savings" method of measuring retention, because the retraining for the person who retains his skill is short compared with that required to bring a person without prior training to the same level.

Suppose that it takes 40 training periods to teach a certain gunnery skill. Four years later, five periods are required to recapture the skill. Saving: 35 periods, or 87 per cent. This training-plus-retraining actually took more time (45 trials) than that needed to train a new recruit (40 trials), but the great advantage is in giving the bulk of the training long before it is needed. The soldier can be trained in peacetime, the school can teach skills of homemaking before the girl attains adult responsibility. Anticipatory training is not efficient unless there is a high probability that the skill will be used subsequently, or unless it has transfer value.

Transfer can be examined in the same way as retention. Suppose the person learns skill A, and after some interval, long or short, is trained on skill B. Again the savings may be examined by comparing his training time on B with that of a person who had no training on A. Consider these hypothetical figures.

Trials to learn A	40	
Trials to learn B after A	25	Savings: 25 trials or 50 per cent
Trials to learn B without A	50	

A evidently has transfer value, because it facilitates the learning of B. We say that interference has occurred if the figures look like this:

Trials to learn A	40	
Trials to learn B after A	60	Savings: −10 trials or −20 per cent
Trials to learn B without A	50	

This so-called negative transfer is likely when cue-response sequences developed for use in performance A are inappropriate in performance B.

TRANSFER OF DISCRIMINATIONS AND CUE-RESPONSE SEQUENCES.   Facilitation is to be expected; the discriminations and cue-response sequences for one skill are usually helpful in others. The boy who can ride a bicycle learns to slow when he observes children at the edge of the street, to correct steering on the basis of visual feedback, to estimate when a car in a side street will reach the intersection he is approaching. When he begins to drive an automobile, all these interpretations will be helpful. The timing of actions will have to be altered, but the old timing does not interfere for long. Comparable facilitation is expected in learning a second language. Ability to listen to another person and to imitate what he says is developed about age 1 in thousands of trials. It is brought forward to the service of second-language learning. Likewise, knowing what sound to make when seeing *t* in English is an aid to learning French.

But there is also interference, because the old cue-response sequences are not entirely appropriate. As Pei (1960, p. 87) points out:

> The written notation may be the same, but the spoken sounds for the most part diverge, sometimes slightly, sometimes to an astounding degree. . . . Any

French grammar, for instance, will warn us to pronounce the written symbol *u* in French with rounded lips, not like the *u* of "union" or "cut"; but comparatively few French grammars will warn us to pronounce French *t* with the tip of the tongue touching the back of the upper teeth, not the upper gums, as we do in English. . . . It is precisely by these trifling differences that a native speaker can be distinguished from a foreigner who has learned the language.

What happens is obvious. When the cue is received, the person makes the response learned to that cue in the past; i.e., he transfers it. If the response is made provisionally, with a lively sense of doubt, the person is likely to perceive differences between the sound he makes and the sound produced by the French speaker. If consequences are less carefully observed, the learner considers his response confirmed. It sounds nearly right and others understand him. Recall the disk-cutting operation, where the worker trained in the ordinary way mastered an imperfect pattern that did produce disks. The instructor can help in transfer, as in original learning, by directing attention to faulty technique at the proper time.

These examples suggest that both facilitation and interference are likely to occur, the balance between them depending on the similarity of the new task to the old. This principle is expressed more formally in Table 15. Cues are classified as identical to those used originally or as entirely novel. In the transfer skill the same response may be used as in the original skill, or it may be connected to the cues in some contradictory manner. The classification of examples in Table 15 is much simplified. Any complex skill consists of many cue-response combinations, including mediating responses and feedback-and-correction patterns. Hence many degrees of similarity and dissimilarity occur between various parts of any two tasks.

Having learned to read English text facilitates any task where the shape of words, their layout in a horizontal line, etc., helps one to bring forth the proper response. If the old response must be suppressed or reshaped, some interference occurs. Being able to read a word as a whole does not interfere with examining single letters during printing (row 2). There is little transfer from reading to learning (row 4) to call one irregular drawing a *prog*, and another a *nerk*; but pronunciation skills will produce some facilitation. While Table 15 classifies situations as if they presented cues identical to former situations, or completely new cues, there is of course a gradation from great similarity between situations to none. Even within the same skill a person is continually learning to respond to cue combinations that are a bit different from those previously used. Adaptation of a skill to a somewhat different situation is itself an example of facilitation.

Interference is especially important in verbal learning. From the teacher's point of view, a fact, a correct spelling, or a formula is a new reaction to a new stimulus. The new response, however, competes with other responses the pupil brings forward from past experience. Suppose the

TABLE 15

Transfer depends on the similarity of new and old tasks (modified from Gagné et al., 1950)

Cue directing new response	New response	Example [1]	Probable transfer
Identical to that directing original response	Same as original response save for detail or elaboration	Reading English organized in tables; reading English verse	Great facilitation; some correction needed
	Unrelated to original response	Printing English letters	Some facilitation through discrimination of cues
	Opposite or contradictory to that given to same cues in the original skill	Reading foreign words having pronunciation unlike English forms (German *Beer* pronounced "bear")	Severe initial interference; with close attention, response is readily corrected so that net effect is facilitation; habit interference likely
Not present in original task	Same as original	Learning names for abstract drawings	Some facilitation
	Unrelated to original response	Drawing geometric forms	Neither facilitation nor interference

[1] Assume that original response is oral reading of English text.

teacher wants stimulus S_a to suggest response R_a to the pupil. Interference will occur when the pupil already has learned some alternative response R_x to stimulus S_a. He has acquired a wrong response which must be supplanted. Interference will also occur when the pupil has learned a response R_x to stimulus S_b, if he cannot readily discriminate S_a from S_b. For example, the response "peach" (*pêche*) is mistakenly used for *péché* ("sin"). The pupil may need special training in distinguishing response R_a from R_x or S_a from S_b. Interference is obviously to be expected in school, since the student inevitably comes to many topics of study with partially incorrect ideas. Indeed, interference between correct interpretations and imperfectly suppressed wrong interpretations appears to be the principal source of forgetting (Underwood, 1957; Ausubel and Blake, 1958).

HABIT INTERFERENCE.   In motor performance we observe *habit* interference more often than interference with learning. Serious interference *with learning* occurs when the new task requires a change in some part of the original response that is not under voluntary, verbally mediated control. After one learns a rhythmic sequence of motions at one speed, these established coordinations make it hard to learn the proper coordination for another speed (Lordahl and Archer, 1958). A response under voluntary control, on the other hand, is easily altered. A person makes some early errors by carrying forward an old interpretation, but he rather quickly overcomes them. The child who has learned to sight-read tunes in the key of C will make some errors when he begins to read in F, where the note on the third line of the staff (B) must be flatted. But he learns to discriminate, and to respond with B or B♭ according to the key of the selection. Learning the extra discrimination is easier than learning to read in the key of F without prior experience with the simple key of C. Interference with learning is small, compared to the facilitation from earlier practice.

When the player feels at home in the key of F, he sometimes plays a B unflatted because he is careless and fails to make a discrimination that he is perfectly capable of making. This is habit interference.

"Careless errors" occur when an old, thoroughly learned habit intrudes into a less-familiar situation as a person relaxes his attention (Wolfle, 1951, p. 1271). Habit interference is especially likely under conditions of stress or fatigue. Smode *et al.* (1959, p. 12) tell of an airline copilot who had just been trained on a four-engine plane, after long two-engine experience:

> On becoming airborne on a night take-off, the command for "wheels up" was given and the copilot reached for the handle to retract the gear. However, on the four-engine craft, the landing gear handle position was different from that on the two-engine aircraft; also, the flap lever on the four-engine aircraft was positioned similarly to the landing gear handle on the two-engine craft. The copilot, who stated that he was fatigued at the time, activated the flap lever for the wheels up command. . . . [Instantly, however] he "felt" a sensation on the lever different from that expected from pulling the landing gear lever. He immediately [corrected his error].

The pilot failed to make the correct initial discrimination but he saved himself because he was alert enough to discriminate the feedback cues. Habit interference is reduced by more thorough training on *both* the old and the new responses. This strengthens both sets of cue-response connections and develops the ability to discriminate between the situations. *Overlearning*—practice well beyond the point of mastery—is highly desirable to reduce interference (Mandler, 1954).

> **35.** If learning of skills is "permanent," how can one account for the big league pitcher who wins twenty games one year and loses his first seven starts the next season?

36. What does it mean to say that sketching or adding fractions is "comprehended as an organized whole"?

37. Show that interference occurs because a response is transferred to a new situation. In what sense is this transfer "negative"?

38. What facilitation or interference would be expected in these situations? Explain with the aid of Table 15.

    a. A child who has learned to read and play simple piano music in the key of C is asked to practice a piece in the key of G.

    b. A boy who has learned to use a hand saw to cut lumber to size starts to use a table-mounted power saw.

    c. A person who has learned to use a table-mounted power saw changes to a portable power saw.

SUMMARY

By *skill* we refer to a performance in which a complex sequence of actions is carried out in a more or less fixed way. There are some skills in which control of movement makes a great difference in the result, and others where judgment and reasoning are more important; this chapter examines particularly the former, psychomotor performances. The expert performs more smoothly and more automatically than others. Skilled performance is a series of actions, each regulated by cues; the expert senses relevant cues quickly, interprets them promptly and correctly, and runs off the sequence without pause.

Between taking in the external cues and the final response, mediating responses often occur. This is especially the case in an unfamiliar, problematic situation. One type of response—encoding—is a verbal, symbolic interpretation, i.e., a conscious recognition of the cue. This recognition is followed by data processing, the interpretation that leads from recognition of the situation to a conclusion about what should be done. The final step, decoding, is a translation of the decision into muscular action. These mediating responses play a large part in immature behavior. As a person becomes more skilled, the mediating responses drop out; he makes a response in the familiar situation without consciously noticing the pertinent cues and without giving himself a verbal order.

A relevant cue is any stimulus from within or without the body that can help to recognize a situation or direct an action. During learning one becomes familiar with more such cues, so that he recognizes a situation when only a few of the usual cues are present. In addition to the fundamental cues, subtler secondary cues guide one in adjusting or regulating the response. The expert gives more of his attention to these secondary cues.

At every moment during a response, information about the results is being returned. This feedback from muscle sensations and the visual impressions of the act regulates an action as it is carried out; performance therefore is a series of sensing-and-correcting acts. The expert's corrections come more promptly, steered by subtler cues than the novice detects.

The skilled movement is a "program" in which each act comes in at the right instant, its timing and force regulated by signals previously received. Many of the cues come from the previous actions. Cues far in advance of the action shape the expert's movements into a smooth sequence.

Expertness is recognized by the stability of response under stress, more than by the score under good circumstances. The expert maintains his level when external interference obscures cues or prevents concentration, and when fatigue, illness, or the like create internal disturbance. The expert, if prevented by circumstances from using the automatic sequence, can shift down to correct mediating responses.

Active practice with knowledge of results is regarded as the most important requirement in learning a motor skill.

This practice provides occasions to discriminate cues, to sense the cues that arise out of one's own action, and to develop a coordinated response. There is no set of rules to regulate amount of practice; the amount should be greater when a response is hard to explain or demonstrate, when the motor responses needed are not already under control, or when cues are hard to discriminate. Sometimes it is undesirable to practice the motor response until the stimulus situation is thoroughly understood; muscular cues only complicate the situation at the outset. Study or "mental practice" is most useful when the external stimuli are fixed, as in a piano selection or a basketball set shot. In memorization and sometimes in other study, overt practice in the form of self-recitation is valuable. In one study with nonsense material the best results were obtained with 60 per cent of the time going to recitation; in another study with more connected material, 33 per cent recitation gave best results.

A skill may be practiced in isolation or in the midst of a larger activity. The larger context adds interest and brings in a greater variety of situations. But such incidental practice may be too scattered or too casual. The practice situation should present the learner with realistic cues, similar to the cues encountered in everyday use of the skill. Simulators used in training attempt to reproduce all the cues likely to be useful in regulating an action. Within the principle of realism, various simplifications are beneficial. It may be desirable to isolate a subskill for practice, to simplify the cues during early learning, or to provide supplementary feedback. These modifications help the beginner discriminate the most pertinent cues. Drill procedures often call for a repetitious response to a fixed situation. More desirable is practice in a naturally varying context, so that the performer learns to recognize recurring cues in an ever-changing setting. The learner should confront as much variety as he can cope with. When the context makes modification of response necessary, the person learns to respond adaptively rather than rigidly.

Trial and error is unlikely to lead the performer to the best pattern of response; a demonstration or an explanation of the desired pattern is therefore beneficial. Students given such advice pay more attention to form and perform better. Cox showed that special exercises designed to focus attention on significant cues and work methods not only help on the task practiced but also transfer into better ability to learn other tasks. Pains must be taken to make demonstrations comprehensible and to make sure that the demonstration gets full attention. Clarification is especially valuable early in learning. Since the learner responds to perceived consequences, he should be helped to perceive accurately. The instructor by monitoring performance can draw attention to errors of technique that the learner would overlook.

Breaking up practice is desirable. An interval between blocks of trials allows for forgetting of shaky responses; weaknesses so revealed can be corrected. Practice periods are too short if they do not allow for warming up, or if they do not allow for the completion of a whole response sequence. Recommendations for teaching skills and regulating practice are listed on page 296.

Learning curves are useful in emphasizing the improvement to be expected and in giving the learner a picture of his own progress. Various aspects of the performance can be scored to give a learning curve. The curves for such subskills may have quite different forms; one subskill may be improving while another remains unchanged or deteriorates. A schematic learning curve exhibits six stages:

1. Little or no progress. During this period, maturation or learning of prerequisite responses may be taking place.

2. Rapid improvement. Mastering a coordination, understanding what is required or how parts of a problem fit together, or seeing the relation between an act and a goal may be the key to rapid improvement.

3. Decreasing gains. After the easier parts of an act are mastered, refinement of control comes slowly.

4. Plateau. In many curves one observes a period of steady or irregular performance in which there is no gain in score. A restructuring of the performance may be taking place during this time.

5. Improvement. If new coordination or new understanding can be achieved, scores can rise to a new level.

6. Approach to limit. While a learner's score ultimately becomes stable, there is no way to decide whether or not this level is the maximum of which the performer is capable.

Retention is best measured by the savings method; the time required to bring performance back to an acceptable level is an index of forgetting. Such studies show that motor skills are well retained over long periods. Transfer is studied by measuring savings in learning a new task, after having practiced a first task; to measure savings, the time required is compared with that of learners who did not practice the first task. Facilitation is generally to be expected because discriminations and coordinations used in one task are helpful elsewhere. But interference can occur when the response correct in one task is wrong in another. Table 15 outlines conditions promoting facilitation and interference. A distinction is made between interference with learning and habit interference. A person who is capable of discriminating one situation from another may carelessly fail to do so; this is habit interference. Interference is frequent in verbal learning; Underwood considers interference to be the principal source of forgetting of verbal associations. Special training in discrimination may be required to overcome interference. Overlearning is also beneficial.

Reading List 9

Arden N. Frandsen, "Teacher-Guidance of Learning Activities," Chapter 4 in *How Children Learn* (New York: McGraw-Hill, 1957), pp. 92–137.

Frandsen's analysis of teaching in the elementary grades gives many examples of the dependence of effective performance on understanding and suggests how to organize practice materials, demonstration, and practice activities. Some of these topics relate to our Chapter 11.

Herbert J. Klausmeier, "Psychomotor Abilities and Skills," Chapter 8 in *Learning and Human Abilities* (New York: Harper, 1961), pp. 226–53.

A textbook presentation covering principles of effective teaching similar to those of this chapter. In addition, psychomotor aptitudes are discussed.

Mark A. May, "The Psychology of Learning from Demonstration Films," *Journal of Educational Psychology*, 37 (1946), 1–12. Reprinted in Seidman *E*, Loree. Adapted in Mark A. May and A. A. Lumsdaine, eds., *Learning from Films* (New Haven: Yale Univ. Press, 1958), pp. 168–80.

May's suggestions for using films in teaching skills will help teachers obtain benefit from these aids, but they will also help in any explanation or demonstration. Compare May's suggestions with the customary use of films in the classroom, as you have experienced it.

George A. Miller, Eugene Galanter, and Karl H. Pribram, "Motor Skills and Habits," Chapter 6 in *Plans and the Structure of Behavior* (New York: Holt-Dryden, 1960), pp. 81–94.

This volume reports frontier thinking about how men plan and regulate their behavior. While the authors have written for psychologists rather than for students, their remarks in this chapter will do much to supplement our statements about "programs" and "feedback," and to clarify the limitations of verbal tutelage in teaching skills. You will also find Chapters 2, 10, and 12 especially relevant to educators.

R. E. Priebe and W. H. Burton, "The Slow Motion Picture as a Coaching Device," *School Review*, 47 (1939), 192–98.

This experiment on teaching the "western roll" style of high jumping exhibits the benefit of films as a supplement to other instruction and practice. Examine the nature of the gains and consider for what skills taught in school this use of films would be economical. Consider also which of their techniques could be applied to TV instruction broadcast to schools.

CHAPTER **10** INTELLECTUAL DEVELOPMENT AS TRANSFER OF LEARNING

As we noted in Chapter 2, most instruction is intended to develop transferable responses. Everyone agrees that transfer of response to new situations (facilitation) is wanted. But when laymen and educators discuss what the school should teach there is violent disagreement about the likelihood of transfer. Some advocate a strictly intellectual curriculum—if the student thoroughly learns history, classical languages, physics, etc., he will cope with future problems wisely, they say. Others contend that learning which remains verbal and abstract has negligible effect on response to concrete situations, and so is worthless. Rather than count on far-reaching transfer, they would have school assignments anticipate as realistically as possible the personal, civic, and vocational tasks of adulthood. The majority of educational planners reject both these extremes. They are convinced that far-reaching transfer can be obtained, but that the courses intended to transfer often have failed to do so. They search for a curriculum and a method of instruction with dependable transfer effects.

The most imperative educational goal is to increase the pupils' ability to think, i.e., to replace trial and error or thoughtless response in a problematic situation with intellectual control of decisions. This outcome can be called many things—reasoning ability, intellectual power, mastery of the great disciplines, functional skill in problem solving—whatever the name, the aim is transfer.

OUTMODED VIEWS ON THE TRANSFER OF INTELLECTUAL ATTAINMENTS

The Decline of Formal Discipline

Some attention to older views on transfer will be profitable. Every educator will encounter the outmoded theories and must know the reasons for rejecting them. Furthermore, this knowledge will help him judge curricula and methods. Many practices current in the school were instituted under the influence of one of these false theories. Even where the theories are recognized to be invalid, traces of them are to be found in the school program like the fossil print of a prehistoric fern on a lump of coal.

The classical curriculum assumed that a response which can be transferred will be transferred. The language teacher who expects the student of Latin grammar to improve his writing of English assumes this, as does the college faculty which demands geometry from every applicant for admission because "geometry teaches one to reason." The theory behind the classical secondary and college curriculum was that of "formal discipline." This theory holds that the mind possesses distinct "faculties" such as memory, reasoning, and concentration, and that the way to improve these faculties is to exercise them on difficult and abstract lessons. A difficult academic curriculum does serve as an effective screen; it passes no one on to higher education who is unlikely to work diligently and ably on abstract tasks.

But does such instruction necessarily improve concentration, abstract thinking, or judgment? Discouraging evidence has come from many sources. Attempts to improve mental functions by direct practice in memorizing and reasoning produced negligible gains. The studies supposed to improve the mind had no more effect on mental test performance or on ability to master other subjects than did the studies believed to lack disciplinary value.

JAMES'S RESEARCH ON MEMORY.   In one of the earliest American psychological experiments, William James and his students tried to determine whether or not mental exercise does any good. They memorized part of a poem by Victor Hugo, timing themselves. Every day for the next month they "exercised" by memorizing works by other poets. For a final test, they timed their memorization of a new poem by Hugo. They memorized this poem a little faster than the first one, but the gain was so tiny that James (1890, I, p. 663) drew the conclusion that "one's native retentiveness is unchangeable. . . . All improvement of the memory lies in the line of elaborating the associates of each of the several things to be remembered. No amount of culture would seem capable of modifying a man's *general* retentiveness."

James advises "elaborating the associates." This means that to remember better a person should learn more about the subject matter, or make fuller interpretations, so that he will understand the material better. James would argue, and more recent studies agree, that learning a great deal about Caesar improves readiness to memorize a passage from Caesar but does not "prepare the memory" for the grind of medical school. We shall see (page 325) that he was wrong in saying that *all* improvement in memory depends on this one method.

Hundreds of experiments of this general character were performed. Consistently, one intellectual activity was found to have little effect on ability to deal with the next, somewhat different task. This put under suspicion most of the academic program previously advocated on the ground that it would promote *general* intellectual functioning, i.e., effective learning and reasoning in *any* new situation.

THORNDIKE'S STUDIES OF GAINS ON MENTAL TESTS.   "The study of history teaches the student to suspend judgment, weigh evidence, and balance many factors in reaching a decision." Such benefits are often claimed without supporting evidence. When challenged to produce evidence that his subject does improve the mind, the advocate can only point out that the most eminent and intellectually distinguished people (including himself!) have studied his subject. E. L. Thorndike (1924) commented on the worthlessness of such testimony:

> The chief reason why good thinkers seem superficially to have been made such by having taken certain school studies, is that good thinkers have taken such studies, becoming better by the inherent tendency of the good to gain more than the poor from any study. When the good thinkers studied Greek and Latin, these studies seemed to make good thinking. Now that the good thinkers study Physics and Trigonometry, these seem to make good thinkers. If the abler pupils should all study Physical Education and Dramatic Art, these subjects would seem to make good thinkers. These were, indeed, a large fraction of the program of studies for the best thinkers the world has produced, the Athenian Greeks.

Thorndike turned to the newly invented mental test as a way of measuring transfer effects. This test was a series of novel problems, perhaps artificial in nature but nonetheless requiring reasoning. If thinking is improved, should not the better problem-solving show up in improved test performance? Thorndike's (1924) results demonstrated that no high-school subject, as then taught, had superior power to improve performance on his tests. Pupils did gain in test score from year to year, but the pupils who took practical subjects gained nearly as much as the pupils who studied subjects said to have disciplinary value. After corrections were made for initial ability, those who took arithmetic or French gained only a trifle more than those who took cooking or sewing (see also Wesman, 1945; J. V. West and Fruchter, 1960).

In addition to the studies using mental tests, there were studies testing the effect of one subject on performance in others. Here, too, little transfer appeared. It is well established that learning to translate Latin words into English does not guarantee heightened appreciation of our historical backgrounds, interest in classic literature, mastery of English vocabulary, or ability to learn to speak a modern language. Study of the rules of English usage may have little effect on ability to express ideas clearly and correctly (Carroll, 1940; Rapp, 1945; Searles and Carlsen, 1960, p. 461: Strom, 1960).

Psychologists and other students of education swung over to Thorndike's view that hard mental work does not accelerate mental development enough for that alone to justify an academic curriculum. Humphreys (1951) voices the general conclusion drawn from Thorndike's work:

> If you need accounting in your occupation, study accounting during your training and preferably the type of accounting you will need. If you want to read Cicero in Latin, by all means study Latin. If, however, you want to learn French, do not spend several years in the study of Latin, since you will be further ahead if you concentrate on French. If you want to learn to solve social problems, spend your time in the social sciences, not in the study of geometry.

Emphasis on Specific Learnings

If one can use only the specific reactions-to-situations he has been taught, the school should list the situations important out of school or in later courses and teach the pupil to cope with each one. Under this view, transfer occurs only from the learning experience to a task containing "identical elements," i.e., identical cue-response combinations. The question asked about each proposed lesson was, "Does this situation contain elements that the student will have to react to later?" If it did not, it lost favor. As a consequence, the arithmetic curriculum was stripped of such quaint, deliberately difficult problems as:

> Reduce to equivalent fractions having lowest common denominator:
> $$\tfrac{3}{8}, \qquad \tfrac{27}{68}, \qquad \tfrac{213}{493}$$

> How many quart, pint, and half-pint bottles, of each an equivalent number, may be filled from a vessel containing 54 gal. 1 qt.?

Practice exercises were based on the arithmetic used in adult affairs. Spelling words were drawn from letters written by adults; reading vocabulary came from words adults read in newspapers; and science topics were judged according to their practical value. This "social utility" curriculum was based on the belief that the more "like real life" the learning situation is, the greater the effect on later behavior. Marriage, job finding, and similar personal problems were the topics studied in "life-adjustment education," likewise reflecting the view that the school achieves maximum effect by anticipating future problems and by teaching directly relevant concepts and prescriptions. This wave of revision had a good effect on the curriculum, insofar as it cleared out deadwood. Much that has been said about making school tasks realistic is quite sound. The approach remains a completely valid orientation for training in certain vocational skills.

But in denying that one situation can be studied so that the student becomes able to think through other problem situations for himself, the curriculum maker takes on a hopeless task. There are countless important problems in each day's headlines—farm prices, overpopulation, highway safety, and so on. Each is a suitable topic for a social-utility curriculum. Under the theory that general transfer is unattainable, the curriculum became an arena in which momentary fads competed for attention with serious, recurring problems.

There is a risk that piecemeal, topical curriculum development may omit fundamentals of a field of knowledge. In 1940, a high-school chemistry teacher who believed in meeting students' future needs for specific information would have taught units on soap, alloys used in home and industry, and the refining of petroleum. Such a curriculum would anticipate concerns of adult life. The topic of atomic structure would not have seemed useful to this teacher. The nonscientist, he would have said, faces no situations where understanding of atoms and electrons would help. The release of atomic energy in 1942 changed all that. Today, few scientific matters are of wider public concern than the atom and its use.

> **1.** Under the assumption that transfer is limited by the principle of "identical elements," how would the curriculum be selected for the following subjects or objectives?
> **a.** English usage
> **b.** citizenship education
> **c.** nursing education
> **d.** industrial arts
>
> **2.** In what sense are the attempts to improve mental ability by preschool training "transfer experiments"? Does our interpretation of those studies agree with Thorndike's conclusion on transfer?

CONDITIONS FAVORABLE TO TRANSFER

The pessimistic position that transfer is unobtainable could not long be sustained. Nearly every experiment (including those of James and Thorndike) showed some transfer; in many experiments, like that of Cox (page 290), for instance, very satisfying transfer appeared. Psychologists modified their views to include in one theory both the successes and failures to get transfer. Whatever disagreements are presently found among experts on educational transfer relate to the issue: "What teaching methods"—*not* "what courses"—"are most capable of producing learning that will facilitate future learning and problem solving?" There are numerous unanswered theoretical questions about how transfer takes place, but it is agreed that all responses are helped or hindered by accumulated experience.

The basic conclusion from all the studies of transfer is this: *Transfer of a behavior pattern to a new situation is likely to occur whenever the person recognizes the new situation as similar to other situations for which the behavior has been appropriate.* Note that this statement allows for in-terference as well as facilitation. We spoke of transfer (facilitation) earlier as an increase in ability to think. We might also speak of it as an increase in ability to learn. Transfer is measured, as we saw, by savings in learning

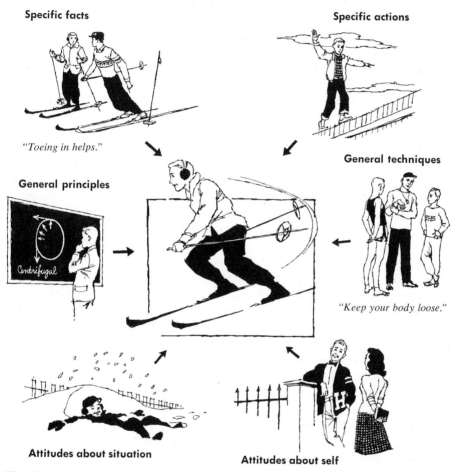

Specific facts

"Toeing in helps."

Specific actions

General principles

Centrifugal

General techniques

"Keep your body loose."

Attitudes about situation

Attitudes about self

72 *Many sorts of response will transfer*

time, i.e., by ability to reach a level of performance more quickly than would be expected without relevant prior experience. A transferable ex-perience does not "strengthen" the mind; it *equips* it, by supplying interpre-tations and response patterns that can be used elsewhere.

All the following types of response transfer beyond the original learning situation:

1. *Specific actions or programs of motor response.* Being able to move each finger to a given spot is prerequisite to typing. Learning to move in

time with an orchestra helps one to learn any new dance step. The more steps learned, the easier it is to master a new routine.

2. *Specific facts or associations.* A single fact may clarify many situations. The pupil learns that *pre* means *before.* He studies the examples *preview, predict,* and *prepare.* Then he can transfer this response to *preheat* (or to *pre-eminent,* where it interferes with interpretation). Information in this category may be descriptive (in the sense of page 58), or it may be a prescription or a generalization of relatively narrow applicability.

3. *Broad concepts and generalizations.* A gardener learns to cope with new insects by classifying them as chewing insects and sucking insects. "Use malathion to spray aphids" is a prescription with a narrow application; "Use malathion on sucking insects" is broader, permitting him to treat an unfamiliar insect. A concept has not been fully learned, and is not transferable, until the learner can recognize the situations where it applies.

To give another example: A teacher helps a student to analyze a tax proposal in terms of general concepts. He learns to consider its effect on economic growth, its fairness to various types of citizens, and the efficiency with which it can be collected. Knowing these concepts in addition to the immediate "How will it affect my pocketbook?" the student is better able to think through other problems of taxation.

4. *General techniques of analyzing situations.* In its simplest form, this consists in becoming aware that certain types of cues are significant. One who learns English comes to rely on word order as a sign of relationship (e.g., *house boat* is interpreted differently from *boat house*). In Latin and other languages, word endings are the chief cue to relations. Pupils familiar only with English try to use word order and "do not see" word endings; this interferes with learning to read Latin (DeWitt, 1960).

More complex skills of communicating, studying, and reasoning also fall in this category. The pupil may learn to look for the topic sentences in paragraphs, or for the major and minor themes in a symphony. He may generalize this into a technique of seeking the central structure in any work of art. In science and mathematics he learns techniques of arranging and criticizing argument. Faulty techniques—for example, copying extensively from a text while studying—can be learned just as easily as good ones.

5. *Attitudes toward subjects or situations.* A boy will not do well in repairing machinery if he assumes that he can locate a difficulty only by trial and error, testing each part in turn. If he believes that he can save time by stopping to reason from the symptoms the machine shows, he will do better. In effect, a change in attitude can raise his "mechanical aptitude." Similarly, pupils learn that foreign language makes connected sense and need not be puzzled out one word at a time. Attitudes are especially important, because a person who *can* make a response will not make it if he is not alert to the possibility of using his past learning.

Ruediger (1908) showed that an attitude of neatness is transferable. Previous studies had showed that if an arithmetic teacher insists on neat papers she gets neat papers, but neatness in other courses does not improve. Ruediger's teacher, however, not only required neat work in arithmetic but discussed neatness as an ideal to be sought in all work; now neatness "trained" during the arithmetic lesson transferred into improvement in all papers. The response did not transfer until other situations were interpreted as resembling the original one.

6. *Attitudes toward one's self, a self-concept.* A pupil develops confidence that he can fix machinery, handle numbers, use tools skillfully, etc. He develops willingness to take a chance. He learns to voice his own opinions, when he doubts an "authority." In a word, his morale improves. Another pupil experiences difficulty in the same learning situation and carries away an equally transferable belief in his own incompetence.

Curriculum activities and content should provide occasions for developing responses of all the types listed above. Two activities may be equally good for teaching a certain specific skill or idea. If so, the teacher will certainly prefer the one that also develops important *general* outcomes such as work methods, broadly significant concepts, interests, social skills, and emotional control.

"Real" problems brought into the school vary in transfer value. To be sure, a lesson dealing directly with the application situation promises to have a relatively large influence on behavior. But there is a great difference between a study of marriage that covers only such specifics as whether or not a young couple should live with their parents and a study that considers the family as a social institution. The latter teaching, at its best, can transfer not only into behavior in the family, but also into a new view of other institutions and other cultures, and so can modify the student's whole world view.

On the other hand, even if the teacher thinks up a fine activity for applying scientific method or developing pride in achievement, the activity is questionable if the specific topic covered is trivial. Almost certainly, work with more significant "content" can promote the same general skills and attitudes, and teach specifics of value as well. An effort to produce transferable general skills need not interfere with mastering the more specific subject matter (e.g., Rudolf, 1949).

Although the debates about transfer have been largely confined to the secondary school, the years from birth to adolescence are full of opportunities for transferable experience. Some of the most widely significant interpretations are to be developed during the childhood years—for example, the concept that events have causes which can be discovered, so that wise decisions give one power over his "destiny." Only the pupil in whom this belief is firmly rooted can resist the superstitions, fallacies, and fatalism of the community ("If God had intended water to have fluorine, He would have put it there").

Even when the school teaches transferable skills and concepts, the student may fail to transfer them. Whether or not a response is used depends on attitudes: what goals the student seeks, what knowledge he thinks he can use, and what confidence he has. Teachers set the stage for transfer partly by pointing out that students should expect their new learning to transfer. Obvious as this seems, it is a rather new concept in teaching. History, for example, is taught because it can shed light on contemporary affairs, but almost never did the old-style text connect the Reconstruction period or the Alien and Sedition Acts with current troubles. Ruediger's study of neatness is a second pertinent example.

3. Which types of transferable response were developed in Cox's experiment on motor skills (page 290)?

4. Which type(s) of transferable response is (are) included in this objective?

a. Students should learn to think quantitatively about relationships observed in business or in nature.

b. Students should appreciate the power of scientific method in investigating social problems.

c. Students should learn to use the semicolon appropriately.

5. What general responses might fourth-graders acquire from a study of Holland? If the prominent minorities in their community are Mexicans and Armenians, what greater transfer value would a study unit on Mexico or Armenia have?

6. A student writes to his Congressman about the proposal to lower the voting age to 18. What responses does this situation have in common with a later one when he wishes to write legislators about changing the Social Security rules? Check each of the six types of response.

7. Is the research on transfer consistent with the following opinion?

Laboratory work and shopwork engender a habit of observation, a knowledge of the difference between accuracy and vagueness, and an insight into nature's complexity and into the inadequacy of all verbal accounts of real phenomena. . . . They confer precision; because, if you are *doing* a thing, you must do it definitely right or definitely wrong. They confer honesty; for . . . it becomes impossible to dissimulate your vagueness or ignorance by ambiguity.

8. One seventh-grade teacher tells the class what lies ahead in mathematics by describing algebra as mysterious and difficult. "Instead of working with numbers, you do problems like this"—and she writes an equation on the board without explaining it. A second teacher does not mention algebra by name, but casually uses various formulas such as $A = lw$ and $i = Prt$ when the class is doing numerical problems on area or investment. Each formula is treated as a shorthand summary of what the group has been expressing in words. What effect would each of these methods have upon readiness for algebra?

9. What experiences in music during the first four grades build readiness for playing an orchestral instrument?

10. How does our principle stating when transfer will occur differ from the theory of "identical elements"? of formal discipline?

THE DEVELOPMENT OF INTELLECTUAL POWER

In our earlier discussion of intellectual readiness, we concentrated on tests of general scholastic aptitude. We now examine a line of research, much of it recent, that looks at intellectual performance in another way. These studies begin to explain what intellect is and how it is constructed. Though the further work required to translate this conception into teaching methods and new mental tests has not yet been done, it nonetheless demands the attention of educators.

Learning to Learn

One of the contributions to this thinking is the work on perceptual development in the blind, which we described on page 100. These studies, and comparable studies of young animals prevented from using their senses by special hoods and gloves, show that ability to use each type of cue is learned. Long-extended practice in discrimination, early in life, forms the machinery that makes it possible to encode and interpret sense impulses. Penfield's discussion of speech production (page 101) points to the similarly early development of machinery to decode intentions into muscular action. Such theories explain the superior ability of Samoans in rhythmic tasks, for example, as a consequence of cumulative attention to rhythmic cues and actions.

A striking feature of Cox's results was that practice on one motor skill, with a suitably designed training method, led to faster learning of a second, quite different motor skill. This type of transfer was christened "learning to learn" by H. F. Harlow (1949). Harlow showed that a monkey, placed in a problem situation, *learns* to take advantage of information obtained by his trial response. From one problem he learns something that improves his performance on a problem where the specific cues are quite different. While experiments with children (e.g., Shepard, 1957) show similar results, studying the monkey has the great advantage that one can control his environment from birth and so know just what cues he has had a chance to use.

For a training session the monkey is placed in a special cage, a shutter

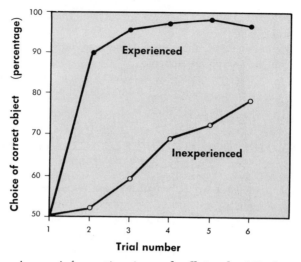

73 *With experience, information is used efficiently* (*Harlow, 1949*)

The lower curve is an average for performance of animals on their first eight
problems. The upper curve is an average of performance after experience
with 200 previous problems. The task is to learn which of the two objects
conceals a food reward.

is raised, and he sees before him two objects, a yellow and a blue cube, say.
Beneath each object is a cup; one cup contains a raisin. The monkey
knocks one object aside, or picks it up. If he exposes a raisin, he gets it
as reward. Then the shutter is lowered to end the trial. How long it takes
the monkey to discover that the raisin is always under the yellow cube
depends on his history. If this is his first problem, he learns slowly (lower
curve in Figure 73). If he has 50 trials with the yellow and blue cubes, and
then 50 trials on a second problem (say, a pyramid vs. an oblong block),
and so on, he eventually becomes expert in solving choice problems. On
trial 1 of a new problem, he has only 50 per cent chance of success, but
if he uses the information this trial gives, he can succeed on trial 2. After
a monkey has done 200 problems, 90 per cent of the time he gets the raisin
on trial 2. He has learned to take advantage of his first-trial experience. It
appears as if he has learned that success depends on his effort to detect
a cue and not on accident. These results, and the less extensive studies with
children, indicate that one develops a general expectancy, perhaps a concept "something about the object indicates the place where the raisin is,"
which leads to active comparison of the objects.

IMPROVED METHODS OF LEARNING. Is there some contradiction between
the finding of "learning to learn" and James's inability to memorize better
after practice? According to the studies following James, practice *alone*

is not likely to "improve memory," but skill in memorizing can be developed. The improvement comes because one can learn effective ways of memorizing.

Woodrow (1927) tested the ability of college students to memorize. Then he gave special training to one group of poor memorizers. He explained superior methods of learning, including learning by wholes, active self-testing, use of rhythm and grouping, attention to meaning, and use of secondary associations. This group practiced the new methods for a short while. A second group "exercised" its memory, memorizing much material but being shown no new techniques. This left a third group of students as a control who received neither training nor practice. Table 16 shows the average scores after students studied the English equivalents of 30 Turkish words for six minutes. The group trained in superior techniques of studying gained in ability to learn Turkish words, historical dates, and connected prose. The essence of "learning to learn" seems to be directing attention toward appropriate parts of the scene and their relationships, not improving "memory" or "concentration" as such.

Woodrow's results are consistent with the view that a student reacts to any situation with particular responses. When asked to memorize, he responds with a definite process: reading the list to himself, trying to recite as many words as he can, or consciously trying to form associations. To help him, we should try to replace his inefficient actions with more efficient ones. The golf pro takes the same steps to improve a man's golf game: he finds out what particular errors the man is making and helps him to correct them, rather than just urging more practice.

By introducing lessons on work-study skills into ninth-grade civics, Leggitt (1934) obtained substantial improvement in eight different areas. The students learned to use reference books, interpret charts, summarize, and outline. Continued practice was helpful. The first introduction to the new methods raised the students' scores, but further gains were made when the students applied the ideas in other civics units. The new methods were learned while the pupils were also learning about legislation, the cost of government, etc., so that the course had both specific and general values.

TABLE 16

Suitable teaching improves ability to memorize (Woodrow, 1927)

Group	Number	Score before training	Score after training	Improvement
Students receiving no training	106	16.2	16.1	−0.1
Students receiving only practice in memorizing	42	14.6	15.1	0.5
Students taught new methods	34	13.6	21.1	7.5

GAINS IN DISCRIMINATION. Discrimination of a specific property is learned. Once the developing individual learns to respond to that property, he can use it as a cue in a new problem. This too can best be observed scientifically at a primitive stage. House and Zeaman (1960) studied the severely retarded (age near 10, MA near 4). It is difficult for such children to use painted or printed patterns as cues. Given 500 choices between a painted black ■ and a yellow **T** , with candy under the **T** on every trial, only one child in five learned to pick the **T** . Three-dimensional objects are easier to differentiate than flat patterns. One group was trained initially with a *cutout* ■ and **T** placed over the reward cups. After a child reached 80 per cent success in choosing the **T** he was shifted to figures painted on a flat plaque. After just 250 trials (trials with objects and with flat patterns were combined in this count), 70 per cent learned to pick the painted **T** . Only 20 per cent in the first group had succeeded with 500 trials on flat patterns. A third group practiced with a cutout red **✚** and a green **●** . As a pupil succeeded at that task, he was shifted to the painted **T** and ■ —a new problem. Even so, there was marked transfer from practice on objects (50 per cent success after a series of 250 trials, counting both object and pattern trials). Evidently some ability to "notice" color or shape was developed in object training that did not emerge in 500 trials on the more difficult judgment of painted shapes.

Here readiness was much advanced by practice on an easier task. The early work on transfer led some people to the much-too-sweeping conclusion that the way to learn a complex response is always to practice that response in a situation identical to that of later application. In the foregoing study greater final learning came from practice on a simplified situation where cues were not identical. Of course, the greater the identity between the practice situation and the use situation, the more certain will be the transfer of whatever is learned. But the learner can transfer no more than he originally learns, and he will acquire only a feeling of inadequacy if the practice task is too difficult.

TRANSFORMING INFORMATION CONCEPTUALLY. In advanced problem solving one transforms information, going beyond direct use of cues. Transformation includes analysis, rearrangement, and translation. The oddity problem is a simple example: Present three objects, two alike (two yellow cubes, one blue); put the raisin always under the odd object. With enough trials, the preschool child will find the solution and go to the blue cube on nearly every trial. Trained on many oddity problems, and then confronted with new objects (two toy dogs and a baby doll), the child can solve the unfamiliar problem on the *second* trial just by observing where the raisin turned up before. This is the gain we have already discussed in ability to use informative feedback. But the child gains something else. After doing many oddity problems, he compares the objects and tries the odd one on the *first* trial. He acts as if he applies a concept of oddity or differentness to whatever set of objects is put before him. His choice is attached to the mediating interpretation ("that one is different") rather than to the object itself.

By school age, children have collected a repertoire of relationships that serve as provisional interpretations: oddity, number, alternation ("if it was the right one last time it will be the left one this time"), relative size ("it's the middle-sized one"), etc. As Figure 74 indicates, responses become attached to the mediating interpretation; when the objects change, the correct response still is made. Having applied the concept "two" to these lights, the person can respond correctly to the lights in any order or any new spatial arrangement, or even to a radarlike display in which he uses the switch to report the number of targets present. The concepts acquired during the school years (e.g., classical vs. romantic, parallel vs. convergent, premise vs. conclusion) have this same power to facilitate analysis of completely new objects and events.

Advanced intelligence is flexible but controlled. The organism conditioned to make response *R* whenever cue *S* appears is an automaton, rigidly set to give that response and at a loss when it fails. But the child who has the oddity concept can pick the yellow cube when it is accompanied by two blue cubes, and can easily shift when there are two yellow cubes and one blue cube.

Concepts work so well that one can apply them in reverse; the response pictured in Figure 74 would carry over with very little retraining if the

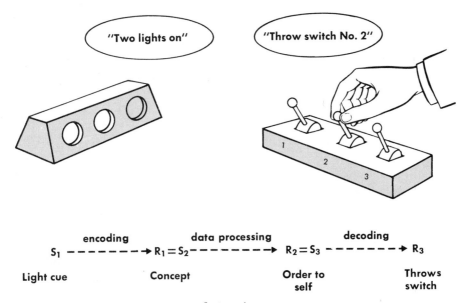

74   *A mediated response is a chain of events*

labels on the switches were changed around. Human adults sorted cards into two bins—cards with red designs to the left, green designs to the right—until they were proficient. When these practiced subjects were asked to sort in the opposite way—red to right, green to left—they very shortly overcame any interference and outdid an unpracticed group. More than that, they outdid a group asked to shift from color sorting to sorting by pattern. It was easier to reverse a response than to use a new mediator (Kendler and d'Amato, 1955).

This result is not found among preschool children. It is easier for them to shift from color sorting to pattern sorting than to reverse the color sorting (Kendler *et al.*, 1960). Only around kindergarten age do children begin to make effective use of verbal mediators to direct themselves. Russian psychologists likewise have found that "in the early stages of child development, speech is only a means of communication with adults and other children. . . . Subsequently it becomes also a mean whereby he organizes his own experiences and regulates his own actions. So the child's activity is mediated through words." (Luria, 1957, p. 116; see also Kendler and Kendler, 1962; Liublinskaya, 1957.)

> **11.** What relation do you see between the idea of "learning to learn" and each of the following?
>   **a.** pre-reading experience to develop readiness
>   **b.** motivation for achievement
>   **c.** ability of a practiced athlete to master a new sport
>   **d.** the study habits of the superior achiever (page 200)
>   **e.** the generalized learning curve of Chapter 9
>
> **12.** Is it reasonable to suppose that there are special techniques of learning for each subject, so that a person with much experience is better able to learn an entirely new body of similar material? For example, can experience in studying Spanish help an anthropologist learn an Indian tongue?
>
> **13.** If an adolescent were exposed to Woodrow's memory training, would his performance on any type of mental test item be improved?

Stages Toward Mature Intellectual Control

The problem-solving behavior of children becomes more complex and more controlled as they grow older. We move on now to reports describing the course of intellectual development from preschool to adolescence. If you are a prospective college teacher, you may be impatient with our talk of monkeys, the mentally retarded, and the school beginner. Or, if you are planning to teach the young child, you may be curious about only the early stages. But every stage depends on its predecessors and leads up to the lessons that follow. Every educational plan must take into account what earlier schooling can do or must leave undone. Especially in these days when college professors are full of plans for starting kindergartners to "think like mathematicians," every teacher needs to understand all that is known about all the stages. There is another reason for not confining attention to one "stage" of thinking. Reports like Kendler's, and others summarized below, speak as if children at age 8 think differently from those at age 5. This is only partly true. A person never leaves the early stages completely. The stranger a problem is, the more he must drop back to primitive performance and work his way toward understanding.

PIAGET'S LIST OF STAGES.   Jean Piaget, in his Geneva laboratory, has spent a lifetime studying the child's intellectual development. He uses many methods: observation of spontaneous behavior, interviews, and tests requiring flexible thinking. In some 20 books Piaget has compiled evidence that the child advances in his reasoning more or less according to this time schedule (Piaget, 1950, esp. pp. 119 ff.; Thomson, 1959; Hunt, 1961, pp. 113 ff.):

Stage O, first two years—acquiring sensorimotor control
Stage IA, 2 and over—extracting concepts from experience
Stage IB, 4 and over—intuitive use of concepts
Stage II, 7 and over—mastering concrete operations (control through perceptual anticipation of consequences)
Stage III, 11 and over—mastering formal operations (control through logical deduction of possibilities and consequences)

This is only a rough statement regarding the periods when one type of performance is beginning to be more prominent than its predecessor. The transition point varies with the concept, the method of instruction, the cultural group studied, etc. (Peel, 1959; Braine, 1959; W. H. King, 1961). The pupil is still having difficulty with certain concrete operations at age 12, when he is already applying formal operations successfully at times.

SENSORIMOTOR CONTROL.   The child initially brings perception and motor response under control by observing and by trial and error. This stage involves little or no thoughtful regulation of response, hence is labeled Stage O. Starting with a visual image that is presumably no more than a disorganized jumble of sensation, he creates an organization. "Fields" of color and pattern that move together he comes to distinguish as objects: his mother, his nursing bottle, his stuffed tiger. He organizes the field by "constructing" objects out of sensory impressions (Piaget, 1954).

The infant practices a thousand times the arm movement toward a dangling object. He is motivated, if we can accept White's views about the "need for competence," by the sheer satisfaction of being able to reach the spot he aims at. He repeats a babbling pattern—apparently satisfied just by the accomplishment—until he can make the sound when he thinks of it. Only then can he imitate what he hears, and learn his family's language.

EXTRACTION OF CONCEPTS FROM EXPERIENCE.   After the child can talk, language helps him to develop concepts. Still he must achieve concepts for himself; they cannot be handed to him. Names for objects can be taught by pointing, but the child has to form for himself even the idea of sameness or identity. His parent may say "the ball," but when this ball is hidden behind a box and pulled out at the other side, the child at this stage does not know it to be the same ball.

During this period, vague relational concepts—bigger, older, more numerous, etc.—are extracted or constructed from experience. Such concepts

75   *The preoperational child cannot maintain a fixed point of view (from Lowenfeld, 1957, p. 136)*

The child was asked to "draw a man"; he shows the parts he knows logically to be present.

can be formed without verbal instruction, through frequent association of a consequence with some aspect of the stimuli, as in the Harlow experiment. A child can form the concept of ledges, high stools, etc. as things he might fall from, even though no name is given. He may make up his own word for such a concept (Roger Brown, 1958b, p. 19).

He also learns by hearing relation-words associated with consequences. His mother says, "Too much water; you'll spill it," and "Mary can stay up because she is older." The child cannot be told directly what the relational word means. He must extract the idea of quantity—"too much," "older"— from the contexts in which it appears (Piaget, 1951).

INTUITIVE THOUGHT.   The child from ages 4 to 7, having inexact relational concepts, reaches conclusions impressionistically. Many small pieces of chocolate he thinks are "more" than one unbroken piece. If the water in a narrow jar rises higher than in a wide jar, for him the narrow jar contains more water. Indeed, when the wide jar is emptied into a narrow one, he maintains that the quantity has increased. To judge a relation he uses correlated cues that usually accompany the relation in question. Higher water levels usually go with more water, so height is an important cue for responding "more" (Piaget and Inhelder, 1940).

When the child in this stage compares objects directly, he makes excellent discriminations by means of unmediated perceptual judgment. He can compare two servings of cake by placing one alongside the other, or two handfuls of candy by pairing off the pieces. Asked to make a bead chain like the one shown—red, yellow, blue, yellow, blue, etc.—he does it well, *if* he can lay his chain alongside the model so as to obtain perceptual feedback (Figure 76). His judgments are performed directly on sensory experience; he does not hold the information in mind or rearrange it mentally. He cannot think of two aspects of an object at once, nor imagine how it would look from a different angle.

Perceptual judgment, unaided by symbolic representation, is often wrong. The child at this age rarely can break a complex impression into perceptual segments and hold their relations in mind. Relations over a distance are hard for him to judge. To compare piles of candy at opposite ends of a long table, pairing off will not work. Not yet able to count objects adequately, he cannot transform his task into a comparison of one symbol with another. When we move the bead model away from his rod (Figure 76b), perceptual point-to-point comparison becomes difficult, because he cannot look back and forth without losing his place, and cannot hold the order in mind as a symbolic pattern. He gradually becomes able to carry information in mind and to transform it (Figure 76, steps c and d).

The child's concepts do not yet permit him to think ahead or to retrace his processes. Piaget (1950, p. 37) cites the experiment of his colleague Rey, who hands out a piece of paper with a three-inch square in the middle, and asks the child to draw the largest and smallest squares he can on the page. The 8-year-old who has advanced beyond the intuitive stage promptly draws a tiny square in the center, and a large one crowding the edge. For him, increase in size is an "operation"; he foresees what will happen when the operation is applied repeatedly. The 6-year-old (who has not mastered the operation) draws just inside and outside the standard, and then makes other squares, moving inward and outward, approaching the goal a little at a time. He shows no anticipation of the final result. He cannot "carry" the idea of square through the series without drawing many intermediate steps.

CONCRETE OPERATIONS.

An operation is a type of action: it can be carried out rather directly by the manipulation of objects, or internally. . . . Roughly, an [internalized] operation is a means of getting data about the real world into the mind and there transforming them so that they can be organized and used selectively in the solution of problems (Bruner, 1960, p. 35).

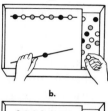

a. Solves by adding one bead at a time, putting copy alongside model to check, regulating by touch or short eye movements.

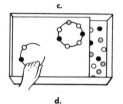

b. Rod is fixed by tester in offset position. Child solves by adding one bead at a time, regulating by back-and-forth eye movements.

c. Child solves by breaking circle into parts. Tends to lose his place and reverse direction. Has no concept of "between."

d. Response is mediated by image of the circle "opened out," transforming the task to one resembling b.

SUCCESSIVE STEPS IN OPERATIONAL THOUGHT (ABOUT AGES 6–7)

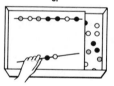

e. Child is told to make chain in reverse order. He must extract the order, neglecting appearance. The performance is regulated by verbal mediators such as "next to" and "between."

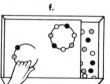

f. Child is told to make chain in reverse order, from a given starting point.

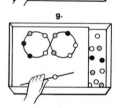

g. Starting point is given. Child mediates response by naming colors in order while working on each section.

76 *The concept of order grows in power*

Problems arranged in the order in which the child masters them, according to Piaget and Inhelder (1956). The child is to construct, on the rod he holds, a chain exactly like the model. The various shadings indicate different colors.

Operations *in thought* make overt physical trial-and-error operations unnecessary. (Recall Meredith's remarks, page 125.)

Somewhere around age 7 the child begins to see each common relational concept as implying a continuous operation that is reversible (growth and shrinkage, adding to and taking away from, rotating to the left and to the right, etc.). Reversibility is the key to precise adjustment. Two quantities can be made the same by up-and-down corrections, as Alice in Wonderland adjusted her height by nibbling the left- and right-hand mushrooms in turn. This reversibility of conceptual operations is very similar to the use of feedback to guide motor performance.

Suppose we ask a child to aim so that a marble, shot from a pivoting tube, will bounce off a wall and strike a target. He will succeed most rapidly if he collects information by shooting from systematically chosen positions that work closer to the target each time. The preoperational child tries shots from haphazardly chosen positions; he has difficulty in finding an exact solution. The older child, making controlled back-and-forth adjustments, gets organized information. He relates the marble's path to the angle of aim. Thinking replaces overt trial (Piaget and Inhelder, 1956).

According to this theory, a concept is fundamentally an imagined action. A relational concept expresses something that can be done with objects; the concept of an object is a prediction about what it will do or what we can do to it.

> To perceive a chair, said Pierre Janet, is to see an object on which one may sit; and to perceive a house, says von Weiszäcker even more emphatically, is not to look upon an image which enters you through your eye, but on the contrary to recognize a solid into which you may enter! (Piaget and Inhelder, 1959, p. 21.)

Thus the infant's operation of turning a toy about in his hands prepares him to rotate an object in imagination and envision the consequences. Only possession of this operation leads one to ask, "What does the other side of the moon look like?" An operation links experiences and makes one aware of gaps.

Just such a discovery was expressed by the writer's daughter, youngest of three, as she extended her 5-year-old idea of "older" to see that it means nothing without a "younger" element. During that year's Christmas vacation, the oldest daughter was home from college full of plans for marriage. The younger girls were impressed by her "graduation" from the family, and by Number Two's moving into the place of Big Sister. Came the day when Number Three left her dolls, sought out her mother, and half in question and half in distress exclaimed: "When *I* grow up and am a Big Sister—why—*I* won't be!" One can almost see her lining up the procession in her mind and working her way up to the front, only to find when she gets there that no one is behind her.

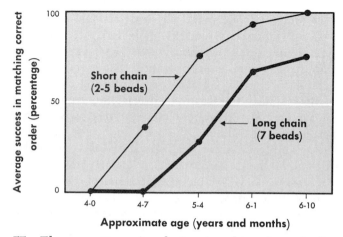

77 *The operation of ordering is achieved gradually (data from Braine, 1958)*

Results were nearly the same for sequences of 2, 3, and 5 beads.

Operational thought develops as one concept after another is disentangled from the vague impressions of earlier days. Some operational thought appears at age 5, and some concrete operations are not yet under control in adulthood. This gradual emergence is to be noted in Figure 77. Braine (1958) asked children to match sets of beads in a way that required them to hold the order of colors in mind. The child can match a short sequence some nine months before he can hold a seven-bead sequence in mind. (See also Wohlwill, 1960b; Elkind, 1961a.)

In concrete operational thought, a person reasons successfully about things that are or have been concretely present before him. Sharp distinctions between related properties (e.g., *weight* and *density*) are a necessary preliminary to operational thought (Ervin and Foster, 1960). A person who cannot distinguish true *distance* from *distance-as-it-appears-from-this-angle* cannot think accurately about distances. When the learner connects each concept with its unique operation, he can separate concepts and attend to one at a time (Elkind, 1961b).

In art and history, as well as in scientific areas, one deals with relations of properties and facts. Lodwich (see Peel, 1959) has shown that keeping two facts or purposes in view becomes possible for the child at this stage. In drawings, parts are coordinated to fit an over-all plan or theme (Lowenfeld, 1957).

When operational thought emerges, a child can understand the so-called *conservation* principles: that breaking up a piece of candy does not change its amount; that changing the shape of plasticine does not change its weight;

that looking at a mountain from a different angle does not change distances on its slopes. Conservation principles are fundamental to disciplined thought: in geometry, the maintenance of shape as triangles are moved; in engineering, the conservation of properties of materials; in history, the search for facts independent of the observer.

FORMAL OPERATIONAL THOUGHT.   A 14-year-old shoots a marble from a tube toward the cushioned edge of a billiard table three times. The following remarks show his logical thought at work (Inhelder and Piaget, 1958, p. 11).

> "The more the target approaches the plunger, the more the plunger must also approach the target. . . . If there were a line here [perpendicular to the cushion], the ball would come back exactly the same way" (i.e., would make equal angles on both sides). Questioned on whether his law always works, he replies, "It depends on the cushion too, . . . it has to be completely horizontal. But if the cushion were oblique, you would have to trace a perpendicular to the cushion and you would still have to take the same distance [angle] from the plunger [to the cushion and] up to the target."

This adolescent is using formal operational thought. He is reasoning accurately about a possibility present only in his imagination.

The early adolescent begins to make logical inferences and to cast his experience into rigorous verbal principles.[1] He begins to ignore the perceptions and prejudices that becloud logical arguments. The transition from concrete to formal operations is illustrated by the child who is asked to draw a rectangle in the same shape as a smaller rectangle. Aids such as rulers are provided (Piaget and Inhelder, 1956, p. 370). During the pre-operational period the child cannot preserve shape; he increases length and lets height come out as it will. He progresses to the point where he can mark off the length and the height, each twice; a concrete operation now keeps the shape under control. Intermediate, fractional enlargements are still beyond him. His next advance is to make a trial enlargement and judge impressionistically whether it is or is not the right shape. Once he can judge, he can attain the right shape by a series of reversible adjustments. Ultimately he becomes able to think of the numerical ratio *Length 1: Length 2* as something that must be preserved. This changes the problem from concrete to abstract form. Now he has a formal operational concept of proportion. He can accurately enlarge the rectangle by any amount. Numbers and arithmetic rules, as mediators, produce the order, "Make the height $5\frac{1}{2}$ inches," which regulates overt response.

Formal operations open the way to systematic consideration of all the

---

[1] Whether the child is capable of logical thought about abstractions and symbols prior to adolescence is not a settled issue. While such thought is not ordinarily exhibited, unpublished studies by Patrick Suppes and by Laymon Allen suggest that it may be possible to teach symbolic logic at ages 8 to 11.

possibilities and combinations, in or out of experience. When the adolescent is asked to observe rods of various sizes and materials and to explain why some bend more than others when weights are applied, he is able to check off possible explanations systematically. He sees that some of the short rods bend and others do not.

Since, unlike the concrete level child, he does not have to limit his consideration to a single relationship at a time, he can then proceed to the consideration of other variables which might determine it. He "feeds" his information into a general mechanism [for comparing and combining statements] . . . which assimilates the facts in the form of propositions and arranges them according to all possible combinations. He can move around among these possibilities [to select an explanation] . . . : for example, that length alone

TABLE 17

Stages in the mastery of operations

Age level	Designation	Principal features
0–2	Acquiring sensorimotor control	Extensive trial-and-error movements develop bodily control and eye-hand coordination. The perceptual field is organized into objects.
2–	Extracting concepts from experience	Words heard are associated with objects. Concepts are formed for recurring experiences.
4–	Intuitive use of concepts	Direct perceptual comparisons are accurate. Associated concepts are confused. Complex situations are reacted to as unanalyzable wholes; conclusions are based on superficial impressions.
7–	Concrete operational thought	Comparisons requiring one to hold information in mind are accurate, if the information is presented concretely. Operations can be imagined and results anticipated. Adjustment by reversal leads to an exact result. Associated concepts are distinguished; one can be changed while the other stays fixed.
11–	Formal operational thought	Operations among symbols or abstract ideas can be carried out in the mind. A complete array of logical possibilities can be systematically considered. Relations involving more than one variable can be comprehended. Accurate comparisons and deductions can be made from information not concretely presented.

does not determine flexibility so that another factor was involved for the short rod that bent. . . . The adolescent both discriminates between parts (variables or specific events . . .) and generalizes to an over-all explanation of the results and to [predictions about] other potential situations. (Parsons and Milgram, 1958, p. xviii.)

The adolescent can construct a theory for a problem situation, arranging and keeping track of complex possibilities. Thought of this kind requires an active exploration of the *structure* of the situation (F. C. Bartlett, 1958, p. 95).

14. In one of Piaget's tests the child sees dolls of three colors (A, B, C) tied on a wire. The experimenter then pulls the wire beneath a box and asks the child which will come out first as he pulls either forward or backward. Explain these results (Piaget, 1950, p. 135):

    a. Three-year-olds correctly give the answer for the forward order.

    b. Three-year-olds cannot give the answer when the wire is pulled backward, but 5-year-olds can.

    c. When the box with the dolls inside is turned through 180° (reversed), 7-year-olds can predict which doll will come out first, but younger children cannot.

    d. Having made several trials in which A or C comes out first, the 5-year-old is likely to predict B as the answer to a new question, because "B is due to have a turn."

15. In the test with the three dolls, where does an "operation" enter? Is anything "conserved" during the operation?

16. A child asked to copy a straight bead chain makes a chain by putting on the beads one at a time, selecting the right colors but not the right number or order. What stage of thought does this represent?

17. Discuss the following concepts as they apply to the development seen in Figure 76:

    a. reversibility (Where is it shown? What is reversed?)

    b. use of a verbal mediator

    c. transformation of information

18. Piaget (1953) describes one of his experiments as follows:

"To study measurement in two dimensions, we give the child a large sheet of paper with a pencil dot on it and ask him to put a dot in the same position on another sheet of the same size. He uses rods, strips of paper, strings, rulers, or any other measuring tools he needs. The youngest subjects are satisfied to make a visual approximation, using no tools. Later a child applies a measuring tool, but he measures only the distance of the point from the side or bottom edge of the paper and is surprised that this single measurement does not give him the correct position. Then he measures the distance from a corner of the paper, trying to keep the same slant (angle) when he applies the rules to his own sheet. Finally, about the age of eight or nine, he discovers that he must break up the measurement into two operations: the horizontal distance from a side edge and the perpendicular distance from the bottom or top edge."

In these results, which of the following is illustrated: impressionistic judgment, concrete operation, formal operation, conservation, reversible operation?

19. Recall the characteristics of the expert from our discussion of motor skills. Which of these characteristics distinguish operational thought from preoperational thought?

20. According to Boehm (1961), one out of four children of 6½ believes that the number of objects changes as they are spread wider. What implications does this have for the primary curriculum?

Interpretation of the Theory

Although Piaget and Inhelder speak of "stages" and locate each stage on the age scale, this is an oversimplification (Kessen and Kuhlmann, 1962). Intellectual development consists of the mastery of one concept after another, through pertinent experience. Each stage prepares for the next, but there are no sharp transitions. While concepts emerge in sequence, it is quite possible to have mastered one operational concept while still using another intuitively, or to apply the concept at one moment and not at another. Conservation of amount appears earlier than similarly rigorous thought about weight, and both of these operate earlier than conservation of volume.

Even the adult, when first trying to understand something new (say, the game of *Go* or the theory of musical harmony), must work his way from intuition to operational thought. He cannot think abstractly without a base of experience. If something in his present repertoire of operational concepts seems to apply, however, he can begin operational thought at once, at least as a provisional try. The theory of crystal structure, for instance, can be studied in a formal way by a person who has mastered the formal structure of solid geometry, because the latter rests on an adequate base of intuitive familiarity. Reasoning in a new field is greatly facilitated by mastery of a pertinent formal theory.

The aim of instruction in educational psychology for teachers is to promote concrete operational thought about teaching methods. The intuitive leap to conclusions should surely give way to controlled adjustment of classroom conditions (a little more of this, a little less of that) to produce the optimum outcome. The operations remain concrete, since the best procedures must be identified by observation of effects, not by theoretical calculations. Formal psychological theory is not, and may never be, able to calculate a prescription for teaching; its service is to point out factors requiring adjustment and to suggest provisional tries.

Sometimes an adult leaps to impressionistic and inexact conclusions merely because he lacks patience or confidence. A group of University of Chicago students worked examination questions orally for Bloom and

Broder (1950). For example, "If the government wished to control an inflationary 'boom' would it be consistent with the policy to have the Federal Reserve System buy securities in the stock market?" A good many students of economics jumped to an impressionistic conclusion—either that the action was consistent or that it was inconsistent—and then sought reasons to support their impression. They gave random associations about such words as "reserve" and "stock market," instead of thinking of the structure of the system and seeing that the action would put more money into circulation.

There is no discontinuity between stages. As we saw in Figures 76 and 77, progress is continuous; a person learns to use his concepts, operations, and sensorimotor controls more expertly and extends their reach. A child playing checkers may be able to think three moves ahead in some plays, one move ahead in others, and not at all when—to his confusion—he is challenged at two points simultaneously.

Intellectual performance proceeds one step at a time through the intuitive recognition of vague properties, the isolation of one relational concept from another, ability to perform the action mentally with anticipation, reversal, and conservation, and, finally, to representation of the operation in a formal symbolic system. Understanding of any single effect or relation starts from very hazy impressions, often logically inconsistent or factually incorrect. One masters a concept only through operating with it in a variety of situations. When a concept becomes "operational," one can treat it imaginatively. A person forms an internal scale of historical time along which he can run, in imagination. Then he can think of social conditions as smoothly changing, rather than static or abruptly changing. Operational thought checks conclusions in advance. The operation replaces the impressionistic leap from data to conclusions with a series of small, reversible steps, each of which the person can judge to be reasonable or unreasonable.

The progress exhibited is primarily a gain in rigor of control. The child gains control of a movement. Then he gains control of an image of a movement: on seeing a triangular block, he can judge whether or not the block, if transported and turned, will fit into a puzzle. This is a provisional try with feedback just as much as if the response were made muscularly. Control through anticipation speeds up the trial and makes overt error infrequent. At a later stage the pupil will be able to measure sizes and angles formally, so as to predict the fit of pieces far too complex for a perceptual judgment. Thought becomes increasingly regulated or disciplined.

Discipline is seen to consist not of a vague mental power but of ability to apply quite specific operations in transforming information. It is not "being bright" that prevents an error in copying a bead chain; it is being able to keep one's place and sense of direction. The correlation between ability to use number concepts operationally and mental age on the

Wechsler scale is only .43 in school beginners (Elkind, 1961a; Dodwell, 1960, 1961). The number scale, the coordinate plane, parallelism, etc., are specific instruments of mathematical thought, not aspects of undifferentiated "mental growth." Biological science has its operational concepts: growth, metabolism, evolutionary development. Similar concepts underlie successful reasoning in geography, economics, and social science. The ideas that seem to matter are very broad concepts, not specifics about the Corn Laws or the parts of a leaf. Mental development comes through practice in which success with a less-controlled impressionistic response builds up conceptual mediators. These have the power to regulate response in confusing circumstances and in circumstances where a radical transformation of information is required. Extensive experience apparently is needed to make a concept truly operational.

The active process of refining motor controls, mental images, and symbolic representations is by no means a matter of "waiting for readiness to develop." But how much the timetable of the stages might be accelerated by suitable training is quite uncertain. Inhelder and Piaget (1958, p. 13) believe that the radical change in thinking observed around age 7 "without doubt corresponds to some alteration in the neural structures." They stress that such neural maturation can do no more than open up new possibilities, and that the realization of operational thought requires learning through active attempts to answer questions. If there is a significant neural change at this age, or some other, it sets a limit to what can be accomplished by early education.

Several small experiments in the Geneva laboratory summarized by Smedslund (1961) and at Leeds (Churchill, 1958) give a strong indication that children make more rapid progress toward operational thought when given direct training. But not all training methods were successful, and older children generally profited more from the training. Children "taught" conservation in a few brief lessons quickly shifted back to incorrect impressionistic reasoning. Training is an opportunity for the child to extend a concept that he has already learned something about, finding a new application for it or discriminating it from related concepts. Each more advanced interpretation is constructed with the aid of an interpretation already present.

THE CUMULATIVE NATURE OF LEARNING

Every success the child has with operational thought is a triumph of transfer. His success arises out of earlier practice-with-feedback at the intuitive level. Formal, symbolic control comes after concrete operations are mastered. Just what does this say to the educational planner? Here we can do no more than anticipate several significant points Chapter 11 will develop more fully.

1. The curriculum should provide repeated opportunities to deal with the most significant general concepts. Each year the child becomes able to comprehend a concept at a higher level. The most basic ideas—the number line, the conservation of energy, the consent of the governed—should appear and reappear in the curriculum, each time more precisely or in a more complicated setting.

2. Operational concepts have an inherent order. One concept is usually based on others that must be developed first. Thus one-to-one correspondence (the operation of matching) is prerequisite to successful ordering. Matching plus mastery of the rote sequence of number names is required for counting. We can think of these concepts as an inverted pyramid, the numerous operational concepts of the 11-year-old having been built upon those attained in each earlier year. At the bottom, the structure rests on the infant's perceptual learning and his first primitive concepts, such as the permanent identity of an object. If one concept is needed for another, then the curriculum should introduce concepts in that sequence. The sequence is not determined by adult logic, but by the process used by the child in attaining the concept.

3. The method and aims of instruction should be suited to the learner's development. Topics that are very difficult to understand when treated as a formal system can make sense to an immature learner when they are presented in a more tangible form. The child's performance should be regarded as good if he is showing progress toward the anticipation of conclusions and reversible operations, even if his answers are not perfect. His formal thought processes should be rewarded when he can derive sound conclusions, even if his verbal formulation is not rigorous. The boy's statement regarding the marble problem (page 335) is clumsy, but his reasoning is not.

There have at times been arguments about whether or not "training in the intellectual disciplines" is appropriate only for the superior, college-bound adolescent (Bestor, 1955, p. 8). This we see is a false issue when we realize that disciplined thinking is developed gradually and not in some one course labeled "mathematics" or "logic." At each school age the child—whether average or superior—should be gaining in intellectual power by adding concepts and mental operations. To be sure, an abrupt plunge into verbal instruction regarding formal operations, without the previous development of concrete operations, will leave all but the verbally adept floundering. And their clever manipulation of symbols may blind the teacher to their deficiencies in encoding and decoding, in connecting abstraction to reality (Ervin, 1960).

4. Intuitive understanding is more to be prized than perfect execution

of a response without understanding. Control can be improved as experience is gained.

5. Comprehension of an abstract concept progresses very gradually, through extremely small steps. Inexact solutions are a sign of progress. Hundreds of applications of a crude analysis may be necessary before the child extends his understanding to a slightly more complex problem. A four- to six-month interval is required between success on one ordering task in Figure 77 and success on the next (though this pace might conceivably be accelerated by special training).

6. Concepts are achieved by the learner's own efforts. Verbal instruction can shorten the process, but only if introduced in the right way and at the right time. Too rapid a translation of observations into "teacher's language" leads to parroting. It cuts short the necessary attention to the events themselves.

The heart of the matter is meaning. If relationships are meaningful to the learner, so that he can judge what is a good response, he will succeed. More than that, he will become able to evaluate early enough to forestall errors.

The pupil who learns a prescription without understanding will make errors because he cannot adapt the presentation to a changing situation. (Recall the example of the tides, page 61; see also Katona, 1950.) A fourth-grader may learn to multiply $\frac{3}{8}$ by $\frac{4}{5}$ even if he does not understand fractions. He can multiply the two top numbers and multiply the two bottom numbers ($3 \times 4 \div 8 \times 5 = \frac{12}{40} = \frac{3}{10}$). Unless he knows why his method works he is almost certain to transfer it blindly when he comes to $1\frac{1}{2} \times \frac{2}{5}$, and get $1\frac{1}{5}$ for the answer. This difficulty would not arise if he had been taught what it means to take one-eighth of four-fifths and then consider what *three*-eighths would be. This indirect process may seem awkward to an impatient teacher, but it divides the problem into steps about which the child can think operationally. The pupil given adequate opportunity to work problems in this way, with full understanding, will develop his own shortcuts—perhaps seeing directly that "$1\frac{1}{2} \times 2$ is 3, so the answer is $\frac{3}{5}$."

THE BROWNELL-MOSER STUDY OF ARITHMETIC. The cumulative value of meaningful instruction is demonstrated by a study of learning and transfer in subtraction. There are two ways to explain how to subtract 27 from 91 (Figure 78). Method D calls for decomposing the larger number. We cannot take 7 from 1; therefore we regard 91 as being the sum $80 + 11$. Or, as we say, we borrow 10 from the 90, and use it to create 11 in the right-hand column. Then we subtract in each column, 7 from 11, and 20 from 80. The second method, called equal additions (EA), is widely used in the British Isles. Again we need 11 in order to subtract 7. We create 11 by adding 10 to both terms. To compensate for the 10 added to the 1 in the top number, we add 10 to the 27. Then we subtract.

It has been claimed that adults who have learned by EA subtract more accurately and rapidly than those who use the D procedure. The only way to decide which to teach is to experiment. Brownell and Moser (1949) divided 41 experimental classes into four groups. Two groups were taught

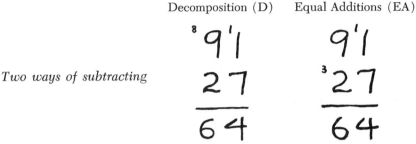

78   *Two ways of subtracting*

Decomposition (D)   Equal Additions (EA)

the D procedure. Half of these were taught borrowing as a meaningful technique; teachers emphasized how the procedure works and why it leads to correct results. The other D classes were taught borrowing as a mechanical procedure. The EA classes were divided similarly.

Judged by the immediate test, the methods gave about the same result (see Figure 79). Even the small differences are of interest, however. First we see that meaningful teaching gave the best results with either the EA or the D technique. Second, we find that when rote teaching—"follow these steps"—was used, the EA method was learned better. Third, with meaningful teaching, D was learned better. Which technique is easiest to learn depends on how it is taught. The D method is easier than EA to explain to pupils. In third grade they know about decomposing a number while conserving the whole amount. Adding equal amounts to two numbers to conserve a difference, however, is a less familiar operation. These findings were confirmed on a retention test six weeks later.

The most important effect was observed on a test requiring transfer.

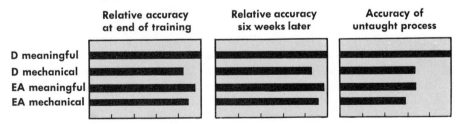

79   *Results of four methods of teaching subtraction* (*data from Brownell and Moser, 1949*)

Based on combined results in 41 classes. Each group is compared with the average performance in the D-meaningful group as a standard.

The pupils had been taught with two-digit numbers. What would happen if they had to subtract three-digit numbers (e.g., 247 from 533)? A three-digit test showed great differences between groups. The D meaningful group, who understood what they had been doing, had a great advantage over the two groups taught without understanding. They were also well ahead of the EA group who had been given explanations but had not understood them.

Here is strong evidence for choosing teaching materials that can be understood, and for teaching by methods that produce insight. In choosing between equally correct procedures or explanations, one that can be more fully and deeply understood at that time is to be preferred. Sometimes it takes additional effort to put the meaning across, and teachers are tempted to take a short cut by teaching a prescription. But in teaching a body of subject matter quick and easy gains are less important than returns over a long period.

While the general implication of the Brownell-Moser study is not to be questioned, their result may not be the final word on the technique for subtraction. The EA method is logically consistent with the operations on negative numbers in algebra, and the D method is not. If the EA method can be taught meaningfully, it might facilitate work in algebra. With this aim, Richard Griggs[2] has prepared new teaching materials that perhaps can make the EA procedure intuitively clear to second-graders. He explains EA in terms of "steps along the number line" that pupils can visualize. The method has been tried with apparent success, but no systematic research has been done to check whether or not it really works better than the unsuccessful EA explanations used in the Brownell-Moser study.

Brownell and Moser point out that readiness in any grade depends on what earlier teachers have done to develop the pupil's understanding:

> It is still common for school people to think of borrowing in subtraction and other such skills as belonging in this or that grade, almost as if the time and place were set immutably by some kind of law. This notion is epitomized in such statements as that children are "ready" for the addition combinations in such-and-such a grade, for subtraction of two-place numbers without borrowing in such-and-such a grade, and the like. Elaborate paraphernalia of testing may be instituted to determine whether children in any particular group have attained the magic state of "readiness for a skill or topic." . . .
>
> Tests in such programs expose "readiness" for what it is, namely, the ability to take on new skills or ideas, that and nothing more. . . . Their readiness is determined, not by their age or by their grade, but by the kind of arithmetic they have had. By manipulating their arithmetical backgrounds we may shift the placement of any arithmetical topic over a range of several years and of several grades.

One school system in the Brownell-Moser study had taught arithmetic meaningfully in the first and second grades; its third graders were able to

[2] Personal communication. University of Illinois Arithmetic Project.

grasp the subtraction procedure quickly. These children asked penetrating questions, and worked out explanations for themselves. Their readiness had been developed.

In another system where earlier work had been mechanical, it was difficult to make *any* explanation of subtraction clear. Prescriptive teaching develops such all-too-transferable attitudes as 6-year-old Sue displays (Risden, 1950):

> Question on a shopping trip: "Five cents for the parking meter and we have only three. How much more do we need?"
>
> KAY: "Two more. That one's easy."
>
> SUE, in triumphant tones: "But that isn't right. My teacher says five and three are eight. My teacher says so and my teacher knows."
>
> KAY, impatiently: "But you don't have five *and* three. You only *have* three and you want five."
>
> SUE: "My teacher says five and three are eight."
>
> Second question a bit later: "Take back these four pop bottles and you may have the deposits. Four bottles, five cents back on each. How much?"
>
> KAY: "Four fives, . . . two tens, . . . twenty cents!"
>
> SUE, stamping her foot: "You're always giving us old problems. You *know* I can't get *your* kind of arithmetic. I can only get school arithmetic."

Sue has learned *not* to learn.

> **21.** Is it fair to state that "readiness is determined *solely* by the kind of arithmetic pupils have had"?
>
> **22.** In planning for a class next year, would you adopt teaching materials that explain subtraction using the D method (Brownell and Moser), or using the EA method (Griggs).
>
> **23.** In a school where the first two years of work have been taught in a rote fashion, should the third-year teacher teach by rote or meaningfully?
>
> **24.** Should reasoning be taught as a separate subject in high school, taught by special units in regular courses, or made incidental to subject-matter lessons or projects?

SUMMARY

Transfer theories range from the highly optimistic theory of formal discipline to the view that transfer is rare and limited. According to the former theory, the mind holds distinct "faculties" that can be developed by difficult academic lessons. Thorndike's research, showing that mental test scores increase by about the same amount no matter what subject the pupil studies, was one of several reasons for discarding this belief. Other studies showed that "exercising" the memory has little or no value, and that academic instruction in grammar, for example, often does little to improve written expression. The theory of formal discipline gave way to the theory of "identical elements," which held that that experience is most likely to transfer which has the most similarity to the application situation. Social utility and life adjustment curricula are based on this principle. This view tends to deny the possibility of far-reaching transfer and provides no basis for choosing among the important problems that might enter the curriculum.

Research consistently shows that transfer (facilitation) is possible, and that transfer is not limited to closely similar situations. Transfer of a behavior is likely whenever the person recognizes a new situation as similar to other situations where the behavior has been appropriate. What is learned and what is transferred depends upon the teaching method; the same subject taught differently may produce great or little transfer. The transferable outcomes include specific actions, specific facts, broad concepts and generalizations, techniques of analyzing situations, attitudes toward the subject or the situation, and attitudes toward the self.

In this chapter we are especially concerned with learning to think and learning to learn, i.e., with increasing the power to cope with unfamiliar situations. Monkeys (and children) receiving practice with one type of problem become more alert in solving later problems involving different cues. They also become aware of mediating concepts that assist in processing information; the "oddity" concept is an example. Woodrow's experiment on memory shows that instruction in techniques of study improves ability to memorize, where mere practice in memorizing does not; that is, improvement takes place through mastery of specific responses, not through a mysterious "increase in memory." Ability to deal with a situation is improved by experience, which makes it easier to detect and discriminate the relevant cues. In the House-Zeaman experiment, it was found that an easy task different from the application situation produced more transfer than a hard task identical to the application situation.

Mediating responses are acquired. A concept such as oddity may be developed without a name, but verbally labeled concepts become increasingly important as a store of possible interpretations. Verbal mediators direct response, but apparently only after preschool ages. The work of Piaget and his associates suggests that thoughtful control of response develops through five stages, summarized in Table 17. The key to Piaget's theory is the concept of *operation*. An operation is originally a physical transformation that changes the situation impulsively or haphazardly. With experience the child learns to reverse the operation to produce a desired result, and then to carry it out in imagination or through operating on symbols. A concept is an imagined action. The conservation principles, important in operational thought, provide a conceptual world that retains its properties as the perceptual appearance of objects varies; the child who understands the constancy of volume knows that the amount remains the same when plasticine is divided and recombined. Although there is a progression of thought with age, at any age several stages of thought appear. The young child shows knowledge of some formal operations; the adult reasons impression-istically when he is inattentive or when he is unfamiliar with a set of con-cepts. Discipline is seen to consist of ability to apply specific concepts operationally in transforming information and regulating action. Each field of study contributes its own powerful concepts. While the evidence sug-gests that progress is slow, and that what can be taught is limited by the stage of a child's development, there is hope that the rate of development toward operational thought can be accelerated by well-designed experiences.

Several suggestions regarding curricular practice are introduced:

1. The curriculum should provide repeated opportunities to deal with significant general concepts, each time at a higher level.

2. The sequence of instruction should observe the inherent order in which concepts rest on one another.

3. The method and aims of instruction should fit the learner, with impres-sionistic thought encouraged early in the learning process, and formal thought encouraged when it first appears, even though it is poorly formu-lated.

4. Intuitive, even crude, understanding is more to be prized than control without understanding.

5. Inexact solutions are a sign of progress toward better solutions.

6. Concepts are achieved by the learner's own efforts.

The pupil who learns a prescription without understanding it will have difficulty in adapting it to a new situation. He may learn rapidly a proce-dure presented in a rote fashion. But the Brownell-Moser study shows that he is then less able to work out the proper procedure in a slightly different situation, and less equipped to understand subsequent explanations. Teach-ing materials that can be understood and teaching methods that foster understanding are needed if learning is to transfer.

Reading List 10

Benjamin S. Bloom and Lois J. Broder, "Variations in the Problem-Solving Characteristics of Students," Chapter 2 in *Problem-Solving Processes of College Students,* Supplementary Educational Mono-graphs, No. 73 (Chicago: Dept. of Educ., Univ. of Chicago, 1950), pp. 22–40. Abridged in Harris.

The study shows why poor students make errors in reasoning, par-ticularly in answering examination questions. Do these errors reflect defects in mental ability, or faulty techniques and attitudes?

Leonore Boehm, "Exploring Children's Thinking," *Elementary School Journal,* 61 (1961), 363–73.

Boehm summarizes the Piaget-Inhelder experiments and theory for the elementary teacher, describing the observed behavior of typical children and the causes of their difficulties with the school curriculum.

Jerome S. Bruner, "Readiness for Learning," Chapter 3 in *The Process of Education* (Cambridge: Harvard Univ. Press, 1960), pp. 33–54.

Bruner summarizes the Piaget-Inhelder report on stages and goes on to recommend curriculum improvements in mathematics and literature. Inhelder contributes a section giving her views on education, especially on elementary education. The entire chapter expands Bruner's assertion that "any subject can be taught effectively to any child at any stage of development."

James Deese, "Transfer of Learning," in *The Psychology of Learning* (New York: McGraw-Hill, 1958), pp. 213–35.

A review of psychological research with particular attention to shifts that have occurred in the theoretical explanations of transfer.

Susan M. Ervin, "Transfer Effects of Learning a Verbal Generalization," *Child Development*, 31 (1960), 537–54.

An experiment testing the transfer obtained following various methods of verbal and nonverbal instruction of 9-year-olds regarding reflection. In addition to its implications for teaching, the paper presents a brief summary of current theory concerning verbal mediation.

Lloyd G. Humphreys, "Transfer of Training in General Education," *Journal of General Education*, 5 (1951), 210–16. Reprinted in Coladarci, Loree.

Humphreys reviews the conclusions from the research of Thorndike and his contemporaries and states what these conclusions imply for the schools. His interpretations pointedly challenge such common educational practices as requiring "a laboratory course in science" of every college student.

J. McV. Hunt, "Implications of Piaget's Stages for Matching Circumstances and Schemata," in *Intelligence and Experience* (New York: Ronald, 1961), pp. 273–88.

In this book Hunt provides the only complete and understandable summary of Piaget's work, describing the major experiments and relating them to evidence from other laboratories. The passage selected here gives Hunt's views on the significant decisions to be made about education at each of the stages of growth.

CHAPTER 11 IMPROVING UNDERSTANDING AND THINKING

Interpretation is the key to appropriate behavior. In the unfamiliar situation, the provisional try is determined either by an impression of its resemblance to some earlier event, or by a conceptually mediated analysis of cues and possible responses. The school, by making concepts and generalizations available to the pupil, improves provisional tries. Ideas are taught not in the hope of strengthening undefined mental powers, but for the sake of solving the problems to which each idea is relevant. Teachers of biology want pupils to apply an understanding of natural processes to questions about health and agriculture. Shop teachers want students to understand what tools can do and why different constructions serve different ends. Knowledge is an instrument for anticipating the consequences of various tries and for inventing novel solutions.

The research of the preceding chapter makes clear that concepts are not handed over ready-made to the learner. He works them out for himself, achieving a mental structure of associations and operations just as he achieves within himself the coordinations for a motor skill. But he can achieve few advanced concepts without aid. The whole point of formal education is to make available to the individual, at the end of some twenty years of his life, the concepts that it has taken all the millennia of human experience to put together. Concept learning is a process of discovery or re-creation, and yet the learner cannot discover for himself all of politics, ethics, aesthetics, and natural science.

Educational methods differ radically in the degree to which they depend on discovery. There are completely didactic procedures, in which knowledge is put before the student in abstract, polished form: the zoology professor lectures about the neatly ordered phyla, the language text carefully explains the declensions and conjugations. Though these methods have some success, teaching which consists chiefly of presenting prefabricated concepts can be distressingly inefficient. The learning is often tedious and incomplete, the facts forgotten or misapplied.

At the opposite extreme is the "do-it-yourself" learning in which the pupil is expected to extract his own concepts and generalizations from experience. Some educators believe, for example, that participating in student government is the best way to gain an understanding of social processes.

Likewise, a language can be learned solely through using it. The principles of proportion can be discovered through numerous attempts to enlarge a figure while preserving its shape. These methods have their successes— but one must doubt their efficiency also, when he watches a pupil fumble with a problem for which a simple rule could be taught, or sees him fail to extract a general principle from his experiences. Some balance between discovery and presentation of concepts is required. No formula will dictate how to teach.

MEANINGFUL LEARNING

Our theory of behavior has emphasized interpretation and feedback. Meaning improves trial responses. In a completely meaningless situation one only acts at random or out of habit; in a meaningful situation one can often work out a reasonable approach which makes the first action successful. Understanding helps one to judge possible responses that come to mind, rejecting those that are inconsistent with some of the facts. In intellectually controlled response, an overt provisional try may be unnecessary. One who can criticize his own ideas intelligently will correct his response before it is actually made.

The value of meaningful teaching has been demonstrated repeatedly in studies like that of Brownell and Moser (p. 342; see also Swenson *et al.*, 1949; Underwood and Schulz, 1960). Greater understanding of what is taught produces more rapid learning, better retention, and better adaptation to new conditions.

Meaning as an Aid to Retention

H. E. Moser (1947) taught fractions to second-graders by a meaningful method. On a retention test several weeks later they did better than they had done at the end of the instruction, even though they were assigned no work on fractions in the interim. Pupils had found fractions so much fun that they made up problems for themselves, "playing" with fractions and so learning more and more. The children understood what they were doing, were successful rather than baffled, and so learned to enjoy manipulating fractions. Learning that breeds more learning is common when pupils enjoy their work and take pride in it.

THE RATE OF FORGETTING.   In discussing motor skill, we reported that the losses due to forgetting are small and rapidly repaired. In studies of verbal learning, quite a different conclusion is frequently drawn. In a typical study, H. E. Jones (1923) tested students on the facts presented in a college psychology lecture, and retested them at intervals. The average on each test is expressed as a percentage of the average score immediately after the lecture:

Interval from lecture to retest	*Percentage retained*
½ week	80
1 week	58
2 weeks	48
8 weeks	36

This steep initial drop and the ultimate leveling off at some low percentage of retention have been reported in many studies of factual learning. Since a similar curve is found in laboratory work with nonsense syllables, this has been described as "the curve of forgetting."

If the facts taught in school are so largely forgotten, much of the instruction is wasted. We are told that 40 per cent of the facts of American history learned in a college course are forgotten after one year, and that only 19 per cent of a high-school chemistry course is recalled five years later (Sterrett and Davis, 1954). Such findings appear to constitute a telling criticism of the academic curriculum that teaches information for future use. But, while these studies are valid and important, so far as they go, it is entirely wrong to conclude that a large amount of forgetting is inevitable.

Even nonsense associations can be well remembered; if this were not true, the leading makers of breakfast foods and detergents would be bankrupt. Underwood (1957) reports that the forgetting curve traditionally reported applies only for learners who have studied many different lists of associations. Past learning interferes with the new responses; where such confusion is present, forgetting is rapid. But when a person is a subject in just one experiment, so that he learns only one list of associations, little interference occurs and the responses are retained with very little loss. This is worth knowing as a theoretical matter.

But as a practical matter the pupil is always asked to learn more than one set of associations. One page of history, one page of geography, one page of conjugations is very like another. Interference is to be expected and a delayed test is likely to show considerable forgetting. The teacher often mistakenly believes that interference has been overcome when the pupil consistently makes the correct response at the end of a lesson. Even though this response is *now* stronger than competing responses arising from past lessons or from misinterpretations, it may not remain stronger. The new response may not be deeply imbedded, with many interconnections to other responses; if so, it can easily be pushed out by a strong-rooted competitor.

Details are subject to interference and most of them disappear rapidly, but general ideas and central thoughts are well retained. English *et al.* (1934) made several studies in which students studied text passages and took immediate and delayed tests. One type of test required them to say whether statements agreed with the text, disagreed with it, or were not covered in the passage. Some statements were isolated verbatim sentences, others were summaries of the main ideas. While there was a modest but steady decline with time in recognition of isolated sentences, there was no forgetting of the main ideas. Indeed, there was a slight improvement in performance on these. R. W. Tyler (1934) reported several retest studies of various outcomes from college science courses (see also Frutchey, 1937; McDougall, 1958). Tests were given before and after the course and again one year later (Table 18). Facts about animal anatomy and classification were almost entirely lost. There was substantial forgetting even of the facts more strongly emphasized. But application of the big ideas of the course was retained at its end-of-course level. And the interpretation of experiments, a high-level reasoning process, continued to improve even after instruction in zoology ended. Broad generalizations and methods of analysis have more meaning than specific facts. They are buttressed by the interconnections of one idea with others. They therefore are better retained.

Before leaving this topic, we should note that even the conclusion that detailed facts are rapidly forgotten is unduly pessimistic. All the studies of school learning are retest studies. They show whether or not facts are available immediately at any moment in later life when a quick question

TABLE 18

Broadly significant ideas are remembered best (R. W. Tyler, 1934)

	Average score at start of course	Average score at end of course	Average score on retest one year later	Percentage of gain retained
Naming structures of animals in diagrams	22	62	31	23
Identifying technical terms	20	83	67	74
Relating structure to function in type forms	13	39	34	79
Applying general principles to unfamiliar situations	35	65	65	100
Interpreting experimental results	30	57	64	125

is asked. But this is an artificial demand. Really significant information can be obtained only by an investigation of "savings" (see page 304). We need to know, for example, how quickly an adult who once studied French for two years can recapture his skill when he plans to go abroad, and how quickly a physician can recapture his knowledge about a rare disease when he encounters his first case of it years after leaving medical school. Practical difficulties block such investigations, but we can be sure that an investigation would show more benefit from course instruction than, for example, the 19 per cent retention of chemistry shown on a hasty retest.

OVERLEARNING AND REVIEW.   Most students are satisfied with their study when they have acquired correct answers. If they stop there, they will not know the material after time has passed. If they continue to deal with the same information over and over, they will learn it so thoroughly that it is most unlikely to be forgotten. Consider the alphabet. As children, we chanted the alphabet, recited it, used it a thousand ways in schoolwork. When the alphabet is called for, it is on the tip of our tongues, for it has been "overlearned." Overlearning results when a person continues to use a response repeatedly, with confirmation.

Nearly all the research on overlearning of intellectual associations has used nonsense syllables or mazes. In one study, college students learned a maze path, then had a chance to forget it, and learned it again (Krueger, 1930). The number of trials required to reach errorless performance the second time is a measure of how much they forgot. On the average, it took 4.6 trials to learn the maze without error the first time. Students who stopped practicing as soon as they got the path correct required 3.6 trials (average) to relearn the maze after four days. Those who practiced four or five extra times on the first occasion needed only 2.3 trials to recapture their learning. Learning was much more firmly established after the extra trials than it was when the "perfect score" was first reached.

In original study or in review, active thought (e.g., self-recitation, looking for meanings, attempts to apply a principle) should continue for a time after one has "caught on" to the correct response. Such extended trials are especially valuable for arbitrary associations such as the alphabet, or for situations where there are "reasonable" incorrect responses.

Forgetting is most to be expected for knowledge that is not used. Forgetting can be virtually eliminated if the teacher provides for continued use of ideas, instead of turning away when the unit ends. Such highly favorable conditions were maintained in one junior-high general science course (Word and Davis, 1939). The course followed the textbook sequence of topics. But "the textbook employed in these general science classes shows integration and correlation of subject matter to an unusual degree. Frequently, items which seem difficult or obscure at the time of presentation become clarified after they have been related to subsequent facts and principles." Each discussion of new ideas renewed acquaintance with previous topics. Tests were designed to encourage review of work covered earlier. Every two weeks an examination was given, made up half of newly discussed content, and half of material presented earlier. The teacher made no effort to provide an end-of-course review. Even so, on the final examination students performed as well on material studied sixteen weeks before as they had immediately after learning it.

RECONSTRUCTION OF IDEAS DURING RECALL.   Forgetting is not just a matter of a fading memory trace. A photograph left in the strong sunlight will fade away evenly, until only some especially strong impression is left. Memory is a reconstruction process, not just a report of what is left after fading. When a person reacts to a situation originally, he makes his interpretation as sensible as he can. When the situation recurs, he makes a new, organized interpretation of the whole situation. This new interpretation is as regular and as logically consistent as he can make it. The process of reorganizing to make sense was most clearly demonstrated by Sir Frederic Bartlett (1932). After exhibiting a sketchy, irregular drawing, he asked a person to draw it from memory. The reproduction, as Figure 80 shows, was made far more regular than the original.

Most errors made by students on examinations result from this same sort of reorganizing. Students rarely miss a question because their brains have gone blank. Rather, having lost some part of the correct interpretation, they put together a new interpretation, making as good sense as possible from the recalled information and the competing responses also recalled. A person reconstitutes his ideas around whatever structure he can remember from the original. If this basic framework is correct, he will reinstate a correct response. If he forgets some significant part of the framework or had an incorrect understanding to begin with, his reconstruction will be in error. Consider the college girl at the concert, obviously playing the intellectual for her young man. "*Coq d'Or—Coq d'Or.* I'm not sure who wrote that. Must be Ravel, because there were so few French ballet com-

80 *Pupils reorganize what they recall (F. C. Bartlett, 1932, p. 178)*

posers." Thus she reached for a logical completion. *Coq d'Or* is an opera, by a Russian who used titles from other languages, and any number of Frenchmen wrote ballet music. She was nonetheless satisfied because she had an answer that "made sense" and that her date could not, with less knowledge, contradict.

81 *Meaningful associations are nearly unforgettable*

If the pupil understands basic facts so firmly that competing responses make no sense to him he is unlikely to accept a false reconstruction. False reconstructions mean failure to achieve a sound basic interpretation because of poor understanding during learning, piecemeal memorization of parts without interconnection, or interference from responses connected to similar stimuli.

Studies of retention and transfer cause us to deny the view of a person's knowledge that is expressed in this quotation (Henderson, 1961, p. 48):

> It is possible, as Ryle (1955) points out, to regard knowledge as either of two kinds: (1) knowledge that something is the case, and (2) knowledge of how to do something. Following Ryle's language, I shall call the first "know-that" and the second "know-how." . . . We can compare knowing-how, but we cannot compare knowing-that. We can speak meaningfully . . . of one person knowing how to play bridge more expertly than another. . . . But we cannot speak meaningfully of one pupil knowing better than another pupil that an approximate value of pi is 3.1416, or of one person knowing more expertly than another person that the dealer in bridge bids first. Knowing-that is a dichotomous variable. Either you know that something is the case or you do not. There is no middle ground.

This writer agrees with our description of expertness in skilled performance, in which we pointed out that even among performers with perfect scores there are differences in mastery. We insist that the same view be taken of factual knowledge. Among those who "know" every one of a series of associations (e.g., rules of bridge), there are differences in speed of response, retention over time, response in confusing circumstances, and resistance to interference from competing associations (e.g., rules of poker). There are also different degrees of understanding. One pupil knows the value of pi better than another if he knows where the value comes from, so that, for example, he knows *why* 3.1416 is preferable to the $2\frac{2}{7}$ he was told to use last year. The teacher should be pleased when a pupil "shows knowledge" by giving a correct answer, but he is dead wrong if he thinks the learning has gone as far as it can go.

Marcus Brown (1961; see also Hartland-Swann, 1958) makes a valuable point in criticizing Ryle and his followers. It is one thing, he says, to "believe" that a statement is true because a teacher has said so; it is quite another to "know," being convinced of the truth by observation or by the relations between ideas. Knowledge of this sort is deepened by extending one's observations or by adding connections to other concepts. Too often the school is content when the pupil has acquired only a belief; tests that ask the pupil to state *what* is true rather than *why* reward believers rather than knowers.

Mastery of a concept comes gradually. The child can copy the order of a straight bead chain some time before he is able to copy the figure ∞ with the order of beads preserved. The depth of understanding, the range of application of a concept, and the precision with which it is used can grow for years after a definition is learned. Take as an example the fact that rubber is elastic. The boy shows minimal comprehension when he gives a few uses of rubber, such as rubber bands. He shows greater comprehension when he thinks of using rubber for tasks where he has not previously seen it used. Perhaps he uses a piece of old inner tube to make a spring for a door. The chemistry student can be expected to explain that rubber stretches because it has very long molecules that can pull out and coil up again. With still deeper understanding the chemist would go on to explain why the molecule is a coil. There is really no end to improving one's understanding of where, how, and why a principle applies.

> **1.** If meaning is an aid to retention, account for the fact that you can recall a meaningless association such as the street address where you lived ten years ago.
>
> **2.** Central thoughts and general ideas are well retained, but in an earlier chapter we learned that poor students do not discriminate general ideas from details. How would this be reflected in their knowledge a year later? What is the implication for the writer of textbooks?
>
> **3.** Describe an experience, such as visiting another city for a second time after an interval of ten years, in which you quickly recaptured "forgotten" knowledge.
>
> **4.** "I know better than you do that it takes five days to get from San Francisco to Hawaii by boat." Is this statement possibly sensible? Explain.
>
> **5.** Which of the following facts seems likely to be overlearned by the time of high-school graduation?
>> **a.** The earth goes round the sun.
>> **b.** A participle is a verb form that modifies a noun.
>> **c.** Columbus discovered America.
>> **d.** The principal of the high school is Mr. Allen.

Meaning as an Aid in Acquisition

Any form of presentation or any experience that makes facts more meaningful and more unmistakable is of great benefit during initial learning. When the pupil has been told a fact, he is expected later to recall it, that is, to select the one correct answer from among all the possibilities. Anything that helps him discriminate the right answer will make learning easier and reduce subsequent interference.

Sometimes meaning can be made so vivid that a single presentation will fix an idea. In early 1945, during World War II, the Army was trying to show soldiers that even though Germany was near collapse a long hard fight in the Pacific would still be required. When the Army tried to teach that the war against Japan had barely begun by reciting statistics of bombings, the teaching had little impact. Sound effects in an orientation film did put across the idea. In the film, a long burst of explosive racket was used to represent the number of tons of bombs dropped on Germany, and a fraction of a second of noise showed, in proportion, the amount dropped on Japan. The contrast was unmistakable and unforgettable.

A single concept may link ideas together in such a way that the amount to be learned is reduced and responses become more quickly available (Shepard and Schaeffer, 1956). Some would teach the one hundred "addition facts," and then have pupils memorize another hundred "subtraction facts." But if addition is made sufficiently meaningful, so that the pupil visualizes $8 + 5$ as an operation performed on the number scale, he can use this same fact when he comes to $13 - 5$. Work with small disks may help him to form an image such as this:

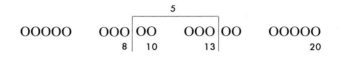

"$8 + 5 = 13$" is locked in place by the "easier" facts $8 + 2 = 10$ and $5 = 2 + 3$. In a second or so, the pupil can check operationally the fact he pulls out of memory. When he thinks in this way, one set of 100 facts serves for both addition and subtraction.

Meaningfulness depends on the learner's belief system. He is less likely to remember a fact that conflicts with his belief system. Levine and Murphy (1943) compared five college students who had Communist sympathies with five equally bright anti-Communists. Each student read a violently anti-Communist selection, and wrote down all he could remember of it. The procedure was repeated with a selection which was strongly pro-Communist. (Some students read the pro-Communist selection first, to balance effects of order.) On three successive weeks, students reread the passages and were immediately tested. Recall tests were made during the next five weeks. Considering "per cent of ideas correctly restated" (Figure 82), the anti-Communist group learned the anti-Communist ideas more rapidly and remembered them longer. The pro-Communists likewise remembered best the selection they wanted to believe. People hold onto the facts that fit their basic ideas of what is true and reasonable.

   6. Brueckner and Bond (1955, p. 264) suggest clarifying the multiplication facts by arranging disks in rectangular arrays, e.g., for $3 \times 4 = 12$:

$$
\begin{array}{cccc}
O & O & O & O \\
O & O & O & O \\
O & O & O & O \\
\end{array}
$$

Is the answer to the multiplication problem now made meaningful? Can you suggest a way of changing the technique so that the answer can be perceived as $10 + 2$ without counting?

Evidences of Meaning

Teaching intended to be meaningful may not be. The teacher needs to make sure that what he is teaching makes sense to pupils, and this is not

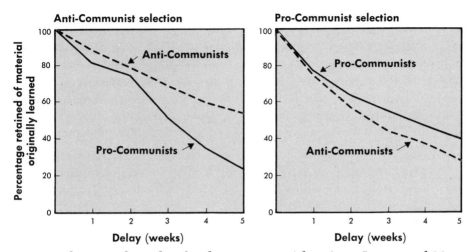

82 *People remember what fits their concepts* (*data from Levine and Murphy, 1943*)

On the anti-Communist selection, the average score of the anti-Communists at the end of the study was 34; of the pro-Communists, 25. On the pro-Communist selection, the averages were 41 and 48, respectively.

easy to judge. Pupils do not necessarily understand a principle when they can "give an example." They may have no clear idea why the League of Nations failed even though they can "give five reasons." These questions are not crucial tests of understanding because the examples and reasons can be memorized without comprehension. A concept, as we said in Chapter 10, is an imagined action, a vision of what can be done in the world and of what the action will accomplish.

The only sure sign that the pupil has command of a principle is transfer: he *operates* with the principle, going beyond the words given by text or teacher and beyond the tasks he previously practiced. A person understands a piece of machinery when he knows its inner workings and can produce reversible changes in its operation. When the boy is taking care of the furnace, and his coal turns to coke instead of ash, he can be told that the fire needs more air. Then, if he understands the structure of the furnace, he will check the blower and dampers and make reasonable changes in them to increase the flow of air. If he understands the principle of incomplete combustion as a result of this experience, he will be able to explain why the inner pages of a magazine tossed on a bonfire do not burn.

The lowest level of understanding is found in arbitrary or "nonsense" associations. An arbitrary association is one that has no reason or explanation. Why shall this stuff be called *iodine?* Why was the discoverer named *Christopher Columbus?* Why does *five* come after *four?* There are no answers. These associations cannot be anything but connections of cue with response. The only way we can test whether or not a pupil possesses an arbitrary association is to ask him to say it back.

Much learning that could be meaningful is taught as an arbitrary association. One of the purest examples of rote learning in the school is the pledge of allegiance. Participating in this ritual is supposed to instill loyalty to American ideals. But how little the ideals are comprehended by the reciting pupil! One principal (A. C. Moser and David, 1936) asked a group to *write* the pledge. Here are some of the formulas the pupils had been repeating:

I pledge the legions to the flag, of the United States and to the legions for which it stands, one nation individual with liberty and justice for all.

I plague the legion to the flag of the United States of America and to the republic for Richlan stand's one nation in indivisible with librty and jesta straw.

Even allowing for spelling, it is clear that these pupils made no sense of the pledge.

Memorization without comprehension is especially likely when pupils are preparing to respond to an unvarying stimulus. If the pupil's goal is to give an instant answer when the teacher demands, "Define parallelogram," he will drill himself to rattle off, "A parallelogram is a quadrilateral whose opposite sides are equal and parallel." His try will be confirmed by approval. Yet he may not realize that a square is a parallelogram or that ⌧ is not. Exercises that can be answered by sheer recall encourage learning without comprehension. If an association is potentially meaningful, as are most of the "facts" taught in school, we should test in ways that require some degree of understanding.

At least superficial understanding is shown when the learner gives examples of a principle, answers a question using the information, or restates an idea in his own words. These responses show that the principle is connected in his mind with real objects or with other principles. Success on a task where information must be transformed by means of a principle is a much more certain demonstration of understanding. The best evidence is application in a new situation (which displays encoding and decoding) or explanation of an unfamiliar phenomenon or set of relationships (which displays theoretical knowledge).

Broudy (1961, p. 84) emphasizes that intellectual knowledge is greatest when "theoretical competence" is reached:

> We say that a physician has a higher level of mastery of medicine than the nurse. His theoretical context is so well developed that the novel, the peculiarities of the individual case, baffle him only until he can fit them into his theoretical framework. Because he may fear the effects of a narcotic on the digestive system of his patient, he may vary its amount or eliminate it altogether. . . . Such adaptiveness based on theory is not expected from the nurse. . . .

Between two physicians, . . . he who is the greater master categorizes faster, more accurately, on fewer cues, and with less [mental] . . . strain.

Tests are rare that indicate whether the pupil has systematically organized knowledge. For the Physical Science Study Committee physics course

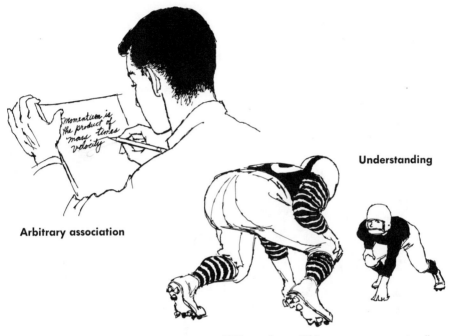

Understanding

Arbitrary association

"If I start faster, I'll have greater momentum."

83   *Understanding is shown in application*

(see p. 62), where disciplined knowledge is an aim, an approach has been made through items such as this (Michels, 1959, p. 20):

> The student is asked to suppose the existence of a number of boxes of identical exterior appearance, each of which is known to contain a single massive disc of metal. The boxes have different interiors, however. Some have smooth frictionless bottoms and others have rough bottoms; some have hard walls from which the disc bounces and others have sticky walls which trap it whenever it strikes. The student is also presented with a series of graphs, each of which shows the motion of a particular box over a horizontal surface as a result of a sharp blow, and he is asked to identify the type of box that corresponds to each graph. These questions cannot be answered correctly unless the student knows about force, mass, momentum, and impulse.

He must encode his image of the box into conceptual terms, and he must transform the graphs either into mental images of the boxes in motion or into conceptual terms—probably both.

When the pupil reaches a correct answer to a problem, it is desirable to check on his method of solving it. If his understanding is imperfect, he may have adopted a procedure that succeeds in spite of being primitive or even incorrect. Brownell and Chazal (1935) point out that speed and accuracy are not the best evidence of sound process in arithmetic:

Suppose that Johnnie is to give the sum of 5 and 4. Suppose further that he obtains his answer by thinking "5, 6, 7, 8, 9." In the typical experiment (and

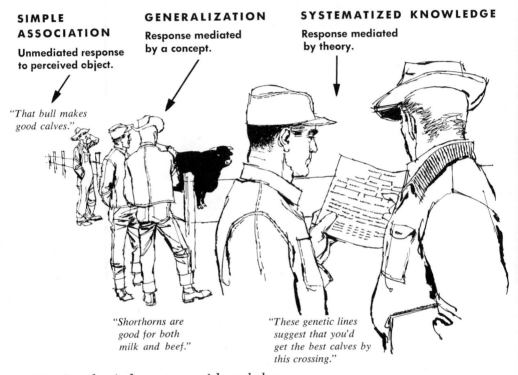

SIMPLE ASSOCIATION

Unmediated response to perceived object.

"That bull makes good calves."

GENERALIZATION

Response mediated by a concept.

"Shorthorns are good for both milk and beef."

SYSTEMATIZED KNOWLEDGE

Response mediated by theory.

"These genetic lines suggest that you'd get the best calves by this crossing."

84   Levels of abstractness of knowledge

in many classrooms), records are made of his time . . . and of the correctness of his answer. The fact that he counted to get the sum is disregarded. Suppose now that George secures the same answer of 9 for the combination in the same length of time . . . but that he does so by thinking "5 and 5 are 10, so this is 9." It is true that Johnnie and George are equal in efficiency, but they are by no means equal in performance. Johnnie is a counter. George is capable of a much more advanced type of quantitative thinking.

We might add that George, with his advanced thinking, is running a greater risk of error until this operation is thoroughly familiar. Meaningfulness is to be observed in the quality of the pupil's errors. Responses far off the target are good if they show that he is using sound principles and paying full attention to the more important aspects of the situation. Within such a sound structure, repairing a few details will remove his difficulty. "Stupid errors" are those in which the form of a solution previously observed is partly reproduced, without the internal connections between parts which show that the essentials have been grasped (Duncker, 1945, p. 7). When Walter writes the word *squrrl* his error is intelligent—more intelligent, perhaps, than the dictionary spelling. Walter knows how to analyze what he hears. When Bob writes *strign* for *string,* his error is either stupid or careless. The response does not capture the essentials of the word.

To the person who understands connections *within* the theory theoretical knowledge is highly meaningful. But there is, in addition, a need for connecting the abstract generalizations to prescriptions for action. Overman (1930) taught second-graders to add numbers, stressing the "meaning" that ones are added to ones and tens are added to tens. But this group did *less* well than a group given the more direct advice to keep the numbers in neat columns. Meaning is complete only when the abstraction can be brought to bear on reality (Ervin, 1960).

There is great need for a readily available mediator to direct action, as Stephens (1961) reminds us:

> . . . students frequently prefer artificial gimmicks to relying upon the intrinsic structure that resides in the material itself. Students of navigation, for instance, must know that there is a compelling structure behind the rule that in going from a compass course to a true course, we should start with the Compass, apply Deviation, get the Magnetic course, and apply Variation to get the True course. Yet generations of midshipmen have ignored the intrinsic considerations and have relied upon Can Dead Men Vote Twice. Conversely, in going from True to Compass, airmen ignore the basic processes involved and recite True Virgins Make Dull Company.

Theoretical knowledge serves like the phonics we spoke of in Chapter 1. It is not used to deal with frequently recurring, routine demands; it is a "low gear" required to deal with the unusual and the problematic.

7. To what extent are these associations potentially meaningful?
   a. A major provision of the Treaty of Versailles was the establishment of an independent Poland.
   b. The planets are, in order, Mercury, Venus, Earth, Mars, Jupiter, Saturn, Neptune, and Pluto.
   c. The English equivalents of the French *arbre, mer,* and *ciel* are, respectively, *tree, sea,* and *heaven.*
   d. Constantinople is now called Istanbul.

8. During the westward expansion the government subsidized the railroads with large grants of land. Would answering the following questions give evidence that the high-school student understands the fact and the reasons behind it?

    a. Are there any businesses today that the government might subsidize for the same reasons that railroads were subsidized?

    b. On this map are shown several railroads that promoters wanted to establish in 1840. Which ones would the government probably subsidize?

    c. Is railroad subsidy an example of socialism? of the free enterprise system?

    9. The principal who found errors in the pledge of allegiance sent a copy of the pledge to his teachers with a request that they teach it to their pupils. One week later the pupils wrote it from memory. Of the nine papers from pupils who had made serious errors on the original test, three were now perfect. There were eight mistakes on the remaining papers, six in punctuation and two in spelling. "This is evidence enough that the pledge is now more than a meaningless formality to the pupils," says the report. Criticize this conclusion.

    10. Why is the physics test using disks in boxes a measure of systematic knowledge rather than merely of knowledge at the "generalization" level?

    11. A girl supposed to be watching over her brothers calls out the window: "Who is chasing who down here?" When questioned about the word usage by an adult, she responds firmly: "You don't change pronouns after *is*." Is this an intelligent error? How might it be eliminated?

Meaning of Verbal Concepts

INTERPRETATION AS SIMPLIFICATION.   Verbal concepts substitute for the complex scene a set of symbols about which one can think more precisely. The person determining the area of a surface must neglect its texture and location; the concepts *base* and *altitude* extract sufficient information to give the solution. Concepts transform, compress, and organize the disorderly world of sensations. Verbal mediators indeed modify perception by sensitizing us to certain cues. Cues for which we lack labels are hard to use (Rosenzweig and Postman, 1958; Carroll and Casagrande, 1958). Learning words for football plays or styles of architecture opens our eyes to the variety in our environment and makes our experience richer. Knowing names for varieties of soil, or personality, aids us in defining and solving problems. We do most of our reasoning by associating and rearranging verbal symbols.

Unfortunately, concepts misrepresent reality and bias our thinking by exaggerating similarities and differences. We generalize about "race differences," for example; but the collection of people for whom the word *race* stands have very little in common. We are told that every dollar paid to the government goes into "government spending"; if a corporation puts money into a new building or a research program, this is called "a capital investment." With such illogical labels as mediators, one is doomed to reach unsound conclusions.

A concept is at first impressionistic, associated with some cues that are truly pertinent, and some that are not sound bases for discrimination. Most of our everyday, nontechnical concepts are left in this primitive stage. A *lake* is a body of water—6-year-olds know that. But how big does the body have to be before that term can properly be applied? How big may it get before we must call it something else? Here is a vast body with no inlet or outlet; can we call it a *lake* even if the map calls it Salton Sea?

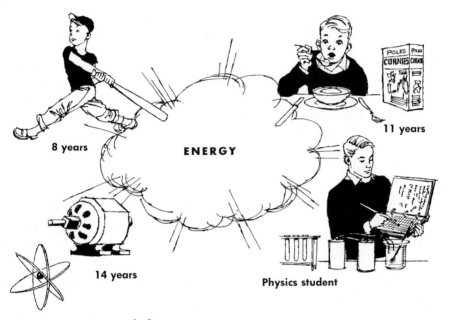

8 years

ENERGY

11 years

14 years

Physics student

85 *A person extends his concepts*

How about Devil's Lake, which has no stream flowing in or out but is said to be filled by an underground river? What shall we call a *lake?*

We observe only as carefully as our immediate goals require. A pupil learns that North and South America are in the Western Hemisphere, that Miami is on the Atlantic Ocean, and Valparaiso, Chile, on the Pacific. Through his years of encounters with maps and globes, he is unlikely to recognize, until somebody tricks him into a bet on the matter, that Miami is west of Valparaiso. He thinks of the continents as arranged on a north-south line, and ignores the general easterly slant as one goes south because he has never needed to examine that relation. When teachers and reading materials use words with a definite meaning, pupils ordinarily make a much vaguer interpretation (Roger Brown, 1958a). They are willing to call Lake Michigan an *ocean* until someone refuses to accept that usage.

Perception is a continual matching of a complex reality to patterns we have learned. Nothing is perceived in exact detail, as a camera plate would register the image. We think of the dots ⋯ as having some pattern; on a football field the pattern leaps to mind as a "**T** formation" even if some men are a bit out of place. Our minds always turn to the simplest pattern that will summarize the main cues we notice. The writer took two children, ages 8 and 7, on an automobile trip through the West; their interest in cowboys enlivened the entire journey. After several days of searching, we actually saw a horseman in a broad hat (probably not a cowboy, but that perception satisfied them). As we passed the rider, they startled us adults by leaning out the window and screaming happily, "Howdy oats!" When, after several repetitions, we objected to such nonsense, they retorted that cowboys always hail each other in that fashion. It finally dawned on us that they were merely acting upon their interpretation of the sound "adiós!" one hears so often from the Lone Ranger and others. Rather than accept the sound as complete nonsense, they fitted it into the best pattern an English-speaking child had available. Similarly, the pupil makes what he can of the words of the teacher, fitting them to a meaning that may be seriously wrong.

TABLE 19

Pupils' concepts grow more precise (*Eskridge, 1939, pp. 52, 58*)

	Percentage of pupils who choose each alternative			
	Grade IV	Grade V	Grade VI	Grade VII
The *capital* of a country means				
1. The chief seaport of the country	2	1	0	2
2. The city which is nearest the middle of the country	7	12	13	4
3. The largest city of the country	28	12	16	7
4. **The city where most of the government work is done**	**42**	**64**	**62**	**86**
I don't know, omitted, or other answer written in	21	11	8	1
If people have *communication* with each other, that means				
1. They write letters to each other	6	4	3	1
2. They telephone each other	8	4	6	3
3. They talk with each other	38	29	31	17
4. **They have some way of exchanging information**	**13**	**17**	**46**	**70**
I don't know, omitted, or other answer written in	35	46	14	9

SHARPENING CONCEPTS.   Before concepts can be used accurately to guide responses, they must be given precise meanings. The children who think of capital cities as large cities (see Table 19) are basing discrimination on a cue loosely associated with the concept instead of the fundamental cue. Their concept is intuitive (page 330) rather than operational. Meanings are sharpened primarily by trials in which misconceptions lead to wrong conclusions.

Fuzzy concepts are disastrous in technical subjects, since technical principles become untrue if words are used loosely. Most applications of prin-

"Which are insects?"

86   *To use a concept, one must discriminate*

ciples require exact interpretations of terms: *friction, denominator, participle, freedom of speech,* and so on. Discriminating "Does this term apply here or doesn't it?" is fundamental to controlling behavior by means of a verbal principle. To multiply fractions, the pupil is told to multiply the numerators, and the denominators. But in $1\frac{3}{4} \times \frac{2}{5}$, what are the numerators? Discrimination is based on some distinguishing character or cue, and to many pupils, the *numerator* is "the number on top." Ergo, the numerators are 3 and 2—and the answer is wrong.

Discrimination is an encoding response connecting a concrete or symbolic situation with a conceptual label that mediates application of a principle. The test of discrimination is to present diverse objects or examples, and to ask the pupil to identify which examples the concept under study fits (Cronbach, 1943). A word is first encountered in a specific setting. Pupils learn to use it for that but may fail to recognize other places where their concept applies. Asked to write what *west coast* means, fourth-graders say, for example, "The west coast of Norway is rocky and hilly." *Natives* are "a black race of people that live in Africa." By the seventh grade, having encountered the word in new settings, the pupils know that natives are of many sorts. They are now more aware of the central meaning: "the people who live in the country where they were born" (Eskridge, 1939).

12. Into what categories is reading matter commonly divided in high-school English teaching? Do these categories influence pupils' attitudes?

13. Show that the category system used in discussing vocations and college majors causes some students to overlook opportunities in fields that cut across the categories.

14. Show that each of the following concepts refers to a common element and disregards details of situations: *lever, paragraph, blonde, motivated.*

15. Choose one of the following pairs of terms and show that a continuous variable would describe the underlying phenomenon better. (Example: *level of business activity,* a continuous variable, is more accurate than the categories *prosperity* vs. *depression.*)

        inherited–acquired   prose–poetry   stable–neurotic

16. To reduce the fraction %, some teachers would speak of "canceling." Others would teach to "divide both numerator and denominator by two." When the student encounters

$$\frac{6x + 2}{4}$$

which concept is most helpful?

17. In discussing the fact that junior high schools usually teach a technique of reading to get main ideas quickly, Mayer (1961, p. 189) says: "All adults guess at words, and all adults skim, not because such procedures are desirable but because the human animal is lazier than he should be. Surely it is not part of the function of the schools to teach children bad habits." How much precision should the school aim for in the pupil's use of skills and concepts?

Experience as the Base for Meaning

The school should do much more than allow the learner to try out his interpretations. We accelerate learning by giving him appropriate explanations and by helping him formulate in words what he has observed (see Chapter 12). Whether or not an explanation is helpful depends on the learner's ability to relate the words to experience. The teacher cannot expect to communicate if he talks about things that have no connection with the pupil's experience. A sea chantey is "a rhythmic song, sung in chorus by a ship's crew"—but this is a pallid image to the pupil who has never heard one. He still wouldn't recognize a chantey. A rainbow, a banana, or a baby defies description; only experience with the real thing acquaints a person with its characteristics. Many concepts deal with relations or abstractions (heredity, kilowatt, a billion dollars) and the teacher cannot point directly to an example. Even these, however, can be connected to familiar experience ("a kilowatt would run ten light bulbs like this").

Images of concrete objects and events are a necessary background for comprehending an abstract relation. Whenever an activity puts the pupil into intimate contact with real objects, he amasses experiences that can clarify theoretical concepts and principles. The boys who make radios acquire images of objects and operations associated with electricity. They know what an added resistor does; they have seen lights dim and have felt wires grow warm. Consequently, they find physics easier to grasp. The class that sets out to persuade the city council to change its bicycle ordinance gains a picture of realities of which the formal chart of government structure is only a reminder.

The child with a garden watches it closely every day and builds up intimacy with soil and insects and rainfall. He knows from digging that water is stored beneath dry topsoil. This illumines facts in his geography which otherwise would have little significance. After the child has waited impatiently for the soil to dry so he can plant a spring garden, reading that the growing season begins two months later in Russia sets meanings rolling in his head. He can draw implications from the facts: how much Russians can produce, why they do not grow slow-maturing corn, why a few weeks of bad weather cause serious concern in Russia.

THE PLACE OF ABSTRACTION.   We have said that experience with the concrete situation is the *base* for understanding. This should not be misunderstood to imply that concrete instruction is invariably better than abstract verbal instruction. The advantages of abstract instruction are probably best illustrated in a series of studies by Ericksen and his co-workers (see Thune and Ericksen, 1960). In these studies, some subjects were trained in a situation where they could use concrete cues, while others were required to learn and apply an abstract pattern. So long as the subjects had enough familiarity with the real situation to understand the abstract scheme, the abstract instruction led to more transfer.

Let us look at the details of one study. Three groups of students were given brief training in operating an electric calculator. All groups had a 20-minute familiarization exercise with a Friden calculator, in which they pushed the buttons and read numbers from the dial. Then there was a 20-minute training period during which Group I did an irrelevant alphabetic puzzle to fill time. Group II (concrete training) did addition, subtraction, and multiplication problems directly on the Friden machine; the tasks proceeded from easy to hard in a sensible instructional sequence. Group III (abstract training) was taught the principles underlying operation of *any* calculator. They worked with a schematic diagram and answered multiple-choice questions about the abstractly labeled parts of the machine. For example: "Which dial shows all addition, subtraction, and multiplication answers? Totals dial, items dial, or multiplier dial?" Questions were arranged in a logical order, so that the student could reason out each answer from the information given. The student did no calculations. At most, he chose the prescription required to accomplish some result (e.g., "Punch 47.2 in the keyboard").

The three groups of students were then tested. Test A called for seven calculations on the Friden machine. Test B consisted of an equally difficult test given on the Friden the next day. Following test B the student was given a 20-minute introduction to the Marchant calculator, where dials and controls are arranged rather differently from the Friden though the theory of operation is the same. Test C required calculations on the Marchant like those already performed on the Friden. The first interesting finding tells something about the confidence produced by the training methods. There was a time limit on each test. The number of subjects finishing the test was as follows (out of 24 in each group):

		GROUP I Familiarization only	GROUP II Concrete Friden training	GROUP III Abstract, general training
Test A.	Friden, immediate	8	23	15
Test B.	Friden, delayed	17	23	19
Test C.	Marchant, after familiarization	13	15	21

The concretely trained group plunged into the Friden test vigorously and successfully (Figure 87). The abstractly trained group was cautious and uncertain, though they did fairly well; on the second day, they did considerably better. But on the transfer task many in the concrete group were at a loss, while the abstractly trained group made an easy and successful adaptation. Evidently, abstract training is beneficial *when it is understood* and

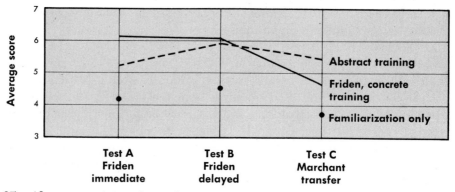

87   *Abstract training has advantages for transfer* (*Thune and Ericksen, 1960*)

when the learning will later be applied in a variety of situations. Concrete training in a single situation can be relied on only if the application situation will be the same.

LEARNING THROUGH ADVENTUROUS PARTICIPATION

The more adventurously the pupil participates and manipulates what he should come to understand, the more he learns and the more flexible are his concepts. Adventurous participation is not the same as imitatively following another's lead. Teachers have not made much use of true problem solving as a teaching method. Much that is called problem solving in the school consists of nothing more than exercises in which the pupil applies textbook prescriptions (Cronbach, 1948). Since you probably have seen little teaching in which the pupil is led actively and curiously to explore the unknown, we shall give several examples from different fields.

SCIENCE AND APPLIED SCIENCE. In the chemistry laboratory, the pupil learns something when he mixes two compounds and observes the "blue-green precipitate" mentioned in the text—but not much. He would learn more if he had no idea what to expect, so that he would face the scientist's problem of describing an observation in a way that communicates (Boeck, 1951). Given no "right answer" in advance, he can be open-minded. He may not see the precipitate as green at all. When this happens the teacher can turn discussion to the problem of obtaining precise, trustworthy observations about color. This is an intellectual challenge within the reach of the high-school student, yet one that realistically represents a recurring difficulty in scientific observation. This discussion calls for scientific thinking whereas routinely verifying that the textbook can be trusted does not.

Indeed, if trust in the book is taught, the science course is generating an unscientific attitude. Schwab (1960) points out that scientific knowledge is transient. Many theories new today will be obsolete 15 years hence, replaced by better conceptions. But few courses prior to graduate school give a valid image of science:

> The traditional course has tended to treat only the outcomes, the conclusions, of inquiry, divorced from the data which support them and the conceptual frames which define—and limit—their validity. The result has been to convey a false image of science as knowledge literally true, permanent—even complete. . . . We tend to provide a structure which admits of no loose ends. We minimize doubts and qualifications. . . .
>
> The student is led to treat conclusions as inalterable truths. When, five or ten years later, this conviction proves false, he retreats from clarity to confusion

and from confusion to generalized suspicion of scientific competence and authority. . . . We need to imbue our courses and our exposition with the color of science and inquiry to give the student an effective glimpse of the vicissitudes of research.

The need for problem-oriented teaching is equally great in applied science. We turn to home economics for a second example of adventurous participation. In conventional teaching the teacher would give a recipe, and expect the pupil to follow it and make a good cake. The intellectual yield of the experience is greatly increased if a question is raised. What does beating do? What happens if we beat the batter less or more, by hand or by machine? Discussion before the cake-making makes the girl a keener observer of the changes in her batter. A controlled plan of dividing the batter, with different batches beaten differently, followed by careful judging of the cakes, will include the experiences of recipe-following and offer much in addition. Such inquiries make the classwork more than a duplication of the girl's apprenticeship to her mother. They teach her that all cakes that taste good are not equally ideal. She begins to see successful baking as a result of controllable operations. She can begin to think about it for herself.

social studies. The pupil cannot perform experiments on social and historical questions, but here too he can be presented with challenges. "What would have happened if . . ." turns abstract concepts and long-dead events into a moving, modifiable system of forces.

Bruner (1960, p. 21) turned sixth-grade geography from memorization to intellectual adventure by showing Boston children an outline map of the Middle West, with a few supplementary facts. "You all know that Chicago is in this region," he said. "Where on the map do you think such a great city would arise?" The pupils fell into hot debate, giving reasonable arguments for many locations: people need food, so one group favored a location in Iowa; water transportation is important, so the city ought to be up where Superior, Michigan, and Huron join; no, said others, a city would surely grow where copious iron ore would bring industry. The prominence of Chicago is actually to be explained by its role as a railroad center, not by any one of the causes the pupils suggested. Previous instruction in geography had taught this class little about the distinctive functions and population patterns of farm areas, sources of raw material, processing centers, and centers of commerce. From Bruner's approach they learned that social facts have causes.

developing mathematical creativeness. Mathematics, especially elementary mathematics, has usually been taught as a set of procedures, definitions, and "correct principles." This is contrary both to the true nature of mathematical thinking and to the psychology of the learner. For a mathematician, the first step in reasoning is curiosity. Galileo was launched on his career when he began to wonder what regularity can be observed in the path of a cannonball. As the creative mathematician puzzles, he turns his problem back and forth, using reversible operations in much the manner of the child adjusting the proportions of a rectangle to match a perceived shape. Only after long familiarity does he create the elegant rule that sums up his experience in a formal operation. And proof comes much later as a secondary step, not unimportant, but worthless until he attains an insight deserving of formal derivation. Galileo required 30 years to move from an impressionistic and incorrect understanding of acceleration to a satisfactory formula (Hanson, 1958, p. 42).

Mathematics has usually been stripped of its adventure in the classroom. Emphasis on prescriptions and proofs has given the student an incorrect idea of its very nature. A "proven" conclusion is not necessarily true. It is merely a result that fits with a set of assumptions, assumptions that the mathematician changes at will.

Ulmer (1942) says:

> From the standpoint of postulational thinking it is unfortunate that reference has so often been made to the great truths of geometry. It is difficult to get individuals to understand the if-then type of thinking if conclusions are regarded as belonging to the absolute, unchanging truths of the universe. For this reason it is strongly recommended that teachers avoid referring to theorems as truths of geometry. In place of a question like, "Do you think such and such a relationship is true?" teachers might substitute "Do you think we can show that it must follow?" The pupils . . . should understand that even a slight change in the set of assumptions may produce changes in the conclusions drawn from these assumptions.

Mathematics has been taught as if it were nothing but a set of formal operations to be mastered and applied. Most pupils never develop deep intuitive concepts of numbers, functions, and probabilities because they are pushed abruptly into formal exercises where the whole emphasis is on moving directly toward the answer. (Note that in the cake-baking and Chicago examples above, the teacher's tactic was to encourage pupils to proceed *indirectly* by entertaining many answers and finding out which fitted the facts.)

Mathematical understanding should rest on intuition. Pupils can solve a problem impressionistically years before they can work out an exact, formally controlled solution.[1] Building familiarity with mathematical ideas through early concrete activities has three virtues: it provides a base of understanding for later instruction, it conveys a sound understanding of what mathematics is like, and it makes the subject fun.

[1] The statements in this section are based on recent, unpublished curriculum studies, particularly the University of Illinois Arithmetic Project, David Page, director.

Starting with geometric objects the pupil can intuitively attain the idea of any triangle as half a rectangle, years before he would understand a direct presentation of "the area equals one-half the base times the altitude." Algebra is perfectly transparent to third-graders if kept within the range of their number experience and treated as a puzzle rather than as a set of prescriptions (UICSM Staff, 1957). It is easy for them to fill the blank in

$$3 + \square = 7$$

and they can quickly learn to solve

$$5 - \frac{\square}{2} = 3$$

The box, of course, is the x of algebra. Pupils must work into such problems gradually; the first successes may be sheer trial and error, but later ones show quick insight. The child will not say, "subtract three from both sides of the equation." He will visualize seven objects regrouped into three and four, and will "see" the answer. If he is moved slowly enough through many, many trials, he becomes able to unravel problems involving several steps, and problems with large numbers.

More remarkable is the child's ability to *create* mathematical generalizations. A rather lengthy description is required to illustrate this. Mr. Palmer hands each sixth-grader a set of centimeter rods. These teaching aids are wooden sticks ranging in length from one to ten units, each length a different color. Mr. Palmer asks everyone to arrange his sticks in order, side by side. Attention is directed to the fact that every stick (save the end ones) is adjacent to two sticks. It is one step away from two others, etc. Pupils are asked to suggest names: "What could we call the sticks next in size to the one I am touching?" Various names are suggested; a vote leads to the term *sideband* ("first sidebands" for closest neighbors, "second sidebands," etc.). By generating terminology in this way, every child is clear as to what the word to be used means. And he is learning the general, transferable idea that mathematical terms are conveniences agreed upon, not truths handed down by some rare intellect.

Next question: "Suppose we take three sticks—1, 2, 3. Can you arrange them so that no stick is next to either of its first sidebands?" When it is agreed that this is impossible, four sticks are tried. Each pupil rearranges his own set and holds up his hand when he thinks he has succeeded. (You should try this with four numbered slips of paper.) The pupil who succeeds early need not sit idle; he can attempt to arrange five or six sticks so that no first sidebands are touching. Mr. Palmer helps a few pupils, but nearly all solve the four-stick problem without help. Now comes the question: "Can you arrange four sticks so that no stick touches its first *or second* sidebands?" This is not possible, and trials show that at least six sticks are required. (The order 3, 6, 2, 5, 1, 4 satisfies the condition.)

Working through a few additional problems, perhaps allowing pupils to work in pairs, or accepting an answer from one pupil and letting him show the others, Mr. Palmer brings the class to the point where they have seen that

> 4 sticks are needed to not touch 1st sideband
> 6 sticks are needed to not touch 1st or 2nd sideband
> 8 sticks are needed to not touch 1st, 2nd or 3rd sideband

88 *Mr. Palmer's pupils worked intuitively*

Now pupils are ready to guess what will happen with any number of sidebands: "What if we do not wish to touch 1st, 2nd, . . . 5th sideband?" There may be some counting on fingers to arrive at the answer "12"; there may be disagreement calling for an experimental trial. Still a further stage is reached when Mr. Palmer asks for the number of sticks required if we want not to touch any sideband through the 100th. (You try to answer!) This requires a formal operation, since counting on fingers is impracticable. A substantial number of pupils arrive at a general rule, in words of their own, to the effect that the sideband number must be multiplied by 2, and then 2 more sticks must be added.

The writer has seen a teacher using this approach bring a demonstration class of sixth-graders, never instructed in this way before, to the solution so smoothly that adult scientists in the audience were unable to keep ahead of the pupils. The pupils are intensely interested. They learn that the world of numbers is lawful and that they can discover (in a sense, they can create) the laws. They gain self-confidence. They learn something about permutations, even though they are a long way from practical applications to statistics or molecular structure. Similar intuitive teaching benefits advanced classes being introduced to unfamiliar relationships.

ART APPRECIATION.   A plan used to teach art appreciation shows another approach that leads the pupil to form his own concepts. The moment a teacher distinguishes Renaissance painters from those who went before, he distracts the pupil from the essential continuity of artistic evolution. Moreover, he tends to block the pupil from later observing the similarities between "modern" art and some "classical" art. Bettelheim (1942), working with junior-high-school pupils, provided postcard prints of many paintings of all periods and schools and asked the pupil to sort them into sets of similar pictures. Each pupil sorted them somewhat differently. This not only called out a discussion of various ways of thinking about art (subject, treatment, color, technique) but also meant that when the group settled down to study one group of paintings, they saw the group in relation to the total field, isolated only for convenience.

LANGUAGE ARTS.   Finally, we can illustrate the place of exploratory problem-solving in the language arts. Roger Brown (1958b, p. 78) recommends asking the first-grader, as soon as he has acquired some sight vocabulary, to note resemblances among (for example) *dog* and *do,* and then to guess what sound probably goes with the unfamiliar words *did* or *dot.* Through this adventurous guessing, the pupil discovers a meaningful phonics for himself.

It is profitable to develop an ear for the word order and structure of a foreign language through extensive conversation, before grammar is taught formally. Fluency and auditory comprehension come from capturing language rhythm at an intuitive level, so that some things "sound right" and others do not. Grammatical analysis, like the formal proof of the mathematician, is a way of criticizing and editing rather than a way of creating. Some complicated expressions, to be sure, can only be worked out correctly by formal analysis; but we are told that out of 2,200 syntactical constructions possible in Spanish, for example, only 70 are commonly used by native writers (Keniston, 1937). It is easier to master these few forms through familiarity than to learn and apply the grammatical system.

Experimentation is much needed to see how ability to construct well-formed English sentences would be affected by experience emphasizing discovery rather than rules or imitation. A fourth-grader could experiment to find how many ways he can rearrange the words "Saturday on the bus the excited boy saw a zebra," and what sense and emphasis each arrangement yields. An older pupil can consider style as a matter for experiment, rewriting the same incident from various viewpoints to convey various attitudes, or to communicate to different audiences. This is comparable to the stage of concrete operations in other thinking; rewriting *is* reversible operation. Most present instruction either asks the child to express himself, with no systematic manipulation and comparison of alternatives, or to apply formal operations for which no concrete base has been prepared.

18. According to Schlesinger (in Bereday *et al.*, 1960, p. 174), early elementary-school instruction in drawing in Russia follows a detailed plan. A schedule indicates what should be drawn in the first lesson, how much should be added in the second lesson, and so on. "The end result of this particular series of lessons was a beautifully drawn and colored tree, with symmetrical branches and leaves; all drawings were exactly alike."

A leading authority on art education, Mme. Shatskaia, is quoted:

"We believe that only children who have mastered the techniques of drawing can be permitted to do any free drawing. Also, children must learn to reproduce what they see around them with reasonable accuracy. This teaches them the correct approach to material reality. This does not mean that the drawings must be photographic reproductions of reality, but it does mean that the significant features of reality must be reproduced."

What assumption does this teaching make about the objectives of art instruction? about the function of discovery? about motivation for drawing?

Does the American school teach any performance with a similar emphasis on skill in technique without concern for self-expression?

Drawing a Verbal Conclusion

Experience ought to lead toward verbal knowledge. A well-formulated principle packs the residue of experience into a small capsule, easily remembered and easily applied. How formal a conclusion should be depends upon the learner's stage of development. The third-grader may very well end his study of problems like $5 + \square = 7$ with a no more profound generalization than, "Find the number of steps on the number line that it takes to go from 5 to 7." A few years later he can be led to a more comprehensive generalization: "An equation remains a true statement when the same operation is performed on both sides of the equation."

It is generally unwise to end a classroom discussion or an experiment without drawing a verbal conclusion. The conclusion may be drawn by the pupil in his own words, but the teacher needs to check the accuracy of his generalization. Otherwise the pupil may miss the point of the experience, extracting no general principle (Corman, 1957). He may arrive at a garbled, unjustified conclusion. ("Big cities grow up where there are railroads." "To solve an equation, move x to one side and everything else to the other side.") There is considerable advantage in having the pupil formulate the generalization in his own words, just because this allows the teacher to detect faulty comprehension. Moreover, the pupil is far more certain to understand what he has stated for himself.

The generalization we wish to teach is an abstraction, a summary expressed in terms of two or more concepts. Generalizations need to be linked to reality, so that they help one deal with concrete events, and they must be connected with other generalizations and theoretical structures so that implications will be seen. The generalization "Mosquitos breed in stagnant pools" is not a guide to action unless one can recognize a stagnant pool (encoding). More than that, he must call on such additional generalizations as "Animals need oxygen" and "Kerosene floats on water" to work out a prescription for killing the mosquitos. The methods of learning through experimentation, described above, are well designed to ensure that concepts are connected to reality. Drawing the verbal conclusion is needed to ensure proper connections between observed facts.

Concreteness is equally important when a principle is presented by the teacher or text, rather than discovered. The verbal presentation ought to be followed by opportunities for application. The application reveals misunderstandings and makes the implications of the principle clear. The principle will not transfer into appropriate concrete situations unless the pupil knows the physical cues that signal where the concept studied is relevant.

PRESENTATION VS. DISCOVERY OF GENERALIZATIONS

In teaching a principle, we have a choice between presenting it verbally and then asking questions about examples, or challenging the pupil to deal with situations from which he can extract the principle. The "adventurous" methods described above all involve a large element of discovery. Should this method supplant instruction by presentation of established principles?

"Learning by discovery" is so frequently recommended to educators that it has reached the status of a slogan. Yet in skill learning we found that the learner profits from direct guidance. And all our discussion of the role of verbal principles and systematized knowledge in facilitating response seems to support verbal instruction in school. To resolve this conflict, we shall have to define just what function discovery plays, and what limitations there are in the faster, more direct teaching by presentation of verbal generalizations.

Perhaps the first comment to be made is that the formal research on discovery is rather insubstantial (Ausubel, 1961). Some of the prominent studies are technically unsound, others are based on casual observation rather than systematic experiment, and practically none of them deals with regular classroom lessons continued over weeks or months. Most of the studies examine the learning of a single mathematical rule, a single card trick, or the solution of some type of puzzle. The following study is a good representative of those that favor learning by discovery; though it deals with relatively meaningless associations, it is an experiment on classroom teaching.

The British Air Force developed a discovery method for teaching aircraft recognition to replace the customary method in which the instructor points out directly the features to look for in each type of plane. The discovery procedure is very simple. Each student is handed a book of over one hundred photographs each showing one of four planes as seen from different angles and distances. For comparison he is given clear, close-up pictures of the four planes with their names. He puzzles out for himself which of the four planes each picture in the book shows; the teacher has only to check his judgments and answer his questions. In the experiment reported, the student worked through several books, covering 20 planes in all. Learning was strikingly better than that from instructor-directed presentation and drill. And students were so much interested in the work that they were reluctant to leave at the end of the class hour (Allan, 1958). (Later, for purposes of contrast, we shall describe how this same task could be taught by presentation, with no provision for discovery; see page 407).

The various studies on discovery (Kittell, 1957; Kersh, 1958; Ray, 1961; Gagné and Brown, 1961; for earlier studies see Hunnicutt and Iverson, 1958) leave us with the following well-established statements:

A discovered response is readily discriminated from alternative responses. Pupils who apply a generalization given by the teacher may learn the mechanics of application without understanding and retaining the principle. If the generalization is given ready-made, the pupil may think he understands it when he does not, hence he may misapply it. When one detail fades from memory his knowledge tends to "fall apart." But if he has constructed the principle for himself, he can reconstruct it fairly rapidly by recalling the underlying experiences.

Pupils are challenged when asked to discover a solution. This motivates them to pay closer attention and to think about the material outside of class. The solution, when achieved, contributes to a sense of competence and to interest in further learning.

When one group has applied a principle given by the teacher, and another has constructed it from experience, the second group is more successful in discovering the principle for solving a further problem. The ability— or the confidence—that enables one to discover generalizations of a particular type is learned.

The first two of these statements are not fundamental arguments for having pupils formulate their own principles. If the teacher's presentation makes adequate use of concrete examples and familiar ideas, it also should be meaningful, well retained, and readily reconstructed at a later date. The second value—superior motivation—is a great advantage, but a "discovery" approach is by no means the only tactic that generates enthusiasm. Even a lecture can inspire further thought "after hours."

The great value of discovery is in two transfer effects: in attitude toward a field of knowledge, and in improved ability to discover principles. The pupil who has discovered a generalization about goldfish, Indian tribes or the use of *who* and *whom* has become less dependent on authority. He has a new sense of his own intellectual power and a clearer view of the nature of knowledge. He expects other generalizations in the field to make sense, and also begins to understand the limitations of knowledge derived from evidence of the sort he used. Each adventure in thinking is expected to make all work in the subject seem more valuable and more intelligible.

As one continues in a field of study he must construct truths for himself. No matter how he is taught, he must recast information into a form that he understands and reconstruct principles half forgotten. Furthermore, as he moves on to advanced problems for which there are no prescriptions (e.g., finding the area of an irregularly shaped field), he must invent a method of attack. Pupils who have once discovered a principle are much less bewildered when they must think for themselves in the next situation. Their superiority lies in specific concepts and techniques (cutting up the irregular figure to form familiar shapes), and also in self-reliance.

From this we conclude that in every field of study *some* of the teaching should be by methods that require the pupil to discover and formulate principles for himself. This way develops a different view of the field than if he always works with principles others have stated for him. Such problem-solving should be spaced throughout the curriculum. An attitude toward history or art or physics is not established at any one point in life. There is a place for discovery in the child's earliest learning in the field, and also in the training of the graduate student. The more mature the student, the smaller the role of the teacher in helping him to formulate and check his discoveries.

A classroom method emphasizing discovery can have serious limitations. Learning by discovery is fine when the pupil succeeds, but pupils often fail to solve the problem set for them (Kittell, 1957; Kersh, 1958). Guidance that helps the learner to concentrate on essentials increases his chance of success (Gagné and Brown, 1961). In Mr. Palmer's teaching, success was ensured by breaking the problem into small steps and by letting pupils share insights with each other. Bruner's pupils participated in framing hypotheses, but the answer regarding the location of Chicago was supplied by the teacher when they were ready for it. In one study (Kimble and Wulff, 1953) pupils learned to read the scale of a slide rule, primarily by trial and

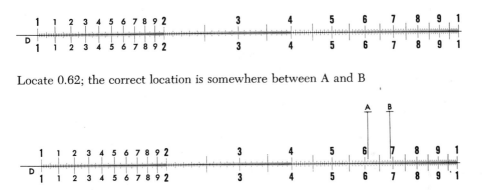

Locate 0.62

Locate 0.62; the correct location is somewhere between A and B

89 *Hints aid discovery (after Kimble and Wulff, 1953)*

> One group was given practice items like that at the top; a second group was "steered" toward correct answers with practice items like that at the bottom. The second group learned more successfully. (*Slide rule courtesy of Keuffel & Esser Co.*)

error. An initial explanation was given, after which students tried many items and were told which answers were correct. In one group the task was simplified by the "helps" shown in the lower panel of Figure 89. The other group responded to the scale in its natural, complex form. The pupils for whom the task had been simplified were more successful on the tasks they had practiced. They also did better than the unguided group on tasks that had not been practiced.

Pupils do not have time to rediscover all of human knowledge. Presentation by the teacher "covers more ground" than learning by discovery. The teacher can present meaningfully many things the pupils could not, within the limits of time, cost, and their research techniques, discover for themselves. Girls discover much about cakes by carrying out the experiment on mixing techniques described above, but the teacher adds to this discovery by showing them enlarged photographs of cakes beaten in various ways. Few of the generalizations about foods necessary to health can be discovered by the pupil. At best, feeding a few experimental animals can form a background for facts the teacher must present. The details of metabolism are beyond the pupil's observation.

Some knowledge is sufficiently arbitrary that it cannot be extracted from experience. To enlarge vocabularies of college students we could ask them to "discover" word meanings from numerous sentences using the word correctly. The student can infer the underlying meaning, and then judge further specimen sentences exhibiting uses or misuses of the word. But students taught this way are less successful than students given a definition of the term along with examples.[2] The difficulty is that if the word *abstruse*, for example, appears in a limited set of sentences, one can guess several meanings all of which make sense. Discovery leads only to a loose, intuitive meaning. A firm, clear definition narrows the meaning more adequately than a hundred examples. Practice in classifying uses of the word as proper or improper is necessary to guarantee that the definition is fully understood.

The basic function of the sequence, "provisional tries first, verbal formulation afterward," is to involve the pupil actively and to make him a reasoner rather than a recipe-follower. The active attitude can be maintained even when the teacher gives considerable assistance. Unless the teacher is extremely skillful, the pupil may lean back, waiting for the teacher to supply so many hints that the answer will come to him without effort. This happens when the pupil feels that the teacher knows the answer and is "holding out" to make him work harder. It does not occur when the teacher is a partner in an experiment where no one knows the outcome in advance. The most successful science projects, at both the elementary and high-school levels, are of this nature. When suitable source materials are available, one can likewise take a research approach to historical questions: e.g., how did the hard life of the pilgrims compare with the life of the common folk in England at that time?

> **19.** How should learning by discovery in the classroom differ from learning by discovery outside of the school? List the responsibilities of the teacher in making this approach profitable.
>
> **20.** Does the possibility of learning by discovery vary according to the subject being taught?
>
> **21.** What assumptions underlie the use of the lecture method of instruction for adults and college students? Can the lecture method be made consistent with the principles of this chapter?
>
> **22.** "The teacher is a partner in an experiment where no one knows the answer in advance." Which of the teaching methods described in the pre-

[2] P. B. Diederich. Personal communication.

ceding section satisfies this requirement? Is it a necessary requirement for adventurous participation by the learner?

23. In what sense does the sentence apply to
   a. a medical-school professor discussing with students the patients under his care?
   b. a second-grade teacher helping pupils compose a note to parents inviting them to a class program?

Verbal Instruction as a Base for Performance

There is another line of research, closely related to the studies of discovery, that inquires regarding the value of verbal instruction. Most knowledge taught in school is verbal; we expect this knowledge to influence action in concrete situations. Yet there is considerable evidence that the person who studies the theory underlying a skill may not thereby become a better performer. Colville (1957) taught certain billiard shots. One group just practiced the shots. Another group spent part of its time studying the underlying physical principles of reflection and momentum, and the rest in practice. The second group had no advantage. Hendrickson and Schroeder (1941) taught boys to shoot at underwater targets with an air rifle; to hit the target, one must correct for refraction, aiming below the apparent target. One group practiced the skill. Two other groups were given verbal instruction about refraction, with a slight difference between the two explanations used. All three groups practiced with a target six inches below the surface of the water, then they were shifted to a target two inches deep. The number of trials required before they could regularly hit the second, shallow target was as follows:

	Mean	*s.d.*	*Approximate range (two s.d. on each side of mean)*
Control group	6.0	2.6	1–11
Explanation 1	5.4	2.3	1–10
Explanation 2	4.6	2.1	0–9

The differences among the groups are barely noticeable. Explanation 2 was a bit more effective, because it came to the point more definitely. But even Explanation 2 stopped with the generalization that the deeper the water, the greater the apparent displacement. Neither explanation provided a prescription for action, hence the boys could not use the knowledge. Few boys understood the explanation well enough to derive a helpful prescription for themselves.

A study by Ervin (1960) suggests that verbal understanding is primarily important in coping with exceptional conditions. She trained children to adjust a tube so that when a ball was shot through the tube and bounced off a backboard it would hit a target. By directing attention to the angles between the path of the ball and the backboard Ervin helped them identify the principle. Children who formulated the principle and children who did not were about equally successful in a transfer task, aiming a flashlight toward a mirror so that its reflection would hit a target. The group that lacked the correct principle adjusted the mirror with the aid of supplementary cues (e.g., aiming at a point on the reflector halfway between the flashlight and the target). On a particularly hard item, however, the mirror was tipped sharply upward so that such supplementary cues were misleading. In this critical situation, only the children who had fixed their knowledge as a precise and correct principle succeeded. In another study (Gagné and Smith, 1962) high-school boys were given a stack of disks on one of three pegs, and asked to move one disk at a time so as to shift the whole stack to a new peg. They were not allowed to place a disk atop a smaller one, and were to execute the transfer in the smallest possible number of moves. Verbalizing gave little or no advantage when there were only three or four disks to be moved, but with five or six disks the verbalizers had a marked advantage. When a problem becomes too complex for intuition and informal use of cues to regulate response, the formal principle is of great value.

Systematic verbal knowledge is an efficient way to summarize experience, not a substitute for it. To act on a concrete situation by means of verbal knowledge, one must encode the physical cues into words; one must, for example, be able to recognize the depth of the water in the airgun experiment. Second, from a general principle one must be able to derive a prescription telling what action to take ("aim above the target") and must be able to decode the prescription into action. Sometimes these steps in applying verbal knowledge are obvious. But ordinarily the teacher who would make a verbal principle useful to the pupil must give particular attention to the encoding and decoding steps (e.g., "How can we decide when the angle of incidence equals the angle of reflection?"). Often it is better to give considerable concrete experience before presenting the verbal rule; the concrete background of trial and error makes it easier to understand the rule and apply it.

    24. This text teaches educational psychology verbally. In what ways does it take the following principles into account?

        a. Concrete experience should come first, verbal formulation afterward.

        b. Meanings are sharpened by trials in which misconceptions lead to wrong conclusions.

        c. Having a general principle, one must be able to derive a prescription for the concrete situation.

    25. One theory advocated by some leading psychologists holds that the secret of success in teaching is to make sure that the pupil makes the correct response from the outset.

        a. How would one teach science according to this theory?

        b. Does this theory agree with our interpretation of Ervin's results?

    c. How does it relate to Piaget's theory regarding the emergence of disciplined thought?

    d. In our discussion of skill, were we concerned to have correct response from the outset? Are skill-learning and conceptual learning governed by the same principles?

IMPROVING REASONING

In one sense, all behavior is problem solving, for one must select appropriate responses and adapt them to the immediate situation. When this choice and adaptation is deliberate, involving conscious criticism of possible responses, the process is called reasoning. Reasoning is the process by which the individual decides on one of several courses of action or explanations without actually trying all the possibilities. It involves recognizing the possible alternatives and judging deliberately which will have the desired consequences. Educators have been especially concerned to improve the way people reason about political affairs, about their work, and about their personal problems.

We have seen how one can improve his thinking about a specific problem or body of content. He learns to look for meaningful connections. He acquires pertinent concepts and generalizations about the subject. But can reasoning be improved in a general way, so that one draws sounder conclusions in dealing with *any* subject?

The effective problem solver shows certain characteristic behaviors, as we said in Chapter 2. He recognizes significant problems and wants to solve them. He has developed values that direct his choices. He has confidence but criticizes his own ideas. He doesn't give up without effort, or accept unchecked conclusions. Attitudes like these, once developed, might affect all reasoning. Reasoning also involves skill, since there are techniques of criticism that can be applied. The good thinker has the information the problem calls for, or can find it. And his thinking is free from emotional interference.

Some of these responses can be taught only by confronting the student with the different kinds of problems he will meet. Studying social problems, he can acquire relevant facts, acquaintance with sources such as *The World Almanac* and the New York *Times,* and concern about slums and illiteracy. He can observe how people form different opinions from the same facts. Pupils who debate whether or not sewer bonds should be approved by the community encounter uncertainty of information and realistic conflicts of interest. Their discoveries *about reasoning itself* can be captured as generalizations. Reasoning about social issues cannot be developed fully by any subject except social studies.

Teaching of Generalizations About Reasoning

There are many generalizations that describe good reasoning: know how much confidence can be placed in each fact you employ; be especially critical of conclusions that agree with your own wishes; define all crucial terms with care; examine the assumptions from which an argument starts, etc. These are just as much "knowledge" to be learned as any fact about trade routes and the Constitution.

Reasoning is improved through practice in reasoning. A problem is presented; the pupil makes an error, and his attention is drawn to the principle of straight thinking that guards against the error. Thus any social issue can bring out the fallacy of assuming that what is true for one person is true for everyone. After the pupil sees that this is indeed an error, he and the teacher can formulate the principle in words appropriate to his maturity. The rule in adult language might be, "Don't reason from the special case to the general case," or "Don't generalize from inadequate samples." For a young child, the rule might be, "Don't expect everyone to act in the same way." When the student is aware of and understands this general principle, he can "practice" it in all his reasoning about people.

A principle does not guide the pupil's action unless he sees what the principle means. "Define terms carefully" is a good rule, but it has to be made meaningful by studying good and poor definitions in settings where faulty ones do obvious harm. Geometry can contribute to this because geometric definitions are concrete and testable. If a pupil defines a *square* as "a figure with four right angles," he and everyone else can see what is wrong much more quickly than if the word defined is *economy* or *race*, even though the latter words will be more used in later reasoning.

Pupils need to see the full range of situations to which a principle applies. Ruediger, you recall, showed that neatness transfers when taught as a general ideal. If "define your terms" is taught only on geometric materials, the student does not regard other reasoning as similar, and may not know how to criticize nonmathematical definitions. Many modern courses combine geometric and nongeometric materials. One type of problem that permits practice in transferring reasoning skill to nongeometric content is the following (Ulmer, 1942, p. 13):

> Telephone rates on residence phones are lower than those on business phones. What is a business phone? Is it likely that the term *business phone* would have the same meaning to everyone? One definition of a business phone is *any telephone used habitually by an individual or an organized group for gain or advancement.* Under this definition, can we say for certain whether telephones in the following places are business phones: the high school; a physician's home; a physician's office; a hotel; the charity ward of a hospital; Mrs. Black, who washes for a living; Y.M.C.A; a church; a courtesy phone at the city library?

The value of this approach is shown in Ulmer's experiment (1939) involving 330 students who took a conventional geometry course, 330 who did not take geometry, and 330 who took an experimental course in which geometric reasoning was connected with reflective thinking about nongeometric problems. The essential difference between the geometric group

Point out the general principle

Give opportunities to apply it

"Dry cells of Brand B last longer."

90   *How to teach for transfer*

and the experimental group was that the former reasoned primarily about geometric derivations and did not discuss methods of thinking apart from that task. The effect of the course was tested by ability to draw sound conclusions from given facts, including some issues where biases might affect reasoning. On the pretest, the groups were very nearly equal. On the final test, the data were:

	Mean	*Range of middle 95 per cent*
No geometry	34	12–64
Conventional geometry	40	13–78
Experimental course	57	25–96

Among the conventional classes, the greatest gains were noted in classes where the teachers had made some attempt to use nongeometric examples of proof. While conventional geometry did improve general reasoning, this effect was confined to pupils with IQs above 100. The experimental course improved reasoning at all levels. It is important to note also that instruction of this sort produces just as much gain in geometry itself as the conventional course (Fawcett, 1938).

Most subjects can contribute to reasoning if taught so as to emphasize the relevant principles (Barlow, 1937; E. E. White, 1936). Science, psychology, English, and practical vocational subjects all involve reasoning, and can be taught so as to obtain this type of transfer. The essential techniques in teaching for transfer are these:

Identify the desirable response in the form of a general principle.

Make that principle very clear to the pupil (helping him to extract it from his experience or providing lucid illustrative material).

Draw the pupil's attention to places where the principle applies.

Give him opportunities to apply it in increasingly varied and complex situations.

These four suggestions apply to the teaching not only of reasoning, but of concepts and scientific principles, attitudes and moral values, mechanical skills, and skills in dealing with people.

Responses That Interfere with Reasoning

Often, attitudes or habits of thought are learned that interfere with reasoning. Rigidity is frequently observed. Instead of reacting to a new situation with fresh thinking, the person automatically treats it like the last situation. This helps him if it *is* like the last situation, but not if it is different. If a pitcher fires five fast balls at a batter, the batter gets set to swing quickly; when the pitcher changes pace and sends up a slow ball, the batter is wound so tight that he cannot adapt. The teacher likewise may pitch similar problems one after another until the pupil gets in a rut—worse, until he believes that following a stereotyped pattern is normal and proper.

Luchins (1942) developed a set of water-jar problems calling for adaptive mathematical reasoning. "If you have a 7-quart jar and a 4-quart jar, how can you get exactly 10 quarts of water?" The teacher showed how to do the following hard problem: Get 100 quarts, given Jar A, holding 21 quarts, B, holding 127 quarts, and C, holding 3 quarts. (Answer: Fill B. Pour from it to fill A and to fill C twice. $B - A - 2C = 127 - 21 - 6 = 100$.) Pupils then worked many more problems with this same structure. When they were asked to get 20 quarts with 23-, 49-, and 3-quart measures, they rigidly applied the formula $B - A - 2C$. They could have obtained the goal more simply: $A - C = 23 - 3 = 20$. The ninth problem in the series gave 28-, 76-, and 3-quart jars, to get 25 quarts. This cannot be solved by the $B - A - 2C$ rule that had been practiced. Though the correct solution should be obvious, 80 per cent of a class sometimes fails to find it. This blindness is as common among college students as among sixth-graders.

When Luchins explored the reason for this failure to think, he found that pupils often had been taught *not* to think about numerical problems. Each day the teacher had demonstrated an arithmetic procedure and told them to do a page of exercises using exactly that procedure. At the end of the water-jar experiment, indeed, they complained. "You should have shown us the other way, too, if you wanted us to use it." Blind imitation was found especially often in tense and competitive classrooms. Pupils urged to work fast were less able to reinterpret. In schools that stressed obedience (said one teacher, "My pupils are very good; they always do exactly as they are told"), pupils were more concerned with doing what Luchins wanted than with getting a sensible answer (see also K. M. Miller, 1957). One can teach just the opposite attitude. Students warned not to stick to the "obvious" method, and told to look for alternatives, were far more flexible than other students not taught this way (Maier, 1933).

There is much other evidence on the importance of variety in the tasks presented during learning (Riopelle, 1953). Schroder and Rotter (1952) had students work problems under two conditions. One group was given problems where one approach always worked. The other group had to find a different method of attack for each problem. On a transfer test, the first group used the method they had practiced even when it gave an incorrect result. The latter group were flexible; they had learned to take an active, questioning attitude, and had learned how to judge the suitability of a proposed solution.

26. In what specific ways is the following statement (Bestor, 1955, p. 83) contradictory to the view of this and the preceding chapter? What conclusion do you reach regarding the issues raised?

"Statesmanship . . . calls for education, and for something more substantial than high-school civics. The men who drafted our Constitution were not trained for the task by "field trips" to the mayor's office and the county jail. They were endowed with the wisdom requisite for founding a new nation by *liberal* education. . . . Through study of the classics they came to the study of history and political philosophy and jurisprudence. And through these great disciplines they reached an understanding of the general problems of government."

27. How did persons like Washington and Jefferson learn to encode and decode the verbal principles of political philosophy? Did they in any sense learn by discovery?

28. What acts by others in the classroom reinforce a student's tendency

to ask a question that implies doubt or criticism of what the teacher has said? What acts provide negative reinforcement?

29. Comment on this statement:

> "Perhaps the best, if not the only way to promote fruitful thinking is to promote knowledge and a deeply set respect for facts. If facts of large or small portent cannot provoke a person to thinking, it is doubtful if a teacher or anything else can."

FLEXIBILITY AND DIVERGENT THINKING

Critical thinking is *convergent* (see page 234). The good thinker approaches his target by feedback and correction. He makes a try and anticipates its consequences. The better he can anticipate, the more certainly he will detect an error. Hence the expert convergent thinker resembles the expert who executes a physical skill under complex, unfamiliar conditions.

There are two important processes in problem solving: the creative formation of trial responses or hypotheses, and the critical process that disposes of unsound proposals. The critical process is negative; it tells what not to do, but it does not generate new plans. The first, creative phase is much less understood though some conclusions have been established. We know that it requires *divergent* abilities that are largely independent of the convergent abilities measured by the usual test. We know that it requires a flexible attitude, and that routine schooling may build up rigid habits that inhibit insight and creative reorganization. We know that emotional tension makes the thinker less able to find new ideas when his first tries fail (page 589).

The superior creative thinker is marked by an active approach. He enjoys exploring and rearranging possibilities. He finds pleasure in variety and in anticipating "what would happen if. . . ." He is, then, independent; he does not wait for someone to show him what to do. He is free to fail; when his idea proves worthless, he loses no self-respect. Much that is known about the creative process can be summarized by saying that the creator is playful. He does not take any one trial seriously. He enjoys the activity even when he is behind in score. His creations emerge from large amounts of "waste effort"—but no one throwing himself into a game tries to conserve his energy.

This playfulness is well illustrated in the data collected by Getzels and Jackson (1960). They compared two groups: pupils high on divergent thinking and not high on the convergent tasks of the Stanford-Binet, and pupils high on the Stanford-Binet and not high on divergent tasks. (Regrettably, no study was made of the equally numerous—and more talented—pupils high on both types of test.) When asked to make up stories about pictures, the pupils selected as better at divergent thinking were very much more likely to use humor and to give an unexpected ending. One picture shows a man in an airplane seat. Here is a typical reasonable, controlled answer from a high IQ pupil:

Mr. Smith is on his way home from a successful business trip. He is very happy and he is thinking about his wonderful family and how glad he will be to see them again. He can picture it, about an hour from now, his plane landing at the airport and Mrs. Smith and their three children all there welcoming him home again.

Contrast this with this story from a high-divergent pupil:

This man is flying back from Reno where he has just won a divorce from his wife. He couldn't stand to live with her anymore, he told the judge, because she wore so much cold cream on her face at night that her head would skid across the pillow and hit him in the head. He is now contemplating a new skid-proof face cream.

These pupils had only four minutes to write a story; the difference shows the creator's intellectual energy, impulsiveness, and willingness to try a response that may not "come off."

Flexibility and originality can be taught. Maltzman (1960) called off 25 common words such as *door* and *sky* six times and required college students to give a different "free association" on each presentation. Thus he required them to reach out, to diverge from the commonplace response. This simple "mind-stretching" exercise produced remarkable transfer to Guilford's Unusual Uses test of creative thinking. Each item in this test is of the form: "List unusual ways in which an automobile tire [or some other object] might be used. Give as many uses as you can." Subjects with experience in making uncommon word associations did much better on this test than others. Maltzman also found that performance on Unusual Uses declined in a group trained to repeat the first association whenever a word was presented twice. These short practice sessions do not teach new techniques of thinking; the results suggest strongly that originality is largely a matter of attitude or mental set. Feeling free to give a "wild" response is most important. The gains produced by Maltzman, while significant, are not so large as to suggest that a dullard can be made creative in a few hours.

At the University of Buffalo, a course in creative problem-solving has been tried (Meadow and Parnes, 1959; Parnes and Meadow, 1960). In this course, students were encouraged to "brainstorm," to toss ideas and proposals into a discussion without hesitation; evaluation of ideas (convergent thinking) was put off until later. There were significant increases in the flow and quality of responses on divergent thinking tests, and these gains persisted over at least eight months.

The teaching methods of Mr. Palmer, described earlier in this chapter, and of Mr. Osborne, an art teacher we shall meet in Chapter 15, are also intended to increase ability to create new ideas. There is too little research at present for us to recommend any one set of teaching procedures for this aim. No one has identified important verbal generalizations about creativity comparable to those used to improve the critical phase of thinking.

The general theme of all the techniques being tried experimentally is to encourage playfulness and the expression of tentative ideas without waiting to criticize them. Much of present teaching—of English, for example—is precisely opposite in spirit: "Know what you want to say before you say it." "Don't be careless." "Outline your ideas before you start writing."

30. What would you expect to happen if, over a semester, a seventh-grade English teacher graded the first draft of every composition on its interest, considering both content and style but completely ignoring grammar, spelling, and other mechanical aspects?

31. Illustrate the divergent and convergent phases of thinking as they appear in making plans for a Saturday evening date.

32. How would the impulsiveness of the creative pupil affect his score on a conventional mental test? Do you think that the Getzels-Jackson adolescent who wrote the flamboyant divorce story is as intelligent as the one who wrote the more controlled story?

33. Explain the finding that when teachers say which pupils they like to have in class, the high IQ pupils tended to be rated higher than the high divergent ones (Getzels and Jackson, 1960). Why should this fact be brought to the attention of teachers?

SUMMARY

Whether principles are presented ready-made or are discovered by the learner, meaning is highly important. A principle is learned faster, is retained longer, and is applied more effectively when it is meaningful. Meaning also contributes to motivation, as in the study of the second-graders who, finding fractions meaningful, made up further problems for themselves and so continued to learn.

Most research on forgetting has measured loss of fragmentary information, using the retest method. Such studies report a "forgetting curve" in which retention drops sharply after learning and then levels off at a low figure. But retention can be very high for major ideas and methods of attack on problems, for overlearned associations, and for factual materials that are appropriately reviewed. Forgetting is to be most expected for knowledge that is not used.

As forgetting takes place, the remaining traces are reorganized to provide a coherent structure that may or may not be correct. When attempting to recall lost knowledge, the person reconstructs a response from this fragmentary structure. The better his initial understanding, the more likely that a sound structure will be retained and the less likely that the reconstructed response will be wrong.

What is meaningful to a pupil is difficult to judge. Ability to recall the words of the text or to give a commonplace example may be developed without understanding. The only sure sign of understanding is transfer: successful response or explanation in a new situation, or construction of an original response. Much learning that could be meaningful is taught in the form of arbitrary associations. This is especially likely if the stimulus to which the pupil is to respond is always the same. Application to an unfamiliar situation shows some understanding. Comprehension is deepest when theoretical competence is reached, i.e., when various principles are organized into a system. While we value theoretical comprehension highly, such knowledge is worthless unless it can be decoded into a prescription for dealing with the concrete situation. The pupil's method of work and the nature of his errors are pertinent in judging whether or not the problem is meaningful. Stupid errors are those in which the parts are correct but internal relations between the parts are lacking. There is no end to improving the precision and depth with which a concept is understood.

Concepts simplify and thus misrepresent reality. Pupils accept much vaguer interpretations than the teacher and text intend, and refine their meanings only when they encounter difficulty. The test of discrimination is to present diverse objects or examples and ask the pupil to apply his concepts to them.

Images from concrete experience are a necessary background for comprehending an abstract relation. Verbal instruction that goes beyond the pupil's ability to visualize the relation and make it concrete is meaningless. Abstract instruction is much more transferable than concrete instruction, provided that it is understood. Concrete, prescriptive teaching is superior only for a fixed situation that is likely to recur.

Numerous examples are given of teaching procedures where the pupil participates in the formation of concepts and the discovery of principles. In true problem solving, the person does not know the answer and cannot find a ready formula in an authoritative source; he works it out for himself. Such problem solving prepares the pupil to recognize how knowledge is developed and to understand that knowledge is constantly being replaced by new principles. It reduces his trust in authority and corrects such mistaken views of knowledge as, for example, that mathematical results are universally "true." Current methods of teaching mathematics place considerable emphasis on intuitive understanding and the arousal of curiosity. Pupils are able to create new mathematical structures for themselves, defining their own concepts and working out generalizations.

It is generally unwise to end a discussion or an experiment without drawing a verbal conclusion. It is often advisable for the pupil to state his findings in his own words, even though his generalization should be checked by the teacher.

A discovered response is readily discriminated from alternative responses and hence better applied. Pupils are motivated when challenged to discover and when successful in doing so. Moreover, those who learn to create or discover for themselves acquire competence in the discovery process and confidence in their own independent intellectual powers. But discovery methods require more time than didactic methods. Also, pupils may not discover successfully, in which case their attitudes and understanding are damaged rather than helped. A certain degree of guidance is desirable in order to make certain that discovery is successful. We conclude that there should be some learning by discovery in every field of knowledge; beyond this minimum, however, adventurous participation is only one of several ways of making educational experience meaningful.

Studying verbal principles often fails to improve performance. In learning billiards, shooting through water, and other skills, verbal instruction produced little or no benefit, even though our theory suggests that a theoretical interpretation ought to improve adaptation. Studies by Ervin and by Gagné and Smith imply that verbal learning is not essential when correct solutions can be attained by informal use of cues, without verbal mediation, but that a verbal formulation is of great use in coping with a complex situation. Verbal instruction is useful only when the pupil can properly encode a concrete problem into a theoretical question and decode the answer given by the theory into an action.

There are many paths to the improvement of thinking. Solving problems in a given subject teaches specific tools and skills of analysis needed in that field. In addition, there are general principles of reasoning to be acquired. These are taught in the same way as generalizations in other fields; through concrete experience in problem solving, reflection on that experience, formulation of the conclusions as a verbal principle, and consideration of where the principle may be applied. Teaching reasoning as if it were itself significant subject matter has marked transfer value. Geometry students so taught improve in nongeometric reasoning, with no less mastery of geometry.

Attitudes that interfere with reasoning are frequently learned. Pupils, indeed, may be taught *not* to think when material is presented in a rote fashion, to be slavishly reproduced. Presenting varied tasks that cannot be treated successfully by a formula encourages flexible thinking and meaningful application of knowledge.

How to promote creative, divergent thinking is only beginning to be understood. Flexibility calls for emotional independence and the freedom to fail without damage to self-esteem. The creative thinker is playful; he does not care much about failure or imperfection. Encouraging wild responses seems to increase fluency of ideas and originality.

Reading List 11

William H. Burton *et al.*, "The Role of Concepts in Thinking," Chapter 9 in *Education for Effective Thinking* (New York: Appleton-Century-Crofts, 1960), pp. 152–69.

Concepts are defined and meaningful use of concepts is discussed. Eleven suggestions regarding teaching method are listed. Other parts of the book are also relevant to this chapter.

Harl R. Douglass and Herbert F. Spitzer, "The Importance of Teaching for Understanding," Chapter 2 in Nelson B. Henry, ed., *The Measurement of Understanding*, Forty-fifth Yearbook of the National Society for the Study of Education, Part I (Chicago: Univ. of Chicago Press, 1946), pp. 7–26.

The authors criticize conventional methods of teaching for excessive "verbalism," and give seven reasons for this overemphasis. They then point to methods of testing understanding which do not reward parroting of symbols that are not understood. In reading, you should try to decide how each of the seven factors they mention can be overcome.

Ellen Frogner, "Grammar Approach *Versus* Thought Approach in Teaching Sentence Structure," *English Journal*, 28 (1939), 518–26.

High-school pupils were trained to judge sentences in terms of their form and clarity, without reference to formal grammatical rules. The method produced ability superior to that of a group trained in formal grammar. Could formal analysis involving rules be expected to supplement the thought method, or would it be undesirable?

Edward M. Glaser, *An Experiment in the Development of Critical Thinking, Teachers College Contributions to Education*, No. 843 (New York: Teachers College, Columbia Univ., 1941).

Detailed results, including comments by teachers and students, show that an experimental program to teach reasoning in relation to language was highly successful. Teaching procedures are described, some of the reasoning tests are illustrated, and an excellent summary of prior research on reasoning is provided.

Gertrude Hildreth, "The Difficulty Reduction Tendency in Perception and Problem Solving," *Journal of Educational Psychology*, 32 (1941), 305–13.

Errors made by pupils in basic school subjects are shown to arise largely from efforts to simplify material into sensible patterns.

Joseph Katz and Nevitt Sanford, "The Curriculum in the Perspective of the Theory of Personality Development," Chapter 11 in Nevitt Sanford, ed., *The American College* (New York: Wiley, 1962), pp. 418–44.

The authors argue that many common practices in the college impede the development of independence, self-knowledge, and the creative use of intellect. They describe adventurous instruction in various college subjects that has the power to release individual talent.

A. S. Luchins and Edith H. Luchins, "A Structural Approach to the Teaching of the Concept of Area in Intuitive Geometry," *Journal of Educational Research*, 40 (1947), 528–33. Abridged in Phillips.

The authors describe discovery methods used with children from age 5 through high school, showing how hints are given and how pupils arrive at solutions based on insight.

CHAPTER **12** COMMUNICATING KNOWLEDGE

MAKING PRESENTATIONS EFFECTIVE

Presenting information is an art; success depends on the teacher's insight into his pupils, his knowledge of the topic, and his use of a style suited to his personality. There is no single pattern or model to be followed, but several general suggestions can be made.

OBTAINING FEEDBACK FROM THE STUDENT. Effective presentation requires the teacher to have a clear idea of the goal and to judge continually whether the class is following him. The teacher cannot assume that what he says is clear to the learner. An invitation to "hold up your hand if you have any questions" is not freely accepted. The teacher can rely to some extent on the pupils' actions and expressions; when they seem puzzled, it is always possible to backtrack and repeat or paraphrase. But unless the teacher knows the precise cause of confusion, the repetition may not remedy the difficulty at all.

Because it provides information regarding the pupils' comprehension, give-and-take discussion is generally better than a lecture in which pupils merely take notes. Likewise, the teacher who pauses to ask a provocative question finds out what has been left vague in the pupil's mind. While the teacher presenting material orally can use feedback from the class to alter his presentation, this is not possible in a written presentation. Questions interspersed in a text, however, have some value in showing each learner what he has and has not grasped. The questions make him more alert and make him more likely to reread sections that were not clear the first time.

Use of Language

The teacher or writer should avoid using a vocabulary more complex than the material requires. Important technical words must of course be introduced (in history, for example, *abolition* and *amendment*), but teachers and texts often use uncommon words that are not essential. "Upon the

TABLE 20

A difficult explanation (*Steward, 1941, p. 491*)

Anthropologists have long recognized that the spread of customs from one group of people to another—"diffusion" in anthropological terminology—accounts for at least nine tenths of the culture of any group. On its face, this would seem to assign any kind of economic determinism an insignificant role. An analysis of this problem, however, in the light of what is known of culture change among primitive peoples, both before and after they have experienced acculturation resulting from contact with European cultures, exposes its considerable complexity. Under certain conditions, subsistence patterns—that is the activities concerned with acquiring food, clothing, shelter and other things indispensable to existence—have imposed very narrow limits on possible variations of social and economic organization. Under other conditions, it is evident that considerable latitude is possible in the socio-economic structure. (Reading difficulty at twelfth-grade level.)

---

accession of Queen Victoria" has no advantage over "When Victoria became Queen." Technical words are appropriate when they communicate a more exact meaning than simpler words. When they are used, their meaning should be developed carefully. What counts in teaching is not how exactly an idea is expressed, but how exact is the meaning the learner gets from the sentence. Use of a word whose meaning for the student is vague causes inexact communication, no matter how precise the thought in the writer's mind.

A simple sentence structure makes ideas much easier to grasp. A passage with long, complex sentences is hard for the learner even when thoroughly clear to someone familiar with the topic. Compare the two versions of a paragraph in Tables 20 and 21. One is highly readable; the other is suited only to superior adolescents and adults. Often a speaker or writer uses a style far more elaborate than is needed to convey his meaning. This is invariably hazardous in educational presentations since the complicated expression is likely to confuse at least a few readers. To be sure, a communication goes too far in the direction of simplicity if it seems like "baby talk" to the student, but few teachers err in this direction.

REDUNDANCY. The teacher should guard against the temptation to "cover ground" rapidly. This phrase itself reveals a false conception of teaching. Exposing the pupil to an idea is not teaching; the exposure must be thorough enough that he comprehends and retains the important part of the presentation. Information can always be presented more rapidly than it can be grasped; language is a highly distilled extract of the speaker's thought.

It is therefore desirable that language intended to teach have much *redundancy*. A redundant communication is one in which there are extra

TABLE 21

Explanation simplified (Flesch, 1943, p. 69)

At least nine tenths of the culture of any group of people goes back to customs spread from another group. Scientists have known this for a long time. So it seems there is not much to the theory that our habits and ideas are shaped by the way we make our living. But it is not as simple as that. We know a lot about how primitive people change their customs. We know how they do that before they get in touch with European ways, and we know how they do it afterwards. In some cases there is very little they can change in the way they live and work together. It is all tied up with what they have to do to get food, clothing, shelter and what else they need. Under other conditions, we can see that the people have much leeway in the setup of their group life and work. (Reading difficulty at seventh-grade level.)

---

words, beyond those essential to carry the thought. Direct repetition is rather ineffective. It is better to restate the same idea in different language, or to elaborate by means of examples. The pupil who misunderstands one part of the communication, either through inattention or because some word is unclear to him, can catch his error if the same thought is echoed in several sentences. When an argument moves from one thought to another with no redundancy, he may not detect his misunderstanding. He has no chance to correct it, and the one distorted idea makes it impossible to make proper sense of the ideas that follow.

Admittedly, a speaker who repeats himself may be called uninteresting. But the main goal of the teacher in enlightenment, not entertainment. Experiments were made comparing nonredundant speeches with redundant versions in which important parts were reiterated. Comprehension and retention were higher for the redundant speeches, even though interest was rated lower (Cantril and Allport, 1935).

The ancient "completion test," usually considered to be a way of testing memory, has been adapted by W. L. Taylor (1953, 1956) to test the comprehensibility of a passage. We think of a message as clear and distinct if we can understand it in the presence of noise. Taylor introduces "noise" into written material by blotting out randomly selected words, and asks a reader to guess the missing words with the aid of the surrounding context. If the passage is sufficiently redundant to overcome this interference, there is a margin of safety for the reader who has trouble comprehending a phrase here and there. Taylor calls this the "cloze" technique, since filling in the blanks demands what the psychologist calls *closure*, the completion of a sensible structure.

Tables 22 and 23 provide examples of the cloze technique. Table 22 was made by rewriting a passage from an outstanding medical text to avoid

TABLE 22

The cloze technique applied to a passage with low redundancy (for key to completions, see page 402)

Several peculiarities of the nervous system —————————— a study of its pathology desirable. The —————————— system is the integrator of activity. Its ——————————, which have extraordinarily long processes called ——————————, make up the conduction apparatus. A minute —————————— may produce extensive effects.

---

redundancy present in the original version. After rewriting, every fifth word—not counting *and, the, of,* and similar words—was replaced by a blank. You can still comprehend much of the passage, but the meaning is not sharply clear. Table 23 presents the passage as it originally appeared. Even with words omitted, the original passage can be almost completely understood. Note how the author expanded the first sentence. The added words do not convey extra ideas. The redundant style echoes the ideas so that the reader is more certain to get the full meaning. Teachers can evaluate teaching materials by mutilating passages in this manner and asking typical pupils to fill in the meaning. This is a more fundamental test of "readability" than inspecting sentence length and other features of style.

1. Redundancy reduces the amount of material a professor can "pack into" a series of lectures. What determines the ideal balance between coverage and redundancy?

2. How is redundancy beneficial in material that is to be studied intensively and repeatedly?

3. What proportion of the words were removed from Table 23 to produce the passage in Table 22? Did any of these words carry meaning the competent reader could not infer from the low-redundancy version?

4. How redundant is each of the following passages? Depending on your answer, rewrite the passage to decrease or increase its redundancy.

"A possible point of departure in analyzing the nature of mental processes in relation to the products of thought is through investigations of problem-solving. Problems can be selected for which only a limited number of solutions are appropriate, although the methods by which the solutions are reached cannot be so easily limited. It is possible to select problems such that some can be solved quickly and simply by the subject, while others tax the subject's mental resources to the utmost" (Bloom and Broder, 1950).

"Allergic disorders constitute a number of reactions occurring in different organs of the body. Eczema, asthma, hay fever, hives, and swellings of the lips and eyelids are the most common manifestations of allergy. There is no general agreement as to what causes allergic reactions, although, with the development of psychosomatic medicine, increasing attention has been paid to psychological factors" (Fouracre, 1960, p. 1002).

TABLE 23

The cloze technique applied to a passage with high redundancy (from Cobb, 1958, p. 158; for key to completions, see page 402)

Neuropathology is, of course, a part of _____ pathology, just as much as the _____ of the blood, but there are several _____ of the nervous system which make a special _____ of its pathology desirable. In the first _____ the central nervous system is the _____ of bodily activity, the special conduction _____ between irritable tissues, i.e., between _____ and effectors. This conduction apparatus is _____ up of neurons—special cells with extraordinarily _____ processes, the axons. An accurate knowledge of _____ conduction paths is essential and of _____ practical importance, because a minute _____ injury may produce extensive, _____ and distant effects.

Organization

The teacher should emphasize main points as explicit generalizations. Students have notorious difficulty in extracting the main points from college lectures. The informal discussion often ends with a blurry impression in the learner's mind, even though the teacher had four specific ideas to bring out. The teacher has many devices for stressing main points so that they provide a structure around which details can be gathered. An outline can be made clear in a text by headings or in a lecture by such signposts as, "And now we turn to the second phase of the cycle, in which carbon dioxide is changed to oxygen." Some teachers put the outline for a lecture on the blackboard before they begin, so that the student knows where he is going. It is nearly always advantageous to write new words and key ideas on the blackboard as they are introduced. The main points should be compiled by the teacher or perhaps by the class to provide a summary.

MEANINGFUL WHOLES. A continuous internal structure is especially important in presentations for the elementary school. The child finds it difficult to arrange a meaningful whole from an experience cluttered with detail (Wohlwill, 1960a). Plot continuity in stories is necessary for him; an adult can keep subplots in order. A continuous, dominant melody is helpful in music a child is to appreciate; an adult can take in more complex counterpoint. In explanations and descriptions for the child, one should give the main ideas in a straightforward way, keeping details and anecdotes clearly subordinate.

When the nature of any detail is determined by the whole—and this is true for machines, scientific theories, literature, and history—then understanding of the part must wait on comprehension of the whole. Before presenting details, it is wise to give a general view of the whole, so that each part will be more meaningful.

Ausubel (1960) has shown the value of an advance organization which provides a structure for the reader. Two groups of students were asked to study abstract text material on Buddhism; two days before, one group had read a short preparatory passage summarizing the main ideas of the text. Those who read the preview were more successful in learning and retaining the content. They were better able to learn even technical facts that had not appeared in the preview.

Working from the whole to a part is preferable to building up the whole bit by bit. Instead of describing the Spanish-American War, the World Court, World War I, and so on, one after the other, it is better to begin with a panoramic view of America's emergence into world leadership. Instead of teaching the radio circuit by going from one tube to the next, the teacher should sketch the major functional blocks, and then move down to smaller details. The whole, when understood, gives meaning to the parts.

The importance of an over-all orientation which "maps" the situation for the learner is nicely demonstrated by a Russian experiment in which children were to learn to push a toy automobile through a maze while blindfolded. Some children were allowed several preliminary trials in which they could "feel out" the general organization of the maze with their fingers. These children, when pushing the auto, had a sense of direction; they made mistakes, but they were never lost. Six-year-olds given ten preliminary opportunities to explore the maze mastered the path for the auto in four trials. Without this orientation, each mistake was disrupting; on the average, 32 trials were required to learn the path (Zaporozhets, 1957).

The organization that seems to be most useful generally is the *whole-then-part* approach, which we can illustrate, as used by a class in studying a play (Dora E. Palmer, 1949). The first step is to get a sense of the whole, the main plot line. The teacher might give a summary, or the pupils might read the play superficially to identify the main action. Having the over-all plot in mind, pupils then can see each act as a unit and look for its basic events. The first act can now be read to comprehend *its* main contributions to the plot or to character revelation. When the pattern of the act is clear, it is time to place attention on particular speeches or single lines. In fact, without the larger setting pupils would find interpretation of these details difficult. The progress from gross structure to detail equips pupils for whatever activity is appropriate: learning lines, staging the play, analyzing the dramatist's technique, or working out paintings to express the ideas. This approach is far different from reading the play line by line, requiring each word to be understood in order. Only when literature is very simple for the

KEY TO COMPLETIONS, *Table 22:* make, central, neurons, axons, injury

KEY TO COMPLETIONS, *Table 23:* general, pathology, peculiarities, study, place, integrator, apparatus, receptors, made, long, these, great, focal, complex reader can he read for both the whole sense and the line-by-line meaning at once.

The "whole" must not be larger than the pupils can comprehend. The proper whole is to be judged by the readiness of the pupils as well as by the subject matter. The character of local and state governments can be seen most logically within the total framework of government services and powers. But the pupil would be hopelessly confused if such a comprehensive picture were his first introduction to government. If the third grade is to understand meteors, the teacher should describe the sun with the earth revolving around it, and the meteor swarms through which the earth passes. This is the minimum "whole" necessary to get a correct picture of the "part," the meteor coming into the earth's atmosphere and blazing up for a moment. This is only a sketchy framework: the moon and the other planets are omitted, and little is said about the universe beyond the solar system. But enough is presented to clarify where meteors come from, why we can't see them steadily, and why they recur in yearly cycles. The explanation would fail unless pupils could comprehend the earth moving around the sun, and some pains would have to be taken with this notion that seems to defy common sense.

5. Does "the whole give meaning to the parts" when
   a. a pupil is memorizing a poem of many stanzas?
   b. a pupil is learning the functions of the parts of a plant?
   c. a pupil is learning the principal parts of an irregular verb?
6. What "whole" might be appropriate if a high-school class is studying the publication of a newspaper? if a third grade is studying it?
7. Fourth-graders are to learn about Egypt from a map. Which of the principles of presentation above can be applied in designing and using the map?

Audio-visual Devices

Sometimes concepts to be learned cannot be described verbally and cannot be introduced concretely into the pupil's life. The Arctic is too far away, the migration of birds covers too much territory, the French Revolution is long past, the marketing of wheat is a complex flow of events. Visual aids bring these to the classroom in a form the pupil can comprehend. A well-planned motion picture can give an experience as vivid as if the pupil had lived through the event. Because photography can take close-up views and long views, can retard motion or telescope time, the camera shows some relations more clearly than direct observation. Dramatic sound recordings (e.g., the "You Are There" series) bring to life the events pupils cannot observe at first hand.

In view of the increasing attention to television as a medium of instruction, we should discuss briefly whether it has any special virtues. Closed-circuit television is primarily a means of giving the student a closer look at whatever the teacher is doing; it multiplies the number of "front-row seats," and sometimes, as in a demonstration of practices in dentistry, brings the student much closer than would otherwise be possible.

Broadcast television, however, seems rarely to have any inherent advantage over teaching by film. Anything that can be televised can be presented on a classroom film, with equally good educational results. The exception is news of the moment, such as a Presidential press conference, where interest is heightened by seeing the event as it happens. The advantages of television over film are that television programs are produced more cheaply and that the teacher finds it convenient to tune in a scheduled broadcast, but finds it a chore to choose and order films, and to thread a projector. The teacher relying on broadcasts is not free to schedule the experience to fit into other class activities, cannot preview the program to judge its usefulness for his group, and cannot rerun part of it when pupil response shows this to be desirable. All these are possible with films.

Whether on film or television, a run-of-the-camera travelogue or laboratory demonstration has less impact than a carefully edited presentation in which segments are repeated, shown from different angles, organized to point out similarities and contrasts, and clarified by supplementary diagrams, summaries of main points, and other expository devices. It is easy to be over-impressed with brilliant technical effects. Studies by Lumsdaine (1958, p. 24) and others indicate that an animated motion picture made from crude sketches frequently teaches as much as a superbly polished color film costing ten times as much to produce. Lumsdaine properly advises the producer to spend more time and funds working out a teachable plan and a clear presentation, and less in the pursuit of technical photographic perfection.

A richly varied concrete or pictorial experience by no means develops all the meanings it could, unless the teacher makes these meanings explicit. Perception is always selective, and the teacher, by directing the pupils' attention, greatly influences what they take from an experience. M. A. May and Lumsdaine (1958, pp. 165 ff.) showed a simple film on the rotation of the earth, in which many photographs and drawings of a globe representing the earth were supposed to make various ideas clear. Fifth-graders learned certain items fairly well. "The axis is an imaginary line" went from 16 per cent knowledge on a pretest to 56 per cent knowledge on a post-test. But other items—"What fraction of the earth's surface is in daylight at any one time?"—showed no gains even though in the picture the fact seemed to be clear. The difference between the well-learned and rarely learned items is that the former were mentioned verbally in the film commentary and the latter were not.

The manner of presentation also makes a difference. What is dramatically presented is well learned.

> The boy in the picture carries the globe around the table to show why the seasons change. During the first part of the demonstration the globe is at the December position in relation to the lamp—the North Pole tilted away from the sun. When the boy carried the globe to the opposite (June) side of the table, he made two mistakes. First, he goes the wrong way around the table and, second, he holds the globe so that the North Pole is always tilted away from the sun. The father corrects these mistakes and emphasizes the counterclockwise revolution of the earth in its orbit. He also stresses the point that the North Pole of the earth's axis is always pointed toward the North Star. In moving the globe to the spring and fall position, the girl starts to make the same mistakes, but corrects them. Mention is made of this fact.

The gains on these items were exceptionally large; e.g., from 37 per cent before the film to 80 per cent after on, "The earth's axis is always pointed toward the North Star." In the previous chapter we recommended drawing a verbal generalization from a project or activity; here we reach a similar conclusion: learning from visual aids should be fixed in words (cf. Menchinskaya, 1957).

The teaching value of audio-visual devices lies not in the gadgetry but in the pupil's thought and feelings. The teacher is often overconfident that pupils have "had an experience" merely because they were shown something that might have been instructive. Venn (1946; see also Wesley, 1962) showed a well-edited film on the nervous system to college psychology students individually. He questioned each one carefully to see how much could be recalled immediately afterward. The students had grasped only a fraction of the content. A second showing taught almost as many additional ideas as the first run. On one run, the viewer literally does not see all that is shown. Some of what he does see has no meaning until the structure of the whole presentation becomes clear. This same effect occurs in reading; that is why we advise students to *study* texts rather than to read them once over lightly. But the idea of *studying* visual aids is strange to teachers and pupils, and often to textbook illustrators and film producers. A picture in the classroom should be an intellectual resource, not a decoration or entertainment.

    8. Television is used in colleges to transmit what is done by the instructor to additional classrooms or to the back of an auditorium. What advantages or disadvantages does this method have compared to each of the following? Can the disadvantages be overcome?
        a. presenting a demonstration several times to separate sections in a small classroom without television
        b. showing a video tape recording of last year's presentation of the same material
    9. A class is puzzled by the fact that a large body of Germans responded eagerly to Hitler's program, swept him into power, and supported his regime

enthusiastically. Knowing that his plans actually led to the disruption of Germany, the class wants to know how he gained such a hold on the people. How could they be helped to realize how the German people felt?

AUTOMATIC, PROGRAMED INSTRUCTION

In the school with which we are familiar, the ideal teacher plans activities and presentations to fit his class, continually watches their progress, and changes his technique artistically as they show understanding or confusion, interest or boredom. This picture of a pupil-teacher relationship as personal as that of patient and physician has been dramatically challenged by the recent rise of teaching machines and other "automatic," highly standardized instructional procedures.

Teaching machines excite some educators and alarm others. Some prophets have visualized a schoolroom in which the pupil spends his whole day happily pushing buttons to answer questions and collecting token rewards from the machine. The critics see the same prospect as a cruel imprisonment, which threatens to mold children in a predetermined pattern and to destroy their creativity. The possibilities of automated teaching are only beginning to be explored (for the history of the movement, see Lumsdaine, 1959).

It is extremely difficult to arrive at a just evaluation of proposals for automated instruction at present. Techniques are changing month by month, and the research studies available provide only sketchy answers to our major questions. We shall describe the devices as they are emerging and consider some of the claims for them. Whether these claims prove to be justified or not, this new line of experimentation is bound to have a lasting effect upon teaching methods and therefore merits careful attention.

Some devices now being promoted are little more than old-fashioned workbooks. At the other extreme there is a system in which the pupil is shown a complex scene, map, or object on a television screen, is asked a question, and punches his answer on a keyboard wired to an electronic computer. The computer evaluates his answer and decides what explanation or question should next appear on his screen. One feature of these devices is *active response by the pupil, immediately scored*, that is, continual trial and correction. Even more important is the sequencing of material so that every question will elicit a response *readily available to the pupil*. The program of instructional material is more significant than the physical device for presenting it.

We have used the word *program* previously, first to discuss the neural programs that direct the speech mechanism, later in discussing skilled performance as a highly organized sequence of activities. It is used here with a similar meaning. A program is a prearranged sequence of explanations and questions. A program for a course is a carefully planned progression of ideas, beginning with elementary notions and working up to relatively complex theories or applications.

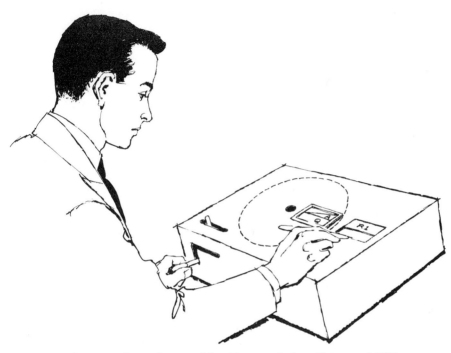

91 *A teaching machine designed by Skinner (after Skinner, 1958)*

The questions are printed on the rim of a disk. One question at a time appears at position Q. After the student has written his answer on the paper tape, he shifts the lever, which moves his answer upward beneath a plastic strip at R1 and exposes the correct answer at A for comparison.

Automatic Procedures

AN ILLUSTRATIVE TRAINING PROGRAM.   As a first example of programed instruction, let us return to the teaching of aircraft recognition (cf. page 379). Suppose that you are to learn to identify four planes. We put you before a machine whose principal features are a screen and four push buttons, and a clip in which we can mount specimen pictures of the four planes, labeled A to D. A projector behind the screen flashes words and pictures onto it. There is no need to discuss engineering details; every machine differs (Galanter, 1959). Our machine will use pictures mounted at the edge of a disk, 20 frames to a disk; it has an automatic changer to slip a new disk into place in the projector.

You turn on the switch, and the first frame appears. It reads: "You are to push the button to show which plane you see on each picture, or to answer whatever question you are asked. Which plane is this?" The frame shows a picture identical to that of plane A in the specimen set. You recognize it easily and press button A, the machine turns the disk, and you see a new picture and a new question. Had you pushed the wrong button, the machine would not have advanced; only a correct response brings the next question. Slightly differing views of the planes make up the initial, very easy set of 20 recognition tasks. The questions gradually become more difficult. Perhaps the sixth panel shows a diagram of a delta wing, and says, "This is called a delta wing. Which plane has a delta wing?" Your attention has thus been focused on one of the significant cues. In the later pictures the planes are seen from angles that make fewer cues available.

When you reach the end of the disk, the machine prints a personal record card: "Disk 1, Feb. 3, 16 correct." The next disk is selected by a rule: If the score is 15 or higher, present disk 2; if below 15, present disk 1A. Disk 2 is more advanced, with the pictures harder to judge. Disk 1A gives further practice on the simple discriminations of disk 1. Instruction continues along these lines. You can work for a reasonable period each day, starting at the level determined by your previous performance. There may be dozens of disks to work through, until the machine, certain that you can recognize the four planes from any angle and distance, "graduates" you.

The procedure ordinarily adopted with machine instruction differs in important ways from the usual classroom teaching (Stolurow, 1960, 1961):

The pupil continually responds. There are no idle moments while someone else recites, while a discussion takes place that he pays no attention to, or while the teacher explains to the laggards something he has already grasped.

The response is overt and in a form to be objectively judged. A class discussion sometimes seems to encourage the pupil even for a vague "contribution." The machine gives no encouragement for mere participation. The pupil must make a definite response; if he is confused, his need for instruction is exposed.

There is prompt feedback. An error is detected at once. The question is not set aside until he has learned the correct answer. Compare this to the usual out-of-class assignment. The pupil does a dozen problems, perhaps making the same error in all of them. The correct answers may not be discussed until the class meets three days later; the teacher does not discover this pupil's trouble until he marks the paper at a still later time.

Sufficient cues and sufficient initial explanation are given to eliminate groping or discovery. The initial items are very easy. Difficulty is introduced by gradually withdrawing some of the cues or by bringing in more complicated examples.

Ideas and questions appear in a carefully planned sequence. Successive questions are pitched just within the learner's reach; if he has done well at one level he should be able to stretch his knowledge to succeed on the next. Questions are pretested to eliminate points of difficulty and to determine the criterion for moving ahead to the next set of questions. Compare this to the traditional class: the teacher decides casually to assign five rather than ten homework problems; the problems form no orderly sequence; a uniform assignment is given to the whole class. The teacher casually schedules three class days for the study of the earthworm.

Measurement of proficiency is instantly used to modify the instruction. The student works at a pace determined by his success. The average student will have to work through, say, two disks at each level in order to meet the standard. If unusually able, he may reach the standard with one disk per level. When he has trouble, he can stay at a particular level until his trouble is overcome. (Perhaps after three tries at one level, the fourth disk will review information from earlier levels that apparently slipped past him.) After two weeks, some students will be ready for graduation, and some may still be working at a fairly elementary level. The pace is adjusted even within the hour; the student is not assigned to a particular group and left there for weeks or months without reconsideration.

The instruction is highly adaptable. The teacher can at any time take a laggard off the machine for special help, or set up a supplementary activity for the student who is ahead of schedule. The machine can be set to require a fast response, if that is a goal. The specimen pictures can be removed so that the learner must classify the planes from memory. Programs can be arranged to require short written responses. When the student has completed his answer, he presses a button and a standard answer appears.

The instruction is automatic, independent of the instructor. In theory, the material could be installed in a room on a military base where no one knows anything about the aircraft pictured. Men could be assigned to the machine for a certain period of time daily. A clerk could collect the record cards monthly and mail them to headquarters to show that the training is moving forward as planned. Assuming that students want to learn, the system takes care of everything else: explanation, special attention to points where the student makes errors, review, and measurement of proficiency.

Aircraft recognition is ideally suited to automatic teaching: the answers are simple; considerable practice is needed to develop accurate discrimination of cues; and the material has little intellectual depth that might demand reflective thought. Historically, the idea of teaching-without-a-teacher originated with such materials. S. L. Pressey suggested (1926, 1927) that multiple-choice tests could be scored as they are taken, and went on to propose that machines which do this could also teach "drill material." Pressey's words at that time anticipate the tone of much current advocacy of machines:

The writer has seen somewhere the statement that education is at present the most inefficiently carried on of any large-scale undertaking in this country. . . . There are at present many things now done in our schools and colleges in very unnecessarily labored and enthusiasm-killing fashion. The writer is convinced that mechanical aids are possible which would do much to relieve the situation. . . . They would leave the teacher more free for her most important work, for developing in her pupils fine enthusiasms, clear thinking, and high ideals. (The writer's suggestions may very likely provoke some sentimentalists to an outcry against "education by machine." What the writer is urging is a freeing of the teacher from the mechanical tasks of her profession—the burden of paperwork and routine drill—so that she may be a real teacher, not largely a clerical worker.)

Pressey's idea, long neglected, was revived by B. F. Skinner. Skinner, an experimental psychologist, had succeeded to a remarkable degree in training pigeons to make complex responses—indeed, to the point of guiding an aerial bomb onto a moving target (1960) and playing ping-pong with another pigeon (1954). Skinner considers that behavior is mostly a matter of selecting a response from one's repertoire. He would say that learning to make one response rather than another comes about through reinforcement, i.e., through trying the response and being immediately rewarded. Judging the pupil's tries and rewarding the desired ones can be reduced to a mechanical process, he says, and hence is no proper task for a professional teacher. "Marking a set of papers in arithmetic—'yes, 9 and 6 *are* 15; no, 9 and 7 *are not* 18'—is beneath the dignity of any intelligent individual" (1954).

Skinner (1958) reports:

At five or six frames per word, four grades of spelling may require 20,000 or 25,000 frames; and three or four grades of arithmetic, as many again. If these figures seem large, it is only because we are thinking of the normal contact between teacher and pupil. Admittedly, a teacher cannot supervise 10,000 or 15,000 responses made by each pupil per year. But the pupil's time is not so limited. In any case, surprisingly little time is needed. Fifteen minutes per day on a machine should suffice for each of these programs, the machines being free for other students for the rest of each day.

While Skinner's proposals were popularized under the name of "teaching machines," the machine is by no means fundamental. Not only do the machines vary widely in what they can do, but all the features of automated instruction listed above can be achieved by printed materials presented without a machine. There are "scrambled" textbooks, for example, that present a short lesson followed by questions. The student scores his answers with a printed key, and is told to turn to another page. If his score is high, he goes to page 212 for the next lesson; if not, he goes to page 296 for a second presentation of the lesson in a slightly different form, with new exercises. Only when he reaches a satisfactory score may he go to page 212. Another device, costing only a few pennies per student, uses a ribbon to pull a mimeographed sheet past an opening in a cardboard folder. The student writes his answer to a question, then pulls the sheet upward until he sees the answer printed two lines below, which provides confirmation. The teacher chooses the next sheet for him to work on, depending upon his score on this page.

When Pressey discussed the possibilities of mechanizing "drill," he had in mind the usual miscellaneous, unordered collection of exercises. Aircraft recognition is often taught in just that way, training being accomplished through hundreds of trial-and-error responses. Skinner's theory of learning emphasizes that one retains the responses that are confirmed; he considers it wasteful to have the student try false interpretations and discover that they are incorrect. Hence Skinner, when he began to teach, sought to arrange the questions so that the pupil was very likely to answer each one correctly. He did this by starting with easy questions, by presenting necessary information, and by advancing the difficulty of questions in "small steps." Skinner's learning theory thus required increasing attention to programing.

10. Which of these features is important in a teaching device?
   a. an arrangement that prevents the pupil from cheating by looking at the answer before responding
   b. an arrangement that requires the pupil to construct the correct response instead of selecting one among several alternatives
   c. a score at the end of every series of questions
11. Classify the following as suited or not suited to automatic teaching.
   a. bidding bridge hands
   b. interpreting a poem
   c. preparing a business letter of a frequently occurring type
   d. understanding how the seasons are determined by the motions of the earth relative to the sun
12. Discuss this statement: "The teaching machine does exactly what an individual tutor would do in helping the student to learn the same material."
13. In programed learning the student is expected to progress as far as he can in the time available, mastering whatever he has covered thoroughly. Skinner (1958) says:

The "grade" will change its meaning. In traditional practice a C means that a student has a smattering of a whole course. But if machine instruction assures mastery at every stage, a grade will be useful only in showing *how far* a student has gone. C might mean that he is halfway through a course. Given enough time he will be able to get an A.

Will such grades serve the usual purposes of grading?
14. What sorts of individual differences does automatic instruction not take into account?

Programing

No other teaching procedure takes the principle of readiness so seriously. The pupil is, ideally, to move to a new idea only when he individually has demonstrated his intellectual readiness for it. And—in theory—no question is presented until sufficient readiness has been developed by the preceding questions to prepare him for almost certain success.

Ideally, the program is a thoroughly orderly arrangement of questions and explanations. Every lesson, and every question within the lesson, is built on interpretations and associations that preceding questions supposedly have taught. In most textbooks the teacher can take up chapters in whatever order he prefers or can omit lessons he considers unimportant. In an integrated program this is impossible. The learner can respond to the tenth unit only if he has mastered the content of the preceding nine units. It is precisely this systematic, cumulative sequence that distinguishes modern programed instruction from old-fashioned repetitive drill on fragments of information. In principle, the programer would like to arrange the learner's encounters with American history, for example, in a cradle-to-graduation sequence such that each new fact would be introduced only after he has acquired the more basic information that would give it meaning.

Skinner stresses a "small step" principle. Each question, he believes,

---

1. **Manufacture** means to make or build. *Chair factories manufacture chairs.* Copy the word here:

     □ □ □ □ □ □ □ □ □ □

2. Part of the word is like part of the word **factory.** Both parts come from an old word meaning *make* or *build.*

     m a n u □ □ □ □ u r e

3. Part of the word is like part of the word **manual.** Both parts come from an old word for *hand.* Many things used to be made by hand.

     □ □ □ □ f a c t u r e

4. The same letter goes in both spaces:
     m □ n u f □ c t u r e

5. The same letter goes in both spaces:
     m a n □ f a c t □ r e

6. **Chair factories** □ □ □ □ □ □ □ □ □ □ chairs.

---

92   *Each step in the program is a tiny one*

A demonstration program for the teaching of spelling prepared by Skinner (1958).

should move only a small distance beyond the questions the pupil has already answered. After providing sufficient cues or hints to call forth a desired answer, the programer can remove some of the cues and ask him to respond again. If this increase in task difficulty were gradual enough, he would never make an error. Figure 92 illustrates how Skinner teaches a spelling word. The pupil answers one question, then compares his answer with the correct one in the manner of Figure 91. It is almost impossible to make an error; one question serves to emphasize the response required by the next. The program is a highly redundant communication. Redundancy is achieved by sheer repetition, by repeating the same thought in new language, and by developing logical interconnections so that the answer to one question follows meaningfully from the preceding explanations and responses.   We do not know how necessary it is to premasticate subject matter. Some programs that cut up the material into tiny bits seem very tedious and take a long time to complete. There can be alternative programs with steps of different sizes; many small steps for the less able pupil, larger steps to challenge the bright one.

In the spelling program there is just one "route" through the material. Every pupil responds to the same questions, save that some pupils must repeat sections where they have made many errors whereas others go straight ahead. In contrast to this "linear" sequence, some programs "branch." The answer the learner gives to a question determines what stimulus he is next presented. If he is correct, he moves forward. If he is wrong the nature of his error suggests where he is confused. He is given a fresh explanation and a series of questions to test and to fix in mind his revised interpretation. Branching procedures assume that there is a reason behind each error, and that the program should make intelligent use of that information just as a live teacher would. The linear program seeks to produce its effects entirely by eliciting correct responses, ignoring errors rather than discussing them.

15. Can one best sequence be found for presenting a body of information about a topic such as the age of the earth?

16. Discuss this proposition: "If the teacher has to work individually with a student who is having difficulty with a program, it is a sign that the program writer did not do his job well."

17. What similarities are there between our suggestions for effective presentation by the teacher (page 420) and the principles used in automatic instruction?

18. What principles demonstrated in the development of programs and automatic presentation and scoring can be applied by the teacher trying to improve a student's composition?

Experimental Results

The present formal evidence on programed instruction is fragmentary, often derived from brief instruction employing hastily developed programs. One of the chief merits of programing is that it specifies each step in teaching so that it can be thoroughly pretested and revised, and standardized in the form that proves best. But few of the programs used in experiments to date have been put through patient tryout and editing, so that programing at its best has not been tested. Furthermore, there has been no adequate test of the claim that when pupils proceed through programs at their own rates, bright pupils progress further than slow learners in the same period of time. Nearly all the experiments have compared groups studying the same instructional material, presented in different ways. We have no adequate histories of long-continued programed instruction in which each pupil is working at his own level, and no adequate observations on the integration of programed instruction with class instruction.

The studies now available suggest that automatic, programed instruction teaches facts and verbally mediated responses as effectively as conventional procedures (Evans *et al.*, 1960; Lumsdaine and Glaser, 1960). There have been, for example, reports of success in teaching factory assembly operations, a highly verbal psychology course, and bridge-playing.

One set of programed textbooks for traditional high-school curricula was developed by mathematicians and tried in dozens of classes. Each pupil proceeded through the book at his own rate, with help from the teacher as needed. His end-of-year performance on a standard test was compared with that in similar groups taught from a conventional text. The preliminary report (Allen Calvin, personal communication) states that when teachers are favorable to the new approach, class performance is at least equal to that of conventional classes, sometimes quite a bit superior; when teachers are unfavorable, class performance on programed materials is inferior. Other studies report that "small-step" programs produce somewhat greater learning than large steps; but the small-step program takes longer, and it appears that making the steps extremely small has a bad effect.

Students do not really reach 100 per cent mastery of the programed material. Indeed, a close scrutiny of some studies shows startling deficiencies of learning. For example, college students worked on a unit from the Holland-Skinner psychology course (Figure 93). After working through the unit, which required one to two hours, they took a 36-item test. The test was also given to a control group which had had conventional class lessons unrelated to the subject of the programed unit. A mean and standard deviation are reported (Coulson and Silberman, 1960):

	Mean	s.d.	Approximate range (two s.d. on each side of mean)
Experimental group	25.1	5.9	36–13 (100%–36%)
Control group (untaught)	17.0	5.2	27–7 (75%–20%)

There is a real difference between groups, not surprising when we recall that the control group had not studied the topic tested. But at least half of the students taught by this very carefully developed program fell within the range of scores made by control students answering on the basis of general background knowledge.

This one result does not warrant any verdict on programed instruction or even on the Holland-Skinner programed text. It does, however, make clear the importance of scrutinizing experimental results. Educators will have to look closely at evidence on programed instruction as it accumulates in the next several years. More than that, they should ask publishers for test data to show the effectiveness of the particular programs they are considering for adoption. One of the chief virtues of programed instruction is that the process of tryout necessarily generates such data.

◢	Technically speaking, a reflex involves an eliciting stimulus in a process called elicitation. A stimulus ——————— a response.	1–8
elicits　　　　　1–8	To avoid unwanted nuances of meaning in popular words, we do not say that a stimulus "triggers," "stimulates," or "causes" a response, but that it ——————— a response.	1–9
elicits　　　　　1–9	In a reflex, the stimulus and the elicited response occur in a given temporal order; first the (1) ———————, then the (2) ———————.	1–10
(1) stimulus (2) response　1–10	A kick of the leg is ——————— by a tap on the patellar tendon.	1–11
elicited　　　　　1–11	The time which elapses between the onset of the stimulus and the onset of the response is called the latency. Thus the time between tap and kick is the ——————— of the knee-jerk reflex.	1–12

93 *Programed instruction in college introductory psychology*

In this text by Holland and Skinner (1961), each question appears on one page; the answer and the next question appear on the following page.

We are not able to greet teaching machines, self-teaching texts, and the other products of this new movement as a great breakthrough comparable to the invention of printing. These devices are designed primarily to impart knowledge, and seem to be neither better nor worse for this purpose than conventional methods of presentation. They are likely to have an important place wherever their administrative convenience is an advantage. In industry, for example, a machine can train one or two newly hired workers much more cheaply than a human instructor can. The high-school pupil may concentrate more if working at a machine that "keeps score" than he does during the usual supervised study. Machines may have special functions in the education of the advanced student or in remedial work.

The evidence now available gives little support for the original view that instruction calling for one active response after another will teach better than a straightforward lecture or text. There are now several studies in which some students had to respond actively to the programed text (e.g., fill in a blank and check against the correct answer), while other students studied the same program with the blanks filled in. That is to say, the second group was merely asked to study the text material in the usual manner. (Sometimes the words that constitute "answers" were underlined.) These experiments showed that reading a programed text produces as much learning as does making active responses to the program. Moreover, the reading accomplishes the same results in less time (Silverman and Alter, 1960; Goldbeck, 1960; Case and Roe, 1961; Goldbeck and Campbell, 1962; Keislar and McNeil, 1962; Krumboltz and Weisman, 1962). Very likely, a well-motivated student will profit more from textbook reading than from an equal time given to programed response-plus-reinforcement.

But this is true only with a very superior textbook. Programed explanations have great clarity; if properly tried out, they must have, since tryout pupils will bog down at any muddy spot. No textbook or lecture is checked out in such detail. Once the program is in good sequential form, with every step of reasonable size, the pupil who is motivated can learn merely by reading it. Overt response is of little importance when a presentation is so highly meaningful that the right response is readily discriminated from all others. The teaching machine is only a technique of classroom management; the programed sequence of ideas is a technique of *instruction*.

The trial-and-feedback step seems most important (a) with learners who have to be kept at the task by artificial controls, (b) with subject matter that cannot be put in words, or (c) with instructional materials that are unclear. Nothing in these findings diminishes the importance of active response in learning sensory discriminations. In acquiring a motor skill, the student cannot possibly learn to respond to cues arising within his own body save by active trial. The findings do imply that active response is less necessary in intellectual learning than psychologists have previously believed (recall the quotation from Pressey and Robinson, page 283).

We have no reason to doubt the claimed advantage of presenting ideas in a tightly knit, carefully sequenced, and pretested program. But there still is the large and unanswered question: What interpretations and responses can be adequately taught through programed presentation? Programing works well for highly structured material where there are fixed stimuli to respond to and a definitely correct response. One can program spelling and vocabulary, and also the more complicated skills of arithmetic, choice among grammatical forms, and balancing chemical equations. We know little about the extent to which programs can develop insight into the nature of a subject or ability to solve problems creatively. A pupil can be drilled to the point of applying the techniques of arithmetic perfectly, yet have little concept of the number line and little ability to organize a new experience in the manner by which Palmer's pupils developed a rule for "sidebands." Skinner's view (1954) that arithmetic is a "drill subject" is violently opposed to the ideas of most psychologists and most mathematicians. The views of Piaget and others discussed in Chapter 10 suggest that trial and adjustment is an essential part of arriving at operational concepts; this conflicts with Skinner's view that only correct responses are educative. Programs, like all other instruction by presentation, are predicated on the identification of a definite right answer, constructed out of responses the learner already possesses. It is very difficult to see how programs can contribute to divergent thinking and creative imagination.

Some programs are attempting to build general understanding and to teach pupils to discover principles for themselves. The most impressive report now available is that of Keislar and McNeil (1961), who used the program illustrated in Figure 94 to teach first-graders the theoretical principles behind condensation. The pictures are in color. A code—taught in the program—shows by the length of the "tail" whether the molecule pictured is moving fast or slow. The pupil hears the text question on a recording, responds correctly, and hears an approving comment. If the pupil makes an error, he hears the question again and makes a new try. Thirteen daily lessons, using 432 items, were given. The extracts shown are from lesson 12. Importantly, the success of the training was judged by the pupil's ability to explain, in a final interview, phenomena he had never studied to which the principles of molecular attraction and coalescence apply. The mean score was 66 per cent; a control group averaged only 22 per cent.

Few of the programs now being tried make any provision for the ultimate transfer of responses to concrete, nonverbal situations. The research on transfer leads us to doubt, for example, that a medical education confined to words, pictures, and tape recordings would prepare the student to recognize, in the flesh, an early case of chicken pox. Nor could it develop in him an encouraging, confident bedside manner. Encoding and

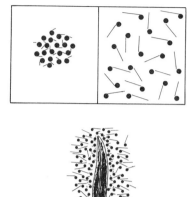

6. Which picture shows how the water vapor molecules would look after hitting something cold?

Yes, the water vapor molecules are attracted to each other when they are slowed down by something cold.

7. Here is a tiny blade of grass that is cooled when the sun goes down. Will the water vapor molecules go faster near the blade of grass?

Good for you! Because the grass is cool, the molecules will slow down near the blade of grass.

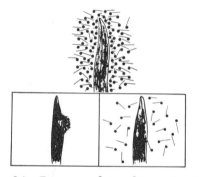

8. Here is a tiny blade of grass. The sun is setting and so the water vapor molecules near the blade of grass are slowing down. What happens to the water vapor when the molecules slow down? Which picture shows?

That's right! If water vapor slows down enough, the molecules will come together or condense.

94   *Programed teaching of scientific theory for first-graders (Keislar and McNeil, 1961)*

The question is presented by tape recorder. When the child gives the correct answer, he hears the approving comment reproduced here. This figure shows the sixth through eighth frames of the twelfth lesson in the program.

decoding cannot be taught entirely from a prepared program. Somewhere verbal concepts must be blended with observations on and responses to concrete reality.

The more "open-ended" the responses to be developed, the less one can teach by presentation. We can judge each response right or wrong when teaching the pupil to avoid grammatical errors. But when we want him to compose interesting sentences in a style suited to his audience and topic, there is no scoring key. Programed teaching can make the pupil a master of the facts about the Fifth French Republic. It can even indoctrinate him with the view of the programer on the desirability of close cooperation between France and West Germany. But interpretation and appreciation of history cannot be reduced to certain "sound" answers. The student ought to form a personal opinion of De Gaulle and of the national collapse that caused his rise to power; there can be as many justifiable opinions as there are students. The program can reward the student only for agreeing with what the programer believes. If composition, literature, languages, social studies, and science are reduced to responses that can be evaluated by a clerk, education will have settled for a good deal less than the aims we set forth in Chapter 2.

We see no danger that the school will reduce itself to a fact-dispensary, with machines in rows like gasoline pumps. Attitudes, reasoning powers, and creative responses will remain important in the minds of educators and parents. The school does have a great deal of factual material to teach, and many definite skills to be developed. These aims do not differ much from school to school, and it is surely possible to prepare standard programs that will be as effective as the lessons a typical teacher might personally prepare. The best hope is that standard programs for presenting material will free the teacher to help the pupil develop intuition and judgment by adventurous participation, as illustrated in Chapter 11.

Let us emphasize once more that not all programs will be equally sound. A program dashed off rapidly is not likely to be truly clear and accurate in what it communicates. It will be slow and expensive—but necessary—to revise every program after tryout, removing sections promoting misconceptions, smoothing out the difficult spots, and quickening the pace where the author's first approach was too leisurely. We will have brilliant programs, and run-of-the-mill programs. The quality of teaching is more important than the form it takes.

19. When a publisher sells a program to a school, what evidence should he offer to provide assurance that the program will be effective?

20. If two programs are offered for World History in the ninth grade, what should a teacher examine to decide which one to adopt?

21. To what extent could the aims of the present chapter be accomplished if the material (appropriately expanded) were put into a machine program and taught without discussion? What can your instructor add to your understanding that a machine cannot?

22. There is a basic conflict between Skinner's view that sound teaching produces mastery at every stage, and the view that there are many behaviors to be developed from any school course, some of which are developed only gradually. Which of these views is wrong? Or, if both are correct, can they be reconciled?

SUMMARY

To be sure that his presentation of material is communicating, the teacher needs to obtain responses from pupils. In a written presentation, questions interspersed in the text help the pupil to check his own comprehension.

It is desirable to keep vocabulary as simple as is consistent with accuracy. Meanings of essential technical terms should be carefully developed. Readability is also improved by using simpler sentences. Redundancy is another desirable characteristic of communicative writing. Saying the same thing over in various words or expressing a thought in more words than are strictly necessary helps to overcome losses from inattention of misinterpretation. Redundant communications are more comprehensible, though sometimes dull. The "cloze" technique of measuring redundancy is illustrated and its application to text materials is suggested.

Stressing main points or providing an outline is an important aid to the student. Presentations should have an internal structure that makes the main meanings prominent and subordinates detail. It is frequently desirable to give an overview of the whole before giving detailed information on subordinate parts. This general orientation makes the parts meaningful. Just what constitutes a psychological "whole" depends upon the background of the learner. The overview should cover all the relations essential for a correct understanding, but should not deal with so large a topic that the pupil cannot follow the explanation.

Audio-visual devices offer vivid experiences. Television as such rarely has any advantage over a filmed presentation. Visual presentations are more effective if carefully edited, but elaborate, polished visualizations may have no more teaching value than crude sketches. Pupils often fail to grasp the full meaning of a visual experience. They may overlook large portions of what is presented. Items mentioned in a verbal film commentary and matters presented dramatically are better retained than others. Pictorial materials should be discussed and reduced to verbal generalizations. The visual experience alone does not fully capitalize on the potentialities of the materials.

Instructional devices whereby the learner answers questions and is automatically rewarded are at present controversial. Not enough evidence is in hand to establish their virtues and defects. The important features of "automatic instruction" are these: continual response, in a form that can be objectively judged; prompt feedback or reinforcement; presentation of sufficient cues to make successful response likely; careful sequencing of materials; regulation of the pace of instruction on the basis of the learner's demonstrated achievement; administration without direct supervision by a qualified teacher.

While such mechanical presentations were first thought of as a way to administer heterogeneous drills, they are now used for systematic programs or sequences of questions. The programer would like to build readiness for understanding each question by increasing difficulty in small steps. Some programs are "linear," in the sense that every student must work through all the questions in the same order, save for repetition of the questions missed. "Branching" programs consider the nature of the student's error, and send him on to an explanation or question designed to eliminate his particular error.

Experimental results on programed instruction are fragmentary, and final conclusions cannot be drawn while the art of designing programs is still emerging. It appears that automatic procedures teach facts as well as conventional instruction does. The "small-step" principle appears to be sound if not carried to extremes. Although it is claimed that students master one question before going on to the next, test scores are usually far below the 100 per cent mark. Some programs are ineffective; the merit of each particular program must be judged from performance data. Several studies cast doubt on the importance of active overt response. Students who merely read through the program, thinking about the content, achieve scores as high as those who fill in the blanks. The chief virtue of programed, automatic instruction may be that the necessity for experimental tryout increases the likelihood that a clear and meaningful presentation will be developed.

Programing works best for definite materials where there is a clearly correct response. Not many programs attempt to teach deep comprehension or creative problem solving. Programs emphasizing verbal stimuli and responses also tend to neglect the encoding and decoding steps in learning. The best hope is that standardized programs for presenting factual, verbal material will free the teacher to plan and direct class experiences that cultivate creativeness, constructive reasoning, and ability to apply knowledge.

Reading List 12

Abraham S. Luchins, "Implications of Gestalt Psychology for AV Learning," *Audio-Visual Communications Review*, 9 (1961), 7–31.

This is one of several chapters in a monograph on learning theory and audio-visual methods. Luchins suggests that although audio-visual presentation is potentially valuable it may interfere with the pupil's verbal or practical learning, and the pupil may take too passive an attitude for the best learning. He indicates how these difficulties may be overcome.

Arthur A. Lumsdaine, "Partial and More Complete Automation of Teaching in Group and Individual Learning Situations," Chapter 13 in Eugene Galanter, ed., *Automatic Teaching* (New York: Wiley, 1959), pp. 147–66.

Lumsdaine shows that many of the principles used in machine teaching are also relevant to instruction by films and workbooks. He emphasizes that any teaching procedure can be systematically varied by the teacher or programer. In the studies he cites, amount of active response by the pupil appears to be the most important single variable affecting learning. Can this be reconciled with the recent evidence indicating that active response had no value?

Mark A. May and J. J. Howell, "Film Evaluation by 'Road Testing,'" Chapter 19 in Mark A. May and Arthur A. Lumsdaine, eds., *Learning from Films* (New Haven: Yale Univ. Press, 1958), pp. 266–82.

An account of procedures used to develop supplementary materials for teaching films and to evaluate the effectiveness of the combination by widespread classroom tryout. A film showing the life of Marie and Pierre Curie is used to illustrate typical problems of the film designer and teacher. This type of detailed criticism can be made of any teaching material, though it is most practical for films and printed materials prepared for national distribution.

Neal E. Miller and others, "Cue: The Student Must Notice Something," Chapter 13 in *Graphic Communication and the Crisis in Education* (Washington: Dept. of Audio-Visual Instruction, National Education Assoc., 1957), pp. 76–88. Also in *Audio-Visual Communication Review*, 5 (1957), No. 3.

Miller emphasizes the importance of confronting the student with the cues that will help him use the knowledge later. There are two particular problems: how to achieve a balance between realism and simplification, and how to get the learner to attend to the significant cues. Although this discussion deals especially with visual presentations, the recommendations apply also to verbal presentations of knowledge and to practice situations for skills.

B. F. Skinner, "The Science of Learning and the Art of Teaching," *Harvard Educational Review*, 25 (1954) 86–97. Reprinted in Fullager, Haimowitz, Loree, Lumsdaine, Rosenblith.

This is the provocative article that led to recent interest in automatic teaching. Skinner makes a serious comparison between the training of pigeons in the laboratory and the teaching of pupils in the school. While the article is one-sided in its emphasis on trial and reward, ignoring the concepts of programing and meaningfulness, it is a closely reasoned condemnation of traditional classroom methods.

CHAPTER **13** IDENTIFICATION AND THE LEARNING OF ATTITUDES

The preceding chapter discussed how explanations help the student make the most suitable interpretation of a situation. The present chapter considers further how meanings are taught, but this time we shall consider a process in which the personal relations between teacher and student play a large part. The acquisition of attitudes is based on an emotional relation between teacher and pupil, and as such contrasts with the more purely intellectual effects of schooling.

When there is just one correct answer whose rightness can be demonstrated, the principal task of the teacher is helping the pupil discriminate and understand that answer. Once the answer is intellectually clear, the pupil guides his behavior by it. When alternative interpretations are intellectually defensible, the pupil usually adopts one of them as a belief. Religious attitudes are one example: no one can prove that being an Episcopalian is better or worse than being a Presbyterian, yet members of each church are loyal to it and would be less satisfied if they could not attend their type of service.

Acquiring a belief cannot be considered simply as intelligent, meaningful learning. Even where science seems to show one answer to be much superior, some people cling to another answer. Is it sheer lack of intelligence that causes people to resist vaccination, to plow in straight lines so that the soil washes away, to drive at unsafe speeds, to write less legibly than they might? In this chapter we find that interpretations are determined by emotional factors as well as by understanding.

Here we encounter again the distinction between ability and typical behavior or habit. A person who possesses knowledge or skill may not use it. It is not enough to know that the speed limit is 35 m.p.h. in this locality; I have learned to drive properly only if I do keep my speed inside that limit. The difference between the person who merely knows what to do and the person who does it is in attitude. Many attitudes affect the behavior of a driver: a love of speed, a wish to save time, a fear of unpleasantness if he should hit someone, carefulness and foresight, or a concept of himself as a law-abiding citizen. Some of these attitudes can be modified by schooling and simple propaganda. Others (e.g., those taught by the authoritarian home) are so deeply rooted that changing them requires remaking a whole personality. Some attitudes are deeply hidden and cannot readily be inferred from behavior; thus a driver who dislikes law and restriction may be very cautious just because he has an exaggerated fear of the law's reprisal.

The learning of attitudes is explained within the same general concepts that explain other learning. The learner confronts a situation, identifies goals, makes a provisional try, and finds his expectations confirmed. In his choice of beliefs he is guided to certain provisional tries by the example of other people. That is, he imitates certain models. The pupil can imitate models who teach the attitudes that the school and community approve. But there are other influential models in our culture who teach attitudes that educators seek to discourage. One of our major questions, therefore, is how teachers can encourage the pupil to adopt the desirable rather than the undesirable patterns he observes.

IDENTIFYING FIGURES AS A SOURCE OF SUGGESTIONS

Whom Does the Learner Imitate?

To say that the child learns by imitation, and that the way to teach is to set a good example, oversimplifies. No child imitates every action he sees. Sometimes he ignores the example his parent wants him to follow and he takes over contrary patterns from some other example. Therefore we must turn to a more subtle theory than "Monkey see, monkey do."

Look at it from the child's point of view. He is in a new situation, lacking a ready response and seeking a response that will gain certain ends. If he cannot reason out what to do, he observes a model who seems able to get the right result. He looks for an authority or expert to imitate. The point is charmingly illustrated by Nevitt Sanford's story (1955) of the 2-year-old, initially terrified of a new puppy, who within a few hours was crawling about, barking, and threatening to bite people—and less charmingly illustrated by Bettelheim's (1943) description of concentration camp inmates adopting the mannerisms of the all-powerful guards. The child sees other persons attain goals or suffer penalties; the consequences they experience modify his subsequent tries much as the consequences of his own behavior do.

There is a second element at work in this situation. The child may attain his immediate goal only to find that his method brings criticism. "Hold your fork properly," he is told. When he shouts across the classroom to deliver a message, he is told emphatically that such a racket is unpleasant, that he should walk across the room and say what he has to say quietly. Thus, the desire to cope with a situation is overlaid with the desire to act properly. The child gets more affection and approval when his parents like his action. Other adults, and peers, reward some actions and criticize others. Consequently the child eventually acquires a conscience, i.e., a desire to act in an approved manner, even when no one else is present to judge his actions.

A person who is repeatedly accepted as an example for conduct and interpretations is called an *identifying figure*. Identification is a complex way of perceiving another person, partly rational and partly emotional. The feeling about the identifying figure includes these ideas: "This person knows what to do and how to act in most situations." "If I do as he does, I will be more likely to attain my goals." "I want and expect him to like and approve of me." In short, you respect, admire, and like your identifying figures, and you model yourself on them (Payne and Mussen, 1956; Kagan, 1958).

Identification occurs from earliest childhood to adulthood. Even the most eminent adults take values and techniques from those they admire. A mark of maturity is a decrease in blind emotional loyalty—"my hero, right or wrong"—and an increased ability to criticize the hero's example. This objectivity depends upon the individual's sense of worth, upon his feeling that "I'm all right even if I disagree with this admirable person."

Figures with Whom the Child Identifies

The child's first identification is normally with his parents. Parents minister to the child, increase his happiness, and take care of things that go wrong. The child's gratification broadens into respect for his parents' wisdom, desire to be like them, and desire for their love in return. As we have seen (page 148), the success of the identification process depends upon the warmth of the home. By the age of 5, the child frequently picks playmates and older members of the family as models: "Johnny showed me how to ride the scooter," or, "Why don't we have the kind of cake I had at Johnny's house?"

Adults outside the home are also identifying figures. Most children see their first teacher as wonderful, the keeper of uncounted delightful surprises. So powerful is the teacher's hold that soon her views are quoted at home in arguments against the once-infallible parents. Children differ in the firmness of their loyalty to the teacher. Some pursue the teacher's example in all things, transferring that loyalty to later teachers so clingingly that they are estranged from their peers. Others come to feel that the teacher "isn't my kind of person." [1]

---

[1] Witness the girl who names a playmate as her ideal, because "she is not too smart and not too dum, not too rich and not too poor, because she is just an average girl."

As reading, television, and community contacts broaden his knowledge of people, the older child has a much wider choice of identifying figures. Some children in the range 8 to 12 seem to identify strongly with fictional characters (the Lone Ranger), historical personages (Lincoln), or famous athletes. Jesus becomes an identifying figure to many. Such identifications are one possible basis for vocational choice, for political attitudes, and for moral standards (Stoughton and Ray, 1946). Everyone the child encounters is a possible identifying figure, yet he identifies with only a few people. His choice reflects the sort of person he is and helps to determine the sort he will become. A teacher may set the best of examples, yet only a few of the students will take over his patterns. Each pupil selects among his teachers; some are his models to a far greater degree than others.

Psychologists do not have adequate methods of finding out who a child's chief models are. Sometimes the child himself does not know whose example he follows. Moreover, when he answers a direct question, he has a fairly good idea of what sort of person he will be praised for naming. In the research on children's ideals, no child names a contemporary criminal as his hero. The reflections of adult criminals, however, show clearly that they identified with unsavory models during childhood.

MODELS CONSISTENT WITH THE SELF-CONCEPT.   Each choice of an identifying figure is based on needs and attitudes already present. If Allen's parents have rewarded him for being quiet and passive, he cannot, on the schoolground, see himself becoming like tough and energetic Rudy. Rudy's conduct would be accepted as an ideal only if Allen were willing to reject everything he had been trying to be. This may happen where there has been such tension between child and parents that he is inclined to reject their standards, that is, when his identification with them has failed.

As the child grows into an adult, his identifying figures represent successive differentiations of his ideal. In his earlier years all adults seem glamorous and powerful to him. By school age some adults seem more "his type" than others. As a boy begins to take pride in his own physique and his ability to oppose others, he is ripe to idolize people who represent a high development of that asset: athletes, daredevil lawmen, stronger boys at school (Bailyn, 1959, p. 15). The medical student rejects as a model the teacher he admires but whose research on animals he sees as inconsistent with his own ideal of serving the patient directly (Hughes, 1959).

A boy who bases his self-respect less on physical attainment and more on intellectual interests is likely to find identifying figures in a field such as science. Clark, who gets from his father a feeling that carpentry is worth doing and is not too hard, is ready for further stimulation along that line. He can attach himself far more comfortably to an older boy whose hobby is telescope-making than he could if craftwork were foreign to him. Identifications overlap, some fading as others grow more intense.

The autobiography of Justice William O. Douglas illustrates how a person seeks a model consistent with his needs and self-concept and takes his provisional trials from this model. As a young boy Douglas had polio, and was left with weak and spindly legs. Tactless comments from boys, plus the solicitous comments of his mother, had left him sensitive and determined to prove himself capable. One of his responses was to plunge into study, driving for grades of 100 in all his courses. He could come near to achieving these grades, but remained dissatisfied with his inability to be like other boys. He stumbled on the story of Sparta in his reading and found that "they were rugged and hardy people, the kind that I aspired to be. So I searched out the literature that described their habits and capacities to see if I could get some clues to their toughness." Unfortunately, these figures did not serve as models, for in Plato Douglas read the devastating fact that the Spartans did away with their weaklings. Then came the model Douglas was ready for (1950, pp. 34–35).

> One day I met another boy, whom I had known at Sunday school, coming in on a fast walk from the country. He was a husky, long-legged chap, to me a perfect physical specimen. I asked him where he'd been, and he replied that he had been climbing the foothills north of town. I asked him why he did it. He told me that his doctor had advised it; that he was trying to correct certain difficulties following an illness. He was climbing the foothills every day to develop his lungs and legs.
>
> An overwhelming light swept me. My resolution was instantaneous. I would do the same. I would make my legs strong on the foothills. Thus I started my treks, and used the foothills as one uses weights in a gymnasium. . . . By the time the next spring arrived, I had found new confidence in myself. My legs were filling out. They were getting stronger. . . . Following these hikes the muscles of my knees would twitch and make it difficult for me to sleep at night. But I felt an increasing flow of health in my legs, and a growing sense of contentment in my heart.

Upon this success and satisfaction, Douglas built a lifelong interest in mountain climbing and the outdoor life.

MODELS OFFERED BY THE SCHOOL

The Teacher

The model is a leader who deliberately or inadvertently demonstrates to the learner how he might behave. The teacher is an influential leader. In staffing a school, one important consideration is to select teachers who will be suitable models for the range of children.

Teachers most admired by students are those who take a personal interest in them. Pupils have been asked by many investigators to tell which teachers helped them most, and why (e.g., Witty, 1947). Invariably high on the list of qualities are phrases like these: "She approaches us as if she considers us intelligent." "She makes you feel you can do the work." "Her class is like a happy family." Other favored traits are patience, wide interests, fairness, and sense of humor. Results like these may seem to imply that a teacher has to be easy or that a teacher's success is to be judged by his popularity. Neither of these follows. The teacher whom the pupils worship is generally also highly regarded by the principal who knows how much the teacher is accomplishing. Pupils respect teachers who keep them pointed toward significant goals, even if the goals require effort. They do not mind insistence on their best effort, but they want the teacher also to recognize their difficulties and help them meet the standards. There is a vast difference between a nagging taskmaster and a teacher who sets the pupils' eyes on a peak and helps them select a path that gets there.

Each teacher appeals to some students more than to others. Miss Shannon, red-haired and bouncing, marriageable and full of ideas, becomes the envy and idol of half the girls in the high school. They swarm to her play tryouts, they cluster round her at dances, they grasp a suggestion tossed out in class and come in the next week with a dozen original "folk ballads" describing school events. For a student who envisions herself as potentially dazzling, willing to make a splash in her crowd, Miss Shannon is a tremendously influential model whose word on necklines or Sherwood Anderson carries great weight. But to retiring, feminine Celia, who would rather be shot than speak before an audience, identification with Miss Shannon would be hitching herself to a rocket. Celia may envy Miss Shannon and those who follow her lead, but she cannot picture herself growing into such a person. She will find a model more consistent with her concept of herself. Perhaps Mrs. van Ness, deliberate and orderly and sensitive, is the one with whom Celia can be comfortable. Mrs. van Ness just teaches French—no dramatics, no chorus, no Athletic Association. But she also is a person, gracious and receptive. If her quiet manner encourages Celia just once to voice a personal problem or an opinion, her respect for Celia's concerns is rewarding and leaves Celia ready to unfold more the next time. Such a relation grows gradually into a firm identification. Mrs. van Ness may be the identifying figure for one pupil to Miss Shannon's twenty, but she reaches some who could never get close to Miss Shannon. A balanced faculty has a variety of personalities to serve as models, so that each student has a good chance of forming an allegiance.

A faculty should include in their number people who exemplify various social roles. The child who lacks a father, or who finds his father unacceptable as a model, will be greatly helped by a supporting masculine figure. Unless the school staff contains suitable men, a boy who craves a masculine idol must seek it elsewhere. His choice may fall on a poolroom character or an adolescent gang leader purely by default of any alternative.

Quiet and intellectual boys may be unable to affiliate with a rugged male, and for them other men are needed as models. If a growing boy forms emotional ties solely with women teachers, the school gives him no help in learning male patterns. Girls need women as models, including women who are adjusting successfully to a career, women who represent primarily the values of the homemaker, and those rarer women who can balance a devotion to both.

Each student reacts to his teachers in his own personal way. Take Jim, for instance. To Mrs. Webster he is an unadulterated tribulation. She objects to his waving his hands and shaking his head when he is reciting. He argues about every topic in history and politics, even though she knows he has half his facts wrong. When the class is making a list of those who have contributed most to American democracy, Jim does not offer the conventional names of Jefferson and Madison as the others do, but nominates a labor leader and relishes the argument the name provokes. Another time, he makes an hour miserable for a student teacher by defending in a logical style the position that capitalism is the same thing as monopoly. Mrs. Webster believes that Jim is unbearable: "Someone should back him up against the wall and tell him a few things."

The facts Mrs. Webster does not know (they are in the office file but she has not looked) tell a good deal about Jim's refusal to accept her attitudes. Jim, for one thing, has an IQ of 140, and Mrs. Webster has not used her class to stimulate initiative and thinking; so Jim is bored. Second, Jim is the son of a woman schoolteacher, his father having died when he was very young. Jim finds it difficult to live up to his mother's demands for perfection and to arrive at any independence at home. His mother encourages him to take on nearly adult responsibilities for jobs, but she checks on him at every turn. She pushes him out of the house to be at work on time, she checks on the way he spends his earnings, she visits the school to confer with his teachers when she finds him to be three days late with an assignment. She is so wrapped up in Jim that she cannot leave him to make mistakes and gain maturity in his own way. Jim reacts to this by striking out against adult authority wherever he can. This accounts for the arguments on social issues, and it also accounts for his resistance to Mrs. Webster. When he has no freedom of choice, all his restiveness comes out in argument.

But Jim's relations to Lyle Harris are just the opposite. Mr. Harris is a young and athletic man who took over the English courses in Jim's junior year. During two years of contact, he has grown into a second father for Jim. On weekends, when Jim is not working, he hangs around Mr. Harris' house, helping him paint his garage, going after pheasants, lying on the porch reading Harris' copies of Hemingway and Steinbeck. Harris, on his part, finds Jim an unusually mature boy who is fun to have around, and who can do almost anything consistent with his need for independence.

Harris, upon his arrival, recognized five pupils among his juniors who were so capable that to keep them in stride with the rest of the group would have been difficult. These five pupils therefore worked out a separate course of study with Harris, planning activities for two weeks at a time and then going off to another room to study their supplementary books and writing projects. This device worked ideally: the three boys and two girls worked seriously because they knew the privilege would be withdrawn if they failed to learn, and they had enough fun in their small and social group to make them want this freedom. Jim became a leader in this group, being

"You're right. He's a swell author."

95 *Mr. Harris was an identifying figure*

the one who on his own initiative kept our friend Bill Chelten in line when he tried to waste group time. The fact that Mr. Harris let him express his drive for leadership and self-direction made him responsible instead of rebellious. It also made him trust Mr. Harris so that he could relax into the dependence that he needed.

    1. Teaching has always tended to attract those who place especial value on intellectual and scholarly achievement, some of whom are shy in social contacts and dislike the competitive rush of the business world. For what pupils would these teachers provide models? If a school contained only this sort of teacher, how would the social learning of pupils be limited?

    2. Elementary schools are making increasing use of "team teaching," in which different teachers teach different subjects or work with a class in different ways. How does this change the possibilities for identification from those found in the single-teacher classroom?

    3. Can the community assume that each girl will develop ideals of home-making by using her own mother as a model?

4. Feelings about the identifying figure were listed early in the chapter. Were these present in the case of Justice Douglas? In the case of Jim?

5. Thelma is the daughter of a professor of astronomy. She does excellent schoolwork, but she is poorly groomed and unattractive, has little social life, and seems depressed. Thelma has taken considerable responsibility for the care of her own younger sisters. The main concern of her brilliant mother is the scholarly journal she edits; she seems alert and well adjusted, but she too is untidy and carelessly dressed. Suggest what the school can do for Thelma.

6. What factors work against an intelligent adolescent's identifying with a distinguished scientist or a President?

Teaching Materials as a Source of Models

While direct personal influence is paramount in the formation of ideals, the school also offers models whenever it describes people. One of the long-appreciated reasons for studying literature, history, and religion is the possibility of following examples of successful living and avoiding the errors others have made. The people we read about suggest ways of living we might otherwise not stumble upon. The girl who decided on her career when she read and identified with the story of an orphanage worker is an example. Why the lightning struck from this story, rather than from Marie Curie or Florence Nightingale, is unknown. Some unfulfilled need or wish evidently made her ready for just the suggestion the orphanage story offered. Munroe (1942) describes how adolescent girls with unsatisfied needs gorge themselves on literature that they can relate to their own conflicts.

A British study of adolescent attitudes (ages 11–16) toward novels read in grammar-school classes has implications going far beyond the ten novels rated. Each pupil marked a scale of 18 statements for each book he had read. Part of the scale appears in Figure 96. Among these superior pupils, there were no important sex differences for the ten books. The books were rated as shown in the table. The features associated with high ratings are worthy of attention. The characteristics of these books—as rated by teachers —correlated as follows with approval of the books by pupils (Whitehead, 1956):

.87 How easily can the reader identify with the hero or heroine?
.78 How much daydream-like wish fulfillment does the book offer?
.71 To what extent is the emotional theme an immature one?
.64 How simple is the language?
−.26 How consistent is the development of plot and character?

The book that commands attention and respect—even in this select group —is the one that has personal meaning for the adolescent. The artistic merit of the book and its depth of theme correlate negatively with approval. To reverse this correlation might well be a paramount objective of the study of literature, though it seems likely that pupils' preferences depend more on their emotional maturity than on their aesthetic judgments.

Just as the school may provide an incomplete selection of live models unless teachers are chosen with this in mind, so the models described in printed materials may not give an adequate range of identifying figures. Texts and reading materials tend to describe people of certain types and to ignore others; to stress certain values and not to illustrate others that are equally worthy. Who appears as a possible model?

First of all, the school's models demonstrate a few roles disproportionately often. Leaders are most often portrayed: generals, presidents, creators. The story of upward mobility—poor boy to president, laborer to magnate —is told over and over. No songs are sung of the office worker or the man who plants 100 acres of soybeans. Where could Mary have read a glam-

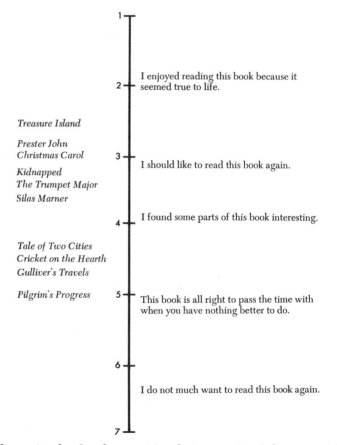

96 *Pupils prefer books that satisfy their emotional hungers (data from Whitehead, 1956)*

orous, teacher-approved account of the secretary-typist, the vocation her talents suited? (For a list of reading materials especially suited to helping pupils with their developmental tasks, see De Boer *et al.*, 1953).

Second, the school stresses dramatic achievement. It is much more exciting to talk of Barbara Frietchie—"Shoot, if you must, this old gray head" —than to visualize the daily life of Barbara's neighbor down the street who did nothing but raise six children so they were happy and useful in their station. The inconspicuous but devoted worker cannot be idealized as easily as the lone pioneer or the lucky discoverer. This is no unique fault of the school. All our literature, our news, and our movies give disproportionate emphasis to conflict, triumph over crises the average man never meets, and exceptional successes.

Third, the picture of life presented is often unrealistic (Warner and Henry, 1948). A well-known example is the tendency to make the criminal dashing and heroic. True, the final scene tries to show that crime does not pay. But meanwhile it often has paid the central figure in power, possessions, and pride. In a teen-ager with unsatisfied needs and little knowledge of the world, reactions like this follow (Blumer and Hauser, 1933, p. 45):

> Knowing that the "bad guy" had plenty of money and an easy way of getting it by robbing and burglarizing, and the good guy was slaving for his money, I thought that the bad guy was the smartest. . . . Thinking it was easy I took up robbery as the best means of obtaining money.

In fairness it should be said that motion-picture makers, partly as a result of such studies, now present the criminal life as less attractive than the pictures of the 1930's made it seem.

Textbooks communicate the value system of the writer. Of considerable interest, in view of our earlier discussion of the rise of affiliation motivation, is a comparison of stories in fourth-grade readers from different generations (Table 24). Stories were scored according to the values (achievement or affiliation) sought by the hero, and the presence or absence of a directly stated "moral." It is evident from the table that moral "preaching" went out of style late in the last century. Achievement imagery was strongly emphasized from 1880 to 1920, and affiliation imagery was most stressed from 1920 to 1940. The study does not report what has become prominent in the past decade.

Sometimes the textbook communicates prejudices without intending to. According to Child *et al.* (1946), the stories in readers show children getting rewards when they carry out the ideas of superiors, but when they act independently they are likely to get into difficulty. Acquiring knowledge by asking an authority is consistently shown as a good thing to do; unrealistically enough, the authorities asked always are able to give the answer. But if the child in the story sets out to discover things on his own, he gets punished fairly often. Time after time the child gets help on a difficult

TABLE 24

Schoolbooks convey the values of the writer (data from deCharms and Moeller, 1962)

Year of Publication	1810	1830	1850	1870	1890	1910	1930	1950
Use of achievement imagery	3	2	4	8	11	9	6	4
Use of affiliation imagery	3	4	6	6	5	7	9	6
Direct moral teaching	16	17	12	6	4	4	1	0

Each number represents the average number of pages, out of 25, where this imagery or teaching appeared.

project by appealing to adults. The stories neglect to provide models of peers helping each other to complete a job, without relying an adults.

In the readers, sex roles are distinct. Women and girls are rarely shown as achieving or striving for recognition; the females are sociable, timid, inactive, unambitious, uncreative, and have an air of helplessness. The males, on the other hand, have a near monopoly on giving information, on effort, and on productivity. The investigators decided that the girl reading these books might well conclude that "being female is a pretty bad thing." If girls do not resign themselves to an inferior position, it is because other social examples and their own experience are more encouraging.

It is not certain how much influence models from books and other mass media have, compared to persons the pupil knows at first hand. In a study of Midwestern adolescents (Peck and Havighurst, 1960, p. 154) it was reported:

> Such people as movie stars, professional athletes, historical and fictional characters appear to have had very little influence on these youth. There was a period in their lives, from about age ten to about age fifteen, when such people were mentioned in the essay "The Person I'd Like to Be Like," but these distant and "glamorous" characters were superseded in the essays by attractive, visible young adults of the community. . . . The great heroes of history seem to have had little or no influence on the youth of Prairie City.

7. In a reader for Russian children, a story tells how a boy tries to do a task in his own way instead of following the plan his group has agreed upon. He fails and is a target of scorn. Then he adopts the group-approved plan, succeeds, and is welcomed back to the group. What effect would this story have on the pupil? Should American readers have stories with such a theme?

8. What models does the elementary and high-school program call to the attention of the student who might later specialize in the social sciences? What steps might be taken to provide additional models?

9. Can the classics of literature provide models for modern adolescents and adults?

DEVELOPMENT OF ATTITUDES
THROUGH EXPERIENCE

Attitudes are important objectives in every school subject. Agriculture aims to teach the boy that land is a resource to be built up by soil treatment, and to make the corn-hog farmer and his son alert to the advantages of diversification. Biology aims to alter attitudes regarding wildlife, community health safeguards, and social problems in which heredity is a consideration. Commercial subjects stress neatness and care of equipment. Attitudes are peculiarly a concern of the social studies, and more research has been done on racial prejudices and social beliefs than on any other type of attitude.

Attitudes as Meanings

Psychologists used to define an attitude simply as a tendency to seek or avoid something. Their early studies of liking and disliking, approval and disapproval were helpful but incomplete. We need to go deeper and understand the reasons behind seeking and avoiding. We therefore have turned to a broader definition of attitude.

An attitude consists of the meanings that one associates with a certain object (or abstraction) and that influence his acceptance of it. These objects may be specific and concrete—my favorite red necktie—or as intangible as monogamy. An element of acceptance or avoidance is present in any attitude, but additional associations are involved. What is your attitude toward coffee? Let's say you drink several cups a day. That implies that you like it. But you drink it regularly for breakfast, never in midmorning except as a social ritual when there is a chance to chat over it, never at night except at a company dinner. Moreover, you never drink coffee unless you can get fresh cream for it. With enough observation we can infer a very complex attitude, perhaps along these lines: you don't care for the taste of coffee alone; you find it acceptable with cream; you feel your start in the morning incomplete without it; it seems "more sociable" than a glass of cold milk.

Attitudes, like other meanings, may be incomplete or inconsistent. Americans have learned to reject totalitarianism. Each person avows with genuine emotion that such government is evil, and applauds "free speech and the fundamental principles of democracy." Yet these same people—some of them—endorse propositions that are totalitarian in spirit (Yates, 1933; Stagner, 1936; Remmers and Radler, 1957). A test of civic knowledge finds that in a national sample of high-school seniors many do not recognize truly democratic practice (Gage *et al.*, 1961). Here are specimen test items: [2]

> Suppose a film company made a movie portraying how our national government put all persons of Japanese descent, who were living in our western states, into special camps during World War II. The film makes this action of our government look very bad. The showing of this film should be
>
> A   prohibited under any circumstances
> B   allowed only if approved by patriotic organizations
> C   allowed only if approved by federal agencies
> D   allowed under any circumstances
>
> The right to hold peaceable public meetings should be given to
>
> A   all groups
> B   most groups, but not those which oppose government policies
> C   only a few groups, providing they support government policies
> D   government-approved groups only

On the first item the correct answer D is given by 33 per cent of the seniors. On the second item A is correct according to the Constitution and 69 per cent of the seniors respond correctly. On the first, more concrete example of civil rights pupils often lose sight of the abstract principle. Its definite associations arouse a value conflict that leads to an intuitive answer rather than an answer controlled by principle.

Evidently pupils fail to apply their abstract conception of democracy to the concrete situation; similar failures of reasoning are also found among older students (Edwards, 1941). It is not enough to develop loyalty to the abstractions *democracy* and *free speech*. These attitudes will not produce democratic judgments unless the concept is a developed system of meanings. As with scientific knowledge, the verbal principle does not direct action unless the pupil has also learned to encode the concrete event so that he knows what abstraction to apply.

10. List several attitudes to be promoted by teachers of primary reading, band, English composition.

11. Many people know correct grammar and usage but do not use it when speaking. What attitudes might account for this?

12. Describe fully your own attitude toward private boys' schools, toward daily comic strips, or toward writing personal letters.

Trial and Confirmation

Attitudes are confirmed or modified through repeated trials. A classic illustration is the child's learning about dogs. The infant reaches out for almost any object to explore it; when he first encounters a dog, it may be just another curiosity. Or the baby's parents may come close at the same time, making pleasant sounds, in effect helping the baby recognize this as similar to other occasions when parents have brought nice things. So the baby pats the dog. An attitude or belief is being tested, and will

"Number work is fun."

"I like arithmetic."

"Does that job use mathematics?"

97 *An attitude is built on previous attitudes*

be confirmed if followed by pleasant results: touch sensations, expressions of parental approval, etc. But if the dog snaps at the fingers or jumps unexpectedly, a new element enters. Many infants retreat crying; having been shocked once, they will next try "dog-avoidance." They have learned a new interpretation.

What results in these encounters is chancy. The pup licks the face of one baby and frightens him into a lasting aversion. The same reaction startles another child but is quickly accepted. A third child reacts instantly with laughter at what the funny object did. This difference in interpreting

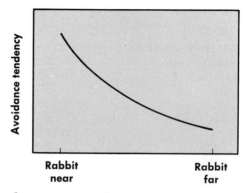

98 *Avoidance tendencies are much stronger when the feared object is close*

the consequence depends on the security of the total situation; one can be much braver in the presence of protecting parents. An even deeper influence is the self-assurance already in the child. If the child has had repeated unpleasant experiences where things worked out badly, he is ready to think the worst of a new ambiguity, to retreat at the first miscue. At the extreme, he develops what Frenkel-Brunswik (1948) calls a "catastrophic view of the world," an idea that unpleasant things are always lying in wait. And as the saying has it, if you look for trouble you are likely to find it.

LEARNING AND UNLEARNING OF FEARS.   An attitude can be confirmed or contradicted by further experience. Watson (1920) taught a child to fear a rat just by clanging a bar every time the child touched the animal. The infant's aversion to violent sound created a fear of the rat. Even the sight of the rat was enough to cause the child to shrink into his corner and begin to cry. The rat had come to mean "horrible sound about to happen."

In this experiment, an important type of transfer appeared. We have seen earlier that a response learned in one situation transfers to other situations recognized as similar. This is a process of *generalization,* even when the generalized interpretation is not verbally mediated. The person who uses the same response for many situations acts as if he had a general concept of situations calling for that action. Thus Watson's boy, fearful of the rat, exhibited similar fears of other furry animals and of a fur collar.

A subsequent study involved both the learning and the unlearning of a fear. Mary C. Jones (1924) trained a boy Peter to fear a rabbit, using Watson's loud-noise technique. After Peter had been made fearful, his responses were more or less like those diagrammed in Figure 98. The closer the rabbit, the stronger the avoidance response. Transfer decreases as resemblance to the training situation decreases. The steepness of the curve

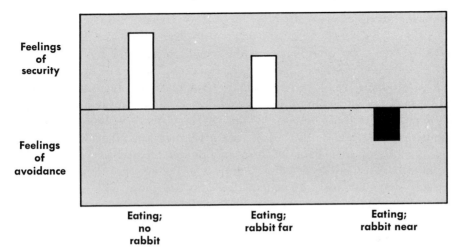

99   *Strong positive feelings outweigh mild avoidance tendencies*

depends on how thoroughly the original response is learned and on other competing responses.

Later, when Peter was in a secure and pleasant situation, the experimenter reintroduced the rabbit. While Peter ate in his high chair, the rabbit was brought into the far corner of the room. Dimly perceived, the rabbit aroused no fear reactions. On successive days the rabbit was pushed closer, and finally released onto the table beside Peter. Peter accepted each further step without observable distress. In effect he was reinterpreting the rabbit as part of a pleasant affair. Before the end of the experiment, Peter was fondling the rabbit, and inquiring for him when he was out of sight. A new meaning had been substituted for the threatening interpretation.

Examine this in the light of Figure 98. The closer the rabbit, the greater the fear. But the more the situation is like the familiar eating situation, the stronger the tendency to feel secure (Figure 99). When the two situations are combined, the security and avoidance tendencies compete. A close rabbit arouses fears that outweigh the pleasant feelings from the eating situation. But a distant rabbit introduces a weak avoidance response, outweighed by the positive response to food. The eating-plus-distant-rabbit is confirmed as a desirable situation. This experience prepares the child for bringing the rabbit a few inches closer.

Many a person who "can't eat" one food has a whole list of foods he cannot enjoy. Attitudes tend to become highly generalized. A particularly important example is attitude toward racial or religious groups. Such attitudes tend to be markedly consistent, dislike for one group going along with dislike for the next (Hartley, 1946; I. A. Taylor, 1960). If attitudes were not so unified, the school could teach tolerance for only one group at a time and would have to build attitudes piecemeal.

Specific attitudes generalize into an attitude toward life (M. B. Smith *et al.*, 1956). The person who has dogmatic racial views also has dogmatic views on scientific questions and on social policy, and tends to accept dictation from authority (Adorno, 1950; Rokeach, 1960). For example, when college students were questioned to obtain advice regarding changes in examination procedures, the prejudiced students resisted any change in procedure and did not even want to be interviewed about possible changes. Giving tests is the job of authority, they said; they wanted to be told the rules rather than to form an opinion themselves (Jacob, 1957, pp. 11, 121 ff.). Conversely, those adults who believe that they, as average citizens, can influence government decisions are those who are generally more secure and more optimistic, and who believe that success depends on effort rather than luck (Douvan and Walker, 1956; cf. the discussion of the achievement ethic, page 48).

The dogmatic person has a system of beliefs that he cannot afford to have shaken. He may be a highly religious person or an atheist; he may belong to the political right or the left. Whatever his beliefs, he protects them by shutting out contrary information and by avoiding discussions that might force the contradictions in his system to his attention. His mind is closed because anything strange is threatening. This makes him hard for the educator to reach. Consider Mikols' (1960) observation of the reaction of dogmatic and nondogmatic students to modern music. The students were classified according to their beliefs about politics, authority, achievement, etc. The groups did not differ in their reaction to the conventional music of Brahms and Saint Saëns, nor in their initial dislike for the strange music of Schönberg. But on a *second* hearing of the Schönberg selection the open-minded students became more favorable while the dogmatic ones rejected it more harshly than they had at first. Open-mindedness is an essential part of readiness for learning and growth.

> **13.** Give examples of attitude generalization shown in the normal course of the development of relations with other persons. Does the similarity of the persons determine the likelihood of generalization?
> **14.** What would be the probable effect of introducing "rabbit far" when the child is eating in a greatly changed situation, say on the grass in a park?
> **15.** A child fears swimming as a result of early experiences in which he lost his balance and choked on water while wading. Suggest a procedure for developing a positive attitude.

SOCIAL REINFORCEMENT.   Each time a person acts on or expresses an opinion, his interpretation is supported or contradicted by events, including the reactions of others. The power of social confirmations or reinforcements is shown in experiments in which the investigator reshapes the subject's conversation by applying slight but consistent reinforcement. The rein-

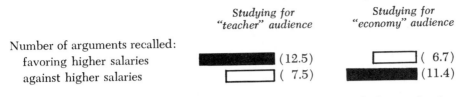

100 *Meanings acceptable to one's audience are most easily learned (data from Zimmerman and Bauer, 1956)*

forcement used is merely to nod one's head, say "O.K.," or grunt affirmatively after the response to be encouraged. Other responses are received with silence and a noncommittal expression; no punishment is used (Verplanck, 1955).

Quay (1959), for example, interviewed college students about their childhood experiences. Everyone received the same general instructions. In one group the student was encouraged (by appropriately placed phrases like "Yes—go on") whenever he told a family incident. Another group were similarly encouraged when they told nonfamily (e.g., school) incidents. The "family" group increased in the number of family incidents, the "nonfamily" group decreased. A similar process operates in everyday conversation to shape one's conversation about labor unions or petting. No doubt, teachers provide selective reinforcement like Quay's even when they think they are open-mindedly encouraging the pupil to express his own views, no matter what they may be.

The teacher is by no means the only person who shapes behavior by his power of reinforcement. Any audience, present or anticipated, may have a similar effect, not only on what one says but on what he learns about the attitude object. Zimmerman and Bauer (1956) assigned college students the task of preparing a talk to be given before the National Council of Teachers on the subject of teachers' salaries. As preparation, they listened to arguments for and against raising salaries and then, a week later, were asked to write down all the arguments they had heard before drafting the talk. These students recalled nearly twice as many arguments for raising salaries as contrary arguments (see Figure 100). Other students heard the same arguments, thinking their talks would be given before the American Taxpayers Economy League.[3] They recalled mostly the arguments against high salaries. One is more sensitive to arguments he will be able to use. Zimmerman and Bauer suggest that an American in a foreign country may hold in mind the facts and incidents he expects his American audience to receive warmly when he returns home and tells his experiences.

[3] Both the teacher organization and the economy league are fictitious. After collecting his data, the experimenter explained to the students that they would not really make speeches, and told what purpose his deception had served.

Attitude Toward Minorities as an Example

Though an attitude is often suggested by a model, one cannot say that an attitude is just accepted at second hand. Like old clothing, we try it on, and if it seems to fit, we keep it. If we can't "be ourselves," if the attitude forces us into positions we see as inconsistent with our other ideas, we seek a new alternative. If attitudes were always accepted from parents our culture would be more conservative in matters of taste than it is. Children would grow up buying clothes and furniture such as their parents chose. Instead, the children take pride in their youth, in living in an advanced century— so they throw out the scrollwork, put the carved walnut in the attic, and lay in a supply of canvas and wrought iron. This fulfills their ideal of sophistication.

To turn to a specific school problem of attitude development, we consider attitudes toward minorities. Discrimination and hostility directed against minorities, particularly the Negroes and Jews, is a major concern of the school. It concerns primary teachers equally with college instructors. As Radke-Yarrow *et al.* (1952) point out, many parents are so confused and emotional about racial issues that they are not able to teach the child tolerance. Deliberate education for interracial understanding has to become a school function.

Our discussion will illustrate the principles so far stated and indicate some of the unresolved problems of attitude education. Before we consider what is known in this area, we need to voice a caution. There are nearly as many theories to explain prejudice, and proposals for abating it, as there are writers on the topic. The urgency of the problem has tempted crusaders to say, "*This* is what's wrong . . . ," and "If schools would only teach *this* way . . ." Some people hold that economic competition is the source of conflict. Others, who note that emotionally disturbed people are often prejudiced, say that we must cure conflicts to eliminate hostility. Still others note that segregation makes it impossible to treat members of minorities as equals. "If we could only mix the groups thoroughly, people would learn to like members of other groups." No one "explanation" of intergroup conflict is correct. The causes of prejudice are many, and not the same for all people. Nearly all the proposed cures have some effectiveness, but no one will dispose of the problem. Teachers and laymen need to see the problem in its full complexity.

When members of a community share a belief, anyone growing up in that community is fairly sure to adopt it too. A child growing up in a family, a neighborhood, and a town tries on their outlooks and behaviors and finds that they work. There is a constant flow of reward for accepting the community point of view as his own or, as we sometimes say, internalizing it. Two fictional cases will show this.

Frank is born the son of a minister of a small Wisconsin town. His beginnings are emotionally successful—he learns to accept restraints and in turn is given affection, encouragement, and respect. He meets his parents' circle of friends. As Frank and his father stop into this or that store, both are greeted warmly. By school age, Frank knows Mr. Schmidt at the grocery, Mr. Levy at the clothing store and Mr. O'Hare the mailman. These men are treated as equals by Frank's father, and Frank never is aware that they might be regarded otherwise. There are only one or two Negroes in the community, workers who are treated no differently from others in like jobs. Frank doesn't know everyone equally well. Mr. O'Hare goes to a different church, and the O'Hares do not visit his home. But Frank meets people as individuals. Tony Paoli is a bully, but Frank doesn't blame Tony's race or religion. Frank's playmates regard Tony as a boy to avoid, but words like "Dago" don't circulate in the group. Probably Frank does hear someone from a more rough-and-tumble neighborhood blast Tony with a string of bad names. This boy does not become a model; he represents what Frank has learned not to be. If Frank were to call Tony a name or two, his teacher and his parents would call his conduct improper. Frank identifies with them enough that this carries weight.

A more conscious social attitude takes shape in later years. The belief is formed into a general verbal principle. Frank's father discusses prejudice at the family dinner table and in church meetings. The immediate subject may be a Sunday text or the complaint of a citizen that a Negro girl is in his daughter's gym class. Frank hears repeatedly an interpretation that stresses the equality of man, the injustice of restrictions based on race, and the responsibility of the individual citizen. The young people Frank knows best are ready to agree with the teachers and ministers. Facts about Negro housing in Chicago will evoke a unanimous "something should be done." Some in the class remain unconcerned by things so remote. But Frank and his friends have no difficulty seeing themselves as potential community leaders. After all, the identifying figures they know best are daily influencing community government. If Frank and his friends circulate a political petition or plan exchange visits with other church groups, they get approval. By now Frank can verbalize a philosophy of tolerance. He may become a crusader in college and adulthood, he may be a passive supporter of others' crusades, or he may lose interest. It is highly improbable that any experience could make him antagonistic to a racial group.

The same smooth course of development produces Ben Blake, who accepts from his community an attitude that Frank would deplore. Ben too was born in a privileged home. For the purposes of our example, we shall make Ben's father a school superintendent. Ben follows Frank's pattern in emotional and social relations. He makes friends, he has a happy childhood, he accepts his father as an ideal. But Ben has no contact with Negroes or Jews as equals. Martha the colored servant is well liked, but Martha's children are not invited to the house. Martha's opinions are not invited when matters more important than tonight's salad are being discussed. Mrs. Blake calls her "Martha," but Martha never uses Mrs. Blake's first name. Ben comes to feel that Martha is there to carry out decisions made by his kind.

This concept is confirmed by hundreds of observations. He learns that Negroes are expected to live in their own area, to attend their own school, to leave the running of the community to the whites. Whom does one consult when a problem arises in daily work? This answer is supplied by his father's references at the dinner table, when he mentions names Ben knows as those of whites. What about Negroes as companions? Ben learns that he is to play within his own neighborhood: The white children who do play with Negroes are spoken of unkindly. It becomes a matter of self-respect to stay distant from Negroes and so prove one's membership in the better element.

This is no pattern of overt hostility or conflict. In fact, Ben is taught to be polite to everyone. Name-calling is as improper for him as for Frank. When questions arise regarding equal treatment for minority groups, Ben does not hear a tirade—not from his parents nor from their friends. When a magazine article raises questions in his mind, he is given answers: "We have worked out these policies of segregation as the best way to avoid conflict. It takes a long time to make change." The people who push for change are spoken of as troublemakers who don't understand the situation. All this is accepted by Ben because he respects his father and likes him, because Ben is rewarded when he echoes this view, and because the facts Ben is shown do fit the community belief. By the end of high school Ben, like Frank, will have verbalized his principles, but the principles will be different.

In these portraits, it is impossible to present Frank and Ben neutrally. The liberal who believes action can hasten social improvement is always easier to show as a sympathetic figure than the conservative who is resigned to slower progress. Both Frank and Ben are intelligent, secure, good citizens. They learned their beliefs the same way—through accepting, trying, and confirming the interpretation of an admired figure. And these beliefs worked well enough to convince each of them of the soundness of his way of acting. If a teacher had bombarded either boy with the other's viewpoint, the odds are that the teacher's ideas would have been rejected. Frank could not incorporate "leave well enough alone" without denying his father's merit and some of his belief in himself. No more easily could Ben become a reformer.

Attitudes certainly can be altered, though the change may be slow. Helfant (1952) reports correlations consistently below .30 between pupil attitudes on international issues and those of their parents. Though other investigators sometimes find higher correlations, it is clear that pupils do

TABLE 25

Pupils' attitudes shift toward the teacher's attitude (after Kroll, 1934)

| | | Pupils' attitude score (average) | | |
| | | Beginning of term | End of term | Change |
Class	Teacher's attitude score			
1	50 (most conservative)	43.8	45.9	2.2
2	52	39.7	41.3	1.6
3	54	43.6	43.8	.2
4	65	44.7	48.7	4.0
5	68	44.7	51.0	6.4
6	69 (most liberal)	45.9	53.4	7.4

collect opinions outside the home and do create a belief system different from that of their parents. One of the important forces in attitude change is the teacher.

Kroll compared six social-studies and English teachers, three of whom held much more conservative beliefs than the others. He administered an attitude scale to their classes (high-school seniors) before and after a semester's work. On the attitude test a high score indicates a liberal opinion. The results are shown in Table 25. You should note several relations. Pupils were, on the average, more conservative than teachers, and in every case the shift of the average was toward the teacher's attitude. The shift toward liberal opinions was appreciably greater under the three liberal teachers than under the three less liberal ones. While the study shows that teachers can modify attitudes, the change accomplished is small, compared to the 60-point range of opinions among pupils.

16. Suppose that Frank and Ben go to a university and are invited to join a fraternity. The invitation is extended by a friend, and the members are likeable and intelligent. How will Frank and Ben react when they find that this group bars some persons on racial and religious grounds?

17. Some homes teach that Darwin's theory of evolution is a false and evil doctrine. Can a college instructor expect to erase this attitude?

Conflicting Influences

Most often, the role of the teacher is to augment the home influence, to capitalize upon and make more definite the pupils' values. But the educator wishes to wean pupils from attitudes learned in the home that are socially undesirable. What happens when a pupil is exposed to conflicting codes, or confronted with evidence incompatible with his beliefs?

People hold tenaciously to systems of attitudes they have built up. If they are strongly committed to a belief, contradictory evidence rarely will shake it; they will find some way to make the evidence conform to the belief (Festinger *et al.*, 1956) or they will ignore the disturbing argument (Kelley and Volkart, 1952). One reads into the words of an admired figure a meaning consistent with his own attitudes. Put into Lincoln's mouth a statement such as, "Negroes are unfit for leadership." The liberal reader will find an explanation that restores consistency: "He means that Negroes have been handicapped and so cannot take their proper station unless given greater opportunities for development." By this means, the reader maintains his views (H. B. Lewis, 1941).

There are other protective devices. One is to attribute attitudes not to the speaker but to his role (Steiner and Field, 1960). When an admired minister speaks against discrimination the prejudiced man in the congregation may react, "You have to say things like that if you're a minister." This accommodation reduces the attention paid to the ideas themselves. (It is illustrated in the relation of teachers and pupils to chewing gum. The teacher censures its use, and even pupils who ordinarily respect teachers' ideas go right on using it. They diminish any feeling of conflict by looking on the teacher's remarks as part of her job, rather than as something she cares about.)

Change is greatest under conditions favorable for emotional learning. This has already been shown in the Jones study with the rabbit and in the Kroll study of high-school teaching. Much more thorough is Newcomb's (1943) study of college students (see also Newcomb, 1958, pp. 265–75). In adolescence, the student's sense of being grown up and independent make him more ready to respond to the challenge of social issues. Voicing an opinion that differs from his parents' is a way of declaring his maturity. This is more pleasurable if taking such a stand solidifies his place in the peer group. College students come to the campus rather like the folks at home in their beliefs. As they encounter concepts from other places, they question certain ideas for the first time. Some of them leave college with viewpoints much different from those of their parents.

This gradual weaning is demonstrated in Figure 101, where attitudes of freshman girls at Bennington College were compared with those of students having a longer exposure to this intellectual melting-pot. At the time of this study (1936) the Bennington curriculum was designed to emphasize current social questions. The freshmen voted as they thought their parents would; the juniors had moved in the direction most favored by the college community as a whole. Other attitude tests showed comparable changes from year to year. The changes were greater than those observed in conventional colleges.

The change in each girl's attitude depended largely on the social satisfactions she attained. One girl who strongly needed the support of a few close associates clung to the attitude her friends shared, even if this was unlike the ideas of her parents. Another girl was striving for independence

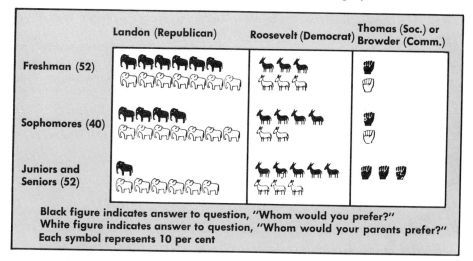

Black figure indicates answer to question, "Whom would you prefer?"
White figure indicates answer to question, "Whom would your parents prefer?"
Each symbol represents 10 per cent

101   *Students in a liberal college move away from their parents' ideas*
(after Newcomb, 1943)

Preferences in the 1936 presidential election. Figures in this chart have
been rounded to the nearest 10 per cent.

from a home where she had learned very liberal ideas. She chose conservative friends, mostly outside the college, and backed away from the intellectual activities of the college: "All I want is to get through and have a
home of my own." Her ideas became more conservative because she did
not try to become one of the general college group. Newcomb's conclusions
from all his cases may be condensed as follows (1943, pp. 155–56; for further evidence see Webster, 1958):

> Those most susceptible were characterized by habits of conformity, with
> varying degrees of passivity or personal initiative. . . .
> Those who were little or not at all susceptible to community influences upon
> attitudes were characterized by negativism, by indifference, or by divided al-
> legiance toward the community. Habits of negativism were in some cases of
> precollege standing, and in others represented a reaction to frustrated hopes
> of social success in college, following some measure of precollege success. . . .
> What seems most clearly to distinguish those who were and those who were
> not susceptible to the community influences thus appears to be the kinds of
> adjustments, already pretty well set on coming to college, in two vital areas,
> viz., toward parents and toward peers. Those who are capable of considerable
> independence from parents find no great obstacle in the fact that dominant
> attitudes at college differ from those of parents. Those who are particularly
> ripe for parental emancipation find in social attitudes a ready symbol. Over-
> dependence upon parents prevents attitude change in two sorts of ways. For
> some, conflict between home and college standards is simply intolerable; to
> embrace the latter would be an act of excessive disloyalty. For others the tie

is so all-absorbing that the college influences are scarcely felt; hence there is no conflict.

As to adjustment toward contemporaries, two sorts of differences may be seen between those who are most and least susceptible to community influences. The first is that of orienting oneself toward a total community rather than toward a limited group within it. Those who choose the latter orientation are almost invariably those whose sense of personal inadequacy in competing with their peers has prevented them from entering the larger arena. Hence they are not influenced by the dominant community attitudes. The second difference is not unrelated to the first. It is the difference between setting goals, phrased

102 *Whose attitudes will be changed?*

in community-wide terms, within or beyond one's limits of achievement. Those who set them too high and fail to reach them are apt to reject the community attitudes, whereas those whose initial goals are not beyond reach tend to raise their standards of achievement, embracing community attitudes more closely with each added success.

METHODS FOR MODIFYING ATTITUDES

The preceding sections have discussed the normal gradual development of attitudes. Because the professional teacher is only one among many molders of attitudes his individual contribution may seem trivial. Yet of the influences that can reach every youngster, the teacher is the only one formally charged to represent society. The teacher therefore has an obligation to intensify his influence by whatever procedures will have greatest effect. Though on first thought you may object to the suggestion that teachers should persuade, or engage in propaganda, part of the teacher's duty is to communicate the ideals of the culture.

Teaching Facts About the Attitude-Object

If attitudes are meanings, perhaps we can use verbal explanations to instill them, just as we do with other concepts. Some teachers assume that students will reconsider their illogical prejudices if given facts about racial groups, including the fact that most so-called races have no biological homogeneity. This view is seen in claims that historical knowledge teaches patriotism and studying French promotes good will toward other nations. Jacob (1957, p. 6), after a review of evidence on attitude change in college, doubts that college *courses* modify beliefs much:

> The main over-all effect of higher education upon student values is to bring about general acceptance of a body of standards and attitudes characteristic of college-bred men and women in the American community. . . . Changes . . . emerge on the periphery of the student's character, affecting his application of values, rather than the core of values themselves. To call this process a *liberalization* is a misnomer. . . . The college man or woman thus tends to be more self-important—more conservative—more tolerant—and less fearful of evil forces in this world and outside than those who have not been "higher-educated." . . .
>
> This study has not discerned significant changes in student values which can be attributed directly either to the character of the curriculum or to the basic courses in social science which students take as part of their general education.

As we saw in Newcomb's study above, change takes place; but the change seems related more to college living than to college lessons.

Teaching facts does not necessarily alter attitudes. Facts alter attitudes when they clarify an unstructured situation, which the person approaches with no clear interpretation; but facts have relatively little impact on the man who has made up his mind. Suppose the daily paper tells you that Senator X, whom you admire, made a deal to pay off an opponent and keep him from running in the next election. The chances are that you will shake your head over this but decide that that is what X had to do to stay in office and carry out his program. Some people will be horrified by the disclosure and say so, but strangely enough, most of them were already opposed to X and welcome this added justification. It takes an overpowering array of facts to change the minds of people who are once set in a belief that has emotional significance (Jahoda and Cooper, 1947; Mead, 1955; M. B. Smith *et al.*, 1956).

On the other hand, if you begin with a blank slate, facts have a great deal of impact. Did you ever hear of W. Morris Hughes, the former Australian prime minister? Probably not. Now suppose I tell you that he is a distinguished Australian observer who has highly favorable views of American institutions and that he stands for scientific progress. Your attitude toward Hughes, if you trust me as an informant, is likely to be favorable at this point. If I tell you instead that Hughes has been attacking the very things you value, such as universal suffrage and the freedom of science, you would disapprove of him. *The Daily Iowan,* a student newspaper, proved this with a series of editorials about Hughes' opinions on a mythical lecture tour of America (Annis and Meier, 1934). Over a four-month period, planted editorials in half the papers favored Hughes. Copies going to the other readers lambasted the visitor. Sure enough, when students were asked what they thought of Hughes, they split down the middle, echoing whichever opinion they had read in the newspapers (see Figure 103). Choose an event that students have not made up their minds about, focus them on facts that support one point of view, and they take on your viewpoint. They learn your attitude regarding the causes of the American Revolution, the value of tonsillectomy, or the sterilization of the mentally weak.

Facts provide a fine starting point for thinking about issues if teachers make a deliberate effort to lead pupils to implications. Bond (1940) made one of the most careful studies of the rational, factual approach to attitude change. He prepared a unit in genetics for college freshmen, as a part of their introductory science course. Certain scientific generalizations were selected for emphasis, such as, "Because of the nature of the process of mutation and the operation of chance, most racial differences are trivial." Students began by defining race and classifying groups on measurable characteristics. In discussion, students commented freely on differences which they thought made some groups inferior or hard to assimilate. This led to distinguishing between biological and cultural qualities, at the end

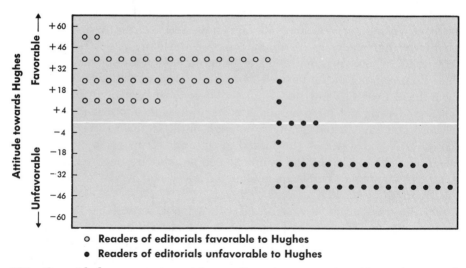

○ **Readers of editorials favorable to Hughes**
● **Readers of editorials unfavorable to Hughes**

103 *One-sided presentation of facts affects interpretation (from Annis and Meier, 1934)*

of the third class hour. The work of Mendel was then introduced, with discussion of theories and examination of hybrid corn specimens. Here the scientific evidence was connected to intermarriage and other questions that had come into the original discussion, so that the facts were seen by the students as significant. The classwork moved into a study of variability and overlap of groups and applied the concepts to skin color, height of Japanese and American soldiers, and other examples. Cultural sources of variation were considered in detail. The final summary at the end of the 15-hour unit was: "Evaluation of an individual should be in terms of individual worth, not of racial or national worth." Meanwhile a control group had studied genetics in a more isolated and traditional manner. They learned the same generalizations, examining more detailed scientific material, but made no deliberate application to racial questions. Both groups read the same sources.

Bond gave both classes 19 tests of attitudes and understanding: the experimental method proved superior on 17 of them, according to Bond's objectives. Specifically,

The experimental group was less favorable to imperialism.

The experimental group was more favorable toward Orientals, Jews, and Italians.

The experimental group was significantly better in reasoning about one set of problems on genetics and heredity, particularly human heredity, but the control group had a slight (insignificant) advantage on a second form of this test.

The experimental group was markedly superior in analyzing and drawing conclusions from an experimental study of mouse heredity.

The experimental method not only improved understanding and reasoning, but also carried over into changed opinions on social problems. No evidence is available on the ultimate question of how much the teaching changed the students' behavior in the community. Even without this evidence, it appears that the 15 hours were well spent.

    18. In the light of Bond's study, how can a French course develop appreciation of and respect for French civilization?

Persuasion

Most of the research on techniques of persuasion—that is, of direct argument for attitude change—has been done through short experiments. Subjects have been shown a single film, or given a single lecture by a stranger, opinions being measured and compared with a control group. This is not much like the persuasion that occurs in the classroom, when a familiar teacher expresses certain viewpoints over an extended period; even so, the experiments have turned up pertinent information.

ONE-SIDED VS. TWO-SIDED PRESENTATIONS.   One group of studies was concerned with the effect of one-sided communications as compared with those that give both sides of an argument. A wartime study (Hovland *et al.*, 1949, p. 215) showed that a two-sided argument which appeared to consider all the facts was somewhat more successful, especially with better educated men. Lumsdaine and Janis (1953) tested both the immediate change of opinion and the persistence of change when subjects heard a counterargument. Two radio programs were prepared arguing that Russia would not be able to produce many atomic bombs in the next five years (the study having been made before Russia's first successful test). One program gave only arguments supporting this belief; the second presented arguments on both sides of the question, but offered the same conclusion, that Russia could not soon make bombs in quantity. Both groups (high-school pupils) heard one or the other program in May. In June, some pupils heard a new speaker argue that within two years Russia would be producing bombs in quantity. All pupils were then asked, "How long do you think it will be before Russia is producing large numbers of atomic bombs?" To measure the effect of the propaganda, the change of estimates from early May to late June was calculated (percentage increasing their estimates less the percentage decreasing). The students who heard either the one-sided or the two-sided argument in May changed about 65 per cent, from the pretest to the test immediately after the May program. When both groups heard, in June, the counterargument that Russia would succeed soon, the group that had heard only one side of the story in May gave ground. The net change from pretest to the test after both the May argument and the June counterargument was:

Group hearing one-sided argument in May	2%
Group hearing two-sided argument in May	61%

Thus only the argument that took into account both sides had a permanent effect. In effect, a two-sided discussion gives an advance basis for ignoring or discounting an opposing communication. Thus "inoculated," the listener tends to retain the conclusion first proposed. For most of the attitudes the school seeks to teach, there will be counterpropaganda from commercial interests or from undemocratic elements in the community. The school should give an appropriate amount of attention to the arguments that might be advanced for believing, for example, that communism will ultimately triumph. Ignoring such arguments leaves the pupil without inoculation against communist propaganda.

A further advantage of considering both sides is that the student is more likely to regard a two-sided communication as fair, and therefore trustworthy. Voice of America broadcasts are more believed by overseas listeners when American mistakes and problems are frankly described, and less believed when the programs insist that American policy is perfect (Carlson and Abelson, 1956).

A propagandist who condemns all your beliefs is clearly no friend; self-respect demands that his arguments be rejected. The communicator who establishes that he and his hearer are agreed on their basic values can become a model. "This fellow thinks as I do. He and I are on the same side." Then the speaker can introduce his "message" that certain attitudes are contrary to the values he and his listener agree on (Carlson, 1956). Mead (1955) tells of the American-trained public health nurse in Mexico who found the native diet extremely unsuitable and condemned it in order to persuade mothers to feed their babies milk. The mothers refused to follow the suggestion. When the nurse dropped her negative tone, and suggested only that babies be fed water in which the family beans had been cooked—a recommendation in harmony with the mothers' beliefs—the suggestion was adopted. The babies did noticeably better, and now the mothers started feeding their babies milk, without further urging. The nurse had become a trusted guide instead of a hostile, uncomprehending outsider.

GROUP DISCUSSION.   We would expect a communication to have greater effect when the person makes some sort of active response to it and that response is reinforced. Mitnick and McGinnies (1958) do report such an effect. A film designed to combat racial prejudice was shown to high-school students; in some classes, but not all, the film was followed by a discussion directed to support the effect of the film. Tests of prejudice were given before and after the teaching, and again a month later. The average scores shifted as shown in Table 26. No attempt was made to change attitudes in the control group; their increased prejudice comes from uncontrolled influences such as the current news. In the experimental groups there was a large immediate change in opinion, but—as is often found in studies of this kind—a later return toward the initial beliefs. Without discussion, two-thirds of the impact of the film was gone a month later. With discussion, only one-fourth of the gain was lost. The effect of discussion here seems rather small, however, and there are other studies in which discussion shows no effect or inconsistent effects (E. B. Bennett, 1955; McGinnies et al., 1958). A truly open discussion may even reduce the intended influence. A member of the group tends selectively to listen to those people whose views he finds congenial; thus a two-sided discussion may help him to resist persuasion (Brodbeck, 1956).

In a discussion group, the active discussants are likely to change more than the listeners (Janis and King, 1954; see also Hovland et al., 1953, pp. 222 ff.). Taking a stand publicly in itself helps fix an attitude. Pupils who wrote an opinion that they expected to be published in a national magazine

TABLE 26

Discussion can make a change of attitude more lasting (Mitnick and McGinnies, 1958)

	Initial test	After teaching	One month later	Net change in prejudice
Film-plus-discussion	70	62	64	6 point decrease
Film only	70	61	67	3 point decrease
Neither (control group)	72	77	75	3 point increase

for teen-agers were much less swayed by later counterarguments than pupils who wrote a similar opinion with no publication in mind (Hovland *et al.*, 1957).

The evidence is too mixed at present to indicate just when a discussion moves attitudes. Among the significant factors appear to be these: How close-knit is the group? Does a speaker receive support from a part of the group when he voices an opinion contrary to that desired by the leader? To what extent do pupils voice agreement merely to escape from the tension of the discussion? For further studies on group influence, see page 485, and also Maccoby *et al.*, 1958, pp. 174–290.

EMOTIONALITY IN PRESENTATION.   Dramatic appeals are effective persuaders (Willis, 1940; Siegel, 1958). Motion pictures can glamorize an occupation or a nationality, capturing the attention and emotions of the viewer. He lives in the characters on the screen for a while, sympathizing with the hero and hating the villian. When the lights go up again he has learned new meanings. Peterson and Thurstone (1933) administered attitude scales regarding various ethnic groups on which pupils could check statements they believed. The statements ranged from extremely favorable to violently unfavorable. Then the pupils were shown one of several Hollywood films. In *The Birth of a Nation* a bestial Negro freed by the Civil War attacks a fair-haired child and is hunted down by an heroically portrayed Ku Klux Klan. After seeing this, the pupils' attitudes toward Negroes became less favorable, and this shift persisted on a retest five months later. In *Son of the Gods* they saw the story of Sam Lee, an admirable young Chinese growing up in a Chinese community, not fully accepted by whites because of his race. A good deal of Chinese life was shown. Before the film, the typical attitude was expressed in such statements as:

> Some Chinese traits are admirable but on the whole I don't like them. I have no particular love or hate for the Chinese.

After the film, opinions had shifted so that the typical attitude was more favorable:

The Chinese are pretty decent.
The Chinese are different but not inferior.

Likewise, in reading a powerful novel a person practices certain interpretations and emotional responses as if he were living the experiences of the character with whom he identifies.

Should an advocate of attitude change try to give his presentation more impact by a strong emotional appeal? Janis and Feshback (1953) tried to persuade high-school pupils to brush their teeth after every meal by stressing the disease and pain that follow improper care. Two other groups were given the same argument, but with little or no attempt to arouse fear. Pupils were later questioned about their behavior in caring for their teeth. The net change toward better practices was as follows:

Strong emotional appeal	8%
Moderate emotional appeal	22%
Very little emotional appeal	36%

The unemotional appeal also tended to inoculate the pupils against later counterpropaganda to the effect that brushing the teeth is not really very important.

Too much pressure defeats the propagandist's purpose. Small amounts of threat may be necessary to make the listener take a proposal seriously, but strong threats arouse resistance. The listener appears to close his mind to the horrors described, and in so doing shuts out also the message telling him how to avoid the horrors. Attempts to gain public attention for civil defense against nuclear attack, and for early tests to detect cancer, have found such resistance difficult to overcome.

19. On which of these topics would you expect one-sided presentation of facts to have the greatest effect on attitudes of a high-school class?
    a. sales taxes vs. property taxes as a source of revenue
    b. laws prohibiting gambling
    c. petting
20. What determines whether a teacher or a text is regarded as a trustworthy source of information?
21. Can a science teacher ever "discuss both sides" of a question on which there is a scientifically accepted conclusion?
22. Discuss this comment: "All this information on how to persuade others to accept your conclusion may be useful if your goal is brainwashing, but not if you are truly an educator."
23. What facts given in this section suggest how education can make people more resistant to influences that run counter to the values and interpretations taught by the school?
24. In a comparison of oral presentation in a quiet, conversational tone

against an excited emphatic, high-keyed style, the conversational tone was less often identified as propaganda by a college student audience. It produced more alteration of attitude (Dietrich, 1946). How can this be explained?

25. Experimenters have obtained "commitment" by having students prepare statements they expect to be published. What less artificial techniques are at the disposal of the teacher?

Activity Programs

Direct experience with the attitude object obviously builds meanings, and activities to provide such experience are advocated as a way to change attitudes. "Students," says Jacob (1957, p. 10), "are often deeply affected by participation in experiences which vividly confront them with value issues, and possibly demand decisions on their part whose consequences they can witness."

Let us compare such an activity with more conventional teaching. In high-school general science, students often study trees. Conventional class activities might include learning the parts of trees, examining a cross section of a trunk, naming trees on lantern slides, talking about the economic value of lumber and conservation, and possibly making a collection of leaves. All this could be done at a high level of understanding and interest. The teacher concerned with developing attitudes might try instead the activity approach described by W. French *et al.* (1948). A class set out to determine how trees improve the community. They studied landscapes pictured in magazines and identified what trees were used in making homes attractive. They learned from their county agent what trees would grow in their locality and what soil conditions were needed. Then they surveyed the school grounds to decide what improvements in landscaping were needed and themselves made many of the improvements. They decided that flowers and lawn were especially needed. They dug a bed for roses, removed the clay top and substituted woods dirt, and nourished rose cuttings to the blooming stage the next year. They leveled the ground where lawn was needed, removed rubbish, and used the extra dirt and clay to fill gullies where soil was being washed away. In addition, pupils surveyed their own homes. Many of them made improvements there.

The merit of this activity can be judged in terms of the often-repeated principle: whatever interpretations are confirmed through trial are learned. The pupils confirmed that it is fun to be outdoors. They probably learned how to handle a shovel, and how deep to set a rose cutting. Understanding about erosion, fertilizer, and soil surely was promoted. If generalizations were explicitly developed, they might have learned much about organizing for community improvement or caring for plants. In addition, as they planned the activity, deciding why it was worthwhile to plant grass and what good would come of it, they were testing and confirming attitudes. The pupils took pride in contributing to the community. Their satisfaction was strengthened by the common spirit of the group and by the praise of adults. As such projects become a tradition, the visibly growing results of previous classes' work will be additional confirmation that community improvement pays. The pupils in the class are learning about conservation problems they can come to grips with. This is far more useful than studying the laws that might somehow conserve trees in the distant Pacific Northwest. Project work is more likely than an academic unit to be thoroughly comprehended, emotionally rewarding, and effective in changing future behavior.

It is not enough to provide a pleasant experience, in which planting is fun; conscious verbal analysis of important judgments and generalizations is important if pupils are to identify similar challenges in the future. One risk in a "real" project is that the work can consume time far beyond its educative value. When pupils spend most of their time loading wheelbarrows with dirt, little intellectual growth takes place. Projects are justified when the pupil is continually improving his interpretations of important situations. Stoddard put it this way: "We learn not by doing, but by thinking about what we are doing."

Are attitudes toward minorities benefited by close contact with members of the minority group? Contact with Negroes may produce favorable attitudes or it may intensify prejudices. If pupils have opportunities to associate with some Negroes on an equal and pleasant basis, this may break down barriers. If a school includes both racial groups, pupils sometimes associate freely only with those of their own race, having formal and limited contacts with the other group. Then they practice only formal politeness, not human friendliness.

Attitudes may shift in an unfavorable direction. Negroes and whites shared cabins at a camp, and a Guess-Who technique was used to obtain information on attitudes. During the first few days, white boys described Negro cabinmates most often by the phrases "one who helps, is kind," "does what he is told," and "bosses others." After two weeks of camp life, Negroes were most often mentioned as "one who bosses others," "gets mad easily," and "is afraid or shy." This perception may be a realistic summary of behavior observed, but the finding casts a shadow on the naive hope that bringing whites and Negroes together will by itself generate admiration and rosy good feeling (Radke-Yarrow *et al.*, 1958, pp. 623–36).

Integrated activities do seem slowly to change attitudes for the better when there are common goals toward which everyone works. Cooperative activities make it possible to practice and confirm desirable attitudes that would otherwise get little encouragement (Sherif *et al.*, 1961).

Some of the clearest work on just what makes contact educative was done in a summer camp to which New York City boys were sent by a social agency (Mussen, 1950). During a four-week period, they worked, played, and lived with other campers, some of whom were Negroes. Subtle and indirect tests showed no average change in the attitude score of white boys. Many individuals changed significantly, some becoming more prejudiced toward Negroes, some less. According to projective tests of personality, the ones who came to the camp with most prejudice had more need to be dominant and aggressive, and seemed possibly to have more hostility to their parents. This suggests that hostility toward parents had generalized to targets safer to attack. During the camping period, the more aggressive boys and those who felt the most maltreated by authority increased their hostility to the Negro. These boys who increased in prejudice were the ones who rather disliked the camping experience, who did not fit in and did not receive social rewards from the mixed group, and who no doubt felt all the more abused and antagonistic as a result. The ones who became less prejudiced were those who fitted into the camp, got along with others, and so found it rewarding to accept group standards. Their personalities were marked by less aggression, less feeling of being mistreated, and more friendliness toward others. Both the boys who changed and the boys who did not change tested and confirmed atttitudes, but only the boys secure in the situation confirmed socially desirable beliefs (see also H. P. Smith, 1955). A similar conclusion was noted in studying prejudiced college students (Adorno *et al.*, 1950).

Highly prejudiced students and adults tend to be those who lack social assurance and self-respect, who feel hostile and find racial antagonism a useful outlet. The most prejudiced people are typically trying to get power and avoid trouble from others who are more powerful. They identify with the strong, have contempt for the weak. And this attitude is traced in many cases to domineering or demanding homes where the parents held firm standards, insisted on obedience, and were admired in a distant, rather cold way. The person learned to be like his parents, demanding of himself and others (see also pages 152 ff. and 626 ff.).

> **26.** What meanings are tried and confirmed in the following programs? How adequate are these activities for teaching attitudes?
> > **a.** A class of fifth-graders prepares a Christmas basket for a needy family. They have been studying underprivileged groups, and specify that the family (known only to the social agency distributing baskets) shall be a Negro one.
> > **b.** Students in a junior high school who descend from different national groups (Greek, Swedish, etc.) participate in an All-Nations pageant in which each group performs a colorful folk dance.
> > **c.** High-school students studying civic problems form a baby-sitting service to look after children on Election Day while parents vote.
> **27.** A prospective teacher spends four months as the part-time leader of a boys' club. What sort of person will acquire desirable attitudes toward boys?

28. Compare Mussen's findings regarding conditions favoring attitude change with Newcomb's.

29. Mussen found that those whose racial attitudes were changed least were hostile to their parents. In another study (page 155) he found that those who were independent of peer opinion saw their parents as having been relatively unfriendly. How are the two studies related? Are they consistent or inconsistent?

What Method Shall the School Use?

If so many approaches have some success, and none works in all situations or on all students, the teacher needs some general principles to guide his choice of method. Students of the prejudice problem (Williams, 1947) point out that re-educational attempts have suffered from adopting a single technique. A school tries lessons on civil rights, or it tries mixed-race recreation, or it tries to instill respect for Negroes by posting a photo of Ralph Bunche and playing spirituals. A more flexible and complex approach is needed since the many aspects of an attitude are learned in different experiences and not all pupils respond to one approach in the same way. Moreover, attitudes develop over many years. This applies not only to intergroup attitudes but to all others.

Some pupils are anxious to conform, readily identify with teachers, and accept whatever values are proposed. Others are rebellious. Bill Chelten would enthusiastically plunge into a reform activity that he views as changing things adults have handled badly, but suggestions from authority would have only a bad effect on him. A pupil who comprehends serious music will be impressed upon hearing the work of William Grant Still, but a pupil who does not value complex art will not respect Negro talent more after this experience. Some young people will be most swayed if a strong consensus is developed in the group as a whole. They need group acceptance, or they take pride in being members in good standing and will adopt values that the majority stand for. Others who take pride in "thinking for themselves" nonetheless become devout conformers in a group with unusual attitudes—a bohemian crowd, an existentialist society, or a radical club.

The attitudes hardest to alter are those rooted in fears and emotional hungers. This is particularly a problem with delinquents; neither punishment nor persuasion relieves the central tensions. The boy or girl turns to delinquency for pleasures he has not found through good conduct. Sexual delinquency among girls often implies a search for love and for a sense of worth; crime among boys reflects, in many cases, a desire for power and a desire to hit back at parents and society for love denied. Unless the basic need for self-respect and power is relieved, it will break out in some other form. A surface treatment that deals only with attitudes toward sex or crime will not produce a stable adjustment. It may teach the person to hide the acts that get him into trouble, but his further tries to satisfy his needs may be equally undesirable.

Attitude instruction is not accomplished in a few classrooms or through a few concentrated doses of indoctrination. Ideas and ideals are developed in personal contacts with peers outside any deliberate program. They are picked out of the casual remarks of a respected teacher. A quite minor story may teach that Indians are cruel, ignoble, and ungrateful. These glimmering, tentative meanings, if not contradicted, become a fixed part of the pupil's interpretative system. Formal instruction can crystallize attitudes already forming. Sometimes it can help the student acknowledge fallacies in his outlook or conflicts among his values. In the long run, though, attitudes are established by living; interpretations are tried, confirmed, and retained accordingly. Each person takes on, for the most part, the attitudes of the people to whom he is loyal. Therefore the principal aim of the school is to make the pupil loyal to his society and to develop his identification with good citizens. If in his school years he forms this allegiance firmly, he can be trusted afterward to work out constructive attitudes on specific issues.

30. Illustrate each of the following generalizations as shown in learning to like symphonic music.
>   **a.** An attitude often begins as a provisional try suggested by the attitudes of an identifying figure.
>   **b.** A model whose attitudes are followed by some learners will not be used as an example by others.
>   **c.** Pleasant experience with a class of objects causes the learner to expect them to be pleasant in the future.
>   **d.** Some pupils are more ready to take on a certain attitude than others because it fulfills personal needs.
>   **e.** A course that gives much information may provide no practice in desirable attitudes toward the subject.
>   **f.** Formal instruction can extend attitudes already forming, which may or may not be the attitudes desired by the teacher.

31. Which of the methods discussed in this chapter can be used for the following purposes?
>   **a.** to interest able pupils in going to college
>   **b.** to encourage children to want a balanced diet
>   **c.** to develop skepticism toward vague, sweeping claims made in advertising

32. "For the teacher to harangue students about what they ought to think or feel is not likely to be effective," says an author. What facts in this chapter indicate that such one-sided presentations have some effect? Could the statement be made more accurate?

SUMMARY

Attitudes are meanings one associates with a certain object, which influence his acceptance of that object. Whereas knowledge can be described as true or false, attitudinal meanings are largely personal, and there is no standard of right or wrong. Nonetheless, since beliefs influence behavior, the teacher of every subject wants to promote certain attitudes and values.

Attitudes develop through trial and confirmation. The responses tried initially are often those suggested by a model or identifying figure. The child observes what others do that seems to produce success or punishment; these observed consequences influence his tries. While any person actually present or encountered in reading may serve as a model for a certain act, the learner is likely to depend consistently on certain identifying figures. A child normally identifies with his parents, and gradually extends his loyalty to persons encountered outside the home. The identifying figure is generally a person regarded as successful and supporting. Moreover, the example he sets must be seen by the learner as within reach and capable of yielding satisfaction; the model, that is, must be consistent with the learner's self-concept.

Teachers serve as models, some teachers being more influential than others. Pupils generally admire teachers who respect them, make demands, support their efforts, and recognize their successes. Since the pupil chooses an identifying figure in the light of his own needs and self-concept, a faculty should include persons of various types. Books and dramatic presentations offer significant models. The book is most likely to be accepted that provides opportunities for identification and wish fulfillment. Models presented in school reading lists are often insufficiently varied, and may present a distorted view of the world. Books read generally feature prominent individuals, and those whose activities are dramatic. Texts may communicate biases, for example, by describing only girls and women who are dependent and sociable. Adolescents seem to take as models primarily those with whom they are personally acquainted rather than the heroes they learned about in school.

In teaching attitudes a distinction must be made between loyalty to a slogan and belief in a well-understood concept. Pupils and adults who say that they believe in democracy or free speech may endorse practices that are quite inconsistent with those ideals.

Pleasant and unpleasant associations are formed by experience with the attitude object, and these associations generalize over other similar objects. The greater the similarity, the greater the likelihood of transfer. A specific fear, formed by a harsh experience, can be eliminated if the feared object is introduced gradually and distantly, while the child is in a satisfying situation. General attitudes are formed, which affect response to a wide range of situations: security, fearfulness, readiness to try a new food, conservatism, tolerance, or prejudice. The person with dogmatic views on race differences tends also to be dogmatic on other subjects, dependent on authority, and resistant to new experience.

Responses that are confirmed by social reinforcement are likely to be retained. This accounts for the fact that children growing up in different homes acquire different attitudes. The teacher, or any other audience, has reinforcing power. Pupils' attitudes are only moderately correlated with parental beliefs because these other influences are at work. Kroll showed that the social attitudes of pupils do move toward their teacher's, even though on the average the movement is not great.

Faced with conflicting influences, people strive to retain consistency. They may ignore disturbing evidence, reinterpret what they hear to fit their preconceptions, or decide that the speaker does not really believe what he says. College students who accept the liberalizing influence of the campus are those who find social satisfaction in the new environment. Those who were emotionally independent of their parents were able to adopt new attitudes. Those who felt socially inadequate, who experienced rejection from others, or who failed to achieve their overambitious goals, did not form new attitudes.

While college social experiences modify beliefs, it appears that academic courses do not usually have much impact. The student may see new ways to apply values he already holds, but he is unlikely to alter the value system itself. Factual teaching is most effective when the student has no clear picture of the attitude object. Even in controversial areas where students have preconceptions, factual teaching can modify attitudes if there is deliberate discussion of attitudinal implications. Bond's teaching of genetics is an example.

Deliberate persuasion has been studied only through small experiments with short communications. The following generalizations emerge from the studies. A two-sided presentation, which considers arguments against the policy recommended, has a more lasting effect than one-sided indoctrination. The two-sided communication is more likely to be considered fair, and inoculates against later counterpropaganda. A communicator who makes it clear that he accepts the basic values of his audience is most likely to be accepted. Discussion sometimes helps fix a new belief more permanently. But the effect of discussion is not always the same. A two-sided discussion may even help the student resist the teacher's persuasion. The person who actively presents arguments contrary to his true beliefs (i.e., who plays a role) tends to change his beliefs in that direction. Dramatic presentations have strong and lasting persuasive influences. But strong appeals—e.g., to fears—may cause the audience to resist the intended message.

Attitude education is not to be accomplished by a few brief efforts at indoctrination. Ideas are developing continually through interpretations offered by teachers and peers, and through concrete experience.

Experiences with the attitude object confirm or reform interpretation. School projects and activities are likely to be comprehended and to provide a source of satisfaction. A prejudiced person working on a project, however, may confirm his prejudices instead of changing them. Moreover, an activity may involve many hours of effort that make no direct contribution to the intended understanding. Lasting change is to be expected when the activity is chiefly a starting point for thoughtful discussion. Attempts to promote racial tolerance through intergroup activities are most successful when all participants work toward common goals. In a summer camp, the more aggressive white boys—those who disliked the camping and did not receive rewards from the group—increased in prejudice. Those who fitted into the camp and received social rewards became less prejudiced.

A consistent program of reinforcing desirable beliefs, and of promoting the pupil's successful membership in groups that reinforce those beliefs, is the foundation on which specific instruction can best build.

Reading List 13

Irving L. Janis and Bert T. King, "The Influence of Role Playing on Opinion Change," *Journal of Abnormal and Social Psychology,* 49 (1954), 211–18. Reprinted in Maccoby.

A full discussion of the value, for attitude change, of having the pupil prepare a talk on a controversial topic. Note the conditions under which this technique has the greatest effect.

Jerome M. Levine and Gardner Murphy, "The Learning and Forgetting of Controversial Material," *Journal of Abnormal and Social Psychology,* 38 (1943), 507–17. Reprinted in Maccoby.

An account of the study on learning about communism discussed in Chapter 11.

Theodore M. Newcomb, "Student Peer-Group Influence," Chapter 13 in Nevitt Sanford, ed., *The American College* (New York: Wiley, 1962), pp. 469–88.

Newcomb reviews studies of the way in which college students influence each other, and of the way in which that influence reinforces or works against the influence of the faculty. His conclusion is, "The social-psychological motors of student life are racing, disconnected from the wheels of intellectual development, and the means of exploiting the power delivered by those motors are at our command."

> Muzafer Sherif *et al.*, "Intergroup Relations: Reducing Friction," Chapter 7 in *Intergroup Conflict and Cooperation: The Robbers Cave Experiment* (Norman, Okla.: University Book Exchange, 1961), pp. 151–96.

Two groups were formed of normal, well-adjusted boys; hostility between groups was generated in the course of competitive activities. This chapter describes the experimental procedure—"introducing superordinate goals"—which overcame hostility. What similar techniques could be used in schools to produce better intergroup relations?

> Howard P. Smith, "Do Intercultural Experiences Affect Attitudes?" *Journal of Abnormal and Social Psychology*, 51 (1955), 469–77.

Smith questioned college students who visited Europe to learn why some changed to more world-minded attitudes than others did. On the basis of his findings, what policies should universities adopt regarding programs that allow a student to study abroad? Should all college students have this experience?

> "Specific Mental Health Implications of Technical Change," Chapter 4 in Margaret Mead, ed., *Cultural Patterns and Technical Change* (New York: Mentor, 1955), pp. 263–88.

The rapid development of remote countries brings a need for radical change in customs and attitudes. Anthropologists and UNESCO workers draw on their experience to indicate why suggestions from experts about, for example, the feeding of infants are rejected. They propose effective methods for this type of teaching. Many of the difficulties have their parallels in teaching Americans to depart from the attitudes of their forebears.

PART FOUR

PLANNING, MOTIVATION, AND EVALUATION

CHAPTER 14 PURPOSES AND ASPIRATIONS

The teacher's eternal question, "How can I motivate pupils?" becomes, on examination, a series of other questions. "What sorts of goals do pupils work toward?" "What causes a pupil to select one goal rather than another?" "How can the teacher influence pupils to choose appropriate goals?" These questions all deal with purposes. A second series of questions deals with consequences: "What effect does punishment have?" "Should competition be encouraged?" and so on. This chapter opens the discussion of such questions as these, discussing particularly the pupil's goals and purposes. The following chapter, on the teacher as classroom leader, discusses specific motivating procedures.

According to our general view of behavior, all activity is directed toward goals. As a person interprets a situation, he recognizes desirable things that can happen to him or certain desirable states that can be brought about. The consequences toward which his efforts are directed are his goals; his trial responses are those that he thinks most likely to produce those consequences. Following his response, the actual consequences confirm or contradict his interpretation. His feeling of success or failure depends partly on his goals, partly on the way he evaluates his action. While an act has many consequences, his feeling about his try depends on what consequences he notices. Two pupils may perform the same way and attain the same objective result, yet one may retain his interpretation on the next trial while the second one alters his. The difference lies in what consequences they noted, and in how these compared to what they had hoped for.

Grace, in the sewing class, chooses a dress pattern and a neat cotton print to make it from. She chooses this pattern because she believes that she will be able to do the required sewing, whereas a more intricate pattern, she fears, would prove unmanageable. She chooses this print rather than another because she thinks that she and her friends will like the result. In these choices, Grace uses concepts and attitudes she has learned; for instance, "Stripes make me look too tall." She places some values ahead of others: perhaps she chooses the print because it is similar to what her friends wear and will make her feel more "in the group" even though she herself admires a solid color. As Grace completes the dress, she will experience confirmations and contradictions of her expectations. Her success will confirm her estimate of her capacity. People praise her, and her friends express the interest she had expected. But the pleats are hard to iron, and she will begin to wish that she had chosen a straight skirt—next time she probably will. There are further consequences that Grace does not notice. Trimming in red gives a less striking effect than trimming in blue would have given. And her mother is impressed by the achievement and begins to treat Grace more as a grownup. If these consequences do not come to Grace's attention or if she does not connect them with the interpretations and decisions she made, they will not modify her next sewing plans.

THE NATURE OF GOALS

Multiple Goals

It is easy to regard each act as directed to one specific goal. The boy makes a kite "because he wants a kite." He does an arithmetic problem in order to get the answer. He and his committee prepare an exhibit on rocks and minerals; finishing the exhibit is indeed a goal. Only in a few simple situations is the goal of the act just to create some one product. Goals usually are complex and multiple. When I shift my posture to relieve a cramped muscle, I appear to have just one goal, very directly related to the action. But the act is guided by my further aim to appear dignified and well-mannered. A learner has some product or end in mind; he prefers also to use certain processes in attaining it. Beyond his immediate aims, he has distant goals toward which this product is only a way station. The wish to win others' respect may provide more incentive to complete the task than the direct wish for the product itself.

A kite-maker may be less concerned with the kite itself and more concerned with getting his parents to praise him for being usefully occupied. The very making of the kite can be socially rewarding, if the maker shares the work with friends. If the boy gets to use his father's tools in this work, the permission proves that his maturity is recognized. Elements of pride or self-respect make the effort worthwhile. He may make the kite unnecessarily complicated in order to use more tools. And since other boys of his age do this sort of thing, he is showing that he fills his proper role, that he is one of the gang. There are many motivations beyond just wanting a kite.

The performer does not wait for the end of his work to judge how he is doing. Any complicated activity involves continual checking to see if the process is going forward according to expectation. The navigator of a plane, having set a course, continues to make celestial observations or listen to the radio range to confirm it. This judging and correcting is a "feedback" process, such as we discussed in connection with skill learning. Information about intermediate consequences alters plans in mid-act (G. A. Miller *et al.*, 1960).

An important step in teaching is to point out proper intermediate goals. We teach learners to watch for the intermediate cues that can redirect action. Thus, one tells a future farmer how to judge if his pigs are feeding properly long before their weights report their growth.

An experiment on typing shows how one can teach the learner to call off an action that would lead to error (Dunlap, 1928). Typists who made the error of writing *hte* were told to practice deliberately striking the keys that way. They practiced their mistake, knowing it was a mistake. Then they practiced the word correctly. Soon they were able to eliminate the error from their regular typing. As their fingers went into the old error, the report from fingers to brain set off the recognition: "Oh, oh! Here comes that mistake." The fingers were stopped in midflight and redirected. Much of learning is learning to recognize when you are on the wrong track.

1. A teen-age girl selects her lunch in the school cafeteria. What goals does she have beyond the desire for food whose taste she likes?

2. What goals are present in a committee preparing a classroom exhibit of rocks?

3. What cues help an actor judge if he is performing well?

4. What process goals might direct a boy in chopping through a tree trunk with an ax?

Remote Goals

For the older person, most of today's tasks are aimed at consequences well off into the future. The college student goes to the library to read two articles. This is, in part, a matter of putting in enough study time to clear his conscience. Another goal is being able to report to the instructor tomorrow that he has completed fifty pages of reading. The pages he reads may fit into material for a paper to be delivered at the end of the term. The hour in the library has still more remote consequences. His work on this course makes him eligible for the basketball team, or keeps him off probation. Even further in the future are job ambitions: good grades will perhaps help him find a good job, and the knowledge acquired from his reading may help him perform the job.

A person's goals are arranged in a plan, which states where he expects to be at a certain time. He has a fairly definite picture of the consequences he expects in the next few minutes, less exact expectations for the next hour or next day, and a few unclear visions of events months or years in the future. A person who has not worked out his eventual aims cannot use them to guide his present conduct. Nor can he do so if he does not pause to connect his present actions to those remote consequences.

In training an animal, it is very difficult to alter responses unless reward or punishment follows the act immediately. But a human can learn to make a correct response even if the reward is long delayed, so long as the correct response is readily discriminated (Noble and Alcock, 1958). Mowrer (1960, p. 383) explains this as follows:

> Human beings, with their remarkable skill in symbolic manipulation, can easily keep, or re-establish, the "connection" between two events (action and reward or action and punishment), even though these events are considerably separated in time. For example, if a subject "knows" that a given response is responsible for a given (delayed) effect, he might say to himself, immediately upon completion of the response: "Although there will be a delay now, before I get the reward, I nevertheless *know* I have done the right thing, so all I have to do is wait."

The ability to foresee consequences thus appears to depend upon the ability to use words and thoughts effectively, and this, as we saw in Chapter 10, develops with age. We would expect the preschool child to be strongly influenced by immediate goals, and insensitive to delayed rewards. Only with the achievement of formal operational thought, established in adolescence, can one trace out all possible consequences of an action in imagination and so develop a high degree of foresight. Foresight depends on knowledge, which assists in prediction, and on alertness to possible consequences. There has been little formal investigation of goal systems, though common observations, and studies of the development of vocational plans (Super and Overstreet, 1960), are consistent with this theory of gradually developing foresight. Mischel (1958), studying 7- to 9-year-olds, found a definite increase with age in the percentage who would rather wait a week for a ten-cent candy bar than have a one-cent bar immediately. Shalemon (1959) and Kuvshinov (1959) showed that increased ability to plan accounts for much of the improvement in problem solving between Grades I and V. The younger child asked to assemble an object works on scattered bits of the task, with little idea where he is going and how the part fits into the whole. Hence he lacks persistence. By the fifth grade, the pupil takes a global view, and perceives each act as a part of the larger whole. Thus actions are more meaningful and each step is well motivated.

By planting the same corn crop this year as last, the farmer achieves his short-term goal. He follows a familiar routine and ends the year with a fine return. That this action depletes the soil, and contributes to surpluses that may someday ruin his market, he considers only if he is well educated. By himself he might never observe this connection between his decision and his long-range goals. At best, to learn the connection by experience would be costly and would take years. Education conveys what others have learned about consequences. Understanding of remote consequences is developed in social studies, literature, and science.

Sometimes a person knows of the remote consequences but does not think about them sufficiently. He lets immediate aims sway each decision. A talented writer, graduating from school, begins to turn out simple pot-

104   *The goals of any learning extend far into the future*

boilers, which have a sure sale. His tries are confirmed by acceptances from publishers, but he fails to develop skill in character portrayal and plot development and in the end must abandon his original aspiration to create literature. Sometimes the person lacks confidence that he can ever attain the remote goal. If so, he does not let that goal influence him as it should. A writer who doubts his own talent is less willing to struggle for years than one who has faith in himself.

REMOTE VS. IMMEDIATE GOALS IN THE CLASSROOM.   The goals to be emphasized in school should fit the maturity of the pupil. For very young children, plans must be quickly fulfilled. The less mature the learner, the less he is influenced by distant goals. "This will help you when you grow up" is a pallid advertisement compared with the immediate enjoyment of a comic strip and a baseball game. Some remote goals are appealing even for young learners. Boys try earnestly to become strong, though it takes a long while to put on muscles. "When I grow up and become a mother" is a conscious

"You're ready to try this advanced pattern."

plan for the 6-year-old girl, which helps shape her interests and her self-concept.

With success in short-range plans, the person gains confidence in his ability and enough interest to sustain a longer activity. The teacher who helps pupils attain clear short-term goals assists them to develop foresight. Short-term goals can provide frequent rewarding accomplishment without the discouraging stretches where the only satisfaction seems unattainably remote. A pupil can get a glimmer of ambition to become a concert musician, but he is more likely to sit down at the piano because he thinks he can *now* play a piece from beginning to end. The small landmarks—playing *Three Blind Mice* by ear, sight-reading *Jingle Bells* and having it sound almost right, overcoming the hurdle of a one-sharp signature in *America*—divide the long pathway into challenging, satisfaction-giving segments. As a person succeeds in attaining one goal, he becomes readier to dedicate himself to a slightly more remote goal. The boy who saves a dollar for a cap gun is more likely to persevere in his next saving than if he starts by saving for an electric train and gives up before the goal is reached.

Remote goals are of little use if they are only hazy fantasy. They become useful for motivation when the path to achieving them becomes clear. Realizing what steps are to be taken reduces a vast ambition to specific activities one can confidently tackle. As Wright (1948) says:

> A goal can be only a point at a distance, with a void in between. Then, all the child can do is dream about it. On the other hand, a goal can be an extended region of activity the finish line of which is tied in closely with steps on the way, so that these steps become parts of the larger goal-structure. John wants to "play in the band." An adult at school has helped to set up this goal, but lets it go at that and, except for tall imagining, so does John. Henry, after exchanging ideas with his teacher, wants to "mow lawns or deliver papers to earn money to spend on a cornet to blow thirty minutes everyday so he can play in the band." He can act with some degree of effectiveness because there is a path to follow. Henry's teacher has helped to arrange a situation in which a "goal with a path leading to it" are defined. Situations like this increase the freedom of children to satisfy their needs.

The planning process in the schoolroom should draw the pupil's attention to appropriate goals. This process involves making him aware of the many different sorts of satisfaction and improvement an activity can lead to. It involves specifying end goals, which direct the activity, and intermediate or process goals. Each block of work should tie into the student's extended plans and ambitions. Practical methods for doing these things will be considered in this and the next chapter.

> **5.** In connection with each of the following situations, illustrate multiple goals, process goals, and remote goals:
>> **a.** A group of fifth-graders write a letter to the town newspaper advertising the school carnival.
>> **b.** A boy scout learns to play bugle calls.
>> **c.** A high-school girl reads her Spanish assignment in *Don Quixote*.

HOW PUPILS SET ASPIRATIONS

A pupil has some expectation in mind when he attempts a task. If he attains the expected results, he is, in one sense of the word, satisfied. If things work out so that he falls short of his expectation, he experiences some degree of failure. This leads to seemingly paradoxical results. A person may do as well as the teacher expected and receive a favorable comment, yet feel thwarted because he aimed higher. Another pupil, who does poorly, accepts that poor performance as inevitable. Thus the one who "fails" objectively is confirmed in his original expectation, and the one who "succeeds" in the teacher's eyes wishes he had done differently. *A response will be used on other occasions, or discouraged, depending on the extent to which the results measure up to the person's expectation.*

Larry bats for the eighth-grade boys, and in four times at bat hits the ball only once. Larry was wrong far more often than he was right. He swung and missed eight times, while connecting with the ball only once. Yet if Larry feels that he has done as well as he should, he will feel pride and pleasure in his batting. Suppose instead that he had the unreasonable expectation of hitting on three out of four chances, or suppose that the group is sarcastic when he strikes out. Then he probably will be annoyed and will start changing his batting form even though it is already good for his age.

In any performance a person has an expectation. He strives to attain what he thinks he *can* attain. Everyone has fantasies about some goals that he knows are unrealistic. Not many people alter their behavior just because it fails to bring them a million dollars. But when a person expects a ten-dollar raise and is turned down, he is genuinely dissatisfied.

The standard a person expects to reach in a particular performance is referred to as his *level of aspiration*. You can measure a level of aspiration by asking a person what score he expects to make on the next trial of a task. But this question focuses unduly on the numerical level of attainment. The person is often just as much concerned with how he will attain this level as with the score itself. One's expectation or aspiration has three aspects:

What characteristics of performance he considers desirable.
How well he expects to perform on each of these characteristics.
How important each of these characteristics is to him.

Consider the pupil giving an oral report on mining to his science class. First, what characteristics does he consider desirable in an oral report? He has probably judged himself in terms of process goals expressed in these questions:

Was I ready on time?
How did the teacher react?
Did I get through without forgetting what I wanted to say?
Did the other pupils seem attentive?

This list ignores other consequences he might consider, including some of those that count most in oral expression outside of school. A report that meets the above standards might not satisfy him if he asked:

Did I interest the other pupils in the topic of mining?
Did the others learn the ideas I presented?
Did I use my voice in a pleasing and effective way?
Did I select the most important ideas for presentation?

Second, how well does he expect to do with respect to each of the outcomes he considers? Some pupils are content if they get through the talk without being openly criticized; some feel that oral reports are bound to bore the class and only hope their friends will accept the talk as no duller than normal; some are out to win acclaim and will be satisfied only with an enthusiastic or admiring response from the class.

Third, which outcomes of his performance are most important to the pupil? Some pupils sacrifice peer approval in order to make a good impression on the teacher. They would be glad to have peer acceptance, but when forced to choose, they have greater need for the teacher's admiration. In judging the quality of the talk itself, some students want to cover much material, whereas others want to present what they do cover with clarity and style.

Aspiration is derived from experience. The typist who has tested himself repeatedly anticipates on his next test a score near his previous average. If he betters it a little, fine; but he will not expect to double his rate immediately. One brings to a new task a self-estimate from other related situations. Roger expects to do better than his peers in any sport he undertakes. He considers himself moderately competent in using tools and expects to complete simple repairs, but does not expect a high order of craftsmanship of himself. Roger expects to be criticized by his teachers—so much so that when a new teacher urges him to study harder he pays no attention. These examples recall our earlier emphasis on the self-concept. Each person carries in his head a notion of what he can accomplish and of how others will react to what he does.

The Influence of Success and Failure

From attempts to take a shortcut, you learn an expectation about muddy paths: you can't walk on them without getting your shoes dirty. You soon know better than to try. As a person makes repeated tries, he builds up an expectation about what is likely to happen to him in the future.

Confirmation encourages one to repeat an interpretation. But this is not the same statement as, "What is rewarded will be repeated; the response that is punished or merely left unrewarded will be dropped." The bowler does not change his technique when he fails to make a strike. Whether or not he reconsiders his interpretation depends on his expectation. If he thinks his best ball will get him about three strikes per game, he may continue in the same way despite the fact that he averages seven "punishments" for every three "rewards." Three strikes per game confirm his expectation.

Experiments using intermittent rewards show that expectancy is more powerful than frequency of reward. D. A. Grant *et al.* (1951) arranged an apparatus that gave a signal, after which a light might or might not go on. The student was asked to guess, after the signal, whether or not the light would go on. Some students were given consistent confirmation when they said "yes"; during their training the apparatus was arranged so that the light came on every time. As the "100 per cent" curve in Figure 105 shows, these students soon were making the "reinforced" response. In another group the light appeared after only 25 per cent of the signals. The learner in this group responded according to this expectancy. On 25 per cent of the trials he said, "Yes, the light will go on."

The most dramatic effect appeared during the "extinction trials" after the experimenter changed the apparatus so that the light would *never* go on. In Figure 105 the points plotted show how many times in a block of five trials the average person said "Yes." We see that as soon as the apparatus was adjusted so that the light did not go on, the group who had had confirmation every time they said "Yes" dropped to saying "Yes" only 40 per cent of the time. From there on, they guesssed "No" after every signal. They had found that the light went on after every signal in the first 60 trials. When the light did not go on for the 61st signal, they

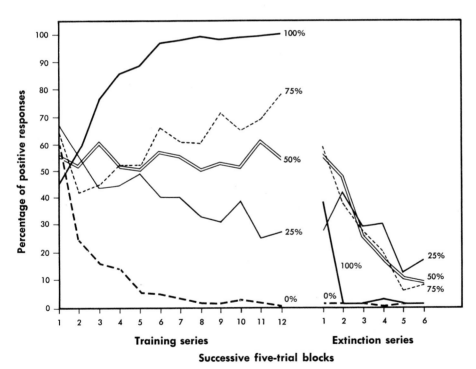

105 *Expectations are established by experience (after D. A. Grant et al., 1951)*

> In the training series, the second light went on 25 per cent of the time for the "25%" group, and so on. In the extinction series, the light never went on, for any group.

promptly interpreted this as a changed situation and gave up their original response. A response confirmed 60 consecutive times was dropped after one or two results contrary to expectation!

The 25 per cent group was very slow to change its responses. In the first five extinction trials they said "Yes" 25 per cent of the time. Then, as the chart shows, they started making the nonrewarded response *more often* because they thought the light was "due" to go on. Discouragement set in only after about 20 extinction trials. The groups with uncertain, intermittent confirmation of the "Yes" response learned to interpret the situation according to a rule: Keep trying; you'll be right a fraction of the time. This expectation was not easily overturned.

Intellectual aspiration is raised and lowered with experience. Jucknat (1938; see also Leshner, 1961) asked a child to tell how rapidly he thought he would do the next puzzle in a series. This was done repeatedly. Then Jucknat gave some children an insoluble puzzle, while others were allowed to succeed. As Figure 106 shows, most of the successful group raised their aspiration on the next trial, confident that they could do the next puzzle even faster. Failing children rarely raised their aspiration. How the person feels about his success affects his motivation. Some of those who succeeded were greatly excited about their success, and their next aim was high. Others who succeeded, but not easily, were hesitant to raise their sights.

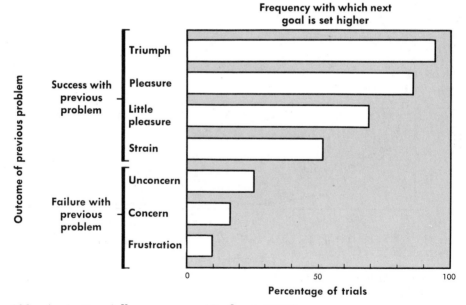

106 *Aspiration follows success* (*Jucknat, 1938*)

In the three failure groups, the child had been asked to solve an insoluble maze.

Jacknut

Among the failures, Jucknat distinguished three degrees of annoyance or disturbance. Among the most upset children almost no one was willing to try for a higher goal the next time. These positive and negative attitudes clearly generalize to other similar tasks. The pupil's whole history of success has a cumulative effect on his self-concept and his expectation. Pauline Sears (1940) studied fourth- to sixth-grade pupils who had been successful or unsuccessful in school. She gave simple word tests (e.g., finding synonyms for easy words). After each trial, she told each pupil his time in seconds. He, being unfamiliar with time scores, could not judge the report as good or poor. Then she asked what score he was going to try for on the next test. She particularly wanted to determine whether or not pupils would set reasonable goals—goals near to or slightly better than their actual performance on the first trial. The same procedure was followed with an easy addition test. Figure 107 shows the results. Children successful in past schoolwork set realistic goals.

The effect of past failures is hard to predict. Pupils who had done badly in school often set unreasonable goals in Sears' study. Some set goals cautiously, much below the score they had already achieved. If adult pressure had been absent, it seemed that many of these pupils, lacking faith in themselves, would have given up entirely. Others with records of past failure set goals so far above their performance as to be unreachable. It is as if they said, "My attainments aren't much, but at least my *goals* are worthy of praise. And failing to reach such a lofty goal as this hardly counts as a failure."

It is not past success alone that encourages effort. A pupil might have a history of success and still back off if he thinks the present work will be more difficult. Teachers alter motivation just by building up expectations of success or failure. Gebhard (1948) presented college girls with a collection of nine puzzles, and asked each girl which puzzle she would most enjoy doing, which next most, and so on. Then the girls worked each puzzle. Gebhard divided the girls into four groups, treating each group differently. As each girl came to the puzzle she had ranked fifth (medium in attractiveness), Gebhard by her comments created an experience of success (or failure) and an expectation of future success (or failure). One girl might be told that she had done very well on the puzzle—"but of course that doesn't show much, since this puzzle was unusually easy. You wouldn't do as well if you tried another puzzle of this type" (success with expectation of future failure). To give an experience of failure with expectation of failure, a girl was told that her score was very low, and that the puzzle she had done so badly on was really quite an easy one for that type. At the end of the experiment, Gebhard again asked the girls to rank the nine types of puzzles, giving the highest rank to the one she would like to do more of, and rank 9 to the least attractive. The special comments intended to modify expectation had been made about whatever puzzle a girl had originally ranked 5.

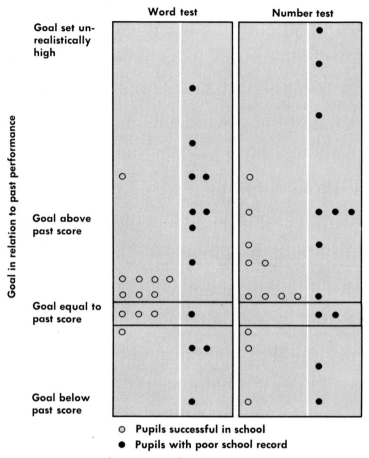

107   *Some pupils set unrealistic goals* (*P. S. Sears, 1940*)

At the end of the study, the average rank assigned to this number 5 puzzle was as follows in each group:

Success on first task, expecting further success   3.9
Failure on first task, expecting future success   4.7
Success on first task, expecting future failure   4.8
Failure on first task, expecting further failure   5.9

Interest was heightened either by past satisfaction or by anticipated future satisfaction. But motivation was highest when both of these were encouraging. It is important to note that failure-with-hope leads to continued interest, for teachers must frequently develop just this attitude in the pupil who is having difficulties.

Figure 108 adds one more important finding from the Sears study. Sears tested one group of pupils who had previously been successful in reading, but who had had trouble with arithmetic. When she told such a pupil that he had done badly on a word test, he set a reasonable goal for his next try. On a number test he shifted his goal unreasonably upward or downward after failure. Obviously these pupils had confidence in their verbal abilities: failure in arithmetic had not lowered their over-all morale.

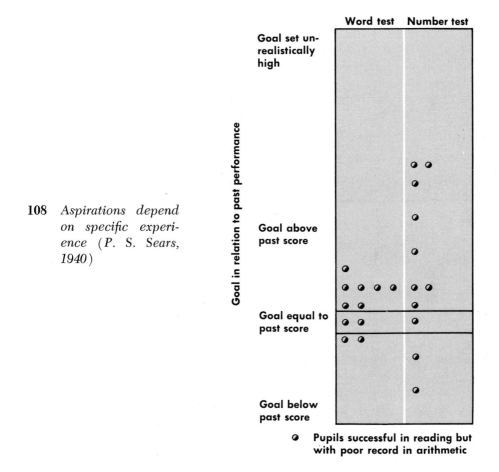

108 *Aspirations depend on specific experience (P. S. Sears, 1940)*

The moral of these and other studies (Israel, 1960; Levin and Baldwin, 1958) is that success or hope of success nearly always increases interest and effort. This has importance beyond moment-to-moment motivation. One of the important objectives of education is to develop a liking for learning so that the pupil will eagerly respond to opportunities for intellectual growth throughout his life. This, indeed, may be the greatest difference between the excellently educated man and the one who is merely trained. The school wants also to encourage interest in specific activities: reading, music, research, outdoor exercise, etc. To develop desire for a goal and enjoyment of an activity, there is no better tactic than to give the pupil a feeling of continually rising accomplishment by arranging tasks that he can master and making sure that he recognizes his gains.

This is not to say that all schoolwork should be "easy." Gewirtz (1959) gave pupils a chance to succeed on one puzzle and then asked which of several puzzles, some similar and some different, each pupil would like to do next. She found that some pupils who succeeded on a puzzle *avoided* further puzzles of that type. They wanted to move on to a new type, which would be more challenging. These, as might be expected, were pupils with strong achievement needs and high ability; they had learned that they could meet challenges, and now they were dissatisfied by tasks only a small step beyond what they had already mastered. Another nice example comes from an experiment in which an 8-year-old girl was asked to guess whether a big or little kangaroo would turn up next in a pile of picture cards. The pack was loaded with big kangaroos, so that they tended to turn up three times out of four, and she divided her guesses in about that proportion (cf. Figure 105). Toward the end of the series she confided to the tester: "I know how to be accurate most often. I only need to guess the big kangaroo all the time. But that wouldn't be any fun" (Messick and Solley, 1957; Solley and Murphy, 1960, p. 159). She was willing to settle for this lower rate while hunting for a successful sequence or pattern of guesses. The secure performer finds fun in accomplishing something the hard way (Atkinson, 1957).

Perhaps the clearest guide to the teacher in adjusting task difficulty is, "Keep tasks within the reach of the pupil." Reaching does, and should, involve effort. In order to maintain self-confidence, the pupil should be able to complete most of his undertakings. But no harm is done if he is challenged also to try for some goals that he has only a small chance of reaching. Reaching an unlikely goal once in five tries can strengthen willingness to try if the one success is satisfying and if the learner understands that his failures are not to his discredit. The reformer, the inventor, the politician, the athlete, the artist, the teacher—all of them must try many times to be rewarded with one triumph. Experience in school can teach one to accept the "failures" that are the inevitable price of daring.

The pupil who fails is not necessarily going to improve. The pupil resigned to getting half his homework correct may continue the same study methods and retain the erroneous responses that lower his score. Long-continued difficulties lead to hopelessness and withdrawal, or to irrational efforts to leap to success overnight. Performance improves when the pupil learns to discriminate the situations where a certain response is correct from those where it is wrong, or learns to make corrections before the response is completed. Merely knowing that one's responses are correct 68 per cent of the time does little to separate the good responses from the bad.

6. What bearing does the foregoing discussion of task difficulty have on the "small-step" principle in programed instruction?

7. A teacher says, "I always grade pupils severely during the first marking period of the semester. Then, when I give higher marks during the second period, they feel successful and are encouraged." Comment.

8. Miss Nagle says, "I never make promises to my second-graders about things we are going to do until I am certain that we will be able to do them." Miss Tompkins says, "I don't think that is so important. They get a lot of pleasure from anticipating things, and they can understand that it is often necessary to change plans. I tell them about pleasant things I have planned, even if they won't always work out." Does the Grant experiment shed any light on this discussion?

Personality and Goal Setting

Difficulty leads one person to strive, another to withdraw. A "4-10 split" on the bowling alley confronts the bowler with two pins on the opposite sides of the lane. From a number of attempts to knock them down, he learns an expectation about me-plus-4-10-splits. He learns that when he tries to topple both pins by making the 4-pin slide across to hit the other, he usually misses both. When he aims only to get one pin, he usually succeeds. With this experience, Bowler A makes no effort to pick up the split. He settles for a score of 9. By not trying he never learns to get both pins. Bowler B, on the contrary, always tries for the two pins and seems not to be discouraged by his failures.

Why does B not conclude that his ambition is hopeless? He gains some satisfaction from near-successes. If, on a rare occasion, he does succeed in getting both pins, the acclaim he wins far outweighs the mild pleasure he might get from consistently hitting one of the two. What intricate personality mechanisms cause people to set conservative or ambitious goals? Does our second bowler love to gamble? Or does he need conspicuous success and so seek it the hard way? Why does B compliment himself on coming close whereas A finds that discouraging?

Goal setting reflects personality. Personality differences between realistic, overstriving, and withdrawing pupils were apparent in Pauline Sears' (1941) results. Self-confident, secure children set realistic goals, expecting slight but regular improvement. The realistic ones

> are self-confident in their attitude toward school subjects, assured in their performance, may show pressure and strong effort but in a realistic fashion which sets socially and self-approved limits on their achievement. They do not react with feelings of failure to poor performance on material which is clearly too difficult for them, nor on the other hand, do they gloat over good performance on easy material.

There is a positive preference among children with a strong need for competence and achievement for tasks where there is some risk of failure. In a ring-toss game, such children choose to stand back from the target so that their success is somewhere near 50 per cent (McClelland, 1957). These children adjust well and eagerly to school.

The overstrivers announce goals way beyond their past attainment. They are uncertain about what they can really expect of themselves (Steiner, 1957). They cannot admit inadequacy, or discriminate the reasonable from the unreasonable. Lacking confidence, they reduce their anxiety by aiming beyond what they can hope to achieve. Thus insecure children often stand far back from the peg in the ring-toss game. If they succeed, their pleasure is great; if they fail, their self-respect does not suffer. Sears finds overstrivers to be apprehensive, inflexible in thinking, and poorly adjusted socially. Not knowing what they can do or how others will regard them necessarily implies a lack of self-respect.

Excessive ambition cloaks many a case of dissatisfaction with self. If a person feels he must prove his merit, he may try to pile up huge production as evidence of accomplishment. Such a person is Howard James, a very intelligent college student who has a sense of inferiority beneath his cheerful and energetic front. His work as a student is just as good as his instruc-

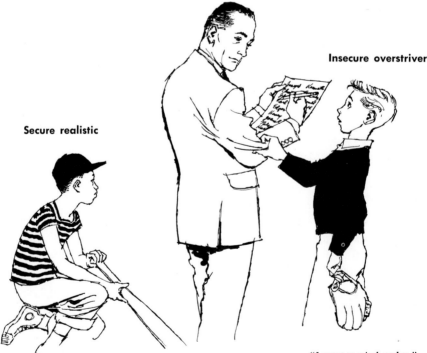

Secure realistic

Insecure overstriver

"I'd like to get on base this time."

"I want to pitch today."

109   *Secure children set realistic goals*

tors require it to be. But instead of trying to do one job well he prefers to dash off several sloppy ones. Howard writes easily and quickly. "But," says his adviser, "his argument is weak beneath the glossy prose. He would rather have it sound impressive than take the pains to make it *right*." If Howard were to do each task for its own sake, rather than hastening to add it to his pile so he can get on to another display of energy, his achievements would be worth more.

Margaret (Chapter 5) represents a withdrawing pattern. Those who set lower goals after failure must reduce pressure on themselves. By never committing themselves to a goal that is hard to attain, they protect themselves from risk and anxiety. They are self-conscious, self-protective, anxious to make a good impression. Whereas the overstrivers are confused in their self-image, those who withdraw have definite and unfavorable self-concepts. They are not merely insecure, they are defeated.

HOW DIFFERENT PUPILS RESPOND TO PRAISE.   We can see from another study what happens when pupils receive approval and disapproval from teachers (Thompson and Hunnicutt, 1944; see also Escalona, 1948). Fifth-graders were asked to work for 30 seconds crossing out certain letters as fast as they could. The work was marked *P* (poor) or *G* (good). These "grades"

Insecure withdrawer

"Please give me easy ones."

were assigned with no relation to actual performance. This procedure was repeated on five days. The pupil received the same grade (*P* or *G*) every day. In another class tested as a control group, pupils received no report on how well they had done.

Scores improved a great deal on the second day, and slightly thereafter. On the final test, the average achievement of the three groups was as follows:

Group *P*	21
Group *G*	20
Controls	15

The groups were equal to begin with, hence final differences must reflect difference in effort. The small amount of practice could not have changed their ability much. The superiority of the experimental groups shows that either favorable or unfavorable evaluation has a motivating effect. The controls who received no external feedback made little improvement.

Personality types were compared: type A is described as outgoing, active, self-assured; type B as more worried, sensitive, withdrawing. Half of the pupils of each type had been marked *G;* and half had been marked *P.* Their average final scores were:

Assured A pupils marked *P*	24
Retiring B pupils marked *P*	18
Assured A pupils marked *G*	18
Retiring B pupils marked *G*	22

The differences here are too great to be chance effects. Evidently the assured pupils strive after meeting failure but coast after success. This confirms Sears' description of the realistic goal-setter. A *good* mark encourages the insecure pupils to their maximum effort, though it may take many successes to overcome their ingrained pessimism (Rychlak, 1960).

Should the teacher conclude that pupils can be typed, and each given praise or reproof according to his type? Certainly not. The available experimental evidence deals with a very limited situation. No test was made of criticism that shows pupils how to improve. No test was made of a mixed sequence of high and low marks, or of the case where, while still doing poorly, the pupil can see that he is making progress. The teacher has to make a judgment about each pupil on each occasion. No formula for rewards and disapproval can be given. The teacher can only try what seems reasonable and watch what happens to a pupil's performance, confidence, and subsequent goal-setting.

> **9.** How can you account for the fact that Bill Chelten (page 145) sometimes sets high aspirations but at other times puts forth little effort?
> **10.** How does a person's self-concept influence his reaction to thwarting?

Group Standards

The standard set by one's group affects his goals. The person who thinks of himself as a normal member of a group will strive for the attainments that go with that status. Goal-setting is influenced by the example of others with whom one identifies or the group to which he feels he "belongs" (Festinger, 1942). College sophomores took an information test. Then each one was told his score and allowed to compare it with a table of norms for college students. Each student then estimated what score he expected to make on a second, similar test. The "norms" were falsified to carry out the experimental plan. The student told that his score was somewhat below the undergraduate average expected to do a little better on the next trial. If told he was below the high-school average, he announced a much higher goal for his next trial. But if told that he fell slightly below the graduate student norm, he raised his expectation hardly at all. Students set goals at the level demanded for self-respect, which is determined largely by what they think others are accomplishing.

GROUP DECISIONS.   The teacher wishing to increase student effort faces a problem like that of the industrial manager who wants more production. The worker usually produces less than he could, and those who do set a fast pace are under pressure to slow down. It is frequently found that allowing workers to participate in setting work goals leads to higher production than when the goals are dictated from above (L. C. Lawrence and P. C. Smith, 1955). Whyte (1955) tells of a factory where girls complained bitterly about the speed of a moving belt that set the pace at which they were to paint toys. The pace had been carefully set at a reasonable level after engineering studies. The girls were paid on a piecework basis, so that they lost money when they did not keep on the pace. When the complaining girls were allowed to adjust the belt speed themselves, changing it from time to time during the day if they wished, complaints disappeared. Moreover, they pushed the speed up so that the average was higher than the speed they complained about when set by the engineers. Group goal setting is not likely to raise the goal, of course, unless the worker sees the higher production as contributing to something he cares about.

Establishing a group consensus was effective in changing housewives' meal-planning. In a time of meat shortage it was necessary to persuade them to serve liver, heart, and other meats they did not ordinarily use. Exhortations and factual lectures had no effect on the meals the women served. A large factor seemed to be their pride in "setting a good table"—which meant providing the roasts and steaks that were scarce and costly. The women felt they were failing as providers if they served the more available but less elegant cuts. When a group of housewives discussed meal-planning and reached a *group* decision to use more liver and heart, the individual women actually did feed these meats to their families. The ideal of being a good cook was redefined by the group so that members had a new basis for judging whether or not they were successful (Lewin, 1958). A group decision about a goal can be expected to lead to superior performance when three conditions are met: the individuals care about holding the approval of the group; the goal truly serves their own interest in a way they can understand; and the group is genuinely free to raise or lower the goal

(J. R. P. French *et al.*, 1960). Consulting the group is a waste of time otherwise.

  11. Show how group standards would cause a bowler to be content with an average of 150 whereas the same bowler in a different group would be discontented.
  12. Could group decision making be used in determining the number of books to be read by high-school English students during a semester?
  13. Could group decision making be used in determining when an assignment is to be completed? (Recall Bill and the German class.)
  14. Why might each of the following practices not work out as intended?
    a. A junior-high-school teacher wants all his pupils to find art pleasurable and interesting, and therefore praises all their work and gives no grade but "A."
    b. A teacher tries to obtain greater effort by telling pupils that unless they improve they will all have trouble with the statewide test to be given a month hence.
    c. A teacher systematically tries to point out the faults of pupils who seem complacent and to provide steady praise for those who have had poor records. He intends for each pupil to set the highest goals he can reach.

THE SCHOOL ATMOSPHERE.   Every school has its own atmosphere, derived from its traditions, its admission policies, the attitudes communicated by the faculty and the community, and the students' spirit as a group. At the high-school and college levels these motivational influences are seen in the stimulation offered to students (more tennis courts or more visiting scientific lecturers?), in the faculty-student relations, and in the activities that command respect. Political interests may mark a person as the campus bore in one school, as one of the moving spirits elsewhere. The student who falls in with the ruling enthusiasms gets many subtle reinforcements. Similar differences in values no doubt appear during the lower grades (Della Piana and Gage, 1955), but differences among elementary-school atmospheres have been studied little.

Especially in private colleges there is self-selection of student bodies so that each group has its own "personality" (Heist and Webster, 1960). Prominent colleges have definite—though not always deserved—reputations among college-bound pupils in their region. As a result, freshmen who enter Antioch look forward to responsibility, freedom from restrictions, and experimental teaching methods. At Swarthmore, the primary expectations are high academic standards, seriousness about intellectual matters, and informal friendliness. The Reed stereotype is the same except that interest in freedom replaces interest in friendliness (Clark, 1959). Such attitudes have serious consequences for the faculty. At Reed, for example, where the entering student anticipates freedom but not responsibility, student government is difficult to maintain; at Antioch, students are ready to take student government seriously and devote energy to it.

The students and faculty combine to produce a distinctive set of pressures, which reinforces certain values and provides opportunities for certain types of learning. These have been investigated by asking students to check on a long list the statements that describe their college (Pace and Stern, 1958). There are notable differences among colleges. On larger campuses, each curriculum provides a different experience. Table 27 makes it evident that the whole environment for learning differs for the liberal arts and the business administration student. Even within a curriculum, the influences on the student vary according to the group he associates with. The Pace-Stern questionnaire, called the College Characteristics Index, is especially useful to a faculty wishing to survey its own campus atmosphere, because a "profile" for the college can be compared with norms for other colleges. Similar instruments for lower grades are needed. To change

TABLE 27

Characteristic environmental pressures make the experience of liberal arts different from that of business administration students (Stern, 1960)

	Percentage of students endorsing this description of their school	
	Liberal arts	Business administration
DEMAND FOR DEFERENCE AND ORDER		
Students are discouraged from criticizing administrative policies and teaching practices	20	92
Students address faculty members as "professor" or "doctor"	13.5	63
In many classes students have an assigned seat	13	99
PRESS TOWARD INTELLECTUAL CONCERNS		
Long, serious intellectual discussions are common among the students	85	22
Most students have considerable interest in round tables, panel meetings, and other formal discussions	75	34
There would be a capacity audience for a lecture by an outstanding philosopher or theologian	76	18
INTEREST IN HUMANITIES		
Modern art and music get considerable attention here	90	41
When students get together, they often talk about trends in art, music, or the theatre	75	18
A lecture by an outstanding literary critic would be well attended	90	34

the campus atmosphere is not easy, but the faculty can do much to provide encouragement for the minority of students who are ready to move in the desired direction.

Coleman (1961a, 1961b) traces some of the effects of different high-school atmospheres on morale and performance. He selected nine public schools in towns and cities in northern Illinois and asked pupils such questions as, "What does it take to get in with the leading crowd in this school?" In every school, personality and good reputation were among the qualities most frequently mentioned. For boys, athletics was considered important. But there were striking variations. In Green Junction, a school of 500 pupils in a community of 5,000, athletics was mentioned as important by 27 per cent of the boys; in the superficially similar Maple Grove, 14 per cent mentioned athletics. In each of these schools, about 11.5 per cent mentioned grades as socially important. Midcity High is the only school where grades were reported to be more important than athletics.

Coleman finds considerable evidence that the social importance of grades influences effort in school. A fraction of this evidence is reproduced in Table 28. We see, first, that the social rewards for a good school record decline with community and school size, though Newlawn and Marketville are exceptions. The average mental ability of boys earning grades of A and A— is expected to be high where the brightest boys are taking their schoolwork seriously. Although the differences from school to school are not large,

TABLE 28

Academic effort depends on peer attitudes (from Coleman, 1961b, pp. 70, 263, 267, and personal communication)

Schools arranged by community size	Enroll- ment	Percentage of boys men- tioning grades as important [1]	Mean ability of boys earning A's [2]	Percentage of boys study- ing at home [3]
Midcity (100,000)	1,935	19	63	40
Millburg (25,000)	1,383	14	62	28
Executive Heights (17,000)	1,862	10	60	42
Newlawn (9,000)	1,053	7	58	10
Elmtown (7,000)	513	12	63	39
Maple Grove (6,000)	421	12	60	26
Green Junction (5,000)	538	11	62	15
Marketville (4,000)	364	16	65	34
Farmdale (1,000)	169	6	56	0

[1] In indicating what is required to be in the leading crowd.
[2] Standard score, relative to the school average of 50.
[3] Counting boys studying two hours or more per night; based solely on boys whose fathers attended college.

there is a significant correspondence between importance of grades and the ability of high achievers. Effort on homework likewise corresponds to other evidence of the social importance of schoolwork, except at Executive Heights. From these and other findings, including rather similar results for girls, Coleman concludes gloomily that

> the adolescent subcultures in these schools exert a rather strong deterrent to academic achievement. . . . Those who are seen as the "intellectuals," and who come to think of themselves in this way, are not really those of highest intelligence, but are only the ones who are willing to work hard at a relatively unrewarded activity.

One of Coleman's questions, which gives evidence of self-respect and morale, was: "If I could trade, I would be someone different from myself. Agree——Disagree" The girl or boy who agrees with this statement is clearly expressing dissatisfaction, not just with his present performance, but with his role in life and his prospects. Table 29 indicates the percentage expressing such discontent among the pupils named by their peers as filling various roles. To be sure, those named as outstanding students are on the average happier than the pupils who have no recognition. But the pupils outstanding in something the peer community cares about are considerably happier than the good scholars. In those schools where grades are unimportant for social acceptance, the high-achieving boys are no happier than the average boys, and the high-achieving girls are distinctly unhappy with themselves. There are similar effects for other achievements: athletic distinction or popularity with the opposite sex contributes much less to self-satisfaction in the school where this value is not rated high by the group.

TABLE 29

The pupil who is socially rewarded has greater self-satisfaction (Coleman, 1961b, pp. 55, 233)

Group of pupils	Percentage wanting to be someone else (low satisfaction)	
	Boys	Girls
All pupils	21	20
Named as popular with opposite sex	12	8
Named as prominent athlete	8	—
Named as "best student"	16	14
Named as "best student" [1] in schools where academic achievement is		
more highly valued	15	15
less highly valued	20	24

[1] Students named as "best student" and also named for another sort of prominence are not counted.

15. In Executive Heights, the qualities needed for being in the leading crowd are as follows: personality, mentioned by over 20 per cent of the boys; athletics, good looks, popularity with girls, and good reputation, 10–19 per cent; good grades, car ownership, and money, less than 10 per cent. How do you suppose their fathers would answer if asked what is needed to be in the leading adult crowd?

16. In what ways can teachers legitimately influence the opportunities a pupil has to be a leader in the school?

17. What steps can a college faculty take to increase "pressure toward intellectual concerns"?

18. What effect do demands for deference and order have on the educational process? What causes may be responsible for the prominence of such demands in business administration departments?

REWARDS AND PUNISHMENTS

According to our view of learning, whether or not an interpretation is retained depends on whether or not the consequences conform to the person's expectation. The expectancy theory is distinctively a theory of human learning; the psychologist performing experiments on animals cannot investigate level of aspiration, self-assurance, group standards, and the other variables that have been prominent in this chapter. Experiments with animals generally lead investigators toward a somewhat simpler "reinforcement" theory. Typical studies of reinforcement examine the effect of rewarding a response with food pellets, or punishing it with shock. The chief motivations in the classroom are those associated with the task itself, and with maintenance of self-respect and the respect of the group; these we have discussed above and shall return to in the next chapter. Since the teacher can administer explicit rewards and punishments, we also should look at the implications of the research on reinforcement.

As the term is used theoretically, *reinforcement* occurs when a response is followed by some pleasant or unpleasant consequence (Ferster and Skinner, 1957; Spence, 1956; Meehl, 1950). We distinguish between positive reinforcement, nonreinforcement, and negative reinforcement. Pleasant consequences constitute positive reinforcements or rewards. They encourage repetition of a response. These rewards include food or a pleasant word from an animal's master; in the schoolroom, the reward might be a gold star, a nod of approval, or a chance to look at an interesting book. Negative reinforcement comes from unpleasant (aversive) consequences, which the person wants to avoid. These include electric shock, loud noise, physical blows, etc. The aversive consequence most used by teachers is scolding. Nonreinforcement occurs when the person responds and "nothing happens"; that is to say, he is not gratified, but neither is he treated harshly.

He has not attained his goal, but the only unpleasant consequence is his own dissatisfaction. The distinction between nonreinforcement and negative reinforcement is illustrated by an experiment in which a person is to learn to follow a small metal target mounted on a phonograph turntable. We can arrange positive reinforcement by having a bell ring every time the person keeps his stylus on target for one second, and negative reinforcement by administering a shock whenever he is off for one second. If we give no shocks, a wrong response is left unreinforced rather than negatively reinforced. This is a disconfirmation, but not a punishment.

EFFECTS OF INCREASED REWARDS.   We have emphasized so often the necessity for indicating to the learner when he performs correctly that little remains to be said about positive reinforcement. We do need to examine what is known about the quantity or intensity of reward. Does one learn faster if, in addition to seeing that his performance is correct, he is given a word of praise, or a ten-dollar bill? Offered a desired prize, a person will try harder. This, however, is not evidence that additional rewards make the correct response more likely to be retained.

Reward during training does give the pupil an incentive to try a task that would otherwise have no appeal. To fulfill this function, it is necessary for the reward to outweigh the rewards from competing activities and to offset the possible unpleasantness of the effort itself. Terrell *et al.* (1959) show that in certain discrimination learning where the correct choice is signaled by a light flash not a single lower-class child in the sample learns as rapidly as the median middle-class child (ages 5–11). Add a simple material reward—a piece of candy along with the light flash—and the middle-class children do no better; in fact, some of them decline. But the lower-class children now learn as rapidly as the others because they are making a real effort. Another study divided college engineering students into two groups—a "compulsive" or striving group accustomed to make stern demands on themselves, and a group with more casual attitudes. In the former group, aptitude was the sole predictor of achievement. Within the latter group, interest in engineering had as much to do with achievement as did aptitude (Frederiksen and Melville, 1954; Frederiksen and Gilbert, 1959). Special incentives and pleasant consequences seem to be unimportant for learners who have a strong desire to win self-respect or approval from superiors, or for those who like the task itself.

Beyond the amount necessary to get a person to engage himself seriously, increases in reward seem to have no effect on learning the response that is trained (Marx, 1960). If the task seems purposeless, so that a person's only satisfaction comes from the added incentive, the learned behavior disappears rapidly when the training ends and the reward stops. A detrimental effect of heightened incentive is that the person narrows his attention to what is strictly relevant to getting the reward. He therefore retains far less "irrelevant" information from the experience (Quartermain and Scott, 1951). Yet facts noticed incidentally while using a reference book or performing an experiment may be significant additions to one's education.

While reward motivates one on an unappealing task, there is a strange converse: on an appealing task, reward can have a bad effect. The clearest evidence is Gately's study of monkeys (see Harlow, 1953). Four monkeys were given a chance to work on complex mechanical puzzles. Four others were given the same opportunity and each was given a food reward as soon as he solved a problem for the first time. The monkeys receiving no special reinforcement continued to explore and manipulate the puzzle after they had taken it apart. The rewarded monkeys never touched a puzzle once the reward had been given. Receipt of the reward became a signal for termination of effort. This phenomenon is not peculiar to the monkey: witness the college student who thoroughly enjoys a course, but who sells his textbook as soon as he has done his duty by the final examination. Hobbies that have no definite reward are often pursued far more persistently.

EFFECTS OF PUNISHMENT.   Aversive stimulation, like reward, is a signal helping the person evaluate his response. The buzzer that comes on when a driver passes a safe speed is such a signal; so gentle a reminder causes no pain, and yet is more compelling than the speedometer needle he had disregarded. This painless monitoring, however, can only technically be called a punishment. Making the punishment stronger would not make it a better signal.

Probably most educators believe that punishing wrong responses eliminates them, so that punishment speeds up learning. One is unlikely to do what will certainly be punished. But does punishing a response during training make that response less likely to occur when the teacher is no longer present to administer punishment? The experimental evidence indicates that mere nonreinforcement eliminates responses more permanently than punishment (E. R. Hilgard, 1956, pp. 109 ff.; Skinner, 1953). Estes (1944) used rats that had been rewarded for pressing a lever. One group was shifted to nonreinforced extinction trials; nothing happened when they pushed the lever. In another group a shock was now given every time the lever was pushed. In the third extinction session, the shocked group made the now "incorrect" response twice as often as the nonreinforced group. More than that, the rats punished every time they pushed the lever were more likely to push the lever when put back into the apparatus on another day than the rats who had been punished only occasionally for the "incorrect" response during the extinction trials. Human response to punishment is not entirely like that of the lower animal. All the evidence together, however, seems to imply that punishment has its chief effect in suppressing a response here and now, where the punishment is encountered. The stronger the punishment, the greater the conflict between hope and fear. Under strong tension, the person is less free to think and to absorb information from the trial.

But adding risk of punishment sometimes makes the person more attentive and more realistic during learning. Reece (1954) projected words onto a screen dimly, one at a time. Some words were followed by shock. If punishment heightens alertness, the subjects ought to be especially keen in recognizing the shocked words each time they reappear. Reece found that this did occur *if the subjects could avoid the punishment* by calling out the word promptly. But the persons who received the shock even if they named the word recognized shock words less well than nonshock words. It is as if they deny the presence of the word that warns of a coming shock, in order to reduce anxiety (Solley and Murphy, 1960, p. 109).

This and other studies emphasize the importance of confidence. Threat makes a person less attentive to subtle cues and less prone to reason closely if he feels that he can do little to avoid punishment. This inattention interferes with learning and adaptation. You will recall that children capriciously rewarded and punished for dependence gave up the effort to discriminate where dependence was appropriate (page 153). Trying to figure out what to do in a conflict situation may arouse intolerable anxiety if the person thinks he is unlikely to judge correctly and the threat is severe. Risk does not damage performance when one feels that he has the situation under control.

Deliberate punishment is most commonly used in school in an effort to improve conduct. If one wishes merely to suppress unwanted responses during the time pupils are under the teacher's eye, consistent punishment would be expected to do the job. If the aim is to teach pupils to regulate their own conduct so that the teacher's pressure can be removed, punishment will not work. Kounin and Gump (1958, 1961) studied response to various control techniques in the kindergarten. The pupil was most likely to do what the teacher wanted when she indicated positively what response she wanted. A teacher's roughness and bad temper in handling a misbehavior disturbed the whole class, not just the child criticized. The pupils' minds were taken off their work and tension rose. A punitive teacher's threats, sharp scoldings, and continual vigilance build up pressures that make children more aggressive. They are also less insightful about the reasons that make good conduct desirable, much less likely to see that they are the losers when misconduct interferes with the class work. Punishment arouses resistance to the teacher and a dislike for the activity; this effect carries forward after the threat of punishment has been removed (Zipf, 1960). The pupil conforms to the demands of the punitive teacher because he has to. He is in conflict over his temptations. The pupil of the nonpunitive teacher may respond to temptation more often, but he is more likely to develop what we shall later describe as rational self-control.

In introducing research on reinforcement, we noted that a reward-punishment theory is not identical to an expectancy theory. The expectancy theory is broader than the reinforcement theory, but not in conflict with it. Response to any single consequence is complexly determined. The taxi driver who scorns a ten-cent tip seems to violate reinforcement theory, unless we are willing to say that small amounts of money are unpleasant. But in dealing with human subjects we have to consider the psychological meaning of a consequence before we can say whether it will be an encouragement or a disappointment.

> **19.** A teacher announces that any pupil who does not complete his homework will be punished by a reduction in his grade. Explain why, even after several experiences with this punishment, some pupils continue to turn in their work late.
>
> **20.** Since pupils who are not strongly motivated to achieve seem to do better when working toward an attractive reward, would you favor a system of rewards such as candy and movie tickets as a way of obtaining greater effort from nonstrivers?

SUMMARY

A person sees in each situation possible sources of satisfaction and ways of making progress toward desirable goals. He is aware of many outcomes that can be attained, some tangible, some social, some connected with maintaining and enhancing self-respect. The possible consequences of his act extend in time. Even within the task itself there are intermediate or process goals, which he uses as a guide. An important step in teaching is to help the person recognize significant intermediate consequences; then he can correct his own actions. Dunlap's experiment shows that deliberately practicing an error brings it to the learner's attention so that it is clearly discriminated from the correct action.

Future hopes and intentions give significance to short-term tasks. Expectations for the near future are definite, while more remote goals are indefinite. But the person who fails to consider remote consequences will often follow an unwise course. Education, by conveying what others have learned about long-range consequences, increases the likelihood that actions will be wise. Young children give little attention to remote consequences, but as they grow older their readiness to work for distant gratification increases. Mastery of the verbal symbols that help one to understand connections between events is necessary for foresight. The teacher cultivates foresight by giving pupils experience in which they attain relatively short-term goals that are satisfying in themselves, and by helping them work out definite plans, which show a well-marked path toward more distant goals.

Whether a trial response is retained depends on whether the consequences measure up to one's expectation. What a person expects to accomplish is referred to as his "level of aspiration," but in addition to his level one must consider the person's image of a desirable performance and the importance he attaches to each consequence. Pupils often fail to consider some significant outcomes and thus may be satisfied with a performance that has serious defects. The expectation is an interpretation established by past confirmations. Reward on every trial produces a response that vanishes as soon as reward is discontinued. A response intermittently rewarded is hard to extinguish because the unrewarded trials do not contradict the expectation.

Aspirations generally rise with success and with the expectation of future success. The pupil with a history of success sets goals realistically, but the pupil with a history of failure is likely to lower his aspiration markedly or to raise it unreasonably. The pupil who finds himself successful in an activity will usually like that activity and put forth more effort in it. But this does not necessarily imply that all tasks should be easy. The pupil often obtains his greatest satisfaction from surmounting a difficulty; this is particularly true of the secure person with strong achievement motivation.

Goal setting reflects personality. A steady but realistic raising of goals is usual among self-confident children. The overstrivers lack a clear self-concept, hence are insecure, apprehensive, and inflexible. Those who withdraw are self-conscious, dissatisfied with themselves, and too ready to take the easy way out. The assured pupil strives in response to criticism, whereas the worried, sensitive pupil seems to respond better to praise.

The person identifies with certain groups, and their performance becomes a standard against which he judges himself. The goal the pupil considers respectable is largely determined by what others are accomplishing. When a group discusses possible goals and agrees on some target, this often results in increased performance. Groups sometimes set higher goals for themselves than they will accept from authority, when the higher output serves their own interest.

The faculty and students give each school an atmosphere of its own. Different colleges and different curricula expose the student to quite different group pressures. The pressure in one course may be toward personal and intellectual conformity, in another toward intellectual independence and aesthetic interests. Coleman finds equally marked differences among high schools. Pupils achieve more nearly in accord with their ability in schools where academic achievement brings prestige. High-achieving pupils have higher morale in those schools where achievement is valued by the group.

Reinforcement is said to occur when a pleasant or unpleasant consequence follows a response. Positive reinforcement (reward) of any magnitude has value as a signal to identify "good" responses. Increasing the reward may make a task attractive so that the pupil will attempt it. Pupils willing to work for approval may not improve when offered a tangible reward. But the pupil who has little desire to achieve will work harder on tasks that are interesting or promise a concrete reward. Beyond the amount necessary to obtain attentive participation, increases in reward seem not to improve learning, and may reduce the learning of whatever does not count toward the reward.

Negative reinforcement (aversive stimulation) following a response the teacher seeks to eliminate has a different effect from nonreinforcement. While punishment does suppress a response in the situation where it is punished, nonreinforcement is more effective in permanently extinguishing the response. Punishment increases conflict and may impair thinking. Learning is much impaired when the punishment is inevitable, but not when the person feels that an alert performance will spare him from punishment. In the classroom, punishment disrupts the class; pupils become tense, antagonistic to the teacher, and antagonistic to the subject under study.

Reading List 14

Arthur I. Gates and Frank G. Jennings, "The Role of Motivation," Chapter 7 in Nelson B. Henry, ed., *Development in and Through Reading*, Sixtieth Yearbook of the National Society for the Study of Education, Part I (Chicago: Univ. of Chicago Press, 1961), pp. 109–26.

Practical approaches to arousing interest and satisfaction in reading.

Ernest R. Hilgard, "Success in Relation to Level of Aspiration," *School and Society*, 55 (1942), 423–28.

The findings of the level-of-aspiration studies are translated into their implications for goal-setting in school. Gives additional illustrations of several points covered in Chapter 14.

Betty L. Mitton and Dale B. Harris, "The Development of Responsibility in Children," *Elementary School Journal*, 54 (1954), 268–77. Reprinted in Remmers, Seidman.

Responsibility is defined as taking goals seriously and accepting the consequences of one's own acts, hence as nearly synonymous with self-discipline. The authors review studies of this trait and extract ten principles regarding the practices by which it can be fostered.

P. M. Symonds, "Classroom Discipline," *Teachers College Record,* 51 (1949), 147–58. Reprinted in Seidman *E.*

Symonds discusses the unfortunate consequences of punishment and describes disciplinary methods consistent with good teaching.

Herbert A. Thelen, "The Triumph of 'Achievement' over Inquiry in Education," *Elementary School Journal,* 60 (1960), 190–97.

A clever—and subversive—argument that present methods of testing and grading interfere with the pupil's education. Examine Thelen's accusations. Which do you consider just? What would be gained and lost if Thelen's remedies were adopted?

CHAPTER 15 THE TEACHER
AS CLASSROOM LEADER

How can the teacher establish an enthusiastic and purposeful work atmosphere? That is the topic of this chapter. Subordinate questions, which teachers often ask, are these: How can the teacher keep a class in order? How can the teacher arouse interest? How can the teacher encourage pupils and give them self-assurance? How can pupils learn to control themselves and to take responsibility for decisions? All of these relate to the function of the teacher as a leader. The teacher is a good leader when he arranges conditions so that pupils want to do something worthwhile, have a chance to try it, and succeed. The benefits of good management are pleasant pupil-teacher relations, good conduct, more satisfaction with classwork, and more learning.

The classroom setting directly affects what the pupil tries to do and what he learns. We refer not to the physical setting of benches and blackboards but to the social and emotional setting. Like the homes described in Chapter 5, classrooms have different atmospheres. Some pupils expect their teacher to drive them and bully them into work, while other classes come in ready to jump into activities and enjoy them. Some teachers are humorous and friendly; others are continually in conflict with the class. In a threatening setting the pupil will do the safest thing he can. In an encouraging climate he will try, and learn; he will take a chance with a daring idea, and create.

Pupils are always motivated; the question is, toward what ends? Their energies run off toward all points of the compass, their work lacks long-term vision, and they lose sight of goals. But they do not lack a will to work, and they enjoy increasing their competence (cf. page 124). Healthy students are coiled springs ready to make something whirl. This may sound like an exaggeration to the teacher who prods and tugs at an indifferent class. Yet these same "indifferent" pupils are spending countless hours planning dances or inventing skits for a carnival. The problem in motivation is not to awaken an inert audience, but to direct the energy of an alert group into constructive channels and keep it there.

Enthusiasm from the teacher helps sell the goals of the classroom. When the teacher thinks it exciting to discuss socialized medicine, the pupils will find the topic lively. Sometimes the teacher can enlist attention just by making each day's work entertaining or by setting short-term goals. The college lecture that states a provocative question and promises to answer it is more effective than one that plods stodgily through the instructor's notes. The kindergartners are given an incentive to pick up scattered beads and crayons when the teacher announces that she will read a story if the task is done in time.

These devices are effective in their way, but they must be renewed every day, and they do not carry outside the classroom. Much better are purposes that direct work over a long period. Class management is principally the art of helping the members of the group find significant and enduring purposes, and satisfaction in their progress.

METHODS OF PLANNING AND CONTROL

Goals may be fully set out in advance or may be left almost to the whim of the moment. Responsibility may be taken entirely by the teacher or may be shared by everyone. Some groups learn to be docile, accepting a leader's proposals and control. Other classes that learn techniques of initiating, planning, and cooperation become more independent of superiors. Too much control gives no chance to plan, to make errors, and then to learn to plan better. Too much freedom leads to frustration because little is accomplished without coordination of effort. We need to inquire just how freedom is useful, how it can be threatening or unfruitful, and how it contributes to developmental learning.

We shall contrast three styles of group operation: undirected activities, teacher-controlled activities, and group-controlled activities. Classrooms are classified according to who sets the goals for the group and evaluates performance. In the undirected program, no one defines the goals and lays out a work plan. The group is turned loose, like children playing in the park. Teacher control means setting of goals by the teacher, and judgment by the teacher that the pupils are or are not doing as they should. Group control, common in adult relationships, is being increasingly used in schools. Goals are selected through group discussion, and the group as a whole decides when things are going as they should. The leader only helps the group to govern itself. In contrasting these patterns, we should remember that most classrooms shift from one style to the other, and that many intermediate styles are found (Cunningham *et al.*, 1951).

Undirected Activities

In a completely undirected activity pupils are told, "You can do just what you want to do." Subsequent questions about what is satisfactory are answered in such terms as, "Do whatever you think best." This utter permissiveness is sometimes intended to promote creativeness and learning "by discovery." It is often used in connection with individual activities (book reports, science projects, etc.), which the teacher sees as "outside the regular work" and therefore suitable for the expression of personal interests. A few theorists (Cantor, 1953) have urged that the teacher retreat to the background and thereby force the student to judge and plan for himself. Cantor has substituted this method of "nonleadership" for the usual lecture and assignment in college sociology classes.

Teacher-controlled Activities

It is hard to describe the second control pattern without arousing prejudices that interfere with observation. Calling it *teacher-controlled* raises visions of a schoolma'am rapping knuckles. To label it *autocratic* is to condemn it. The orderly, systematic, planful teacher is often the best teacher; do not prejudge this pattern because of its name.

A teacher who seeks to maintain unwavering control will use his judgment at all points: in deciding what shall be done, who shall do it, when it is done well, and when reward or criticism is called for. He sets the goals, determines how the work is to proceed, and administers the social rewards. This teacher outlines his course in advance, selects the techniques of evaluation, and sets the standards that determine an *A* or a *C* grade. This is the style also of the teaching machine, which leaves the learner free only to pay attention or not to pay attention, and to pull levers more rapidly or more slowly. A demand for conformity is not unreasonable when the instructional material is carefully prepared and specific knowledge is the intended outcome.

Fromm (1941) makes the valuable distinction between rational authority and irrational authority. In rational authority the superior directs so that both he and his subordinate satisfy their needs. In irrational authority, the superior attempts to satisfy his own needs, at times sacrificing the satisfaction of his subordinate. Many studies on leadership seem to assume that dominant leadership will be harsh and irrational. But dominant teachers can be warm—even jovial—considerate, and intelligent.

Group-controlled Activities

The scheme of organization that allows a group to direct itself is often called "democratic" leadership. Actions recognized as signs of democratic teaching are listed in Table 30. It is especially important that time be devoted to reviewing past accomplishments and deciding on future plans. The

TABLE 30

Behavior of teachers using group control (Heil et al., 1960, Appendix, p. 70)

1. Encourages children to use democratic procedures (discussing, voting, acting as chairman).
2. Uses teacher-pupil planning in organizing classroom activities.
3. Encourages children to accept responsibility for achieving goals the group establishes.
4. Permits children to establish and enforce regulations for behavior in the classroom.
5. Permits children to work without direct supervision.
6. Speaks less than 50 per cent of the time.
7. Welcomes questions from pupils.
8. Encourages expression of more than one viewpoint.

emotional climate must be such that the pupil is free to express opinions that conflict with those of the teacher and of his classmates. Group planning is less a matter of putting everything to a vote than of considering openly feelings of satisfaction or dissatisfaction, and future aims.

Control is not merely turned over to the class. The teacher judges each plan to make sure that it accords with the mission of the school and with his own competence as instructor. The time available also limits the degree of group responsibility; too much planning leaves no time to reach any satisfying goal. Therefore the teacher has to make sure that the limits on group decision are understood by everyone. He encourages the group to decide only those issues where he is willing to abide by the decision.

The undirected pattern can be pleasant. Pupils may find useful things to do, make friends, and teach themselves valuable lessons. But the school should arrange more educative activities than the ones the pupils fall into by themselves; therefore the *laissez-faire* policy falls short. Moreover, as we shall see, pupils tend to find the disorganized, utterly permissive setting annoying because they feel they are accomplishing little. The benefits claimed for intelligent teacher planning and teacher control are these:

More time can go into the activity itself if none is spent in planning.
The teacher's decisions are wiser than those the group makes.
The teacher represents the judgment of society and cannot properly pretend that questions about what and how to study are open for the pupils to decide. Hence group control is always a dishonest form of teacher control.

Others who have thought about the problem are equally convinced that:

Those who share in goal setting become more eager to reach the goals.
When activities reflect pupils' interests, and when purposes are clarified

through group planning, more intelligent cooperation results. Pupils are more likely to continue work "on their own" after the class ends.

Learning to make group decisions and to plan for oneself is as important as mastering "lessons."

Domination often does deaden spirit, causing pupils to regard their activities as pointless. Domination frequently discourages initiative and decreases friendliness and cohesiveness. On the other hand, teacher control can arouse well-directed, enthusiastic effort and produce learning at a high level. On the evidence available, we can support neither the extreme, "What is the teacher for if not to make the decisions?" nor the opposite, "Learning suited to a democratic society can take place only under group control."

Style in leadership is highly personal. The two classroom descriptions that follow will show some of the complexities of pupil response to teachers. Then we can go on to formal research without the risk of a stereotyped conclusion that there is just one good teaching style.

1. How might each of the control patterns contribute to the satisfaction of
   a. an achievement-oriented teacher with a need to be recognized for his intellectual brillance
   b. a teacher who is fearful that others will not approve of and like him
2. In your opinion, should the teacher make each of the following decisions, explaining it to the group, or open the matter for group discussion and decision? Does your answer depend on the nature of the group?
   a. What textbook shall be used?
   b. What type of examination questions shall be used?
   c. What proportion of the class shall receive A's, B's, etc.?
3. To what extent could group decision making be used in the following situations if the teacher desired?
   a. a physical education course taken by tenth-grade boys
   b. a college freshman mathematics course required of all prospective engineers
   c. a fifth-grade unit in science where no topic has been prescribed in advance by the course of study
4. Discuss the following statement both from the viewpoint of a believer in teacher control and from that of a believer in student participation in decision making.

When I was 14—just at the age when I believe a child needs discipline and adult guidance the most—I attended a school that allowed almost perfect freedom, not only in choosing a curriculum, but in standards of behavior.

For example, I hated mathematics. At this school I didn't need to take math. I recall I had a far-from-vague feeling of "Why doesn't someone *make* me take algebra?" The adult firmness that was lacking in those formative years is a vital adjunct of growing up.[1]

[1] *New York Times Magazine*, April 2, 1961, p. 4.

Case Study of an Undirected Classroom (Art)[2]

Mr. Osborne had previously taught art to eighth-graders by spending the semester on water-color painting. The assignments began with simple drawings of objects, then moved on to more complex still life, and ended with some imaginative painting. As the class did its work, Mr. Osborne watched and criticized, encouraged and explained. After taking a summer-session course that urged development of more independence in pupils, he set up a new plan. To his next class he said in effect, "You're here to learn about art. Art consists in working out ideas in pleasing and appropriate form. You can only do that by trying. We will use this semester in any way you wish. You can use any medium"—he displayed several—"and try any idea you want. I'm here to help and to answer your questions."

His experimental semester proved interesting; originality and individual differences blossomed as never before. The first weeks were wasted as the class waited for directions that never came. Then some of the students with more experience in art began sketches; someone else became fascinated with the potter's wheel and started rolling clay under Mr. Osborne's instruction; and working groups gradually began to form.

After six weeks, when Mr. Osborne would normally have been looking over a lot of plates showing two apples, with uniform composition and execrable coloring, he had finished works from only a few pupils. These were sketches, bowls, a house exterior—the work of pupils who had an interest at the start or who were trying hard to get back into the familiar groove of turning-in-a-paper-and-getting-a-grade. Most of the class were midway in something. Some had torn up two attempts and started over. Some had left their first medium and taken up another. A few still wandered around watching the others. At the opposite extreme, one girl who had been drawing as a hobby for several years had begun a self-portrait in crayon.

Following his plan of letting pupils set their own goals, Mr. Osborne neither approved nor disapproved when Penny made six identical bowls, one after the other, nor when Ned and Herb spent a week without a trace of effort. The pupils who were busy were happy. They looked at each other's work and provided plentiful praise for each success. They crowded round Mr. Osborne to show him each step of Charlotte's miniature stage setting for *Romeo and Juliet*. Some asked how to get this effect or why that color was muddy or whether the sky should be blue or green. They were given assistance and saw Mr. Osborne's pleasure in their progress, without, however, being told that this product was good or that one bad.

Ned and Herb, out of the group entirely by now, had to be suppressed when they passed the limits of tolerable behavior and took to making and

[2] This report is based in part on research by Herbert A. Thelen and John Withall.

sailing paper airplanes. It required only the proof that Mr. Osborne meant his rule against disturbance to end that try for attention. The boys' next effort was a construction project (woodworking was allowed as art). During two weeks of sketching and conferring the plan was a secret. Then, with the air of producing a white rabbit, they announced they were building

110 *Mr. Osborne's pupils were free*

a guillotine! Now they wanted Mr. Osborne's help. And he gave it gravely, however much he wondered whom the boys had in mind as their symbolic victim. His invited criticisms of the design were accepted, and off the boys went to make their machine.

Report-card time could scarcely be handled by routine grading. Mr. Osborne and the class agreed that what counted was working out creative ideas, making improvement rather than necessarily having a perfect product to show. (Here their procedures verged on group control.) Each pupil rated himself on such questions as, "Have I used my time wisely?" and, "Have I become more skilled in using some art medium?" Then Mr. Osborne talked to each pupil, going over the ratings and deciding if they were sound. It was hard to accept some pupils' overestimates of their work, or others' self-depreciation. As much as he could, Mr. Osborne kept to provocative questions: "Do you think it was wise to try both modeling and drawing, or would you have gotten more out of staying with one?" "Even though you don't like this picture now, do you feel that you learned anything that will help you from here on?" And, since the goal was to teach pupils to judge themselves, he did accept their answers and the summary grade they claimed. Ned and Herb created no problem here. They claimed only a *D*, and seemed pleased to be able to say that they had changed to a better use of time.

To shorten the story, we recount only a few more observations. The work went on through the semester in the same way, most pupils finishing one project and starting another. Sometimes the new project was a redoing of the old one with a revised design; sometimes it was a shift of medium. Marcia's self-portrait proved to be a thorough unlikeness. Having tinkered with nose and eyes and chin and having followed Mr. Osborne's suggestions as well as she could without making it any more a success, she came in one day with a grim look, tore it neatly in four pieces, and took her French book off in the corner to read while the class stood back as if she had attempted suicide. After three days, she came to Mr. Osborne with a grin, said she was glad she'd torn it up, and what was wrong anyhow? Mr. Osborne silenced his thoughts about why an adolescent, concerned with visualizing her changing self, would have special motives to do a self-portrait. He said instead that self-portraits are exceptionally difficult and require skill Marcia had not built up. His suggestion that she might work on some of the techniques of catching facial lines by making sketches from photographs appealed to her. Next day she brought in a publicity photo of a movie star who, not surprisingly, had Marcia's coloring and plumpness and a good deal more of mature sex appeal.

When the end of the course came, Mr. Osborne's feelings were mixed. Watching the unpredictable projects come to life had been much more fun than watching uninspired painters draw uninspired fruitbowls. Discipline problems had been few. Some of the pupils had discovered real intricacies in art and were genuinely mastering one or another medium. Some pupils had done the best their talent permitted, others had settled for cheap and sketchy products. The boys finished their guillotine and showed it to everyone in the building. But there had been no follow through, and their effort to make copper paper cutters during the last six weeks had no heart in it. Art meant no more to them than it had at the start of the term.

The student reactions were unanimous in praise of Mr. Osborne. They liked him, said he'd been helpful and patient and the other things one likes to hear. The majority said the same thing about art. It had been fine, they'd learned a lot, and they wished other courses gave them more chance to try things. Then some doubts crept into the replies. "I wish," said Marcia, "you'd told me a self-portrait was too hard. I could have learned a lot more by starting with something easier." Penny thought she hadn't learned much, that if Mr. Osborne had made her do something harder she'd have tried more than she did on her own. Many of the pupils said it was unpleasant to not know what to choose. And Mr. Osborne should have told them if they were doing their projects well. Ned and Herb were violently negative. Mr. Osborne hadn't told them what to do; they'd have done it if he had. The guillotine was all right—(defiantly) they'd earned a C—but that wasn't what they were in school for.

All in all, Mr. Osborne felt that *he* had learned a lot. Enough so that he wouldn't teach the same way again. Accepting pupil ideas and letting pupils learn from mistakes had worked. They had begun to realize just what they could properly bite off. His method had done rather well in providing for the range of talent. There was more original and much more meaningful art than in the fruit arrangements. Personal relations had been good, and fewer pupils found art frustrating. But his sphinx-like refusal to express his own ideas had left some pupils unsure, feeling that he was hiding his true opinion. He had offered a bewildering range of choice, and pupils had not chosen wisely in view of their talents. Too many had given up painting when, by starting out to paint an easier subject, they would have had encouraging success. He had thrown them too abruptly on their own, made them act like mature art students. Independence cannot be forced into flower overnight.

    5. If you were Mr. Osborne, what plan would you adopt the next time?

    6. Summarize what appear to you the values and limitations of an undirected classroom program as seen in this example.

    7. Suggest how a comparable undirected program might be attempted in science, English, or Spanish at either the elementary or the secondary level.

Case Study of Group Planning (English)

Miss Simmons organizes so that her class plans part of the work but with some teacher control. Her general style of teaching is rather firm and orderly. She gets the group to make definite plans and sees to it that they are followed. Some teachers are more content to let activities work out as they go along. Within this businesslike procedure, Miss Simmons gives pupils a large measure of responsibility, establishes a pleasant and energetic group spirit, and responds flexibly to individual talents and problems.

In Branner High School, students expect a certain routine. A book is assigned as the text, a list of supplementary reading is passed out, and the class shuffles off down the track seeing no vista beyond tomorrow's assignment to "take pages 13 to 20 and be able to answer the questions on page 21." Miss Simmons, though, greets them the first day from behind a desk strangely free of a pile of texts to pass out, and says, "We're going to spend several days deciding what to work on this term." (Looks of puzzlement exchanged by pupils.) "Naturally, since this is an English class, we are going to study ways of using language. You have been learning in other grades to write clearly and to talk effectively. We will try to develop more skill along those lines. But we can do that while we work on other tasks. A second reason for a course in English is that it is important to become familiar with the many methods of communication people use. Both for information and for entertainment, we use books, newspapers, plays, and other forms of language. English courses in this school give you a chance to study these tools so you can enjoy them more and use them better. Let's begin by listing the forms of communication we know of, since we will select one of them as a topic for study for the next several weeks." Miss Simmons, as you see, did not leave the choice of goals wide open. She stated firmly what she was there for. She assumed that the pupils would study. But she gave them latitude to voice their interests before specific goals were fixed.

The choice that followed was not fixed quickly by vote among alternatives that the class had little feeling about. Discussion was used to warm up interests and awaken ideas. First there was the listing on the blackboard of communication media. A mixed list which ranged from magazines to encyclopaedias, from advertisements to operas, was gradually assembled. Miss Simmons listed every medium proposed, fearing that too critical a scrutiny of suggestions would make some pupils hesitant to talk.

On the second day, Miss Simmons asked the class what questions would be important to study in order to understand the media better. This inquiry, as she expected, brought bewildered silence. Having no experience in setting problems for themselves, the group could not respond. Miss Simmons then described learning as a process of solving problems, a new view to students who thought of schoolwork as soaking up statements from books. There are many problems connected with communication, she commented. Some communications have little effect because no one pays attention to them. Some people do not know where to find interesting things to read, to see, or to listen to. She mentioned as a typical problem the then-current controversy as to whether certain TV channels should be turned over to a service reaching only paying subscribers. "What other questions about any of these communication methods might be important?"

A somewhat dragging discussion followed, in which a total of four problems came out. "Shouldn't there be more good plays on television instead of such trashy stuff?" (This from Mary. Is she trying to curry favor?) "Why do some books get to be best sellers?" "Wouldn't we get better publishing and broadcasting if the government took charge?" "Why is it that all the literature and stuff they call 'good' is so dull?" (Thelma's offering seems to be on the rebellious side, but at least she speaks up. Acceptance of that comment should make others a little bolder.)

As soon as she had sufficient discussion to illustrate what might be suitable questions about forms of communication, Miss Simmons divided the group into committees. Each pupil indicated which medium he wanted to work on during this planning stage. Six committees were formed to deal with magazines, novels, radio, newspapers, television, and motion pictures. Each group was assigned the task of finding important questions about its

"Movies aren't true to life."   *"That's not what I found."*

111 *Miss Simmons' pupils discussed things they cared about*

medium by talking about it and by reading in periodicals to see what current controversies there were. The class meetings for the next few days were devoted to the work of these committees. Some groups went to the library while others used reference books and magazines Miss Simmons had assembled in advance.

Miss Simmons used discussion to start her pupils on a process in which they had had no experience and could not do well. She steered a course between giving so many hints that she was doing the planning and letting the discussion coast to a halt for lack of ideas. She payed out rather little rope at any time, showing pupils how to accomplish each step. In a group that knew more about planning, she might have counted on more self-direction and a greater flow of ideas. These pupils could not express their interests in the communication arts, although such interests surely did exist. Sending the committees to current periodicals was shrewd, for it emphasized that this course could be up to date and that pupils would face problems of adult importance.

Each committee was to bring in a list of questions on its medium. Miss Simmons' suggestions had made it possible for most of the groups to get under way with some feeling of success. The most fruitful lead proved to be her suggestion that students go through issues of a news magazine, reading articles in the appropriate section (press, TV and radio, books, etc.). As each committee assembled to exchange reports on what members had read, it turned out that some topics aroused genuine interest. An article on a famous comic strip pointed out how the writer used it to convey his social attitudes. The newspaper committee was intrigued and made a bit uneasy by the idea that they had been absorbing this indoctrination without knowing it. The TV-radio group read a glowing account of British radio, especially the Third Programme, and greeted it with a vigorous echo of Thelma's comment that these cultural things are always dull. The motion picture committee began to wrangle when a student read a review of a movie she had seen and thought just wonderful: the review was of a bitingly different opinion. "Who are these people who write these reviews? Why does anyone care what they think when they are so wrong?" This argument blazed hotter after someone found evidence that reviewers disagree among themselves.

Early in the second week the committees were ready to report to the whole class. Some committees had long question lists, others short. With so many questions now before the group, there was danger of losing the planning mission in scattered debates on the questions themselves.

Miss Simmons brought thinking to a focus by pointing out that the same question had been asked by many committees. Every committee had asked, in one form or another, whether or not censorship to elevate taste would be desirable. The companion question, "Who sets standards of taste?" came up equally often. The class worked on consolidating the ideas under major headings, and after two days came up with a list which included

> Should we have censorship?
> Do stars make too much money?
> How can we tell what is good in books or movies?
> Should propaganda be allowed in entertainment?
> Can educational communications be interesting?

As must be evident, Miss Simmons thought some of the questions far more significant than others. She knew that the planning sessions had succeeded, not so much from the questions as from the spirit of the discussion.

Now a choice among the topics was due. The majority sentiment quickly lined up behind motion pictures, and the class turned to setting goals in that area. Most of the group wanted to debate, here and now, the issues of taste and censorship. Out of this, Miss Simmons suggested that the next four weeks be devoted to preparing standards for judging a movie. That is, the class would try to decide what qualities make a desirable movie. As intermediate activities to help in setting the standards, she suggested viewing films as a class, writing reviews and comparing them to see if the standards used agreed, and viewing films by committees, to see if those rated good or bad by the critics seemed to deserve those opinions. These activities were introduced by the teacher, and in that sense Miss Simmons was dominating the group. But the pupils had made a choice and that decision was being carried out. Their planning was being used. In a class with more experience in a flexible program, more of the procedures would be suggested by the group.

In two weeks of stage setting, Miss Simmons had achieved several things. In the first place, she built group spirit. These pupils had more social interaction than they would have had in months of some other classes. Everyone had become involved, talking about things he knew and saying things he wanted others to believe. Oral communication, then, was being used for a purpose rather than as a colorless exercise. In the reviews to be written, the pupils would again be using language to convey ideas rather than to deliver a composition on demand. The long-range plan, set up with the group and made clear to them, would provide the motivation for weeks of activity.

The planning was not complete, since goals regarding language skills were left undefined. Miss Simmons would discuss the improvement of written language with the class after the first reviews had been done and after their content had been discussed. In the general framework that "we are here to learn to use language better," she and the group could come to an agreement on the characteristics of a superior review. The class would also need criteria of good class discussion and of good group planning. So long as these were lacking, the students would not become capable of noting the consequences of their own performance and improving it. Miss Simmons properly did not stress these goals at the outset when students were entirely strange to the process of taking responsibility.

Group planning must be free to go in many directions and cannot be confined to the ordered pages of a text. Nothing could be further from the technique and aims of the programed instruction examined in Chapter 12. Instead of using prepackaged materials, Miss Simmons drew on various resources. Her group was reading current periodicals on the second day of the course and later learned from movie reviews, from reading material about movies, and from the films themselves. The resources of Branner High were fairly good in this respect. A few older films could be rented, including some based on important literature, and others appeared on television. Local theater operators supplied a pair of passes to each pupil, which permitted discussion of a few recent pictures and did wonders for pupil enthusiasm. If these resources had not been available, Miss Simmons would have needed a different plan. Perhaps it would have been necessary to work on television rather than motion pictures just because it is more available. If so, this would have been a factor to introduce into the initial planning.

8. Recall Mr. Wells's classroom (Chapter 3). What degree and method of control was illustrated there?

9. Which of the following are developed in Miss Simmons' classwork: motor skills, study methods, problem solving, concepts, attitudes, self-confidence, social behavior?

10. Among Miss Simmons' instructional aims, which could be achieved by means of programed instruction?

11. Does adopting a textbook for a course prevent planning by the group? What is the advantage in having a definite textbook?

12. In an experiment, one group of college teachers was to act "democratically," and another "autocratically." The results of the two methods were to be compared. The factors listed below defined the autocratic pattern. How do they differ from sensible but firm teacher control?

a. The aims and procedures were dictated by the teacher. The students were given no chance to help decide them.

b. The teacher selected the tasks to be done and chose the people to do them.

c. The teacher remained detached, and acted defensively if his decisions were questioned.

d. When the group had at some earlier time reached a decision, some of these group decisions were reversed abruptly by the teacher.

e. Appointments were made at the convenience of the teacher only.

f. The teacher announced that students' papers would not be returned. He reported neither comments nor grades on the papers.

EFFECTS OF VARIOUS STYLES OF CONTROL

Emotional Security

Happy pupils are preferable to pupils who are confused or discontented. Pupils who enjoy their activities put forth more effort and are less likely to develop antagonism toward school, the subject, or the teacher. Relations are friendlier when pupils have frequent occasion to work together. A teacher-controlled classroom may not permit much group activity, but friendly interaction is almost certain to occur when the group takes responsibility. Group planning can produce important changes in social relations. Cliques fade away as the group begins to work together. At the end of the work friendship choices are likely to be spread thoroughly among the group (Rehage, 1951; R. K. White and Lippitt, 1960b, p. 241). What is not so obvious is that friendliness grows more rapidly in a group working toward a common goal than in a group that is less work-oriented (Berkowitz *et al.,* 1957).

Pupils prefer thoroughly planned activities. In an undirected program, members do not know what is expected of them. This is disturbing, first because pupils have learned that unless they do what is expected they face unpleasant consequences; they are insecure until they know the teacher's expectations. Second, when pupils are not sure they are doing the right thing, their sense of worth begins to suffer. No one likes to feel that he is wasting his time. In the teacher-controlled class, the firmly set goal helps pupils to get started. They do not mill around aimlessly, for the way to go is clearly marked. The pupil has no doubt about how he is doing, for the firm leader evaluates promptly. The price paid for such clear guidance is that pupils may never learn to set up goals for themselves. Many pupils dislike group control. They feel insecure in taking responsibility for decisions and find it hard to be sure that they are doing what they should to win approval.

Effort and Efficiency

Pupils who know the goal can select provisional tries better than pupils who follow instructions they do not see the point of. They can contribute better suggestions and judge their own progress. Moreover, as the last chapter reported, a group that participates in setting goals is more likely to strive for those goals. Once a goal becomes the group's rather than the teacher's, effort follows. Pupils enjoy work that seems to be going somewhere, and they are kept at work by their sense of responsibility to each other (Raven and Reitsma, 1957; Berkowitz and Levy, 1955).

Some of the evidence for this conclusion comes from a famous study made in the late 1930's by Kurt Lewin and others (R. K. White and Lippitt, 1960a, b). Four clubs for 10-year-old boys were established under the leadership of college students. The leaders were trained to employ certain patterns: undirected activities, leader domination, or group control. Each club received different treatment at different times.

Each club set to work on a project. For example, some of them made plaster casts of footprints in the manner of Dick Tracy, and some worked on model planes. The groups that had little or no direction and planning spent little time on the project (Figure 112). The groups that worked out plans cooperatively used a much larger proportion of their time constructively. When an adult leader dominated, reactions varied. Some groups reacted aggressively to the leader, resisting his control. We chart their results with the heading "Dominated A." Other groups ("Dominated S") were submissive to the leader. As the figure shows, these boys spent far more time in their work.

The most important difference was observed when the leader left the room. A hidden observer reported the percentage of time spent in effective work with and without the leader. For the Dominated A group, these were the results:

	Effective work
Leader present	50 per cent
Leader absent	15 per cent
Leader returns	60 per cent

In the Dominated S group, the trend was similar: 75 to 30 to 80. Evidently the group did not care a great deal about the goals imposed by the leader, and escaped from the task when it could.

In the group that worked out its own goals, the results were:

	Effective work
Leader present	50 per cent
Leader absent	50 per cent
Leader returns	40 per cent

These boys were certainly nowhere near top efficiency, but they continued to work whether the leader stayed or not. The group that accepts the goals is less dependent and needs less supervision.

The undirected group gave unexpected results. Effort rose when the leader left the room and dropped when he returned: 30 to 50 to 20 per cent. When the designated leader left, some of the boys began to provide direction. These boys suggested goals and obtained cooperation but stopped their efforts as soon as the adult came back.

Confirming evidence is seen in Ryans' (1952) classroom observations of 275 third- and fourth-grade women teachers. The teachers were rated during the observations, and the behavior of the pupils was also rated. The classroom was given a total score, taking into account the following pupil qualities: alert rather than uninterested, orderly rather than unruly, responsible rather than dependent, constructive rather than obstructive, participating rather than withdrawn, and initiating rather than passive. The teacher

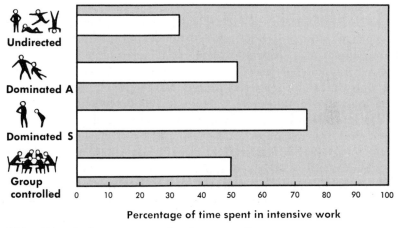

Undirected

Dominated A

Dominated S

Group controlled

Percentage of time spent in intensive work

112 *Directed groups put forth more effort*

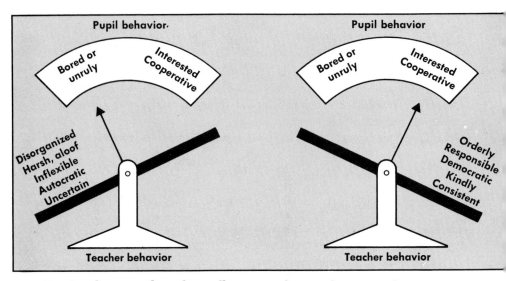

113   *Pupils respond to the well-organized, considerate teacher*

who obtains such desirable pupil behavior is more often rated as democratic, understanding, kindly, systematic, consistent, responsive, etc. The appearance in this list of *systematic, consistent,* and similar terms emphasizes the importance of having definite goals; disorganized, unpredictable teaching tends to generate poor conduct. Both for efficiency and for security it is necessary for pupils to know where they are going and why.

Ryans' data tell us something about the "flavor" of the classroom as well as its over-all excellence. The classes with the same over-all score (i.e., equally alert and interested) were arranged on a scale from those where pupils were orderly, passive, and restrained to those where pupils took initiative and participated vigorously. The teachers with docile classes tended to be more systematic and inflexible, more constant and predictable, more responsible—but more autocratic. Where the greatest pupil initiative was found, the teacher was more democratic, more understanding of pupils, and more original—but also less responsible and less organized.[3] The teacher who works out goals and procedures adaptively, taking class views into consideration, obtains more active and independent pupil response. The orderly teacher who follows her own plans rigidly can establish cooperation, but the response is likely to be less vigorous. To encourage initiative, it is probably necessary to tolerate some looseness of system.

Ryans and Wandt (1952; see also Ryans, 1960) made another study in the high school. They found that the classes with desirable behavior had teachers who were understanding, systematic, stimulating, and responsive.

---

[3] These interpretations are based on the original data. Ryans makes slightly different interpretations from tables produced by factor analysis.

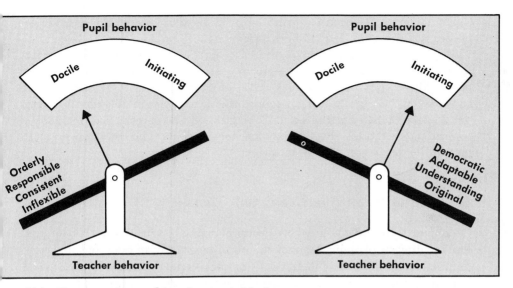

114 *Democratic teaching fosters initiative*

This chart pictures findings regarding elementary classrooms that were alike in the behaviors represented in Figure 113.

This is consistent with other studies. But the remaining findings are strange. Neither greater democracy nor greater kindliness seemed to have an important effect on the behavior of high-school classes. Teacher qualities were strongly correlated with pupil response in business education and foreign language classes, but not in four other academic areas. Further research must explain these puzzling results, or disconfirm them.

Learning of Course Material

"Which method teaches the most?" remains the big question; the evidence (Deutsch, 1949; Flanders, 1951; Perkins, 1951; D. M. Johnson and H. C. Smith, 1953; Haigh and Schmidt, 1956; R. C. Anderson, 1959) points fairly consistently to these conclusions:

Classes under teacher control and classes with group planning learn course material equally well.

When the subject matter requires that the student examine and clarify his own emotional reactions (as in some psychology courses), encouraging the student to express his ideas freely promotes learning.

The first of these conclusions means that teachers can afford to take time for group planning. Time used for this purpose is evidently repaid by more effective learning in the time that remains.

The second conclusion is illustrated by a study of two college psychology classes (McKeachie, 1951). Both groups saw "The Feeling of Rejection." This is the filmed treatment of the case of Margaret, the emotionally disturbed girl we discussed in Chapter 5. After the showing, each class discussed the causes of Margaret's difficulties. The group who had learned to work together freely had far more insight and were better able to bring out their emotional reactions about the girl and her parents. Patton (1955), confirming this, adds the finding that the students who take the greatest part in the discussion change most.

Learning to Be an Effective Group Member

We now turn to the area where group planning has its greatest advantage. Participating in planning teaches the pupil how to make decisions and how to be effective in group interaction. For social effectiveness one must learn to identify relevant cues in the social situation, discover appropriate actions, and take advantage of feedback. It has taken educators a long time to realize that social abilities, like other processes of interpretation and reaction, have to be learned. Schools used to make no provision for developing respect for others' views, concern for group goals, ability to settle disagreements amicably, and all the talents needed for living among people and working in teams. Leaving social learning to chance is not adequate. Somewhere the school must provide experience in working democratically in a self-directing group. Moreover, since attitudes and skills develop progressively, this must stretch over all the years of schooling.

Group activities do not automatically teach desirable attitudes. An attitude must be confirmed through trial to be retained. For maximum transfer, verbal generalizations should be reached through deliberate discussion of the group process itself. A class may review its work and decide whether or not it planned wisely, what caused the discussion to ramble off the subject, and what fears might have kept some members from speaking up (Cunningham, 1951; Rehage, 1951; Thelen, 1952; see also page 293).

These remarks reopen the debate about other-directedness in socialization. Some will argue that effort to teach social skills is inconsistent with a proper emphasis on individual achievement. We, however, have taken the position that the individual's intelligence is not fully effective unless he can take responsibility in a group. Being a skilled group member is in no way incompatible with being skilled in self-direction; indeed, planning and evaluation are much the same in both cases. Thus Kemp (1961) finds that cooperative planning leads second-graders to greater self-control and improves their comprehension of what self-control means.

The cumulative results of the research on planning techniques are shown in Table 31; these results will be amplified by a later discussion of teacher personality. The findings do not add up to a sweeping conclusion that "democratic, pupil-centered" methods are invariably superior.

TABLE 31

Effects of three control patterns: a summary

	Effect of undirected activities	*Effect of teacher control*	*Effect of group-controlled activities*
Emotional security	Often disturbing because of low accomplishment	Relieves anxiety by setting definite standards	Frustrating if group feels planning wastes time
Enjoyment	Enjoyable until anxiety appears	Enjoyment depends on the work; little social satisfaction	Enjoyable if group feels it is progressing; promotes friendly interaction
Effort and efficiency	Frequently wasteful of energy; pupils easily distracted and disorderly	Effective if group accepts direction and if leadership is maintained; group may resist direction	Leads to greater acceptance of goals, and continued effort when leader is absent; leads to responsible self-direction
Learning of course material	No direct evidence; probably ineffective compared to other approaches	As good as group control	As good as teacher-control; encourages free expression of ideas and feelings, hence possibly superior for altering attitudes
Learning skills of group membership	No better than spontaneous play	Little opportunity for social learning	Provides directed training in planning, teamwork, and leadership; improves self-control

Harsh domination has undesirable consequences. But the teachers who plan without consulting their pupils produce an effective atmosphere for learning when they make the plans clear to the pupils and remain responsive to pupils' needs, difficulties, and suggestions. The only doubt cast on teaching through the exercise of "rational authority" is that it may reduce the pupils' chance to learn the skills of group planning.

13. What would prejudice some educators either for or against the teacher-control pattern?

14. In a secondary school, which teachers should take responsibility for developing pupils' skill in group membership?

15. If supporting dominative teaching were compared with restrictive and antagonistic domination, what differences in results would you expect?

16. Wispé found some evidence that below-average students learned more psychology from question-and-answer recitations than from free discussion, even though the methods worked equally well for most students (Wispé, 1951). What explanation can you suggest?

17. In educational activities outside the group lessons (e.g., science projects, creative writing for the school magazine), is it wise to leave the pupil to do whatever he wants without teacher direction?

18. Most of the argument in the text points to the fact that some part of the educational program should give experience in planning. Suppose that you teach in a school where other classes develop the skills of group membership. What, if anything, is to be gained by the use of group planning in your class?

FACTORS LIMITING THE TEACHER'S CHOICE OF CONTROL PATTERN

What determines the style of the classroom? Is the teacher free to adopt any style he chooses? One's role is inevitably controlled by the expectations of others; for the teacher, these expectations are defined by his colleagues, his pupils, and the community. Anyone who departs too far from the role these people have in mind for him will encounter difficulties. Others expect him to act in a certain way and they prepare to respond in the appropriate manner. When he does something unexpected, they are unprepared and insecure.

Suppose, to take a simple example, that a science teacher decides to spend every class hour on films. Suppose also that he does away with homework and tests. Some pupils would resist because they have learned to fit into the conventional pattern and win praise for good marks. The new plan will disturb them because they no longer know how to win rewards. Some teachers will be critical because the science teacher is abandoning the methods they rely on; this implies that he thinks their methods are poor. Further, they fear that he may set a pattern which pupils will expect of their other teachers. Parents may complain about the new fashion of teaching, and even if they do not, the school administrator may discourage the radical departure because *he* fears criticism.

The pupils' expectations include some idea as to what the teacher's *legitimate* power is. The group accepts a decision they regard as within the responsibility of the teacher, whereas they may resent the same decision if they do not regard it as legitimate (J. R. P. French and Raven, 1959). Pupils believe that the teacher's role legitimately includes a great deal of control and judging. Pupils at all grade levels expect the teacher to direct and to maintain standards, but also to treat them pleasantly and to listen to their suggestions (Louis M. Smith, 1960). Hence the teacher who exercises control in a nonarbitrary way will find his classes ready to conform. He will have to prepare them much more carefully if he wants them to take unusual responsibility or if he wants to use power in a way to which they are not accustomed.

Subject matter limits the teacher. If his responsibility is to teach French, he cannot open the semester by letting pupils decide whether to study French culture, to learn to read, or to learn to converse in French. They will progress to other courses in French, hence they must reach a certain proficiency in reading and writing. The algebra teacher cannot let the group decide whether to take up factoring or spend additional time on solving equations; some later teacher will expect these pupils to be competent in all the fundamental skills of algebra. The more the curriculum is structured as a definite sequence of concepts and skills, the less are the teacher and his group free to discuss what to study. But even where the important general objectives are fixed—as in Miss Simmons' English course —many different approaches may be considered for reaching those objectives, and the class can reasonably participate in planning. Group planning has been used successfully in every subject from Latin to homemaking.

A third limitation is within the teacher himself. No one is equally comfortable in every style of teaching. Some professors dislike facing a college class unless they have a completely outlined lecture. Other professors would find this dull, and do their best only when engaged in give-and-take with students. As Thelen (1952) points out, the leader who lets the group take responsibility necessarily becomes anxious that things will go wrong. There is always the risk that the group may plan poorly, become frustrated, and become hostile toward the leader. Plan-as-you-go teaching is full of stress for the teacher; some teachers enjoy this uncertainty and some do not.

The teacher always has freedom to work toward a method of teaching that satisfies him. Never is his role so completely specified that he must do precisely as everyone else does. The freedom is small under some administrators and in some positions; in other positions, there are almost no constraints. The best evidence that the teacher is free to teach in his own way is the variety you find among classrooms in any state. Teachers find many innovations possible, especially when they introduce drastic changes slowly, and help their pupils and other teachers understand what they propose.

WARMTH AND ACCEPTANCE OF THE PUPIL

In studies of teacher success, warmth consistently appears as one of the two most important qualities (orderliness being the other). Some teachers make a great deal of emotional contact with pupils; they express their own feelings freely and welcome the pupils' open emotional response. Some teachers are far more remote and impersonal. Thus one teacher-pupil relation is friendly and considerate, and one is businesslike. Emotional involvement does not depend on the method of control; one can find warmth (or impersonality) in a teacher-controlled class or in one where group planning is used (Christensen, 1960).

Descriptions of Impersonal and Supporting Teachers

The impersonal teacher may like pupils but interpret the role of the teacher as a remote work-director. There are other impersonal teachers who keep their distance because they fear pupils. A few who come into teaching have had years of difficulty in peer relations, especially if as bookworms or independent thinkers they did not share the fads of the majority. They see teaching as a chance to elevate pupils to their own interests and standards, but they rather expect pupils to resist their attempts at friendship just as their peers did earlier.

The impersonal teacher expresses no interest, or only perfunctory interest, in what the pupil does when it is not a part of "the schoolwork." He insulates the work from pupil friendships, requiring that friendships be parked outside so they don't "interfere with the work." He may deliberately keep friendships from forming, for instance by seating pupils who support each other as far apart as possible.

The impersonal approach gives the pupil little assurance that his tries will have pleasant consequences. Although the teacher may conscientiously dispense praise when it is merited, the impersonal atmosphere can quickly degenerate into a harsh and critical one for the pupil who lacks talent and interest (de Groat and Thompson, 1949). Miss Simmons, however, is an example of the businesslike, impersonal teacher who keeps emotional interaction with her pupils at a minimum and yet makes the classroom highly stimulating.

Different writers mean different things when they speak of "warm" teachers. The phrase may refer to any or all of these qualities:

Spontaneous expression of feeling. The teacher colors classroom relationships with a continual expression of his own enthusiasm and liking for his pupils.

Support and encouragement. Reinforcement is noncontingent; the teacher approves of the pupil as a person, whatever he does, persuades him that he can reach his goal, and helps him over obstacles.

Contingent social reinforcement. The teacher gives plentiful praise, but only when he judges the pupil's actions to be meritorious. Approval is given when it is earned, not otherwise.

Tact and considerateness. Criticism or rejection of a pupil's proposal is presented in such a way that the pupil does not feel blamed or inferior.

Acceptance of pupil's feelings. The teacher encourages the pupil to express his interests, fears, etc., and takes them seriously.

These combine in many ways. Miss Apple lavishes love on her primary group and gushes over their performances (noncontingent reward). So fearful is she of prodding and discouraging them that she simplifies activities and gives them more help than they need. Miss Tremaine is not at all averse to pressing for achievement, but she does it with a continual rush of enthusiasm and optimism. She convinces the child that he can do the arithmetic problems as much by her own cheerful say-so as by her explanation. She can be patient while a child works at a difficulty, but her praise and pleasure (contingent reward) are known to everyone when he makes good. The supporting teacher need not be hearty and vocal. A quiet teacher who puts a hand on this one's head and glows when that one brings up some finished work may be fully as supporting as Miss Tremaine with her vigor.

Support can be carried to the point of indulgence where the child gets his way, his path is always smoothed for him, and no standards of performance are maintained. He dwells in a padded cell where he cannot hurt himself but where he does not face reality. Such a cushioning environment often reflects the teacher's need to win affection, loyalty, and trust. Miss Apple is a 53-year-old kindergarten primary teacher, intelligent and well-trained. She tells us that she wishes she had married. Being a wife and mother is the most important role in life for a woman; too many women, she feels, sacrifice their children to have a career. As a teacher, she hopes to supply the love that is so necessary. Teachers, she says, are likely to push children too hard. They give children too much information and outrun the child's mind. She turns to the other extreme, letting interest govern the child's growth, humoring him when he is uninterested, and standing by to give full help when he expresses a want. Because the most important thing to her is minute-by-minute friendship with the child, she does practically no long-range planning of schoolwork. She wants children to learn, but she also enjoys them as babies. She reconciles this conflict by a faith that if a child is emotionally healthy, "things will work out all right."

Effects on Pupil Behavior

The investigations of teacher characteristics do not clearly separate the effects of different types of warmth. Each investigator defines warmth in a different way, and few studies carry us beyond the obvious finding that considerateness is better than harshness.

One clear advantage of the supporting environment is that the pupil is encouraged to try, and is therefore more likely to learn. As the likelihood of disapproval lessens, inhibitions disappear. Inventiveness and self-expression are released. This view is supported by several findings: warm, considerate teachers get an unusual amount of original poetry and art from children (Cogan, 1960), generate a greater interest in schoolwork (Reed, 1961), and may produce more proficiency in vocabulary and arithmetic (Christensen, 1960).

The warm, more acceptant teacher is usually better liked by pupils; we would expect a well-liked teacher to have more influence, especially on attitudes and interests. Most of the studies find that pupils give high ratings to teachers who respect their rights and wishes and encourage their growth toward independence (Leeds, 1950; Flanders, 1959; Ryans, 1960). But not all classes are concerned with emotional relationships. Della Piana and Gage (1955) divided elementary classes according to the pupils' choices on such questions as

Which do you want more?

1. a teacher who doesn't make us afraid
2. a teacher who explains so that we can understand

In some classes the average pupil was mostly concerned with feelings and personal relationships (i.e., emotionally oriented). Pupils of this type prefer teachers who are more acceptant and supporting (correlation of the average rating given the teacher with the teacher's attitude = .60). This is the usual finding. But Della Piana and Gage considered separately the classes where pupils were achievement-oriented; these pupils were concerned with how well the teacher explained and helped them learn. The ratings from these pupils correlated only .20 with the teacher's warmth and sympathy. Among pupils motivated to achieve, warmth may not be very important. French's study (page 50) leads to the same conclusion.

A study on level of aspiration points to another way the teacher affects motivation. Lehmusvuori (1958) divided teachers according to a questionnaire, separating the considerate ones from those less concerned with their pupils' feelings. He took pupils from the classrooms of these teachers and tested them individually. Each pupil did a simple intellectual task and then stated what score he expected to make on the next task in the set. Before he stated his next goal, he was told that he had done well or badly on the task just finished. He was alternately praised and criticized. The pupils who had been taught by nonacceptant teachers changed their goals on every trial. Each moment's success or failure moved their expectation up or down. They were weather vanes with no firm self-concept, dependent entirely on evaluation by authority. The pupil who had a more acceptant teacher paid little attention to what the investigator said on each new trial. He set a goal on the basis of his experience over several trials, and stayed with that goal regardless of a momentary setback. The considerate teacher had evidently confirmed the habit of independent self-evaluation.

Sarason *et al.* (1960) give a further argument for being responsive to the pupil's feelings. Unless feelings are brought into the open, the teacher has little insight into the child and therefore is unable to help him. Merely helping him acknowledge his weaknesses is an important step in bringing him to work on them. Sometimes the pupil refuses to admit he needs help if he expects the teacher to be critical of his weakness. The pupil's self-evaluation may be quite wrong, especially when he becomes discouraged over difficulties that are normal for the beginner.

> **19.** Can you recall, among your high-school and college teachers, examples you would class as supporting or as impersonal? What effect did each have on your method of work, your interest, and your learning?
>
> **20.** It is said that some teachers sacrifice the needs of their pupils in order to satisfy their own emotional needs. What does this mean? Illustrate.
>
> **21.** Pupils striving to achieve seem to care little about the warmth of their teachers. What sort of emotional relations do those with a strong need for achievement have with their parents (Chapter 4)? Do you see any connection?

The Interaction of Teacher Style and Pupil Needs

A study of teacher personality by Heil and others (1960) merits close attention. The study involved nine elementary schools, 50 teachers, and over 700 fourth- to sixth-graders. Exceptionally complete data were collected. On the basis of personality questionnaires, Heil was able to classify the teachers into three categories, which we may label spontaneous, orderly, and fearful. Additional description will fill out the picture of each type:

Spontaneous. Self-expressive, turbulent, accepts own impulses, has strong preferences. Likes humor, dislikes routine. Satisfaction more from ideas than from relations with other persons. Low drive toward leadership, low self-aggrandizement, strong independence.

Orderly. Severe self-control, avoids impulsive action, submissive to authority. Secure when things run smoothly. A planner de luxe, ambitious and likes to lead.

Fearful. Perceives environment as threatening. Dependent, dislikes being alone, severely conscientious. Protects self by adhering closely to rules and precedents.

In the community he studied, Heil found 12, 15, and 23(!) teachers in these categories, respectively. Classroom observations were also made to determine the extent to which the teachers used democratic and flexible practices; differences among the three types of teachers in this respect were not significant. In an analysis of results, democratic, warm, responsive teachers were classified as superior.

The effect of each teacher was judged chiefly by the changes on a stand-ardized achievement test from October to June. Statistical corrections for school and neighborhood differences, and for class differences in IQ, were made. In Table 32 we have expressed gains on a scale such that the gain of the average pupil is 100 points. The right-hand column of the table indicates the over-all effectiveness of each type of teacher. Since the num-ber of teachers of each type is small, some of the differences observed would not reappear in other groups of teachers, and cautious interpretation is advised. It appears that orderly teachers get relatively good results and fearful teachers are relatively ineffectual. Among the spontaneous and orderly teachers, those who were most democratic and warm had better results than the others. Supplemental data indicate that pupil anxiety was highest under fearful teachers, lowest under orderly teachers. The pupils' readiness to accept responsibility for their actions was lowest under orderly teachers, highest under spontaneous teachers. These results are generally consistent with Table 31.

TABLE 32

Achievement depends on both teacher and pupil personalities (data from Heil et al., 1960, p. 51).

Teacher type	Number of teachers	Average achievement by pupils of each type			
		Strivers	Docile conformers	Opposers	All pupils
Spontaneous, superior	6	**130** [1]	**162**	75	101
Spontaneous, inferior	6	105	84	52	85
Orderly, superior	7	118	146	**135**	**125**
Orderly, inferior	7	126	91	123	106
Fearful, superior	11	114	95	69	91
Fearful, inferior	11	98	105	80	100
All teachers	48	113	111	86	100

[1] The highest average in each column is in **boldface.**

The effect of each teaching style varies with the pupil's personality. Pupils were classified into three major groups:

Strivers. Strong need for self-respect or for positive approval, want to do well in school, concerned with the task more than with affectional relations.

Docile conformers. Concerned with maintaining smooth personal relationships, avoiding adult disapproval.

Opposers. Conflictful, anticipate rejection. Resistant or withdrawn from authority.

The most noteworthy findings in the table are these:

The strivers do about the same under all teachers. They do fairly well even under some of the fearful teachers.

The conformers make very marked gains under the encouraging spontaneous teachers, but do badly under the spontaneous teachers whose classroom practices are less democratic and supporting.

The opposers do best under the firm authority of the orderly teachers and quite badly under the spontaneous and fearful teachers.

22. Shy and fearful teachers are more inclined to be dominative and less inclined to share planning with their classes. How can this be explained?

23. Can you make any connections between Heil's three types of teacher personality and Mead's three types of teachers (page 45)?

24. What would tend to generate pupil anxiety under fearful teachers? Under spontaneous teachers?

25. Which of the differences in Table 32 are most likely to be chance differences attributable to peculiarities in this small sample of teachers?

26. If you were selecting a teaching staff for Grades IV–VI, which of Heil's types of teacher would you prefer?

CLASSROOM MOTIVATION

Our view in these three chapters can be summarized in several principles of good motivation, which we can use to examine critically such school practices as grading, testing, and competition.

Every activity should lead toward goals that the pupils are aware of and will want to attain.

Goals should be within the pupils' reach, and should seem attainable to them.

The pupils should be able to judge whether or not they are attaining their goals and how they are falling short.

Classroom activities should lead to satisfactions that pupils will also seek outside the classroom so that the learned actions will be used in non-school situations.

A striking example of sound motivation is the project method used in agricultural education. The student plans his work and uses his knowledge functionally. He judges his success by his crop and is not dependent on teacher approval for a confirmation of correct actions.

Setting Definite Goals

For efficient and energetic work, goals should be clear. As soon as purposes and standards of performance are made definite, the pupils can direct their energies constructively. They can judge which procedure is probably best, instead of waiting for the teacher to steer them. They check on their own accomplishment and therefore have a more continuous sense of progress. If the goals seem worth reaching, either because they are immediately interesting or because they serve some need, the pupils will mobilize their energies toward those ends without prodding.

Definiteness is particularly important in assignments. Some teachers end the class hour with such a statement as, "In tomorrow's work we will consider the rise of labor unions in relation to big business. Read the next five pages in the book." What reasons can the pupil have for doing this? Perhaps he has a chance interest in unions. Or he may be one of those omnivorous students who enjoys reading almost anything. Or, if he has formed responsible habits of work, he will feel obligated to do as told and will have the task on his conscience until he does it. Admittedly, any pupil is remotely aware of future praise and grades to be obtained, but if the question is whether to study or go to a show, it is easy to rationalize that he can strive for grades some other night. None of these motives seems to call for more than a cursory reading of the text, enough to satisfy mild curiosity or to ward off self-reproach.

More vital motives lie dormant. It is probable that many pupils really care about labor unions. They are not eager now to read about Sam Gompers and the ancient Haymarket riot, but Dad is a union member and everyone at home is strong for the union. A chance to argue about the matters Dad is always talking about will appeal to some boy's interest in taking an adult role. The teacher might have turned the class loose on the topic of unions with a "what-do-you-think?" opening. One pupil states the idea, perhaps an echo of a parental prejudice, that labor unions are making it impossible for business to show profit. This provokes another pupil who identifies with skilled labor. Airing prejudices and counterprejudices promotes a willingness on the part of everyone to probe more deeply into the topic.

Having aroused interest, the teacher must harness it to study. The pupil can listen to harangues about labor or business without any gain in insight. If the teacher helps the group summarize the discussion by listing major points of disagreement, the next question becomes how to settle specific disputes. Many issues will be factual; for instance, "Businessmen treat their help well" vs. "Without unions, workers are exploited." This can be examined only by going to proper sources. Some will be magazine reports of current labor relations; some will be history books, which tell what conditions gave rise to unions; some could be statements made by a labor leader

1   **2**   **3**   **4**

1   *"I'd like to show Dad I'm as smart as he is."*

2   *"Why don't girls have as much opportunity as boys?"*

3   *"I wish I understood people better."*

4   *"What do I care about history? I'm going to be a scientist."*

115   *Vital motives lie dormant*

or a businessman who visits the class, or of adults whom the class interviews about local working relations. Pupils gather material for a purpose they have accepted as worth their effort. In contrast, the traditional manner of motivating assignments pointed only to goals far removed and indefinite: "when you know this you'll be ready for college," or "you'll understand history." When trying to answer a question, a person reads differently than when he is trying to complete a chore. When he wants to explain to the class what he has learned rather than just to appease the teacher with a recitation, he will really strive to understand.

It is legitimate to argue that history assignments which devote one period to labor and another to the Bull Moose campaign or some other topic cover more ground than does a whole unit of work on one social issue. Pupils learn more, however, when they see the purpose of an assignment and when each day's work adds meaning to the work that went before. In a problem-oriented unit the teacher does not merely inflate one day's topic into three weeks' talking. He uses the question about labor to get at fundamental matters: How determine a fair return on capital? Should laborers have as good a living standard as owners and managers? Has government a proper place in business negotiations? These questions could not even be raised clearly in a one-day discussion about the days of Sam Gompers.

27. In the study of unions, how might the activities and goal-setting procedures provide for individual differences in ability and motivation?

28. Seventh-graders became interested in a contemporary Sicilian bandit described in a news story. One pupil reported that he was a Robin Hood helping the poor; another challenged the report. After considerable disagreement because the class had few facts, they decided to hold a "trial for murder." A judge, defendant, and prosecutor were appointed, and a search for evidence began. For facts not available in published sources, the pupils wrote to news services, to Italian officials, to the Italian Embassy, even to the bandit's relatives in Italy. The judge visited courts to learn proper legal procedure, and the class prepared detailed reports on topics such as *habeas corpus* and the jury system in American law.

Discuss this activity considering responses that could be learned, pupil interest, clarity of purposes, practice with understanding, and provision for individual differences. In what ways might the method be inferior to more traditional lessons on trial by jury?

29. Are the general principles stated above identical to the generalizations about reward presented on pages 490–92?

30. How do our principles differ from the statement, "The subject matter for any class should be determined by what pupils are interested in"?

Competition

Pitting pupils against one another is often used as a motivating technique. There is a prize for the best essay on liberty, gold stars for those who keep their desks neatest, fellowship awards for those who make the best showing in advanced study. Competition does spur people on to greater efforts, as is seen every day in the American culture, but the limitations of competitive motivation are often overlooked.

Does competitive activity provide known and desired goals? Certainly the immediate goal is known. The attractiveness of the goal is another matter. The rewards offered are rarely of great value in themselves. They are mostly symbolic of approval from authority, and as such appeal to the conformer. Others enjoy the game of testing their powers against their peers Some of those who respond most strongly to a competition need evidence of superiority to sustain their self-respect. Defeating others is more important than doing the task well. In some pupils, competition arouses conflict; the threat of losing or the tension induced by working against others prevents wholehearted participation. Some of the most talented pupils like to express their ideas and satisfy their curiosity but care very little about the prizes an adult offers.

Can everyone be confident of reaching the goal? Competition violates this second principle. When most participants are likely to lose, many pupils protect themselves by setting a low level of aspiration, i.e., by not trying. In a spelling match, some pupils are pleased if only they are not the first to make an error; winning is far from their minds.

A competitive program tends to help only the better performers. The capital athlete is encouraged to train to his very peak. The average player gets little attention from the coach and may sit out the season on the bench. The topmost spellers stay in the spelling competition, and some wind up in a national contest in Washington. The weaker spellers are eliminated early and become an audience while the others continue to practice and learn.

Competition usually makes poor provision for examining one's own performance. When prizes are awarded, the winner does not learn why he did well, and the losers have no idea how to do better the next time. Prizes are attached to products, not to processes. A pupil who wins a gold star for doing his arithmetic rapidly may be using processes that will prove a disadvantage in later work. An art student who tries to satisfy contest judges may be sacrificing the development of his own style. Competition is not a good teaching situation, but it may cause the learner to take more seriously the noncompetitive teaching sessions that prepare him for the competition.

Winning a competition does teach pride in an accomplishment. The boy who wins some races begins to think of himself as a potential athlete and starts training seriously. The farmer whose corn wins a ribbon at the county fair works even harder to be a winner thereafter. If an achievement becomes a source of self-esteem, a person is likely to engage in it when there are no special prizes. But pride is developed by doing something well; a person can learn to take pride in his skill without the spur of organized competition.

Competition has harmful effects. Focusing the spotlight on the very best, it damages the self-respect of the mediocre. The boy whose craftsmanship is limited needs to practice and to believe in his capability just as much as the boy who can win prizes. The student who is hopelessly outclassed in public-speaking competitions will avoid speech activities; the school should be developing his skill and confidence as a speaker. Class discussions, panels, and noncompetitive talks would provide practice without threat. Competition is not the way to bring each person to his full potentiality. By emphasizing the false standard that one should take pride where he excels, it discourages the pupil from developing his lesser talents. Competition should not be made so important that failure to win is emotionally disruptive. When there are many activities in which pupils have a chance to excel, no single defeat takes on a special importance.

The student learns to be a competitor. Because competition plays a part in our culture, the person's socialization should include learning to be a good loser, to push to his limit when in competition, and to win gracefully.

It should be possible to teach these behaviors without teaching such harmful attitudes as, "Why work when there's no prize?" A person who is competitive in all his activities is as maladjusted as a person who is never aroused.

Competitions reflect the desire of the school to encourage the ablest. But the twentieth-century school has accepted the responsibility for developing every pupil as fully as possible. A "star" system in music and speech, for example, has given way to a program designed to make competent performance a source of satisfaction for every pupil. (One cannot say the same thing about the athletic program.) Features of the music program include much ensemble work, admission to the ensemble of any player who can perform the selected music, attention to beginners, and interschool "competitions" in which every chorus that enters can go home with a first-class rating if it performs creditably.

An interesting proposal regarding competition comes out of Coleman's studies of prestige in high school. The athlete holds the spotlight, says Coleman (1961b, p. 72), because he is the only pupil who does something conspicuous to enhance the prestige of the school and the pride of its members.

> He is doing something for the school and the community, not only for himself, in leading his team to victory, for it is a school victory. The outstanding student, by contrast, has little or no way to bring glory to his school. His victories are always purely personal ones, often at the expense of his classmates. . . . It is no wonder that his accomplishments gain little reward, and are often met by such ridicule as "curve raiser" or "grind," terms of disapprobation which have no analogues in athletics.
>
> One obvious solution is to substitute interscholastic (and intramural) competition in scholastic matters for the interpersonal competition for grades which exists at present. . . . Such a change would make it necessary to create, with considerable inventiveness, the vehicles for competition—intellectual games, problems, group and individual science projects, and other activities. Yet there are some examples which show that it can be done, as in the debate teams, music contests, drama contests, science fairs (though science fairs as now conducted are ordinarily competitions between individuals . . .).
>
> . . . social rewards from the student body as a whole are only forthcoming in response to something the individual or team has done for *them*, such as bringing glory to the school by winning over another school.

While public attention to academic accomplishment would encourage the able students, the hazards of Coleman's proposal appear to be considerable. The mob emotions of the statewide basketball tournament have not contributed to the physical fitness of pupils generally, and basketball gambling scandals remind us of the moral hazards involved when schools seek to capture the public eye. We should never get in the position where all the class time goes to the topics expected to count in a tournament or where all the science teacher's attention goes to "preparing the team for the tournament" to the neglect of the other pupils.

We cannot say flatly that competition is either good or bad in the school. Kept in proper proportion, it can make work more attractive and can lead to the conspicuous success that instills pride. The danger arises when competition serves only a minority and interferes with the school's obligation to give every pupil pride in what he can become. In the writer's opinion, the best policy is to set up worthwhile school programs in which pupils attain satisfactions through meeting high standards. Intelligently regulated competition added to such a program seems likely to be a beneficial stimulant.

31. Architecture students in their senior year are assigned a project set by a national committee (say, a design for a nursery school). This serves as classwork, and the completed project is judged in a national competition. In what ways is this procedure potentially beneficial? Could it interfere with learning?

32. A national magazine for students offers a poetry prize. The English teacher announces that everyone in the class is to write a poem for the contest. What determines how much effort various members of the class will put forth?

33. In a statewide science fair what is gained by having prizes for the best projects? What evaluation might be provided that would have educational value?

34. Should student elections for class and school offices be competitive?

Marking

The school needs an official record of the pupil's performance, particularly for guidance. Grades and report cards also fulfill the school's responsibility to tell the parent how Johnny is getting along in the world. For those purposes marks should be an emotionally neutral, factual account—but no one regards them that way. Pupils treasure them or worry over them; parents beam or scold. Teachers use marks deliberately as a means of reward and punishment.

As a motivating device, marks do meet the first of our criteria; they serve as definite goals, though not all pupils will work for high marks. The student has a level of expectation when he enters the course, and he will work seriously to reach that level. The teacher who lists extra work that can be done to earn an A will get that work from students who regard themselves as potential A students. Those content to plug along at an average level will ignore the higher goal.

The motivating effect of marks is limited by the feeling of many pupils that high grades are out of reach. This is especially the case when the same standard is set for every pupil regardless of his initial ability. If a mark compares the pupil with others of the same ability, every pupil has a chance for a high mark. But where the mark is first and foremost a record of level attained, as it must be to serve its administrative purposes, the pupil who starts at a superior level is fairly certain to have a high final mark whether or not he pushes himself. Marks are meaningful as a reward only if they measure progress during the course, which is not the same as level of final performance. Marking practices may or may not promote self-judgment. At the worst, there is occasionally a teacher who collects papers or observes pupils at work, makes records that they never see, and at the end of the term issues marks with no explanation. Until the final blow falls, the pupil has no idea whether or not his work is satisfactory. Not knowing how to judge his own work, he may feel that he is doing badly when he is not, or he may be too confident. Marks serve better when they are the end product of a series of judgments about progress made cooperatively by pupil and teacher. If the pupil is continually judging his work in terms of standards that he understands, he is fully aware of the improvement desirable. These frequent judgments, starting early in the course, arouse little tension and encourage a hopeful attitude.

A particular fault of traditional marks is that they grade the performance as a whole. A person who receives a *B* knows that he has done reasonably well but has not done everything perfectly. The mark tells him nothing about how to do better and is not an aid to further learning.

Table 33 shows a report card which provides for a descriptive evaluation that keeps the goals of the course before the pupil and gives him a differentiated picture of his standing.

That the mark by itself has only a small influence on subsequent effort is shown by the extensive experiment of E. B. Page (1958). In high schools and junior high schools, a number of teachers agreed to mark objective tests in a special way. After marks had been placed on an objective test, the teacher randomly assigned each paper to one of three groups. The Group I pupil was given his paper back with no comment save the mark. Every Group II pupil was given a stereotyped comment, ranging from "Excellent!" if his score was high, to "Let's raise this grade!" Every *C* student, for example, received his mark with the notation, "Perhaps try to do still better?" In Group III the teacher wrote on every paper a personal comment, saying whatever she thought would encourage that particular pupil. On the next objective test, Groups II and III outperformed Group I. The personalized comments seemed to have greater effect than the standardized comments, especially with older pupils. Even the very short "pep talk" scribbled on the paper produced measurable improvement. Before the experiment the teachers had expressed the mistaken belief that only superior students respond to personal encouragement. But the greatest improvement was that of the *F* students in Group III, who received a personal encouraging note.

TABLE 33

A report card consistent with sound motivation

PROGRESS REPORT SOCIAL STUDIES
University of Illinois High School
Urbana, Illinois

___ 1st quarter - November ___ 3rd quarter - April

___ Semester - February ___ Final Report - June

RATING SCALE: + - Outstanding, S - Satisfactory, U - Unsatisfactory, O - Inadequate basis for judgment.

+	S	U	O	Respects rights, opinions and abilities of others
+	S	U	O	Accepts responsibility for group's progress
+	S	U	O	Is careful with property
+	S	U	O	Uses time to advantage
+	S	U	O	Is attentive
+	S	U	O	Follows directions
+	S	U	O	Makes regular preparations as required

	S	U	O	Evidences independent thought and originality
	S	U	O	Seeks more than superficial knowledge
	S	U	O	Evidences growth in orderly and constructive group discussion
	S	U	O	Keeps informed on current affairs
	S	U	O	Discriminates in the selection and use of social studies materials
	S	U	O	Demonstrates growth in the skills of critical thinking
	S	U	O	Places people and events in their chronological and cultural setting
	S	U	O	Demonstrates social responsibility

ACHIEVEMENT

The grade below is a measure of achievement with respect to what is expected of a pupil of this class in this school, and in relation to what is expected in the next higher course in this subject.

___ 5 excellent ___ 2 passing, but weak

___ 4 very good ___ 1 failing

___ 3 creditable ___ 0 inadequate basis for judgment

EFFORT

The grade below is an estimate, based on evidence available to the teacher, of the individual student's effort.

___ 5 excellent ___ 2 weak

___ 4 very good ___ 1 very weak

___ 3 creditable ___ 0 inadequate basis for judgment

Teacher: _____

COMMENTS:

35. If letter grades are used, should a fixed percentage of the class be allowed *A*'s?

36. In a certain college, grades are filed in the office and not released to the student or to other instructors until he graduates or leaves school; he is informed only if he fails a course. What can be said for and against this policy?

37. In the arithmetic class that discovered a general principle regarding "sidebands" (page 374), participation was highly enthusiastic. What did Mr. Palmer do to "motivate" his pupils? What style of leadership did he use? Does his success illustrate the principles of this chapter, or is it an exception?

38. A teacher taught a social studies class by a group project method, in which all members worked together on the plan, collected evidence, and organized their conclusions into a team report. The teacher reported the same grade for all members of the team. What is your opinion of this marking procedure? Can you suggest any alternative marking procedure, assuming that grades must be reported and that the teaching method itself is not to be changed?

DISCIPLINARY PROBLEMS AS A FAILURE OF LEADERSHIP

Classroom discipline is a condition where pupils are using their time in educationally desirable ways. The teacher who cannot establish this condition cannot teach. Good discipline does not require every student in his place, every pupil silent save one, everyone focused on the speaker. In such a classroom the listeners may be learning nothing. Discipline has not failed when six eager children burst out with an idea at once, so long as they are willing to listen to each other. It is good for a class to break up into groups doing different things, all humming with busyness and work-related conversation. The test of discipline is whether or not the behavior of the group permits everyone to work effectively.

Groups waste time and, in rare instances, rebel against the teacher. If this happens only occasionally, the causes are likely to be beyond the teacher's control: fatigue, a wave of colds, excitement over a holiday, a conflict carried over from the preceding class. These difficulties can be handled sometimes by reducing pressures, sometimes by an activity of special interest.

Persistent disorder or confusion means that the group does not know what to do or does not want to do it. The teacher therefore should re-examine his methods of establishing goals. If the goals seem unrewarding to the students and not worth attaining, only continual cajoling and threats will keep them at work. Perhaps the students could not be convinced of the value of the goals—if so, maybe they have no real value. Possibly the goals are reasonable but have been poorly explained to students. If so, the teacher should find out what the pupils are trying to do and explain where they are on the wrong track, or clarify the limits of allowable behavior. This applies both to the end in view and to the work methods employed.

If the goal is accepted by the class and understood, why should they not do what the end requires? One cause is boredom; monotonous and repetitive tasks are an invitation to mind-wandering and trouble-making. Pupils have interests and needs, which continually steal their attention. The girl across the aisle attracts the attention even of a boy who really wants to know what the text says about the solar system. That is why teachers seek to arrange work which permits students to satisfy nonintellectual needs while they learn ideas. The boy can get to know the girl while they work together on a committee. She may keep his mind from total attention to the subject matter, but that was happening anyhow. Fear of failure is another reason for not "tending to business." The group that is baffled and expects to remain baffled will prefer any diversion. Setting goals that can be reached is one obvious answer. The other treatment for discouragement is to go back and make the work clear, even if deficiencies piled up years before have to be treated one by one.

The problems of individual misconduct are comparable to the problems of group disorder and have similar causes. Does the pupil know where the group is heading? Does the goal seem worthwhile to him? Does he think he can do what is expected of him? If these questions are answered affirmatively, the only remaining explanation is that some individual need is interfering. We shall discuss maladjustment at length in Chapter 17.

When an individual pupil fails to use his time constructively, the invariable solution is to make a study of him as a person. Determine his readiness patterns, and your treatment will be determined accordingly. If penalties for misconduct are unthinkingly imposed on the pupil who deviates, the teacher may be adding new stresses where there were already too many.

SUMMARY

The problem of motivation is to direct the pupils' energies toward worthwhile goals. Class management should help them find enduring purposes and satisfaction in their progress. Undirected activity, teacher control, and group control are contrasted. In the first, no one defines goals or plans the work; in the second, the major decisions are handed down by the teacher. In group control the class governs itself, making plans and decisions with the aid of the teacher. Group planning is less a matter of taking formal votes than of openly considering the pupils' opinions and feelings. The teacher must make clear the limits within which the group is free to operate. The style of teachers using group control is summarized in Table 30. Mr. Osborne's teaching illustrates the advantages and weaknesses of undirected activity; Miss Simmons uses group control in teaching English.

The major results from comparisons of control techniques are summarized in Table 31. Additional noteworthy findings include the following: Friendly relations develop more rapidly in a work-oriented group with a shared goal than in a group that has no task. In an undirected group, performance may improve when the adult supervisor leaves because group members then supply some leadership. Elementary teachers who obtain more alert and enthusiastic participation are observed to be well organized and considerate. Where the teacher is more democratic and less conventional in procedure, the pupils show more initiative; the highly "responsible" teacher may produce docile pupils. The results of democratic teaching in high-school classes are inconsistent. Group activities do not automatically teach effective group membership; verbal review of the group process during and after the activity promotes transferable learning. Experience in group planning fosters self-discipline. The research leads to the conclusion that organized, thoroughly planned teaching is best, and that in some part of the school experience planning by the pupils should be used to teach the skills of group membership. We do not conclude that group control is universally superior.

What style the teacher can adopt depends on the expectations of others. Pupils have an image of the teacher's legitimate exercise of power; they expect the teacher to control activities, to set standards, and to be open to their suggestions. A second limiting factor is the curriculum to be taught. The teacher's own needs and personality also make some techniques more satisfying than others.

The teacher may apply any control technique warmly or impersonally. The impersonal teacher is work-centered, just rather than indulgent, and unconcerned with pupils' feelings. "Warmth" takes different forms: spontaneity, unconditional encouragement, lavish praise contingent on "good" performance, considerateness, or acceptance of pupils' feelings. These do not have identical effects, though any form of warmth encourages the insecure pupil to try, and increases interest. Some classes strongly prefer teachers who are acceptant and supporting. Other classes—where achievement motivation is strong—judge a teacher by his success in clarifying the material to be learned; to them, the teacher's warmth makes little difference.

The study of Heil and others indicates that pupils of different personalities profit from different teaching styles. Orderly teachers get the best over-all results, and fearful teachers get the poorest results. Strivers do much the same no matter what the teacher's style. Conformers do exceptionally well under the supporting, spontaneous teacher. Pupils who oppose authority do poorly under spontaneous or fearful teachers, but do well under orderly teachers.

Four principles of motivation are emphasized:

Every activity should lead toward goals the pupils are aware of and want to attain.

Goals should be within reach, and the pupils should regard them as attainable.

The pupils should be able to judge how well they are progressing.

Classroom activities should lead to satisfactions that pupils will also seek outside the classroom.

We have discussed how these principles are applied in making assignments, in evaluating competition, and in marking systems.

Classroom discipline is effective when pupils are using their time effectively. Good discipline does not call for perfect order, but it does call for cooperation and self-restraint. Persistent disorder implies that the goals of the work are not clear to the pupils or are not acceptable. Making the goals more attainable and the work more interesting alleviate the causes of inattention and frustration rather than the symptoms.

Reading List 15

Nathaniel Cantor, *The Teaching-Learning Process* (New York: Dryden, 1953).

Cantor attacks the conventional methods of teacher control and instruction by presentation of knowledge. This book consists of extracts from a course for teachers taught by Cantor using an acceptant, undirected procedure. Transcripts of discussions illustrate his technique and also reflect what the teachers in the class think about discipline and the tensions of teaching. It is important to decide just what portion of Cantor's argument is consistent with the evidence we have reviewed.

Jules Henry, Barbara Biber, and Leah Levinger, "The Teacher's Role in Creativity," *American Journal of Orthopsychiatry,* 29 (1959), 266–97.

Henry charges that attempts to make pupils spontaneous lead to classroom disorder. He discusses tactics that teachers use to reduce friction and noise in the class; the tactic frequently is one that expresses the teacher's needs. Biber speaks strongly for a teaching style that fosters contributions from the group. Levinger contrasts and criticizes the two papers.

David H. Jenkins, "Characteristics and Functions of Leadership in Instructional Groups," in Nelson B. Henry, ed., *The Dynamics of Instructional Groups,* Fifty-ninth Yearbook of the National Society for the Study of Education, Part II (Chicago: Univ. of Chicago Press, 1960), pp. 164–86.

Jenkins defines the sources of the teacher's authority and the leadership responsibilities the teacher must take. He offers seven maxims regarding control of the class and development of harmony.

Ronald Lippitt and Ralph K. White, "Major Differences in Boys' Behavior," Chapter 5 in *Autocracy and Democracy: An Experimental Inquiry* (New York: Harper, 1960), pp. 61–88. Similar material in Coladarci, Maccoby, and Charters.

This is a summary of the experimental findings in the classic study of boys' clubs treated by different control techniques. Both statistical results and individual boys are discussed. As you read, try to decide whether the experiment proves that the group-control pattern is best generally, best for some groups and some purposes, or not particularly advantageous. What further experiments would you as a teacher like to have performed?

Wilbert J. McKeachie, "Procedures and Techniques of Teaching: A Survey of Experimental Studies," Chapter 8 in Nevitt Sanford, ed., *The American College* (New York: Wiley, 1962), pp. 312–64.

McKeachie reviews studies on all aspects of college instruction, some pertinent to this chapter on control patterns, and others dealing with television, lecture, and other instructional techniques.

Nevitt Sanford, "Dominance Versus Authority and the Democratic Character," *Childhood Education*, 23 (1946), 109–14.

A summary of research on class direction, which draws a careful distinction between legitimate direction of activities and arbitrary suppression of the pupil. Relates leadership policy to the maturity and character of the child.

William L. Wrinkle, *Improving Marking and Reporting Practices in Elementary and Secondary Schools* (New York: Rinehart, 1947).

This is an account of the experiences of a school changing from A, B, C, D, F marking to a system intended to have fewer logical and psychological faults. Try the author's "attitude test" on grading, and examine the special record forms illustrated. The author considers which grading procedures suggested by theory are really practicable.

CHAPTER 16 JUDGING PERFORMANCE

Evaluation is the process by which teacher and student judge whether or not the goals of schooling are being attained. The swimmer who is able after some instruction to move away from the edge of the pool knows that he is progressing. The fourth-grade teacher notices that his pupils are regularly checking their addition, turning in few papers with undetected errors. The home economics teacher observes that many girls in her cooking class are not measuring ingredients with care. Testing is only one of many evaluation procedures. Daily assignments, class discussions, and shopwork exhibit ability and typical behavior. The student can judge himself with respect to responsibility, neatness, etc.; opinions collected from other students can help him see his actions objectively. A finished project is a tribute to competent performance, or a glaring evidence of lapses.

We shall in this chapter consider how evaluation aids in teaching and the value each method of evaluation has. We shall discuss the limitations of tests and how these may be overcome. We shall compare short-answer tests with discussion questions and look at some new varieties of tests.

FUNCTIONS OF EVALUATION

Evaluation has five functions:

It helps the learner realize how he should change or develop his behavior (feedback to learner).

It helps the learner attain satisfaction when he is doing as he should (reinforcement).

It provides a basis for subsequent decisions about the learner: what courses he is ready for, what remedial treatment he needs, what job or college to recommend him to.

It helps the teacher judge how adequate his teaching methods are (feedback to teacher).

It provides information for administrative judgments.

The first two of these will be our primary concern in this chapter. The third was considered adequately in Chapter 7 on readiness. The last two need only a few sentences of elaboration.

The teacher who gives an examination not only tests his class, but also tests himself. If the history class misses some questions about tariffs, learning was incomplete. Perhaps tariffs have not been explained clearly, or perhaps pupils did not recognize their importance and did not study them. Such evidence suggests what should be retaught; it also suggests whether or not a teaching method is effective enough to use the next time the teacher wants to attain the same objectives.

The administrator uses evaluative information to review the total school program and policies. He may find, for example, that the range of performance in English is so great that a remedial program or an honors program is needed. He may decide that the schedule needs to be arranged to provide more time for the art course or for mathematics. He may decide, after consulting with the teachers, that a foreign language laboratory must be provided to improve comprehension of spoken language. Evidence arising from evaluation, properly interpreted to the community, also has value in building support for the program and for needed changes.

Evaluation is primarily important, however, as feedback to the learner. Provisional tries, we have said, lead to changed performance *if* the performer is dissatisfied with the consequences he notices. When a pupil is trying to master something, he makes an effort to judge himself. The boy on the basketball floor welcomes a chance to take a shot. When he finds a weakness he practices hard to overcome it and looks for the precise cause of his error. Academic tests likewise give the pupil a chance to find out where to improve. The pupil's attitude toward a classroom test, however, is not at all like his attitude toward basketball practice. The chance to try in the classroom is often evaded; many pupils try to stay out of a discussion and most of them groan when a test is announced. Pupils see tests as a threat, as something the teacher does *to* the pupil for *his* purposes. In the right classroom atmosphere, pupils will see tests as an aid in reaching their own goals.

After the pupil leaves the schoolroom, he will have to judge for himself how well he is doing. Through experience in self-evaluation he learns to judge himself. Therefore many teachers ask the pupil to appraise his own adequacy with respect to each of the course objectives. The pupil, with the teacher, decides what further progress he should try for. This new aim is developed from evidence he understands. He knows what his specific goals should be and recognizes his progress toward them. Duel (1958) checked the value of self-evaluation procedures in a technical school. At the start of the course and at the end of each unit of instruction students rated themselves on such questions as, "How proficient are you in using a multimeter to measure output voltages and currents of a vacuum tube?" Two groups were taught in precisely the same way, save that one group filled out this form, which focused attention on important outcomes. In every unit of the course the group using the form was superior on objective proficiency tests.

If a person feels that he has reached a satisfactory level of performance, he will make little further change. Sometimes the pupil is satisfied with inadequate performance. When study or the rewriting of a theme is tedious, it is much pleasanter to say, "This is acceptable," than to admit the inadequacies of the work. If the pupil judges his performance accurately, he will know when he has truly done well enough to go on to something else.

Students frequently have very limited insight into their own weaknesses. Kooker and Williams (1959) asked college psychology students to indicate which of their answers to objective examination questions they were "certain of," with the understanding that this report would not affect their grades. On true-false items, these students were correct in about 85 per cent of their "certain" answers to true-false items and in about 75 per cent of their "certain" answers to four-choice items. On answers not called "certain," the corresponding percentages were about 60 and 50. The value of the test as a direct means of overcoming misinformation is shown in an experiment with high-school English classes (Plowman and Stroud, 1942). The pupils studied a passage and took a multiple-choice test; a week later they were retested. They eliminated nearly half their errors as a result of looking over their corrected test papers for just five minutes on the day after the first test. This occurred even though the pupils had no reason to expect a retest. It is important to note that the teacher not only indicated which items the pupil had missed but also which response to each question was correct.

TABLE 34

The pupil learns from inspecting his corrected test paper (from Plowman and Stroud, 1942)

Condition	Content studied	Mean score on day 1 (per cent)	Mean retest score on day 7 (per cent)	Difference
First test inspected on day 2	A	72	84	12
	B	71	83	12
No feedback from first test	A	68	67	−1
	B	73	68	−5

1. Which purposes of evaluation does each of the following practices serve?
   a. A final examination is given on the last day of a college course. No report on the test is returned to the student.
   b. After a series of lectures on existentialism, students fill out a quiz at home. Each one marks his own paper at the start of a section meet-

ing, after which the hour is devoted to discussion of controversial or confusing questions.

c. Eight issues of a school newspaper are submitted to a "clinic" operated by the state university. A rating is returned along with comments on the good and the poor features of the paper.

2. What evaluation procedures could a history teacher employ to improve the oral expression of his students?

3. In the light of the Plowman-Stroud study, evaluate each of the following statements:

a. It would be good classroom practice to give every test twice, allowing the pupils to inspect their corrected papers.

b. Since the questions in any test are only a small sample of the material studied in a course, no significant gain in knowledge results from going over them.

c. As much learning results from discussing the correct answer to every question in class as from allowing the pupil to examine his own corrected paper.

Evaluation Clarifies Objectives

What the learner tries depends on his goals. The goals of learning are supposed to be established during planning, but actually the learner's goals depend on what evaluation he anticipates. Goals not reflected in evaluation procedures will be neglected. Progress toward some objectives affects marks; the pupil pays only lip service to other objectives not represented in the evaluation. A main objective in history may be "to understand that present-day problems have a historical basis." If tests deal only with facts about the past and not at all with the present-day significance of those facts, the objective is forgotten. Pupils do not study by asking themselves, "How does this chapter bear on current problems?" They learn about Continental currency because it is in the book, never connecting it with contemporary controversies about how to pay for armaments. They are failing to get what they should from the course.

Donald wants to learn chemistry. He is enthusiastic about science, plans to continue science courses in college, and probably will find a career in science. His day-to-day study calls for continual decisions about what is important. Shall he try to remember the names of discoverers? technical terms like *adiabatic* and *aliphatic?* the formulas for chemicals? the industrial technique for making sulfuric acid? Unless he happens to need some bit of knowledge for an immediate purpose like setting up a darkroom, he can only decide what is important according to what the teacher appears to "count."

Donald performs an exercise in the laboratory. The directions call for adding 10 cc. of silver nitrate to a solution. When he pours in an amount he guesses to be about right, he gets a bulky precipitate. He records the result in his notebook and writes the equation that explains it. The teacher circles in red where Donald wrote Ag_2NO_3 instead of $AgNO_3$ but makes no other comment. So Donald is confirmed in his neglect of laboratory procedure, but is warned that formulas are important. Another teacher might have observed Donald's laboratory operations and cautioned him against guessing at amounts. Then Donald would have learned that technique is important in science.

It is appropriate in classroom planning for both teacher and pupils to think about the changes in observable behavior that are intended. If the tests (or other methods of evaluation) then measure these behaviors, pupils will see what is meant by objectives that might otherwise be overlooked or forgotten. In history it would be appropriate for both daily discussions and tests to ask about current implications of past events. Miss Simmons' class (see page 506) could properly make an effort to improve its committee work. By setting up criteria—"What do we mean by good committee work?"— the class could develop a check list of specific goals. With this check list all committees could rate themselves periodically. Everyone would know what was meant by the objectives. The boy who tried to do the whole job himself instead of sharing responsibility would be called into question. Evaluation by test alone might have rewarded him for monopolizing the learning opportunities.

Evaluation procedures can teach new ideals. The student of agriculture learns to judge cattle or corn, and in that way discovers what qualities to strive for on his own farm. A recording of his playing shows the music student that his volume is uneven; as he plays for his own pleasure, he will henceforth be judging himself and correcting his volume. Dubin (1946) developed the drawing ability of preschool children simply by looking at each drawing and making comments. Each comment suggested appropriate things for the child to think about. Scribblers were asked what their drawings represented. Those who were already drawing representatively were asked what the obscure parts of their drawings represented. With the most advanced children, the teacher discussed the use of color, or organization. These pupils improved much faster than a control group that received no such directing evaluation.

Merely giving tests has a motivating effect. Frequent testing has special value for the weaker students. A quiz every week leads to greater improvement than similar teaching with few quizzes (Kirkpatrick, 1939; Ross and Henry, 1939; Fitch *et al.*, 1951). The same principle is applied in the teaching machine where feedback follows each response. With adequate measurement of performance, the pupil knows what he is accomplishing and what he has failed to grasp. Pupils so tested do more than study what they have missed. Given a clearer sense of purpose and progress, they study more

TABLE 35

Sixth-graders can set definite goals

1. The conversation should be kept going.
   a. Keep on main points.
   b. Change the subject smoothly.
2. The people should be polite.
   a. Boys should stand when girls enter.
   b. If a boy and a girl start to talk at the same time the boy should let the girl go ahead.
   c. If two girls or two boys start to talk at one time, the girl or boy who has talked more gives place to the one who has talked less.
   d. Only one person should talk at a time.
   e. Usually questions should be addressed to the group instead of to individuals.
   f. The people in the audience should not attract the attention of the people in the conversation group.
3. The host or hostess should be polite to the guests.
   a. The host or hostess should talk only to encourage the guests to talk.
   b. The host or hostess should talk only when the conversation drags.
   c. The host or hostess should greet the guests cordially.
4. Only people who have studied the *Weekly Reader* and read the local papers and listened to radio reports should accept an invitation.
   a. People should think as they read.
   b. People should be able to locate on the map places mentioned.
   c. People should look up difficult words.
   d. People should be able to give the source of their information.
5. People should talk about topics that are important now and will probably be important for some time to come.
   a. About the causes of the war and how the war affects people.
   b. In connection with disasters, about means of preventing them.
6. People should discuss sensible, interesting, and pleasant topics.
7. People should use good English.
   a. People should make themselves heard.
   b. People should pronounce words correctly.
   c. People should use correct expressions, e.g., *the reporter* instead of *it*, and *interesting conversation* or *a pleasant conversation* or *a lively conversation* instead of *a nice time*.
   d. People should omit unnecessary words.
   e. People should try to add to their vocabularies all the time.

This is a list of standards set by sixth-graders, for use in judging their own panel discussions of current events. From Walter W. Cook, *Grouping and Promotion in the Elementary School* (Series on Individualization of Instruction, No. 2). Minneapolis: University of Minnesota Press. Copyright 1941 by the University of Minnesota and reproduced by permission.

diligently, and acquire a better knowledge even of the items not mentioned in the test. But the effect of the test is to direct effort, not just to increase it. Keislar (1961) presented paragraphs containing two kinds of information to sixth- and seventh-graders, and immediately after they had read each paragraph tested them on one kind of information only. After they had been put through 20 paragraphs in this way, he tested them on both kinds of information from the next paragraph. The pupils who had been tested on the first type of information learned more of the first type of information from the final paragraph; those who had been tested on the second type learned more of the second type. The test had defined what was worth attending to.

To summarize, tests motivate and direct learning by providing short-range goals, by reducing broad objectives to definite aims, and by rewarding good tries.

    4. How does the list of current-events standards (Table 35) differ from the standards a teacher might prepare for judging the discussions? Which list would most assist learning?

    5. Donald discovered what to value in laboratory work only from the way the teacher criticized his report. How might a proper planning session before he entered the laboratory have better equipped him to recognize important goals?

REQUIREMENTS OF AN EVALUATION PROCEDURE

Many evaluation methods as now used are not effective aids to learning. Some methods have limited value because they give an untrue estimate of the pupil's behavior or consider only part of his performance. Other methods measure well enough, but are used in such a way that the information leads to no improvement. We amplify here the discussion begun in Chapter 7; you may need to review pages 209–15. There we were primarily concerned with tests, but here we consider the requirements of evaluation procedures generally.

Validity

The foremost requirement is validity. A procedure is valid for evaluation if it describes truthfully an aspect of the pupil's performance that is a goal of instruction. A method valid for some purposes is not valid for all other appraisals. A simple test of knowledge of electrical terms and practices might be a good way to determine what a junior-high-school boy has learned from a unit of shopwork and what readiness he has for a further course. Such a limited test would certainly not measure whether a high-school graduate knows enough about electricity to be hired as a repairman. A valid test for hiring purposes would have more questions, would cover more difficult topics, and would require performance rather than verbal knowledge.

The evaluation procedure examines a sample of behavior. Occasionally one can test pupils on every specific fact in a course; in the teaching machine, the course of study and the "test content" are almost identical. But when one wishes to test ability to use knowledge, one cannot possibly observe the pupil in every situation where his learning would be useful. Many objectives are stated in terms of typical behavior. To appraise citizenship one can observe only a sample of the actions that show good or poor skills and attitudes. A valid test for an objective must sample adequately the situations included within the objective.

A German test illustrates problems of sampling. If the test includes a large number of words that can be guessed because of their similarity to

22 Where could a person live most independently?

    1 on a farm
    2 in a city of 25,000 people
    3 in a city of 100,000 people
    4 in a small town

22   1 2 3 4 ○○○○

23 Who invented the telegraph?

    1 Clinton   3 Howe
    2 Bell   4 Morse

23   1 2 3 4 ○○○○

24 In most civilized countries, a person who refuses to obey the law is —

    1 kept away from other free people
    2 sent out of the country
    3 put to death
    4 put in the army

24   1 2 3 4 ○○○○

25 Mulberry trees do not grow well in the United States. For that reason, the United States produces very little —

    1 silk   3 linen
    2 nylon   4 rayon

25   1 2 3 4 ○○○○

26 The first extensive explorers of the ocean were the people of —

    1 Japan   3 the Indies
    2 Western Europe   4 Australia

26   1 2 3 4 ○○○○

116

A sample of content in the social studies

Items from *Stanford Achievement Test*, Intermediate II Battery, Complete, Form X, copyright 1963 by Harcourt, Brace & World, Inc. Reproduced by special permission.

English, such as *Hund* and *Licht*, the class may get many items right even though their vocabularies are poorly developed. Too many questions on the subjunctive might make the group seem weak in grammar. If no items require the dative case, teacher and pupils may remain unaware of a serious weakness at that point. Until very recently, all language tests were written, demanding neither listening comprehension nor speaking ability. A systematic attempt to cover the important subskills and types of content is necessary for validity.

Sometimes a test may validly sample an area and yet not be suitable for a particular classroom. The teacher often wants to determine how well the class has learned what it has been taught, rather than its ability over a whole field. A test is said to have *curricular validity* if it samples adequately the behavioral objectives of the curriculum the pupil has been pursuing. A German test that samples the whole German language would have poor curricular validity for a course in scientific German. If a class does not study subjunctives because the teacher chooses to emphasize something else, there is little point in testing knowledge of subjunctives. You will recall from Chapter 1 that when elementary classes using activity methods of instruction were evaluated, they failed to show any superiority on traditional tests. On tests suited to their new objectives, however, they were superior to the classes taught more traditionally. Whenever new curricula are introduced, or old curricula are modified to fit local conditions, evaluation procedures must be re-examined. The distribution of emphasis, the order of presentation, and the thought processes practiced are often altered; consequently, tests suitable to the old curriculum no longer give a just appraisal.

Validity depends on the form and wording of items, as well as on their content. Pupils who know the material studied will miss an ambiguous question; contrariwise, a student who does not understand the material may get the question right because an unintended clue is given. For example, students expect true-false items containing the word "always" to be false. They can answer such an item correctly when they are ignorant of the pertinent facts.

The objectives of learning are rarely confined to facts to be learned. The important aim is to change the way the pupil reacts to situations. A class studies foods because it is agreed they should choose foods more wisely. No written test shows whether they have learned this. The test item, "Vitamin ____ is sometimes called ascorbic acid" would tell nothing about food habits. It would be better to ask, for instance, "What essential food element (or elements) is missing from a lunch composed of a hot dog and a milk shake?" Even this question determines only whether or not the pupils have the desirable response available. The only way to obtain fully valid evidence of the pupils' *typical* responses would be to observe what they select in the cafeteria. Less accurate but useful information would be compiled by having the pupils keep a diary of what they eat each day. Such a diary would encourage them to judge and correct their own behavior.

Too often the evaluation program determines only whether or not a pupil knows what the teacher wants. Fred Henry, taking an education course, believes firmly that the high-school mathematics curriculum should emphasize manipulative skill in algebra. But if asked, "What should the mathematics curriculum include, and why?" Fred knows that he will be rewarded if he repeats the instructor's arguments favoring a general mathematics program suitable for pupils of average ability. The instructor, receiving this answer, can have no confidence that Fred has altered his attitude.

6. If seventh-grade boys have been learning to play basketball in their physical education class, would a valid measure of learning be obtained by having each one throw a total of 20 shots from various positions (free throw, lay-up shot, long shot, etc.), counting the number of baskets made?

7. Why might each of the following procedures lack validity when used to evaluate student progress?

  a. Progress in a typing course is judged solely by performance on speed tests.

  b. Progress in arithmetic in fourth grade is tested solely by exercises in the four fundamental operations, such as $21 \times 14 =$ _____.

  c. A college English class is learning to read poetry orally. As a written examination, the students are given several unfamiliar selections on which they are to mark where the accents would be placed.

8. Under what circumstances and for what purposes is it proper to measure students on a task they have not studied?

9. A new English curriculum for junior high schools emphasizes creative composition. While good form is a desired outcome, formal grammatical terms (e.g., parts of speech) are never used; pupils are taught to judge whether or not each sentence is clear and sounds well. Can one compare fairly the effect of this curriculum with the effect of a curriculum that teaches formal grammatical analysis? Can the same test have curricular validity for different curricula?

10. What sort of intermediate-grade program would prepare a pupil to make a high score on the social studies section of the Stanford Achievement Test (Figure 116)? Can you describe a good social-studies program that would lead to below-average scores on this test?

11. To what extent does this test measure recall of specific facts? general understanding of concepts and principles? reasoning?

12. In Chapter 2 we listed five qualities of the socialized person which may be regarded as the major objectives of education. Do the school evaluation procedures cover all of these qualities? Answer for the elementary school, the high school, or the college.

13. A course is intended to teach teachers how to aid children who have personality difficulties. As a means of evaluating learning, what are the limitations of the question: "What would you do with a child who has a feeling of inferiority?"

Accuracy

Accurate measurement is desirable but costly. To improve accuracy one must devote more effort to developing tests and other procedures and more time to testing or observation. Accuracy is a primary consideration when important and irreversible decisions are to be made, for example, in college admissions. In day-to-day decisions (whether to move to a new topic or to review, for example) teachers rely on casual scraps of evidence. This does no harm if the teacher remains alert to indications that the decision was wrong.

The assessment of behavior calls for the same precautions as the accurate measurement of height or weight: testing everyone under comparable conditions, scoring carefully, and the like. Mental measurement encounters an additional difficulty. A single observation of height or weight is dependable, but a single question is an insufficient sample of ability. To get a dependable measure of knowledge or skill, it is necessary to use a large number of items. We determine a student's knowledge of German vocabulary only very roughly by a ten-word test; some average students might, by chance, know all the words in the test and some very good students might miss one or two words. With 100 words, we could rank class members with considerable accuracy and could determine gains from month to month.

> **14.** In a teaching-machine program, a decision that the pupil should go ahead to the next fact is based on his response to a single question. If he misses, he must repeat. Is such information accurate enough for this purpose?
>
> **15.** If a very accurate measure of leadership skill were desired (perhaps for a Peace Corps assignment), how could it be obtained?

Usefulness for Diagnosis

Since evaluation should point out ways of improving, the most valuable procedures will indicate specifically what the pupil is doing incorrectly. In some courses, the instructor marks a test and posts the grades. This ends the evaluation. When a student looks at the list and finds his grade of C, he can resolve to do better, or he can brush off the result as "about all I expected." The test has given him no aid in improving. He does not know what he missed, what he studied inadequately, or what misconceptions he has.

Almost any observation or test can have diagnostic value. A diagnostic evaluation tells what has been accomplished correctly and what is wrong, instead of merely assigning a grade or score. It examines what questions about chemistry a student missed, what faults in speaking form he is displaying, or at what step in long division he goes astray.

FORMAL TESTS AS EVIDENCE OF PERFORMANCE

Nearly all teachers test skills and knowledge. Tests can also identify changes in attitudes, study habits, and interests. In our earlier discussion (Chapters 6 and 7) we stated the following principles of testing:

A test appraises the pupil's performance by observing his work on a sample of tasks or items. The sample must be representative of the area and large enough to give dependable evidence.

Ability tests measure what the pupil can do. It is much more difficult to appraise his typical behavior.

To obtain information on typical behavior, personal observation, self-reports by the pupil, and reports by his peers are generally superior to tests.

Norms provide a basis for interpreting scores of the individual or the class. They indicate what average pupils do, not necessarily what pupils *should* do.

To obtain dependable evidence, tests must be given in the same way to all students.

THE VALUE OF TESTS IN SELF-EVALUATION.   Tests are an especially good way to help the learner gauge his own progress. If the teacher judges his performance and tells him that he is performing poorly, he may only rationalize: "Mr. Blake just has it in for me," or "You have to talk in class a lot to get a good grade; I know the stuff all right." This does not lead to any effort to improve. By contrast, a test is impartial, especially if graded objectively. The student can see just which tasks he handles ineffectively. He may be able to administer the test to himself. When a series of equivalent tests can be given, week after week, the exactly measured gain in score from test to test makes his progress evident. All these advantages make a test a valuable feedback procedure.

Teachers have various biases, which enter into their impressionistic evaluations, and objective measurement provides a much needed corrective. The most evident of these biases is the assignment of higher marks to girls even when this is not warranted by the girls' proficiency. In one of several studies on this topic, R. S. Carter (1952) examined the marks in beginning algebra classes given in the same school by six experienced teachers, three men and three women. We see in Table 36 that there was little difference in the mental ability of the boys and girls, and a standardized end-of-semester achievement test revealed no important, statistically significant difference between pupil groups. But the teachers' marks were not fair indications of performance. The three men teachers gave appreciably lower

TABLE 36

Teachers' reports are not impartial (*R. S. Carter, 1952*)

Group	Mean IQ	Mean achievement test score	Difference	Mean grade	Difference	Correlation of marks with achievement
Boys taught by men	107	30.8		76.6		.78
Girls taught by men	109	29.2	1.7	79.5	−2.9	.57
Boys taught by women	108	29.5		82.6		.37
Girls taught by women	107	30.5	−1.0	86.7	−4.1	.35
All boys	107	30.2		79.3		.59
All girls	108	29.7	.5	82.5	−3.2	.45

marks than the three women teachers. Girls received significantly higher marks than boys. Girls' marks, and marks given by women teachers, had relatively little correlation with achievement. There is no evidence in this study as to why marks were inaccurate, but other reports indicate that teachers often grade on conduct, neatness, and other matters far removed from course achievement. Any form of credit for docility (for example, credit for consistently prompt and complete homework) will favor the girl.

LIMITATIONS OF TESTS.   Tests have notable limitations, most of which arise because the teacher and the students tend to regard them as the only really important evidence of accomplishment. Yet tests cover only a few of the school's objectives. As illustrated earlier, skills in committee work, in expressing ideas orally, and in using the library are major objectives of education. These need systematic evaluation that pencil-and-paper tests cannot provide. Likewise, there is no formal way to test curiosity, intellectual alertness, and enjoyment of elegant reasoning or superior literary style. Unfortunately, the accomplishments not included in formal tests are slighted in teaching, in studying, and in forming a self-concept.

When tests are elevated into the one important index of accomplishment, they distort the learning process. The student crams for the final examination because he wants his record to be *un*representative of his learning during the semester. The test under these circumstances is not likely to be highly valid. Information loaded aboard at the last minute is likely to be poorly integrated, and if so it will be forgotten as soon as the test is over. Performance under do-or-die pressure, moreover, is likely to be below the student's true level. The test ought to be no more than a way of judging formally what has been judged informally all along. Periodic, low-pressure evaluation gives the truest picture of attainment.

The typical end-of-course examination loses the main educative value of an evaluation procedure. It sets no goals for future learning; the student puts the course behind him when he turns in the test paper. It gives no diagnostic report to augment his self-knowledge or point to faults he could correct; the student never sees his paper, never tries to determine what his grade means. It does not guide reteaching; the instructor never sees the student after the paper is graded.

Tests tend to hold all pupils to the same standard. Everyone is asked the same questions, which implies to the pupil that he is expected to perform the same tasks as everyone else. This negates all the high-sounding principles about setting goals in line with individual readiness and giving everyone a sense of worth. The pupil who is making progress from his initial level is discouraged if he can do only a fraction of the items in the test. The bright pupil who succeeds on nearly all the items is unimpressed when the teacher scolds him for working below his capacity. The teacher who would like to encourage a pupil to spend extra time on independent reading or creative literary work hesitates, when he knows that this will lower his score on examinations covering the "regular" classwork. Only when tests are reduced to their proper role as one among many evidences of accomplishment can the teacher adapt short-term goals to individual readiness.

A plan is needed to salvage the values of the test without letting it undermine the educative process. The answers appear to be:

Use tests prior to and continually during learning.

Emphasize diagnosis; do not attempt to grade over-all merit, or at least keep such composite scores subordinate to the descriptive breakdown.

Make balanced use of all types of evaluation techniques.

Compare scores with the individual's prior performance rather than with the performance of others.

Evaluation throughout the year is part of the teaching process; it teaches self-appraisal, it gives steady encouragement and helps define goals. Tests that tell what needs to be learned next or reviewed further are constructive and motivate future work; tests given because the class is ready to leave a topic are only appropriate to a Judgment Day. Over-all grading leads to an undifferentiated feeling of satisfaction or dissatisfaction rather than to an awareness of strengths and weaknesses. A balanced program is one in which all genuine goals are taken into account, each type of accomplishment being judged either by a test or by some other procedure. This reinforces planning by making all objectives seem important. Because the diverse types of performance so observed are not highly correlated, the average pupil is likely to be very good on a few of them, which provides important encouragement. And the very superior pupil finds that he has weak spots. Evaluation in terms of improvement from one test to a later equivalent test guarantees that most pupils receive a favorable report most of the time. When each week's measure is in terms of the percentage of answers correct, with each test moving on to new material, the pupil has little sense of growth; he comes to think of himself as consistently pegged around 75 per cent, or some other level. A grade that compares him with others is equally uninspiring. Most of the class will be in the average range, passable but not distinguished enough to generate enthusiasm. Average though he may be, the golfer can be highly enthusiastic when he lowers his score from 100 to 90. School evaluation should make progress equally exciting for the pupil, but it rarely does.

16. How could final examination procedures be modified to eliminate some of their faults?

17. What are the differences and similarities between tests suitable to measure readiness for fourth-grade geography and tests used to evaluate accomplishment in geography at the end of the year?

18. To what extent does teaching by machine with programed material conform to the description of a good evaluation program?

Effective Forms for Teacher-made Tests

Making valid tests is an art. It is hard to prepare questions that are a good sample of the subject matter, are free from ambiguity, and test understanding as well as memory. Developing tests is inventive, in the same sense that preparing a clear and interesting explanation calls for invention. What is known, however, about effective tests helps the teacher avoid common mistakes.

SHORT-ANSWER TESTS.   The short-answer test was designed to overcome two major faults of the traditional discussion question. An essay test filling a class period covers from one to five questions, rarely more. It is thus a skimpy sample of content, and a pupil who happens to be ignorant on one topic suffers severely if that topic constitutes a large part of the test. Students who do well on one essay test often do badly on another supposed to test the same abilities. The second fault is invalid scoring. Sometimes the same paper receives an entirely different grade when marked by a second teacher. Scorers are influenced (sometimes unconsciously) by neatness of writing, flow of words, sentence structure—until the score can almost be said to measure everything but knowledge. One scorer gives a high grade to a terse, outlined answer, which covers the main points; another gives a high mark to a discursive paper, full of examples, which covers fewer specific issues. The short-answer test—presenting far more items per test and reducing all answers to a form that can be readily scored—avoids both these problems.

Some short-answer tests call for completion of sentences or recall of a single fact. Others, called recognition tests, use true-false, multiple-choice, and matching items. Although numerous item forms have been devised, the multiple-choice form is overwhelmingly superior to other recognition tests in adaptability and accuracy. Published tests use this form almost exclusively.

Short-answer questions reduce a topic to specific elements. These are typical simple recall questions:

The Southern states used slave labor principally to grow _____ and _____.

In a right triangle, the side opposite the right angle is called the _____.

A scoring key lists the accepted answer to each question; it can be used by anyone, even the student himself. Alternative answers can be listed if more than one phrasing is to be allowed credit. Recognition items are even easier to score, since the student has only to check the best answer. Examples of the multiple-choice item are:

The Southern states used slave labor principally to produce cotton and
   a. wheat
   b. tobacco
   c. corn
   d. wool

All halogens
   a. combine readily with metals
   b. are gases at room temperature
   c. are found abundantly as free elements

A test of the short-answer type can cover a great deal of ground. Dozens of facts can be included in a brief quiz, hundreds in an examination. Scoring is quick so that pupils can immediately identify their errors and start relearning. If each question deals with a specific point, the pupil knows directly where his trouble lies. A test of grammatical usage, for example, can include subsections on capitalization or use of the apostrophe, so as to identify what the pupil does not understand. The pupil's composition would perhaps reveal the same faults, but only after the teacher himself had scored the paper and classified the errors.

Are recognition tests less trustworthy than recall tests? Many teachers believe so, because a pupil can recognize answers that he could not himself produce. There are three important counterarguments, however. One is that a pupil who misses a recognition item indeed needs to think more about the point involved. In that sense the easily administered recognition test does give valid diagnosis. Second, recognition items take less time than recall items and therefore can sample more thoroughly. Third, pupils who score high on recognition tests also are likely to score high on recall tests of the same ability. This has been demonstrated repeatedly. On a mathematics test used for college entrance, ability to recognize answers to algebra problems is highly related to performance in solving problems where no alternative answers are given (Plumlee, 1947). Ability to plan scientific experiments "from scratch" is correlated with ability to select which of several suggested plans is best (R. W. Tyler, 1934). Students who can recognize the better of two pronunciations on a recording of French speech are themselves superior in pronunciation (Tharp, 1935). This is logically to be expected, in view of the important part feedback has in skilled or conceptually mediated performance; the recognition test is a direct sample of this evaluative step in the performance. Obviously, critical ability is not the whole of performance, and the recognition test does not answer all questions about accomplishment.

Recognition tests are objectionable when they restrict testing to bits and pieces of information. Understanding, judgment, and reasoning can be tested with short-answer questions, though this is much more difficult than merely rephrasing textbook sentences to make half of them false. Our discussion in Chapter 11 of evidences of meaning will be recalled. Arbitrary association, without meaning, leads to a perfect score when every question presents the same stimuli as were encountered during instruction. Meaning is demonstrated by transfer, by successful transformation of information to cope with an unfamiliar problem or to explain a phenomenon.

Concrete details are rarely the important outcomes of instruction. When tests are confined to details, students prepare by cramming on these minor points to the neglect of main ideas and deeper interpretations (Terry, 1933). What type of test is used determines who will be rewarded in school and encouraged in his study habits. While performance on a test requiring verbatim recall of a text correlates positively with a test on main ideas, the correlation is below .50 (English *et al.*, 1934). Many students who earn an *A* on one type of test earn a *C* on the other. Tyler reported similarly weak correlations between tests of factual knowledge and ability to apply principles. McKeachie (1959) reported that among the various sections of a college psychology course, the instructors whose students did best on a fact-loaded objective test were average or below as judged by their classes' performance on an essay test measuring reflective understanding and integration.

The same question is asked in evaluation as in formulating objectives originally: What are the situations to which we want the educated person to respond, and what response is desired? For evaluation, we need to present a situation simple enough to be dealt with in the available time and complex enough to require a thoughtful response.

A door chime is made of an electromagnet, with the design shown in the picture.

In this chime, a tone is produced

    a. at the moment the doorbell button is pressed
    b. as long as the button is held down
    c. at the moment the button is released

The wire marked B has come loose.
Where should it be fastened?

    a. position 1
    b. position 2
    c. position 3

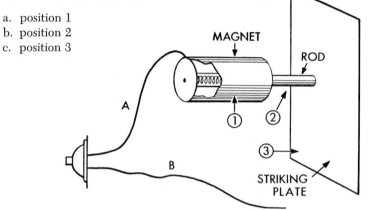

117   *A test of application*

In a junior-high-school unit dealing with electromagnets, one objective would be to develop understanding of devices using magnets. Recall items testing simple facts are easy to write ["The core of a magnet is (a) copper (b) iron (c) steel (d) any metal"]. To test comprehension, the teacher might introduce a magnetic device never before seen by the students, and require them to figure out how it works. For example, the item shown in Figure 117 might be used. The student can answer the questions only by recognizing how the parts function. He has to remember, for instance, that turning on the current will pull the striker, not push it. This is a test of comprehension and reasoning, not of memory alone.

Probably the greatest development of applicational tests has been in law, medicine, nursing, and other professional education. Hurst *et al.* (1961) discuss a test for educational psychology students, which describes Redwood School (an eight-grade, one-room school), its community, its teacher, and five individual pupils. Various incidents occurring in the classroom are briefly described, and statements about the incident are presented. The student agrees or disagrees with each statement, credit being given if he agrees with "experts." While no one question can be appreciated without seeing its entire context, an example will give the flavor of the test.

Following geography, Miss Branson took the first-grade reading class to the corner of the room where she worked with them. As each child read orally, she recorded their errors. At the end of the session each pupil was required to print ten times each word he had misread or missed during his turn at reading aloud.

In having the pupils in the first grade print the words they missed in reading several times, Miss Branson was making effective use of the principle of practice. (Agree——Disagree)

In teaching pupils to write, the important objective is intelligible and graceful communication. Multiple-choice items that merely ask the pupil to select correct grammatical forms have an important place, but both effective and ineffective expressions may be formally correct. Effectiveness of expression can be judged from the pupil's writing, but fair comparisons are hard to make. The daring pupil who tries to express complex thoughts or ventures into unconventional sentence structure gets into far more difficulties than the pupil who says less and sticks to tried-and-true forms. There is no way to compare these pupils because each one has defined the task differently. A large part of effective style is the ability to judge which expressions should be retained; in writing, as in other skills, self-evaluation during the act is important. To measure this, the items in Figure 119 present alternative ways of saying the same thing. When pupils are asked to select the most appropriate wording, every pupil is compared on the same task.

Assume that it is possible to drill a small tunnel completely through the earth from the North Pole to the South Pole as shown in the diagram.

A standard mass M is to be weighed at various positions relative to the earth's surface, using a spring balance to measure the gravitational force on the mass, as shown in the diagram. With no mass attached to the spring, the pointer is at **A**. With the mass M, the spring deflects to scale reading **C** when a measurement is taken at Point 1. Assume that the mass of the spring is negligible in comparison with that of mass M. For each of the following conditions, select the reading on the scale to which the pointer would be *closest*.

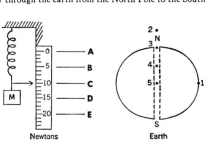

6 The mass M is weighed in a stationary position at Point 2, which is 2000 miles above the earth's surface.

7 The mass M is weighed at Point 3 on the earth's surface.

8 The mass M is weighed at Point 2, while moving freely in a circular orbit 2000 miles above the earth's surface.

9 The mass M is weighed at Point 5, at the center of the earth.

10 The mass M is weighed at Point 4, midway between the surface of the earth and the center of the earth.

118 *A test of theoretical understanding (Copyright, 1959, by Educational Services, Inc. Reproduced by permission.)*

From Test 10, Tests of the Physical Science Study Committee.

I LIKE THE WIND

1 I love the wind. **2** When it blows in the summertime. **3** Because it is so hot in the summer, you need wind, and it helps to have on short pants and a swimming pool nearby. **4** The thing about the wind is that there is always a breeze to keep you cool and fresh.

5 My mother likes a good breeze. **6** Often when I am inside reading a comic on a hot, muggy day, she will say go on out and get some fresh air. **7** That reminds me that there is a fine breeze outside, and I take my comic. **8** I go outside with the comic and suddenly I know that I like the breeze and the moving trees better than any comic. **9** Anyway, it's always better to listen to my mother when she gets that way. **10** One day my brother didn't, and was he ever sorry!

11 Another thing I like about the wind, it makes such wonderful sounds. **12** Sometimes it is a friendly whisper, sometimes a beastly howl and whine, sometimes a boyish bang and crack at a teaparty.

13 The wind isn't always so enjoyable. **14** Once it blew a new hat of mine into the ocean. **15** Another time it carried off the roof of our tent on a camping trip. **16** But the worst thing it did was to knock a tree right through the roof of our house.

17 I like the wind. **18** I would rather suffer the damage it does than never enjoy its refreshment, its excitement, and the music it brings.

13 Which is the best way to write Sentence 3?

  A You need wind, and it helps to wear shorts because it is so hot in summer, and you need a swimming pool.

  B Shorts and a swimming pool nearby, with the wind, help because summer is so hot, but the wind is the most.

  C Shorts, a nearby pool, and the wind all help you to stand the summer heat.

  D You need wind because it is so hot in summer, to stand it, and wearing shorts with a swimming pool nearby helps too.

14 Which way of writing Sentence 11 is most effective?

  E Another thing I like about the wind, it makes such wonderful sounds. (As it stands)

  F I like the wind, too, for the wonderful sounds it makes.

  G Wonderful sounds that the wind makes are another thing that makes me like it.

  H The wind! Such wonderful, wonderful sounds! How I love them!

15 A better connecting link between Paragraphs 3 and 4 is needed. What would be the best way to provide this link?

  A Begin Sentence 13 with *But*

  B Before Sentence 13 put *This isn't the whole story.*

  C Before Sentence 13 put *All the same, another side to this whole question, which I should mention, and that is this.*

  D Before Sentence 13 put *Big Boys at a teaparty may be all right, but listen to this.*

16 Which way of writing Sentences 14, 15, and 16 is clearest and simplest?

  E Once it blew a new hat of mine into the ocean. Another time it carried off the roof of our tent on a camping trip. But the worst thing it did was to knock a tree right through the roof of our house. (As they are written now)

  F Once it blew something of mine into the water. Another time it damaged our property on a trip. But the worst thing was when it harmed our house.

  G I will mention three things it did. It did them to my new hat, the roof of our tent, and our house. One was blown into the ocean, the next was carried away, and the third had a tree knocked through its roof.

  H It blew a hat, carried off a tent roof, and knocked a tree. Where? Into the ocean, far away, and through our house roof!

119 *A test of judgment about writing (Copyright, 1957, by the Cooperative Test Division of the Educational Testing Service and reproduced by permission.)*

From the Sequential Tests of Educational Progress, Form 3A, Grades VII–IX.

To be sure, not every pupil who is a good critic is a creative writer; selecting among alternatives is not the same thing as imagining the alternatives to begin with. Short-answer tests can measure convergent thinking even in the most advanced fields, but no test that pretends to include *the* right answers can measure divergent thinking.

19. The Redwood School test correlates only .23 with a multiple-choice test of textbook knowledge in educational psychology. How may this be explained? Which test, or what combination of the two tests, would be best to use as a course final examination?

20. Prepare a test item to measure understanding of the principle that acquired characteristics cannot be passed to one's children by heredity.

21. The score on a recognition test is not affected by the student's ability to express his ideas. When is this an advantage, when a disadvantage?

22. In recognition tests for high-school and college courses, is it wise to allow time for everyone to finish? Or should the test be timed?

23. Which of these aspects of appreciation of poetry can be measured by a recognition test?

    a. knowledge of forms: sonnet, iambic meter, epic
    b. ability to create verbal images to depict an experience
    c. ability to point out similarities in style among poems
    d. enjoyment of poems of many different types
    e. judgment of the originality and artistic appropriateness of metaphors

DISCUSSION QUESTIONS. Short-answer questions cannot replace discussion questions in which the student formulates his own answer. To learn what problems he is sensitive to, how he attacks a problem, and what range of intellectual resources he can bring to bear, something beyond the short-answer test is needed. Free-response questions produce data of value in evaluation and instruction:

Read this poem and criticize it in terms of the author's success in achieving his purpose.

Starting from this list of rules for a mathematical game, decide what is the best opening move and explain why.

This passage criticizes the American foreign aid program of the 1950's as wasteful and unnecessary. Read, and discuss what information should be examined to determine whether or not the criticisms are justified.

From this map showing the physical geography of a region and these diagrams showing the nature of the soil and rocks (or better, actual specimens), what hypotheses about the geological history of the region seem reasonable?

We have have not included in this list the common informational questions with which you are surely familiar. Nor have we worded questions in a form suitable for the elementary grades. In the lower grades, written tests rarely ask for more than short answers because the pupil's ideas are more advanced than is his skill in written expression.

At any grade level, direct observation is the ideal way to evaluate. We would like to study ability in composition by having the pupil prepare an essay before our eyes, preferably working aloud so that we would become aware of even the thoughts he does not put on paper. This would be a work sample of the process of composition rather than a product sample alone. Such observing is too time-consuming to be used frequently, and

120   *Observation collects information on both divergent and convergent processes*

there is a risk that the student will not behave "naturally" in the presence of the observer. Nonetheless, direct observation has the same advantage for studying intellectual and artistic performances as it does for studying physical skills.

Only their greater practicality makes discussion questions preferable to observations. The discussion question requires a verbal response, and usually asks for a reaction only to a verbal stimulus. Because of time pressure, the response often is merely a first provisional try, rather than the best performance the student could produce. On the other hand, if ample time is allowed the final product may not reveal the confusions and errors that observation would disclose. Even with these limitations, discussion questions are important in evaluating reasoning, expression, and other accomplishments.

The chief fault of the essay test is that it is too easy to prepare bad questions. In a minute or two a teacher can dash off enough questions to occupy his class for an hour. It takes far longer to prepare an hour test in short-answer form. More questions are needed, and the teacher is far more critical of ambiguities because he knows that pupils will challenge the answer key. These "advantages" of the essay test are illusory. The time saved in test preparation is more than offset by the time required for thoughtful scoring, and the ambiguities in the hastily prepared questions impair the accuracy of measurement.

The teacher preparing a discussion question must have clearly in mind what he wishes to observe. "Discuss the causes of World War II" can be interpreted in as many ways as there are readers. One student thinks it wise to list all the events he knows that had any effect on the war. Another lists two or three causes and tells why he thinks them important. One writes on the years just before the war, another goes back 20 years. Some students stress economic strains; some stress political and diplomatic maneuvers which hastened the outbreak of the conflict. The papers cannot be compared because everyone was trying to do a different thing. To permit fair scoring of responses for quality, a discussion question must set a clear task. It must indicate both the content to be covered and the form or style wanted. Understanding of basic conflicts underlying World War II can be fairly assessed by such a question as: "State four continuing economic or political problems on which the aims of the German and French governments differed during the years 1925 to 1939. Tell what each government desired." [1]

Comparing students on a quality scale is not, however, the significant aim in using discussion questions. If nothing is desired save a "grade," the short-answer test is likely to serve much better. It samples more thoroughly; it is on balance more practical; and its score correlates so highly with a quality score for free response that in most cases it leads to the same decisions regarding pupil merit as a long and searching essay test. The real virtue of the discussion question is in the descriptive information it provides. To know that Albert's style is conventional and colorless, that his generalizations are cautious and qualified, that he sees a problem in a very broad context, etc.—these are findings ripe with suggestions for Albert and his teacher. Albert needs to be freed to experiment with metaphor. He should be encouraged to make vigorous, sweeping statements. If his inhibitions can be relaxed, he will hereafter be able to choose between a forceful and a qualified style, to suit his subject matter and his audience. When the main result of the test is a rewarding grade of *A*, or a discouraging *C*,

---

[1] Excellent detailed suggestions for writing effective test questions, with many examples, are given by Robert L. Ebel, "Writing the Test Item" (on objective questions), and John M. Stalnaker, "The Essay Type of Examination," in E. F. Lindquist, ed., *Educational Measurement* (Washington, Amer. Council on Educ., 1951), Chapters 7 and 13.

everyone loses sight of the subtler information that justified essay testing. For many characteristics revealed by the essay, any rating of merit is arbitrary. Who can say that a "light" style is better than a ponderous one, that sensitivity to political problems is more creditable than sensitivity to economic implications, that a pessimistic conclusion is wiser than a cheerful one? Yet knowledge of these preferences, habits, and blind spots is important for the teacher.

Discussion questions should be aimed at relatively complex understanding and reasoning. A memory test ("List the agreements of the Munich conference," or "What are three principal advantages of the city-manager form of government?") can be passed without any understanding. To make sure that the student understands, he should be confronted with unfamiliar material, which he has not been told how to answer. For instance, he may read a description of government and civic problems in a community having aldermanic government and be asked to tell how a city manager would be expected to change conditions. The discussion question, indeed, has its greatest advantage in testing interpretations of situations that are so complex that there is no single "right answer." It is in those situations that the student's originality, special interests and biases, and judgment come to the fore.

Having asked a question, it is necessary to decide what aspects of the answer to look at. These aspects will be chosen in the light of course objectives. For one course, we might want to determine if students place their thoughts in good order. In another, what matters is how many sound suggestions are advanced, regardless of the form of presentation. When a test is to be scored, it is wise to prepare a guide that lists the ideas which a good answer is expected to contain, or the characteristics expected of an A, B, or C answer. Rather than jumbling everything into a single score, it is desirable to judge separately the content, organization, grammar, and whatever other aspects are important. Such a report points out improvements and weaknesses. A descriptive note by the teacher is likely to be more useful as feedback to the pupil than a numerical grade.

24. In what subjects and for what purposes can discussion questions profitably use other than verbal stimuli?

25. In most mathematics courses the pupils are asked to work out answers, for example, solving for the missing side of a triangle, or determining where two lines intersect. Is a test of this sort more like a discussion test or a short-answer test?

26. We distinguish four types of knowledge: description, prescription, generalization, and systematized knowledge. For which types are discussion questions most likely to be superior to short-answer questions?

27. Write a better question on the central theme of this chapter to replace this one: "Discuss the function of examinations in education."

28. A reader says, "The English teacher's job is to help the student say

whatever he wants to say. Whether he is cautious or daring, conservative or liberal, optimistic or pessimistic is not the teacher's business." What do you think?

PERFORMANCE TESTS.   The third important type of formal work sample is the performance test. The person performs the task he has been learning to do instead of writing about it. The typing test is a commonplace example. If the student is learning about reference books, a suitable performance test might send him to the library to find out the population and principal industries of Cincinnati. It is desirable to observe and record specific actions. When the observer fills out a check list the learner has a permanent record of what he did. Table 37 shows a check list for recording the handling of a microscope. Where observation is impractical, the product itself can often be judged.

TABLE 37

Portion of a check list on use of the microscope (from Tyler, 1930)

The botany student is asked to find a yeast cell. The observer writes numbers, in order, indicating what right and wrong actions the student does.

Student's actions	Sequence of actions
a. Takes slide	1
b. Wipes slide with lens paper	
c. Wipes slide with cloth	
d. Wipes slide with finger	
e. Moves bottle of culture along the table	
f. Places drop or two of culture on slide	2
g. Adds more culture	
h. Adds few drops of water	
i. Hunts for cover glasses	3
. . . .	
m. Adjusts cover with finger	
n. Wipes off surplus fluid	
o. Places slide on stage	
p. Looks through eyepiece with right eye	
. . . .	
w. Adjusts concave mirror	
x. Adjusts plane mirror	
y. Adjusts diaphragm	
z. Does not touch diaphragm	
aa. With eye at eyepiece turns down coarse adjustment	
ab. Breaks cover glass	
ac. Breaks slide	
ad. With eye away from eyepiece turns down coarse adjustment	
ae. Turns up coarse adjustment a great distance	

Performance tests are more valid than typical written examinations. When workers who have learned to repair machinery take a written test, those who score best are often the ones with the greatest verbal fluency, not the ones who do best on the bench (Stuit, 1947, p. 307). Regrettably, performance tests are relatively expensive, time-consuming, and for some skills completely impractical. A performance test in cooking is easy to set up; a performance test in building happy family relations is next to impossible.

The Use of Standardized Tests

Standardized tests are available to measure attainment of the objectives accepted by schools generally. These supplement the tests made up by the teacher. There are published tests of skill in language usage, knowledge of current affairs, reading comprehension, understanding of scientific principles, and ability to interpret literary passages, for example. Most standardized tests are carefully prepared, contain well-edited items, and attempt to sample fully the types of behavior to be tested. The published norms indicate the range of scores among typical pupils of each grade.

Published tests are generally more accurate than the tests put together by the classroom teacher. The norms make it possible for the teacher and the school administrator to judge how the development of their pupils compares with that in other schools. If the local curriculum neglects certain widely accepted objectives, this fact is pointed out for attention. These advantages suggest that published tests have an important place in any school program.

Published tests have the following important limitations:

They deal with only a portion of the common objectives of education. Adequate standard tests are not available for important behaviors such as independent self-direction, selection and organization of materials for a report, understanding of other persons, responsiveness to music, etc.

They do not cover the special objectives of the local school, and may be unfair to pupils who have not studied the usual text materials. Understanding the community and the region where one lives is an important goal of social studies, yet this is necessarily missing from the standard test. There may be excellent reasons for a class to read *1984* instead of *A Tale of Two Cities*, but the standard test is likely to report that these students are ignorant about literature other pupils know, giving them no credit for their uncommon knowledge. The published test confines attention to content stressed in schools generally.

Some schools enroll pupils with superior readiness. It is unreasonable to expect the pupils in a particular school to do just as the standardizing group did; perhaps they should do better, or perhaps they should not hope to reach the norm.

None of these difficulties is serious if standardized tests are wisely selected and wisely interpreted. The teacher who selects tests can examine items in advance and decide whether or not the content represents what his class has dealt with. If not, he can find a better test, stick to tests of his own construction, or use the test in a frank spirit of "let's see what happens."

The greatest difficulty arises when tests control instruction. Administrators sometimes impose tests without examining their curricular validity; teachers are threatened when scores on such tests are taken as an indication of their merit. College Board tests loom large in the minds of some teachers; the fact that in foreign language, for example, such tests call for reading and writing rather than listening and speaking has undoubtedly altered the balance between oral and written work in the classroom. When a test is imposed from without, the teacher's attitude is entirely different from his attitude when he selects the test in the light of his own instructional aims. Sometimes, thinking that the test indicates what he should strive to teach, he begins to select assignments to prepare for the tests and to neglect whatever the test omits. At worst, the teacher drills the student on the specific sample of questions included in the test. Then the test determines what is taught.

The function of standardized tests is to show what level pupils have reached on certain undoubtedly significant objectives so that future work can be planned to give additional attention where it is needed. Increasingly, standardized tests are being used at the start of the school term, or during the term when the group is ready to plan new activities. The tests are used then for stock-taking: "Let's see where we stand in order to decide where emphasis should be placed." To help in this process, tests must measure clearly defined behaviors. A report that the group is "below average in scientific knowledge" does not suggest how to improve. A report that the group makes errors in interpreting data from experiments or knows little about genetics can be used in deciding what to study next. The test score becomes a base line from which progress can be measured. When it is recognized that individual progress is the important thing, teacher and pupils become interested in applying the same test or one of comparable difficulty later in the year to find out what progress has been made.

29. In a certain county the superintendent sends a standard test to all schools to be given at the end of the term. School averages are published in the local newspaper. In this county the boys dislike school and drop out as soon as they reach the legal age. The boys in one school are especially critical of the English course, and they much dislike the reading selections studied. Their English teacher points out that this particular literature is the basis for the questions in the superintendent's test. She says that if material related to the boys' interests (perhaps bulletins on farming or auto mechanics) were used instead as reading material, their scores on the standard test would be even lower. In this situation, what would be the most appropriate changes?

30. List important objectives of a fifth-grade unit on South America (in which pupils learn about geography, customs, legends, trade, etc.) that you would not expect a standard test to measure.

31. Critics of the schools frequently propose that a national examination be required for high-school graduation, in order to force all pupils to meet certain standards in "worthwhile" subjects. What assumptions does such a proposal make regarding the purpose of education? Would there be valid objections to the plan if the test were prepared by competent teachers and testers, under the direction of a board of well-informed citizens?

32. A state university wishes to encourage better instruction in written English for college-bound students. It considers two alternatives: requiring that all applicants have four years of English instead of the three now required, or requiring an English proficiency test of all applicants in addition to a scholastic aptitude test. What facts would help in this decision? What can be said for and against each proposal?

HOW TO JUDGE EDUCATIONAL PROGRESS

Evaluation in Elementary Grades

BASIC SKILLS AND CONCEPTS.   In the elementary school, one aim is the development of the so-called fundamental skills of reading, quantitative thinking, and communication. Most of the teachers' evidence comes from observation of daily performance. Standardized tests are used occasionally for accurate measurement of these abilities. The better tests are designed to measure understanding rather than mechanical performance. Questions about reading try to determine whether the pupils grasped the sense of the story ("Why did the Indians fight Daniel Boone?") rather than whether they simply followed the words ("What was Peter's sister called?"). Arithmetic skill is best tested with problems that require understanding of numerical relations rather than routine computations. Speed tests are used to appraise skills that should have reached a near-automatic level, but most authorities recommend that demand for speed be delayed until understanding is well developed.

Diagnostic evaluation is of great importance. Though special diagnostic tests are available (see page 196), the teacher relies heavily on observations. He watches the pupil or asks him to solve the problems aloud. Thus he can note faulty processes that would not be clear in the written product. He discovers that one child seems mostly to need confidence, since he makes few errors when he plugs away step by step. Another is misled by the cue phrase "How much is left?" and tries to subtract when a percentage problem requires division. Still another is tripping himself by writing 4's that look like 7's. Similar analysis is made for reading, speech and writing.

Class discussions and written work provide an opportunity to determine how well concepts are understood. A workbook can be designed to give valuable practice in thinking through new materials and in discovering one's difficulties. But if the pupil merely copies words from a text, he fails to gain any useful practice in interpretation and skill. It is important that a large proportion of the questions the student works on, whether in a recitation, a programed lesson, or a project, require him to think about meanings. Questions that can be answered just by remembering yesterday's conversation word for word are poor evaluation devices. An example of good evaluation and bad in the same incident is the story told by William James (1920, p. 150).

> A friend of mine, visiting a school, was asked to examine a young class in geography. Glancing at the book she said: "Suppose you should dig a hole in the ground, hundreds of feet deep, how should you find it at the bottom—warmer or colder than on top?" None of the class replying, the teacher said: "I am sure they know, but I think you don't ask the question quite rightly. Let me try." So, taking the book, she asked: "In what condition is the interior of the globe?" and received the immediate answer from half the class at once: "The interior of the globe is in a condition of igneous fusion."

SOCIAL-EMOTIONAL DEVELOPMENT.   The teacher can observe interests, attitudes, and social development. The choices pupils make when given free time, the ideas they contribute to a discussion, and the materials they display to others in the class are all indications of preferences and special interests. This means that the teacher who gives pupils the freedom to make choices will learn the most about them. Social learning and social difficulties are displayed continually. When the pupils are free to move around and interact, the teacher may observe helpfulness, leadership, supportive behavior, and conflict. Jimmy wants his own way. Carol is belligerent when tired. This is evidence on social growth and social needs, but such evidence is not at all standardized.

It is possible to design standard situations that permit comparison of classes or measurement of gains. The Russell Sage Social Relations Test (Damrin, 1954) consists of a puzzle. The class is to build a house according to a pattern, using variously shaped pieces. One or two pieces are given to each child. After the task is stated the teacher or examiner retires to the side lines and leaves the pupils to work. Classes differ greatly in their efficiency and maturity of work. Some decide early that they need to organize their efforts, name a chairman, and have him systematically call for pieces as they are needed. Some classes break into competitive clusters, each trying to beat the others by somehow fitting its handful of pieces together. Some classes remain lost and aimless without the teacher. Inefficient social behavior is not confined to the young; some adult groups take longer than children to build the house, because every person is thinking about his individual contribution.

Emphasis should be placed on the integration of all information into a value judgment and a plan for action. A low score in arithmetic might by itself seem to say that immediate concentration here is urgently required. Seeing this in relation to other facts, the teacher might conclude that the pupil is at this time making rapid strides toward gaining acceptance by the group and that playfulness during the arithmetic period is, for the moment, a good sign. A very fine performance in drawing might in one child be something to encourage; in another child, the result would suggest a one-sided interest. Persistence we normally regard as healthy, but when a usually perfectionist student gives up on some half-done project, this may be a good sign. He may be seeing his efforts in better perspective. Ruth Munroe tells of the college teacher who had the good sense to congratulate one rigid, too controlled girl on "attaining a little confusion" in one of her papers. Similarly, an elementary teacher set down the following plan for an excessively inhibited girl (P. S. Sears, 1957, p. 324):

> One of the goals for Yvonne is to get her to relax and have a little more fun in life. Therefore, I decided to seat her in a rather lively social setting. At first she resisted the temptations all about her, but slowly she has loosened up a bit and once or twice I have watched her pass a note or whisper (rather self-consciously). When she notices me watching her she looks very guilty and waits for my reaction. She seems to be waiting for some censure but I have been merely smiling and letting her enjoy some of the social goings on in the classroom.

Much of the evaluation the teacher keeps to himself. Barry is offered a book in which he can get the facts about airplanes the group needs for its project; the teacher need not mention that the task was chosen to increase his interest in reading. Paul is asked to work with the teacher in arranging the class visit to the newspaper office—without any open statement that evaluation showed he needed to feel important and accepted by adults.

Other findings are brought into the open for discussion, especially when the pupils can improve themselves as soon as they understand the goal. Thus it would be appropriate for a class to discuss the reasons for school regulations and to keep track of its own improvement in living by them, or perhaps to criticize its own performance after taking the Russell Sage test.

> **33.** Knowing that the grammatical usage of a fifth-grade class (punctuation, capitalization, tenses, etc.) is below the national norm for that grade, what facts would you look for in deciding whether or not an increased emphasis on that ability is desirable?
>
> **34.** The Russell Sage test measures the behavior of the group, not of the individual. In what sense is change in the behavior of a particular group an objective of instruction?
>
> **35.** How could a school principal judge whether or not a fourth-grade teacher is effective? Should test results play a part in the judgment?

Evaluation in High School

In high school, the responsibility for evaluation is divided among many teachers, and there is some risk that no one will obtain a comprehensive view of the pupil. Individual teachers judge progress in a particular subject, and the more expert teachers will consider a wide range of objectives in that evaluation. But evaluation of performance not peculiarly pertinent to one particular subject (e.g., work habits) is likely to be overlooked, and important questions about the relations among the pupil's various achievements may not be asked.

The tests used for guidance, such as interest tests, measures of adjustment, sociometric tests, and tests of reading and study skills, also tell about the effectiveness of instruction. Teachers can observe important facts about adjustment and intellectual functioning. When these data are brought together where the teachers, counselors, and administrators can and will use them, they answer many questions and raise others. For example, it will be seen that many boys are developing interests along scientific lines, but that none is developing interest in writing or art. This implies that the school program is failing to reach and stimulate those boys who might develop artistic or literary talents.

Guidance at its best is not restricted to a few hurried decisions. It is the process of appraising needs and readiness, and helping the pupil to understand what he is like and what he can do for himself. Seen in this way, guidance is inseparable from evaluation. An administrative structure that leaves guidance to a "guidance department" and expects evaluation to be done within each classroom misses the best possibilities of both.

Too often, test results are used only in the course for which the test was designed. They are not used by the pupil's other teachers during the same year or later. It is better if the science teacher learns what trouble the pupil has had in mathematics. The English teacher ought to find out which students are using language effectively in other subjects. Recording a grade in the office will not circulate this type of information. Ideally, each teacher will file a statement on each pupil, commenting on any significant characteristics noted (see page 171).

Common practice falls far short of the ideal, both in breadth of evaluation and in use of results. If measurement is intended to obtain marks for administrative purposes, better evaluation would not lead to many changes. We take the larger view that evaluation is an essential part of learning and of educational planning. It then follows that improved evaluation is the key to a more effective school.

36. Many instructors regard the test as a judgment upon the pupils, not upon the educational program. The quality of instruction, they say, is to be evaluated by the content of the curriculum, which can be appraised only by scholars in the various content fields. Contrast that position with the view taken in this book.

37. The goal of education is to change behavior throughout the life of the pupil. What facts might be collected ten years after pupils leave high school that would help to evaluate the instruction and the guidance program?

38. What facts collected in the high school would be useful for evaluation of the elementary schools from which the pupils come?

SUMMARY

Evaluation is not just a matter of assigning marks. It is the process by which both teacher and pupil judge what is being learned. The five functions of evaluation are providing feedback for the learner, reinforcing the desired responses, providing information on readiness for future work, judging the teaching procedure used, and providing information useful in reviewing the total school program.

Evaluation procedures clarify the goals of instruction; the pupil takes most seriously those objectives that are counted in marking. Self-evaluation is important both as an aid to learning and as a skill needed to regulate one's own performance outside of school. Students often fail to realize their own inadequacies; tests make these clear. The pupil who looks over a corrected test paper is more likely to learn what he has missed. Frequent tests produce greater learning. The test increases effort to learn the type of material tested.

An evaluation procedure is valid if it describes truthfully an aspect of the pupil's performance that is a goal of instruction. Responses are observed in a sample of the situations to which the objective is relevant. Curricular validity must be judged in terms of the objectives of the particular class. Verbal items usually indicate knowledge of the response desired rather than typical behavior, yet many school objectives are concerned with typical behavior. Accurate measurement is most important for final, irreversible decisions. Accuracy is increased by taking a larger sample of behavior. For teaching purposes, it is desirable to obtain diagnostic information from the evaluation.

Tests are objective. They are therefore more satisfactory than reports from teachers. It is a mistake, however, to focus attention on tests as the sole measure of accomplishment, since they do not appraise all significant attainments. The end-of-course examination does not promote further learning.

These recommendations for using tests are made:

> Use tests prior to and continually during learning.
> Emphasize diagnosis rather than total score.

Use all types of evaluation techniques.
Compare the individual with his own earlier performance.

Short-answer tests present a larger sample of content than essay tests and are more dependably scored. The multiple-choice test is more satisfactory than other recognition tests. Recognition tests correlate highly with recall tests. Identifying a correct solution correlates with ability to produce the solution for oneself. But creative performance calls for fluency in suggesting solutions as well as in criticizing them; the recognition test measures only the second of these processes. Tests on detailed facts encourage neglect of deeper interpretations. Recognition tests can call for comprehension and application of principles. Free response tests are also valuable, especially for assessing ability to interpret. Such tests are most useful when the style as well as the quality of the pupil's response is considered. Performance tests, though expensive and in some situations impractical, are more valid than typical written examinations.

Standardized tests have norms based on typical classes. This permits useful comparisons if one bears in mind the objectives not covered by the test, the special objectives of the local school, and the ability level of the local pupils. The function of the standardized test is to show what level pupils have reached on certain significant objectives, as a basis for planning future work.

In the elementary school, most of the teacher's evidence on fundamental skills comes from observation. The better standardized tests measure understanding rather than speed in a mechanical performance. Social development is likewise judged by observation. The action to be taken when a faulty performance is identified depends on all the facts about the pupil. In high school, objectives not identified with one subject are likely not to be considered in evaluation. The tests used for guidance contain information on the effect of instruction that is often overlooked. Information obtained by one teacher is not available to other teachers. Integration of evaluation with guidance and instruction is called for.

Reading List 16

J. Stanley Ahmann *et al.*, "Evaluation in the Language Arts," Chapter 11 in *Evaluating Elementary School Pupils* (New York: Allyn and Bacon, 1960), pp. 248–75.

Objectives in language use are stated and methods of testing are described. What uses should be made of these tests? How much time should go into such evaluation?

Benjamin S. Bloom, ed., "Application," *Taxonomy of Educational Objectives* (New York: Longmans, 1956), pp. 120–43.

One advanced evidence of understanding is ability to apply a principle in a new situation. The authors discuss the mental activities involved in application and illustrate how the ability is tested.

Robert L. Ebel, "Writing the Test Item," Chapter 7 in E. F. Lindquist, ed., *Educational Measurement* (Washington, Amer. Council on Educ., 1951), pp. 185–249. Abridged in Seidman *E.*

A brief and thorough "handbook" of types of items, difficulties to be avoided, and ways of testing interpretation skills. A large number of sample test items are presented.

Edgar Z. Friedenberg, "The Measurement of the Insight of Graduate Students into the Methods of the Social Sciences," *Educational and Psychological Measurement*, 12 (1952), 350–67.

Friedenberg presents a complex test designed to require high-level reasoning about an experiment. The test is of interest as an example of what can be done with multiple-choice items. The study also shows how an expert test constructor tries out and criticizes a new test.

PART FIVE

EMOTIONAL LEARNING

CHAPTER 17 HEALTHY ADJUSTMENT TO DIFFICULTIES

A person trying to realize a vision, trying to build a satisfying personal life, trying to deal with the daily tasks of his job or his schoolwork, inevitably encounters thwarting. We call his responses provisional tries just because he cannot be sure how they will work out; only in the most repetitive type of activity will one try after another be confirmed by the expected consequence.

As we noted in Chapter 3, the contradiction of expectations may be followed by a reinterpretation, which ultimately produces an acceptable result, or it may be followed by some other, nonadaptive reaction. Our discussion of aspirations in Chapter 14 mentioned some of the factors that cause the pupil to lower, maintain, or raise his goals unrealistically following failure on one try. Adaptation depends both on the immediate situation and on the person's long-standing attitudes toward himself. In this chapter we are ready to examine more thoroughly adaptive behavior, adjustment, and mental health. The teacher must be able to recognize the various types of reaction to thwarting that occur, and must understand the conditions under which each one is desirable. This calls for value judgments, but these judgments can be aided by experimental findings regarding stress and emotional learning.

As Jahoda (1958, p. 8) points out, there are both short-term and long-term aspects of adjustment. Some questions about adjustment refer to momentary responses in a particular situation. Thus we can ask whether a pupil's reaction is healthy or not if, after two tries at translating a paragraph in his German assignment lead to no sensible result, he drops it and turns to the television set, saying that he'll have to get help from the teacher in class tomorrow. A quite different question is involved when we ask whether or not a boy deeply disturbed over the death of his mother is emotionally healthy. His response to the immediate situation is normal even though distressing; indeed, it would be a bad sign if he maintained a cheerful front. The question is whether or not his personality is stable enough that he will recover his effectiveness and satisfaction in life. These two types of judgment—about the soundness of a response to an isolated difficulty and the soundness of the personality structure—will be considered in turn. The distinction must be kept in mind, because a style of response that is entirely healthy in a single situation may indicate serious disturbance if it is frequent.

Each blocking is more than an incident in itself. While the pupil is reacting to a specific failure he learns a way of reacting to failures generally. Adjustment patterns are formed through emotional experiences. Such learning can produce an individual with faith in himself and readiness to take obstacles in stride. If the process takes a less benign course, the person may become fearful and ineffectual, or, in extreme cases, neurotic or psychotic.

IMMEDIATE REACTIONS TO THWARTING

When a person tries to deal with a situation and does less well than he expected, we say that he is *thwarted*. The thwarted person either acts on the situation again or withdraws. These alternatives may be further subdivided:

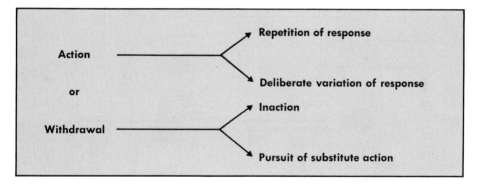

To clarify the alternatives, our cookie-jar illustration from Chapter 3 may be recalled. Even if the boy's stick knocks the jar over, he may continue to jab at the shelf in the hope that his jabbing will knock off a cookie (repetitive action). He may reinterpret the situation and try a different response such as climbing (variation of response). Some children would retreat from the problem. They would perhaps sit on the floor and gaze wishfully at the distant jar (inaction). The fourth alternative is to turn to a different goal. The boy might go after an apple, which satisfies the same need, or go outdoors to fly his kite (substitute goal).

Regarding each of these reactions we have two inquiries: What effect does this reaction have upon a person's learning? What causes a person to react this way? You should review the discussion in Chapter 14, which showed that pupils react differently to failures, according to their experience and makeup.

1. Does the definition of thwarting say that any person who fails to reach a goal is thwarted?

2. Define thwarting, making use of the concept of level of aspiration.

121   *Possible reactions to thwarting*

Repetitive Response

Sometimes we find the performer trying to do again the very thing that he has just tried unsuccessfully. For example, the motorist's car fails to start. He continues to press the starter at intervals, hoping that the motor will fire. He does not, of course, repeat his response identically. Variations in coordination and attention, and changes in the situation, make each trial a little different from the last. But he makes no new interpretation and does not deliberately alter his action.

Repetition helps if the learner's original interpretation was approximately correct. Minor variations in the situation or unintentional changes in his response will permit success on some subsequent trial. At its best, repetition of a response is wise perseverance.

When the learner repeats his response without pausing to look for other interpretations, he perhaps overlooks superior courses of action. A reader translates a foreign word the wrong way and finds that it does not fit into the sentence; he may continue trying to rearrange the words when the only way to get the meaning is to translate the word differently. At its worst, repetition becomes rigid, mechanical action, continued because any action is more comfortable than admitting defeat or starting over. Even after repeated trials have shown that the response is not going to work, the learner may keep on with it. The lock refuses to yield to the key, but the stubborn man continues until he bends the key in the lock and has the added problem of extricating it.

A noteworthy example of blind repetition is the action of the parent who, failing to control his child with a particular tactic, becomes even more determined to make that tactic work. In such a heated contest of wills he damages his whole relation with the child. The Mitchells are farm parents whose first interpretation is always that parents have to keep children under control. They expect and demand obedience, and when Charley or Diana does not give in, neither of the Mitchells stops to reinterpret. Diana has submitted to this pressure. The parents have made her into a plodding, lackluster, unhappy girl who when nagged sufficiently gives in to their demands. Charley completely defeats his parents by being tough enough to resist them. Thwarted, the Mitchells react by repetition rather than by reinterpretation. The observer reports (Baldwin *et al.*, 1945, p. 28):

> Mrs. Mitchell told of an incident which occurred recently—she had told Charles to go and stay in his room as punishment for some trivial offense. Charles flatly refused to go, and Mrs. Mitchell finally whipped him up the stairs with a fly swatter—Charley maintaining all the time that he wouldn't stay. The child did come straight downstairs, and the same thing happened again. About the third time he came down, Mrs. Mitchell grabbed him, said she knew one place where he couldn't get out, and locked him in the cellar. . . . Another time she spanked Charles seven times in succession because he wouldn't stay in his room and remarked hopelessly to the visitor that she can't lock him in the closet as punishment because Charles says he likes it in there.

Do not dismiss this as merely a bizarre family. The Mitchells are not unusual. Both parents have a college education and undoubtedly love their children when they are not exasperated. It simply never occurs to the Mitchells to re-examine their insistence on control and give the children more independence. When a sitter puts Diana's hair up in curls, Diana shows her good feelings next day by cheerfully volunteering for housework. This doesn't give Mrs. Mitchell any new ideas about how to handle the girl—it only proves that children are unpredictable!

What conditions cause a person to repeat after thwarting? These answers may be listed (Robinson, 1940):

Past experience has convinced the person that he is likely to succeed on further trials.

He may not know how to find any other response.

The goal is important to him.

He would lose self-esteem if he changed to a new response or a new goal.

Regarding hope for success, recall the evidence that children who have succeeded in past reading keep their level of aspiration high after a blocking (page 479). Pupils who have a history of reading difficulty drop their goals the instant they encounter trouble. We can expect the learner to persevere only if his previous experience has taught him confidence.

Second, to change a response, one has to know how to reinterpret. Most problems can be reasoned out, but a person must have the attitude that reasoning will pay off. If mechanical things are mysterious to him, a person can find a new response only by trial and error. He will not pause to reason because he feels it hopeless for him to try to understand the device. A person who feels he cannot reinterpret mathematics will not discover a new and better line of attack on a problem. One reason for the Mitchells' failure is that they think children are incomprehensible. An active, hopeful search for new responses is necessary for problem solving (cf. pages 388–89).

The third condition favoring repetition is self-evident: A person tries harder and longer when a goal is important. The fourth statement, however, that repetition is used to preserve self-esteem, needs explanation. People sometimes stick with very minor goals in order to save face. The motorist's significant goal is to get to his office. But if being unable to start his car touches his pride, he will not be happy to call a serviceman or take a bus. He would be especially embarrassed if the serviceman were to start the car immediately. For this reason he struggles with the car instead of calling for help.

Sometimes a person feels threatened if he has to reinterpret. To cope with Charley, Mr. Mitchell would have to re-examine his whole concept of parental authority. No wonder he prefers not to face the problem analytically.

Some people would lose self-respect if they did not persist after difficulty. Escalona (1948) says:

The average frequency of raising the level of aspiration after failure has been found to be consistently higher in American subjects than in European subjects. This may be ascribed to a difference in general ideology. In the American culture great stress is laid upon the ability to "take it." In the United States most expressions of what may be called the standard cultural attitude toward failure (as in proverbs, motion pictures, magazines, and in the more formal teachings of schools and churches) stress the necessity of overcoming failure. "Failures are stepping stones to your successes," "Never say die," and the like are characteristic expressions of the American attitude toward failure. This is in sharp contrast to the European, specifically the pre-Hitler German attitude, which stressed acceptance of individual limitations and placed a positive value on being satisfied with one's lot and on submission to the inevitable.

Failing may bring some satisfaction. Mrs. Mitchell seems to enjoy telling how unmanageable her children are. She takes pleasure in her martyrdom. There are other reasons why repeating a wrong response may be enjoyed. For instance, a boy who tries for the football squad but never makes it feels that he has done his bit, and escapes having to face real athletic competition in some sport where he could make the team.

    3. In each of the following fields describe a situation where repetition of a response after thwarting would be helpful, and one where it would be undesirable:
        a. sports
        b. writing a composition
        c. teaching reading
    4. Might a student find satisfaction in "proving" that chemistry is too difficult for him?
    5. A farmer has planted corn in the same field several years in succession, and his last crop was very poor. His son learns in school that rotation to alfalfa would be wise. What threats might keep the father from following the son's suggestion?
    6. Knowing the conditions that foster repetition, what can a teacher do if a pupil persistently makes the same mistake?

Altered Response

If the learner's original interpretation is wrong, the only way he can solve the problem is to try something different. The stalled motorist might do better, instead of stepping on the starter, to discover that his ignition is not turned on. Adaptation based on reinterpretation is the common method of improving a response.

Altering the response is not necessarily the best reaction when a provisional try fails. If the goal is unattainable, lowering one's aim or shifting to a new goal is wiser. If the first response was based on an adequate interpretation, vacillating through other alternatives only delays success. At the extreme, "trying something different" degenerates into disorganized trial and error (Sherman and Jost, 1942). The pilot jams and jerks controls to get out of a tailspin; the pupil guesses wildly in response to a teacher's question. Trying new translations for the word that will not fit is helpful if the first try was based on a misunderstanding but unwise if the first suggestion will fit sensibly when the right arrangement of ideas is found.

Repeating a response indicates some faith in one's plan and one's ability to execute it; altering the plan indicates faith that some better plan can be discovered. Thus alteration may either imply confidence in one's adaptive powers, or merely lack of confidence in the previous try.

Repeated shifting of response almost invariably indicates lack of understanding. If a situation seems senseless, all one can do is guess. If a person feels incompetent, any try will be more comfortable to him than staring blankly at the difficulty.

Withdrawal

The least painful way out of many difficulties is to stop trying. Lowering one's aspiration is a sensible adaptation when the odds against success are great. At the extreme the person may withdraw passively, retreating into a corner to do nothing, or he may actively flee from his difficulties. Withdrawal gets him out of an intolerable situation, but is not usually a desirable reaction because it leaves him feeling defeated. Moreover, when he stops trying, he loses all chance of learning to handle the situation.

Freshmen who attempt premedical courses lacking readiness for the work should withdraw into some more feasible program. A boy who cannot make the football team should use his afternoons in a more fruitful activity than riding the bench. Whether or not goals should be changed after thwarting is not a moral issue; it is a question of whether or not the person has accurately judged the possibility of his eventual success. Withdrawal without a substitute endeavor is no improvement over the original inappropriate activity.

Withdrawal is less likely if a person is self-assured or has a strong commitment to the goal. If the probability of success seems low and attaining the goal is not very important, the struggle is not worthwhile to him.

Paradoxically, a person who expects to fail may withdraw from a goal he wants very much. A girl desperately desiring boys' attention nonetheless refuses a date because she fears she would not carry it off successfully. Better to withdraw and leave the issue unproved, she thinks, than to fail irrevocably. Hamlet, who weighed his fateful alternatives until the right hour for action was past, is a subtler case of withdrawing. The person who gives up has decided that trying and failing is too costly, compared with whatever rewards he expects to win.

Pursuit of a Substitute Goal

The student who cannot find material for a report on medieval weapons may make a fine report on castles. John, who couldn't catch crawfish, prepared a basket for them instead of retreating to the side lines. Seeking satisfaction in one place when it is denied in another is sometimes called *compensation.*

Abandoning one goal and substituting another has both advantages and disadvantages. If the original goal is indeed beyond the person's reach,

122　*Compensation through a substitute activity*

changing is the only possible constructive reaction. But often the original goal is attainable, even though hard to reach. Although the boy who shifts from weapons to castles because he knows where to locate material on castles will produce a good report, he may not get the very practice he needs at digging out material on obscure topics. Either topic serves if the goal is to develop skill in oral presentation.

TWO TYPES OF SUBSTITUTION.　We may distinguish two types of substitution. When a try is blocked, the person may substitute a new goal that will attain the *same* basic ends. If rain spoils a picnic, the crowd may go to someone's basement to eat and dance. The companionship, courtship and eating are as satisfying as they would have been in the original plan. An undersized boy who wishes he could be an athlete may satisfy the same need for approval by becoming the school's sports writer. The second type of substitution involves dropping efforts to obtain one sort of satisfaction and pursuing another. For example, the unmarried woman denied sexual satisfaction can substitute no goal that will lead to the same satisfaction;

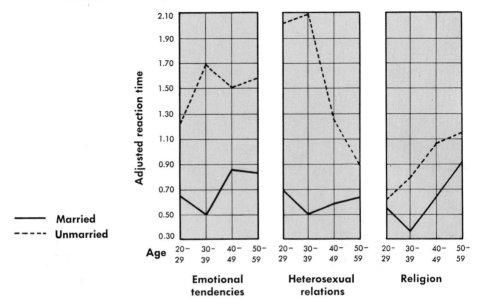

123   *The sources of tension vary with age and marital status (Powell and Ferraro, 1960, p. 96)*

Higher reaction time is taken as an indication of greater emotional arousal.

she must find other rewards, perhaps in caring for children or taking pride in her efficiency.

The development and abatement of tensions is well demonstrated by a study of 200 women teachers, half of them unmarried (Powell and Ferraro, 1960). To measure the strength of tensions in various areas, the investigators presented a series of words such as *lighthouse, shadow, worry, afraid, apple, window, dance, kissing, second, tree, church, God, leaves, fender*, etc.—a mixture of neutral words and words that relate to areas of possible emotional conflict. The teacher was asked to respond to each word with any association that came to mind, and her reaction time was recorded. While the investigators analyzed both the reaction time and the degree of disturbance shown by the association, we shall consider here only the former data (see Figure 123). There was no difference between married and unmarried teachers in their reaction to neutral words. But the unmarried teachers were slower to respond to emotionally significant words and hence were presumably more aroused than the married teachers. (Exception: the area of teacher-supervisor relationships, where both groups showed long reaction times!) Relations with men (present or absent) are a source of tension for the younger unmarried teachers; this problem is much less intense after 40. Concern over the vocational future, greater in the un-

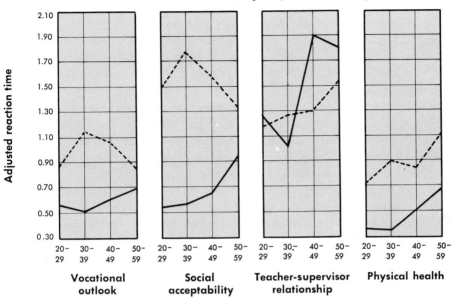

married teacher, likewise drops in later years. This study demonstrates the possibility of studying emotion objectively, but it leaves many questions unanswered. Since different teachers were tested at each age, the changes observed may reflect the fact that women who remain in teaching have different initial adjustment from the ones who drop out before 40. We have no indication in this study as to whether the longer reaction times represent serious maladjustment or merely a reasonable concern. And the study sheds no direct light on the way in which goal substitution, lowering of aspiration, and other mechanisms helped to reduce tensions for these teachers.

There are some dangers in goal substitution, where the person abandons efforts to achieve one type of satisfaction. If the person replaces the hard-to-attain goal with another goal of an entirely different kind, his ultimate development is likely to be unbalanced. Some developmental task is likely to go unaccomplished. The pupil who cannot work smoothly with the committee because others disregard his suggestions may go off on an independent project. He gains independence and self-respect, but he learns also to expect not to get along with his peers. Soon he is working by himself all the time.

Peculiarly difficult philosophical issues are involved in judging whether or not the substitution of one goal for another is desirable. A person who continually retreats to one area may develop great proficiency and self-confidence in it. He may make tremendous contributions even if his development is unbalanced. Many brilliant and productive men have had severe social maladjustments. Van Gogh, Beethoven, the scientist Cavendish are well known for their moodiness, eccentricity, and temperamental outbursts, as well as for their work. These men achieved, but they appear to have been far from happy. A remarkable contemporary portrait of a discontented achiever is Ginzburg's (1962) interview with Bobby Fischer, the 18-year-old who has been called the greatest chess player that ever lived. We do not yet understand the relation between adjustment and creativeness, but da Vinci, Brahms, and Jefferson are evidence that admirable social adjustment does not interfere with the making of major contributions. Should we pry a boy away from intellectual affairs because we feel that his social development will be handicapped by such concentration? We surely ought to teach him skill in communicating with others. Beyond that the teacher probably should try to bring the student out of his withdrawal into smoother social relations. Any other course is equivalent to saying that it is all right to leave his left arm paralyzed since he will develop exceptional dexterity with his right.

We have considered in each previous section the conditions that make each response to thwarting especially likely. There is little to add regarding substitution of goals. Abandoning the original goal involves either lack of confidence or lack of commitment. Taking up a substitute shows that the person expects to gain some satisfaction from it. Thus substitution, unlike withdrawal, implies that the person has self-confidence in at least one area. Comparisons of the possible reactions are summarized in Table 38.

7. Demonstrate that each of the following might be a substitute activity after thwarting.
a. A boy becomes a delinquent.
b. A young woman joins the armed forces.
c. A woman presses her children toward high achievement.
d. A man dedicates his life to the service of people with incurable handicaps.
8. What socially desirable substitutes could the teacher make available to the child who fails in primary reading and for the present cannot keep up with the reading activities of the group?
9. A pupil is preparing a dish of agar-agar for the cultivation of bacteria and is supposed to keep his plate free of impurities. Others in the group are successful but his first plate is unusable because dust has gotten on the surface and started small growths. Illustrate how this thwarting might be followed by repetition, altered response, withdrawal, or substitution of a new goal. What factors would make each response especially likely?

An Example of Reactions to Thwarting

In order to observe persistence and withdrawal, J. R. P. French (1941) presented three puzzles to a team. The team could try whichever puzzle it wished, and could change to another one at any time but was told to try

TABLE 38

Reactions to thwarting: a summary

Reaction	This reaction is likely when—	This reaction is desirable when—	This reaction is undesirable when—
Repetitive response	Person expects response to succeed. Person cannot withdraw or re-interpret, or dislikes trying the more appropriate response.	Person re-examines situation before deciding to repeat.	Person is "forcing" without re-examination. Repetition is long continued.
Altered response	Person has little faith in his original response. Person has confidence in his ability to reinterpret and carry out a new action.	The new response is based on reinterpretation; the old response is given due consideration.	New response is chosen thoughtlessly.
Withdrawal	Person does not expect to succeed. Person finds trying unpleasant, or does not value the goal.	Person has little chance of succeeding. Goal is unimportant.	Person withdraws when reasonable effort will bring success.
Substitution	Substitute is available. Other conditions as in withdrawing.	The new goal satisfies the same needs as the original goal. The new goal permits useful learning. Other conditions as in withdrawing.	Person fails to satisfy a basic need, so develops in unbalanced manner. Person must learn to cope with original situation. The substitute undertaking is unrealistic.

to finish some puzzle as soon as possible. French tells what happened in a team that tried the Hindu disk problem: There are three pegs, with a pyramid of disks on one of them; the task is to move the disks one at a time so as to transfer the whole stack to a different peg. Putting a large disk on top of a smaller one is never allowed. The stack can be moved, but since very many moves are required, the task could not be finished in the time allowed.

The team made some progress at the start, but student R, who understood the logic of the problem, soon said, "Wow, this thing isn't as easy as it looks." "We're not going to get anywhere," he announced during the fifth minute, and continued thereafter to comment on the likelihood of failure. The others were still making progress, and when R urged them to change to another problem they ignored him. When R announced that it would take three days to finish the problem, Y retorted, "Don't be a rebel." Three members continued to work hard and openly rejected R's comments. Two other members said little and helped little; they had withdrawn from the task.

After about 20 minutes, the group had become entangled in the extreme difficulty of shifting nearly the entire stack back and forth, one disk at a time. R announced that it would require 2,014 moves to finish. (He had shifted from the task of doing the problem to the task of proving his reasoning superior. His proposal to withdraw and substitute a new goal was at first wise and realistic. The persistence of the rest of the group in the face of his analysis was unwise. After he had failed to win converts, R persisted in his attempts to get the group to change tasks. Thus both sides were stubbornly repeating.) R's computation was greeted with sarcasm: "Think of the exercise!" and "Let's shoot the mathematician and continue." R did point out the difficulties firmly enough so that the group paused to vote on a shift of problems, but decided not to. By this time some members were sticking to the problem not because they believed they could do it, but in order to resist R, trying to avoid admitting that R had been right all the time.

> **10.** What psychological factors kept the group from substituting goals when R first pointed to the difficulty ahead?
> **11.** What can we infer about R's self-concept from his actions? Could he have acted more wisely than he did?

Implications for Teaching

All four types of reaction may now be examined in a single learning situation. For our example we return to Margaret and her failure in the play tryout (see page 163). When a pupil tries to recite a memorized speech and fails, he may make another trial after an interval, and this trial may indeed succeed. He may go back and study further. He may try the speech on a group of friends before facing the larger audience. Some pupils, while giving up a particular goal, might try for another. One girl might decide that she could not be the leading actress but would try for a less demanding part. Another might give up acting but would seek to participate by working on the costumes. Margaret withdrew; she did not try again for this or any other part. The teacher wants every pupil to learn to speak before groups; withdrawal and substitution defeat this purpose even when they are adjustive. When the response does not save self-respect, thwarting can have a ruinous effect, as this and other incidents did with Margaret. The ways to reduce frustration and conflict are these:

Eliminate blockings that have no educative aim.
Reduce the emotional penalty attached to failure of a trial response.
Make it possible for the child to overcome the obstacles.

SETTING ATTAINABLE STANDARDS.   Thwarting is decreased by setting appropriate goals. If there are enough rewarding parts to go round, either in this play or in a series of plays, there is no need to choose one pupil ahead of another. If the girls set goals they can reasonably expect to attain, few of them will fail. If they all seek to be princesses, most of them will fail.

A blocking is unnecessary when it does not help the pupil learn. It is similarly unnecessary if with better teaching the pupil could learn to respond easily and rapidly. Pupils should be assigned the tasks they are ready to master. When a school demands that every entering 6-year-old learn to read, some pupils with limited mental development are confronted with a demand they cannot meet, but which they could meet easily if allowed to postpone reading for six months or a year. Even when a school postpones reading for some pupils, these pupils may be punished for their deficiency. If most of the class effort is centered on reading, the "poor unfortunates" in a nonreading group will feel as inferior as if they were being forced to try primer reading every day.

Excessively high standards increase the frequency of thwarting. When a pupil is learning for the first time to stand before a group and speak, criticizing his posture is much less important than encouraging him to state his main idea. "You did well *but—*" is all too likely to make him feel that he never can do right.

Some classrooms (and some college campuses) have too many standards of conduct, so that no active pupil can hope to avoid criticism (Williamson, 1956). The teacher may prohibit whispering or moving about the classroom, when a moderate amount of either would facilitate the classwork rather than upset it. When pupils become restless the teacher reprimands them. Soon friction becomes the rule rather than the exception. The teacher with fewer regulations to enforce is freer to teach, and the pupils with fewer regulations to obey have fewer temptations.

ENCOURAGING RESOLUTE TRYING.   Commitment to the goal in view is required if the person is not to give up at the first obstacle. Teachers increase the pupils' commitment by sound planning with the class. Acceptance of a goal is increased if the pupil perceives reasonable subgoals, recognizes how the specific learning fits into his long-range ambitions, and feels that the rest of his group want him to succeed. A pupil may make a halfhearted try if the teacher dictates that he should learn a part. Save as he needs the teacher's praise, it means nothing to him whether he succeeds or gives up after a gesture of conformity. But when he had a part in deciding that the class should give the play and wants it to succeed, he has strong motivation to make a good try.

The pupil who hopes to master a task can afford to persist or to reinterpret. The pupil who feels doomed to fail is bound to become tense or apathetic. At some points the most helpful way to reduce tension is to provide a clear explanation or demonstration; at other times, to diagnose and provide remedial treatment. When a pupil is making some progress, the teacher should help him recognize the progress he has already made. All these suggestions are in extreme contrast with the too common pattern where the student who is having difficulty is merely scolded for lack of effort or pushed to one side as hopeless.

Confidence is built up by accumulation of successes. Margaret was demoralized, not because someone else was made princess, but because many other experiences had convinced her that she did not have ability. Teachers build confidence by introducing new challenges gradually. Taking up a little dramatics at a time assures success in the small steps and makes the big steps easier. A girl who delivers a single line in a first-grade skit is building readiness for a long part a few years later. What matter if she does forget and has to be prompted in a fifth-grade tryout? That has happened to her before with no disastrous final outcome.

If a pupil fails at one thing, the teacher will often substitute another chance for success. Substituting costume-making for acting contributes nothing to dramatic ability. Nonetheless, there are bound to be occasions when a pupil cannot achieve a particular goal. Then he is helped by a substitute goal that attains the same major ends. If he helps the group, he can enjoy the activity, learn something valuable through the duties themselves, and, more important, feel that others think him competent at something. Margaret, after her failure, could only think, "I'm no good and the others know it." In a substitute responsibility she could have developed a sense of worth and belonging.

REDUCING EMOTIONAL PENALTIES.   The play tryout was a crushing experience for Margaret just because this one play was elevated into special importance. If this had been one of dozens of plays, she could have tried in a more relaxed fashion, and could have accepted her defeat more easily because there would be a next time. Teachers encourage resolute trying by making the trying nonpunishing. The emotional intensity of a failure depends on how it affects self-respect. Emotionality is increased when failure endangers one's acceptance by others. If criticism or unkind comparisons follow your best effort, escaping attention is likely to become your primary

124 *A path toward success*

goal. Ridicule is especially threatening. But the too-solicitous teacher may make a pupil feel as conspicuous as one who bluntly rebukes an error.

12. We warn against making it punishing for the pupil to try, and there is substantial evidence of the detrimental effects of harsh, sarcastic teachers. Laymen, however, challenge this view, describing highly influential teachers who carried sternness to or beyond the point of brutality. Is it possible to reconcile our principles with anecdotes such as the following?

Gann (1961, esp. pp. 53 ff.) was an airline copilot, being trained by his captain for the pilot's responsibilities. There is no doubt that Captain Ross was an excellent pilot and made an equally precise and resourceful pilot out of Gann. Yet here is a partial description of his manner in the flight cabin:

As the weeks turned into months, he became continually harder and less forgiving. . . . Ross never relented in his instruction, which had the quality of ceaseless pounding, so that frequently at the end of a flight my brain seemed to hang limp between my ears, twisted and bruised. My percentage of mistakes fell away rapidly, a condition which caused those few remaining to stand out even more sharply. Punishment was always quick and sure. An acid tongue-lashing, at which Ross was wonderfully adept, would be followed by a hard blow on my shoulder or whatever other part of my anatomy was convenient. The free-swinging blow served as a sort of punctuation mark to his verbal acrimony. . . .

Ross's demand for perfection remained a match for the remarkable stiffness of his shirts. He was not satisfied with the allowable fifty feet of difference between chosen cruising altitude and that actually flown. . . . A variation of even twenty feet either above or below brought forth a searing admonition to sit up and fly right. Rough air was no excuse.

He teased, bullied, inspired, threatened, and connived until by the full heat of summer it came to pass that I could occasionally please him.

TENSION

As a person works toward a goal, he may develop any degree of tension from mild interest to utter panic. Tension in one setting may be carried forward to the next. Many individuals carry tensions with them into whatever they do. While tension can be a source of inefficiency and unhappiness, it need not be. Tension can improve performance and intensify enjoyment. The proper aim for educators is not to keep the student free from tension and emotion, but to teach him to manage it.

Tension arises when a person is uncertain of success and cares about the goal. Even when the goal is trivial, there may still be tension if failure would damage self-esteem. If failure would make the person seem inferior to the standard he sets for himself, then the prospect of failure is harder to bear and tension mounts. With neither threat nor desire, there is no tension.

Tension may be specific or generalized. The child breaking the cookie jar feels guilty about that specific act, but he may also feel a generalized guiltiness: "I am the sort of boy who is always getting into serious trouble." Being forgiven for the act may dispel the specific tension, but the generalized tension persists, intensifying the child's emotional reaction after his next misdemeanor.

Fear, anger, and a sense of rejection may likewise generalize into fearfulness, hostility, or a feeling that "no one loves me." Other generalized tensions are anxiety, discouragement, and moodiness. Such standing tensions may be active even in the absence of any recent thwarting. A tense child bursts into tears or strikes an inoffensive playmate "without cause." The cause, of course, lies in the past events that created emotional disequilibrium and so made a tiny irritation unbearable.

Tension is reflected in behavior in various ways: problem-centered exertion, direct discharge, displaced discharge, or suppression. In problem-centered exertion the person stays with the problem, bearing down hard. By direct discharge we refer to the overt expression of emotion through complaints, weeping, or the like. In displaced discharge, one withholds his fear, anger, or depression at the time of disturbance, but reacts with disproportionate emotion to some later event. Suppression refers to the bottling up of emotional reactions, even to the point of pushing them out of mind. As we shall see, suppression may be accompanied by significant nonadaptive reactions.

Problem-centered Exertion

A person gives more of his attention to a problem as his tension mounts (unless he withdraws from the challenge). The person struggling to make a speech despite his fears will be unable to spread his attention. While simply trying to get his words out one after the other, he may forget his gestures, forget to watch the clock, even forget some of the ideas. The experienced and secure speaker, not so much aroused, thinks on his feet, and adapts to his audience. Concentration of attention can be an asset. But when a person shuts out cues that he should take into account, he responds less effectively. Moreover, tension aroused by one problem interferes with concentration on the next task; the first difficulty keeps returning to mind. Thus an embarrassing error during social studies may impair thinking during the next hour's science.

REACTION TO STRESS. An effective person does not remain eternally cool and unmoved. Threat generates greater drive and more pointed mobilization of effort. The effective performer bears down more than usual, but he does not panic or let his responses escape conscious control. A driver is suddenly threatened by a car that pulls out of the oncoming traffic into the wrong lane. Instantly, the driver's state changes from passive awareness to total arousal. He tightens every muscle, slams on the brake, jerks the steering wheel, and gets past the obstacle. This is an alerting, as can be observed by the stiffness of his whole system for minutes thereafter, his greater talkativeness, higher-pitched voice, and increased rate of smoking. Depending on the degree of stress, moments or hours may pass before these symptoms are fully abated. This driver remained a thinking mechanism, working rapidly and keenly but not stupidly. Had he swung too far to the right, or braked into a skid, his vigorous exertion would have been worse than a completely calm response. Sometimes emotions do "run away," mobilizing the person so intensely that his muscles become hard to control.

Absence of tension means absence of effort. Moderate tension promotes alertness, effort, and learning. But with further increases in tension, performance begins to deteriorate. Tension becomes irrationally extreme when a person expects punishment no matter what he does. The only way he can reduce tensions is to bull his way through to the conclusion, taking his punishment in the process. As we saw earlier (page 282), under these circumstances he is less sensitive to cues, and hence less intelligent in his behavior.

An experiment with college students gives a somewhat controlled comparison of behavior under normal problem-solving conditions and under stress. The student was to find his way out of a room having four doors. He understood that one door was unlocked on each trial, but he was not told that the door unlocked on one trial would never be the unlocked one on the next. In a long series of trials, an alert subject could be expected to discover and use this principle. One group of students was put through 100 trials with no special motivation, then through stress trials. In each of the stress trials, the student was subjected to an electric shock through the floor (strong enough to cause a "lively prance"), a cold shower from an over-

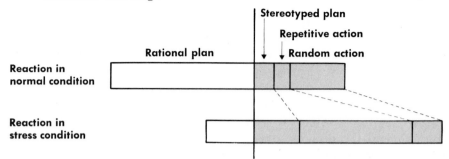

125   *Stress makes problem solving inefficient (data from Patrick, 1934)*

head sprinkler, or a continuing blast from a loud horn. These annoyances led to rattled, hit-or-miss behavior even in subjects who had formerly understood the problem. Actions were classified into four types:

Rational plan (subject does not push any door twice in succession)
Stereotyped plan (subject tests doors in 1-2-3-4 order)
Repetitive plan (subject pushes same door repeatedly after it fails to open)
Random, irregular trial and error (subject pushes doors unsystematically, including door that was correct last time)

Figure 125 shows the percentage of responses of each type in each group. Under tension, the students made many more overt door-pushing reactions, with fewer pauses for thought. The quality of their reactions deteriorated, with more repetitive action and stereotyped action. The number of random responses increased, though in this study their percentage did not. The students acted as if in panic (Patrick, 1934):

> A marked increase was found in the number of efforts made, showing a definite increase in excess activity . . . under the influence of emotional stimuli. This would seem to establish just what one observes in the nature of "random," "useless," "repetitious" responses . . . when [people] are disturbed and excited due to some mix-up in everyday life. A concrete example would be the reactions of men under a "hard-boiled" foreman set over them when they are in the beginning stages of learning a job; or the random reactions of pupils made under a teacher who "snaps" at her pupils while they are learning the use of certain formulae in algebra.

TENSION AND CREATIVE INCUBATION.   A certain degree of tension is necessary to solve an intellectual problem. When he encounters an unexpected check, the able scientist neither shrugs it off nor broods over it. He reinterprets if he can. If he does not arrive at a reinterpretation that makes sense, he will carry the problem with him (Zeigarnik, 1927). This residual tension—"incubation"—keeps the problem "in the back of his mind." Suddenly, seemingly out of nowhere, the solution pops into his mind (Humphrey, 1948).

This experience is reported by numerous discoverers, as in the story of Kekulé, who was fruitlessly trying to explain the chemical mystery of benzene. Benzene has six carbon atoms and six hydrogen atoms, even though the normal combining rate is four to one. Kekulé could no more explain this than his predecessors could, but he kept the problem in mind. One evening while he was dozing by the fire, there flashed into his mind an image of the atoms dancing in the air before him in a hexagonal ring. This hexagon, a completely new concept in chemistry, accounted for the facts about benzene. The solution had in some way grown by itself in Kekulé's mind. Incubation of ideas is little understood. One crucial element, however, appears to be the person's tension or his involvement with the problem. Many a chemist had encountered Kekulé's problem and dismissed it. Kekulé was sufficiently committed to the problem to build up tension, keep the problem alive, and eventually solve it.

The ability to live with a problem, tolerating some stress instead of settling for an inadequate solution or giving up, is essential for original, creative thought. It is an aspect of the "playful" attitude toward ideas that we discussed earlier. These remarks ("Creativity," 1961) are based on Stein's observations of creative chemists:

> We speak often of "attacking" a problem, and that is precisely what most of us do. But highly creative men . . . are not so likely to try to force or pull out a solution; they tend to become part of the problem field, sensing its forces and following its leads, and thus to let the problem "solve itself."
>
> Less creative workers seem more oriented toward quick achievement. The more creative work more slowly at first, marshaling resources. Then they move quickly, with an air of certainty, to a synthesis.

Short-term assignments in school do nothing to encourage a patient, exploratory attitude, which permits one to waste time in blind alleys or to "stew over" an unsettled problem. The teacher presses the student to lay out a schedule, to work forward according to a plan, and to set a terminal date for his work. This type of guidance has obvious merits, and indeed it is essential in much teaching. But provision should also be made for longlasting involvement in a problem, for "setting it on the back burner" while more routine work continues. The teacher can encourage creative thinking, for example, by posing a problem and encouraging pupils to return to it from time to time, bringing in questions and hunches whenever they occur. This is not possible if in February the teacher rules out any discussion of November's topic because the class has moved on to another section of the course.

EFFECTS OF ANXIETY.   Attitudes toward one's self account for much of the success and failure in problem solving. Numerous studies of the relation between anxiety and intellectual performance have been made, the most extensive being the work of Sarason *et al.* (1960, pp. 159 ff.). Elementary pupils responded to questions of this sort:

When you are home and you are thinking about your reading lesson for the next day, do you worry that you will do poorly on the lesson?

After you have taken a test do you worry about how well you did on the test?

Pupils at the two extremes of the scale are described as having high and low "test anxiety." When HA (high anxiety) and LA children with equal

126 *The anxious pupil shines when the task is clearly structured*

scores on a general mental test took more specialized ability tests, there were several differences, which may be summarized as follows: On tasks requiring flexible and creative interpretation (e.g., drawing a person), the less anxious pupils were superior. They tended to be more spontaneous and more productive, and showed better judgment; they enjoyed the task more. On a mental test designed so that cautious, self-critical alertness to errors raised the score, the HA group was somewhat superior. Dull HA children did notably better on this test than dull LA children. Other studies indicate that anxious subjects learn better than nonanxious subjects when the material is simple and can be mastered by sheer diligence (Spence, 1954; Castenada *et al.*, 1956). Recalling our earlier discussion of the school as a selecting agency, we can see that one type of instruction may identify the anxious pupil as superior and encourage him, whereas in another program the nonanxious pupil will look best.

Gaier's (1952) case studies of University of Chicago students are consistent with these experimental studies. He found that the anxious, rigid

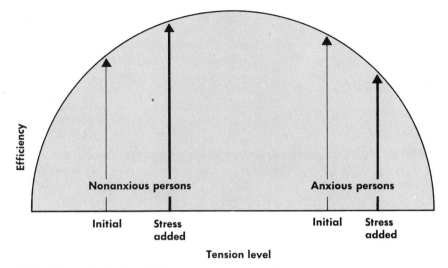

127 *Hypothetical relations of anxiety and external pressure to performance*

students tend to do better than others on tests calling for straight recall of material assigned for study. Given definite material to absorb, they bear down and learn. Required to reorganize ideas creatively, they do less well than the others. During a class discussion on intellectual issues, the HA students give far more attention to objects in the classroom (and hence less to the discussion) than LA students. When the task is diffuse, their minds withdraw from it.

Anxiety built up by past failures produces a sort of built-in motivation. But anxiety inhibits interpretation. The anxious pupil tends not to trust himself and turns to authority for guidance. He is more likely to refuse to answer when in doubt. He is more readily confused (Lucas, 1952). Anxiety therefore tends to facilitate performance in a task where carefulness and reliance on authority pays off. It tends to interfere with original thought, which always implies a departure from the safe, well-marked path. The anxious person is more likely to "go to pieces" when the situation piles up extra stresses, whereas the nonanxious person frequently improves under stress (e.g., Gordon and Berlyne, 1954).

The effects of arousal and anxiety are not the same in every study, but they tend to support the conclusion that there is an optimum level of tension for any particular task. Anxious persons start at a fairly high tension level. Merely setting a task in front of them may elicit their best performance; stronger pressure or incentive may push them over into excessive tension. A mild degree of threat, on the other hand, may move the nonanxious person closer to the optimum tension level.

13. What studies described elsewhere in this book have shown relations between personality and response to threats or incentives? Are these studies consistent with the interpretation of this section?

14. Why is a higher level of tension desirable for some performances than for others?

Direct and Displaced Discharge

A direct emotional outburst interrupts all progress toward the original goal. Reasoning is partly suspended when one is venting his feelings. Fine

128 *Displaced discharge of tension*

motor skills become jerky and erratic. Since emotion disrupts the more complex forms of learned and intelligent behavior, we teach children to "control" their emotions. Outbursts are regarded as a form of immaturity. There is another side to the question, however. Unhelpful as overt emotion can be, displaced emotion or the suppression of reactions can be more damaging.

Whenever a person cannot freely admit his feelings, he is likely to discharge the tension toward safe targets (Dollard, 1938; Dollard *et al.*, 1939). This we call displaced discharge of tension. Displaced emotion sometimes shows up later, long after the original blocking.

Displaced hostility is a well-known phenomenon. Mark picks on Wesley, but Wesley cannot attack Mark safely because Mark is bigger or because Wesley fears to fight him. If the latter is true, Wesley's shame about cowardice increases his tension. Wesley might burst into tears, or attack Mark by tattling—but his teachers and peers have already taught him that these are "not done." With tension high and no way to resolve the original conflict, Wesley is a bomb ready to explode. The victim may be little Clyde or Mary, who seem safe to attack. If Wesley has found that he can get away with attacks on certain children, they are a likely outlet for his antagonism.

Little children attack openly and physically. Expressions of aggression become subtler with age. If a child cannot fight back against his parents, perhaps he can safely attack the teacher by asking troublesome questions, by making smart remarks that upset class procedure, or by resisting suggestions. Verbal attacks may be highly indirect. Among the common ways of releasing hostility are these:

physical attacks on persons or property
verbal attacks, swearing
combativeness and competitiveness carried beyond the limits of sportsmanship
symbolic aggression through stories or art products that portray conflict or injury (e.g., the guillotine in Mr. Osborne's class)
marked preference for stories involving attack and injury
blaming one's difficulties on others
negativism, i.e., taking the opposite side wherever possible
resistance to law and order in any social group
vindictiveness, often nobly disguised as a demand that the guilty be punished

The school should reduce aggression where it can by helping the pupil satisfy his needs. But we cannot say flatly that all displaced aggression is undesirable. We profit from the scientist who finds pleasure in proving others wrong, from the warrior who cuts up the enemy line with more than merely professional gusto, and from the businessman who outdoes his competitors.

Emotions other than hostility are also displaced. The 7-year-old who wishes to be dependent and receive condolence may know better than to cry about a scolding from the teacher. To voice his self-pity directly is taboo. But when he falls and hurts himself an hour later, he can "justifiably" cry and seek sympathy. Some "sensitive" children make much ado over slight injuries. Excessive grief—compared to the normal response to a given insult—is best regarded as a spilling over of tensions and dependency needs arising elsewhere that could not be expressed directly. Displacement of a positive emotional reaction was illustrated by Miss Apple (page 521), who desired to give and receive affection but lacked a husband and family. She could displace sentiment onto the pupils in her classroom. This outlet is socially approved; many other love-making behaviors would not have been.

Suppression and Related Reactions

When emotional expression is prohibited by social standards, people learn to suppress their feelings. However angry or sad they become internally, they keep the evidence hidden (Doob and Sears, 1939). Ordinarily the student who suppresses emotional reactions continues dutifully at work or withdraws quietly from the scene of his troubles. The more significant effects of suppression are observed over longer periods of time, for suppression carries tension forward into new situations and may eventually build conflict to a level the person cannot tolerate. Some people characteristically hold in their emotions. The adult Margaret could not stand up for her rights or express resentment. Suppression is seen in a less painful form in overly conservative students who never allow themselves the pleasure and risk of acting impulsively.

In the last century or two Western man has looked on emotion as a base reaction, a barbaric enemy to the intellectual life (R. May, 1950). While uncontrolled emotion indeed does great damage, so do the methods used to suppress it. Usually emotional control is taught by taboos on emotional expression: "Nice boys don't fight." "You're too grown up to cry." Sometimes the threat to withdraw affection is direct: "No one will like you if you do that." If the child will stay calm, he is told, he will be praised, loved, and treated well, but if he lets his emotions show, he will lose these blessings. Soon he learns his culture's ideal of emotional suppression.

Recently we have turned more to the view that emotion, constructively used, makes life rich and purposeful. Emotion inspires even the activities once thought to be purely intellectual. Current practice in child-rearing and education aims to harmonize emotional reactions with intellectual ones. Therefore we encourage children to acknowledge their emotions rather than deny them. Of course, one must learn to suppress overt expressions of emotion that would interfere with social relations.

REPRESSION.   Suppression takes the extreme form known as *repression* when the person pushes the thought of his emotion from his own mind and in effect denies to himself that he ever had such attitudes. Repression is especially likely when a person feels guilty. He may believe that no good person feels aggressive, or that sexual impulses are shameful and immoral. If so, the most comfortable way to handle such impulses is to "forget" them. Feeling anxious about his hostility or fear, he may wish to deny to himself that he has it. The fear or dislike is then swallowed into the depths of the mind.

Acknowledged fear or anger can be dealt with. Knowing the object of his fear or hate, the person can avoid it. Better, he can learn more constructive responses. When he represses knowledge of the specific stimulus for his emotion, a generalized and inaccessible tension results. Much of the work of psychiatrists consists of interviewing a patient for hours on end, getting him to retrace his remotest memories. In dredging up childhood expe-

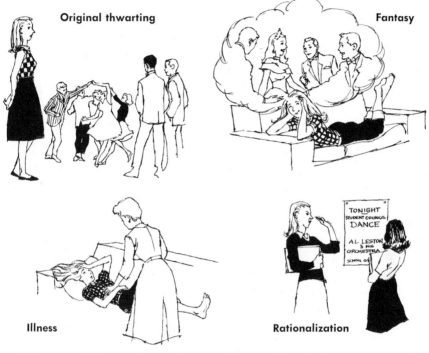

Original thwarting

Fantasy

Illness

Rationalization

"Ooh, my head! I just can't go to the dance."   *"I don't like that orchestra."*

129 *Some reactions related to suppression of emotion*

riences, the patient eventually recalls emotional incidents long absent from his conscious mind. Interpreted by the specialist, these incidents indicate the originally repressed (dangerous) attitude. Treatment then helps the person to face himself and acknowledge his attitudes. He learns from the emotional support of his therapist that even with his "faults" he can be a well-liked, worthy person.

Repression is harmful because the tension remains alive and contributes to lasting maladjustment. A person who fears authority may deny this fear even to himself if he regards it as weakness. Having repressed the fear, he will act as far as possible the role of a person who fears no man. But this action must constantly bring him in contact with that authority which he fears. In denying his fear he places himself continually in situations where conflict is aroused. (See the case of Mack, page 630.)

15. What are the "emotional styles" of our culture?

16. Distinguish among displaced emotion, suppressed emotion, and repressed emotion as possible ways of handling aggressiveness. Illustrate how they might appear in a student who feels that his assignments are too difficult but does not want to change to another course.

ILLNESS AS A CONSEQUENCE OF REPRESSION.   Repressed emotion can lead to illness or bodily disorder, such as ulcers or high blood pressure. Sometimes there is no detectable physical change, but the person suffers from painful headaches, nausea, or indigestion. Other ailments that are at times traced to emotional causes include paralysis, sexual impotence, skin irritations, asthma, and blindness (Dunbar, 1954).

Teachers cannot diagnose or treat these ailments any more than they can treat diseases. They will, however, suspect that psychological causes lie behind the ills of some of their students. In such a case an examination by a psychiatrist or clinical psychologist is desirable. If the teacher suspects that emotional difficulties are causing illness, it is wise to examine the pupil's school situation to see what pressures and sources of distress can be removed.

Headache or nausea may be a way of withdrawing from a crisis. To avoid an examination one needs a more respectable reason than fear of failure; a headache supplies just that. Psychologically convenient illness is by no means the same as a garden-variety falsehood. Untrue excuses are at times useful, and you probably have used them yourself. But a psychogenic headache is not a lie. It hurts, as it must if the person is to maintain his self-respect while he withdraws.

Such an ailment may be a quest for pity and protection. An adult cannot regain the sort of affection and solicitude he had in his pleasant childhood; by becoming ill he can retreat to that state again, eliciting sympathy. Those who suggest this theory do not imply that the pain is unreal, or that the person is shamming illness. They would only argue that the person's very disorder is one that satisfies otherwise unfulfilled needs.

17. Should a college teacher tell a student that his illness may have an emotional origin and that he should see a psychiatrist?

18. Explain how Margaret's headaches might be regarded as a withdrawal or a seeking for dependence.

19. Margot made trouble in high school by escapades and disorderly conduct. Upon her graduation and entrance into college, the high-school principal recommended that the college give her as little of the limelight as possible, so as to cure her exhibitionism (Munroe, 1942, p. 66). What theory about substitute behavior did the principal have? Do you agree?

FANTASY.   Some people, having suppressed their emotion, use fantasy to gain satisfaction. The boy who cannot swim must sit on the bank while the others cavort out in the pool; there is more pleasure in daydreaming about being a great swimmer than in any action he can take. Sylvia's boy friend may not look like much, but she can find a rosy future by dreaming that a really romantic character becomes fascinated by her. Occasional

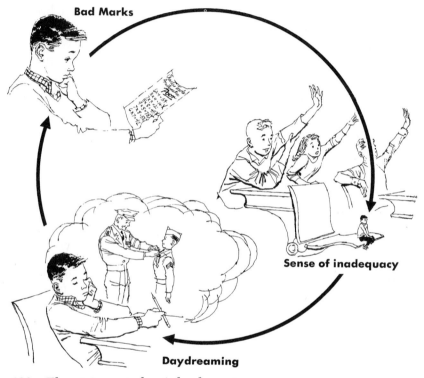

130   *The vicious circle of daydreaming*

fantasy does no harm. In fact, it helps the person to visualize his program of goals and imagine his future. Anticipating future pleasures gives determination to strive toward remote ends.

Fantasy does harm when it removes one from the stimuli he ought to deal with. The boy on the bank is not learning to swim, as he would if he entered the water and tried his best. Sylvia, daydreaming instead of being attentive to her escort, runs the risk of boring him and losing what male attention she has. If a pupil escapes the arithmetic problem by floating off into an imagined success, he is using time he can ill afford to waste.

Fantasy is habit-forming because it is peculiarly satisfying: one can always make the story come out right. Overt aggression gets one into some fights he loses, and adaptation through illness brings pain. But fantasy, while it lasts, is completely absorbing and rewarding. So it is that some people come to rely more and more on fantasy. They spend less and less time facing their real problems—and these consequently grow more serious. This vicious circle creates severe mental disorders. Psychotic patients are distinguished by their lack of contact with reality. They are unable to keep the facts of a situation in focus. They substitute their own wishes for reality.

This inability to discriminate between truth and fantasy creeps upon a person slowly. Tendencies established in childhood may not break over into diagnosed mental disorder until adolescence or adulthood. Psychotic breakdown has complex causes, and the satisfaction obtained in fantasy is only one contributing element. Perhaps certain genes predispose a person toward this type of disorder. But some studies find that psychosis springs up most often in impoverished sections of the community where family ties and community organizations are weakest. These blighted areas breed mental disorder because society has found no way to give the children of the area a sense of well-being, accomplishment, and emotional attachment.

RATIONALIZATION.   Rationalization might be regarded as a special type of fantasy more openly reported than daydreams. Rationalizing is simply the process of reinterpreting a disappointment so as to save self-respect. "The test questions were unfair," "I didn't want to go to the dance anyway," "People would like me if I had a car and nice clothes"—these rationalizations make thwarting more bearable. In fact, they assist in the normal lowering of aspirations after thwarting. When a young man discovers that he will not be satisfied in business management and switches to a general course, he may wonder secretly whether he is running from competition or from a masculine role. His arguments about the importance of obtaining a well-rounded education make him feel better about the shift.

The difficulty with rationalization is that a person may distort the facts in making up a pleasing tale. And when one disregards facts, he runs the risk of aggravating his problem. It is normal to respond to praise with self-approval, and to take criticism seriously and try to change the response criticized. But delinquents, according to McDavid and Schroder (1957), are likely to dismiss criticism with a rationalization—"I didn't have time," "He has it in for me," etc. When praised, they often explain it away with some such suspicious interpretation as, "He's just trying to build me up and make me feel good." They have had so much difficulty in relations with others that they cannot take social feedback at face value. Even praise, while pleasant, is too inconsistent with their expectations to be accepted. Consequently, the social reinforcement loses its power to guide their responses. They are not able to learn how to keep out of trouble.

In considering the various reactions that can follow thwarting one should remember that a reaction undesirable in one pupil is likely to be desirable in another. For Margaret it was unrealistic to try for the lead in the play—but it is significant that she tried at all. Such a burst of ambition in this retiring girl should have been a signal for the teacher that Margaret

131 *Reactions undesirable in one pupil are desirable in another*

had suddenly become ready for a new activity. Even though her goal was "unreasonable," it was a healthy try.

    20. Illustrate a rationalization that might be used by a pupil who
        a. does not finish his work because of failure to concentrate
        b. calculates from his experimental data that copper sulfate crystals

contain 5.3 water molecules whereas the theory indicates 5.0 as
the correct figure

c. submits a story that the school literary magazine judges unworthy
of publication

d. fails to convince other committee members that his ideas are right

EVALUATING MENTAL HEALTH

In the last few sections, we have begun to shift attention away from
isolated reactions and to consider consistent styles of reaction to frustration.
We may recall the styles exhibited by the pupils in Chapter 5: Margaret
usually withdrew; Clark turned to substitute activities; Bill was quarrelsome. What styles should be encouraged?

By way of introduction to this discussion, Table 39 invites you to examine your present opinions about traits which might be considered undesirable. On a separate sheet of paper, write three columns of numbers:
1–10, 11–26, 27–36. Then arrange the traits in order of their seriousness,
assigning rank 1 to the most serious. Do not devote much effort to working out a precise order in the middle column, but give careful attention to
rankings at each end of the list. Base your judgment solely on how serious,
as a sign of emotional disturbance and possible breakdown, this behavior
would be in a 10- to 12-year-old if it occurred repeatedly. Your own up-
bringing, your psychology courses, and your professional reading should
make your judgments better than guesses, but you probably also have
misconceptions. Later you can compare your ranking with a ranking by
experts.

TABLE 39

Which traits mark the maladjusted child?

Carelessness	Inquisitiveness	Sullenness
Cheating	Interrupting	Suspiciousness
Cruelty, bullying	Masturbation	Tardiness
Destroying materials	Profanity	Tattling
Disobedience	Obscene notes, talk	Temper tantrums
Domineering	Restlessness	Thoughtlessness
Dreaminess	Shyness	Truancy
Enuresis	Silly, smartness	Unhappiness
Fearfulness	Smoking	Unreliable
Heterosexual activity	Stealing	Unsocial withdrawing
Imaginative lying	Stubbornness	Untruthfulness
Impertinence	Suggestible	Whispering

Different personalities are developed for different roles. An aggressive and overbearing manner is appropriate to the lord of the manor; the serf is compliant. The whole outlook of the culture leaves its mark on the drive and aggressiveness of the members. Navaho culture, according to Kluckhohn and Leighton (1946, p. 226; cf. the quotation from Escalona, page 578 above), is steadily conscious of the threats and dangers of life rather than its opportunities. Each Navaho regards the world as full of forces man cannot hope to control.

> When in a new and dangerous situation, do nothing [is the Navaho rule]. If a threat is not to be dealt with by ritual canons, it is safest to remain inactive. If a Navaho finds himself in a secular situation where custom does not tell him how to behave, he is usually ill at ease and worried. The white American under these circumstances will most often overcompensate by putting on a self-confidence he does not in fact have. The American tradition says, "When danger threatens, do something." The Navaho tradition says, "Sit tight and perhaps you may escape evil."

The Navaho cannot readily stand off and judge his own adjustment patterns. We, too, in evaluating alternative styles of life, are blinded by our own training. We may therefore perpetuate weaknesses of our culture just because they seem normal to us.

Even within our own culture, there are several rather different concepts of what constitutes a healthy style of life. Jahoda (1958), reviewing the writings of psychiatrists, philosophers, and men of religion, as well as behavioral scientists, concludes that many distinct personality patterns must be judged as mentally healthy. She warns against blurring the concept of mental health by making it synonymous with all goodness. One can be well adjusted in his pursuit of almost any set of values. It is with this thought in mind that we have separated character for treatment in Chapter 18.

All the school does for a pupil is wasted if, in the end, emotional conflicts incapacitate him. A socialized person is a contributor and a problem solver. He uses his knowledge and skill to act wisely on his environment. Excessive timidity or aggressiveness can prevent him from making this contribution. *The adjusted person is one who commits himself to a consistent set of goals and uses his energies effectively in working toward them.* We emphasize effectiveness; the person who is consistently effective, and so fulfills his needs, will be happy as well.

The list of 36 traits which you ranked earlier has been used in a number of studies of professional opinions, starting with Wickman (1928). Authorities on emotional development have ranked the symptoms using instructions like those given above. While the ranking varies a little from study to study, depending on its date and the experts chosen, the consensus is

TABLE 40

How experts judge symptoms of adjustment (from Henderson, 1949)

10 most serious	10 least serious
Unhappiness	Whispering
Fearfulness	Profanity
Unsocial withdrawing	Smoking
Cruelty, bullying	Interrupting
Enuresis	Tardiness
Shyness	Heterosexual activity
Suspiciousness	Masturbation
Suggestible	Carelessness
Temper tantrums	Inquisitiveness
Domineering	Thoughtlessness

always much like that given in Table 40. Compare that ranking with yours, studying particularly any large discrepancy. Unhappiness is rated the most serious of all signs, thoughtlessness the least serious.

This table serves as a summary of what mental hygienists judge to be symptomatic of bad adjustment, i.e., as likely to foreshadow breakdown or serious malfunctioning. The traits most serious in the eyes of the experts are signs of unhappiness and tension. Violent discharge of emotion (direct or displaced) is represented by cruelty and tantrums. Withdrawal and repression are indicated by several adjectives high on the list: unsocial, fearful, shy. The experts are concerned when the pupil has recurring trouble in relations with others or in meeting everyday demands. A pupil can have trouble, however, and still respond to life toughly and optimistically. Serious emotional strain is implied when cheerfulness gives way to depression and passivity replaces vigor. Most of the symptoms rated very serious show lack of confidence and lack of forward motion.

The school and community disapprove of many of the actions on the "least serious" list. They will get the pupil into trouble, and he should learn to avoid most of them. But do these actions imply personality disturbance? The question is not whether profanity, say, is morally good or bad. The question asked is empirical: Is this behavior especially common among those who show a progressive disorganization of personality, which leads to breakdown? The experts say not. Smoking, profanity, whispering, sex experimentation are all goal-seeking tries made by normal children at one time or another. The act is disapproved, or it is approved in their social group; they develop their ultimate responses accordingly. The children who smoke are no more maladjusted than those who do not. Indeed, it is a reasonable guess that the boyhood smoker shows healthy toughness by daring to break the rules. Interrupting, inquisitiveness, and whispering are signs of energy and eagerness. They may inconvenience others, but they are not signs of something basically wrong.

Good adjustment calls for emotional balance. It is an outlook on life that keeps the person effective within the limits of his resources and on good terms with himself. The ideal is not a person so contented with what he is that he never wants to improve. Self-acceptance is present when the person thinks that he is progressing toward his ideal. The three cores of good adjustment are realism, commitment, and self-acceptance.

21. Why might domineering be an unhealthy sign?
22. Would the traits be rated the same way by the experts if they were considering high-school pupils?
23. Of the various ways of handling tension (direct discharge, displaced discharge, suppression), which do the experts seem most to disapprove of?

Realism

The realist makes use of facts in setting goals, choosing responses, and predicting his chances of success. He criticizes his own plans. He recognizes hazards, but he neither exaggerates nor underrates them. He may be fearful if there is some real danger, but his fear is a reaction to that specific danger and not a general attitude to all demands and difficulties.

The realist controls his behavior because he will receive less reward if he is thoughtless. Whenever there are facts to be used, the person who fails to use them is to some degree acting blindly. Sometimes, to be sure, facts are ignored because a problem is not worth close analysis or the time is short. Such "intelligent" neglect of facts is readily distinguished from lack of realism.

When a person insists on ideas that are provably false, we say that he has lost contact with reality. The psychotic who distorts the world to fit his fancies and the college student who continues in an unsuitable career plan are both lacking in realism. Exaggerating one's difficulties, overestimating one's own power, and rejecting without study ideas that conflict with one's established beliefs are milder forms of unrealism. These occur among the average run of pupils and adults; they imply ineffectiveness, but not mental disorder.

Commitment

Realistic awareness does not alone produce adjustment. A person must be willing to commit his energies to a plan of action, sometimes to an action more likely to fail than to succeed. Problem situations are ambiguous, and facts alone rarely permit one to decide with certainty what he should do. The pupil who waits until enough facts are available to *ensure* success will pass up his opportunities. He will lag behind more daring leaders.

Excessive "realism" means caution and inhibition. When faced with a risky decision, a person should not remain idle forever. Some people are paralyzed by uncertainty. To avoid error, they do nothing. If a person thinks an action has a good chance of attaining his goal, he should be able to commit his energies to a trial. He must positively *invite* thwarting by accepting risk.

Commitment to a goal is the key to persistence. The person has to value the goal so much that the possibility of attaining it outweighs the risk of failure. A missionary commits himself to try a difficult and improbable feat of re-education, at the risk of poverty, isolation, perhaps even death. The people who make no history have their commitments too. A mother commits herself to keeping a home happy; the committed farmer tries to reclaim a "hopeless" plot where nothing has flourished.

Because of the multitude of roles in our society and the variety of value systems, there is little agreement as to what a person should commit his energies to. From the point of view of mental hygiene, the important thing is that each person have some commitment. Without the feeling that *something* matters, the person lacks the positive pleasures of overcoming obstacles and building toward an end. In the intervals when his environment is presenting no problems to him, he has no goals and no plans. He becomes apathetic and colorless, safe but dull.

CONFLICT BETWEEN GOALS.   Conflict between values makes adjustment difficult. The person whose goals pull him in opposite directions is under continual strain. Sometimes the conflict is between two threatening alternatives: "Shall I fight with other boys and risk physical pain, or shall I run from the fight and suffer both shame and scorn?" A choice between two positive commitments may also cause conflict. When life has invested both goals with intense emotional significance, the pressure becomes disorganizing.

A dramatic report by Hunt (1938) supports the view that conflict rather than thwarting alone is the cause of breakdown. Some people maintain mental health in the most grinding, debasing environment. Fifteen boys grew up in such an environment in a suburb of Washington, D. C., at the turn of the century. From birth they suffered from poverty, alcoholic and quarreling parents, and neglect. In adulthood five of the 15 were committed to a hospital for psychotic disorder and alcoholism. A sixth died on the streets in young manhood, with a history of alcoholic excess. In retracing childhood influences, Hunt found two to be particularly significant: the seduction of the boys by homosexuals and their conversion to a religion of strict and emotional beliefs.

Every one of the six boys who became disorganized had participated in both these irreconcilable activities. Of the nine boys who did not break down, only one tried to follow both standards, and he tried only occasionally. The boys who had once learned to participate in a homosexual crowd returned again and again to the gang. But the church revivals were powerful, even irresistible. These boys, with their sense of sin, pledged at each revival meeting to follow the church's standards. Thus, each time they went back to the gang, they experienced overwhelming disgust with themselves. "In later adolescence the boys were almost continuously miserable. Most of this ring lost interest in school. They quit, did odd jobs, or 'mooned about' in their misery." This history does not prove that conflict was the sole cause of breakdown. There is some reason to believe that the boys who formed close identification with their parents were the ones who did not succumb when the other boys were seduced by adult laborers. Emotional security and a clear self-concept make resistance to temptation possible.

Self-acceptance

Realism and commitment are surface signs of adjustment. Self-acceptance is a deeper characteristic which to some extent explains why a person functions well. In earlier chapters self-confidence and self-respect have repeatedly been key concepts. Aspiration, interests, reasoning, understanding, and so on—all these desirable behaviors are made possible by the person's feeling that he can succeed and that if he fails he will still be worthy of approval. A person must live with his limitations. His body has its weaknesses and imperfections; so do his talents. If he is superior in popularity or wisdom, he is still inferior in something else. A person shapes a self-concept out of his knowledge of what he is and how he compares with others, and at the same time shapes an ideal of what he should be.

The person who accepts himself (Sheerer, 1949)

> has faith in his capacity to cope with life
> considers his worth as a person equal to others'
> does not regard himself as queer or abnormal; does not expect others to reject him
> is not shy or self-conscious
> assumes responsibility for his own behavior
> follows his personal standards instead of conforming to external pressures
> accepts praise or blame objectively
> does not condemn himself for his limitations, or deny his superior qualities
> does not deny his impulses and emotions, or feel guilty about them

Anxiety—that is to say, generalized fearfulness not attached to a specific threat—is best understood as a sign of inadequate self-acceptance. Every person will from time to time fail at something important. In the anxious person the conflict between the ideal "I must succeed at this to be worthy of approval" and the prediction "I may fail" is ever present. The self-accepting person takes a different stance. "I am worthy of respect even if I do not attain this goal." He is not forced to strive for unattainable perfection, nor is he complacent.

Emotional control should be achieved without burdening the child with shame and self-doubt. "Only babies cry" damages the child's self-concept. "It must hurt a lot. Let's see what we can do for it" accepts the feeling as natural but does not reward the weeping itself. Shaming a child because he has not learned a desired emotional response is as detrimental to his personality as ridiculing him for physical or intellectual retardation.

All that we have said regarding good adjustment is a conclusion based on two generations of psychiatric progress. It marks a great change from the old notion that faultless, inhibited behavior shows ideal adjustment. It departs also from the later doctrine that spontaneous letting-oneself-go is advisable. But our view of adjustment is not really new. The concept has not been expressed better than in the ancient advice of Polonius:

> This above all: To thine own self be true,
> And it must follow, as the night the day,
> Thou canst not then be false to any man.

A person loyal to his own self knows his worth and trusts his potentialities. He asks himself to do all he can and expects others to respect his effort and accomplishment. He works for what he values and believes in, being swayed neither by the fashions others set nor the opposition he meets. Yet for all his confidence and sense of direction he keeps his eyes open. He serves himself ill if he expends his energies on the truly impossible or clings to his beliefs and attachments heedless of changes in the world. Bringing facts and purpose together, he accomplishes. He gives, in Kurt Goldstein's words, "an affirmative answer to the shocks of existence."

Adjustment is judged in terms of the total life pattern. We cannot judge a single act as showing adjustment or maladjustment. It is for this reason that we cannot classify single emotional reactions as good or bad.

One boy reads comic books or daydreams when he gets free time. He also enters energetically into work, and plays eagerly with others. His relaxation by means of fantasy implies no maladjustment. At worst, he can be accused of spending time pleasantly rather than profitably. Another boy withdraws into a comic book whenever there is an occasion for free play among pupils. Perhaps he is "well adjusted" by many standards: eager participation in classwork, absence of visible tension, quick recovery from mistakes. Yet if he consistently backs off from his peers, his fantasy appears to be a route of escape from a threat. This withdrawing can only be regarded as a bad sign. Teachers should try to bring him back into the group. There is no threat of emotional breakdown, for he shows too many positive signs of realistic commitment and self-acceptance. His handicap is confined to a specific area. Similarly for the other types of reaction. A person who gives way to his temper may be better or worse adjusted than one who does not. Better, perhaps, if he goes on from the outburst to solve his problem; worse, if he lets the explosion take the place of constructive effort. The degree to which a person is "adjusted" or "maladjusted" is judged by the extent to which he is, as a whole, realistic, committed, and self-acceptant.

132 *Mental health appears in many forms*

Writings about mental health have been attacked on two flanks. Some critics regard the demand for adjustment as a demand for placidity and conformity. The concern of psychologists about the damaging consequences of failure is seen as a relaxation of "standards" and an encouragement to "softness" (Mowrer, 1947). The concern for relations with others is misread as condemnation of the individualist. But the mental hygienist is not speaking for passive conformity; indeed, the second group of critics attack him for defining adjustment in egocentric terms. These critics point out that the major problems of contemporary life can rarely be solved by individual action. If adjustment is thought of solely as commitment to individual goals and belief only in one's individual powers, it does stop short of effectiveness. Egocentric and competitive individuals are often unwilling to sacrifice prestige and freedom in order to take part in group decisions about goals and group action; but this implies a lack of respect for others which is unrealistic. By our argument, neither individualism nor affiliation is virtuous in itself. The person who cannot shift from one to the other is seriously handicapped.

24. Which of the "serious" symptoms in Table 40 show lack of realism? lack of commitment? lack of self-acceptance?

25. Why does R. R. Sears (1953) list the following as signs of *desirable* emotional development in the 9-year-old?

> Failure at schoolwork elicits *openly* disappointed reaction, but there is some indication of renewed effort toward accomplishment.
> Mild physical injury is reacted to with brief (not intense) grimacing and crying.
> Reacts to teacher's disapproval with some slight signs of independence, e.g., snickering covertly with intimate friend when disciplined.
> Competes for teacher's approval, mainly by more effective school work.

26. Comment on this statement arising out of an international conference on the mental health of college students: "Mental health is not characterized by adjustment under all circumstances, nor by freedom from anxiety and tension, nor by freedom from dissatisfaction, nor by conformity or constant happiness."

27. There is disagreement among specialists as to whether "mental health" can be defined as anything more than "the absence of mental disorder." Does the description given above discuss a set of symptoms to be avoided, or does it point out positive responses to be learned?

SUMMARY

A person is said to be thwarted or blocked when his action fails to produce the consequence he expected, or some other equally satisfactory consequence. He may then repeat his response, try a new response, turn to some other goal, or become inactive. Table 38 evaluates each reaction and lists the factors making it likely. The effect on adjustment of a failure to achieve a goal is suggested by a comparison of married and unmarried teachers. The unmarried teachers show greater emotionality regarding various life problems. A second study, of short-term thwarting, describes performance and social relations in a group working on an impossible task.

The teacher should eliminate blockings that have no educative aim, reduce penalties attached to an unsuccessful try, and aid the child in overcoming obstacles. This calls for setting attainable goals, for criticizing only serious faults, for reducing regulations to a minimum. The teacher encourages resolute trying by making goals clear, by explaining how the work is to be done, and by feedback that develops self-confidence.

Tensions may be specific to a single situation or they may build into generalized guilt, fearfulness, hostility, etc. Tension may be expressed in problem-centered exertion, direct discharge, or displaced discharge; or it may be suppressed.

Narrowing one's attention and pressing harder is often detrimental to performance. The person may fail to notice some of the significant cues. As Patrick's experiment (see p. 591) showed, he is likely not to use principles he understands, and instead makes unthoughtful or even panicky tries with little intellectual control. Stereotyped, nonadaptive action also increases.

Moderate tension is necessary if a problem is to be solved. Scientific problems often are resolved through an "incubation" process. Having clearly identified his problem, the scientist carries the problem in the back of his mind; a solution often comes to him at a time when he is not giving the problem his attention. The more creative worker does not press for a quick solution; rather, he immerses himself in the problem, becoming acquainted with it from all angles. School assignments for work to be delivered the next day, or a long-term project to be fully outlined in advance, give no opportunity for this type of creative exploration.

Highly anxious children are superior when goals can be achieved through self-critical, diligent effort, dependent on authority. Low anxiety leads to greater success when flexibility, originality, and independent judgment are required, and greater ability to keep attention on relatively unorganized discussions. The person with low anxiety is likely to respond positively to pressure that disrupts a person who starts with high tension. This implies that for every task there is some optimum tension level, and that a certain incentive or pressure may be desirable with some pupils and detrimental with others.

Discharge of emotions on a "safe" target is illustrated by the hostility seen in negativism, in artistic productions, in competitiveness, and sometimes in stern morality. Other emotions—fear, self-pity, etc.—may similarly be bottled up until some socially acceptable excuse for the emotion appears.

Bottling up—suppressing—emotion is demanded by the culture. Often the person is trained to deny his emotions even to himself; this is called repression. Acknowledged impulses are easier to control than repressed wishes and fears. Much of psychotherapy consists in bringing repressed thoughts forward for examination. Repressed tensions may crop out in the form of psychogenic illnesses. Fantasy and rationalization are minor forms of defensive retreat from difficulties; carried to extremes they remove the person from reality into a false, psychotic world.

Any definition of "adjustment" expresses cultural values. It is important to avoid irrelevant criteria that make the term indistinguishable from "goodness." We identify the adjusted person as one who commits himself to a consistent set of goals and uses his energies effectively in pursuing them. Good adjustment consists of realism plus commitment plus self-acceptance. The person who lacks these is ineffective and unhappy. Mental hygienists rate violent discharge of tension and certain types of withdrawal as especially serious symptoms of possible breakdown (see Table 40). The pupil's mental health is judged by his response to difficulties, not by the fact that he has difficulties or by the fact that he is a nonconformer.

The self-accepting person does not see himself as perfect. He does consider himself to be responsible, respectable, and capable. He regards his impulses as normal. He regards his transgressions and failures as errors rather than as signs of unworthiness. He is true to his own values.

Critics of the mental-health movement make two somewhat contradictory charges. It is said that those who seek to promote adjustment encourage passive conformity. It is also said that adjustment is defined in terms of egocentric satisfaction even though today's world calls for cooperative living. We accept neither conformity nor inconsiderateness as indicative of adjustment. Both affiliation and individualism have a place in effective living.

Reading List 17

Pearl H. Berkowitz and Esther P. Rothman, "The Teacher and the Disturbed Child," in *The Disturbed Child* (New York: New York Univ. Press, 1960), pp. 116–30.

Every teacher occasionally must deal with a seriously disturbed, aggressive, or withdrawn child. This chapter gives a compact list of recommendations intended to increase the teacher's insight into herself and the child.

Alexander Mintz, "Non-Adaptive Group Behavior," *Journal of Abnormal and Social Psychology*, 46 (1951), 150–59.

Groups of volunteers worked on a cooperative task where the prospect of individual punishment (fines for poor performance) made the task threatening. The performance is compared with that in a group who were solely concerned with doing a good team job. The deterioration of reasoning under tension is demonstrated, and the author compares this to such panic behavior as a run on a bank. What school procedures arouse comparable tensions?

O. Hobart Mowrer, "Discipline and Mental Health," *Harvard Educational Review*, 17 (1947), 284–96. Reprinted in Mowrer, *Learning Theory and Personality Dynamics*, in Coladarci, and in Loree.

Mowrer argues that discipline is necessary if a person is to develop self-acceptance, ambition, and integration. He therefore denies that the treatment of children should be supportive and nonpunishing. Although this article is directed toward parents, you can judge whether the five reasons given for discipline apply in school, and you should try to decide what school procedures the author would advocate.

Lois B. Murphy, "Effects of Child-Rearing Patterns on Mental Health," *Children*, 3 (1956), 213–18. Reprinted in Seidman *C*.

Murphy lists aspects of American culture that in her opinion are threats to emotional security, and also lists types of stimulation and support that build mental health. Her position appears to be in conflict wih Mowrer's. She also implies that a school program stressing "excellence" can harm the child. Do you agree?

C. H. Patterson, "The Classroom Teacher and the Emotional Problems of Children," *Understanding the Child*, 21 (1952), 67–72. Reprinted in Fullagar.

Symptoms of tension are described, together with recommendations for the teacher. The author's emphasis on allowing controlled expression of emotion should be noted.

Fritz Redl and William W. Wattenberg, "Diagnostic Thinking in the Classroom," Chapter 12 in *Mental Hygiene in Teaching* (New York: Harcourt, Brace, 1959), pp. 326–43.

This chapter describes reactions of pupils to frustration, demonstrating particularly how excessive emotionality, aggression, cheating, and other disturbing responses arise. Identification of the basic frustration is shown to be essential to handling such problems. Note other chapters in the book also.

CHAPTER **18** CHARACTER DEVELOPMENT

Perhaps you have thought of character as a moral quality quite separate from intelligence, knowledge, or emotional maturity. Character, however, is evidenced in the way a person behaves when faced by a conflict, especially one where his wishes run counter to the interests of other people. The choice he makes depends on his concepts, attitudes, needs, and feelings. For this reason, a discussion of character gives us an opportunity to review and integrate principles we have been developing throughout the earlier chapters.

How would *you* propose to develop the character of the young? Do you think of character as habit, so that providing opportunity to practice good behaviors and win reward for them would be the best method? Or do you think character is primarily composed of ethical concepts? If so, you would explain important concepts and have pupils interpret situations by means of them. Or is character a reflection of emotional adjustment? That would suggest that good character is to be achieved by making pupils emotionally secure.

Character is not really a cumulation of separate habits and ideas. Character is embedded in the total structure of personality. Beliefs, feelings, and actions are linked together, so that to change character calls for reorganization of the personality. Tiny "lessons" on principles of good conduct will not be effective if they cannot be integrated with the personality system. Thus to gain an understanding of character we must examine the very structure of personality. Then we shall turn to educational methods.

A DEFINITION OF CHARACTER

To probe fully into what character is and should be we would have to confront unsettled philosophical issues. We can give a sufficiently definite answer, in keeping with the beliefs of present-day America, without pretending that we know finally what are the best values and the best forms of living. Many sources of knowledge contribute to current views on character: folk experience, religious teaching, anthropological observations, controlled experiments, and clinical examinations of personalities.

We shall define character in terms of the choices the individual makes when his actions affect the welfare of others: the person of good character chooses an act that promotes the welfare of others as well as himself. By such a definition we exclude temperamental qualities, which give the personality flavor but are not especially relevant to the good of the community. We exclude energy level, for example, and matters of preference and taste. Behavior that reveals character expresses a choice between major satisfactions; the choice is usually between gratifying the self and helping others. We would call an act generous only if it involves an element of sacrifice, for a person does not display character in giving away something he does not want. As character develops, a person learns to take more pride and pleasure in considerate action than in impulsive and selfish behavior. "Good" behavior is motivated by its connections with affection, self-respect, and other needs.

Our definition makes it exceedingly difficult to evaluate a pupil's character. Only if we know how he makes his judgments and what motivates them can we decide whether or not a given act represents considerateness and maturity. But this is precisely the point to be made in a psychological study of character: We cannot judge the goodness of an act unless we know what it means to the individual. As we shall see, the very best behavior, judged by its conformity to community standards, may be a symptom of *lack* of moral judgment.

1. How would a New England Puritan of 1650 react to our definition of character? Does our definition neglect any values that present-day Americans should teach to their children?

2. Show that each of the following character traits requires sacrifice of some gratification: loyalty to friends, honesty, defense of an unpopular principle, consideration for others' feelings.

3. Could truthfulness sometimes be motivated by a desire to hurt another person? Would it then be a virtue?

FIVE LEVELS OF CHARACTER

Five levels of character development can be recognized (Peck and Havighurst, 1960):

    a. the amoral
    b. the self-centered, expedient
    c. the conforming, conventional
    d. the irrational-conscientious
    e. the rational, altruistic

A person acts amorally when he does not recognize the good or bad effects of his choice on other persons. A self-centered act is one where the person does what he prefers, considering others only in order to attain his ends. A conventional act is one where the person does what his group usually does, without reflecting whether it is good or bad. Behavior is classified as conscientious when the person follows some rule of good conduct that he firmly believes in. At the fourth level of development the application of the formal rule is rigid, without intelligent recognition of variation in circumstances. In rational, altruistic behavior, conscience dictates an aim rather than a rule of action. At this highest level the person is interested in the welfare of everyone affected by his acts and decides for himself what action will produce the most satisfactory result.

This scheme of analysis should not be allowed to oversimplify a complex subject. Anyone, somewhere in his actions, shows behavior at each of these levels, though one level is usually most prominent. The development of character follows this order only approximately. Some moral judgments are rational, even in the 6-year-old. Perhaps some persons develop to this level without going through an irrational-conscientious stage. There is no sharp transition from selfish behavior to considerate behavior and no age when the child suddenly "becomes responsible." On tests of character, change in self-regulation appears to be gradual (Hartshorne and May, 1928). The important reason for distinguishing among the five levels is that educators who propose to develop character have to be clear about their aim. Education that encourages conforming or irrational-conscientious conduct may interfere with the ultimate emergence of rational character.

The Amoral Level

Amoral behavior is that where the performer is unaware of or disregards the effect his act has on others. The newborn infant has no concept of good or bad. The young child reaches for attractive objects on impulse and is outraged when his will is blocked. Soon, in the process of normal socialization, he will be taught not to reach for what belongs to others and to control emotional expression. If a 3-year-old pulls up a flower from someone's yard, he is not necessarily choosing a disapproved act. On the contrary, probably he does not know that picking the flower is frowned on. So far as he knows, he is making no choice between self-interest and community interest. Amoral behavior is rare among school-age children and adults. A person who is purely egocentric, out for every gratification he can get, is "emotionally retarded" in the same sense as others are "mentally retarded." In an adult amoral disregard of others is a serious abnormality, recognized in psychiatry under the diagnostic label "character disorder."

The Expedient Level

The expedient person is also self-centered, but his behavior is far more controlled. He chooses to gratify his own wishes, but he knows the importance of considering others' reactions in order to come out ahead in the long run. The self-centered person may do things that benefit others; indeed, according to Peck (Peck and Havighurst, 1960, pp. 5–6):

> his outward behavior may often be honest and responsible, in the main, so far as others can see. The key to his low-level morality is his "me-first" attitude in a critical situation, where an unmoral act may bring advantages that outweigh any disapproval. . . .
>
> . . . many very young children . . . have learned to behave correctly when an adult is around. . . . In the absence of such controls, they immediately relapse into doing what they please, even if this involves shoving other people around, taking what they want, or otherwise gratifying their self-centered desires.

An older expedient person gratifies his impulse even when he knows the action is not "good." He sizes up the risk of detection and the penalties that might follow. If these are small, he goes ahead. It is not the impulse to do something unwise that shows immature character; at any age a person has impulsive desires for pleasures and possessions. The impulse may be to lie down for a nap instead of returning to work, or to scribble a smart rebuttal in a library book. A male teacher might have an impulse to ask a high-school girl for a date or to punch an impertinent boy in the nose. A person may acknowledge such wishes without guilt and still know that to act on them would be unwise.

The Conventional Level

Conventional or conforming behavior is learned fairly early in life. A person learns to make a choice that differs from his own first impulse if that choice is normal in his group; this is part of learning a role. When distressed, we hide our tears more out of an attempt to behave properly than for any moral reasons. How fast we drive is determined mostly by how fast we see others driving. There is a strong element of expediency in conventional behavior. One can be sure that if he follows the pack he will be safe from disapproval. He does not gratify so many of his idiosyncratic impulses as the person we have classified as expedient does, but he also is acting in terms of what is "the best policy."

Character should develop beyond the conventional level, so that the person knows why a certain group norm is desirable to imitate and when to reject the norm as a model. But many "good citizens" who do the right things operate at the conventional level. They act to get social approval. Faced with a choice between what the group wants to do and what their judgment tells them is best, they are more likely to go along with the group. They become passive supporters of those who persecute minorities. They follow the fads in political opinion, in consumption, and in child rearing.

"Everybody jaywalks."

133   *Conforming behavior*

When, carried on the tide of changing popular sentiment, they find themselves acting in a way inconsistent with their old beliefs, they feel discomfort rather than guilt.

The Irrational-Conscientious Level

Conscience is the name given to internal self-criticism, which makes the person dissatisfied with some conduct even though that conduct attains his external goals. Freud proposed that we distinguish between two types of self-criticism—*ego and supergo*. We can sketch this useful distinction without developing these concepts fully. The ego may be thought of as the attitude that keeps a person realistic, that helps him foresee consequences and move toward his goals. Superego judges whether his plans are morally worthy or unworthy. Ego knows that buying votes is a way to win elections but superego keeps a candidate from using that route to win. Thus superego (the conscience or system of values) judges any provisional try against the standard of moral goodness, whereas ego judges the proposed behavior in terms of its efficiency. This seems to describe the nervous system as a place where two little men named Ego and Superego wrestle. Such a metaphor, though fanciful, helps us to distinguish moral learning from realistic learning. Before our discussion ends, we shall see that the two do not have to be in opposition.

Behavior is irrational-conscientious when a person acts in the light of values held emotionally rather than rationally. It is easier to illustrate this behavior than to define it. Consider the person who cannot tell a lie. Many people learn just this attitude in early childhood through identification with a parent who insisted on truthfulness. A person subjected to severe punish-

"*I never cross against a light.*"

134 *Irrational-conscientious behavior*

ment or the threat of it for untruthfulness attaches emotion to falsehood. If the child's first innocent alterations of the truth bring severe punishments, he is likely to have some of the internal sensations of fear when the thought of falsehood tempts him later. The temptation to untruth is threatening for him as the rabbit became threatening for the child who came to associate it with loud noise (page 439). His anxiety will bar him from lying even when there is no possibility of his being detected and punished. It will bar him from lying when lying might serve others well. If, because of some strong temptation, he does lie, he will feel guilty afterward. Guilt is a sense of unworthiness, "of having violated one's own moral integrity" (Peck and Havighurst, 1960, p. 7). It is quite different from the feeling of the person who believes he has made a mistake and can act more wisely next time. The latter person is learning to discriminate where lying is bad. The first person, subjected to severe punishment on some occasions, develops a conflict that prevents discrimination (page 153).

Some people might argue that inviolable values represent the best in character. The person who is irrevocably attached to truth-telling, however, is limited. He will lack the gracious social lies, which make it possible to get along with others in some circumstances. "How did you like my daughter's performance in the school play, Mr. Jones?" If Jones cannot evade or stretch the truth, his candid comment will make him unpopular and needlessly wound the matron and her daughter. Jones could never fill a role— e.g., espionage agent—where "the whole truth and nothing but the truth" is not a prime value. One value competes with others; a person cannot solve a problem where his irrationally held values do not all lie on one side. An irrational value system may be self-defeating because it insists on a single principle of action regardless of circumstances. The rule of behavior transfers, but not adaptively.

Self-defeating actions caused by irrational values contribute to neurotic maladjustment. It is neurotic, for example, for a person to drive himself toward a standard of perfection he can never attain. Yet we observe this behavior in intelligent people, as in the man who never completes a report on time because he is always dissatisfied with the loose ends. We observe it in the student who spends hours retyping a theme because he does not want to turn in pages with erasures; he would be far wiser to turn in the theme typed less perfectly and get on to more profitable tasks. The person who resolves his conflict by violating a deeply conditioned value pays the penalty afterward in feelings of guilt. Self-acceptance and guilt are incompatible; the person who defines his best performance as a failure condemns himself to endless discontent.

Many irrational conformers adjust well to the community. The values that parents pound into children do aid in social living. Nothing is to be said against truthfulness, cooperation, generosity, and neatness considered as abstract values. They combine into a comfortable and useful style of life. It is in the exceptional situation that conventional values are inadequate guides to action. It may be necessary to attack others boldly to bring a community problem into the open; then excess of considerateness is a vice. When neatness means delay, or when to cooperate means to abandon one's principles, the person who cannot violate these abstract standards is weak rather than admirable.

The rational conscience has its greatest advantage over the irrational conscience in facing tough decisions. For each person some values are more important than others. A man might arrange values in this order: protection of his family, responsibility in his work, kindliness in dealing with others, entertainment of his children, avoidance of debt. He has few difficulties in deciding what to do when a conflict arises between a high-ranking and a low-ranking value. He keeps his home warm and pays his doctor bills, even if he goes into the red to do it. In any such hierarchy, some values have very nearly equal importance. This man's desire to be generous to an employee may be as strong as his desire to spend the firm's money wisely. If these values are founded in emotional conditioning rather than rational judgment, he will be left with no basis for making a decision. He can escape the dilemma only by an impulsive plunge into an action he cannot justify intellectually.

The Rational, Altruistic Level

Most standards of conduct are encountered first at the conventional level, then verbalized into a policy to be followed without a clear reason, and finally, much later, understood. So the child upon entering school finds that it is the custom to spend a certain period each day picking up materials. He conforms, first to be sure of approval, then because he finds it comfortable to do things that fit into his role as class member. The teacher criticizes a piece of work as untidy. The student council sends out the word that there is too much trash on the school ground. Such incidents coalesce into an abstract concept of neatness. If he accepts his teacher and peers as models, this abstract ideal will become a value for him. Skilled teaching can gradually bring him to question why neatness is desirable, and how one can decide what is "neat enough."

He will recognize that an untidy paper is hard to read, that an untidy school yard is ugly. But he will not have impulses to square the corners of the papers on his desk. When he must do a job rapidly, he will subordinate neatness to the greater end.

To arrive at rational solutions to conflict, he must be clear which values are subordinate. Destruction of life is undesirable, so war is undesirable; but oppression is undesirable and sometimes willingness to make war may be the only way to prevent oppression. When one's system of beliefs is organized so that he knows which are the most important and why, he may regret having to choose but he does not feel guilty about foregoing the less important outcome. He is emotionally tied to his basic goals, not to trivial short-term gratifications. His sense of right and wrong is in harmony with his goals and his chosen paths. Such a person is integrated. Wish, knowledge, and conscience are allies rather than antagonists. The ideal of moral education is to free a man's mind so that it can serve his highest values.

A value is a principle comparable to those discussed in Chapter 11. It is an aid to interpretation. *One understands a value if he knows what consequences are likely to follow when it guides conduct in various situations.* One understands a conflict between values when he sees what more remote values each value serves. Thus in the long run having a philosophy makes one's conduct realistic. If a person is clear about what is of highest importance and knows that he must sacrifice minor values in order to achieve it, both ego and superego are satisfied. If, in addition, he is concerned for the welfare of others, we speak of him as altruistic.

It is unlikely that any of us becomes totally rational about his conduct. Personal needs have sufficient force to keep us from carrying out some moral decisions. Socialization will never be so ideally directed as to free a man from all inhibiting fears and blind loyalties. One can be rational in some areas more than in others, and at some times more than at others. The rational, altruistic character is an ideal to be approached, perhaps never to be attained save in myth.

One might distinguish among the five levels in this way. The amoral person ignores values beyond immediate pleasure and displeasure. The

"It may be safe, but it confuses the drivers if we cross against the light."

135   *Rational, altruistic behavior*

expedient person has become aware of ethical values or group standards but does not use them to judge himself. For him conformity may be a means, but not an end. The conventional person wants to do as others do, and this aim is more compelling for him than any abstract moral idea. When the group abandons some value, he also abandons his attachment to it. Conscientious individuals are emotionally attached to value ideals, which they use to judge proposed actions. The irrational conscience is emotionally bound to a collection of sometimes incompatible verbal principles. This is different from the rational conscience, which is concerned with real effects.

The person with rational character is firmly committed to some basic values, but he knows how they fit together and holds few standards inviolable. The rational, altruistic person adheres neither to the group example nor to abstract "laws" of morality; for him, a conflict situation calls for reasoning. Fromm (1947, p. 130) has argued cogently that the person who most considers others is also the one who has the deepest self-acceptance.

Character differences are readily observed even among prominent, successful adults. School superintendents were judged as "moralists" or "expedients" on the basis of interview data (Gross *et al.*, 1957, 1958). These classifications overlap those used above; the moralists fit our descriptions of rational or irrational-conscientious behavior, and the expedients include both our selfish expedients and conformers. These men were asked how they would resolve a conflict, for example, between pressure from a school board which wants the budget held down, and pressure from a group of teachers who want salaries raised. What the superintendent recommended depended on whether or not he perceived each pressure as legitimate and proper, and on whether or not he expected to encounter serious trouble if he rejected either recommendation. Here are representative results:

CASE 1. If the superintendent sees Pressure A as *legitimate* and *threatening* trouble if he does not comply, and Pressure B as *illegitimate* and *threatening* trouble if he does not comply:

> Among moralists, 3 choose course A and only one compromises
> Among expedients, 3 out of 3 compromise

CASE 2. If the superintendent sees Pressure A as *legitimate* and not *threatening*, and Pressure B as *illegitimate* and *threatening*:

> Among moralists, 4 out of 4 choose course A
> Among expedients, 4 out of 4 choose course B

(This specific result is based on a small number of responses; we have neglected the numerous superintendents placed in an intermediate category between expedient and moral.) Whether or not the school superintendent should bow before some realistically perceived threats is arguable; there is some wisdom in living to fight another day. But the fact that on important matters these men frequently bowed to threatening, illegitimate demands is an indictment.

4. Classify the following statements or actions according to the level of development the action represents:

> a. James, 11, thinks that criminals are crazy because "crime does not pay."
> b. Martha insists on inviting a Japanese schoolmate to her party because if she is not invited her feelings will be hurt.
> c. Martha's mother suggests that Martha limit her list to children of her own class and ethnic group, on the grounds that people in her neighborhood don't usually mix with people from other parts of town.
> d. Sunny, a white girl age 4, goes to nursery school and immediately starts playing with a Negro boy.
> e. When a Negro boy turns out for football, he does well and the coach places him on the first team; the remaining boys, reared under a policy of segregation, threaten to quit the team. The coach defies them to quit, tells them the school can go without a team before he will permit discrimination within it.
> f. To teach responsibility, a college formulates with the students an

"honor principle" which replaces all other rules. The students are free to do what they choose, "consistent with the welfare of the entire community." After five years of successful operation, with a few cases of honor violations disposed of by a student-faculty review committee, the system is threatened with breakdown. Reserve books are taken from the library without being signed out. Equipment is broken in dormitory scuffles for which no one admits blame. Though the persons responsible are known to many fellow students, these students choose not to report them as "honor violators."

5. Is a person with a "strong ego" egotistical?

6. Would it be possible to have a rational, selfish character?

7. Can you think of a situation where waste, i.e., ignoring economy, would contribute to good ends?

8. Which of the five levels of character integration is most likely to make a person happy?

HOW CHARACTER IS UNIFIED

An adult's character depends on the entire process by which he has learned his personality and his values. The structure of needs and attitudes of a college student represents twenty years' cumulated learning. It is important to recall the process of personality development introduced in Chapters 4 and 5, for this long series of connected experiences is the basis of character formation. Those earlier chapters concentrated on factors creating readiness for learning. We now re-examine the process in a broader setting to see how the individual develops his outlook on the world.

When a person fails in a major developmental learning, he then has increased difficulties of adjustment. If such a failure is followed by compensatory success, the person may be happy. But the failure leaves a vulnerable area. Buried doubts about his worth may undermine his judgment and assurance in later conflicts. His self-respect may be impaired even when he has overcome the original difficulty. The shape of his personality is a consequence of the competence he thinks he has, the desires and fears he has acquired (whether acknowledged or repressed), the persons he has identified with, and his ideas about the world. To understand impulses and the controls that hold them in check, any character trait must be seen as part of the whole personality.

Mack, a Case Study of Character Structure

Our case studies of Chapters 5 and 13 demonstrated some of the ways in which developmental problems press each personality into its own shape.

We now examine another case report, richer in some ways than the earlier ones.

Mack came under examination by investigators studying antiminority prejudice in young adults (Adorno *et al.*, 1950). Mack, though unusually hostile, is no "crackpot," nor is he in difficulties by usual school or community standards. Because he is so normal in many ways, the deep flaws in his character are a useful illustration of effects of fairly typical home and school experience on development. At the time of the study, Mack was a

136   *Mack is a model citizen on the surface*

college freshman preparing for a law career. Needing money, he had held a job as a responsible clerk in the War Department for some time before returning to school.

Mack's salient problems center around his attitudes toward authority and toward his sex role. He has conflicts between what he feels he is—his self-concept—and what he thinks it necessary to try to be—his ideal self. He has always tried to conceal his doubts about himself, and he has learned just those attitudes and behaviors that make this suppression easier. Here we can only summarize the personality picture, giving none of the detailed evidence from which the original analyst, Nevitt Sanford, reasoned.

RELATIONS WITH PARENTS.   The most basic forces shaping Mack's history are his weak physical constitution and his relations with his parents. Mack was loved by his mother and in early childhood got some affection from her. Mack's father was fifty years older than he, emotionally distant, demanding good conduct but giving little affection. He was, as Mack recalls him, un-

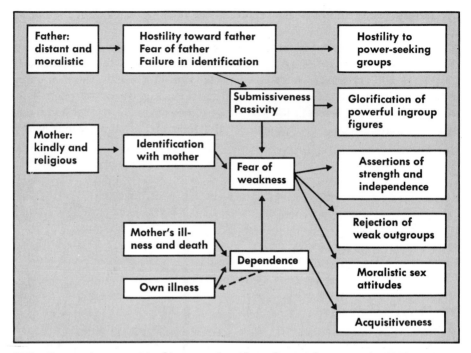

137 *Forces forming Mack's attitudes (based on Adorno et al., 1950, p. 801)*

ambitious, a nonsmoker, and a strictly honest man. (He regarded having a charge account as taking unfair advantage of the merchant.) Mack's chance of gaining secure affection was wrecked when his mother became seriously ill. She had two operations, returning from each to care for Mack and his sister as well as her strength allowed. She died while Mack was still a child. This left Mack in the care of an aunt with a separate home of her own, and of his sister who was only four years older.

A second strain was put on this boy who never felt a continuing and warming love. From the age of 12, Mack was continually in poor health: first, anemia, later, stomach trouble. During most of his adolescence and early adulthood he was weak and unable to exert himself. His disorder was severe enough to cause his discharge from the Army. Quite possibly his illness had psychological causes. It appears that Mack would like to depend on someone and be free not to strive; perhaps illness was a useful way of withdrawing when he could not quit outright.

RELATIONS WITH PEERS.   Mack had good relations with boys, and a close companion in his cousin Bud. He engaged in sports of many kinds. He joined DeMolay and rose to the post of Master Councillor. His high-school mates elected him vice-president of the student body, and in business school he was president. He won acceptance readily.

Mack was not especially at ease in dating, and describes himself as "always the backward boy." He did have sexual relations in his late teens, and speaks of his initiation with some guilt and an apparent need to blame the girl. At the time of the interview (his age was 24), Mack was going with a schoolteacher. His remarks about her may have special interest for some readers, as well as reveal Mack more fully (Adorno *et al.*, 1950, p. 789).

> I hope to get married to the girl I'm going with now. She is an awfully nice companion. Most girls are interested only in a good time and want fellows with lots of money to spend. . . . I talked with her uncle about an automobile that she was interested in. I looked it over for her, since I knew something about cars, and told her it was in good condition. I got started going with her that way. I found out that she wasn't interested in money, but was interested in me in spite of my discharge from the army, my poor health and prospects. She's just very good—not beautiful, but a tremendously nice personality. . . . She has a nice figure and is very wholesome. When we get married depends on circumstances. It's quite a responsibility. . . . We're both at the proper age. I intend to work part time. I don't like her teaching; I like to support my wife. . . . She is a good cook, and that is an asset, what with my stomach condition.

As the investigators pieced together Mack's attitudes and history, they arrived at the "stream of influence" diagram we present (much simplified), in Figure 137.

EMERGENCE OF SUBMISSION AND DEPENDENCY NEEDS.   Mack responded to his older, impersonal father with both admiration and hostility. He neither took his father as an ideal, nor did he become an outright rebel. Mack did not feel free to violate his father's wishes or to attack him, yet he had no wish to follow his father's ways.

Unable to rebel or to identify fully, Mack submitted to his father's authority; a dutiful person is safe from punishment. Mack now treats other men the same way. He admires and approves distinguished and powerful figures, such as certain generals prominent in policy-making. His philosophy stresses the importance of authority and control. And he wishes to be a powerful figure himself. He sees every organization as a hierarchy of power, composed of the lowly who are directed and the key figures who rule. Having repressed his hostility toward "father figures," he thinks of prominent and powerful men as benign, just, and supporting. Mack is essentially an appeaser, hoping to win some measure of acceptance from the powerful figures whose potential to crush him he covertly fears. Mack criticizes anyone who is scrambling for power, suspicious of anyone who would try to get ahead of him. This is one underpinning of his antiminority feelings, for he thinks minority groups are plotting to gain power.

Mack's mother, while alive, communicated religious values. She saw to it that her children attended Sunday school, and Mack accepted some of the teachings. He speaks of God with conviction and reads the Bible thoughtfully. Mack's mother was a model he could imitate. She rewarded him with affection and offered him guidance, but did not threaten when disobeyed as his father did.

All the forces in Mack's life came together in a hunger for dependency. If he could only get more love, instead of the little attention his bed-bound mother could give. If he could only return to her care, after her death left him to the hurried ministrations of his sister and aunt. If, sick as he was, he could be comforted and told to take life easy. Even in marriage, Mack appears mostly to want someone who will replace his mother. Mack does not admit his wish to be dependent, and therein lies his greatest conflict.

FEAR OF WEAKNESS.   Fear of weakness is the chief attitude that pulls Mack out of the role of spineless conformer. Much of his conduct is motivated by a desire to appear masculine, independent, and strong. For self-respect, he must appear to stand on his own feet. Mack's dependency was punished by his father, to the point where Mack could not express it. On a conscious level, Mack deeply resented his later illness. To be physically strong became a conscious ideal, and he could not admit having the dependency wishes of a little boy. When Mack speaks of dependence, he justifies it by referring to his illness. "She will cook for me, because of my illness."

Given this deep-seated conflict between an ideal of strength and a craving to be cared for and directed, what does Mack do? He stresses the symbols of independence and strength: he finds pleasure in a good rifle, insists on being sole support of his wife, and is tough and aggressive in presenting his political views. Abhorring softness in himself, he condemns it in others. "He thinks of people in rigid categories of weak versus strong. . . . His main concern is not to be in any way identified with weakness." Thus we find him unsympathetic to the persecuted. He must push them away, and find reasons to condemn them rather than align himself with them.

Sex is dangerous. Mack never had constructive sex education, and he has not succeeded in any previous affectional relation. Speaking of his present girl, his tone is remarkably unimpassioned. Mack tries to withhold sexual feeling and condemns women who are sexually enticing. Mack had little to do with girls when in school, and seems to lack respect for them as individuals, yet he is nearly ready to marry. This is understood by seeing that Mack thinks of "two kinds of women." Sanford summarizes the types: "The bad, weak, dangerous, exploitive, sexual women who drag one down, and the good, wholesome, asexual one who gives." Mack is able to accept his schoolteacher because he can think of her as pure and mothering, inspiring rather than exciting. With Mack's expectation in view, Sanford seems entirely correct to say: "One cannot be very optimistic about the prospects for Mack's forthcoming marriage. While on the one hand he wants more than any woman can give him, on the other hand, he feels it would be weak to ask his wife for anything at all. And this is not to mention the problem of how sex is to be introduced into the picture without spoiling it altogether."

Mack's wish that women would take care of him is part of his more general wish that he could get things from the world. Having property is important; he is quick to praise those who help him get ahead. At the same time he holds his grasping in check, for he has the conventional disapproval of selfishness. Mack's strongest desire is "to raise myself physically, financially, and socially." But he is too fearful to contend against established power. Law is an ideally chosen route of advancement where he can be on the side of authority. He expects his training to "unlock doors." Competition disturbs him: nearly twenty years later, he still recalls that in the seventh grade a girl defeated him in a spelling bee. He is a trend-spotter, who likes to see who or what will be powerful and attach himself to that bandwagon. He wants to be carried to a position of power.

In the final analysis, Mack's ideas are inconsistent with reality and conflicting within themselves. He expresses clearly false ideas about minorities, political affairs, and human nature. He seems closed to learning anything about others that would make him less submissive to power figures and less suspicious of women and of competitors. His emotions are so torn between his hunger for love and his fear of weakness, his wish to relax and his urge to get ahead, that he cannot use his intellect freely. Unless therapy helps him face his conflicts and solve them openly, he is condemned to continue his desperate juggling of rationalizations, and repressions. In final summary of his character, we have Sanford's remark (p. 808) that he is

> in danger of being overwhelmed by emotional impulses from within or authoritative commands from without. Since the inner impulses are more to be feared than the outer authorities there is rigid adherence to the standards of the latter, but since these authorities are not accepted in any fundamental way, this adherence could be given up altogether in circumstances that made it safe to do so.

AN EVALUATION OF MACK'S CHARACTER. Departing now from Sanford's comments, we can look at Mack from the viewpoint of our analysis of character. There are good attributes to note, especially Mack's leadership and responsibility. His insistence on shouldering his own responsibilities probably makes him a most dependable employee. His fear of authority and his submissiveness probably make him careful and thorough. But in human relations we find him intolerant and suspicious where he might better be sympathetic.

Mack has no convictions, he has only policies. If he were at the ego-centric level, he would be gluttonously acquisitive. Knowing selfishness is criticized, he holds his material desires in check. He shows respect for others not because he feels kindly, but for self-protection. Almost all Mack's behavior is conforming, conventional. He does what strong figures show him to do, and has no secure beliefs with which to criticize their example. If a fascist movement led by a strong and successful man were to gain power, Mack would rush to serve him even if the movement was cruel and stupid. Mack is not going to be a martyr to any principle. He is bright enough to state high-sounding ideals, but these are not the springs of his conduct.

Just one strongly embedded value acts as a censor on Mack's conduct, and that is his rejection of dependency. Feeling that his urges toward dependency are dangerous, he makes himself outwardly as vigorous and independent as possible. If his repressed dependency wishes are indeed a cause of his illness, his irrational need to seem independent is clearly damaging him. Thus in the one area where Mack acts at the irrational-conscientious level, his insistence on independence is basically neurotic.

Mack's character remains immature because conforming has been continually rewarded. Lacking an accepted model, he did not internalize moral values in childhood. His strong unconscious needs forced him to cling to unrealistic interpretations. Mack had the advantages of fairly good education, sports, religious influence, and experience in student government. All these are claimed to contribute to character, but they failed to some extent with Mack.

> **9.** Which of Mack's expectations or attitudes may have been confirmed in school classrooms?
>
> **10.** Which of Mack's attitudes may have been confirmed in seeking election and serving as a student-body officer?
>
> **11.** What does Sanford mean in saying that Mack does not accept authorities "in any fundamental way"?
>
> **12.** If you were Mack's law-school adviser, would you urge Mack to apply for psychotherapy?

Evidence from Character Tests

Our first statement regarding character spoke of it as a unit or system, but the case of Mack shows that character is not wholly good or wholly bad. Any person has some desirable attitudes and some undesirable ones. Even "delinquents," who are overtly in conflict with society, cannot be described by labeling their character bad (Healy and Bronner, 1936).

> Delinquency is no small part of the total stream of the individual's life activities and represents, equally with all other behavior, a response to inner

and outer pressures. In common with all voluntary activities, it is a variety of self-expression.

The terms by which delinquency is designated—larceny, truancy, breaking and entering, and so on—are descriptions of behavior which do not in the least indicate what is expressed by the offender in the delinquent act. While it seems necessary to have labels for such types of conduct, yet it must be recognized in all common sense that naming the offense reveals nothing of the determinants of the behavior. . . .

Contrast cases of the simple offense, truancy. One boy may be avoiding a situation in which he feels inadequate and discouraged; another has developed out of family life antagonism to all forms of authority—school representing one form; another has such need of recognition that, even though he does not dislike school, he truants in order to be "a regular fellow" with his companions; still another is the victim of peculiar anxieties which make the classroom hateful to him.

Even statements in terms of traits seem sometimes to imply more uniformity than is observed in behavior. A pupil's honesty, for example, varies from situation to situation, as is shown when the pupil is offered various temptations.

BEHAVIORAL TESTS.   The Character Education Inquiry of Hartshorne and May (1928, 1929, 1930) is an investigation of unusual interest. The study was distinguished from virtually all man's previous attempts to find out about character because in this work the investigators actually observed character in action. While later research has gone beyond the interpretations of Hartshorne and May, none of their carefully gathered facts has been contradicted. Most judgments of character are based on reputation, or on the casual impressions of teachers and other acquaintances. The C.E.I. instead built tests in which pupils were actually confronted with conflicts. What the child did was an indisputable measure of his character in that setting. Here are tests of honesty, generosity, and cooperation:

Pupils were asked to do as well as they could on an impossible task, such as placing dots in small circles while blindfolded. This is so difficult that any pupil who succeeded certainly peeked.

Pupils worked at an arithmetic game where each one experimented at his seat with a box of coins. Afterward, while placing his coins in the box and returning them to the front of the room, the pupil had a chance to sneak out some money. Hidden marks on the box told the research workers which children took money.

Each pupil was given as a present a pencil box full of attractive things. A box was provided into which he could deposit, unobserved, whatever objects (if any) he wished to donate to poor children. Covert markings allowed the investigators to score the child on generosity.

Each pupil took some arithmetic tests when working "for himself," i.e., with his name on the paper and a prize offered for high score. In another set of tests his scores were to be counted in the group's score, but he did not sign his individual paper. The similarity in the two scores presumably represented how much effort he put out for the group good.

Other tests dealt with self-control and persistence. The tests were intended only for research, and were not made part of the school record.

The value of using measurements instead of opinions is suggested by the scores of the two sexes. Two comparisons were made: how honestly the boys and girls behaved, and how teachers rated their honesty. As Table 41 shows, more boys than girls resisted temptation on most of the tests. In contrast, teachers rated girls as more honest than boys by a wide margin. Girls' measured conduct was slightly better than boys' in some traits, but in reputation they were undeservedly far above the boys. This is reminiscent of the bias found in teacher's academic marks (page 551).

On the character tests, an average score was computed for the whole series. This average measure of resistance to temptation and altruism is an index of character, but it has little meaning. Even if we consider only tests of honesty, we find many pupils with scores near 50 per cent. With such a score, we cannot predict whether this pupil will or will not yield to the next temptation he encounters. The child ranges from honest to dishonest depending on what the situation means to him (unless honesty is an "irrationally" ingrained value). Some children took coins because they wanted money badly and felt that they hurt no one in stealing school money. The same children might never take another child's unguarded lunch money. Others no doubt enjoyed the sense of daring in taking money under the teacher's nose; they found no such reward in the dotting test. Hence their conduct was not determined by honesty alone. If two situations present different goals and different threats to a pupil, it is unreasonable to expect that he will react to them in the same way.

TABLE 41

Performance of boys and girls on character tests (from Hartshorne and May, 1928)

| | Percentage who cheated | | |
Test	Boys	Girls	Difference
Peeping in dotting test	79	85	6*
Peeping in a party game	38	68	30*
Cheating in grading own school papers	31	34	3
Cheating in grading own schoolwork at home	30	37	7*
Working on speed test after time is called	39	35	−4

* Difference between sexes too large to have occurred by chance.

To catalog actions in terms of a trait name is to give an external description. Acts that spell "honesty" or "bravery" to an observer may mean something quite different to the performer. When a character is examined for its own consistency, rather than by the observer's idea of what things should go together, unity is found. Mack's respect for honored American figures seems inconsistent with his antagonism for less distinguished individuals. When we see this in terms of Mack's need to be independent and his fear of competitors, it is thoroughly consistent. Margaret is persistent in working on a job in an office, but not at all persistent in her personal life. The explanation that unifies the seeming inconsistency is Margaret's neurotic fear of doing anything that might cause her to lose love.

JUDGMENTAL TESTS.   The character tests described above are behavioral, designed under the assumption that character consists of broad or narrow habits, i.e., of acts. But we have looked on character as a decision-making operation. To test the deeper aspect of character we need to investigate how the child reasons when confronted with a moral problem. The most practical way to proceed is to use verbal questions like those of a general mental test; indeed, a few such items are included in the Binet and Wechsler tests of "intelligence." Durkin (1959a, b), following the lead of Piaget (1932), presented questions like these in an interview:

> One morning in school a boy named Keith took a ruler off Russell's desk and wouldn't give it back to him. What should Russell do? Why? What if Keith had taken the ruler and broken it in two? What should Russell have done then? Why?

In using such questions, one must keep in mind that people who give "good" verbal responses may not act nobly (see Corey's study, page 646). But one can assume that a person who recommends a selfish or aggressive act is likely to act in that way.

Piaget, it will be recalled, has been interested in the "conservation principles" shown in intellectual development. The child learns to adjust quantities, weights, and the like to restore balance. Piaget has suggested that

TABLE 42

The child's moral interpretation varies with the situation (Durkin, 1959b)

	Percentage of pupils recommending "reciprocal" action in Grade		
Type of injury	II	V	VIII
Refusal to share property	72	39	17
Defaming one's character	50	21	6
Taking one's property	7	5	3
Destroying one's property	11	10	0

the childish behavior of "getting even" can be looked on as a similar restoration of equilibrium. Durkin classified pupils' responses according to whether or not they used the reciprocity principle—"treat him as he treated you." The results (Table 42) show a marked trend with advance in grade, and marked differences from one type of conflict to another. With maturing, new principles are acquired. The pupil does not apply a newly learned abstract principle uniformly over every situation.

13. How can you explain the behavior of a child who did not take money or cheat on arithmetic tests, but who did peek on the dotting test?

14. How can you explain the girls' greater tendency to cheat in a party game than in the dotting test?

15. Pupils who cheated on an arithmetic test were not the same ones who cheated on a spelling test (McNally, 1950). Explain.

16. Bright children display higher scores on behavioral character tests than average children. Explain.

17. How would a conformer be expected to respond on Durkin's test? A child with a rigid conscience?

18. In one character test, pupils check a list of words, marking those whose meaning they know. Then a test is given to see if they really know the words. Does the number of words checked but not truly known indicate the same sort of dishonesty that the dotting and coin tests show?

CHARACTER AND AUTHORITY

The way the child comes to terms with authority is at the center of personality and character formation. One child may reject authority if he cannot receive rewards by doing as authority demands. Lacking identification, he may never become committed to moral values, and may defy them. Margaret is at the other extreme of reaction to authority. She found it so necessary to do what authority suggested that she completely denied herself freedom to pursue her own course. She showed neither commitment nor self-acceptance.

Defiance and Delinquency

Delinquency represents a failure of learning, and mental ability can be a predisposing factor. But delinquent behavior arises out of the interaction of multiple factors, as Vernon Jones (1946, p. 717) makes clear:

. . . neither feeble-mindedness nor dullness in and of itself produces juvenile delinquency. There are always mediating factors. It is probable, for example, that low mental ability leading to difficulties and frustrations at school is one important mediating factor. It is possible that abilities to foresee consequences of one's acts are dimmed and the capacities to visualize possible punishment ahead are weak as a result of dullness. This may be a second factor. Moreover, when dullness is combined with the inferior home background that ordinarily accompanies it, the training is likely to be defective, the prestige of the family as a restraining force is likely to be negligible, and the individual aspiration level is likely to be low.

Statistically, delinquency is about equally likely at any ability level. The majority of delinquents are normally bright, and some are superior; one or two criminals show up even in Terman's collection of mentally gifted cases.

Delinquents are frequently self-centered, though more often at the superior, more realistic expedient level than at the amoral level. Those who violate social norms are usually antagonistic to them. A hidden observer watched students at work on a series of tasks. When the tests became difficult and frustrating, some students cheated and some did not. Thirty-one per cent of the cheaters were openly angry about the problems. None of the noncheaters showed resentment; if anything, they seemed to blame themselves. We get a picture of the cheaters as quick to rebel, to express emotion, and to expect the world to impose on them (Mackinnon; see Murray, 1938, pp. 491–95).

Glueck and Glueck (1950) compared delinquents in an institution with a matched group of boys in school (Figure 138). Each personality was assessed by an expert who studied the boy's projective test records, the two groups of records being mixed so he could not identify which was which. The difference between the two groups was marked. The delinquents were far more independent, more excitable, and less controlled. The nondelinquents were more submissive, their impulses more controlled. A serious fault of the study is that it describes only the delinquents in a corrective institution. Perhaps they differ from the delinquents who do not get sent to institutions. Nor can we rule out the possibility that treatment in prison has altered their personalities.

The solitary law-breaker is usually expressing in his behavior the tensions arising from poor childhood relations with authority. The aggressive delinquent has failed to find satisfactory affection at home, and has failed to achieve self-respect in school and work (Healy and Bronner, 1938, p. 201). His most rewarded tries have been his aggressions. Violence confirms his pride in his toughness and independence, brings him admiration from some of his peers and a sort of "revenge." In a follow-up study of boys reared in a slum neighborhood, McCord *et al.* (1959, p. 169) found a substantial relation between home discipline and likelihood of becoming a criminal. Their findings echo those of Bandura and Walters and R. R. Sears *et al.* (pages 148–56 above).

Consistent discipline, whether of a punitive or love-oriented nature, tended to prevent criminality. Lax discipline resulted in a relatively high proportion of

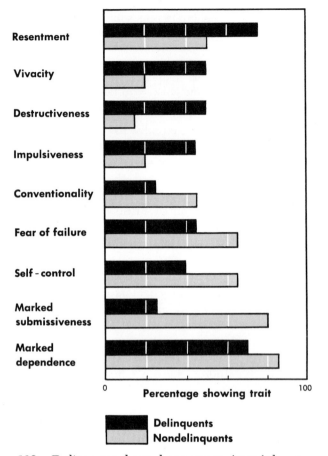

Resentment

Vivacity

Destructiveness

Impulsiveness

Conventionality

Fear of failure

Self - control

Marked
submissiveness

Marked
dependence

0   Percentage showing trait   100

◼ Delinquents
▨ Nondelinquents

138   *Delinquent boys have more forceful per-
      sonalities (after Glueck and Glueck, 1950)*

criminals. . . . Nevertheless, criminals disciplined in a lax manner were more
likely to reform than criminals disciplined in an erratically punitive way. . . .
Boys disciplined in this manner were most likely to commit every type of crime,
except traffic violations.

The relations of home backgrounds to types of crimes committed led to
these interpretations (McCord *et al.*, 1959, p. 151):

Property crimes seem to be motivated primarily by a desire for attention and,
to some extent, for material welfare. Property criminals had been emotionally
and materially neglected by both their mothers and fathers. . . . [One can
argue that] early family neglect gives rise to deep feelings of rejection and
deprivation; the lack of consistent discipline leads to a rebelliousness unchecked
by internalized inhibitions. . . .

Crimes against the person appear to be a reaction against maternal domination or paternal rejection. Retaliation against the cruelty or neglect of their fathers and the overprotectiveness of their mothers seems to be the primary motivation. . . .

Sexual crimes apparently stem from thwarted desires for maternal affection. . . . The socially accepted modes of expressing affection are inhibited in the child. He then turns to deviant ways of expressing affection, because these patterns of behavior have not been forbidden in early life by the parents.

The motivation for *traffic crimes* appears to be a search for mastery or power. On the one hand, the traffic criminal may be seeking an escape from the domination of an overprotective mother. On the other hand, he may be seeking recognition to compensate for the emotional passivity of his mother.

A part of the supporting evidence for these conclusions is the accompanying table. Other information—particularly the moral strength and the attitude of the father, and the character of the social environment—must be added to these facts on the mother's role to understand the genesis of delinquent personality. It is clear that criminality is most likely if the boy has been unable to establish emotional security and independence.

Some clinical studies (Wattenberg and Balistrieri, 1950; Hewitt and Jenkins, 1946) indicate that not all delinquents are maladjusted and emotionally at odds with authority. The gang delinquent may be a secure person conforming to the subculture in which he finds himself. His peers accept and reward him, and lead him into conduct that the larger society disapproves. His lack of firm values which would cause him to reject this conduct as improper can perhaps be traced to ineffectual parents or parents who themselves have weak moral standards. McCord *et al.* (pp. 195 ff.),

TABLE 43

Delinquency expresses tensions arising in the home (from McCord et al., 1959, p. 153)

Attitude of mother	Percentage of boys convicted of each type of crime			
	Property crimes	Crimes against the person	Sex crimes	Traffic violations
Neglecting	**64**	**16**	**16**	16
Passive	45	0	14	**50**
Cruel	32	5	0	27
Overprotective	31	**10**	5	**42**
Loving	27	2	2	20
All mothers	34	6	5	28

Figures in **boldface** are significantly higher than the average, considering the number of cases in the group.

on the other hand, insist that even the gang delinquent is aware of moral standards but selfishly chooses to ignore them. Whether all delinquents are maladjusted is therefore a controversial question.

Conformity

The conforming character fits in easily to his group, whether the group be "good" or "bad." Getting along with others is his principal guide to conduct. Such a personality is obviously formed by successful experience in gaining acceptance from others. A child who feels secure with his parents will expect to be approved when he follows their example. If he has been consistently accepted by his social group, he will expect satisfying consequences when he continues to use their standards as his own. Some persons never grow beyond a conforming level. Their moral complexion changes as they go from group to group. Pupils of this pliable type tend to be optimistic, confident, popular, and active in school affairs (Havighurst and Taba, 1949; F. J. diVesta, cited by Woodruff, 1951, pp. 339–51). They tend not to drive toward great school achievement, though they get along fairly well. Jeanne (see Chapter 4) had many of these characteristics. But our study of her was made early (eighth grade); an articulate moral philosophy is not to be expected at this point. The fact that conformers are usually at ease is not entirely a good sign, according to results on the "conformity test," which asks the subject to tell which of three lines is longest, after two other subjects have spoken. These others are confederates of the experimenter, trained to agree on a clearly false answer. The subject who gives the same false answer is obviously conforming to group pressure instead of responding realistically. College students who admit to various worries and dissatisfactions with themselves conform only half as frequently as students who have low anxiety scores (Mangan *et al.*, 1960).

The irrational-conscientious have a strong need to come to terms with authority. Doing what is right is essential to their self-respect. Temptations to violate moral rules arouse fear of punishment. Therefore we find a large group of submissive people who have firmly learned a code and who get along well with authority. They often are timid and self-critical, though they may instead be like Mack's father, overbearing and self-righteous (Peck and Havighurst, 1960, p. 95).

> They are "pillars of the church and of the community"; and often seem just about as warmly human as so many stone pillars. . . . They do not have any very positive or warm self-acceptance. . . . They take some cold satisfaction from rigorously observing the letter of the law. That is about the extent of their joy in living.

Rational Self-discipline

We complete this résumé of the way relations with others channel character development by considering the rational, altruistic. We lack studies of rational adult character, for work on adult character has largely been confined to neurotics and criminals. We do have studies of adolescents in whom personal moral standards are still developing (Havighurst and Taba, 1949; Peck and Havighurst, 1960). The rational adolescent is continually shuttling between conformity and independence. He has enough self-respect to think for himself, but enough respect for others to feel uncertain when he disagrees with them. His home is harmonious, reasonably lenient, democratic, and highly consistent, all of which help him learn discriminations between good and bad conduct. He has identified with parents and learned to want to do right. He has not become so dependent on parent approval or peer approval that he fears to disagree. This results from balanced developmental learning.

To summarize: The self-centered person fails to accomplish developmental tasks of relating to authority and winning self-respect in normal ways; independence is disproportionately important. The conformer places too much importance on peer approval. The irrational-conscientious person has wanted adult or community approval, and finds self-respect in following the code endorsed by authority. He remains dependent on the rules set down by his identifying figures, even after they have left the scene. The rational character permits one value or another to take precedence according to the situation. Such a person finds self-respect in self-direction. He does not, however, slip into that neurotic independence which makes a person do things just because they are unconventional, nor into a "Bohemian" independence that is just another form of conformity.

As a way of bringing the preceding sections together, Table 44 provides a brief outline. The amoral character is omitted, since truly amoral cases have been removed from school before adolescence. It is important to remember that the chart indicates some common combinations. Each individual works out a relationship all his own. One can certainly not conclude that every person with high ability and a democratic home will have a rational character in adolescence.

19. Recall the following case reports and discuss the probable character level of each individual:

a.	Clark	(page 137)	**d.** Olive	(page 141)
b.	Diana Mitchell	(page 577)	**e.** Barbara Singer	(page 152)
c.	Charley Mitchell	(page 577)		

TABLE 44

Summary of common constellations of adolescent character

Level of character integration	Factors predisposing to this pattern	Feeling about parents	Feeling about peers	Feeling about self
Self-centered, expedient	Rejectant or neglecting home	Feels rejected and rejecting	Rejects most of group but may find some supporters	Discontented, strives actively for power, independence, or momentary goals
Conventional, conforming	Pleasant appearance and good physique	Feels loved and secure	Feels loved and secure	Self-satisfied No apparent anxiety
Irrational-conscientious	Any handicap that might arouse inferiority feeling Dominant, severe home	Feels likely to be rejected if conduct is bad Little open conflict	Not close to peers Thinks of them as vaguely threatening	Secure if able to live within his code, but anxious when conflicting aims arise
Rational, altruistic	High mental ability Democratic home or mildly dominant home Bases for approval and disapproval made clear	Respects and loves parents but feels safe in acting independently	Often feels somewhat isolated	Believes in own ability but not complacent

20. What changes in conduct would you anticipate if an adolescent of each of the four common types moved from a strict, religious small town to a large city high school where group standards are much less strict?

21. Which type of pupil would teachers usually enjoy most?

22. From all the information you now have, what age seems most important for character formation?

23. Peck and Havighurst (1960, p. 151) find that moral character as rated by psychologists on the basis of tests and interviews correlates .70 with marks of high-school pupils. How can this very high correlation be explained?

24. In a small community adolescents were asked individually to name adults who represented desirable qualities. Those at the lower levels of character development appear to select less admirable persons as models; some adults named are shiftless and a bit disreputable (Peck and Havighurst, 1960, p. 153). How is this choice of models to be explained?

PROCEDURES FOR TEACHING CHARACTER

Providing Repetitive Practice to Form Habits

One of the popular conceptions of character is that it consists of specific habits and that frequent repetitive practice is the method of making sure such habits are fixed. This idea has never been more eloquently put than by William James (1890, I, pp. 121 ff.) in his famous essay on habit:

> Habit is thus the enormous flywheel of society, its most precious conservative agent. It alone is what keeps us all within the bounds of ordinance, and saves the children of fortune from the envious uprisings of the poor. It alone prevents the hardest and most repulsive walks of life from being deserted by those brought up to tread therein. . . . It is well for the world that in most of us, by the age of thirty, the character has set like plaster, and will never soften again. . . .
>
> The great thing, then, in all education, is to make our nervous system our ally instead of our enemy. It is to fund and capitalize our acquisitions, and live at ease upon the interest of the fund. For this we must make automatic and habitual, as early as possible, as many useful actions as we can. . . . There is no more miserable human being than one in whom nothing is habitual but indecision, and for whom the lighting of every cigar, the drinking of every cup, the time of rising and going to bed every day, and the beginning of every bit of work, are subjects of express volitional deliberation. Full half the time of such a man goes to the deciding, or regretting, of matters which ought to be so ingrained in him as practically not to exist in his consciousness at all. . . .
>
> Never suffer an exception till the new habit is securely rooted in your life. Each lapse is like letting fall a ball of string which one is carefully winding up; a single slip undoes more than a great many turns will wind again. Continuity of training is the great means of making the nervous system act infallibly. . . .
>
> As a final practical maximum. . . : Keep the faculty of effort alive in you by a little gratuitous exercise every day.

An extract scarcely does justice to the full panorama of James's argument, but the point of view is clear. Whereas this chapter has stressed reason and feelings as the great flywheels, James saw most action as the running off of automatic habits.

The educational methods consistent with this doctrine called for practice and more practice. One can train the pupil to head every paper in exactly the same way, with a neat one-inch margin on all sides. If the teacher is consistent enough with reinforcement, the pupil will perform this little trick perfectly every day. But the great fault of repetitive practice is that it will not transfer adaptively unless the teaching is directed toward understanding.

Suppose the pupil is to "form the habit of generosity." How might the habit theory suggest that he be taught? He would be given occasions to be generous in charity drives, to prepare Thanksgiving baskets, and the like. Theoretically, each time he places his dime or his can of food on the class pile, his "habit of giving" is strengthened. But what does the act mean in the light of our theory of learning? What is the child's goal? What interpretation does he make? The pupil, confronted with the announcement of a drive, knows that he must choose between getting the money and not contributing. Some get the money easily by asking at home; they face no conflict. Consider, however, the pupil who knows that his father will be angry at the request, or embarrassed by a lack of funds. This child sees that not contributing will be conspicuous and unpleasant. (While teachers surely do not want to embarrass the poorer child, the daily reminder that some pupils have "forgotten" the campaign is a punishment.) In the end, to avoid a specific unpleasant consequence at school, the child gets the money if he can. This try is confirmed: no one bothers him until the next drive. He does not, however, form a habit of being generous. When he will be criticized for not giving publicly, he will give publicly. If no criticism seems likely, he will not be generous, for giving was a response intended solely to avoid criticism. Giving acquires no positive value for him. In fact, the tension aroused may make charity drives unpleasant to him.

The picture in the school is scarcely as black as this, partly because educators now recognize that the *idea* of self-sacrifice can be developed without drill. Discussions communicate values to those pupils who identify with the teacher. Activities are selected that involve doing something for others that the child can do and will enjoy doing. This is better than using him as an intermediary to collect money from home. Proper experiences make contributing satisfying, rather than a way of escaping from annoyance.

"Habits of conduct" may not transfer. In the boys' club (page 512) where boys were strongly directed so that they "practiced" persistence and co-operation, the orderly atmosphere disintegrated as soon as the leader left. For the expedient, an act loses its point when the promise of reward or the threat of punishment is removed. The conformers and the conscientious are more likely to retain the behavior, not because of extensive practice but because a new aim was communicated which they were willing to adopt. To teach standards of conduct is to teach new meanings for situations, not to instill thoughtless habits.

    25. Describe school procedures that employ repetitive practice to teach
        a. patriotism
        b. responsibility in carrying out duties

Teaching General Verbal Principles of Conduct

Talking and reading about good behavior has been relied on to build character by both religious and secular educators. School readers have generally used stories designed to inspire high ideals, McGuffey's series being the most famous example. Educators have always hoped that history, literature, and other subjects would contribute to character, though we have nothing beyond anecdotes to show that such hopes are sometimes realized. The place of verbal education in attitude formation was discussed at length in Chapter 13; here we review principles along with a limited amount of new evidence.

Explicit value generalizations can be formed through verbal education. Discussing, for example, why everyone's ideas should be considered in group planning formulates an abstract concept. The concept clarifies why the policy is expected to work. Unless principles are pulled out for explicit examination, pupils can learn desirable conduct in one situation without ever forming a general concept of honesty, foresight, or democratic practices, or without making the subtle discriminations that help them to know where a generalization applies.

Some of the earliest experiments on character education (Voelker, 1921) confirmed the importance of verbal concepts. Fifty-seven boys were divided into six small patrols. First the experimenter tested character with instruments of the sort we described earlier (page 633). Then two patrols were given the usual boy scout training, which mentioned honesty and other such concepts but primarily provided "practice" in group activities. Two "experimental" patrols were given many opportunities to discuss moral principles along with their activities. A continual effort was made to clarify and emphasize a code of good conduct. The last two groups, used as a control, received no scout training and no discussion of good conduct. By far the greatest gains on final tests were made by the experimental group. The patrols that merely experienced an activity program made only slight gains over the control group. So also, a study of neatness (Ruediger, 1908) demonstrated that requiring pupils to do their arithmetic lessons neatly did not improve their other work. When the practice was supplemented by class discussion about the value of neatness, pupils began to examine their work in other situations to see that it conformed to this ideal. That is, they accepted a new goal and they used it to judge their conduct when no authority was insisting that they do so. The experiments cited in connection with group planning (Chapter 15) confirm the merit of making aims conscious.

Verbal education runs a great risk of being verbalistic education. A pupil can learn the words without learning the sense and without accepting the principle as his own. The learner should surely try his principles in real situations so that he can see how they operate. Many adults who endorse civic participation, for instance, do not actually participate because they have no realistic idea of how to get things done for the good of the community. The pupils who set out to change the city bicycle ordinance learned a great deal about what civic participation is like and what consequences can be expected. They learned, for instance, that a moment of dabbling does not get results, that civic change comes only with persistent endeavor. Students thus acquire a level of aspiration that fits the facts. When as adults they perceive a civic problem, there is a good chance of their attacking it realistically (Douvan and Walker, 1956).

Verbal principles have only a surface influence unless the person incorporates them into his ideal. Too many studies have found, as Corey (1937) did, that what people say is better than what they do. Some pupils who express high standards still act selfishly when it is safe. Corey asked college students what they thought about cheating on tests, and to no one's surprise they stated that cheating is sinful and contrary to the cheater's best interests. The next step was to find out if they would cheat, given a good chance. After each Friday quiz, Corey left the papers unmarked and passed them out in class on Monday for each person to grade his own. Then Corey compared the scores on the papers with the grades he had secretly recorded before returning them on Monday. In five weeks, only one-quarter of the class consistently refrained from changing answers to raise their scores. Whether or not a person was honest had no relation to the attitude he expressed (correlation of .02). Indeed, in another study delinquents were found to have *more* moral and religious knowledge than nondelinquents (E. R. Bartlett and Harris, 1936).

> **26.** Does having a student government promise that students will practice democratic attitudes? that they will acquire these attitudes as conscious ideals?

Efforts to Improve Emotional Adjustment

A large part of the behavior we consider undesirable is a reflection of tension and insecurity. Hence anything the school does to enhance self-acceptance promotes good conduct.

REDUCTION OF FRUSTRATION.   The first concern of the school should be to make sure that its policies and techniques do not create or intensify emotional strains. The youngsters who *cause* difficulty in school are those who have *had* difficulty in school. Mullen (1950) studied pupils aged 9 to 16 who had caused classroom discipline problems or who had been truants. Of this group of over 1,000 pupils, an impressive number had suffered from remediable physical and educational handicaps. The two types of maladjustment to school seemed to have different determinants (see Table 45). The truants came from unsatisfactory home situations: families on relief, broken homes, crowded homes, and the like. The children who caused discipline problems were merely restless and impulsive. These findings are consistent with other research on delinquents reported above, and also with Ullman's study of high-school boys who do and do not graduate (page 184).

Children from reasonably well-to-do homes, especially children bound for college, are given much more emotional support and more teacher approval; they capture the class offices, and they predominate in the extracurricular activities (except athletics). All too often school life is a source of irritation rather than support for the less favored pupils.

Esther, is 16, beginning to date boys and to hold a part-time job. She had been merely an obscure and average participant in school, but as a junior she and a friend tried out as cheerleaders. Three popular girls went out for the activity, helped each other practice, and easily won the tryout from Esther and her friend. This one thwarting could not have been the sole cause of Esther's irritation, but it was soon followed by truancy, which resulted in complaints from the school to her parents. At this point a field worker interviewed Esther and obtained this comment (Havighurst and Taba, 1949, p. 39):

> The way a lot of us girls are treated here, you just can't blame us for the way we feel. Frankly, for a lot of us, there's nothing but just coming to classes,

TABLE 45

Disorder and truancy reflect deeper frustrations (Mullen, 1950)

| | Percentage showing each factor among preadolescents | |
Background factor	Truants	Classroom discipline problems
Repeated one or more grades	64	60
Interrupted attendance	34	21
Reading disability	27	25
Defective teeth	49	41
Defective vision	30	28
Broken home	53	31
Poor work habits	14	53

and listening to the teacher, and reciting our lessons, and studying, and going home again. We're just pushed out of things. There are a group of girls here who think they're higher than us, and they look down on us. I won't mention any names, but they're a group of girls from the wealthier families. They have a club that's supposed to be outside the school, but it's really in the school. They can do things that we can't afford, and they hog all the offices and are in all the activities. They just won't pay any attention to us. I've almost quit going to church because some of this same group go to the church that I used to go to, and there's only one girl besides myself who goes there that's not in that group. They snub us, and they won't talk to us. Now, I know that we're not rich. Dad's only a factory worker, and we can't afford to do a lot of things, but we'd like to be in the school activities and the school games, and things like that. But they just make us feel like we're not wanted. I went to some of the activities when I first started high school, but they just ignored us. . . . They just dance among themselves and have a good time, and we're just nobody. We're made to feel out of place, and that's just the way it is.

Many other girls expressed similar attitudes. Esther is turning more and more to dates with young men out of school. She stays out fairly late and her reputation suffers. This makes it harder for her to get dates with the "better" boys. Thus programs that are good in principle, like clubs, offices, and dances, intensify the emotional difficulties of some pupils unless teachers continually guard the educational values of the programs.

Making the instructional program more meaningful and better suited to pupil readiness, diagnosing the individual and helping him to remove his handicaps, adopting an acceptant teaching style—all the recommendations we have made regarding sound teaching lead to greater success and thereby contribute to mental health.

HELPING PUPILS ACCOMPLISH THE DEVELOPMENTAL TASKS.   A girl may go through school without learning to spell, and suffer only routine annoyance; but if she remains ill at ease with boys during adolescence, she must continually become more isolated and self-conscious. Failure in a developmental task leads to continued punishment. Anything the school can do to help satisfy the basic needs—affection, adult approval, peer approval, independence, competence, and self-respect—promises to improve adjustment.

In the earliest years of schooling, the teacher may offer affectionate support to the child who has not felt enough affection at home. The teacher can give the child friendship, which makes him feel comfortable and valuable. Teachers in later grades express their liking for pupils less overtly, but the adolescent too needs an adult friend with whom he can share his problems.

Warmth is especially valuable in dealing with people who feel guilty or incompetent. Therapists regard establishing friendship with the patient as an essential step in treating him. A friendly relation does not mean an indulgent one in which the pupil can "get by with anything," nor does it mean singling out a particular pupil as a favorite. A teacher can be on friendly terms with every pupil in a class and yet hold all of them responsible for worthwhile activity and for judging themselves. For the child who has always been in trouble with authorities and who feels that no one at home understands him, finding someone who expects him to do well offers him his first hope.

If school regulations seem arbitrary, or if the demands seem always to be out of reach, the pupil must regard authority as an enemy. He may come to terms by giving up his own aims and waiting to be told what to do, or he may become a rebel.

Relation to authority is the heart of character. Feeling rejected leads either to defiant selfishness or to a hangdog anxiety to appease. If a child comes to school already at odds with his parents, the teacher has difficulty serving as an identifying figure. But every teacher does win the respect and trust of some pupils who enter antagonistically. The teacher encourages such identification, as Chapters 13 and 15 explained, by approving of the pupil as a person, treating him warmly, and correcting him in a way that maintains his understanding of the standards applied and his hope for improvement. In a school where adult decisions are explained, and where pupils know that their interests and arguments will be taken into consideration, pupils learn to get along with authority. When authority is rational and directed to purposes everyone accepts, the learner sees authority as an ally. He can make a countersuggestion without the guilt feelings of a mutineer. Even some defiant pupils are won over to a cooperative, productive relationship.

Some pupils become unduly dependent. Instead of relying on their judgment, they may learn that the only safe thing to do is to follow what the teacher says. Whenever the sincere question, "What do *you* think?" is asked, the pupil who thinks for himself is rewarded. Whenever a conflict in values or interests is settled by open discussion rather than by a flat-footed decision from on high, the pupil is helped toward the precious idea that reason, not power, makes standards for conduct. This generalization is built over the years. Just as the pupil learns, if properly taught, that scientific principles make sense and can be reasoned about, so he learns that values are reasonable.

From early childhood reasoning about values can be encouraged. If a person once incorporates a slavish attitude toward ethical values set down by authority, his readiness to reason will be set back. Teaching is never neutral. Either the school from the start encourages independence of thinking, security, and maturity, or it teaches the opposite: irrational dependence and anxiety.

A second foundation of character is attitude toward peers. If the pupil rejects the group, he will not profit from their standards and may remain at the self-centered level. If he conforms anxiously, he will not be free to dissent even when others are wrong. He may need prestige so badly that he becomes hostile in competition or cheats to win. The school should give the pupil a chance to win group acceptance. We need only to list some of the procedures already discussed:

Group activities give pupils a chance to contribute and feel approved. Sociometric evidence can be used to place the student among those

"Should we help Martha pick up her things?"

139 *No age is too early for reasoning about values*

likely to give him emotional support. Isolates can be diagnosed and given special help.

The teacher can minimize competition and other practices that make some pupils feel inferior.

Curriculum units devoted to problems of social relations are helpful.

In adolescence, learning to get along with the opposite sex is a problem, sometimes a disturbing and discouraging one. Corey (1948) says,

It is common knowledge that these sexual adjustments are difficult for American youth for a number of reasons. In the first place, while they mature physiologically along about the age of fifteen, sixteen, or seventeen, a very large number of boys and girls cannot behave consistently with this physiological maturity for six or seven years. . . . This situation makes for a great deal of strain.

A second reason for the difficulty high-school children have making wholesome heterosexual adjustments is that many of their parents won't give them helpful counsel for fear of losing face. A mother who might be able to talk realistically to her daughter about the pleasures and hazards of premarital lovemaking is reluctant to do so. This would risk the fiction of parental perfection, narrowly defined, that most fathers and mothers try to perpetuate. Unmarried high-school teachers are even in a more compromising position. They are not supposed to know much about sex other than what comes out of books, and anyone can read. The consequence is that high-school boys learn about heterosexual relations from each other or from pornographic literature. Both of these sources are interesting, but neither is dependable. The interest of high-school boys and girls about sexual matters is genuine and the problem is important.

Sex is one of the areas where the rules of our society intensify emotional difficulties. Conflict and confusion can be relieved to some degree by open discussion in the classroom, and even more by a personal counselor who can talk confidentially with pupils.

Self-acceptance is enhanced by every success, and damaged by anything that makes a pupil feel ashamed or inadequate. The teacher helps by giving him satisfaction in his accomplishments and by making all criticism constructive. The latter phrase is too often a cliché. But there is a vast difference between calling an action unsatisfactory and teaching a pupil just how to reach his goal.

A common failing of schools is to save all the praise for those few pupils who are most conspicuously successful. Those who accomplish intellectual, symbolic tasks easily gain self-respect, while those who fail in such work receive no encouragement. The teachers who establish a variety of class activities so that everyone does something well foster self-respect in all pupils.

On the other hand, social achievement may get more conspicuous reward from the community than intellectual achievement (Coleman, 1960). The school newspaper exalts the socially elite, the athletes, and the political leaders. Characteristically two-thirds of the student body go through school without being known personally to the bulk of their classmates or their teachers. Some of the anonymous students are adequately self-assured and committed to their own goals; others wonder whether or not their work is really worthwhile when no one seems to care about it. One college sophomore received a certificate complimenting her excellent marks. Said she, with almost tearful pleasure. "In two years, this is the first time anyone has said anything about my work."

27. In the program you expect to teach, how can the child of limited scholastic aptitude be given a chance to develop self-respect?

28. Is it wise or unwise to require pupils to do average schoolwork, or better, before they can

    a. serve as traffic-patrol boys

    b. participate in high-school athletics

    c. attend school dances

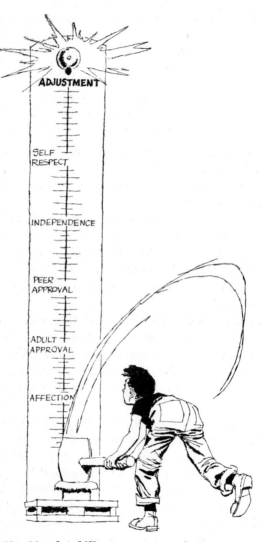

140 *Need fulfillment means adjustment*

29. Corey's statement favors "education for life adjustment." How much of the school's effort should be devoted to goals of this type?

30. In a Nebraska city there was for about 30 years a plan of rewarding junior-high-school pupils with efficiency certificates if they achieved near their ability level, participated in a range of activities, were rated high by teachers on character traits (one was nonsmoking), and, to top off the record, wrote a letter to a civic leader about a current problem. Former pupils were studied 20 years after graduation to appraise their civic conduct (Bath, 1948). What are the implications for character education of the following findings?

- a. The adults who had won certificates had sounder credit, paid their bills more promptly, participated more in church affairs, and had better jobs than those not given awards.
- b. Smoking was equally frequent among those who had won certificates and those who had not.
- c. Those who received certificates were in general those who had shown the desired traits before reaching junior high.

The Role of the School

Our chapter opened by showing that whether or not a person adopts community standards depends on his attitude toward authorities, peers, and himself. The formation of personality begins in infancy, in the emotional interaction of the person with his parents. The home lays a good foundation for the school's work in some cases and a very unpromising foundation in others.

As teachers we should not dream that we are omnipotent. The vital emotional influences of the early years instill fears and enthusiasms that are not easily changed in high school and college. The correlation of conscientiousness at age 10 with conscientiousness at age 13 is about .80; likewise for emotional independence and academic performance. Between 13 and 16, the stability of these traits is estimated at .91 to .98 (Peck and Havighurst, 1960, p. 156). The dull usually remain relatively dull, the

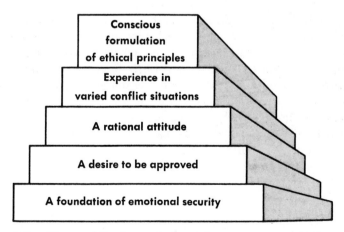

141 *The architecture of character*

selfish relatively selfish. Stephens (1961) makes this straight-from-the-shoulder comment on the teacher's handicaps in promoting moral behavior:

> Most algebraic behavior will be under the teacher's eye and he can apply as rigid a schedule of reinforcement as he chooses. This is not true for sexual behavior. In applying his schedule of reinforcement to algebraic responses, the teacher encounters little competition from other people or other agencies. If other agencies do contest his decision about the adequacy of a response, the teacher has abundant prestige to bolster his position in these matters. In sexual behavior the teacher has no such monopoly of social reinforcement.

The school cannot outweigh all the other influences on the pupil. Influence on character is personal, and the pupil is far more deeply involved with parents and peers than with the average teacher. Nonetheless, every pupil has a range of potentiality; the teacher can do much to make sure that he swings toward the best of that potentiality rather than toward the worst.

This means, first, that the school builds emotional readiness by making the pupil secure. Second, it reinforces his desire "to be good." Third, it teaches him to see ethical conflicts as problems to be solved intelligently. Then the school provides opportunities to deal with such conflicts and to gain experience in solving them. The fifth aspect of building character is to translate the experiences into conscious generalizations. The verbal summary may be brief and simple with young children; with older ones there will be occasions for discussing complex dilemmas. Out of this thinking they will create properly complex philosophies of life.

Special thought needs to be given to covering the range of important problems. For example, a program where students always interact with the teacher, having no occasion to work in groups, will confront them with none of the problems of settling disputes or delegating responsibility. Extracurricular activities and student government are of special value because they introduce problems the school subjects do not.

A person who learns to reason about his conduct and what he holds most dear can adapt to new strains and new uncertainties. We would disagree with James's view that character is "set like plaster at thirty." Character begins to set almost at the time of birth. Some of the underlying fears and pleasures are firmly set before school entrance, and the later structure of character does grow around this framework. But a person can acquire new understandings and attachment to new ideals throughout his life, if at his core he likes the world, feels that the world likes him, and believes in the power of his own intelligence.

SUMMARY

Character is imbedded in personality, and as such expresses the person's beliefs, his social relationships, and his intellectual development. The person of good character chooses acts that promote the welfare of others, and are at the same time consistent with his own goals. One cannot judge character from an act alone; one must consider the basis on which it is made. An act that merely conforms to community standards may show lack of moral judgment.

Following Peck and Havighurst we describe five levels of character: amoral; self-centered, expedient; conforming, conventional; irrational-conscientious; and rational, altruistic. The child starts at the amoral level and proceeds to some higher level on this scale. Not all of an individual's acts are at the same level, and it is not necessary to advance through the stages in order. Educators should seek to encourage rational character rather than irrational conscientiousness or conformity. The descriptions of the stages may be summarized as follows: the amoral person is unaware of or unconcerned about the effects of his acts on others, and therefore gives no consideration to their welfare. Amorality in an older person is a sign of a failure in socialization. The expedient person deliberately disregards the welfare of others when it is to his advantage to do so; he succumbs to temptation. The conformer follows the standard set by his group rather than any moral principle. He will follow his impulses, whether or not they are harmful to others, if they do not run counter to the group norm. He changes his standards when the group norm changes. The person who is irrationally controlled by his conscience is unable to violate taboos because of emotional conditioning. Thus his decisions are not free choices adapted to the realities of the situation. Rigid moral standards can contribute to maladjustment. The irrational-conscientious person has no basis for dealing with conflict situations where he must choose between values. The rational person adopts standards of conduct that he perceives to have beneficial effects, considering both his own welfare and that of others. He has a clear hierarchy of values. Even prominent, successful adults in our society make many decisions on an expedient or conforming basis.

The case of Mack demonstrates that character is a unified structure, not a collection of isolated good habits. The shape of Mack's personality was formed through his lack of maternal care and support, his need for strong masculine identification, and his success in conforming to peer standards, among other influences. Religious organizations and experience in school government seem to have reinforced his insecure conforming to authority. His need to avoid dependency adds a note of irrationality, though it also makes him effective in his work.

Character tests observe how pupils act and reason in conflict situations. The Hartshorne-May studies with objective "temptation" tests indicate that girls behave little better than boys, though they receive much more favorable ratings from teachers. A child's response varies from situation to situation. The unity of character is to be found not in a trait label such as "honest" but in the meanings of various situations for the individual. The developing child acquires new intellectual principles for analyzing social situations; the reciprocity principle, for example, is very strong in primary grades and fades out later.

Delinquency involves defiance of authority. Delinquents are bolder, more energetic, and more hostile than the average boy. Delinquency has little to do with intelligence, though failure to achieve self-respect at school may be one source of resentment against the world. Home discipline is undoubtedly far more significant. Neglect or inconsistent punishment has particularly damaging consequences; harsh but consistent discipline seems not to produce an unusual rate of delinquency. Although the greater proportion of criminals are inconsiderate and hostile, a substantial number are conformers who have adjusted successfully and passively to the subculture of a gang.

Many "good" pupils obtain such gratifying reward from doing what others do that they never develop high standards of independent morality. There is evidence that pliant conformers are less anxious than nonconformers. The irrational-conscientious are also conformers of a sort, anxiously obeying a standard from which they fear to depart. The rational character is developed by the home that encourages independence and makes it easy to discriminate between good and bad conduct. Characteristics of adolescents at each level of development are summarized in Table 44.

Character education has taken many forms. William James saw character as mere habit, and recommended practice of a good act until it becomes fixed. In schools, this theory is seen in attempts to provide practice in generosity, for example, by frequent collections for charity. Practice may develop no understanding of values, may not produce satisfaction from "good conduct," and may not transfer. Deriving principles of good conduct from the pupil's activities is helpful in forming conscious ideals. On the other hand, many people who can describe good conduct do not behave well.

Since conduct is rooted in personality, the starting point for character education is the reduction of tensions. Any activity or relationship that helps the pupil accomplish the developmental tasks and gain self-acceptance lays a foundation for rational altruistic conduct. School programs not suited to pupil readiness, on the other hand, intensify frustration and interfere with socialization. The school makes a particularly important contribution to character by helping the pupil come to terms with authority. This means that he must see authority as reasonable rather than threatening, so that he is not pushed into defiance or fearful conformity. The school is not able to overcome all the distortions of personality and values that the pupil learns in the home and the peer group. Character in late adolescence is very strongly correlated with character at age 10. But every pupil has a range of potentiality, and the school that promotes emotional security and understanding of values can help him make the most of his life.

Reading List 18

Erich Fromm, "The Emergence of the Individual and the Ambiguity of Freedom," Chapter 2 in *Escape from Freedom* (New York: Rinehart, 1941), pp. 24–39.

A thoughtful, simply written attempt to distinguish between good conduct and conformity. Freedom, says Fromm, is "freedom to"—not "freedom from." Be sure as you read that you know what common definitions of good character he would disagree with. Then decide which you yourself accept, since this is a philosophical, not a scientific, choice.

Robert J. Havighurst and Hilda Taba, "Objectives for Prairie City," Chapter 18 in *Adolescent Character and Personality* (New York: Wiley, 1949), pp. 190–204.

After studying adolescents in a midwestern high school, the authors propose a program of character education that involves contributions to the pupil's emotional, social, and intellectual growth. Detailed procedures are suggested. Other chapters in the volume offer other interesting material: descriptions of character tests, case studies of character types, and statistical findings.

Helen Heffernan *et al.*, "The Organization of the Elementary School and the Development of Personality," *California Journal of Elementary Education*, 20 (1952), 129–53. Reprinted in Fullagar.

Starting from the theory of Erikson presented in one of our readings for Chapter 4, these authors describe hazards to mental health that can be removed by changes in promotion policy, and other practices. Consider especially the authors' arguments against "departmentalization," a practice that is coming into prominence with the use of special teachers for science and some other subjects in the lower grades.

William C. Kvaraceus, *Juvenile Delinquency. What Research Says to the Teacher*, No. 15 (Washington: National Education Association, 1958), p. 32.

A survey of knowledge on delinquency, which emphasizes the importance of diagnosis and of school-community cooperation. Of special interest is the check list of 65 items developed by Mackie describing the teacher effective with potential delinquents. Would anything have to be added to or subtracted from this list to make it a sound description of the good teacher for pupils with mature character?

Gerald H. Read, "Character and Moral Education in a Collectivist Society," Chapter 18 in George Z. F. Bereday *et al.*, eds., *The Changing Soviet School* (Boston: Houghton Mifflin, 1960), pp. 405–49.

"A naive view of the Soviet Union pictures every citizen operating at the level of social conformity." This chapter describes the philosophy and practice of character education in Russian schools. Consider how the Russians would regard our definition of character and our five levels. Are their goals sufficiently different from those in the United States to make different techniques of character education desirable there? Precisely where would ideal character education for the United States differ from the practices recommended by Russian leaders?

Nevitt Sanford, "Developmental Status of the Entering Freshman," Chapter 6 in Nevitt Sanford, ed., *The American College* (New York: Wiley, 1962), pp. 253–82.

Sanford discusses typical character patterns of college freshmen, finding the majority to show what we call the irrational-conscientious pattern, lacking a mature sense of their own identity. He discusses aspects of college life that can promote or hinder future growth of character.

BIBLIOGRAPHY

Abegglen, James C. "Personality Factors in Social Mobility." *Genetic Psychology Monographs,* 58 (1958), 101–59.

Abernethy, Ethel M. "Relationships Between Mental and Physical Growth." *Monographs of the Society for Research in Child Development,* Vol. 1, No. 7 (1936).

Abrahamson, Stephen. "Our Status System and Scholastic Rewards." *Journal of Educational Sociology,* 25 (1952), 441–50.

Adorno, T. W., and others. *The Authoritarian Personality.* New York: Harper, 1950.

Allan, Mary D. "Learning Perceptual Skills: The Sargeant System of Recognition Training." *Occupational Psychology,* 32 (1958), 245–52.

Ames, Louise B. "The Sense of Self of Nursery School Children As Manifested by Their Verbal Behavior." *Journal of Genetic Psychology,* 81 (1952), 193–232.

Ammons, Robert B. "Effects of Knowledge of Performance: A Survey and Tentative Theoretical Formulation." *Journal of General Psychology,* 54 (1956), 279–89.

Ammons, Robert B., and others. "Long Term Retention of Perceptual-Motor Skills." *Journal of Experimental Psychology,* 55 (1958), 318–28.

Amos, Robert T., and Reginald M. Washington. "A Comparison of Pupil and Teacher Perceptions of Pupil Problems." *Journal of Educational Psychology,* 51 (1960), 255–58.

Anderson, G. Lester, and Arthur I. Gates. "The General Nature of Learning." In Nelson B. Henry, ed. *Learning and Instruction,* Yearbook of the National Society for the Study of Education, Vol. 49, Part 1. Chicago: Univ. of Chicago Press, 1950.

Anderson, R. C. "Learning in Discussions: A Résumé of the Authoritarian-Democratic Studies." *Harvard Educational Review,* 29 (1959), 201–15.

Anderson, Theresa. "A Study of the Use of Visual Aids in Basket Shooting." *Research Quarterly of the American Association for Health, Physical Education, and Recreation,* 13 (1942), 532–37.

Angiolillo, Paul F. "French for the Feebleminded: An Experiment." *Modern Language Journal,* 25 (1942), 266–71.

Annett, J. "Learning a Pressure Under Conditions of Immediate and Delayed Knowledge of Results." *Quarterly Journal of Experimental Psychology,* 11 (1959), 3–15.

Annis, A. D., and N. C. Meier. "The Induction of Opinion Through Suggestion by Means of 'Planted Content.'" *Journal of Social Psychology,* 5 (1934), 65–81.

Asch, Solomon E. "Studies of Independence and Conformity." *Psychological Monographs*, Vol. 70, No. 9 (1956).

Astin, Alexander W., and Sherman Ross. "Glutamic Acid and Human Intelligence." *Psychological Bulletin*, 57 (1960), 429–34.

Atkinson, John W. "Motivational Determinants of Risk-Taking Behavior." *Psychological Review*, 64 (1957), 359–72.

Ausubel, David P. "The Use of Advance Organizers in the Learning and Retention of Meaningful Verbal Material." *Journal of Educational Psychology*, 51 (1960), 267–72.

———. "Learning by Discovery: Rationale and Mystique." *Bulletin of the National Association of Secondary School Principals*, 45 (December, 1961), 18–58.

Ausubel, David P., and E. Blake, Jr. "Proactive Inhibition in the Forgetting of Meaningful School Materials." *Journal of Educational Research*, 52 (1958), 145–49.

Ausubel, David P., and others. "A Preliminary Study of Developmental Trends in Sociempathy: Accuracy of Perception of Own and Others' Sociometric Status." *Child Development*, 23 (1952), 111–28.

Bahrick, H. P., and others. "Learning Curves—Facts or Artifacts?" *Psychological Bulletin*, 54 (1957), 256–68.

Bailyn, Lotte. "Mass Media and Children: A Study of Exposure Habits and Cognitive Effects." *Psychological Monographs*, Vol. 73, No. 1 (1959).

Baker, Robert A., and Stanley W. Osgood. "Discrimination Transfer Along a Pitch Continuum." *Journal of Experimental Psychology*, 48 (1954), 241–46.

Baldwin, Alfred L. "Socialization and the Parent-Child Relationship." *Child Development*, 19 (1948), 127–36.

———. "The Effect of Home Environment on Nursery-School Behavior." *Ibid.*, 20 (1949), 49–62.

Baldwin, Alfred L., and others. "Patterns of Parent Behavior." *Psychological Monographs*, Vol. 58, No. 3 (1945).

Bandura, Albert, and Richard H. Walters. *Adolescent Aggression*. New York: Ronald Press, 1959.

Barker, Roger. "Ecology and Motivation." In M. R. Jones, ed. *Nebraska Symposium on Motivation, 1960*. Lincoln: Univ. of Nebraska Press, 1960, pp. 1–49.

Barlow, M. C. "Transfer of Training in Reasoning." *Journal of Educational Psychology*, 28 (1937), 122–28.

Bartlett, Edward R., and Dale B. Harris. "Personality Factors in Delinquency." *School and Society*, 43 (1936), 653–56.

Bartlett, F. C. *Remembering: A Study in Experimental and Social Psychology*. Cambridge, England: Cambridge Univ. Press, 1932.

———. "The Measurement of Human Skill." *Occupational Psychology*, 22 (1948), 30–38, 83–91.

———. *Thinking*. London: George Allen and Unwin, 1958.

Bath, John A. "A Study of Selected Participants and Non-Participants in a Program Designed and Directed Toward the Development of Initiative and Good Citizenship." *Journal of Experimental Education*, 16 (1948), 161–75.

Battig, W. F., and others. "Transfer and Retention of Bidimensional Compensatory Tracking After Extended Practice." *American Journal of Psychology*, 70 (1957), 75–80.

Bayley, Nancy. "Consistency and Variability in the Growth of Intelligence from Birth to Eighteen Years." *Journal of Genetic Psychology,* 75 (1949), 165–96.

———. "Mental Development." In C. W. Harris, ed. *Encyclopedia of Educational Research.* New York: Macmillan, 1960, pp. 817–23.

Benedict, Ruth. *Patterns of Culture.* Boston: Houghton Mifflin, 1934.

Bennett, Edith B. "Discussion, Decision, Commitment and Consensus in 'Group Decision.'" *Human Relations,* 8 (1955), 251–74.

Bennett, George K. "The DAT—A Seven-Year Follow-up." *Test Service Bulletin,* No. 49. New York: Psychological Corporation, 1955.

Bennett, George K., and Jerome E. Doppelt. "A Longitudinal Study of the Differential Aptitude Tests." *Educational and Psychological Measurement,* 11 (1951), 228–37.

Bennett, George K., and others. *Counseling from Profiles. A Casebook for the Differential Aptitude Tests.* New York: Psychological Corporation, 1951.

Bereday, George Z. F., and others, eds. *The Changing Soviet School.* Boston: Houghton Mifflin, 1960.

Berko, Jean, and Roger Brown. "Psycholinguistic Research Methods." In Paul H. Mussen, ed. *Handbook of Research Methods in Child Development.* New York: Wiley, 1961, pp. 517–57.

Berkowitz, Leonard, and Bernard I. Levy. "Pride in Group Performance and Group Task Motivation." *Journal of Abnormal and Social Psychology,* 53 (1955), 300–06.

Berkowitz, Leonard, and others. "Effects of Performance Evaluations on Group Integration and Motivation." *Human Relations,* 10 (1957), 195–208.

Berlyne, D. E. *Conflict, Arousal, and Curiosity.* New York: McGraw-Hill, 1960.

Bestor, Arthur. *The Restoration of Learning.* New York: Knopf, 1955.

Bettelheim, Bruno. "The Evaluation of the Appreciation of Art." In Eugene R. Smith, Ralph W. Tyler, and others. *Appraising and Recording Student Progress.* New York: Harper, 1942, pp. 276–306.

———. "Individual and Mass Behavior in Extreme Situations." *Journal of Abnormal and Social Psychology,* 38 (1943), 417–52.

Bills, Robert E. "Nondirective Play Therapy with Retarded Readers." *Journal of Consulting Psychology,* 14 (1950), 140–49.

Bilodeau, Edward A. "Some Effects of Various Degrees of Supplemental Information Given at Two Levels of Practice upon the Acquisition of a Complex Motor Skill." *Research Bulletin,* 52-15. San Antonio: Human Resources Research Center, 1952.

———. "Acquisition of Two Lever-Positioning Responses Practiced over Several Periods of Alternation." *Journal of Experimental Psychology,* 46 (1953), 43–49.

Bilodeau, Edward A., and others. "Some Effects of Introducing and Withdrawing Knowledge of Results Early and Late in Practice." *Journal of Experimental Psychology,* 58 (1959), 142–44.

Bilodeau, Edward A., and Ina McD. Bilodeau. "Motor-Skills Learning." *Annual Review of Psychology,* 12 (1961), 243–80.

Bloom, Benjamin S., and Lois J. Broder. "Problem-Solving Processes of College Students." *Supplementary Educational Monographs,* No. 73, 1950.

Blumer, Herbert, and Philip M. Hauser. *Movies, Delinquency, and Crime.* New York: Macmillan, 1933.

Boeck, Clarence H. "The Inductive-Deductive Compared to the Deductive-Descriptive Approach to Laboratory Instruction in High School Chemistry." *Journal of Experimental Education,* 19 (1951), 247–54.

Boehm, Leonore. "The Development of Independence: A Comparative Study." *Child Development,* 28 (1957), 85–102.

———. "Exploring Children's Thinking." *Elementary School Journal,* 61 (1961), 363–73.

Bond, Austin De M. "An Experiment in the Teaching of Genetics." *Teachers College Contributions to Education,* No. 797. New York: Teachers College, Columbia Univ., 1940.

Bonney, Merl E. "Personality Traits of Socially Successful and Socially Unsuccessful Children." *Journal of Educational Psychology,* 34 (1943a), 449–72.

———. "The Relative Stability of Social, Intellectual, and Academic Status in Grades II to IV, and the Interrelationships Between These Various Forms of Growth." *Ibid.* (1943b), 88–102.

Bradley, Beatrice E. "An Experimental Study of the Readiness Approach to Reading." *Elementary School Journal,* 56 (1956), 262–67.

Bradway, Katherine P., and Clare W. Thompson. "Intelligence at Adulthood: A Twenty-five Year Follow-up." *Journal of Educational Psychology,* 53 (1962), 1–14.

Braine, Martin D. S. "The Ontogeny of Certain Logical Operations." *Psychological Monographs,* Vol. 73, No. 5 (1959).

Brodbeck, May. "The Role of Small Groups in Mediating the Effects of Propaganda." *Journal of Abnormal and Social Psychology,* 52 (1956), 166–70.

Bronson, Wanda C. "Dimensions of Ego and Infantile Identification." *Journal of Personality,* 27 (1959), 532–45.

Broudy, H. S. "Mastery." In B. O. Smith and Robert O. Ennis, eds. *Language and Concepts in Education.* Chicago: Rand McNally, 1961, pp. 72–85.

Brown, Marcus. " 'Knowing and Learning.' " *Harvard Educational Review,* 31 (1961), 1–20.

Brown, Ralph R. "The Time Interval Between Test and Retest in its Relation to the Constancy of the Intelligence Quotient." *Journal of Educational Psychology,* 24 (1933), 81–96.

Brown, Roger. "What Shall a Thing Be Called?" *Psychological Review,* 65 (1958a), 14–21.

———. *Words and Things.* Glencoe, Ill.: Free Press, 1958b.

Brownell, William A. "The Evaluation of an Arithmetic Crutch." *Journal of Experimental Education,* 2 (1933), 5–34.

Brownell, William A., and Charlotte B. Chazal. "The Effects of Premature Drill in Third-Grade Arithmetic." *Journal of Educational Research,* 29 (1935), 17–28.

Brownell, William A., and Harold E. Moser. "Meaningful *Versus* Mechanical Learning: A Study in Grade III Subtraction." *Duke University Research Studies in Education,* No. 8, 1949.

Brueckner, Leo J., and Guy L. Bond. *The Diagnosis and Treatment of Learning Difficulties.* New York: Appleton-Century-Crofts, 1955.

Bruner, Jerome S. "Learning and Thinking." *Harvard Educational Review,* 29 (1959), 184–92.

Bruner, Jerome S. *The Process of Education.* Cambridge: Harvard Univ. Press, 1960.

Bryan, William L., and Noble Harter. "Studies in the Physiology and Psychology of the Telegraphic Language." *Psychological Review,* 4 (1897), 27–53.

Buck, J. V. "The Sociometric Technique and the Teaching of General Science." *School Science and Mathematics,* 52 (1952), 456–61.

Buros, Oscar K., ed. *Fifth Mental Measurements Yearbook.* Highland Park, N. J.: Gryphon Press, 1959.

Buswell, Guy T. "Fundamental Reading Habits: A Study of Their Development." *Supplementary Educational Monographs,* No. 21, 1922.

Cannon, Kenneth L. "Stability of Sociometric Scores of High School Students." *Journal of Educational Research,* 52 (1958), 43–48.

Cantoni, Louis J. "Guidance: Four Students Ten Years Later." *Clearing House,* 28 (1954), 474–78.

Cantor, Nathaniel. *The Teaching-Learning Process.* New York: Dryden, 1953.

Cantril, Hadley, and G. W. Allport. *The Psychology of Radio.* New York: Harper, 1935.

Carlson, Earl R. "Attitude Change Through Modification of Attitude Structure." *Journal of Abnormal and Social Psychology,* 52 (1956), 256–61.

Carlson, Earl R., and H. I. Abelson. *Factors Affecting Credibility in Psychological Warfare Communications.* Washington, D. C.: Human Resources Research Office, George Washington Univ., 1956.

Carroll, John B. "Knowledge of English Roots and Affixes As Related to Vocabulary and Latin Study." *Journal of Educational Research,* 34 (1940), 102–11.

Carroll, John B., and Joseph B. Casagrande. "The Function of Language Classifications in Behavior." In Eleanor E. Maccoby and others, eds. *Readings in Social Psychology.* New York: Holt, 1958, pp. 18–31.

Carter, Harold D. *The California Study Methods Survey.* Los Angeles: California Test Bureau, 1958a.

———. "The Mechanics of Study Procedure." *California Journal of Educational Research,* 9 (1958b), 8–13.

Carter, R. S. "How Invalid Are Marks Assigned by Teachers?" *Journal of Educational Psychology,* 43 (1952), 218–28.

Case, Harry W., and Arnold Roe. "An Evaluation of Auto-Instructional Techniques." Paper presented to American Psychological Association, 1961.

Castenada, Alfred. "Effects of Stress on Complex Learning and Performance." *Journal of Experimental Psychology,* 52 (1956), 9–12.

Castenada, Alfred, and D. S. Palermo. "Psychomotor Performance as a Function of Amount of Training and Stress." *Journal of Experimental Psychology,* 50 (1955), 175–79.

Castenada, Alfred, and others. "Complex Learning and Performance as a Function of Anxiety in Children and Task Difficulty." *Child Development,* 27 (1956), 327–32.

Chance, Erika. *Families in Treatment.* New York: Basic Books, 1959.

Child, Irvin L. "Socialization." In Gardner Lindzey, ed. *Handbook of Social Psychology,* Vol. 2. Cambridge: Addison-Wesley, 1954, pp. 655–92.

Child, Irvin L., and others. "Children's Textbooks and Personality Development:

An Exploration in the Social Psychology of Education." *Psychological Monographs,* Vol. 60, No. 3 (1946).

Christensen, C. M. "Relationships Between Pupil Achievement, Pupil Affect-Need, Teacher Warmth, and Teacher Permissiveness." *Journal of Educational Psychology,* 51 (1960), 169–74.

Churchill, Eileen M. "The Number Concepts of the Young Child: Researches and Studies." *University of Leeds Institute of Education Bulletin,* 17 (1958), 34–49.

Clark, Burton R. "College Image and Student Selection." In *Selection and Educational Differentiation.* Berkeley: Center for the Study of Higher Education, Univ. of California, 1959, pp. 155–68.

Cobb, Stanley. *Foundations of Neuropsychiatry.* Baltimore: Williams and Wilkins, 1958.

Cogan, Morris L. "The Behavior of Teachers and the Productive Behavior of Their Pupils." *Journal of Experimental Education,* 27 (1958), 89–124.

Coleman, James S. "The Adolescent Subculture and Academic Achievement." *American Journal of Sociology,* 65 (1960), 337–47.

———. "Social Climates in High Schools." *Cooperative Research Monograph No. 4.* Washington, D. C.: U. S. Office of Education, 1961a.

———. *The Adolescent Subculture.* Glencoe, Ill.: Free Press, 1961b.

Colville, Frances M. "The Learning of Motor Skills as Influenced by Knowledge of Mechanical Principles." *Journal of Educational Psychology,* 48 (1957), 321–27.

Cook, Walter W. *Grouping and Promotion in the Elementary Schools.* Series on Individuation of Instruction, No. 2. Minneapolis: Univ. of Minnesota Press, 1941.

Corey, Stephen M. "Professed Attitudes and Actual Behavior." *Journal of Educational Psychology,* 28 (1937), 271–80.

———. "Designing a Curriculum for Student Development." *Bulletin of the National Association of Secondary School Principals,* 32 (March, 1948), 101–10.

Corman, Bernard R. "The Effect of Varying Amounts and Kinds of Information as Guidance in Problem Solving." *Psychological Monographs,* Vol. 71, No. 2 (1957).

Coulson, J. E., and H. F. Silberman. "Results of an Initial Experiment in Automated Teaching." *Journal of Educational Psychology,* 51 (1960), 135–43.

Cox, Catharine M. *Genetic Studies of Genius.* II. The Early Mental Traits of Three Hundred Geniuses. Stanford: Stanford Univ. Press, 1926.

Cox, John W. "Some Experiments on Formal Training in the Acquisition of Skill." *British Journal of Psychology,* 24 (1933), 67–87.

"Creativity." *Carnegie Corporation of New York Quarterly,* 9 (1961), 1–7.

Cronbach, Lee J. "An Analysis of Techniques for Diagnostic Vocabulary Testing." *Journal of Educational Research,* 36 (1943), 206–17.

———. "The Meanings of Problems." *Supplementary Educational Monographs,* No. 66, 1948, pp. 32–43.

———. "The Two Disciplines of Scientific Psychology." *American Psychologist,* 12 (1957), 671–84.

———. *Essentials of Psychological Testing.* New York: Harper, 1960.

Cronbach, Lee J., and Goldine C. Gleser. *Psychological Tests and Personnel Decisions*. Urbana: Univ. of Illinois Press, 1957.

Culler, Elmer, and Edward Girden. "The Learning Curve in Relation to Other Psychometric Functions." *American Journal of Psychology*, 64 (1951), 327–49.

Cumming, Elaine, and others. "Disengagement—A Tentative Theory of Aging." *Sociometry*, 23 (1960), 23–35.

Cunningham, Ruth, and others. *Understanding Group Behavior of Boys and Girls*. New York: Bureau of Publications, Teachers College, Columbia Univ., 1951.

Damrin, Dora E. "The Russell Sage Social Relations Test." *Proceedings, 1954 Invitational Conference on Testing Problems*. Princeton: Educational Testing Service, 1955, pp. 75–84.

Davies, Dorothy R. "The Effect of Tuition upon the Process of Learning a Complex Motor Skill." *Journal of Educational Psychology*, 36 (1945), 352–65.

Davis, Allison. "Socialization and Adolescent Personality." In Nelson B. Henry, ed. *Adolescence*. Yearbook of the National Society for the Study of Education, Vol. 43, Part 1. Chicago: Univ. of Chicago Press, 1944, pp. 198–216.

Davis, Allison, and Robert J. Havighurst. *Father of the Man*. Boston: Houghton Mifflin, 1947.

Dawe, Helen C. "A Study of the Effect of an Educational Program upon Language Development and Related Mental Functions in Young Children." *Journal of Experimental Education*, 11 (1943), 200–09.

Dearborn, W. F. "Experiments in Learning." *Journal of Educational Psychology*, 1 (1910), 373–88.

DeBoer, John J., and others. *Reading for Living*. Springfield, Ill.: Illinois Curriculum Program, 1953.

de Charms and Gerald H. Moeller. "Values Expressed in American Children's Readers." *Journal of Abnormal and Social Psychology*, 64 (1962), 136–42.

de Charms, Richard, and others. "Behavioral Correlates of Directly and Indirectly Measured Achievement Motivation." In D. C. McClelland, ed. *Studies in Motivation*. Princeton: Van Nostrand, 1953, pp. 414–23.

de Groat, A. F., and G. G. Thompson. "A Study of the Distribution of Teacher Approval and Disapproval Among Sixth-Grade Pupils." *Journal of Experimental Education*, 18 (1949), 57–75.

De Haan, Robert F., and Robert J. Havighurst. *Educating Gifted Children*. Chicago: Univ. of Chicago Press, 1961.

Deighton, Lee. "A Plea for Cooperative Effort in the Study of Language." *English Journal*, 38 (1949), 218–22.

Della Piana, Gabriel M., and N. L. Gage. "Pupils' Values and the Validity of the Minnesota Teacher Attitude Inventory." *Journal of Educational Psychology*, 46 (1955), 167–78.

Deutsch, Morton. "An Experimental Study of the Effects of Cooperation and Competition upon Group Process." *Human Relations*, 2 (1949), 199–232.

Dewey, John. *Democracy and Education*. New York: Macmillan, 1916.

——. *Experience and Education*. New York: Macmillan, 1938.

DeWitt, Norman J. "Classical Languages." In C. W. Harris, ed. *Encyclopedia of Educational Research*. New York: Macmillan, 1960, pp. 211–21.

Dietrich, John E. "The Relative Effectiveness of Three Modes of Radio Delivery in Influencing Attitudes." *Speech Monographs,* 13 (1946), 58–65.

Dillon, H. J. *Early School Leavers—a Major Educational Problem.* New York: National Child Labor Committee, 1949.

Dodwell, P. C. "Children's Understanding of Number and Related Concepts." *Canadian Journal of Psychology,* 14 (1960), 191–205.

———. "Children's Understanding of Number Concepts." *Ibid.* 15 (1961), 29–36.

Dollard, John. "Hostility and Fear in Social Life." *Social Forces,* 17 (1938), 15–25.

Dollard, John, and others. *Frustration and Aggression.* New Haven: Yale Univ. Press, 1939.

Dolto, Francoise. "French and American Children As Seen by a French Child Analyst." In Margaret Mead and Martha Wolfenstein, eds. *Childhood in Contemporary Cultures.* Chicago: Univ. of Chicago Press, 1955, pp. 408–23.

Doob, L. W., and R. R. Sears. "Factors Determining Substitute Behavior and the Overt Expression of Aggression." *Journal of Abnormal and Social Psychology,* 34 (1939), 293–313.

Douglas, William O. *Of Men and Mountains.* New York: Harper, 1950.

Douvan, Elizabeth, and Alan M. Walker. "The Sense of Effectiveness in Public Affairs." *Psychological Monographs,* Vol. 70, No. 22 (1956).

Dubin, Elizabeth R. "The Effect of Training on the Tempo of Development of Graphic Representation in Preschool Children." *Journal of Experimental Education,* 15 (1946), 166–73.

Duel, H. J. "Effect of Periodic Self-Evaluation on Student Achievement." *Journal of Educational Psychology,* 49 (1958), 197–99.

Dunbar, Flanders. *Emotions and Bodily Changes.* New York: Columbia Univ. Press, 1954.

Duncker, Karl. "On Problem-Solving." *Psychological Monographs,* Vol. 58, No. 5 (1945).

Dunlap, Knight. "A Revision of the Fundamental Law of Habit Formation." *Science,* 67 (1928), 360–62.

Dunn, Lloyd M. "Mentally Retarded Children." In C. W. Harris, ed. *Encyclopedia of Educational Research.* New York: Macmillan, 1960, pp. 835–48.

Dunnette, Marvin D. "Personnel Management." *Annual Review of Psychology,* 13 (1962), 285–314.

Durkin, Dolores. "Children's Concepts of Justice: A Comparison with the Piaget Data." *Child Development,* 30 (1959a), 59–67.

———. "Children's Acceptance of Reciprocity as a Justice Principle." *Ibid.* (1959b), 289–96.

Dynes, Russell R., and others. "Level of Occupational Aspiration: Some Aspects of Family Experience as a Variable." *American Sociological Review,* 21 (1956), 212–15.

Edgerton, Harold A. *Should Theory Precede or Follow a "How-To-Do-It" Phase of Training?* New York: Richardson, Bellows, Henry, 1956.

———. *The Relationship of Method of Instruction to Trainee Aptitude Pattern.* New York: Richardson, Bellows, Henry, 1958.

Edwards, Allen L. "Rationalization in Recognition as a Result of a Political Frame of Reference." *Journal of Abnormal and Social Psychology,* 4 (1941), 224–35.

Eichorn, Dorothy H., and Harold E. Jones. "Maturation and Behavior." In Georgene J. Seward and John P. Seward, eds. *Current Psychological Issues.* New York: Holt, 1958, pp. 211–48.

Elkind, David. "The Development of Quantitative Thinking: a Systematic Replication of Piaget's Studies." *Journal of Genetic Psychology,* 98 (1961a), 37–46.

————. "Children's Discovery of the Conservation of Mass, Weight, and Volume." *Ibid.* (1961b), 219–27.

Elkins, Deborah. "Some Factors Related to the Choice-Status of Ninety Eighth-Grade Children in a School Society." *Genetic Psychology Monographs,* 58 (1958), 207–72.

English, Horace B. "Chronological Divisions of the Life Span." *Journal of Educational Psychology,* 48 (1957), 437–39.

English, Horace B., and others. "Studies in Substance Memorization." *Journal of General Psychology,* 11 (1934), 233–60.

Erikson, Erik H. *Childhood and Society.* New York: Norton, 1950.

Ervin, Susan M. "Transfer Effects of Learning a Verbal Generalization." *Child Development,* 31 (1960), 537–54.

Ervin, Susan M., and Garrett Foster. "The Development of Meaning in Children's Descriptive Terms." *Journal of Abnormal and Social Psychology,* 61 (1960), 271–75.

Escalona, Sibylle K. "An Application of the Level of Aspiration Experiment to the Study of Personality." *Teachers College Contributions to Education,* No. 937. New York: Teachers College, Columbia Univ., 1948.

Eskridge, Thomas J., Jr. "Growth in Understanding of Geographic Terms in Grades IV to VII." *Duke University Studies in Education,* No. 4, 1939.

Estes, William K. "An Experimental Study of Punishment." *Psychological Monographs,* Vol. 57, No. 3 (1944).

Evans, J. L., and others. "A Preliminary Investigation of Variation in the Properties of Verbal Learning Sequences." In A. A. Lumsdaine and Robert Glaser, eds. *Teaching Machines and Programmed Learning.* Washington, D. C.: National Education Assoc., 1960, pp. 446–51.

Fairbanks, Grant, and Newman Guttman. "Effects of Delayed Auditory Feedback upon Articulation." *Journal of Speech and Hearing Research,* 1 (1958), 1–11.

Faust, Margaret S. "Developmental Maturity as a Determinant in Prestige of Adolescent Girls." *Child Development,* 31 (1960), 173–84.

Fawcett, Harold P. *The Nature of Proof.* Yearbook, National Council of Teachers of Mathematics, Vol. 13. New York: Teachers College, Columbia Univ., 1938.

Ferster, Charles B., and B. F. Skinner. *Schedules of Reinforcement.* New York: Appleton-Century-Crofts, 1957.

Festinger, Leon. "Wish, Expectation, and Group Performance as Factors Influencing Level of Aspiration." *Journal of Abnormal and Social Psychology,* 37 (1942), 184–200.

Festinger, Leon, and others. *When Prophecy Fails.* Minneapolis: Univ. of Minnesota Press, 1956.

Fitch, Mildred L., and others. "Frequent Testing as a Motivating Factor in Large Lecture Classes." *Journal of Educational Psychology,* 42 (1951), 1–20.

Fite, Mary D. "Aggressive Behavior in Young Children and Children's Attitudes Toward Aggression." *Genetic Psychology Monographs,* 22 (1940), 151–318.

Fitts, Paul M., and others. *Skilled Performance.* New York: Wiley, 1961.

Flanders, Ned A. "Personal-Social Anxiety as a Factor in Experimental Learning Situations." *Journal of Educational Research,* 45 (1951), 110–13.

———. "The Effect of Teacher Influence on Student Attitudes." Mimeographed. Minneapolis: University of Minnesota, 1959.

Flesch, Rudolf. "The Marks of a Readable Style." *Teachers College Contributions to Education,* No. 897. New York: Teachers College, Columbia Univ., 1943.

Ford, Joseph B. "Some More on the Samoans." *American Psychologist,* 12 (1957), 751.

Fouracre, Maurice H. "Physically Handicapped Children." In C. W. Harris, ed. *Encyclopedia of Educational Research.* New York: Macmillan, 1960, pp. 995–1008.

Frankel, E. B. "The Social Relationships of Nursery School Children." *Sociometry,* 9 (1946), 200–25.

Frazier, Alexander, and Lorenzo K. Lisonbee. "Adolescent Concerns with Physique." *School Review,* 58 (1950), 397–405.

Frederiksen, Norman B., and Arthur C. F. Gilbert. "Replication of a Study of Differential Predictability." *Educational and Psychological Measurement,* 20 (1960), 759–67.

Frederiksen, Norman B., and Donald S. Melville. "Differential Predictability in the Use of Test Scores." *Educational and Psychological Measurement,* 14 (1954), 647–56.

French, Elizabeth G. "Some Characteristics of Achievement Motivation." *Journal of Experimental Psychology,* 50 (1955), 232–36.

———. "Effects of the Interaction of Motivation and Feedback on Task Performance." In J. W. Atkinson, ed. *Motives in Fantasy, Action, and Society.* Princeton: Van Nostrand, 1958, pp. 400–08.

———. "Motivation as a Variable in Work-Partner Selection." *Journal of Abnormal and Social Psychology,* 53 (1956), 96–99.

French, John R. P., Jr. "The Disruption and Cohesion of Groups." *Journal of Abnormal and Social Psychology,* 36 (1941), 361–77.

French, John R. P., Jr., and Bertram H. Raven. "The Bases of Social Power." In Dorwin Cartwright, ed. *Studies in Social Power.* Ann Arbor: Inst. for Social Research, 1959, pp. 150–68.

French, John R. P., Jr., and others. "An Experiment on Participation in a Norwegian Factory." *Human Relations,* 13 (1960), 3–20.

French, John W. "Aptitude and Interest Score Patterns Related to Satisfaction with College Major Field." *Educational and Psychological Measurement,* 21 (1961), 287–94.

French, Will W. "Secondary School Programs for Improved Living." *Bulletin of the National Association of Secondary School Principals,* 32 (May, 1948), 3–100.

Frenkel-Brunswik, Else. "A Study of Prejudice in Children." *Human Relations,* 1 (1948), 295–306.

———. "Differential Patterns of Social Outlook and Personality in Family and Children." In Margaret Mead and Martha Wolfenstein, eds. *Childhood in Contemporary Cultures.* Chicago: Univ. of Chicago Press, 1955, pp. 369–405.

Friend, Jeannette G., and Ernest A. Haggard. "Work Adjustment in Relation to Family Background." *Applied Psychology Monographs,* No. 16, 1948.

Fries, Margaret E. "The Child's Ego-Development and the Training of Adults in His Environment." In *The Psychoanalytic Study of the Child,* Vol. 2. New York: International Universities Press, 1946, pp. 85–112.

Fromm, Erich. *Escape from Freedom.* New York: Farrar and Rinehart, 1941.

———. *Man for Himself.* New York: Rinehart, 1947.

Frutchey, F. P. "Retention in High School Chemistry." *Journal of Higher Education,* 8 (1937), 217–18.

Fuchs, A. H. "The Progression-Regression Hypothesis in Motor-Skill Learning." *Journal of Experimental Psychology,* 63 (1962), 177–82.

Gage, N. L., and others. *Principles of Democracy Test.* Chicago: Science Research Associates, 1961.

Gagné, Robert M., and Larry T. Brown. "Some Factors in the Programing of Conceptual Learning." *Journal of Experimental Psychology,* 62 (1961), 313–21.

Gagné, Robert M., and Ernest C. Smith, Jr. "A Study of the Effects of Verbalization on Problem Solving." *Journal of Experimental Psychology,* 63 (1962), 12–18.

Gagné, Robert M., and others. "On the Relation Between Similarity and Transfer of Training in the Learning of Discriminative Motor Tasks." *Psychological Review,* 57 (1950), 67–79.

Gaier, Eugene L. "Selected Personality Variables and the Learning Process." *Psychological Monographs,* Vol. 66, No. 17 (1952).

Galanter, Eugene, ed. *Automatic Teaching: The State of the Art.* New York: Wiley, 1959.

Galperin, P. Y. "An Experimental Study in the Formation of Mental Actions." In Brian Simon, ed. *Psychology in the Soviet Union.* Stanford: Stanford Univ. Press, 1957, 213–25.

Gann, Ernest K. *Fate Is the Hunter.* New York: Simon and Schuster, 1961.

Gardner, John W. *Excellence.* New York: Harper, 1961.

Gates, Arthur I. "Recitation as a Factor in Memorizing." *Archives of Psychology,* No. 40, 1917.

———. "The Necessary Mental Age for Beginning Reading." *Elementary School Journal,* 37 (1937), 497–508.

———. *The Improvement of Reading.* New York: Macmillan, 1947.

Gebhard, Mildred E. "The Effect of Success and Failure upon the Attractiveness of Activities as a Function of Experience, Expectation, and Need." *Journal of Experimental Psychology,* 38 (1948), 371–88.

Getzels, J. W., and P. W. Jackson. "The Study of Giftedness: A Multidimensional Approach." In *The Gifted Student.* Cooperative Research Monograph No. 2. Washington, D. C.: U. S. Office of Education, 1960, pp. 1–18.

Gewirtz, Hava B. "Generalization of Children's Preferences as a Function of Reinforcement and Task Similarity." *Journal of Abnormal and Social Psychology,* 58 (1959), 111–18.

Ginzburg, Ralph. "Portrait of a Genius as a Young Chess Master." *Harper's Magazine,* 224 (1962), 49–55.

Glueck, Sheldon, and Eleanor Glueck. *Unravelling Juvenile Delinquency.* New York: Commonwealth Fund, 1950.

Gold, Martin, and Carol Slater. "Office, Factory, Store—and Family: A Study of Integration Setting." *American Sociological Review,* 23 (1958), 64–74.

Goldbeck, Robert A. *The Effect of Response Mode and Learning Material Difficulty on Automated Instruction.* Pittsburgh: American Inst. for Research, 1960.

Goldbeck, Robert A., and V. N. Campbell. "The Effects of Response Mode and Response Difficulty on Programed Instruction." *Journal of Educational Psychology,* 53 (1962), 110–18.

Goodenough, Florence L., and Clara R. Brian. "Certain Factors Underlying the Acquisition of Motor Skill by Pre-School Children." *Journal of Experimental Psychology,* 12 (1929), 127–55.

Goodlad, John I. "Research and Theory Regarding Promotion and Nonpromotion." *Elementary School Journal,* 53 (1952), 150–55.

Goodlad, John I., and Robert H. Anderson. *The Nongraded Elementary School.* New York: Harcourt, Brace, 1959.

Gordon, C. W. *The Social System of the High School.* Glencoe, Ill.: Free Press, 1957.

Gordon, W. M., and D. E. Berlyne. "Drive-Level and Flexibility in Paired-Associate Nonsense-Syllable Learning." *Quarterly Journal of Experimental Psychology,* 6 (1954), 181–85.

Grant, David A., and others. "Acquisition and Extinction of Responses with Different Percentages of Reinforcement." *Journal of Experimental Psychology,* 42 (1951), 1–5.

Grant, Eva I. "The Effect of Certain Factors in the Home Environment upon Child Behavior." *University of Iowa Studies in Child Welfare,* 17 (1939), 61–94.

Gronlund, N. E. *Sociometry in the Classroom.* New York: Harper, 1959.

Gross, Neal B., and others. *Explorations in Role Analysis.* New York: Wiley, 1957.

———. "Role Conflict and Its Resolution." In Eleanor E. Maccoby and others, eds. *Readings in Social Psychology.* New York: Holt, 1958.

Guilford, J. P. *Personality.* New York: McGraw-Hill, 1959.

Gulliksen, Harold. *Theory of Mental Tests.* New York: Wiley, 1950.

Haggard, Ernest A. "Socialization, Personality, and Academic Achievement in Gifted Children." *School Review,* 65 (1957), 388–414.

Haigh, Gerard V., and Warren Schmidt. "The Learning of Subject Matter in Teacher-Centered and Group-Centered Classes." *Journal of Educational Psychology,* 47 (1956), 295–301.

Hanson, Norwood R. *Patterns of Discovery.* Cambridge, England: Cambridge Univ. Press, 1958.

Harlow, H. F. "The Formation of Learning Sets." *Psychological Review,* 56 (1949), 51–65.

Harlow, H. F. "Mice, Monkeys, Men, and Motives." *Ibid.*, 60 (1953), 23–32.

Harlow, H. F., and Clinton N. Woolsey, eds. *Biology and Biochemical Bases of Behavior*. Madison: Univ. of Wisconsin Press, 1958.

Harlow, H. F., and others. "Learning Motivated by a Manipulation Drive." *Journal of Experimental Psychology*, 40 (1950), 228–34.

———. "Performance of Infant Rhesus Monkeys on Discrimination Learning, Delayed Response, and Discrimination Learning Set." *Journal of Comparative and Physiological Psychology*, 53 (1960), 113–21.

Harmon, John M., and Arthur G. Miller. "Time Patterns in Motor Learning." *Research Quarterly of the American Association for Health, Physical Education, and Recreation*, 21 (1950), 182–86.

Harmon, Lindsey R. "High School Backgrounds of Science Doctorates." *Science*, 133 (1961), 679–88.

Hartland-Swann, John. *The Analysis of Knowing*. London: George Allen and Unwin, 1958.

Hartley, E. L. *Problems in Prejudice*. New York: Kings Crown Press, 1946.

Hartshorne, Hugh, and Mark A. May. *Studies in Deceit*. New York: Macmillan, 1928.

———. *Studies in Service and Self-Control*. New York: Macmillan, 1929.

———. *Studies in the Organization of Character*. New York: Macmillan, 1930.

Hartson, L. D. "Contrasting Approaches to the Analysis of Skilled Movement." *Journal of General Psychology*, 20 (1939), 263–93.

Havighurst, Robert J. *Human Development and Education*. New York: Longmans, 1953.

Havighurst, Robert J., and Douglas M. More. "Recommended Objectives in Personal Development and Social Maturation." In *Supplement to "Elementary School Objectives."* Princeton: Educational Testing Service, 1953, pp. 84–102.

Havighurst, Robert J., and Bernice L. Neugarten. *Society and Education*. Boston: Allyn and Bacon, 1962.

Havighurst, Robert J., and Hilda Taba. *Adolescent Character and Personality*. New York: Wiley, 1949.

Healy, William, and Augusta Bronner. *New Light on Delinquency and Its Treatment*. New Haven: Yale Univ. Press, 1936.

Hebb, D. O. *A Textbook of Psychology*. Philadelphia: W. B. Saunders, 1958.

Heil, Louis M., and others. Characteristics of Teacher Behavior Related to the Achievement of Children in Several Elementary Grades. Cooperative Research Project No. 352. Mimeographed. Brooklyn: Brooklyn College, 1960.

Heist, Paul, and Harold Webster. "A Research Orientation to Selection, Admission, and Differential Education." In Hall T. Sprague, ed. *Research on College Students*. Berkeley: Center for Higher Education, Univ. of California, 1960, pp. 21–40.

Helfant, Kenneth. "Parents' Attitudes vs. Adolescent Hostility in the Determination of Adolescent Sociopolitical Attitudes." *Psychological Monographs*, Vol. 66, No. 14 (1952).

Helping Teachers Understand Children. Washington, D. C.: American Council on Education, 1945.

Henderson, Kenneth B. "Uses of Subject Matter." In B. O. Smith and R. O. Ennis, eds. *Language and Concepts in Education.* Chicago: Rand McNally, 1961, pp. 43–58.

Henderson, Richard L. A Comparison of Three Methods of Organizing and Administering Child-Study Programs in Rural Twelve-Grade Schools. Unpublished doctoral thesis. Univ. of Chicago, 1949.

Hendrickson, Gordon, and W. H. Schroeder. "Transfer of Training in Learning to Hit a Submerged Target." *Journal of Educational Psychology,* 32 (1941), 205–13.

Henry, Jules. "Docility, or Giving Teacher What She Wants." *Journal of Social Issues,* 11 (1955), 33–41.

Herr, Selma E. "The Effect of Pre-First-Grade Training upon Reading Readiness and Reading Achievement Among Spanish-American Children." *Journal of Educational Psychology,* 37 (1946), 87–102.

Hess, Robert D., and Irene Goldblatt. "The Status of Adolescents in American Society: A Problem in Social Identity." *Child Development,* 28 (1957), 459–68.

Hewitt, L. E., and R. L. Jenkins. *Fundamental Patterns of Maladjustment.* Springfield: State of Illinois, 1946.

Highet, Gilbert. *The Art of Teaching.* New York: Knopf, 1950.

Hilgard, E. R. *Theories of Learning.* New York: Appleton-Century-Crofts, 1956.

Hilgard, Josephine. "Learning and Motivation in Preschool Children." *Journal of Genetic Psychology,* 41 (1932), 36–56.

Hill, Winfred F. "Learning Theory and the Acquisition of Values." *Psychological Review,* 67 (1960), 317–31.

Hoffman, Lois W., and others. "Parental Coerciveness, Child Autonomy, and Child's Role at School." *Sociometry,* 23 (1960), 15–22.

Hoffman, Martin L. "Power Assertion by the Parent and Its Impact on the Child." *Child Development,* 31 (1960), 129–44.

Holland, James G., and B. F. Skinner. *The Analysis of Behavior.* New York: McGraw-Hill, 1961.

Holland, John L. "Creative and Academic Performance Among Talented Adolescents." *Journal of Educational Psychology,* 52 (1961), 136–47.

Horn, Thomas D. "A Comparison Between Correct Spelling in School Assignments and Correct Spelling As Measured by Spelling Tests." Paper presented to American Educational Research Association, 1961.

House, Betty J., and David Zeaman. "The Transfer of a Discrimination from Objects to Patterns." *Journal of Experimental Psychology,* 59 (1960), 298–302.

Hovland, Carl I., and others. *Experiments on Mass Communication. The American Soldier,* Vol. 3. Princeton: Princeton Univ. Press, 1949.

———. *Communication and Persuasion.* New Haven: Yale Univ. Press, 1953.

———. "The Effects of 'Commitment' on Opinion Change Following Communication." In *The Order of Presentation in Communication.* New Haven: Yale Univ. Press, 1957, pp. 23–32.

Huey, Edmund B. *The Psychology and Pedagogy of Reading.* New York: Macmillan, 1912.

Hughes, Everett C. "Stress and Strain in Professional Education." *Harvard Educational Review,* 29 (1959), 319–29.

Humphrey, George. *Directed Thinking.* New York: Dodd, Mead, 1948.

Humphreys, Lloyd G. "Transfer of Training in General Education." *Journal of General Education,* 5 (1951), 210–16.

Hunnicutt, C. W., and W. J. Iverson, eds. *Research in the Three R's.* New York: Harper, 1958.

Hunt, J. McV. "An Instance of the Social Origin of Conflict Resulting in Psychoses." *American Journal of Orthopsychiatry,* 8 (1938), 158–64.

——. *Intelligence and Experience.* New York: Ronald Press, 1961.

Hurst, John G., and others. "An Approach to Evaluation in Educational Psychology Courses and Its Instrumentation." *Educational and Psychological Measurement,* 21 (1961), 445–56.

Inhelder, Bärbel, and Jean Piaget. *The Growth of Logical Thinking from Childhood to Adolescence.* New York: Basic Books, 1958. (Originally published in French, 1955.)

Israel, Joachim. "The Effect of Positive and Negative Self-Evaluation on the Attractiveness of a Goal." *Human Relations,* 13 (1960), 33–48.

Jacob, Philip E. *Changing Values in College.* New York: Harper, 1957.

——. "Social Change and Student Values." *Educational Record,* 41 (1960), 338–46.

Jahoda, Marie. *Current Concepts of Positive Mental Health.* New York: Basic Books, 1958.

Jahoda, Marie, and Eunice Cooper. "Evasion of Propaganda: How Prejudiced People Respond to Anti-prejudice Propaganda." *Journal of Psychology,* 23 (1947), 15–25.

James, William. *The Principles of Psychology.* New York: Holt, 1890.

——. *Talks to Teachers on Psychology.* New York: Holt, 1920.

Janis, Irving L., and Seymour Feshback. "Effects of Fear-Arousing Communication." *Journal of Abnormal and Social Psychology,* 48 (1953), 78–92.

Janis, Irving L., and Bert T. King. "The Influence of Role Playing on Opinion Change." *Journal of Abnormal and Social Psychology,* 49 (1954), 211–18.

Johnson, Donald M., and Henry Clay Smith. "Democratic Leadership in the College Classroom." *Psychological Monographs,* Vol. 67, No. 11 (1953).

Johnson, G. Orville, and Samuel A. Kirk. "Are Mentally Handicapped Children Segregated in the Regular Grades?" *Exceptional Child,* 17 (1950), 65–68, 87–88.

Jones, Daisy M. "An Experiment in Adaptation to Individual Differences." *Journal of Educational Psychology,* 39 (1948), 257–72.

Jones, Harold E. "Experimental Studies of College Teaching." *Archives of Psychology,* Vol. 10, No. 68 (1923).

——. "Physical Ability as a Factor in Social Adjustment in Adolescence." *Journal of Educational Research,* 40 (1946), 286–301.

Jones, Mary C. "The Elimination of Children's Fears." *Journal of Experimental Psychology,* 7 (1924), 382–90.

——. "The Later Careers of Boys Who Were Early- or Late-maturing." *Child Development,* 28 (1957), 113–28.

Jones, Mary C., and Nancy Bayley. "Physical Maturing Among Boys As Related to Behavior." *Journal of Educational Psychology,* 41 (1950), 129–48.

Jones, Mary C., and Paul H. Mussen. "Self-Conceptions, Motivations, and Inter-personal Attitudes of Early- and Late-maturing Girls." *Child Development*, 29 (1958), 491–502.

Jones, Vernon. "Character Development in Children—An Objective Approach." In Leonard Carmichael, ed. *Manual of Child Psychology*. New York: Wiley, 1954, pp. 781–832.

Jucknat, Margarete. "Leistung, Anspruchsniveau, und Selbstbewusstsein." *Psychologische Forschung*, 22 (1938), 89–179.

Kagan, Jerome. "The Concept of Identification." *Psychological Review*, 65 (1958), 296–305.

Kagan, Jerome, and Howard A. Moss. "The Stability of Passive and Dependent Behavior from Childhood Through Adulthood." *Child Development*, 31 (1960), 577–91.

Kahl, Joseph A. "Education and Occupational Aspirations of 'Common Man' Boys." *Harvard Educational Review*, 23 (1953), 186–203.

Katona, George. *Organizing and Memorizing*. New York: Columbia Univ. Press, 1950, pp. 108–36.

Keislar, Evan R. "Shaping of a Learning Set in Reading." Paper presented to American Educational Research Association, 1961.

Keislar, Evan R., and John D. McNeil. "Teaching Scientific Theory to First Grade Pupils by Auto-Instructional Device." *Harvard Educational Review*, 31 (1961), 73–83.

———. "A Comparison of Two Response Modes in an Autoinstructional Program with Children in the Primary Grades." *Journal of Educational Psychology*, 53 (1962), 127–31.

Keliher, Alice V. *Life and Growth*. New York: Appleton-Century, 1938.

Kelley, H. H., and E. H. Volkart. "The Resistance to Change of Group-Anchored Attitudes." *American Sociological Review*, 17 (1952), 453–65.

Kelly, E. Lowell. "Consistency of the Adult Personality." *American Psychologist*, 10 (1955), 659–81.

Kelly, E. Lowell. "Multiple Criteria of Medical Education and Their Implications for Selection." In Helen H. Gee and John T. Cowles, eds. *The Appraisal of Applicants to Medical Schools*. Evanston: Assoc. of American Medical Colleges, 1957, pp. 185–98.

Kemp, C. Gratton. "Children's Perception of and Performance in Self-Control." Paper presented to American Educational Research Association, 1961.

Kendler, Howard H., and Tracy S. Kendler. "Vertical and Horizontal Processes in Problem Solving." *Psychological Review*, 69 (1962), 1–16.

Kendler, Howard H., and May F. d'Amato. "A Comparison of Reversal Shifts and Nonreversal Shifts in Human Concept Formation Behavior." *Journal of Experimental Psychology*, 49 (1955), 165–74.

Kendler, Tracy S., and others. "Reversal and Nonreversal Shifts in Nursery School Children." *Journal of Comparative and Physiological Psychology*, 53 (1960), 83–88.

Keniston, Hayward. *Spanish Syntax List*. New York: Holt, 1937.

Kersh, Bert Y. "The Adequacy of 'Meaning' as an Explanation for the Superiority of Learning by Independent Discovery." *Journal of Educational Psychology*, 49 (1958), 282–92.

Kessen, William, and Clementina Kuhlmann, eds. "Thought in the Young Child." *Monographs of the Society for Research in Child Development*, Vol. 27, No. 2 (1962).

Keyes, Daniel. "Flowers for Algernon." In Judith Merrill, ed. *The Year's Best S-F.* New York: Simon and Schuster, 1960.

Keys, Noel B. "The Underage Student in High School and College." *University of California Publications in Education*, 7 (1938), 145–272.

Kimball, Solon L. "The New Social Stratification and the New Restraints on the Child in School." Paper presented to American Psychological Association, 1961.

Kimble, G. A., and J. J. Wulff. "The Effect of 'Response Guidance' on the Value of Audience Participation in Training Film Instruction." Washington, D. C.: USAF Human Factors Operations Research Laboratories, Report No. 34, 1953.

King, Richard G. The Prediction of Choice of Undergraduate Field of Concentration in Harvard College. Unpublished doctoral thesis, Harvard Univ., 1958.

King, W. H. "The Development of Scientific Concepts in Children." *British Journal of Educational Psychology*, 31 (1961), 1–20.

Kirk, Samuel A. *Early Education of the Mentally Retarded.* Urbana: Univ. of Illinois Press, 1958.

Kirkpatrick, James E. "The Motivating Effect of a Specific Type of Testing Program." *University of Iowa Studies in Education*, 9, No. 4 (1939), 41–68.

Kittell, J. E. "An Experimental Study of the Effects of External Direction During Learning on Transfer and Retention of Principles." *Journal of Educational Psychology*, 48 (1957), 391–405.

Klausmeier, Herbert J., and others. "Comparison of Organismic Age and Regression Equations in Predicting Achievements in Elementary School." *Journal of Educational Psychology*, 49 (1958), 182–86.

Kluckhohn, Clyde, and Dorothea Leighton. *The Navaho.* Cambridge: Harvard Univ. Press, 1946.

Knapp, Clyde, and Harry Combes. "Does Basketball Belong in Grade School?" *Illinois Education*, 38 (October, 1949), 64–66.

Knezevich, Stephen J. "The Constancy of the IQ of the Secondary School Pupil." *Journal of Educational Research*, 39 (1946), 506–16.

Kooker, Earl W., and Chester S. Williams. "College Students' Ability to Evaluate Their Performance on Objective Tests." *Journal of Educational Research*, 53 (1959), 69–72.

Kounin, Jacob S., and Paul V. Gump. "The Ripple Effect in Discipline." *Elementary School Journal*, 59 (1958), 158–62.

———. "The Comparative Influence of Punitive and Non-Punitive Teachers upon Children's Concepts of School Misconduct." *Journal of Educational Psychology*, 52 (1961), 44–49.

Kroll, Abraham. "The Teacher's Influence upon the Social Attitude of Boys in the Twelfth Grade." *Journal of Educational Psychology*, 25 (1934), 274–80.

Krueger, W. C. F. "Further Studies in Overlearning." *Journal of Experimental Psychology*, 13 (1930), 152–63.

———. "Influence of Difficulty of Perceptual-Motor Task upon Acceleration of Curves of Learning." *Journal of Educational Psychology*, 38 (1947), 51–53.

Krumboltz, John D., and Ronald G. Weisman. "The Effect of Overt Versus Covert

Responding to Programed Instruction on Immediate and Delayed Retention." *Journal of Educational Psychology,* 53 (1962), 89–92.

Kuvshinov, N. I. "Reshenie prakticheskikh zadach uchashchimisia nachal'nykh klassov na urokakh truda." *Voprosy Psikhologii,* 5 (1959), 48–58.

Laughlin, F. *The Peer Status of Sixth- and Seventh-Grade Children.* New York: Teachers College, Columbia Univ., 1954.

Lawrence, C. H. "The Endocrine Factor in Personality Development." *Educational Record,* 23 (1942), 88–89.

Lawrence, Douglas H. "Acquired Distinctiveness of Cues: II. Selective Association in a Constant Stimulus Situation." *Journal of Experimental Psychology,* 40 (1950), 175–88.

———. "The Transfer of a Discrimination Along a Continuum." *Journal of Comparative and Physiological Psychology,* 45 (1952), 511–16.

Lawrence, Douglas H., and W. Richard Goodwin. "Transfer in Tracking Behavior Between Two Levels of Speed." *Research Bulletin* 54-70. San Antonio: Air Force Personnel and Training Research Command, 1954.

Lawrence, L. C., and P. C. Smith. "Group Decision and Employee Participation." *Journal of Applied Psychology,* 39 (1955), 334–37.

Lawson, Reed. *Learning and Behavior.* New York: Macmillan, 1960.

Lazarus, Richard, and others. "The Effects of Psychological Stress upon Performance." *Psychological Bulletin,* 49 (1952), 293–317.

Leeds, Carroll H. "A Scale for Measuring Teacher-Pupil Attitudes and Teacher-Pupil Rapport." *Psychological Monographs,* Vol. 64, No. 6 (1950).

Leggitt, Dorothy. "Measuring Progress in Working Skills in Ninth-Grade Civics." *School Review,* 42 (1934), 676–87.

Lehmusvuori, Heimo. "The Effect of Teachers' Authoritarian and Democratic Attitudes on the Children's Level of Aspiration After Success and Failure." *Research Reports, Department of Psychology, Jyvaskyla Institute of Pedagogics,* No. 13 (1958), pp. 7–20.

Leshner, Saul S. "Effects of Aspiration and Achievement on Muscular Tensions." *Journal of Experimental Psychology,* 61 (1961), 133–37.

Levin, Harry, and Alfred L. Baldwin. "The Choice to Exhibit." *Child Development,* 29 (1958), 373–80.

Levine, Jerome M., and Gardner Murphy. "The Learning and Forgetting of Controversial Material." *Journal of Abnormal and Social Psychology,* 38 (1943), 507–17.

Lewin, Kurt. "Behavior and Development as a Function of the Total Situation." In Leonard Carmichael, ed. *Manual of Child Psychology.* New York: Wiley, 1946, pp. 791–844.

———. "Group Decision and Social Change." In Eleanor Maccoby and others, eds. *Readings in Social Psychology.* New York: Holt, 1958, pp. 197–211.

Lewis, Helen B. "Studies in the Principles of Judgment and Attitudes: IV. The Operation of 'Prestige Suggestion.' " *Journal of Social Psychology,* 14 (1941), 229–56.

Lindahl, Lawrence G. "Movement Analysis as an Industrial Training Method." *Journal of Applied Psychology,* 29 (1945), 420–46.

Lippitt, Ronald, and others. "The Dynamics of Power." *Human Relations,* 5 (1952), 37–64.

Liublinskaya, A. A. "The Development of Children's Speech and Thought." In Brian Simon, ed. *Psychology in the Soviet Union.* Stanford: Stanford Univ. Press, 1957, pp. 197–204.

Lordahl, Daniel S., and E. James Archer. "Transfer Effects on a Rotary Pursuit Task as a Function of First-Task Difficulty." *Journal of Experimental Psychology,* 56 (1958), 421–26.

Loree, M. Ray, and Margaret B. Koch. "Use of Verbal Reinforcement in Developing Group Discussion Skills." *Journal of Educational Psychology,* 51 (1960), 164–68.

Lorge, Irving. "Social Gains in Special Education of the Gifted." *School and Society,* 79 (1954), 4–7.

Lortie, Dan C. "Laymen to Lawmen: Law School, Careers, and Professional Socialization." *Harvard Educational Review,* 29 (1959), 352–69.

Lowell, Frances E. "A Study of the Variability of IQ's in Retest." *Journal of Applied Psychology,* 25 (1941), 341–56.

Lowenfeld, Viktor. *Creative and Mental Growth.* New York: Macmillan, 1957.

Lucas, J. D. "The Interactive Effects of Anxiety, Failure, and Interserial Duplication. *American Journal of Psychology,* 65 (1952), 59–66.

Luchins, A. S. "Mechanization in Problem Solving—The Effect of Einstellung." *Psychological Monographs,* Vol. 54, No. 6 (1942).

Lucito, Leonard J. A Comparison of the Independence-Conformity Behavior of Intellectually Bright and Dull Children. Unpublished doctoral dissertation. Univ. of Illinois, 1959.

Lumsdaine, A. A. "Pictorial Quality and Color." In Mark A. May and A. A. Lumsdaine, eds. *Learning from Films.* New Haven: Yale Univ. Press, 1958, pp. 18–30.

———. "Teaching Machines and Self-Instructional Materials." *Audio-Visual Communication Review,* 7 (1959), 163–81.

Lumsdaine, A. A., and Robert Glaser, eds. *Teaching Machines and Programmed Learning: A Source Book.* Washington, D. C.: National Education Assoc., 1960.

Lumsdaine, A. A., and I. L. Janis. "Resistance to 'Counterpropaganda' Produced by One-Sided and Two-Sided 'Propaganda' Presentations." *Public Opinion Quarterly,* 17 (1953), 311–18.

Luria, A. R. "The Role of Language in the Formation of Temporary Connections." In Brian Simon, ed. *Psychology in the Soviet Union.* Stanford: Stanford Univ. Press, 1957, pp. 115–29.

McCarthy, Dorothea. "Research in Language Development: Retrospect and Prospect." *Monographs of the Society for Research in Child Development,* 24, No. 5 (1959), 3–24.

McClelland, David C. "Risk Taking in Children with High and Low Need for Achievement." In J. W. Atkinson, ed. *Motives in Fantasy, Action, and Society.* Princeton: Van Nostrand, 1957, pp. 322–39.

———. "Review and Prospects." In David C. McClelland, ed. *Talent and Society.* Princeton: Van Nostrand, 1958, pp. 234–68.

———. "Encouraging Excellence." *Daedalus,* 90 (1961), 711–24.

McClelland, David C., and others. *The Achievement Motive.* New York: Appleton-Century-Crofts, 1953.

Maccoby, Eleanor E., and others, eds. *Readings in Social Psychology*. New York: Holt, 1958.

McCord, William, Joan McCord, and Irving K. Zola. *Origins of Crime*. New York: Columbia Univ. Press, 1959.

McDavid, John, Jr., and Harold M. Schroder. "The Interpretation of Approval and Disapproval by Delinquent and Non-Delinquent Adolescents." *Journal of Personality*, 25 (1957), 539–49.

McDougall, W. P. "Differential Retention of Course Outcomes in Educational Psychology." *Journal of Educational Psychology*, 49 (1958), 53–60.

Macfarlane, Jean W., and others. "A Developmental Study of the Behavior Problems of Normal Children Between Twenty-one Months and Fourteen Years." *University of California Publications in Child Development*, Vol. 2 (1954).

McGinnies, Elliott, and others. "The Effects of Sound Films on Opinions About Mental Illness in Community Discussion Groups." *Journal of Applied Psychology*, 42 (1958), 40–46.

McGraw, Myrtle B. "Maturation of Behavior." In Leonard Carmichael, ed. *Manual of Child Psychology*. New York: Wiley, 1946, pp. 332–69.

McKeachie, Wilbert J. "Anxiety in the College Classroom." *Journal of Educational Research*, 45 (1951), 153–60.

———. "Procedures and Techniques of Teaching: A Survey of Experimental Studies." In N. Sanford, ed., *The American College*. New York: Wiley, 1962, pp. 312–64.

McKeachie, Wilbert J., ed. *The Appraisal of Teaching in Large Universities*. Ann Arbor: Univ. of Michigan Press, 1959.

Mackinnon, D. W. "What Do We Mean by Talent and How Do We Test for It?" In *The Search for Talent*. New York: College Entrance Examination Board, 1960, pp. 20–29.

McMurray, Foster, and Lee J. Cronbach. "The Proper Function of Text Materials." In Lee J. Cronbach, ed. *Text Materials in Modern Education*. Urbana: Univ. of Illinois Press, 1955, pp. 28–58.

McNally, J. "A Study in Classroom Cheating in Arithmetic and Spelling." *British Journal of Educational Psychology*, 20 (1950), 137–39.

Maier, N. R. F. "An Aspect of Human Reasoning." *British Journal of Psychology*, 24 (1933), 144–55.

Maltzman, Irving. "On the Training of Originality." *Psychological Review*, 67 (1960), 229–42.

Mandler, G. "Transfer of Training as a Function of Degree of Response Overlearning." *Journal of Experimental Psychology*, 47 (1954), 411–17.

Mangan, G. L., and others. "Taylor MAS and Group Conformity Pressure." *Journal of Abnormal and Social Psychology*, 61 (1960), 146–47.

Marks, J. B. "Interests, Leadership and Sociometric Status Among Adolescents." *Sociometry*, 17 (1954), 340–49.

Marshall, Helen R. "Relations Between Home Experiences and Children's Use of Language in Play Interactions with Peers." *Psychological Monographs*, Vol. 75, No. 5 (1961).

Marx, Melvin H. "Motivation." In C. W. Harris, ed. *Encyclopedia of Educational Research*. New York: Macmillan, 1960, pp. 888–901.

May, Mark A., and A. A. Lumsdaine. *Learning from Films*. New Haven: Yale Univ. Press, 1958.

May, Rollo. *The Meaning of Anxiety*. New York: Ronald Press, 1950.

Mayer, Martin. *The Schools*. New York: Harper, 1961.

Mead, Margaret. *The School in American Culture*. Cambridge: Harvard Univ. Press, 1951.

Mead, Margaret, ed. *Cultural Patterns and Technical Change*. New York: Mentor, 1955.

Mead, Margaret, and Martha Wolfenstein, eds. *Childhood in Contemporary Cultures*. Chicago: Univ. of Chicago Press, 1955.

Meadow, Arnold, and S. J. Parnes. "Evaluation of Training in Creative Problem Solving." *Journal of Applied Psychology*, 43 (1959), 189–94.

Medinnus, Gene R. "The Relation Between Several Parent Measures and the Child's Early Adjustment to School." *Journal of Educational Psychology*, 52 (1961), 153–56.

Meehl, Paul E. "On the Circularity of the Law of Effect." *Psychological Bulletin*, 47 (1950), 52–75.

———. *Clinical Versus Statistical Prediction*. Minneapolis: Univ. of Minnesota Press, 1954.

Menchinskaya, Natalia A. "Some Aspects of the Psychology of Teaching." In Brian Simon, ed. *Psychology in the Soviet Union*. Stanford: Stanford Univ. Press, 1957, pp. 190–96.

Meredith, G. P. "The Space, Time, Language and Intellect of the Young Child." In Kenneth Soddy, ed. *Mental Health and Infant Development*, Vol. 1. New York: Basic Books, 1956, pp. 251–63.

Messick, S. J., and C. M. Solley. "Probability Learning in Children: Some Exploratory Studies." *Journal of Genetic Psychology*, 90 (1957), 23–32.

Meyer, William J. "The Stability of Patterns of Primary Mental Abilities Among Junior High and Senior High School Students." *Educational and Psychological Measurement*, 20 (1960), 795–800.

Meyer, William J., and A. W. Bendig. "A Longitudinal Study of the Primary Mental Abilities Test." *Journal of Educational Psychology*, 52 (1961), 50–60.

Meyer, William T., and George G. Thompson. "Sex Differences in the Distribution of Teacher Approval and Disapproval Among Sixth-Grade Children." *Journal of Educational Psychology*, 47 (1956), 385–96.

Michels, Walter C. "Some Lessons from High School Physics." *1958 Invitational Conference on Testing Problems*. Princeton: Educational Testing Service, 1959, pp. 17–26.

Mikol, Bernard. "The Enjoyment of New Musical Systems." In Milton Rokeach, ed. *The Open and Closed Mind*. New York: Basic Books, 1960, pp. 270–84.

Miller, D. R., and G. E. Swanson. *The Changing American Parent*. New York: Wiley, 1958.

Miller, G. A., and others. *Plans and the Structure of Behavior*. New York: Holt, Rinehart and Winston, 1960.

Miller, K. M. "Einstellung Rigidity, Intelligence, and Teaching Methods." *British Journal of Educational Psychology*, 27 (1957), 127–34.

Miller, Robert V. "Social Status and Socioempathic Differences Among Mentally

Superior, Mentally Typical, and Mentally Retarded Children." *Exceptional Child*, 23 (1956), 114–19.

Mintz, Alexander. "Non-Adaptive Group Behavior." *Journal of Abnormal and Social Psychology*, 46 (1951), 150–59.

Mischel, Walter. "Preference for Delayed Reinforcement: An Experimental Study of a Cultural Observation." *Journal of Abnormal and Social Psychology*, 56 (1958), 57–61.

Mitnick, L. L., and Elliott McGinnies. "Influencing Ethnocentrism in Small Discussion Groups Through a Film Communication." *Journal of Abnormal and Social Psychology*, 56 (1958), 82–90.

Morse, Arthur D. *Schools of Tomorrow—Today.* Garden City: Doubleday, 1960.

Moser, A. C., and B. B. David. "I Pledge a Legion." *Journal of Educational Sociology*, 9 (1936), 436–40.

Moser, Harold E. The Concept of Arithmetic Readiness; An Investigation on the Second-Grade Level. Unpublished doctoral thesis, Duke University, 1947.

Mowrer, O. Hobart. "Discipline and Mental Health." *Harvard Educational Review*, 17 (1947), 284–96.

———. *Learning Theory and Behavior.* New York: Wiley, 1960.

Mullen, Frances A. "Truancy and Classroom Disorder as Symptoms of Personality Problems." *Journal of Educational Psychology*, 41 (1950), 97–109.

Munroe, Ruth L. *Teaching the Individual.* New York: Columbia Univ. Press, 1942.

Murray, Henry A. *Explorations in Personality.* Cambridge: Harvard Univ. Press, 1938.

Mussen, Paul H. "Some Personality and Social Factors Related to Changes in Children's Attitudes Toward Negroes." *Journal of Abnormal and Social Psychology*, 45 (1950), 423–41.

Mussen, Paul H., and Luther Distler. "Child-Rearing Antecedents of Masculine Identification in Kindergarten Boys." *Child Development*, 31 (1960), 89–100.

Mussen, Paul H., and Mary C. Jones. "The Behavior-Inferred Motivations of Late and Early Maturing Boys." *Child Development*, 29 (1958), 61–67.

Mussen, Paul H., and Jerome Kagan. "Group Conformity and Perceptions of Parents." *Child Development*, 29 (1958), 57–60.

Nelson, C. Donald. "Subtle Brain Damage: Its Influence on Learning and Language." *Elementary School Journal*, 61 (1961), 317–21.

Newcomb, Theodore M. "The Consistency of Certain Extrovert-Introvert Behavior Patterns in 51 Problem Boys." *Teachers College Contributions to Education*, No. 382. New York: Teachers College, Columbia Univ., 1939.

———. *Personality and Social Change.* New York: Dryden Press, 1943.

———. "Attitude Development as a Function of Reference Groups." In Eleanor E. Maccoby and others, eds. *Readings in Social Psychology.* New York: Holt, 1958, pp. 265–75.

Newman, H. H., and others. *Twins: A Study of Heredity and Environment.* Chicago: Univ. of Chicago Press, 1937.

Noble, C. E., and W. T. Alcock. "Human Delayed-Reward Learning with Different Lengths of Task." *Journal of Experimental Psychology*, 56 (1958), 407–12.

Northway, Mary L. *A Primer of Sociometry.* Toronto: Univ. of Toronto Press, 1952.

Overman, J. R. "Experimental Study of the Effect of the Method of Instruction on Transfer of Training in Arithmetic." *Elementary School Journal,* 31 (1930), 183–90.

Owens, William A. "Age and Mental Abilities: A Longitudinal Study." *Genetic Psychology Monographs,* 48 (1953), 3–54.

Pace, C. Robert, and George G. Stern. "An Approach to the Measurement of Psychological Characteristics of College Environments." *Journal of Educational Psychology,* 49 (1958), 269–77.

Page, Ellis B. "Teacher Comments and Student Performance." *Journal of Educational Psychology,* 49 (1958), 173–81.

Palmer, Dora E. "The Play's the Thing." *English Journal,* 38 (1949), 568–71.

Palmer, H. O. Tachistoscopic Training for Beginning Typing Students in a Secondary School. Unpublished doctoral dissertation, Oregon State College, 1955.

Parnes, Sidney J., and Arnold Meadow. "Evaluation of Persistence of Effects Produced by a Creative Problem-Solving Course." *Psychological Reports,* 7 (1960), 357–61.

Parsons, Anne, and Stanley Milgram. "A Guide for Psychologists." In Bärbel Inhelder, and Jean Piaget. *The Growth of Logical Thinking.* New York: Basic Books, 1958, pp. vii–xxiv.

Parsons, Talcott. "Family Structure and the Socialization of the Child." In Talcott Parsons and Robert F. Bales. *Family, Socialization and Interaction Process.* Glencoe, Ill.: Free Press, 1955, pp. 35–131.

———. "The School Class as a Social System: Some of Its Functions in American Society." *Harvard Educational Review,* 29 (1959), 297–318.

Patrick, James R. "Studies in Rational Behavior and Emotional Excitement. II. The Effect of Emotional Excitement on Rational Behavior in Human Subjects." *Journal of Comparative Psychology,* 18 (1934), 153–95.

Patton, J. A. A Study of the Effects of Student Acceptance of Responsibility and Motivation on Course Behavior. Unpublished doctoral dissertation. Univ. of Minnesota, 1955.

Payne, Donald E., and Paul H. Mussen. "Parent-Child Relations and Father Identification Among Adolescent Boys." *Journal of Abnormal and Social Psychology,* 52 (1956), 358–62.

Peck, Robert F., and Robert J. Havighurst. *The Psychology of Character Development.* New York: Wiley, 1960.

Peel, E. A. "Experimental Examination of Some of Piaget's Schemata Concerning Children's Perception and Thinking and a Discussion of Their Educational Significance." *British Journal of Educational Psychology,* 29 (1959), 89–103.

Pei, Mario. *The Story of Language.* Philadelphia: Lippincott, 1949.

Penfield, Wilder, and Lamar Roberts. *Speech and Brain-Mechanisms.* Princeton: Princeton Univ. Press, 1959.

Pentony, P. "Home Environment and Nursery School Behavior." *Australian Journal of Psychology,* 8 (1956), 61–65.

Perkins, Hugh V. "Climate Influences Group Learning." *Journal of Educational Research,* 45 (1951), 115–19.

Perry, William G., Jr. "Students' Use and Misuse of Reading Skills: A Report to a Faculty." *Harvard Educational Review,* 29 (1959), 193–200.

Peterson, H. A. "Recitation or Recall as a Factor in the Learning of Long Prose Selections." *Journal of Educational Psychology,* 35 (1944), 220–28.

Peterson, Ruth C., and L. L. Thurstone. *Motion Pictures and the Social Attitudes of Children.* New York: Macmillan, 1933.

Physical Science Study Committee. "A Planning Conference Report." *Physics Today,* 10 (1957), 28–29.

Piaget, Jean. *The Moral Judgment of the Child.* New York: Harcourt, Brace, 1932.

———. *The Psychology of Intelligence.* London: Routledge and Kegan Paul, 1950. (Originally published in French, 1947.)

———. *Play, Dreams, and Imitation in Childhood.* New York: Norton, 1951. (Originally published in French, 1945.)

———. *The Origins of Intelligence in Children.* New York: International Universities Press, 1952. (Originally published in French, 1936.)

———. "How Children Form Mathematical Concepts." *Scientific American,* 189 (1953), 74–79.

———. *The Construction of Reality in the Child.* New York: Basic Books, 1954. (Originally published in French, 1937.)

———. "Logique et équilibre dans les comportements du sujet." *Études d'épistémologie génétique,* 2 (1957), 27–72.

Piaget, Jean, and Bärbel Inhelder. *La développement des quantités chez l'enfant.* Neuchatel: Delachaux and Niestlé, 1940.

———. *The Child's Conception of Space.* London: Routledge and Kegan Paul, 1956. (Originally published in French, 1948.)

———. *La génèse des structures logiques élémentaires.* Geneva: Delachaux and Niestlé, 1959.

Piaget, Jean, and A. M. Weil. "Le développement chez l'enfant de l'idée de patrie et des relations avec l'étranger." *Bulletin internationale des sciences sociales* (UNESCO), 3 (1951), 605–21.

Piaget, Jean, and others. *The Child's Conception of Geometry.* New York: Basic Books, 1960. (Originally published in French, 1948.)

Pitman, I. J. "Learning to Read." *Journal of the Royal Society of Arts,* 109 (1961), 149–80.

Plowman, Letha, and J. B. Stroud. "The Effect of Informing Pupils of the Correctness of Their Responses to Objective Test Questions." *Journal of Educational Research,* 36 (1942), 16–20.

Plumlee, Lynnette B. "Comparison of Problem-Types in the Comprehensive Mathematics Test." *College Board Review,* 1 (1947), 17–31.

Polya, Gyorgy. *Mathematics and Plausible Reasoning.* Princeton: Princeton Univ. Press, 1954.

Porteus, S. D. "The Validity of the Porteus Maze." *Journal of Educational Psychology,* 30 (1939), 172–78.

Powell, Marvin, and Charles D. Ferraro. "Sources of Tension in Married and Single Women Teachers of Different Ages." *Journal of Educational Psychology,* 51 (1960), 92–101.

Prescott, Daniel A. *The Child in the Educative Process.* New York: McGraw-Hill, 1957.

Pressey, Sidney L. "A Simple Apparatus Which Gives Tests and Scores—and Teaches." *School and Society,* 23 (1926), 373–76.

———. "A Machine for Automatic Teaching of Drill Material." *School and Society,* 25 (1927), 549–52.

———. "Educational Acceleration: Appraisals and Basic Problems." *Bureau of Educational Research Monographs,* No. 31. Columbus: Ohio State Univ., 1949.

———. "Development and Appraisal of Devices Providing Immediate Automatic Scoring of Objective Tests and Concomitant Self-Instructions." *Journal of Psychology,* 29 (1950), 417–47.

Pressey, Sidney L., and Francis P. Robinson. *Psychology and the New Education.* New York: Harper, 1944.

Priebe, R. E., and W. H. Burton. "The Slow Motion Picture as a Coaching Device." *School Review,* 47 (1939), 192–98.

Psathas, George. "Ethnicity, Social Class, and Adolescent Independence from Parental Control." *American Sociological Review,* 22 (1957), 415–23.

The Pursuit of Excellence (Rockefeller Report on Education). Garden City: Doubleday, 1958.

Quartermain, David, and T. H. Scott. "Incidental Learning in a Simple Task." *Canadian Journal of Psychology,* 14 (1960), 175–82.

Quay, Herbert. "The Effect of Verbal Reinforcement on the Recall of Early Memories." *Journal of Abnormal and Social Psychology,* 59 (1959), 254–57.

Radke-Yarrow, Marian, and others. "The Role of Parents in the Development of Children's Ethnic Attitudes." *Child Development,* 23 (1952), 13–53.

———. "Interpersonal Dynamics in Racial Integration." In Eleanor E. Maccoby and others, eds. *Readings in Social Psychology.* New York: Holt, 1958, pp. 623–36.

Rapp, Albert. "The Experimental Background of the Problems of Learning." *Classical Journal,* 40 (1945), 467–80.

Raven, Bertram H., and Jan Rietsma. "The Effects of Varied Clarity of Group Goal and Group Path upon the Individual and His Relation to His Group." *Human Relations,* 10 (1957), 29–44.

Ray, Willis E. "Pupil Discovery vs. Direct Instruction." *Journal of Experimental Education,* 29 (1961), 271–80.

Reece, Michael M. "The Effect of Shock on Recognition Thresholds." *Journal of Abnormal and Social Psychology,* 49 (1954), 165–72.

Reed, Horace B., Jr. "Teacher Variables of Warmth, Demand and Utilization of Intrinsic Motivation Related to Pupils' Science Interests." *Journal of Experimental Education,* 29 (1961), 205–29.

Rehage, Kenneth J. "A Comparison of Pupil-Teacher Planning and Teacher-Directed Procedures in Eighth-Grade Social Studies Classes." *Journal of Educational Research,* 45 (1951), 111–15.

Remmers, H. H., and D. H. Radler. *The American Teenager.* Indianapolis: Bobbs-Merrill, 1957.

Riesen, Austin. "Effects of Stimulus Deprivation on the Development and Atrophy of the Visual Sensory System." *American Journal of Orthopsychiatry,* 30 (1960), 23–36.

Riesman, David. *The Lonely Crowd.* New Haven: Yale Univ. Press, 1950.

———. "Teachers Amid Changing Expectations." *Harvard Educational Review,* 24 (1954), 106–07.

Riopelle, Arthur. "Transfer Suppression and Learning Sets." *Journal of Comparative and Physiological Psychology,* 46 (1953), 108–14.

Risden, Gladys. "When Thinking Is Stimulated." *Childhood Education,* 27 (1950), 24–25.

Robinson, Else E. "An Experimental Inventory of Two Factors Which Produce Stereotyped Behavior in Problem Situations." *Journal of Experimental Psychology,* 27 (1940), 394–410.

Rokeach, Milton. *The Open and Closed Mind.* New York: Basic Books, 1960.

Rosen, Bernard C., and Roy d'Andrade. "The Psychosocial Origins of Achievement Motivation." *Sociometry,* 22 (1959), 185–218.

Rosenthal, Fred. "Some Relationships Between Sociometric Position and Language Structure of Young Children." *Journal of Educational Psychology,* 48 (1947), 483–97.

Rosenzweig, Mark R., and Leo Postman. "Frequency of Usage and the Perception of Words." *Science,* 127 (1958), 263–66.

Rosenzweig, Mark R., and others. "A Search for Relations Between Brain Chemistry and Behavior." *Psychological Bulletin,* 57 (1960), 476–92.

Ross, C. C., and Lyle K. Henry. "The Relation Between Frequency of Testing and Progress in Learning Psychology." *Journal of Educational Psychology,* 30 (1939), 604–11.

Rudolf, Kathleen Brady. "The Effect of Reading Instruction on Achievement in Eighth Grade Social Studies." *Teachers College Contributions to Education,* No. 945. New York: Teachers College, Columbia Univ., 1949.

Ruediger, W. G. "The Indirect Improvement of Mental Function Thru Ideals." *Educational Review,* 36 (1908), 364–71.

Ryans, David G. "A Study of Criterion Data." *Educational and Psychological Measurement,* 12 (1952), 333–44.

———. *Characteristics of Teachers.* Washington, D. C.: American Council on Education, 1960.

Ryans, David G., and Edwin Wandt. "A Factor Analysis of Observed Teacher Behaviors in the Secondary School." *Educational and Psychological Measurement,* 12 (1952), 574–86.

Rychlak, Joseph F. "A Socio-Psychological Theory of Performance in Competitive Situations." *Human Relations,* 13 (1960), 157–66.

Ryle, Gilbert. *The Concept of Mind.* New York: Barnes and Noble, 1955.

Sandiford, Peter. *Educational Psychology.* New York: Longmans, Green, 1928.

Sanford, Nevitt. "The Dynamics of Identification." *Psychological Review,* 62 (1955), 106–18.

Sanford, Nevitt, ed. *The American College.* New York: Wiley, 1962.

Sarason, Seymour B., and others. *Anxiety in Elementary School Children.* New York: Wiley, 1960.

Schachter, Stanley. *The Psychology of Affiliation.* Stanford: Stanford Univ. Press, 1959.

Schoeppe, Aileen, and Robert J. Havighurst. "A Validation of Developmental and Adjustment Hypotheses of Adolescence." *Journal of Educational Psychology,* 43 (1952), 339–53.

Schoeppe, Aileen, and others. "Some Factors Affecting Sixteen-Year-Olds' Success in Five Developmental Tasks." *Journal of Abnormal and Social Psychology,* 48 (1953), 42–52.

Schroder, Harold M., and Julian B. Rotter. "Rigidity as Learned Behavior." *Journal of Experimental Psychology,* 43 (1952), 141–50.

Schwab, Joseph J. "Inquiry, the Science Teacher, and the Educator." *School Review,* 68 (1960), 176–95.

Searles, John R., and G. Robert Carlsen. "English." In C. W. Harris, ed. *Encyclopedia of Educational Research.* New York: Macmillan, 1960, pp. 454–70.

Sears, Pauline S. "Levels of Aspiration in Academically Successful and Unsuccessful Children." *Journal of Abnormal and Social Psychology,* 35 (1940), 498–536.

———. "Level of Aspiration in Relation to Some Variables of Personality: Clinical Studies." *Journal of Social Psychology,* 14 (1941), 311–36.

———. "Problems in the Investigation of Achievement and Self-Esteem Motivation." In M. R. Jones, ed. *Nebraska Symposium on Motivation, 1957.* Lincoln: Univ. of Nebraska Press, 1957, pp. 265–339.

Sears, Robert R. "Ordinal Position in the Family as a Psychological Variable." *American Sociological Review,* 15 (1950), 397–401.

———. "Recommended Objectives in Personal Development and Social Maturation." In *Supplement to "Elementary School Objectives."* Princeton: Educational Testing Service, 1953, pp. 124–31.

Sears, Robert R., and others. *Patterns of Child Rearing.* Evanston: Row-Peterson, 1957.

Seashore, Harold. "Academic Abilities of Junior College Students." *Junior College Journal,* 29 (1958), 74–80.

———. "Some Implications of Differences Among Colleges in the Abilities of Their Students." *California Journal of Educational Research,* 10 (1959), 105–07.

Sells, Saul B., and others. "Evaluative Studies of the Activity Program in the New York City Public Schools: A Preliminary Report." *Journal of Experimental Education,* 9 (1941), 310–22.

Shalemon, E. "O vozrastnykh osobennostiakh èlementarnogo konstruirovaniia u schkol'nikov I, III, V klassov." *Voprosy Psikhologii,* 5 (1959), 100–06.

Sheerer, Elizabeth. "An Analysis of the Relationship Between Acceptance of and Respect for the Self and Acceptance of and Respect for Others in Ten Counseling Cases." *Journal of Consulting Psychology,* 13 (1949), 169–75.

Shepard, Winifred O. "Learning Set in Preschool Children." *Journal of Comparative and Physiological Psychology,* 50 (1957), 15–17.

Shepard, Winifred O., and Maurice Schaeffer. "The Effect of Concept Knowledge on Discrimination Learning." *Child Development,* 27 (1956), 173–78.

Sherif, Muzafer, and others. *Intergroup Conflict and Cooperation: The Robbers Cave Experiment.* Norman, Okla.: University Book Exchange, 1961.

Sherman, Mandel, and Hudson Jost. "Frustration Reactions of Normal and Neurotic Persons." *Journal of Psychology,* 13 (1942), 3–19.

Shock, N. W. "Growth Curves." In S. S. Stevens, ed. *Handbook of Experimental Psychology.* New York: Wiley, 1951, pp. 330–46.

Shuttleworth, Frank K. "The Physical and Mental Growth of Girls and Boys

Age Six to Nineteen in Relation to Age at Maximum Growth." *Monographs of the Society for Research in Child Development,* Vol. 4, No. 3 (1939).

Siegel, Alberta Engvall. "The Influence of Violence in the Mass Media upon Children's Role Expectations." *Child Development,* 29 (1958), 35–56.

Silverman, R. E., and M. Alter. "Note on the Response in Teaching Machine Programs." *Psychological Reports,* 7 (1960), 496.

Skapski, Mary K. "Ungraded Primary Reading Program: An Objective Evaluation." *Elementary School Journal,* 61 (1960), 41–45.

Skeels, H. M., and H. B. Dye. "A Study of the Effects of Differential Stimulation on Mentally Retarded Children." *Proceedings of the American Association for Mental Deficiency,* 44 (1939), 114–36.

Skinner, B. F. *Science and Human Behavior.* New York: Macmillan, 1953.

———. "The Science of Learning and the Art of Teaching." *Harvard Educational Review,* 25 (1954), 86–97.

———. "Teaching Machines." *Science,* 128 (1958), 969–77.

———. "Pigeons in a Pelican." *American Psychologist,* 15 (1960), 28–37.

Slater-Hammel, Arthur T. "An Action Current Study of Contraction Movement Relationships in the Tennis Stroke." *Research Quarterly of the American Association for Health, Physical Education and Recreation,* 20 (1949), 424–31.

Smedslund, Jan. "The Acquisition of Conservation of Substance and Weight in Children." *Scandinavian Journal of Psychology,* 2 (1961), 1–10, 71–84, 85–87, 153–60, 203–10.

Smith, Howard P. "Do Intercultural Experiences Affect Attitudes?" *Journal of Abnormal and Social Psychology,* 51 (1955), 469–77.

Smith, Louis M. "Pupil Expectations of Teacher Leadership Behavior." Cooperative Research Project No. 570. Mimeographed. St. Louis: Washington Univ., 1960.

Smith, M. Brewster, and others. *Opinions and Personality.* New York: Wiley, 1956.

Smith, M. Drury. "Periods of Arrested Progress in the Acquisition of Skill." *British Journal of Psychology,* 21 (1930), 1–28.

Smith, William M., and others. "Delayed Visual Feedback and Behavior." *Science,* 132 (1960), 1013–14.

Smode, Alfred F., and others. *Motor Habit Interference.* Stamford, Conn.: Dunlap and Associates, 1959.

Solley, C. M., and Gardner Murphy. *Development of the Perceptual World.* New York: Basic Books, 1960.

Sontag, Lester M., and others. "Mental Growth and Personality Development: A Longitudinal Study." *Monographs of the Society for Research in Child Development,* Vol. 23, No. 68 (1958).

Spence, Kenneth W. "Current Interpretations of Learning Data . . ." In *Learning Theory, Personality Theory, and Clinical Research: The Kentucky Symposium.* New York: Wiley, 1954, pp. 1–21.

———. *Behavior Theory and Conditioning.* New Haven: Yale Univ. Press, 1956.

Sperry, R. W. "Mechanisms of Neural Maturation." In S. S. Stevens, ed. *Handbook of Experimental Psychology.* New York: Wiley, 1951, pp. 236–80.

Stagner, Ross. "Fascist Attitudes: Their Determining Conditions." *Journal of Social Psychology,* 7 (1936), 438–54.

Steiner, Ivan D. "Self-Perception and Goal-Setting Behavior." *Journal of Personality,* 25 (1957), 344–55.

Steiner, Ivan D., and William L. Field. "Role Assignment and Interpersonal Influence." *Journal of Abnormal and Social Psychology,* 61 (1960), 239–45.

Stember, C. H. *Education and Attitude Change.* New York: Institute of Human Relations Press, 1961.

Stern, George. "Student Values and Their Relationship to the College Environment." In Hall T. Sprague, ed. *Research on College Students.* Berkeley: Center for Higher Education, Univ. of California, 1960, pp. 67–104.

Sterrett, Marvin D., and Robert A. Davis. "The Permanence of School Learning." *Educational Administration and Supervision,* 40 (1954), 449–60.

Stephens, J. M. Unpublished manuscript. Baltimore: Johns Hopkins University, 1961.

Steward, Julian H. "Determinism in Primitive Society." *Scientific Monthly,* 53 (1941), 491–501.

Stolurow, Lawrence M. "Teaching Machines and Special Education." *Educational and Psychological Measurement,* 20 (1960), 429–48.

———. *Teaching by Machine.* Cooperative Research Monograph No. 6. Washington, D. C.: U. S. Office of Education, 1961.

Stolz, Herbert R., and Lois Meek Stolz. "Adolescent Problems Related to Somatic Variations." In Nelson B. Henry, ed. *Adolescence.* Yearbook of the National Society for the Study of Education, Part 1. Chicago: Univ. of Chicago Press, 1944, pp. 80–99.

———. *Somatic Development of Adolescent Boys.* New York: Macmillan, 1951.

Stoughton, M. Louise, and Alice M. Ray. "A Study of Children's Heroes and Ideals." *Journal of Experimental Education,* 15 (1946), 156–60.

Strodtbeck, Fred L. "Family Interaction, Values, and Achievement." In D. C. McClelland, ed. *Talent and Society.* Princeton: Van Nostrand, 1958, pp. 135–94.

Strom, Ingrid M. "Research in Grammar and Usage and Its Implications for Teaching Writing." *Bulletin of the School of Education, Indiana Univ.,* Vol. 36, No. 5, September, 1960.

Strong, Edward K., Jr. *Vocational Interests 18 Years After College.* Minneapolis: Univ. of Minnesota Press, 1955.

Stuit, Dewey B., ed. *Personnel Research and Test Development in the Bureau of Naval Personnel.* Princeton: Princeton Univ. Press, 1947.

Super, Donald E., and Phoebe Overstreet. *The Vocational Maturity of Ninth-Grade Boys.* New York: Teachers College, Columbia Univ., 1960.

Swenson, Esther J., and others. *Learning Theory in School Situations.* Minneapolis: University of Minnesota Press, 1949.

Taba, Hilda. *School Culture.* Washington, D. C.: American Council on Education, 1955a.

———. *With Perspective on Human Relations.* Washington, D. C.: American Council on Education, 1955b.

Tanner, James M. *Growth at Adolescence.* Springfield, Ill.: Thomas, 1955.

Taylor, Edward A. "Some Factors Relating to Social Acceptance in Eighth-Grade Classrooms." *Journal of Educational Psychology,* 43 (1952), 257–72.

Taylor, I. A. "Similarities in the Structure of Extreme Social Attitudes." *Psychological Monographs,* Vol. 74, No. 2 (1960).

Taylor, W. L. " 'Cloze' Procedure: A New Tool for Measuring Readability." *Journalism Quarterly,* 30 (1953), 415–33.

———. "Recent Developments in the Use of 'Cloze Procedure.' " *Journalism Quarterly,* 33 (1956), 42–48.

Terman, Lewis M., and Maud A. Merrill. *Measuring Intelligence.* Boston: Houghton Mifflin, 1960.

Terman, Lewis M., and Melita H. Oden. *The Gifted Group at Mid-Life.* Stanford: Stanford Univ. Press, 1959.

Terrell, Glenn, Jr., and others. "Social Class and the Nature of the Incentive in Discrimination Learning." *Journal of Abnormal and Social Psychology,* 59 (1959), 270–72.

Terry, Paul W. "How Students Review for Objective and Essay Tests." *Elementary School Journal,* 33 (1933), 592–603.

Tharp, James B. "A Modern Language Test." *Journal of Higher Education,* 6 (1935), 103–04.

Thelen, Herbert A. "The Experimental Method in Classroom Leadership." *Elementary School Journal,* 53 (1952), 76–85.

Thompson, George G., and C. W. Hunnicutt. "Effects of Repeated Praise or Blame on the Work Achievement of Introverts and Extroverts." *Journal of Educational Psychology,* 35 (1944), 257–66.

Thomson, Robert. *The Psychology of Thinking.* Baltimore: Penguin Books, 1959.

Thorndike, E. L. "Mental Discipline in High School Studies." *Journal of Educational Psychology,* 15 (1924), 1–22, 83–98.

Thorndike, Robert L., and Elizabeth Hagen. *10,000 Careers.* New York: Wiley, 1959.

Thune, Leland C., and Stanford C. Ericksen. Studies in Abstraction Learning: IV. The Transfer Effects of Conceptual vs. Rote Instruction in a Simulated Classroom Situation. Mimeographed. Nashville: Vanderbilt Univ., 1960.

Tolman, Edward C. "Principles of Purposive Behavior." In Sigmund Koch, ed. *Psychology: A Study of a Science.* New York: McGraw-Hill, 1959, pp. 92–157.

Torrance, E. Paul. "Explorations in Creative Thinking in the Early School Years: A Progress Report." In C. W. Taylor, ed. *Third Research Conference on the Identification of Creative Scientific Talent.* Salt Lake City: Univ. of Utah Press, 1959, pp. 58–71.

Tryon, Caroline M. "Evaluations of Adolescent Personality by Adolescents." *Monographs of the Society for Research in Child Development,* Vol. 4, No. 4 (1939).

Tryon, Caroline M., and William E. Henry. "How Children Learn Personal and Social Adjustment." In Nelson B. Henry, ed. *Learning and Instruction.* Yearbook of the National Society for the Study of Education, Vol. 49, Part 1. Chicago: Univ. of Chicago Press, 1950, pp. 156–82.

Tuddenham, Read D. "Studies in Reputation, III. Correlates of Popularity Among Elementary-School Children." *Journal of Educational Psychology,* 42 (1951), 257–76.

Tuddenham, Read D. "Studies in Reputation." *Psychological Monographs*, Vol. 66, No. 1 (1952).

———. "The Constancy of Personality Ratings over Two Decades." *Genetic Psychology Monographs*, 60, No. 1 (1959), 3–29.

Tuddenham, Read D., and M. M. Snyder. "Physical Growth of California Boys and Girls from Birth to Eighteen Years." *University of California Publications in Child Development*, No. 2, 1954.

Turner, Ralph H. "Preoccupation with Competitiveness and Social Acceptance Among American and English College Students." *Sociometry*, 23 (1960), 307–25.

Twining, W. E. "Mental Practice and Physical Practice in Learning a Motor Skill." *Research Quarterly of the American Association for Health, Physical Education, and Recreation*, 20 (1949), 432–35.

Tyler, Leona. "The Stability of Patterns of Primary Mental Abilities Among Grade School Children." *Educational and Psychological Measurement*, 18 (1958), 769–74.

Tyler, Ralph W. "A Test of Skill in Using a Microscope." *Educational Research Bulletin*, 9 (1930), 493–96.

———. "Permanence of Learning." *Journal of Higher Education*, 4 (1933), 203–04.

———. *Constructing Achievement Tests*. Columbus: Ohio State Univ., 1934.

UICSM Project Staff. "Arithmetic with Frames." *Arithmetic Teacher*, 4 (1957), 119–24.

Ullman, Charles A. "Teachers, Peers and Tests as Predictors of Maladjustment." *Journal of Educational Psychology*, 48 (1957), 257–67.

Ulmer, Gilbert. "Teaching Geometry to Cultivate Reflective Thinking." *Journal of Experimental Education*, 8 (1939), 18–25.

———. "Some Suggestions for Teaching Geometry to Develop Clear Thinking." *Kansas University Studies in Education*, Vol. 2, No. 7, 1942.

Underwood, Benton J. "Interference and Forgetting." *Psychological Review*, 64 (1957), 49–60.

———. "Ten Years of Massed Practice on Distributed Practice." *Psychological Review*, 68 (1961), 229–47.

Underwood, Benton J., and Rudolph W. Schulz. *Meaningfulness and Verbal Learning*. Chicago: Lippincott, 1960.

Vandell, R. A., and others. "The Function of Mental Practice in the Acquisition of Motor Skills." *Journal of General Psychology*, 29 (1943), 243–50.

Vander Meer, A. W. "The Economy of Time in Industrial Training." *Journal of Educational Psychology*, 36 (1945), 65–90.

Venn, E. Grant. Unpublished Master's thesis, State College of Washington, 1946.

Vernon, Madeline D. *A Further Study of Visual Perception*. Cambridge, England: Cambridge Univ. Press, 1954.

Vernon, P. E. "Education and the Psychology of Individual Differences." *Harvard Educational Review*, 28 (1958), 91–104.

Verplanck, W. S. "The Control of the Content of Conversation: Reinforcement of Statements of Opinion." *Journal of Abnormal and Social Psychology*, 51 (1955), 668–76.

Voelker, P. F. "The Function of Ideals and Attitudes in Social Education." *Teachers College Contributions to Education,* No. 112. New York: Teachers College, Columbia Univ., 1921.

von Senden, M. *Space and Sight.* Glencoe, Ill.: Free Press, 1960. (Originally published in German, 1932.)

von Wright, J. M. "A Note on the Role of 'Guidance' in Learning." *British Journal of Psychology,* 48 (1957a), 133–37.

————. *An Experimental Study of Human Serial Learning.* Helsinki: Finnish Scientific Society, 1957b.

Waldfogel, Samuel, and others. "The Development, Meaning, and Management of School Phobia." *American Journal of Orthopsychiatry,* 27 (1957), 754–80.

Wall, W. D., and K. M. Miller. Motivation and Countermotivation. Paper presented to International Congress of Applied Psychology, Copenhagen, 1961.

Warner, W. Lloyd, and William E. Henry. "The Radio Day Time Serial: A Symbolic Analysis." *Genetic Psychology Monographs,* Vol. 37, No. 1 (1948).

Waterland, J. C. The Effect of Mental Practice Combined with Kinaesthetic Perception. . . . Unpublished Master's thesis, Univ. of Wisconsin, 1956.

Watson, John B. *The Psychological Care of the Infant and Child.* New York: Norton, 1928.

Watson, John B., and Rosalie R. Watson. "Conditioned Emotional Reactions." *Journal of Experimental Psychology,* 3 (1920), 1–14.

Wattenberg, William W., and James J. Balistrieri. "Gang Membership and Juvenile Misconduct." *American Sociological Review,* 15 (1950), 744–52.

Webster, Harold. "Change in Attitudes During College." *Journal of Educational Psychology,* 49 (1958), 109–17.

Wechsler, David. *Wechsler Intelligence Scale for Children, Manual.* New York: Psychological Corporation, 1949.

Weinstein, Eugene A. "Development of the Concept of Flag and the Sense of National Identity." *Child Development,* 28 (1957), 167–74.

Weir, Morton W., and Harold W. Stevenson. "The Effect of Verbalization in Children's Learning as a Function of Chronological Age." *Child Development,* 30 (1959), 143–49.

Werner, Emmy. Report of the Stress Study. Unpublished manuscript, Institute of Child Development and Welfare, Univ. of Minnesota, 1959.

Werner, Heinz, and Edith Kaplan. "The Acquisition of Word Meanings: A Developmental Study." *Monographs of the Society for Research in Child Development,* Vol. 15, No. 1 (1950).

Wertheimer, Rita R. "Consistency of Sociometric Status Position in Male and Female High School Students." *Journal of Educational Psychology,* 48 (1957), 385–90.

Wesley, Frank. "Silents, Please." *Audio-Visual Communication Review,* 10 (1962), 102–05.

Wesman, Alexander G. "A Study of Transfer of Training from High School Subjects to Intelligence." *Journal of Educational Research,* 39 (1945), 254–64.

West, Joseph V., and Benjamin Fruchter. "A Longitudinal Study of the Relationship of High School Foreign Language Study and Mathematics Study to Freshman Grades." *Journal of Educational Research,* 54 (1960), 105–10.

West, Leonard J. "Review of Research in Typewriting Learning with Recommendations for Training." *Research Report* TN-57-69. San Antonio: Air Force Personnel and Training Research Center, 1957.

West, Leonard J. "An Experimental Comparison of Nonsense, Word, and Sentence Materials in Early Typing Training." *Journal of Educational Psychology*, 47 (1956), 481–89.

Wheeler, Lester R. "The Intelligence of East Tennessee Mountain Children." *Journal of Educational Psychology*, 23 (1932), 351–70.

———. "A Comparative Study of the Intelligence of East Tennessee Mountain Children." *Ibid.*, 33 (1942), 321–34.

Whipple, G. M., ed. *Intelligence: Its Nature and Nurture.* Yearbook of the National Society for the Study of Education, Vol. 39, Part 2. Bloomington, Ill.: Public School Publishing Co., 1940.

White, Ernest E. "A Study of the Possibility of Improving Habits of Thought in School Children by a Training in Logic." *British Journal of Educational Psychology*, 6 (1936), 267–73.

White, Ralph, and Ronald Lippitt. "Leader Behavior and Member Reaction in Three 'Social Climates.'" In Dorwin Cartwright and Alvin Zander, eds. *Group Dynamics.* Evanston: Row-Peterson, 1960a, pp. 527–53.

———. *Autocracy and Democracy: An Experimental Inquiry.* New York: Harper, 1960b.

White, Robert W. "Motivation Reconsidered: The Concept of Competence." *Psychological Review*, 66 (1959), 297–333.

———. "Competence and Psychological Stages." In M. R. Jones, ed. *Nebraska Symposium on Motivation, 1960.* Lincoln: Univ. of Nebraska Press, 1960, pp. 97–141.

White, Verna E. *Studying the Individual Pupil.* New York: Harper, 1958.

Whitehead, Frank. "The Attitudes of Grammar-School Pupils Toward Some Novels Commonly Read in School." *British Journal of Educational Psychology*, 26 (1956), 104–11.

Whyte, W. F. *Money and Motivation.* New York: Harper, 1955.

Whyte, W. H. *The Organization Man.* New York: Doubleday, 1956.

Wickman, E. K. *Children's Behavior and Teachers' Attitudes.* New York: Commonwealth Fund, 1928.

Williams, Robin M. *The Reduction of Intergroup Tension.* New York: Social Science Research Council, 1947.

Williamson, E. G. "Preventive Aspects of Disciplinary Counseling." *Educational and Psychological Measurement*, 16 (1956), 68–81.

Willis, E. E. "The Relative Effectiveness of Three Forms of Radio Presentation in Influencing Attitudes." *Speech Monographs*, 7 (1940), 41–47.

Winger, F. E. The Determination of the Significance of Tachistoscopic Training in Word Perception As Applied to Beginning Typewriting Instruction. Unpublished doctoral dissertation, Univ. of Oregon, 1951.

Winterbottom, Marian R. "The Relation of Need for Achievement to Learning Experiences in Independence and Mastery." In John W. Atkinson, ed. *Motives in Fantasy, Action, and Society.* Princeton: Van Nostrand, 1958, pp. 453–78.

Wispe, Lauren G. "Evaluating Section Teaching Methods in the Introductory Course." *Journal of Educational Research*, 45 (1951), 161–68.

Witty, Paul A. "The Teacher Who Has Helped Me Most." *Elementary English,* 34 (1947), 345–54.

Wolfenstein, Martha. "French Parents Take Their Children to the Park." In Margaret Mead and Martha Wolfenstein, eds. *Childhood in Contemporary Cultures.* Chicago: Univ. of Chicago Press, 1955a, pp. 99–117.

———. "Fun Morality: An Analysis of Recent American Child-Training Literature." In Margaret Mead and Martha Wolfenstein, eds. *Childhood in Contemporary Cultures.* Chicago: Univ. of Chicago Press, 1955b, pp. 168–78.

Wolfle, Dael. "Training." In S. S. Stevens, ed. *Handbook of Experimental Psychology.* New York: Wiley, 1951, pp. 1267–86.

Wohlwill, Joachim F. "Developmental Studies of Perception." *Psychological Bulletin,* 57 (1960a), 249–88.

———. "A Study of the Development of the Number Concept by Scalogram Analysis." *Journal of Genetic Psychology,* 97 (1960b), 345–77.

Wood, Ben D., and Frank N. Freeman. *An Experimental Study of the Educational Influence of the Typewriter in the Elementary School.* New York: Macmillan, 1932.

Wood, K. S. "Parental Maladjustment and Functional Articulatory Disorders." *Journal of Speech Disorders,* 11 (1946), 255–75.

Woodrow, Herbert. "The Effect of Type of Training upon Transference." *Journal of Educational Psychology,* 18 (1927), 159–72.

———. "The Ability to Learn." *Psychological Review,* 53 (1946), 147–58.

Woodruff, A. D. *Educational Psychology.* New York: Longmans, Green, 1951.

Worcester, D. A. *The Education of Children of Above-Average Mentality.* Lincoln: Univ. of Nebraska Press, 1955.

Word, Aubrey H., and Robert A. Davis. "Acquisition and Retention of Factual Information in Seventh-Grade General Science During a Semester of Eighteen Weeks." *Journal of Educational Psychology,* 30 (1939), 116–25.

Wright, Herbert F. "How the Psychology of Motivation Is Related to Curriculum Development." *Journal of Educational Psychology,* 39 (1948), 149–56.

Wrightstone, J. Wayne. "Demonstration Guidance Project in New York City." *Harvard Educational Review,* 30 (1960), 237–51.

Yates, Ida M. "Concepts and Attitudes Concerning Slander and Freedom of Speech." *Journal of Educational Research,* 27 (1933), 283–97.

Young, P. T. *Motivation and Emotion.* New York: Wiley, 1961.

Zaporozhets, A. V. "The Development of Voluntary Movements." In Brian Simon, ed. *Psychology in the Soviet Union.* Stanford: Stanford Univ. Press, 1957, pp. 108–14.

Zborowski, Mark. "The Place of Book-Learning in Traditional Jewish Culture." In Margaret Mead and Martha Wolfenstein, eds. *Childhood in Contemporary Cultures.* Chicago: Univ. of Chicago Press, 1955, pp. 118–41.

Zeigarnik, B. "Über das Behalten von erledigten und unerledigten Handlungen." *Psychologische Forschung,* 9 (1927), 1–85.

Zimmerman, Claire, and Raymond Bauer. "The Effect of an Audience upon What Is Remembered." *Public Opinion Quarterly,* 20 (1956), 238–48.

Zipf, Shiela. "Resistance and Conformity Under Reward and Punishment." *Journal of Abnormal and Social Psychology,* 61 (1960), 102–09.

AUTHOR INDEX

Abegglen, J. C., 159, 659
Abelson, H. I., 453, 663
Abernethy, Ethel M., 94, 659
Abrahamson, S., 161, 659
Adorno, T. W., 440, 458, 627–30, 659
Ahmann, J. S., 571
Alcock, W. T., 469, 680
Allan, Mary D., 379, 659
Allen, Laymon, 335
Allport, G. W., 399, 663
Alter, M., 416, 686
Ames, Louise B., 117, 659
Ammons, R. B., 293, 304, 659
Amos, R. T., 7, 659
Anderson, G. L., 85, 245, 659
Anderson, R. C., 515, 659
Anderson, R. H., 252, 257, 262–66, 670
Anderson, Theresa, 290, 659
Angiolillo, P. F., 248, 659
Annett, J., 293, 659
Annis, A. D., 450, 659
Archer, E. J., 308, 677
Asch, S. E., 155, 660
Astin, A. W., 56, 660
Atkinson, J. W., 167, 660, 668, 677, 691
Ausubel, D. P., 176, 307, 379, 402, 660

Bahrick, H. P., 299, 660
Bailyn, Lotte, 426, 660
Baker, R. A., 288, 660
Baldwin, A. L., 148, 152, 157, 166, 243, 479, 576, 660, 676
Bales, R. F., 687
Balistrieri, J. J., 638, 690
Bandura, A., 149, 150, 155, 660
Barker, R., 107, 108, 660
Barlow, M. C., 388, 660
Bartlett, E. R., 646, 660
Bartlett, F. C., 280, 282, 337, 354, 660
Bath, J. A., 653, 660
Battig, W. F., 304, 660
Bauer, R., 441, 692
Bayles, E. E., 86
Bayley, Nancy, 94–97, 228, 238, 240, 661
Becker, H. S., 167
Bendig, A. W., 240, 679
Benedict, Ruth, 34, 661

Bennett, Edith B., 453, 661
Bennett, G. K., 225, 227, 240, 661
Berdie, R. F., 184
Bereday, G. Z. F., 377, 658, 661
Berko, Jean, 293, 661
Berkowitz, L., 511, 512, 661
Berkowitz, Pearl, 614
Berlyne, D. E., 124, 125, 595, 661, 670
Bestor, A., 39, 63, 341, 389, 661
Bettelheim, B., 376, 424, 661
Biber, Barbara, 537
Bills, R. E., 245, 661
Bilodeau, E. A., 277, 293, 661
Bilodeau, Ina McD., 277, 293, 661
Blake, E., 307, 660
Bloom, B. S., 338, 347, 400, 572, 661
Blumer, H., 433, 661
Boeck, C. H., 371, 662
Boehm, Leonore, 105, 134, 338, 347, 662
Bond, A. De M., 450, 662
Bond, G. L., 231, 358, 662
Bonney, Merl E., 117, 179, 662
Bradley, Beatrice E., 245, 662
Bradway, Katherine, 228, 662
Braine, M. D. S., 329, 334, 662
Brian, Clara R., 290, 670
Brodbeck, May, 453, 662
Broder, Lois J., 339, 347, 400, 661
Bronner, Augusta, 632, 637, 671
Bronson, Wanda C., 114, 662
Broudy, H. S., 58, 63, 66, 360, 662
Brown, L. T., 379, 381, 669
Brown, M., 356, 662
Brown, R., 28, 293, 330, 365, 376, 661, 662
Brown, R. R., 238, 662
Brownell, W. A., 295, 342–44, 362, 662
Brueckner, L. J., 231, 358, 662
Bruner, J. S., 61, 67, 88, 201, 249, 331, 347, 372, 662, 663
Bryan, W. L., 303, 663
Buck, J. V., 180, 663
Buros, O. K., 186, 663
Burton, W. H., 290, 294, 313, 395, 683
Buswell, G. T., 9, 10, 663

Calvin, A., 414
Campbell, V. M., 416, 670

Cannon, K. L., 179, 663
Cantoni, L. J., 219, 663
Cantor, N., 500, 537, 663
Cantril, H., 399, 663
Carlsen, G. R., 316, 685
Carlson, E. R., 453, 663
Carmichael, L., 676, 678
Carroll, J. B., 28, 29, 316, 364, 663
Carter, H. D., 200, 663
Carter, R. S., 550, 551, 663
Cartwright, D., 691
Casagrande, J. B., 364, 663
Case, H. W., 416, 663
Castenada, A., 282, 594, 663
Chance, Erika, 150, 663
Chazal, Charlotte B., 362, 662
Child, I. L., 32, 433, 663
Christensen, C. M., 520, 522, 664
Church, J., 135
Churchill, Eileen M., 340, 664
Clark, B. R., 486, 664
Cobb, S., 401, 664
Cogan, M. L., 522, 664
Coleman, J. S., 488, 489, 530, 651, 664
Colville, F. M., 383, 664
Combes, H., 98, 675
Cook, W. W., 544, 664
Cooper, Eunice, 449, 673
Corey, S. M., 29, 646, 650, 664
Corman, B. R., 378, 664
Coulson, J. E., 414, 664
Coweles, J. T., 674
Cox, Catharine M., 126, 664
Cox, J. W., 290, 664
Cronbach, L. J., 58, 178, 194, 236, 255, 371, 664, 665, 678
Culler, E., 298, 665
Cumming, Elaine, 103, 665
Cunningham, Ruth, 176, 499, 516, 665

d'Amato, May F., 328, 674
Damrin, Dora E., 567, 665
d'Andrade, R., 158, 684
Darley, J. G., 192
David, B. B., 360, 680
Davies, Dorothy R., 290, 665
Davis, A., 157, 159, 665
Davis, R. A., 351, 353, 687, 692
Dawe, Helen C., 245, 665
Dearborn, W. F., 276, 665
De Boer, J. J., 433, 665
de Charms, R., 159, 434, 665
Deese, J., 347
de Groat, A. F., 520, 665
De Haan, R. F., 254, 665
de Hirsch, Katrina, 231
Deighton, L., 289, 665
Della Piana, G. M., 12, 486, 522, 665

Deutsch, M., 515, 665
Dewey, J., 31, 60, 665
DeWitt, N. J., 320, 665
Diederich, P. B., 382
Dietrich, J. E., 456, 665
Dillon, H. J., 218, 666
Distler, L., 114, 149, 680
di Vesta, F. J., 29, 640
Dodwell, P. C., 340, 666
Dollard, J., 596, 666
Dolto, Françoise, 48, 666
Doob, L. W., 598, 666
Doppelt, J. E., 240, 661
Douglas, W. O., 427, 666
Douglass, H. R., 395
Douvan, E., 440, 646, 666
Dubin, Elizabeth R., 543, 666
Duel, H. J., 540, 666
Dunbar, Flanders, 600, 666
Duncker, K., 363, 666
Dunlap, K., 468, 666
Dunn, L. M., 254, 666
Dunnette, M., 302, 666
Durkin, Dolores, 635, 666
Dye, H. B., 245, 686
Dynes, R. R., 157, 666

Ebel, R. L., 561, 572
Edgerton, H. A., 236, 666
Edwards, A. L., 436, 666
Edwards, W. G., 303
Eichorn, Dorothy H., 99, 667
Elkind, D., 334, 340, 667
Elkins, Deborah, 117, 118, 667
English, H., 109, 352, 555, 667
Ennis, R. O., 66, 662, 672
Ericksen, S. C., 369, 370, 688
Erikson, E. H., 113, 134, 667
Ervin, Susan M., 334, 341, 347, 363, 383, 667
Escalona, Sibylle K., 482, 578, 667
Eskridge, T. J., Jr., 366, 368, 667
Estes, W. K., 492, 667
Evans, J. L., 414, 667

Fairbanks, G., 280, 667
Faust, Margaret S., 97, 667
Fawcett, H. P., 388, 667
Ferraro, C. D., 582, 682
Ferster, C. B., 490, 667
Feshback, S., 455, 673
Festinger, L., 446, 484, 667
Field, W. L., 446, 687
Fitch, Mildred L., 543, 668
Fite, Mary D., 120, 668
Fitts, P. M., 282, 668
Flanagan, J. C., 173
Flanders, N. A., 515, 522, 668

Flesch, R., 28, 398, 668
Ford, J. B., 242, 668
Foster, G., 334, 667
Fouracre, M. H., 400, 668
Frandsen, A. N., 312
Frankel, E. B., 120, 668
Frazier, A., 91, 167, 668
Frederiksen, N. B., 491, 668
Freeman, F. N., 251, 692
French, Elizabeth G., 49, 157, 668
French, J. R. P., Jr., 486, 518, 584
French, J. W., 227, 668
French, W. W., 67, 456, 668
Frenkel-Brunswik, Else, 155, 156, 167, 438, 669
Friedenberg, E. Z., 192, 572
Friend, Jeannette G., 116, 669
Fries, Margaret E., 113, 669
Frogner, Ellen, 395
Fromm, E., 500, 624, 657, 669
Fruchter, B., 316, 690
Frutchey, F. P., 352, 669
Fuchs, A. H., 282, 669

Gage, N. L., 194, 436, 486, 522, 665, 669
Gagné, R. M., 379, 381, 384, 669
Gaier, E. L., 594, 669
Galanter, E., 313, 407, 422, 669
Galperin, P. Y., 292, 669
Gann, E. K., 589, 669
Gardner, J. W., 38, 231, 669
Gates, A. I., 85, 196, 245, 250, 284, 496, 659, 669
Gebhard, Mildred E., 477, 669
Gee, Helen, 674
Getzels, J. W., 390, 669
Gewirtz, H. B., 480, 670
Gilbert, A. C. F., 491, 668
Ginzburg, R., 584, 670
Girden, E., 298, 665
Glaser, E. M., 395
Glaser, R., 414, 677
Gleser, Goldine C., 255, 665
Glueck, Eleanor, 637, 638, 670
Glueck, S., 637, 638, 670
Gold, M., 36, 670
Goldbeck, R. A., 416, 670
Goldblatt, Irene, 121, 672
Goldstein, K., 610
Goodenough, Florence L., 290, 670
Goodlad, J. I., 252, 257, 262, 263, 266, 670
Goodwin, W. R., 288, 676
Gordon, C. W., 118, 670
Gordon, W. M., 595, 670
Grant, D. A., 474, 475, 670
Grant, Eva, 243, 670
Griggs, R., 344
Gronlund, N. E., 118, 176, 178, 179, 670

Gross, N. B., 625, 670
Guilford, J. P., 233, 234, 391, 670
Gulliksen, H., 211, 670
Gump, P. V., 493, 675
Guthrie, A. B., 104
Guttman, N., 280, 667

Haganah, Theda, 192
Hagen, Elizabeth, 194, 222, 226, 688
Haggard, E. A., 116, 156, 669, 670
Haigh, G. V., 515, 670
Hanson, N. R., 373, 670
Harlow, H. F., 99, 124, 323, 324, 492, 670, 671
Harmon, J. M., 295, 671
Harmon, L. R., 219, 671
Harris, C. W., 661, 665, 666, 668, 678, 685
Harris, D. B., 496, 646, 660
Harter, N., 303, 663
Hartland-Swann, J., 356, 671
Hartley, E. L., 439, 671
Hartshorne, H., 618, 633, 634, 671
Hartson, L. D., 280, 671
Hauser, P. M., 433, 661
Havighurst, R. J., 36, 37, 106, 108, 122, 123, 154, 157, 161, 254, 266, 434, 617–25, 640–47, 653, 657, 665, 671, 681, 684
Healy, W., 632, 637, 671
Hebb, D. O., 100, 671
Heffernan, Helen, 657
Heil, L. M., 501, 523–25, 671
Heist, P., 36, 486, 671
Helfant, K., 444, 671
Henderson, K. B., 356, 672
Henderson, R. L., 606, 672
Hendrickson, G., 383, 672
Henry, J., 42, 537, 672
Henry, L. K., 543, 684
Henry, N. B., 85, 86, 134, 266, 395, 496, 537, 665, 687, 688
Henry, W. E., 97, 433, 688, 690
Herr, Selma E., 245, 672
Hess, R. D., 121, 672
Hewitt, L. E., 639, 672
Highet, G., 6, 672
Hildreth, Gertrude, 395
Hilgard, E. R., 73, 124, 492, 496, 672
Hilgard, Josephine R., 99, 100, 672
Hoffman, Lois W., 151, 672
Hoffman, M. L., 155, 672
Holland, J. G., 415, 672
Holland, J. L., 38, 672
Horn, T. D., 282, 672
House, Betty J., 326, 672
Hovland, C. I., 452, 454, 672
Howell, J. J., 422
Huey, E. B., 8, 672

Hughes, E. C., 426, 672
Humphrey, G., 593, 673
Humphreys, L. G., 317, 347, 673
Hunnicutt, C. W., 379, 490, 673, 688
Hunt, J. McV., 238, 244, 329, 347, 608, 673
Hurst, J. G., 556–673

Inhelder, B., 331–40, 673, 682
Israel, J., 479, 673
Iverson, W. J., 379, 672

Jacob, P. E., 49, 440, 449, 456, 673
Jackson, P. W., 390, 669
Jahoda, Marie, 449, 574, 605, 673
James, W., 5, 315, 568, 643, 673
Janet, P., 333
Janis, I. L., 452, 453, 455, 463, 673, 677
Jenkins, D. H., 537
Jenkins, R. L., 639, 672
Jennings, F. G., 496
Johnson, D. M., 515, 673
Johnson, G. O., 254, 673
Jones, Daisy M., 259, 260, 673
Jones, H. E., 91, 99, 351, 667, 673
Jones, Mary C., 94, 96, 97, 438, 673, 674, 680
Jones, M. R., 267, 685, 691
Jones, V., 636, 674
Jost, H., 580, 685
Jucknat, Margarete, 476, 674

Kagan, J., 155, 425, 674, 680
Kahl, J. A., 48, 219, 221, 674
Katona, G., 342, 674
Katz, Joseph, 396
Kearney, N. C., 67
Keislar, E. R., 416–18, 544, 674
Keliher, Alice V., 94, 674
Kelley, H. H., 446, 674
Kelly, E. L., 169, 189, 674
Kemp, C. G., 516, 674
Kendler, H. H., 328, 674
Kendler, Tracy S., 328, 674
Keniston, H., 376, 674
Kersh, B. Y., 319, 380, 674–75
Kessen, W., 338, 675
Keyes, D., 247, 675
Keys, N. B., 256, 675
Kimball, S. L., 36, 675
Kimble, G. A., 381, 675
King, B. T., 453, 463, 673
King, R. G., 227, 675
King, W. H., 329, 675
Kirk, S. A., 244–46, 254, 673, 675
Kirkpatrick, J. E., 543, 675
Kittell, J. E., 379, 380, 675
Klausmeier, H. J., 86, 94, 312, 675

Kluckhohn, C., 605, 675
Knapp, C., 98, 675
Knezevich, S. J., 211, 675
Koch, Margaret B., 293, 677
Kooker, E. W., 541, 675
Kounin, J. M., 493, 675
Kroll, A., 445, 675
Krueger, W. C. F., 298, 353, 675
Krumboltz, J. D., 416, 676
Kuhlmann, Clementina, 338, 675
Kuvshinov, N. I., 469, 676
Kvaraceus, W. C., 657

Laughlin, F., 179, 676
Lawrence, C. H., 98, 676
Lawrence, D. H., 288, 676
Lawrence, L. C., 485, 676
Lawson, R., 72, 676
Lazarus, R., 282, 676
Leeds, C. H., 522, 676
Leggitt, Dorothy, 325, 676
Lehmusvuori, H., 522, 676
Lee, Dorothy, 167
Leighton, Dorothea, 605, 675
Leshner, S. S., 476, 676
Levin, H., 479, 676
Levine, J. M., 358, 359, 463, 676
Levinger, Leah, 537
Levy, B. I., 512, 661
Lewin, K., 152, 485, 676
Lewis, Helen B., 446, 676
Lindahl, L. G., 278, 294, 298, 676
Lindquist, E. F., 561, 572
Lindzey, G., 663
Lippitt, R., 91, 511–13, 538, 677, 691
Lisonbee, L. K., 91, 668
Liublinskaya, A. A., 328, 677
Lodwich, A. R., 334
Lordahl, D. S., 308, 677
Loree, M. R., 293, 677
Lorge, I., 254, 677
Lortie, D. C., 189, 677
Lowell, Frances E., 243, 677
Lowenfeld, V., 330, 334, 677
Lucas, J. D., 595, 677
Luchins, A. S., 388, 396, 421, 677
Luchins, Edith H., 396, 677
Lucito, L. J., 156, 677
Lumsdaine, A. A., 292, 312, 404, 414, 421, 422, 452, 677, 678
Luria, A. R., 328, 677

McCarthy, Dorothea, 149, 677
McClelland, D. C., 39, 157, 159, 161, 167, 482, 665, 677
Maccoby, Eleanor E., 454, 663, 676, 678, 680
McConnell, T. R., 36

McCord, Joan, 637–39, 678
McCord, W., 637–39, 678
McDavid, J., Jr., 602, 678
McDougall, W. P., 352, 678
Macfarlane, Jean W., 97, 116, 169, 678
McGinnies, E., 453, 454, 678, 680
McGraw, Myrtle B., 99, 678
McKeachie, W. J., 236, 516, 538, 555, 678
Mackinnon, D. W., 38, 637, 678
McMurray, F., 58, 678
McNally, J., 636, 678
McNeil, J. D., 416–18, 674
Maier, N. R. F., 389, 678
Maltzman, I., 391, 678
Mandler, G., 308, 678
Mangan, G. L., 640, 678
Marks, J. B., 120, 678
Marshall, Helen R., 150, 678
Marx, M. H., 491, 678
May, M. A., 292, 312, 404, 422, 618, 633, 634, 671, 679
May, R., 598, 679
Mayer, M., 55, 246, 368, 679
Mead, Margaret, 34, 45–46, 167, 449, 464 666, 669, 679, 691, 692
Meadow, A., 391, 679
Medinnus, G. R., 151, 679
Meehl, P. E., 7, 490, 679
Meier, N. C., 450, 659
Melville, D. S., 491, 668
Menchinskaya, Natalia A., 405, 679
Meredith, G. P., 125, 679
Merrill, Judith, 675
Merrill, Maud, 203, 238, 688
Messick, S. J., 480, 679
Meyer, W. J., 240, 679
Meyer, W. T., 115, 679
Michels, W. C., 361, 679
Mikol, B., 440, 679
Milgram, S., 337, 681
Miller, A. G., 295, 671
Miller, D. R., 47, 51, 67, 679
Miller, G. A., 73, 313, 468, 679
Miller, K. M., 221, 389, 679, 690
Miller, N. E., 86, 422
Miller, R. V., 254, 679
Mintz, A., 614, 680
Mischel, W., 470, 680
Mitnick, L. L., 453, 454, 680
Mitton, Betty L., 496
Moeller, G. H., 434, 665
Moore, O. K., 247, 251
More, D. M., 122, 671
Morse, A. D., 246, 266, 680
Moser, A. C., 360, 680
Moser, H. E., 250, 342–44, 350, 662, 680
Mowrer, O. H., 469, 611, 614, 680
Mullen, Frances A., 647, 680

Munro, Rona, 11
Munroe, Ruth L., 431, 568, 680
Murphy, G., 358, 359, 463, 480, 493, 676, 686
Murphy, Lois, 615
Murray, H. A., 637, 680
Mussen, P. H., 97, 114, 149, 155, 425, 458, 673, 680, 681

Nelson, C. D., 198, 680
Neugarten, Bernice L., 106, 266, 671
Newcomb, T. M., 169, 446–48, 463, 680
Newman, H. H., 241, 680
Noble, C. E., 469, 680
Northway, M. L., 118, 681

Oden, Melita H., 236, 256, 688
O'Donnell, Mabel, 11
Osgood, S. W., 288, 660
Overman, J. R., 363, 681
Overstreet, Phoebe, 112, 188, 470, 687
Owens, W. A., 228, 681

Pace, C. R., 487, 681
Page, D., 373
Page, E. B., 532, 681
Palermo, Dora S., 663
Palmer, D. E., 402, 681
Palmer, H. O., 287, 681
Parnes, S. J., 391, 679, 681
Parsons, Anne, 337, 681
Parsons, T., 113, 221, 681
Passow, A. H., 266
Patrick, J. R., 592, 681
Patterson, C. H., 615
Patton, J. A., 516, 681
Payne, D. E., 425, 681
Peck, R. F., 154, 434, 617–24, 640–43, 651
Peel, E. A., 329, 334, 681
Pei, M., 60, 305, 681
Penfield, W., 101, 681
Pentony, P., 157, 681
Perkins, H. V., 515, 681
Perry, W. G., Jr., 201, 231, 682
Peterson, H. A., 283, 682
Peterson, Ruth C., 454, 682
Physical Science Study Committee, 62, 682
Piaget, Jean, 104, 125, 289, 329–40, 673, 682
Pitman, I. J., 10, 682
Plowman, Letha, 541, 682
Plumlee, Lynnette B., 555, 682
Polya, G., 38, 682
Porteus, S. D., 209, 682
Postman, L., 364, 684
Powell, M., 582, 682
Prescott, D. A., 170, 175, 192, 683

Pressey, S. L., 256, 283, 409, 683
Pribram, K., 313
Priebe, R. E., 290, 294, 313, 683
Psathas, G., 152, 683

Quartermain, D., 492, 683
Quay, H., 441, 683

Radke-Yarrow, Marian, 442, 457, 683
Radler, D. H., 121, 435, 683
Rapp, A., 316, 683
Raven, B. H., 512, 518, 668, 683
Ray, Alice M., 426, 687
Ray, W. E., 379, 683
Redl, F., 615
Reece, M. M., 493, 683
Reed, G., 658
Reed, H. B., Jr., 522, 683
Rehage, K. J., 511, 516, 683
Remmers, H. H., 121, 194, 435, 683
Rey, A., 331
Riesen, A., 100, 683
Riesman, D., 44, 47, 49, 52, 67, 684
Rietsma, J., 512, 684
Riopelle, A., 389, 684
Risden, Gladys, 345, 684
Roberts, L., 101, 681
Robinson, Else E., 578, 684
Robinson, F. P., 283, 683
Rockefeller Report, 39, 40, 681
Roe, A., 416, 663
Rokeach, M., 440, 684
Rosen, B. C., 158, 684
Rosenthal, F., 117, 684
Rosenzweig, M. R., 99, 364, 684
Ross, C. C., 543, 684
Ross, S., 56, 660
Rothman, Esther P., 614
Rotter, J. B., 389, 684
Rudolf, Kathleen B., 321, 684
Ruediger, W. G., 321, 645, 684
Rummel, J. F., 194
Ryans, D. G., 513–15, 522, 684
Rychlak, J. F., 484, 684
Ryle, G., 356, 684

Sandiford, P., 303, 684
Sanford, N., 54, 396, 424, 538, 627, 631, 658, 678
Sarason, S. B., 182, 523, 594, 684
Schachter, S., 114, 684
Schaeffer, M., 358, 685
Schlesinger, Ina, 377
Schoeppe, Aileen, 123, 127, 684
Schmidt, W., 515, 670
Schroder, H. M., 389, 602, 677, 685
Schroeder, W. H., 383, 672
Schulz, R. W., 350, 689

Schwab, J. J., 371, 685
Scott, T. H., 492, 683
Searles, J. R., 316, 685
Sears, Pauline S., 267, 477–79, 481, 568, 685
Sears, R. R., 23, 149–53, 598, 612, 666, 685
Seashore, H. G., 220, 685
Sells, S. B., 15, 685
Shalemon, E., 470, 685
Sheerer, Elizabeth, 609, 685
Shepard, Winifred O., 323, 358, 685
Sherif, M., 458, 465, 685
Sherman, M., 580, 685
Shock, N. W., 98, 685
Shuttleworth, F. K., 94, 686
Siegel, Alberta E., 454, 686
Silberman, H. F., 414, 664
Silverman, R. E., 416, 686
Simon, B., 669, 692
Skapski, Mary K., 262, 686
Skeels, H. M., 245, 686
Skinner, B. F., 407, 410–19, 422, 490, 492, 667, 672, 686
Skinner, C. E., 85
Slater, Carol, 36, 670
Slater-Hammel, A. T., 280, 686
Smedslund, J., 340, 686
Smith, B. O., 66, 662, 671
Smith, E. C., Jr., 384, 669
Smith, E. R., 661
Smith, H. C., 515, 673
Smith, H. P., 458, 463, 686
Smith, L. M., 519, 686
Smith, M. B., 440, 449, 686
Smith, M. D., 301, 686
Smith, Patricia C., 485, 676
Smith, W. M., 281, 686
Smode, A. F., 308, 686
Snyder, M. M., 94, 689
Soddy, K., 134
Solley, C. M., 480, 493, 679, 686
Sontag, L. W., 243, 686
Spence, K. W., 490, 594, 686
Sperry, R. W., 100, 686
Spindler, G. D., 67
Spitzer, H. F., 395
Sprague, H. T., 671, 687
Stagner, R., 435, 687
Stalnaker, J. M., 561
Stein, M., 593
Steiner, I. D., 446, 482, 687
Stember, C. H., 55, 687
Stephens, J. M., 363, 654, 687
Stern, G. G., 487, 681, 687
Sterrett, M. D., 351, 687
Stevens, S. S., 685, 686, 692
Stevenson, H. W., 16, 17, 690

Steward, J. H., 398, 687
Stoddard, G. D., 457
Stolurow, L. M., 408, 687
Stolz, H. R., 91, 93, 134, 687
Stolz, Lois M., 91, 93, 134, 687
Stone, L. J., 135
Stoughton, M. Louise, 426, 687
Strodtbeck, F. L., 47, 48, 157, 159, 167, 687
Strom, Ingrid M., 316, 687
Strong, E. K., Jr., 189, 192, 687
Stroud, J. B., 86, 541, 682, 687
Stuit, D. B., 564, 687
Super, D. E., 112, 188, 470, 687
Suppes, P., 335
Swanson, G. E., 47, 51, 67, 679
Swenson, Esther J., 350, 687
Symonds, P. M., 497

Taba, Hilda, 161, 179, 180, 192, 640, 641, 647, 657, 671, 687
Tanner, J. M., 93, 94, 687
Taylor, C. W., 232, 688
Taylor, E. A., 179, 688
Taylor, I. A., 439, 688
Taylor, W. L., 399, 688
Terman, L. M., 203, 232, 236, 238, 256, 688
Terrell, G., Jr., 491, 688
Terry, P. W., 555, 688
Tharp, J. B., 555, 688
Thelen, H. A., 497, 503, 516, 519, 688
Thompson, Clare, 228, 662
Thompson, G. G., 115, 490, 520, 665, 679, 688
Thompson, Laura, 292
Thomson, R., 329, 688
Thorndike, E. L., 316, 688
Thorndike, R. L., 194, 222, 226, 688
Thune, L. C., 369, 370, 688
Thurstone, L. L., 454, 681
Tolman, E. C., 73, 688
Torrance, E. P., 234, 688
Tryon, Caroline M., 97, 117, 688
Tuddenham, R. D., 94, 117, 169, 177, 688, 689
Turner, R. H., 121, 689
Twining, W. E., 284, 689
Tyler, Leona, 239, 689
Tyler, R. W., 352, 555, 563, 661, 689

UICSM Project Staff, 374, 689
Ullmann. C. A., 184, 689
Ulmer, G.. 373, 386, 689
Underwood, B. J., 295, 307, 350, 351, 689

Vandell, R. A., 284, 689
Vander Meer, A. W., 290, 689

Venn, E. G., 405, 689
Vernon, Madeline D., 8, 689
Vernon, P. E., 242, 689
Verplanck, W. S., 441, 689
Voelker, P. F., 645, 690
Volkart, E. H., 446, 674
von Senden, M., 100, 690
von Wright, J. M., 284, 288, 690
von Weiszäcker, V., 333

Waetjen, W. B., 232
Waldfogel, S., 153, 690
Walker, A. M., 440, 646, 666
Wall, W. D., 221, 690
Walters, R. H., 149, 150, 155, 660
Wandt, E., 515, 684
Warner, W. L., 433, 690
Washington, R. M., 7, 659
Waterland, J. C., 285, 690
Watson, J. B., 51, 438, 690
Watson, Rosalie R., 690
Wattenberg, W. W., 615, 639, 690
Webster, H., 447, 486, 671, 690
Wechsler, D., 208, 690
Weil, A. M., 104, 682
Weinstein, E. A., 104, 690
Weir, M. W., 16, 17, 690
Weisman, R. G., 416, 675
Werner, Emmy, 158, 690
Wertheimer, Rita R., 199, 690
Wesley, F., 405, 690
Wesman, A. G., 316, 690
West, J. V., 316, 690
West, L. J., 288, 292, 301, 690, 691
Wheeler, L. R., 242, 691
Whipple, G. M., 247, 691
White, E. E., 388, 691
White, R. K., 511–13, 538, 691
White, R. W., 124, 125, 691
White, Verna E., 112, 192, 691
Whitehead, F., 431, 432, 691
Whyte, W. F., 485, 691
Whyte, W. H., 47, 691
Wickman, E. K., 605, 691
Williams, C. S., 541, 675
Williams, R. M., 459, 691
Williamson, E. G., 587, 691
Willis, E. E., 454, 691
Winger, F. E., 287, 691
Winterbottom, M. R., 157, 691
Wispé, L. G., 691
Withall, J., 503
Witty, P. A., 428, 692
Wohlwill, J. F., 334, 401, 692
Wolfenstein, Martha, 34, 48, 167, 666, 669, 679, 692
Wolfle, D., 308, 692

Wood, B. D., 251, 692
Wood, K. S., 149, 692
Woolsey, C. N., 49, 670
Woodrow, H., 325, 692
Woodruff, A. D., 640, 692
Worcester, D. A., 256, 258, 267, 692
Word, A. H., 353, 692
Wright, H. F., 472, 692
Wrightstone, J. W., 246, 692
Wrinkle, W. L., 539
Wulff, J. J., 381, 675

Yates, Ida M., 435, 692
Young, P. T., 124, 692

Zander, A., 691
Zaporozhets, A. V., 402, 692
Zborowski, M., 159, 692
Zeaman, D., 396, 672
Zeigarnik, B., 592, 692
Zimmerman, Claire, 441, 692
Zipf, Shiela, 493, 692
Zola, I., 678

SUBJECT INDEX

Abilities, 194–263; correlation among, 202, 223, 555; interaction with instruction, 235–36; occupational differences, 222–27; profile stability, 239; *see also specific abilities*

Ability grouping, 235, 252–57

Abstract instruction, 369

Acceleration, 256

Accuracy of tests, 210–12, 548–49

Achievement, evaluation of, 531–33, 539–69; and personality, 117, 156, 523, 594; prediction of, 206–08, 215, 219–27

Achievement motivation, 46–51, 157–61, 221, 433, 480, 482, 488, 522; *see also* Striving

Achievement tests, 195–202, 252–53, 539–72

Activity methods of teaching, 15, 285, 456

Adaptive behavior, 70, 74, 575–84

Adjustment, appraisal of, 168–90, 568, 583, 603–11; definition of, 574, 605; improvement of, 646–51; teachers' opinions, 604–06

Adolescence, developmental tasks, 109, 110, 650; physical changes, 94

Adulthood, mental ability in, 227–28

Affection, need for, 110, 113, 521

Affiliation, 46–51; *see also* Peers

Age grading, 248

Aging, 103–227

Aggression in children, 149–55, 597; *see also* Delinquency

Aim, *see* Aspiration, Goal, *and* Objective

Alteration of response after thwarting, 70, 74, 579

Amoral character, 617–18

Anecdotal records, 171–74

Anxiety, 593–95, 609, 640; over achievement, 159, 594

Approach-avoidance conflict, 153, 439, 492, 608

Arbitrary association, 353, 359

Arithmetic, teaching of, 250, 362; methods, 342–45, 350, 358, 363; contrasted with mathematics, 38, 249

Art, teaching of, 376

Art ability in small children, 330

Art class, case study, 503–06

Aspiration, 472–85, 522, 578

Assignments, 526–28

Atmosphere, classroom, 498–531; home, 147–61; school, 486–89

Attitudes, 423–60; definition of, 435; learning of, 320, 345, 424–60; as a school objective, 44–51, 53–55; teaching methods, 427–34, 444–60, 645–60

Audio-visual methods, 286, 290, 294, 357, 403–05, 454

Augmented Roman alphabet, 11

Authoritarian attitude, 435, 440, 458, 626–32

Authority, relations with, 111, 115, 151–56, 425–30, 500, 636–41, 649

Autocratic home, 148, 152, 156

Autocratic leadership, 500–02, 511–17

Automatic instruction, 260, 406–11

Barbara Singer, 152

Behavior, elements in, 68–70; habitual, 53, 643; observation and diagnosis of, 169–74, 560

Behavioral definition of objectives, 52

Belief and learning, 358; *see also* Attitudes

Belief distinguished from knowledge, 356

Bill Chelten, 145–47, 430

Blocking, *see* Thwarting

Brain, development of, 98–102

Brightness, provision for, 254, 256

California Study Methods Survey, 200

Case studies, 24; list of, xiii

Character, 21–23, 154, 616–54; definition of, 617; levels of, 617–25; tests of, 632–36, 646; unity of, 626–36

Character Education Inquiry, 633

Charles White, 225

Cheating, 634, 637, 646

Chemistry, 351, 371, 542; *see also* Science education

Childhood, early, emotional and social development, 103, 111, 113; intellectual development, 101, 104, 125, 329; physical development, 99–101

Clark, 137–41

Class, social, 35–38, 152, 161, 491, 647

Clerical perception, 225

Cloze technique, 399

Collateral learning, 31

College, aptitude for, 205–08, 219–21; attitude change during, 446–49

College atmosphere, 486

College enrollment trends, 37

College Characteristics Index, 487

Commitment, 587, 607

Compensation by substitution of goals, 581

Compensation in abilities, 202, 223

Competence, need for, 111, 124–28

Competition, 528–31

Concentration in studying, 201

Concepts, formation, 330–34, 367–69; operational, 331–34; use in interpreting, 272, 326, 340, 349, 357–79

Concrete experience, 368, 403–05

Concrete operational thought, 331

Conduct, teaching of, 516, 609, 643–46

Confidence, 42, 126, 474–84, 587

Confirmation, 69, 74, 80

Conflict, approach-avoidance, 153, 439, 492, 608

Conforming character, 447, 619, 625, 639, 640

Conformity, in American culture, 46–51, 105, 121; encouragement in school, 38–42; test of, 155

Conscientiousness, and home discipline, 21–23; irrational, 620–23, 640; rational, 623–25, 641

Consequence as element in learning, 69, 74, 80, 275–81, 466–94

Conservation principle, 354

Contradiction of expectations, 69, 74, 80, 472–80, 574–80

Control, experimental, 15

Control of class, 115, 493, 498–528, 534, 587

Convergent thinking, 223, 390, 559

Coordination, motor, 92, 275–80

Correlation coefficient, 20–22

Correlational studies, 19–23

Creative thinking, 28, 234, 374, 390–92, 583, 592

Crime, *see* Delinquency

Cue, 273, 284, 285, 364

Cultural deprivation, 242–47

Cultures, comparison of, 105, 121, 578, 604

Curricular validity, 547

Curriculum, implications for, 340–44, 456–60, 650; psychological issues, 12–14, 81, 233–37, 244, 314–18

Daydreaming, 600

Defense mechanisms, 596–603

Delinquency, 433, 602, 632, 636–40

Democratic attitudes, 435–36, 440, 442–44, 446–48, 516

Democratic relationships, in classroom, 500–02, 511–17; in home, 148, 157, 243

Demonstration, 290–93

Dependence, *see* Conformity, Independence

Descriptive knowledge, 58

Development, 88–164; *see also specific developments*

Developmental tasks, 108–28; and school program, 648–51

Diagnosis, achievement, 196–98, 548, 566; reading, 196; skill, 294

Differential Aptitude Tests, 223–26

Differentiation of instruction, 236, 258–61

Disciplinary methods, in classroom, 115, 493, 534, 587; in home, 21–23, 149, 151, 637

Disciplinary problems, 534, 606, 647

Discipline, formal, 314

Disciplined knowledge, 60–63, 360

Discovery, 378–84

Discrimination, and conceptual learning, 330, 364–68; and emotional learning, 151; sensory, 242, 245, 326; and skills, 273, 282–89, 293

Discussion as teaching method, 293, 452, 507, 516, 544

Discussion test, 559–62

Divergent thinking, 223, 390, 559

Domination, *see* Home atmosphere, Leadership

Dropouts, 218

Dullness, 242; provision for, 254

Educational psychology, purposes, 1–26, 338

Emotion, 438, 590–611; discharge of, 595; in persuasion, 454; suppression of, 598; *see also* Stress, Anxiety, *and* Adjustment

Emotional difficulties, remedial treatment, 599, 646–51

Emotional security, *see* Adjustment *and* Anxiety

Encoding, 272, 327, 367

English, teaching of, 288, 316, 376, 412, 558; *see also* Language, Speech

English class, case study, 506–10

Environment, effect on intellectual development, 125, 241–47; expansion of, 103–08

Error of measurement, 211

Essay test, 201, 559–62

Evaluation, 531–33, 539–69; diagnostic,

196–98, 548, 566; programs, 552, 566–69; purposes of, 539–45

Experience as aid to interpretation, 125, 330–35, 368–70

Experimental studies, 14–18

Expert, characteristics of, 271–82, 360

Explanation, 290, 368, 378–84, 397–405

Eye movements, 8–10

Facilitation, 305–07; *see also* Transfer

Factual learning, effect on attitudes, 449; as objective, 58–62, 349, 355–63

Faculty theory, 315

Failure, effect on aspiration, 474–80; *see also* Nonpromotion *and* Thwarting

Fantasy, 601

Fatigue, 282, 295

Fear, 438, 590, 598, 606

Feedback, 275–81, 408, 468

Flag, concept of, 104

Foreign language, *see* Language

Foresight, 468–72

Forgetting, 304–06, 350–57

Formal discipline, 314

Formal operational thought, 335

Formative periods, 89

Frustration, *see* Thwarting

Generalization, 30, 320, 335, 377–84; of attitude, 154–56, 438–40, 443

Glutamic acid, 56

Goal, 466–94, 522, 587; clarified by classroom planning, 512, 526–28; clarified by evaluation, 540–44; conflict between, 608; as element in behavior, 69, 72; remote, 468–72; substitute, 575–84

Grade-equivalent scale, 215, 252

Grade placement of experiences, 248–51, 344

Grading, *see* Marking

Group control, 500–02, 511–17

Group membership, learning skills of, 516

Group standards, 484–89

Grouping of pupils, 252–63

Growth, mental, 221, 228, 238–43, 328–36; neurophysiological, 98–102; physical, 90–98

"Guess Who" test, 176

Guidance, 188–90, 218–27

Habitual behavior, 53, 643

Height, 91–94, 241

Heredity and mental ability, 238, 241

Home influence, on attitude, 442–44; on character, 21–23, 154, 626–32; on intellectual development, 221, 243; on readiness, 147–61

Homogeneous grouping, 252–57

Identification, 424–34

Illness, psychogenic, 600

Impersonal teachers, 520

Incentive, *see* Goal *and* Reinforcement

Incubation, 592

Independence, 111, 121–23, 151–56, 649

Individual differences, 83–97, 136–65, 168; adapting schooling, 236, 248–63, 412, 484, 568; *see also* Mental ability, Personality

Indoctrination, 433, 451–55, 460

Industrial arts, 277, 290, 564

Information as educational goal, 58–62, 349, 355–63

Intellectual development, *see* Mental development

Intelligence, *see* Mental ability

Intelligence quotient, 204–10, 216–19

Interaction of instruction with pupil characteristics, 235–36, 483–84, 523–25

Interest inventory, 187–90, 211

Interests, development, 188–89; as an objective, 44

Interference and forgetting, 305–08, 355

Interpersonal relations as an objective, 43, 46–51; *see also* Authority *and* Peers

Interpretation, 58–63, 68–72, 80, 83, 349–84; verbal, 17, 272, 292, 328, 364–68, 83, 645; *see also* Explanation

Intuitive thought, 38, 373; as stage of development, 330

Iowa Test of Work Study Skills, 199

Irrational-conscientious character, 153, 617–18, 620–23, 625

Jeanne Allison, 128–30

Jim, 429

Judgment, moral, 635

Judgment by teachers, 7, 170–74, 184, 550, 604–06, 634

Junior high school, 246–62

Kekulé, 593

Knowledge, degrees of mastery, 356, 359; kinds of, 58–63; *see also* Understanding

Knowledge of results, 277, 293

Kuder Preference Record, 187

Kuhlmann-Anderson test, 206–07

Language, as a discipline, 60, 62; learning of, 252–53, 282–305, 320, 555; second, as school subject, 248

Leadership, classroom, 498–528

Learning, definition, 71; elements in, 72–83; stages, 298–301; *see also* Attitudes, Skills

Learning curves, 297–303

Learning theory, 73

Learning to learn, 323–26
Legal profession, 189, 226
Level of aspiration, 472–85, 522, 578
"Life adjustment" education, 317, 650
Literature, learning from, 431–34

Mack, 626–32
Manipulation and exploration, 124–26, 329–33, 492
Margaret, 162–65
Marking, 531–33, 550; of essay tests, 562
Masculinity, 114, 117, 428
Mathematics, 249, 272–76, 386, 555; *see also* Arithmetic
Maturation, 98–102, 340
Meaningfulness, of explanation, 397–405; and learning, 342–63; and retention 350–57
Mechanical reasoning, 223–27
Mediation, 271, 295, 327, 335, 363
Medical students, 189, 426
Memorizing, 283, 315, 325; *see also* Retention
Mental ability, 202–57; and achievement, 206, 208, 219; adult, 227; basis for grouping pupils, 235, 252–57; development of, 101, 104, 125, 227, 238–43, 329; distribution of, 217, 219; effect of experience on, 219, 238–47; heredity and, 238–41; home influences on, 221, 243; improvement of, 243–47, 316; measurement of, 202–27; stability of, 237–47
Mental age, 215
Mental health, *see* Adjustment, Emotion, *and* Thwarting
Mental Measurements Yearbook, 186
Mental practice, 284
Minnesota Counseling Inventory, 184
Minorities, attitude toward, 442–44, 450, 454, 457–58
Mobility, social, 35–38
Models, 424–34
Monitoring, 293–95
Mooney Problem Checklist, 7, 181
Moral concepts, 645; *see also* Character
Moral judgment, 635
Motion pictures, learning from, attitudes, 433, 453–55; concepts, 403–05; skills, 286–90, 294
Motivation, 81, 112, 124, 160, 466–535; *see also specific motivations*
Multiple-choice test, 554–59

Neatness, 321, 645
Needs, 108–28, 646–49; *see also specific needs*
Neural maturation, 98–102, 340

Nonadaptive behavior, 70, 74, 574–83
Nongraded school, 261–63
Nonpromotion, 257
Normal distribution, 93–94, 217
Norms, in goal setting, 484; for tests, 214–18, 564

Objectives, 12–14, 30–63
Observation of pupils, 169–75
Occupations, aptitude, 222–27; interest, 187–90
Olive, 79, 141–44
Operational thought, 331–40
Originality, 234, 390
Osborne, Mr., 503–06
Overlearning, 308, 353

Palmer, Mr., 374
Parents, attitude to achievement, 157–61, 220–21; feelings about adolescent, 121; handling of children, 21–23, 113, 147–61; identification with, 114, 425
Parts vs. wholes, 401
Pascal, Blaise, 126
Patterns, perception of, 8, 365, 402
Peers, approval by, 110, 116–21, 489; influence on attitudes, 105, 120, 446–48, 486–89; ratings by, 175–81
Percentile, 215
Perception, 8, 100, 365
Performance, effects of stress, 281, 590–95; records of, 278, 297–303
Performance test, of achievement, 563, 567; of mental ability, 204
Personal characteristics of learner, 69, 73, 79
Personality, and achievement, 117, 156, 523, 594; appraisal, 168–90, 568, 583, 604–11; and attitudes, 426, 438, 447, 457–58; consistency of, 116, 123, 169, 179, 653; and goal setting, 481–84; related to physique, 91–97
Persuasion, 451–55
Philosophy of life, 48, 440, 623
Physical development, 89–102
Physical education, 97, 280, 284, 290
Physical Science Study Committee, 62, 251, 361, 557
Planning, 470–72, 485, 506–10, 516, 544; *see also* Goals
Plateau, 301, 303
Popularity, 91, 116–21, 151, 489
Practice, 283–98, 410–16; amount and spacing, 295–96; mental, 284; importance, 283, 416
Praise, *see* Reinforcement
Prediction, college marks, 208, 220

Preschool, and intellectual development, 244–47
Preverbal understanding, 58, 330
Principles, 377–88; as kind of knowledge, 59–60, 335; teaching of, 352, 416
Problem solving, emotional interference, 339, 585, 591; effective, 41, 388; improvement of, 316, 340, 371–82, 385–91
Problems, personal, inventory of, 181
Profile interpretation, 211, 222–27, 239
Program, neural, 101; skill learning, 279
Programed instruction, 406–19
Projective methods, 185
Promotion policies, 256–57, 261–63
Provisional try, 74, 436
Psychology, relations to education, 3–12; research methods, 12–24; teaching and learning of, 405, 414, 516, 555, 556
Puberty, 94–97
Punishment, 492

Questionnaires, personality, 181–85

Rate of learning, 297–301
Rational character, 617, 623–25
Rationalization, 602
Reaction to thwarting, *see* Thwarting
Readability, 397–401
Readiness, 73, 88–263; adapting to, 233–63; assessing, 168–263; elements in, 88–90; increasing, 244–47, 340, 344
Reading, eye movements in, 8–10; methods of teaching, 8–12, 201, 245–47, 250, 544; phonetic analysis, 3; tests of, 195–97, 252–53
Realism, and adjustment, 481, 607; in curriculum, 285–89, 317, 321
Reasoning, improvement of, 340, 385–91; *see also* Problem solving
Recall, *see* Retention
Recall test, 553–55, 559–62
Recitation, as aid to learning, 283, 397
Recognition test, 554–59, 561
Records, anecdotal, 171–74
Redundancy, 399–401, 413
Reinforcement, 472–93; inconsistent, 151, 474; social, 440, 489; negative, 490, 492
Reliability of tests, 210–12, 548
Reorganization in recall, 354–56
Repetitive response, 289, 575–79, 643
Repression, 598
Research on education, 6–24
Retardation, mental, 244–47, 254, 326, 636
Retention, facts and ideas, 350–57; motor skill, 304–06; savings method, 304
Review, 353
Reward, *see* Reinforcement

Rigidity, 388–91, 576–79, 591, 594
Role, 103, 106–08

Sampling in testing, 209, 545
Scholastic aptitude, 202–57; prediction of achievement, 206–08, 215, 219–27
Scholastic Aptitude Test, 205–06
Science education, 352, 353, 371, 450, 542, 555, 563; *see also* Physical Science Study Committee
Scores, 215–26
Self-acceptance, 609; *see also* Self-respect
Self-concept, 126, 479, 481; and choice of models, 426; testing of, 181–86
Self-report test, 181–90
Self-respect, 42, 126; competence and, 124–28, 488–89; enhancing, 258–63, 588; physique and, 90–98
Sensorimotor control, 99–102, 289, 329
Sentence Completion Test, 185
Sex attitudes, 34, 650
Sex differences, 114, 117, 150, 550, 634
Sex role, 114–17, 428, 434
Simmons, Miss, 506–10
Simplification, in interpretation, 354, 364–66; of task, 11, 286
Situation, 73, 81, 285–89; similarity and transfer, 305–08, 318–22
Skills, 270–308; definition, 271, 280; *see also specific skills*
Social class, 35–38, 152, 161, 491, 647
Social development, influences on, 91, 104–23, 150–56, 511, 516, 646–51; as an objective, 43, 46–51
Social mobility, 35–38
Social Relations Test, 567
Social studies, 325, 372, 405, 436, 533
"Social utility" curriculum, 317
Socialization, aims of, 39–51; role of school in, 33–38
Sociogram, 118–19, 177–81
Sociometric techniques, 118–19, 175–81
Space relations test, 223–27
Special abilities, 222–27
Speech learning, 149, 280, 293, 305
Standard deviation, 216
Standard error, 211
Standard score, 216
Standardized testing, 195, 565–66
Stanford-Binet Scale, 203
Stress, effects on behavior, 584, 590–611; and intellectual performance, 53, 595; and skilled performance, 281–82
Striving, 51, 159, 481, 491, 524
Study techniques, 198–202, 283, 325
Substitute goals, 575–84
Success, effect on aspiration, 474–80

Superior ability, and adjustment, 236, 256, 583; provision for, 254, 256, 530

Supporting teacher, 428, 520

Suppression of emotion, 598

Systematized learning as kind of knowledge, 60

Talent, screening of, 33–38, 233–37; *see also* Abilities

Teachers, differences among, 45, 428, 498–525; influence on pupil attitudes, 425–30, 445; judgments of pupils, 7, 170–74, 184, 550, 604–06, 634; as leaders, 115, 493, 498–528; as models, 425–30; tensions of, 582

Teaching machine, 406–19

Tests, 175–267; achievement, 195–202, 252–53, 539–69; character, 632–36, 646; college selection, 205, 208, 219–21; conformity, 155; discussion questions, 559–62; effect on learning, 541–43, 565; general mental ability, 202–08, 210; motivating effect, 541, 543; personality, 181–90; reading, 195–97; short-answer questions, 553–59; sociometric, 118–19, 175–81; special ability, 222–27; standardized, 195, 564–65; teachers' responsibilities, 194; *see also* Evaluation, Guidance, *names of particular tests*

Text materials, clarity, 397–419; source of models, 413–34

Thought, concrete, 331; convergent, 390; divergent, 390; formal, 335; intuitive, 330, 373; operational, 331–40; preoperational, 330; *see also* Reasoning

Thwarting, 574–611; management in school, 586–89; reactions to, 575–603

Transfer of learning, 314–92; conditions favoring, 318–22; as educational aim, 56; teaching for, 290–392

Truancy, 633, 647

Typical performance, 53, 200, 213

Typing, 247, 292, 301–03, 468

Typing class, case study, 76–83

Uncertainty band, 211

Understanding, importance of, 61, 342–45, 350–63; evidence of, 358–63, 555–60; teaching for, 358, 368, 401

Undirected classroom, 499, 504–07, 511–13

Validity of tests, 209, 545–47

Value assumptions in education, 13

Values, and adjustment, 604–11; in different cultures, 45, 578, 605; of teachers, 45; *see also* Attitudes

Verbal ability, 223

Verbal interpretation, 17, 328, 364–68, 377, 645; and motor performance, 272, 292, 383; *see also* Concepts

Vision, maturation, 100

Visual aids, 286, 290, 294, 403–05, 454

Vocabulary, 364–68, 397

Vocational choice, 112, 188–90

Warmth, in classroom, 520–23; in home, 148–57, 639

Wechsler test, 204

Wells, Mr., 76–83

Whole-then-part method, 402

Withdrawing, 481–82, 575–84, 606

Work sample, 209, 545